Results-Oriented Interviewing

Principles, Practices, and Procedures

Wallace V. Schmidt
Rollins College

Roger N. Conaway
The University of Texas at Tyler

Allyn and Bacon

Boston ▪ London ▪ Toronto ▪ Sydney ▪ Tokyo ▪ Singapore

Vice President: Paul Smith
Series Editor: Karon Bowers
Series Editorial Assistant: Leila Scott
Marketing Manager: Susan E. Ogar
Composition and Prepress Buyer: Linda Cox
Manufacturing Buyer: Megan Cochran
Cover Administrator: Jenny Hart
Photo Researcher: Susan Duane
Production Administrator: Mary Beth Finch
Editorial-Production Service: Shepherd, Inc.
Electronic Composition: Shepherd, Inc.

Copyright © 1999 by Allyn & Bacon
A Viacom Company
Needham Heights, MA 02494

Internet: www.abacon.com

Library of Congress Cataloging-in-Publication Data

Schmidt, Wallace V., 1946–
    Results-oriented interviewing : principles, practices, and
procedures / Wallace W. Schmidt, Roger N. Conaway.
        p. cm.
    Includes bibliographical references and index.
    ISBN 0–205–26710–6
    1. Employment interviewing. 2. Interviewing. I. Conaway, Roger
N. II. Title.
    HF5549.5.I6S353   1998
    658.3′ 1124—dc21
                                                                              98–24287
                                                                                    CIP

Printed in the United States of America

10 9 8 7 6 5 4 3 2 1   03 02 01 00 99 98

*To my wife, Susan, and son, Matt, for their love and patient support;
to my parents, Clarence and Sylvia, who encouraged me to mindfully
question, probe, and persistently explore; and to Wally and Ruth whose
faith, confidence, and hope always uplift my spirits.*
—WVS
*To my wife, Phyllis, who encouraged me throughout this project;
to my children, Scott and Grant, for pretending interest in "Dad's" work;
and to my parents, Ed and Marge, who encouraged me to pursue
excellence to the finish.*
—RNC

ABOUT THE AUTHORS

Dr. Wallace V. Schmidt

Dr. Schmidt is a professor of organizational communication at Rollins College/Hamilton Holt School, Winter Park, Florida, where he teaches courses in communication theory, organizational communication, interviewing, conflict resolution, and intercultural communication. Previously, he has taught at Hofstra University, Texas Tech University, and The University of Texas at Tyler. He holds an M.A. from the University of Nebraska and a Ph.D. in Communication from New York University. Wally is a past president of the Florida Communication Association and an active member of the National Communication Association, Association for Business Communication, and the American Society for Training and Development. He has presented professional papers at international, national, regional, and state conferences and conducted business workshops in the areas of managerial leadership, interviewing, creative problem solving, and presentational power. In 1992, he received the Walter E. Barden Distinguished Teaching award from Rollins College.

Dr. Roger N. Conaway

Dr. Conaway is an associate professor of communication at The University of Texas at Tyler where he teaches courses in business and professional speaking, interviewing, free speech, and research. Previously, he has taught at Central Missouri State University. He holds an M.A. from Stephen F. Austin State University and a Ph.D. in interpersonal and public communication from Bowling Green State University. Roger is a past president of the Southwest Regional Association for Business Communication and an active member of the National Communication Association, Association for Business Communication, International Listening Association, and Texas Speech Communication Association. He has presented professional papers at national, regional, and state conferences and served as a consultant to business and industry. He also has conducted workshops and seminars in the areas of team building, interviewing, customer service, and effective listening. In 1992, he was nominated by the faculty of The University of Texas at Tyler for the Minnie Stevens Piper Professor Outstanding Teaching award.

CONTENTS

FIGURES

VIDEOTAPE CONTENTS

PREFACE

Why do we always emphasize the wrong stuff? During the two years I spent getting an MBA at Stanford in the early 1970s, I probably crunched a million numbers. But I never had 30 seconds worth of counsel about interviewing techniques. My subsequent experience as a management consultant leads me to conclude that lots of people can crunch numbers and do problem analysis effectively. Damn few, however, are excellent interviewers. . . . I'll be blunt: For youthful analysts in finance and for VPs of marketing alike, little is of greater importance than interviewing skills.

—Tom Peters*

Next to social conversation, the interview is undoubtedly the most common form of interaction between people, regardless of the situation or context. Whereas social conversation is casual and incidental, an interview requires intent; it is planned and prepared for before it occurs. Interviewing, then, represents a planned system of information gathering and assessment.

Whether you are an employer or employee, buyer or seller, teacher or student, counselor or client, newsmaker or newsgatherer, undoubtedly you will participate in interviews throughout your life. Each day, millions of people engage in job interviews, appraisal interviews, counseling interviews, negotiation/sales interviews, survey interviews, and journalistic/broadcast interviews, to name only a few. Interviewing may be considered a management, research, and media tool.

It is a process used in a variety of contexts that frequently merge and overlap. James Burke, Chief Executive Officer of Johnson and Johnson's Tylenol division, had avoided media attention for some seven years, never appearing on television. Then, on September 30, 1982, in the suburbs of Chicago, three people died as a result of contaminated Extra Strength Tylenol capsules. Now, Burke and his management team actively pursued the press and television with a clear media strategy to calm the public and restore Tylenol's market credibility. They also used focus groups and survey interviews to assess public opinion. Ultimately, Tylenol introduced tamper-free packaging and regained much of its marketshare. The Tylenol example clearly illustrates the need to understand interviewing in its various contexts. Increasingly, the lines between business, research, and media contexts are becoming blurred, requiring an expanded awareness and understanding of the interviewing process by interviewers and interviewees alike.

We live in an organized society and spend most of our lives working for organizations. Organizations routinely use interviews to conduct business—to select employees, appraise performance, counsel and coach, discipline misconduct,

*Tom Peters, *The Pursuit of WOW!* (New York: Vintage Books, 1994), 75.

negotiate contracts, and smoothly supervise the exiting of workers. Moreover, they regularly use interviews to gather information—the survey interview, telephone interview, focus group interview, organizational audit, and computer-assisted interview. Finally, since organizations are open systems, they must invariably respond to media inquiries—journalistic and broadcast interviews.

Results-Oriented Interviewing: Principles, Practices, and Procedures approaches interviewing from a communication perspective and explores interviewing in terms of the multiple contexts in which it occurs—business practices and procedures, research practices and procedures, and media practices and procedures. Each context is examined, with its unique characteristics and dimensions being identified. Emphasis is given to the notion that interviewing, in whatever setting, constitutes individuals interacting with one another in a highly mobile and changing environment. Axiomatic to our investigation is that *interviewing is an art one can learn and a tool one can use.*

What This Book Will and Will Not Do

You may have certain expectations about what a book such as this should do for you. A magical formula providing "techniques" and "strategies" would be nice. It is fashionable today to reduce complex phenomena to a few simple premises that can be distilled further into several sequential steps. Unfortunately, interviewing is both an art and a science requiring a combination of background knowledge and theory based on practice and research, plus guided application. Each interview type is unique in purpose and structure, placing different responsibilities on the parties involved. It is with this in mind that we propose an integrated approach and videotape learning package intended to develop interviewing competencies that address contemporary demands and pressures, and contribute to effective information sharing and information gathering.

Our approach to developing effective interviewing skills is based on the belief that understanding theory, observation, and analysis are antecedent steps to performance. Interviewing skills are best learned by grasping the principles and observing and sifting out what works from what does not work. Thus, this book has several unique aspects:

- *It is integrative in orientation.* Interviewing research and theory is integrated with real-life situations and practical applications. Each chapter begins with a detailed case study, which is discussed and analyzed throughout the chapter.
- *There is a focus on taking responsibility for the interview.* We describe what your responsibilities are toward others and what theirs are toward you. Interviewing is depicted as a complex, dynamic, yet personalized process.
- *It is results oriented or action focused.* Emphasis is placed on what one can *do*, both as an interviewer and interviewee. Interviewing, grounded on established principles and tested procedures, is presented as the basis for information collection and problem solving. Video segments critically focus attention on each of the interview types discussed.

Here, the necessary knowledge, sensitivity, and skills involved in interviewing are linked to the situation and contextual demands. We examine the reasons for conducting interviews and study and analyze the roles and relationships as they commonly occur in various contexts. Interviewing is evaluated in terms of both the interviewer and interviewee, and the appropriateness to specific contexts and desired results. The absence of context, or the frame of reference that gives meaning to a situation, can be a formidable barrier to successful interviewing.

The Uses and Benefits of a Videotape Package

Combining our approach with a video package to teach interviewing is not so much a novel idea, as an idea whose time has come. Just two decades ago "futurists" described a society where information would be the primary commodity. They predicted an "Electronic Age" of computers and telecommunications for both business and personal use. Currently, we are moving boldly into this information society, driven by advances in electronic communications. These changes require that we recognize and embrace new approaches.

Clearly, videotape is becoming another tool for speech communication and can be integrated with other teaching materials, including the text and lectures that rest with individual instructors. The use of a video learning package strengthens the interviewing course in a number of ways:

- The video segments present the broad spectrum of interviewing, typical of contemporary society. They illustrate interviewing in business, research, and media contexts.
- Real-life interviewing situations are used to narrow the "theory-to-skills gap" and permit you to observe, speculate about, and even emulate behavior that may lay outside your normal framework. Role-played situations are presented for observation, analysis, and evaluation. In this way, the video learning package can help you experience, not just intellectualize about, the interviewing process. Students can use the video package to transform textual material into skills that will benefit them, while instructors can use it as a basis for class discussion.
- The video segments provide an "instructional window" for learning. Through theory and activity, through the verbal and the visual, you are encouraged to learn by doing, observing, and experimenting; by thinking, experiencing, and taking chances. As an ancient Chinese proverb states: "Tell me, I forget; show me, I remember; involve me, I understand."

The video learning package can enrich instructionally the interviewing course and stimulate the learning environment. It helps make for a better fit between content, application, and needs.

The accompanying videotape is available for purchase separately or in a package with the text.

Return on Investment

Results-Oriented Interviewing: Principles, Practices, and Procedures explores the factors affecting interviewing in its various contexts and identifies the tools and skills fundamental to functioning effectively. Ultimately, however, the return on investment of time and energy rests with you. The interviewing process presented in this book is not a passive one. You can't just thumb through pages, reading words, nodding to yourself when you encounter things you like and then moving on to the next chapter. In order to become an effective interviewer/interviewee, you will have to respond actively to what you read and observe in the video segments. Specifically, this involves several activities:

- *Connect new ideas to what you already understand.* Make this material fit into your life, your values and attitudes, your unique situation.
- *Talk with others about what you are reading.* In order to make new ideas part of you, use them in your daily interactions with others. Ask others what they think about these matters. Conduct your own research studies to confirm or refute what you have read. Focus group discussions and interviews with experts in the field can provide you with "up close and personal" information and reflections on areas of study.
- *Practice.* Thinking and talking are fine, but also take action. Experiment with new ways to make your interviewing more viable and purposeful. Actively assume the responsibility for effective interviewing.

We would recommend that you not "see" this material as a book, in the sense that it is something to read once and put on a shelf. In fact, we have left room in *Results-Oriented Interviewing* for you to complete this book. We hope that you will read and write between the lines and improve what we have done. In effect, this is a personal journey, enhancing awareness, sharpening assessment, and improving application. By the end of the journey, you not only will know how to be a more effective interviewer/interviewee, but also will have learned how to become more accountable for results. We quote Emerson: "That which we persist in doing becomes easier—not that the nature of the task has changed, but our ability to do has increased."

Acknowledgments

Results-Oriented Interviewing: Principles, Practices, and Procedures could not have been possible without the encouragement, generous support, and participation of a number of people. For their acceptance of our ideas and candid, timely suggestions for improving the text, we thank the following reviewers who read early and late editions of the manuscript: Steven Ralston, East Tennessee State University; Vernon Miller, Michigan State University; E.W. Brody, University of Memphis; Jim Schnell, Ohio Dominican College; Barry Brummett, University of Wisconsin—Milwaukee; Hank Flick, Mississippi State University; and Peter G. Ross, Central Michigan University. The book benefited immensely from their comments. We thank Dr. Wilson Renfro and Dr. Charles Fries for their help with the counseling interview. We also acknowledge Tom Watson and Barbara Huggins for their willing participation in the video. Tom, you are a true professional, and as a communication consultant, your help has been invaluable. Barbara, your interest and care for children and how you express that care through interviewing is truly inspiring.

We thank our students at the Hamilton Holt School of Rollins College and The University of Texas at Tyler. Their personal experiences and interviewing stories served as windows to the world of work, and we profited greatly from their informal observations. They have taught us much by eagerly applying interviewing knowledge and skills in the workplace. Thanks also to our colleagues at both institutions who expressed confidence in the project and gave invaluable feedback throughout the development of the manuscript. Furthermore, we express a debt of gratitude to those who initially ignited and fanned our curiosity in communication—Professor Emeritus Raymond K. Tucker at Bowling Green State University and the faculties at Midland Lutheran College, the University of Nebraska, and New York University.

The word *very* is usually superfluous, except in expressing our very special thanks and gratitude to Carol and Don Tuttle of Tuttle Associates, who suggested the title for this text and shared with us their insights and understanding and reminded us what "return on investment" means. Moreover, we would be remiss if we did not express our indebtedness to Terry James and Jeff Miller for producing the video package accompanying the text. We were fortunate to have their professional experience and careful, competent services.

We greatly appreciate Carla Daves and Karon Bowers of Allyn and Bacon who championed the project, and Paul Smith, Editor in Chief of Communication, who offered valuable editorial advice while directing the project. Recognition must be given to Andrea Geanacopoulos, Kathy Rubino, and Leila Scott for gently and wisely pushing us to completion. Also gratitude to Kelly Bechen, our masterful copyeditor, whose tactful criticism and suggestions helped shape the book in a very positive way. Finally, thanks to Bill Barke, President of Allyn and Bacon.

Most of all we would like to acknowledge the patience, helpful input, and never-ending encouragement of our wives. To Susan and Phyllis, who lived through each stage of the manuscript with us, we say thank you. We could not have done this without your support and your participation. You were both wonderfully tolerant of our moods and a particular source of strength, since writing is a lonely business most of the time.

SECTION ONE

Interviewing:
Basic Principles

1 The Nature of Effective Interviewing

Interviewing is an important and integral part of our complex society. It is a routine component of our Information Age and crucial to information gathering and information sharing. Interviews are an exchange of information, opinions, attitudes, or experiences from one person to another. They are efforts to solve problems or bring about change by questioning and talking to other people.

Chapter 1 defines the interviewing process and explores the differing types and functions of interviews. The interview situation is examined and the basic anatomical features of an interview outlined. This chapter is designed to accomplish three objectives:

1. *Awareness*. You will learn the special role of interviews and the multiple functions they serve.

2. *Assessment*. You will be able to analyze an interview and determine its effectiveness.

3. *Application*. You will be able to identify the situations that give rise to interviews and those features common to all interviews.

* * * * *

The Interviewing Challenges at Southwestern State University

Southwestern State University is one of the many state-supported institutions of higher learning in the southwestern part of the United States. It was founded in the last decade of the nineteenth century when the area was only a U.S. Territory and in almost one hundred years has grown from a one-building, one-curriculum school to an institution of twenty-two thousand students offering undergraduate and graduate degrees in all major academic disciplines. All of the programs at Southwestern State are fully accredited by the appropriate academic associations, and the university commands a reputation for quality teaching. Southwestern State University also supports a School of Medicine and School of Law. The Board of Trustees hope that Southwestern State will someday become one of the three most influential state-supported institutions of higher learning in the southwest.

Dr. Melissa Ortiz was selected as the first female, Hispanic President of Southwestern State University three years ago. At the time, she knew she would be particularly visible as a Hispanic woman assuming the top position at an institution with a history of male leadership. However, she was not intimidated by challenges, and prior to being asked to apply by the Chair of the Board of Regents she had been Southwestern's Vice President of graduate programs. Moreover, Dr. Ortiz's strong academic background included a variety of administrative positions at West Coast universities before coming to Southwestern. She is task oriented and well respected among faculty, staff, and students. The regents had been glowing in their praise of her and were unanimous in their support for her candidacy. She is now pleased to be able to acknowledge that support through the receipt of a sizable financial gift which will be used to establish a School of Communication.

As Melissa Ortiz waits for the press conference to begin, she reviews the upcoming challenges. First, she and a Curricular Task Force need to review the academic requirements for the School of Communication and determine the emphasis programs would assume. Working with faculty and students, she hopes the Task Force can identify a distinct focus which will characterize the School of Communication and draw attention to Southwestern State University. Second, she knows she will have to work with a Search Committee to select a dean for the newly established School of Communication. There are several possible internal candidates, but perhaps an external choice will better serve the interests of the university. Third, the state and the university are facing many financial exigencies, and to maintain viable programs she will have to encourage the community, alumni, and friends to generously support Southwestern State University through donations. She believes this and future press conferences can generate the enthusiasm needed to support new faculty positions. She is relying on her charm and personal negotiation skills to win support for several endowed chairs and visiting scholar positions from prominent alumni, community leaders, and national foundations. Finally, she realizes the School of Communication represents a major commitment and risk which can only succeed through carefully gathering and sharing information.

Melissa Ortiz quietly contemplates the desired tone for the press conference announcing the School of Communication and privately begins to think about the data collection process and decisions to be made in the near future.

Discussion Questions

1. How would you describe the interviewing challenges facing Melissa Ortiz and Southwestern State University?
2. What types of interviews will occupy the Curricular Task Force and for what purpose? The Search Committee? Melissa Ortiz and selected alumni, community leaders, and foundations?
3. Describe the various situations characterizing the interviews. How are they similar? How do they differ?
4. Identify the critical issues the various interviews must address and the questions involved parties must ask/answer.
5. How should Melissa Ortiz, the Curricular Task Force, and the Search Committee communicate their decisions regarding the School of Communication?

Interviewing Defined

People's efforts to adapt to and to influence their environment depend substantially on their abilities to communicate with other people concerning their problems and those of the groups to which they belong. Our ability to communicate and our methods of doing so are unique among the world of living organisms in that we can share experiences by means of sophisticated sets of signs and symbols. We live in a world of talk—talk that influences our lives. While we often regard our ability to communicate as casually as we fold our arms, communication is a critical component of our social system.

We communicate daily on a one-to-one basis with friends, colleagues, and associates. We regularly participate in social and work groups. We occasionally listen to speakers who, in sharing their visions, can inspire and motivate. We are the subjects of countless mediated and electronic messages, which influence our thinking and effect our behavior. Communication is basic to how we relate in our society.

Interviewing is both similar to and different from other types of communication. Certainly the communication skills that make one an effective communicator in "everyday" life will also assist in interview situations. However, interviews are a distinct form of interpersonal communication and represent something more than casual conversation. Although good interviews may appear to be highly conversational, there are some important points that distinguish them from mere conversation.

The term *interviewing* as commonly used may refer to many different kinds of interactions; thus, it is difficult to write one definition that will precisely and accurately accommodate all of them. However, by focusing on the essential features or characteristics of interviews, we can create a general definition useful as a frame of reference. We define an **interview** as *a unique interpersonal process whereby two parties purposefully interact with one another, asking and answering subject-specific questions, in an effort to gain and share information which can contribute to the solving of problems* *and/or change for the mutual benefit of the participants.* A discussion of the key concepts contained within this definition will make it more meaningful.

Interviews are a unique interpersonal process representing a dynamic, ever-changing interaction, with many variables operating with and acting upon one another. Two principal dimensions of this process are content and relationship. Content is *what* is said; relationship is *how* it's said.[1] We conduct interviews to get information or to give information. Therefore, at one level, the content or information exchanged occupies our attention. The content of messages includes such factors as quantity, accuracy, and believability of information. Both verbal and nonverbal language codes may be used to convey content. While the emphasis is usually on the former as the primary language used, the nonverbal messages must not be overlooked. These visual messages can reinforce the verbal ones, or at other times, they may contradict them. The content of information also defines relationship—how the information is to be interpreted—and this interpersonal relationship between the parties is equally important. This structured relationship is often described in terms of roles that define the prescribed behaviors of the participants. The two roles that people occupy in an interview are that of the interviewer and the interviewee. The interviewer may be a single individual or just as likely may be several people, a team, or a panel. The interviewer role identifies the person or persons with the responsibility and power to plan, schedule, and execute the interview. The interviewer initially establishes the interactional relationship between the involved parties. However, it must be stressed that the interviewer and interviewee roles are supplementary and that you can only view the interviewer role in terms of its relationship to the interviewee role. Interviewees comprise the second part of the relational equation and typically have less power than the interviewer, although each role often is shaped by very personal interpretations. Interviewees possess information which is necessary for the interviewer to obtain if the interviewer's objectives are to be achieved and problem solving or change is to occur. The interviewer and interviewee are integral participants in the interviewing process and interdependently influence one another, as well as the final outcome.

The two parties involved in an interview purposely interact with one another; there is a definite reason for conducting the interview. People interview for task-related purposes; they have something they want to accomplish—select a person for a job, appraise and apprise an employee, correct disruptive behavior, help someone solve a personal problem, determine the undermining causes of organizational unrest, influence another person's beliefs or actions, report a news story, conduct a press conference, or collect research data necessary for decision making. Each party in the interview has a purpose and some content to communicate, either planned in advance or developed during the interview. The degree to which each party's purpose is achieved is a measure of how productive and successful the interview is.

Asking and answering subject-specific questions is central to the interviewing process. For the interviewer and interviewee to interact effectively, both must possess communicative skills and an interviewing strategy. By strategy, we do not mean to imply the use of manipulative or deceptive behavior. Rather, we mean that each participant has a positive, constructive plan for interacting and uses that plan as the basis for skillful communication. The most important communication skills in interviews are (1) planning, (2) question asking, and (3) question answering. The use of questions and answers gives direction to the interview structure and contributes to achieving the mutual purpose of the participants.

People interview to gain and share information. Information gathering interviews are designed to obtain facts, opinions, attitudes, reasons for actions, or trends of belief. They are an exchange of information, opinions, or experiences with the skillful interviewer looking for a revelation or an insight, a thought or a viewpoint that is interesting, not commonly heard, and not already known. Equally important in an interview is the basic need to share information. Therefore, the people involved are encouraged and motivated to alternately speak and listen, to share information, probe, clarify answers, and provide feedback. However, we need to qualify this generalization because modern technology has created some interesting new situations. One familiar example is the telephone interview, but computer-assisted communication networks are becoming standard practice in government, industry, and many universities. These networks provide relatively complete control over the amount and kinds of information transmitted, the people to whom the information is addressed, and the times at which messages will be exchanged. Our modern technology represents a powerful means of exchanging information.

Finally, the object of any interview is to provide information of mutual benefit while furthering the goals of the participants. Both parties in an interview contribute to the interaction, and the effectiveness of their efforts depends on their mutual cooperation. Neither party has exclusive control over the communication behavior of the other, and consequently, each must work to create a supportive and positive communication climate.

* * * * *

Given this definition of interviewing, we can begin to describe the challenges facing Melissa Ortiz and Southwestern State University. She and the Curricular Task Force will want to talk with faculty, students, and curricular experts about the curriculum for the new School of Communication. Together, they will want to gain information which can contribute to developing a mission statement, strategic goals, and a plan of courses. Melissa Ortiz and the Search Committee will have to interview candidates for the position of Dean of the School of Communication. This will be a vital hiring decision, requiring a clear understanding of the position and a careful examination of the applicants. It is equally critical that the candidates understand the demands of the position and the institutional culture at Southwestern State University. Finally, Melissa Ortiz will want to gain support for the new School of Communication from constituencies outside Southwestern State University. This will necessitate meeting with news reporters, as well as selected individuals and groups. She will have to publicly and privately encourage enthusiasm and exert a positive influence. Clearly, the effective use of interviewing will directly contribute to the success of the new School of Communication and mutually benefit Southwestern State University and the community. However, what types of interviews will yield the mutually desired outcomes?

Types and Functions of Interviews

Despite the way we sometimes talk, it is a mistake to speak in terms of *the* interview. There are many different situations in which two parties interact that can be called an interview, and consequently, there are many different types of interviews serving different functions. Likewise, it is a mistake to identify one kind of interview as being relevant to only one kind of job. As we examine the different types and functions of interviews, you will begin to realize that interviews are function specific rather than occupation specific, and all are used in the many professional arenas comprising society.

The Selection Interview

The selection interview is used for screening, hiring, and placing applicants, employees, and members of the organization. It is the most common form of interview in organizational life with over 99 percent of today's organizations relying on the selection interview as part of their hiring procedures.[2] Although numerous tools and procedures are used to select and recruit new employees, the interview is consistently the most frequently used selection device. The selection interview provides an opportunity to obtain information about the candidate that might not be obtained otherwise. Moreover, the interviewee can gain a better understanding of the position and get a sense of the working atmosphere and of the people in the organization. The selection interview is crucial to the hiring process.

The Appraisal Interview

Performance appraisals are a key component in maximizing organizational efficiency and effectiveness. Studies indicate that 89 percent of companies with more than five hundred employees and 74 percent of smaller companies employ performance appraisal systems.[3] Properly conducted appraisal interviews can (1) improve employee job performance by revealing training needs; (2) facilitate objective decision making regarding employee retention, promotion, and/or transfer; (3) increase employee motivation and personal growth by providing feedback regarding job performance; (4) reduce the potential threat of legal complications by providing documentation; and (5) enhance attainment of organizational goals and objectives by providing a means to foster and monitor goal directed behavior.[4] The appraisal interview is inherent to the employer-employee relationship and is an essential communication link between employer and employee.

The Discipline Interview

The discipline interview occurs when the employer perceives an ongoing problem of which the employee is aware and which is in clear violation of organization policy, rules, or regulations. Today, more and more companies are proactively including a discipline process as an integral part of their personnel policies and procedures in an effort to avoid potential litigation.[5] Discipline is a serious business designed to *correct behavior, not to punish*. A constructive attitude will do much to soften a discipline report and contribute to a productive discipline interview.

The Counseling Interview

The counseling interview typifies the helping or coaching relationship essential to sound organizational management. Its main objective is to change the counselee's behavior or the attitudes that motivate the behavior and contribute to a greater understanding of his or her talents, roles, or performance in the organization.[6] Counseling is a process which occurs on many levels of responsibility, and the reasons for counseling vary greatly. Counseling is often remedial, but coaching is also part of a larger sphere of counseling activities. Counseling is an important managerial/supervisory role designed to help others improve their job-related performance, enhance their career opportunities, and find greater satisfaction in doing their jobs.

The Exit Interview

The exit interview can be a helpful instrument in understanding who is leaving, why, and whether the loss will be a plus or a minus. It has several specific functions: (1) to discover why the employee is leaving; (2) to discover any problems within the organization which may be causing employees to leave; (3) to discover causes external to the organization responsible for employee turnover; (4) to discover possible means for improving the organization; and (5) to enhance the "goodwill" image of the organization by showing concern for the future career of the individual leaving.[7] The exit interview can contribute much information about operational situations and lead to suggestions regarding necessary changes.

The Negotiation Interview

Negotiations represent a special form of social interaction or reciprocal give-and-take where the parties hold some potentially conflicting interests, as well as common interests. An apt description of negotiation is mutual persuasion, since each party tries to influence the other to modify a position. Negotiation interviews take place in many different contexts, ranging from sales presentations to contract negotiations; therefore, there will be some unique features and strategies that should be adapted to these different situations. Nevertheless, there are many characteristics that all of these contexts share. A negotiation interview takes place whenever an interviewer seeks to affect an interviewee's perceptions and thus bring about changes in ways of thinking, feeling, or acting.

The Sales Interview

Selling is such a common activity that it is unusual for a day to pass without our observing at least one sales interview. Consequently, you are probably not surprised to hear that more than 6.5 million people in the United States make their living in activities officially classified as sales occupations. However, it could be argued that we are all involved in sales interviews, since we are often selling ourselves and our ideas.

The Survey Interview

Surveys and polls are an integral and essential tool used for information gathering by individual researchers, business firms, political parties and organizations, government bureaus and agencies, and social service institutions devoted to education, public health, and social welfare. Survey Interviews are used in a particular kind of data collecting known as **descriptive research.** Surveys and polls are often used for the practical purpose of better understanding the attitudes, needs, and desires of a particular audience in order to guide decision-making and executive actions. Students and professors, and researchers and professionals within the social and behavioral sciences, the humanities and arts, business and public administration, and a wide variety of other professional studies also use surveys to test hypotheses regarding the people who comprise our society. The information gained from such survey information is used to enhance the literature and the state of current thought within a particular discipline. Because surveys and polls can be designed to effectively and efficiently capture a wide variety of information on many diverse topics, they represent a principal research instrument.

The Telephone Interview

The telephone interview has become a popular research tool because it is quick and economical. The telephone interview is a most useful tool in data collection and research. While often used as the primary data collection technique, it is also a very good supplement to personal interviews. Low refusal rates and quick access to reliable information from a large geographical sample make telephone interviews highly advantageous.

The Focus Group Interview

The focus group interview is an unstructured, free-flowing interview with a small group of people. A focus group might intensively examine a problem area, probe attitudes and opinions given a specific topic, generate new ideas, or have participants react to a particular situation. As a form of qualitative research, it is more subjective, more "human," and more informal than quantitative research. The setting may range from a living room to a more formal conference room, depending upon the degree of informality and self-exploration desired. The moderator or facilitator occupies a key role and must be able to distinguish between a *directed* interview and interviewing *directively.* Direction must exist in the moderator's mind as a series of exploratory goals, but the interviewer must not put words into respondent's mouths. In essence, the focus group represents a temporary community of people formed for the purpose of discovery. The focus group interview can be an excellent means of securing subjective information that has rich explanatory value.

The Organizational Audit

The organizational audit identifies strengths and weaknesses, reveals potential problems, and permits organizations to develop and implement remedial steps before problems can escalate beyond control. It is principally a diagnostic technique answering the questions: What characterizes this organization? What does it do well and what needs improving? The diagnostic design provides for tailored, systematic observation and analysis of all organizational areas considered important.

The Computer-Assisted Interview

Computer-assisted communication networks add enormous flexibility and power to currently available communication channels and create unique avenues for interviewing. These networks facilitate the transmission of large quantities of information and make it possible for people separated by time and distance to communicate with one another. Although many aspects of computer networks are very technical, one does not need to know a great deal about how they work to use them. The most commonly used computer network options are electronic mail, computer databases, computer billboards, and interactive computer conferencing.

Computer networks create important new opportunities for communication generally, and interviewing in particular. Clearly, computer-assisted interviews will not replace face-to-face interviews but will "expand greatly the human and information resources to which one has constant and convenient access."[8]

The Journalistic Interview and Investigative Reporting

The journalistic interview is an integral part of the news reporting process and represents the primary means of gathering those bits and pieces of information and fact that form an investigative report. Interviews account for 80 to 90 percent of a journalist's research. The reporter-interviewer is the reader's surrogate whose role, as Hugh Sherwood says, is to be a "catalyst" who asks the right questions at the right time to get facts, anecdotes, and emotional responses from the person being interviewed.[9] The traditional who, what, when, where, how, and why model for investigative reporting outlines the basic criteria and agenda for journalistic interviews. Kris Gilger of The (New Orleans) Times-Picayune says, "skillful interviewing is the basis for all good reporting," and Bill Endicott of the Los Angeles Times observes, "it's probably the most important thing reporters do."[10]

The Broadcast Interview

The broadcast interview is essentially a planned conversation between two parties for the purpose of gathering information on behalf of a viewing and/or listening audience. The goals of the broadcast interviewer are not just to conduct an interview and to elicit information, but to address the technological, journalistic, and artistic demands of radio and television. It's important for the parties involved in broadcast interviews to understand the electronic medium and the challenges posed by electronic news gathering while satisfying the audience's need for interesting or entertaining material.

The News Conference

The news conference is an effective, timesaving vehicle for disseminating legitimate and important information to the general public on a timely basis. Meeting the press in a public forum allows an immediate response to potentially hundreds of reporters who otherwise may be seeking individual interviews. To ensure that the news media receive a consistent message from a responsible spokesperson, news conferences are focused and controlled by the interviewee, with a statement or news release given to reporters at the start of the conference.

*   *   *   *   *

Having outlined the different types of interviews, it becomes clear that Melissa Ortiz and others at Southwestern State University will have to engage in varying interviews, each serving different functions. The Curricular Task Force will want to consider using survey interviews, telephone interviews, and focus groups to gather needed information to make their decisions. The Search Committee will use the selection interview to assess desirable candidates interested in being the new Dean of the School of Communication. Melissa Ortiz will use personal influence and negotiation interviews to persuade alumni, community leaders, and foundations to contribute financial support. She will hold news conferences to focus public attention and to encourage enthusiasm. Journalistic interviews and broadcast interviews will report the ongoing developments and flurry of activities associated with creating the new School of Communication. Finally, with educational institutions becoming more integrally linked in their common mission to provide quality learning, computer network interviews may be used in a variety of ways to gather and share important information. Certainly, the interviewing challenges at Southwestern State University are multiple and require careful planning and consideration. How should the varying interview situations be orchestrated?

A Situational Perspective

Interviewing demands intellect, patience, empathy, and a keen understanding of the interviewing situation. An *interviewing situation* is one in which people, places, and events combine to create an opportunity for an interview to take place. Based on the previous discussion, it is obvious that interviewing occurs in many situations and for a variety of purposes. What distinguishes a skilled from an unskilled interviewer is the ability to analyze a situation, determine the possible options and alternatives, and then choose how to proceed. Felix Lopez compares the skilled interviewer to a master musician:

> Interviewing is very much like piano playing—a fair degree of skill can be acquired without the necessity of formal instruction. But there is a world of difference in craftsmanship, in technique, and in finesse between the amateur who plays "by ear" and the accomplished concert pianist. The self-instructed player mechanically reproduces on the keyboard certain melodies that have been committed to memory, the artist, by skillfully blending mastery of musical theory, countless hours of practice, is pleasing to the audience, and expressive to the pianist's inner feeling.[11]

Certainly, the novice or moderately competent interviewer/interviewee can experience some success, but a lack of understanding and critical insight causes important information to be lost or not communicated. Focusing on the interviewing situation, however, allows the involved parties to effectively accomplish the desired goals and objectives.

Trying to identify a single pattern that characterizes the number of participants and settings in which interviews occur would be impossible. However, we can describe general features of situations in which interviews take place. There are three categories of relatively discreet variables that, individually and in combination, strongly influence the effectiveness of an interview: (1) the nature of the situation, (2) the interviewer and interviewee roles, and (3) the climate of communication.

The Nature of the Situation

All interviews arise out of an *exigency*—a combination of people, places, and events marked by a degree of urgency requiring resolution. The nature of interviewing situations change with differing combinations of people, places, and events affecting the behaviors of the participants. Some situations naturally invite cooperation, while other situations naturally invite conflict. The majority of situations fall between these extremes, and the nature of the situation depends on how the participants define it. Therefore, it is important to define the situation and select an environment which is most conducive for interviewing. With a knowledge of what to expect along with preparation, the parties can keep the situation in perspective and prevent the interview from becoming "The Great Confrontation." Thus, when analyzing the interview situation, one must recognize what has preceded or will proceed from the interview and consider: (1) the physical setting, (2) the social setting, (3) the time dimensions, (4) the psychological climate, and (5) the legal/ethical constraints.

Architecture, furnishings, room dimensions, temperature, lighting, noise, privacy, physical placement of participants, and territoriality all contribute to the setting and affect the interview situation. A well-lighted, moderate-sized room which is pleasantly decorated and set at a comfortable temperature with proper ventilation creates a positive climate that encourages communication among the participants. An environment free of noise and distractions enhances concentration and

Setting, social or cultural customs, and the nature of the occasion influence the interview situation.

helps maintain lines of thinking. The spatial and territorial dimensions dictate control and influence the formality or informality of the situation. The actual physical setting creates the desired atmosphere or mood needed to encourage dialogue and move the interaction beyond surface exchanges. Fortunately, the interviewer has considerable freedom to plan and arrange the interview and adjust the physical characteristics of the meeting place.

Social or cultural customs and the nature of the occasion influence the communication climate and the personal relationship established between the participants. In order to avoid interpersonal problems, both parties must be sensitive to the other's sociocultural background, as it is often easy to offend the other unconsciously. While this can be difficult when cultural customs differ, the parties must particularly make an effort to appreciate and be open, understanding, and tolerant of diversity. It is also important to remember that each person comes to an interview with unique perceptions of the situation. The interviewer may consider the interview routine, however, the interviewee may see it as a major event in their life. It is in the social setting where the necessary credibility and trustworthiness are established to prompt a candid, truthful exchange of information and ideas.

The length of the interview and its time of occurrence may also influence its outcome. People feel more alert and motivated at different times of the day/week/month/year. Some prefer to deal with important matters early in the morning and early in the week, while others prefer midmorning or early afternoon and later in the week. Selection interviews are often inappropriately scheduled for Mondays, when motivation is low, or Fridays, when interviewers are looking forward to the weekend and anticipating relaxing. Holidays, such as Christmas, Chanukah, Thanksgiving, and Yom Kippur, are particularly poor occasions for reprimands or dismissals but may prompt more counseling, since people experience more loneliness during these times of the year. Press conferences and news interviews need to be scheduled with reporter deadlines, printing, and broadcast airing times in mind. Time dimensions should be carefully considered since they affect concentration, mood, and ability to communicate.

The most common way of thinking about psychological climate in an interview is in terms of comfort or stress. Comfort represents the degree to which the parties feel at ease. Stress is the degree of anxiety experienced by the interviewer or interviewee. Shyness, communication apprehension, nervousness, and ego threats are potential problems that plague interviews and reduce their effectiveness. Tact, patience, sensitivity, and language skills can help alleviate these tensions. Whatever can be done to build a congenial relationship will positively affect the psychological climate and be a powerful motivator in the interview. It is here where rapport building becomes important. Perhaps the overriding principle for constructing a comfortable psychological climate is for the participants to engage in **healthy communication,** expressing genuine consideration for one another's needs. Here, *healthy* refers to *involved* and *concerned* communication with one another and is evidenced in "one who is other-oriented, while at the same time maintaining the ability to accomplish his/her own interpersonal goals. This other-orientation is demonstrated by being empathic, affiliative, and supportive . . . adapting [ones] behavior as the situation within an encounter changes."[12]

Constraints establish the parameters of the situation, limiting what can be done in an interview. They define what you can say or do during an interview, restrict the questions you can ask, and/or determine how you can use the information you obtain during an interview. The amount of time available and your relationships with the other person may limit the topics discussed in an interview. However, participants may have some control over these factors. Other, less-flexible constraints are established by factors over which the participants have little or no control. Legal constraints apply to many interviews. Equal employment laws prohibit certain topics from being discussed in selection interviews and in appraisal interviews. Slander and liable laws regulate the conduct of reporters and broadcasters, restricting their use of information. Organizations having electronic message systems and computer billboards may restrict the kinds of topics that may be discussed "on line." Finally, ethical and moral standards influence how the parties conduct themselves. Many professional societies and associations have adopted codes of conduct intended to regulate the behavior of their members. However, our personal ethics, developed by the time we become adults, more directly influence how we deal with other people. These constraints help define the interview situation and deserve attention whenever planning, participating in, or evaluating an interview.

Interviewer and Interviewee Roles

The term **roles** refers to sets of behavior that we associate with particular situations. Roles are important in interviewing situations, and common expectations are necessary to make any interview go well. Among other things, roles determine who will initiate the interview, who will do most of the talking, what subjects will be discussed, and how the interview will come to an end. Our ability to interact with other people in useful and satisfying ways depends on our finding roles in which all the participants are comfortable.

The skilled interviewer is keenly sensitive to planning options, questioning strategies, and the alternative role of interviewee/respondent. This is not meant to imply that the interviewer can or should anticipate everything that is going to happen in an interview. It does stress, however, the *proactive* role of the interviewer. It is the interviewer who sets the course, taking the initiative in scheduling the interview, identifying the topics to be discussed, establishing the purpose of the interview, and preparing questions. The interviewer must probe analytically and thoroughly, being aware of personal interpretations of what the interviewee says and tempering personal biases or prejudices when making decisions.

Regardless of interviewing type, interviewers select a communicative style characterizing the extent to which they try to control the nature and content of the interviewee's answers. Using a **directive style,** the interviewer establishes the purpose of the interview, defines and analyzes the situation, gives opinions and information, makes suggestions, and assertively controls the pacing. The **nondirective style** involves probing and the use of questions to indirectly influence the interview process rather than the content. Here, the interviewee may assume greater control of purpose, subject matter, and pacing. At one extreme, some interviewers adopt a rigidly controlling style, limiting the interaction, while at the other end of the continuum, interviewers make little or no effort to control the content of the interview, acting more as facilitators or advisors. The choice between the two is one of the most important decisions that any interviewer makes, because it influences every other behavior in the interaction.

Which style is better—directive or nondirective? The answer is neither one. They are simply two basic alternatives at either end of a graduated continuum that are available to the interviewer. Each approach can be appropriately applied and has its own advantages and disadvantages. Typically, selection interviews, discipline interviews, news conferences, surveys, and opinion polls tend to be more directive, while appraisal interviews, counseling interviews, exit interviews, and focus group interviews are more nondirective. Rarely is an interview completely directive or completely nondirective, yet these different orientations affect the structure of the interview, the amount of participation, and the role that the interviewer plays. In choosing which style to use you keep in mind your personality, your objectives, your relationship with the interviewee, the amount of time and energy you can spend, and most importantly, the interviewee's expectations of you.

The primary responsibility of the interviewee is to provide accurate information. Interviewing is a two-way process requiring a balance in turn-taking, meaning interviewers must also be listeners and respondents. Part of the coordinated action in interviews comes from the orderly interchange in which both parties know when they can speak and when they should listen. The desired or specific balance varies with each particular interview situation and type of interview. Participants with highly developed social and communication skills will enjoy a more balanced exchange than those who are more introverted and less articulate.

In addition to interpersonal skills and communication competency, the type of interview influences the balance. The selection and journalistic interviews often reveal a 70/30 balance, with the interviewee dominating the speaking, while the discipline interview and negotiation or persuasive interview may require an 80/20 balance, with the interviewer dominating the speaking. Appraisal interviews are frequently a 50/50 balance, with counseling and focus group interviews permitting the interviewee the greatest freedom to speak. No interview can be successful without meaningful feedback.

The importance of listening is self-evident. The skilled interviewer/interviewee listens to comprehend, analyze, and interpret information while displaying interest and concern. This requires placing oneself in the situation of the other party and listening with a "third ear" to what is not said. John Stewart and Gary D'Angelo observe that genuine understanding "involves grasping fully what the other person is trying to say—from her or his point of view—and how he or she feels about it. It comes about when you are able to interpret accurately and empathically the cues the other person makes available."[13] Active listening is a mutual responsibility that cannot be taken for granted or given too much attention.

Finally, it is important to note that the roles of interviewer/interviewee are not arbitrary. Roles are determined by the situation and may change when participants move to other situations. This requires that we be **rhetorically sensitive** to our changing surroundings. Roderick Hart and Don Burks conceived the concept of rhetorical sensitivity and define a rhetorically sensitive person as one who will:

1. Be able to alter roles in response to the behaviors of others and accept their role adaptations.
2. Be able to appropriately adapt communication behavior to people in varying social conditions.
3. Be able to adapt to multiple others, each struggling to adapt as well and contribute to a better definition of selves.
4. Be able to monitor communication with others in order to make it purposive rather than expressive.
5. Be able to modify personal behaviors and adapt to others in a rational and orderly way.[14]

Hart and Burks are attempting to demonstrate that the variables of public rhetoric also apply to private interactions. We believe that effective interviewing is correlated with rhetorical sensitivity. Interviewer and interviewee roles require being attentive, understanding, caring, empathetic, and trustworthy.

Climate of Communication

The climate of communication arises out of our understanding of the nature of the interview situation and the roles we assume while engaged in interviewing. The basic tenet of communication climate is that a party's cognitive and affective perceptions of an interview situation influence that party's behavior during the interview. The concept of communication climate might be thought of as the spirit or tone that dominates an interview and is responsible for the interpersonal relationships that exist among the involved parties. These relationships may be friendly and produce mutually positive effects benefiting both parties, or they may be hostile and produce negative effects upon those involved. Thus, the communication climate of an interview may range from supportive to defensive and can be measured by the degree to which the participants find formal and informal communication systems to be open or closed.

Jack Gibb distinguishes between supportive and defensive communication climates and personal communication styles.[15] A **supportive climate,** contributing to a supportive style, is characterized by:

1. *Description* (nonjudgmental, asking questions for information, presenting feelings, events, perceptions, or processes without calling for or implying change on the receivers)
2. *Problem orientation* (defining mutual problems and seeking solutions without inhibiting the receiver's goals, decisions, and progress)
3. *Spontaneity* (free of deception, unhidden motives, honest and straightforward)
4. *Equality* (mutual trust and respect, participative planning without influence of power, status, appearance)
5. *Empathy* (respecting the worth of the listener, identifying, sharing, and accepting problems, feelings, and values)
6. *Provisionalism* (willingness to experiment with one's own behavior, attitudes, and ideas)

On the other hand, a **defensive climate,** contributing to a defensive style is characterized by:

1. *Evaluation* (passing judgment, blaming, praising, and questioning standards, values, and motives)
2. *Control* (trying to do something to another, attempting to change an attitude or behavior of another)
3. *Strategy* (manipulation and tricking others)
4. *Neutrality* (expressing lack of concern for another's welfare)
5. *Superiority* (an attitude of superiority in wealth, intellectual ability, physical characteristics)
6. *Certainty* (dogmatic, needing to be right, wanting to win)

The importance of fostering a supportive communication climate rather than a defensive climate cannot be overstated.

The distinctive features of an open climate are a great willingness to trust, an avoidance of evaluation, and an apparent willingness to accept whatever information the interviewee wants to give. Essentially, the interviewee experiences a certain freedom of expression. A closed climate is the antithesis of an open one. Communication basically goes in one direction, with the interviewer being highly directive. There is little desire on the part of the interviewer to create rapport or a cohesive relationship, and participation is highly controlled. One needs to stay keenly aware of the communication climate being created.

* * * * *

The interviewing situations facing Melissa Ortiz and committee members at Southwestern State University share a number of common characteristics. All will necessitate establishing a positive rapport with the other parties and creating an open, supportive communication climate. All will require a rhetorical sensitivity regarding the other parties and a sharing of accurate information. Each of the individual interviews, however, must be carefully planned and the unique situational demands considered. Melissa Ortiz will want to plan news conferences and journalistic/broadcast interviews on a timely basis with reporters' deadlines in mind. She will want to select an appropriate site on campus for photo opportunities and video taping. The negotiation or persuasive interviews with selected alumni, community leaders, and foundations will be largely conducted off campus. These will be more directed interactions designed to secure financial support for the new School of Communication. The Curricular Task Force will want to give serious attention to developing a survey questionnaire and training interviewing assistants to help with the follow-up telephone interviews. The focus groups will be more nondirective and involve the faculty in a free exchange of ideas. This will require an informal atmosphere with the faculty having the greater balance of message exchange. The Search Committee will use a more directive approach when interviewing potential candidates for the position of Dean of the School of Communication. Both committees are engaged in a lengthy interviewing process, which will take six months to a year to complete. The information gathered will have to be collated, interpreted, and evaluated. To be successful, those involved in the many interviews must attend to the anatomical features comprising any interview situation.

Anatomy of an Interview

It is not practical to partition an interview arbitrarily into discreet parts, because an interview requires fluid interaction between the parties. However, for purposes of discussion, we can identify certain common parts of any interview. Regardless of their specific purpose, all interviews have many of the same features—planning, opening, questioning, turn taking, closing, reporting, and evaluating.

Planning

Successful interviewing requires careful planning. Like any other communication event, an interview can be no better than the preparation which precedes it. This includes determining the purpose of the interview, formulating questions that will provide the necessary information needed to make decisions, assessing the interview situation, and considering what information the other party might request. The important point is that you go into the interview with a predetermined plan, even though you might alter it during the course of the interview itself. *Without a plan, you succeed only by luck.*

Opening

The interviewer will want to establish rapport and create a positive, supportive atmosphere. A brief statement or summary of the problem the issues that prompted the interview can be helpful. In the opening, clearly communicate both the general and the specific purposes of the interview, specify how long the interview will take, and provide something that will make the other party want to participate.

Questioning

The ability to use questions effectively is the key to successful interviewing. Several factors need to be taken into account when preparing questions. You need to consider how *broad* they are in scope, how *leading* they are in directing the interviewee toward or away from one or more answers, and how *personal* they are in their potential for creating a supportive or defensive communication climate. There is a great difference between merely asking questions and making questions work for you effectively. The skillful interviewer understands the rationale for selecting certain types of questions over others, knows their functions, and phrases questions that produce useful information. Different kinds of information require different types of questions and questioning techniques.

Turn Taking

Rather than one person doing all of the talking and another doing all of the listening, as might be found in a public speaking situation, the interview requires each participant to take a turn. This turn taking enables the interview to flow, with both parties probing or following up on answers and moving the conversation from one topic to another. There are no rules governing the turn taking, although the interviewer will usually lead the direction of the interview. You need to carefully monitor turn taking and the balance of message exchange.

Closing

The interviewer should find an appropriate way of closing the interview. Generally, it is considered courteous to thank the respondent for participating. The interviewer might summarize the interview, and if some action has been promised or is anticipated, indicate when the action will be taken. In any case, at this point you want to provide information needed to ensure a clear understanding of what has transpired and end on a cordial note.

Reporting

The information gained during the interview needs to be organized, collated, and reported. The ultimate purpose for interviewing is to gather information that can be used for decision making or shared with a larger audience. Reporting the information gained is a vitally important step that determines the usefulness of interviewing as a tool.

Evaluating

The interview "isn't over until it's over." Simply put, following the interview, each party must pursue follow-up and evaluation activities. This evaluative process provides each an opportunity to assess their skills and determine the effectiveness of the interview. This can be helpful when you conduct future interviews.

Interviewing is a particularly important form of communication because it provides the greatest opportunity for effective communication. However, taking advantage of this opportunity requires some special skills and also requires that the involved parties are able to identify exactly what their purposes are.

*   *   *   *   *

Melissa Ortiz, the Curricular Task Force, and the Search Committee must review their respective purposes and examine the issues that will influence and guide their interviews. They will want to prepare agendas, draft questions, and plan the interviews. Melissa Ortiz will want to maintain public enthusiasm through her news conferences. Through negotiated or persuasive interviews, she will want to motivate selected individuals and targeted groups to action. She will also want to anticipate and be prepared to respond to questions posed by reporters during journalistic and broadcast interviews. The Curricular Task Force will give serious attention to planning questions that will define the educational program offered by the new School of Communication. What should be the admission requirements? What about core courses? Major tracks of study? Elective courses? What should be the distinctive mission of the new School of Communication? These interviews will demand active listening and require that care be given to turn taking. The Search Committee will explore the academic/experiential backgrounds of candidates and examine their strengths and weaknesses. They will have to assess the leadership potential of candidates and determine their ability to provide direction for the new School of Communication. The planning and conducting of these interviews will be time consuming and require considerable energy, but the resulting information from effective interviewing is invaluable to decision making, problem solving and change.

To be useful, information must be shared. How should Melissa Ortiz, the Curricular Task Force, and the Search Committee share their information and communicate decisions they made regarding the School of Communication?

Critical Focus

Watson Communications International, Inc. (WCI) is a management consulting and training company headquartered in Longview, Texas, with offices in San Jose, California, and Guam. Its founder and president, Dr. Thomas R. Watson, received his Ph.D. in communication studies from the University of Nebraska and was a college professor in the Texas A&M University System for ten years. Dr. Watson has over twenty years experience in consulting and training. He and his training team bring depth of experience from such fields as communications, education, management, marketing, and publishing.

Dr. Watson's clients include businesses, such as AT&T, Texas Instruments, North American Coal Corporation, El Chico Restaurants, and TRW. He has also consulted for government and business entities internationally, including the Government of Guam, the Bank of Hawaii, the Government of Saipan, Pacific Marshall, Inc., and Pacific International Marianas. Since forming his own firm, he and his team have trained thousands of managers—from first line foremen to chief executive officers—in programs ranging from basic management skills to highly sophisticated programs for senior executives. Watson Communications International, Inc. specializes in team building, quality customer service programs, communications assessment and training, management training, crisis communication, sales communication, public speaking training, and employee motivation. Dr. Watson believes that "when managers and employees become more effective, work as a team, communicate better, become better problem-solvers, focus on and meet customer needs, and when supervisors get more done through others, a company makes money and this is the *bottom line.*"

Dr. Tom Watson is a confident, professional trainer and experienced communicator. His successful company has grown as a result of hard work and the ability to gather and share information through interviewing.

To help you apply your understanding of interviewing, consider the following questions. These questions direct your attention to the potential of interviews and provide a means to initially analyze interviews.

1. How does interviewing differ from other forms of communication?
2. Under what conditions is an interview the most appropriate vehicle for gathering information?
3. What types of interviews are used to gather information? What kind of information is being elicited by each of the types?

4. What environmental or context factors influence the selection of an appropriate style for an interview?

5. How would you evaluate an interview? What questioning techniques were used? Notice particularly the interviewer's probing techniques. How can questioning techniques affect the relationship between the two parties? What techniques of turn taking were used by the interviewer and the interviewee? What participant behaviors, message components, and climate caused the situation to be positive? What impressions do you get of the interviewer and interviewee?

Summary

Interviewing is an interaction between people asking and answering questions in an attempt to solve problems for the mutual benefit of both parties. It is a special form of communication used in a variety of contexts to gain and share information. The different types of interviews frequently used include the selection interview, appraisal interview, discipline interview, counseling interview, exit interview, sales interview, negotiation interview, survey interview, telephone interview, focus group interview, organizational audit, computer-assisted interview, journalistic interview and investigative reporting, broadcast interview, and news conference.

Effective interviewing requires planning. If the planning takes the form of consideration of alternatives, it will be an excellent prelude to the actual interaction. Thus, interviewing requires analyzing each situation and deciding which strategies and techniques are most appropriate. Moreover, interviews are a joint process, and therefore, to be productive, careful attention must be given to creating an open, supportive communication climate. Finally, it becomes evident that linked to these considerations are such features as the opening, questioning, turn taking, closing, reporting, and evaluating. These points will be further amplified in each of the chapters that deal with specific types of interviews, since effective planning needs to take place before every interview.

An interview cannot be reduced to a formula or single "how-to-do-it" recipe. Thorough preparation, developed communication skills, adaptive flexibility, and a willingness to face the risks involved in intimate, person-to-person interaction contribute to interviewing effectiveness and yield the personal, as well as mutual, rewards sought. This chapter introduced you to the importance of interviewing and focused on selected features. Chapter 2 will elaborate on the interviewing process and more specifically examine the communication skills required to be effective.

SHARPENING YOUR FOCUS

1. Compare and contrast communication in the interviewing process with the interpersonal process. Be specific. Include a definition of each.

2. Define and discuss the nature and function of the following types of interviews: (a) selection interview, (b) appraisal interview, (c) counseling interview, (d) discipline interview, (e) exit interview, and (f) negotiation/sales interview.

3. Identify ways that interviewing can be used as a research tool.

4. Differentiate the purpose(s), demands, and challenges of the journalistic interview with the broadcast interview.

5. Compare and contrast *The New York Times, USA Today,* and *The Wall Street Journal* with tabloids and such magazines as *Time, People,* and *Sports Illustrated.* Which are news? Entertainment? Next, compare and contrast NBC's *Today,* CBS's *This Morning,* and ABC's *Good Morning America* with *60 Minutes, 48-Hours,* and *Prime Time Live,* as well as such programs as *Geraldo, Jenny Jones,* and *The Oprah Winfrey Show.* Which are news? Entertainment? How does each use interviewing and treat its interviewing responsibilities?

6. Make a list of different interviewing experiences you have had. Indicate the nature of the interview, the context or environment in which it occurred, the outcome, and whether you communicated as effectively as you would have liked to during the encounter. During these interviews, rate your effectiveness as l, 2, 3, 4, or 5, with 1 representing *extremely ineffective* and 5 representing *extremely effective.* From your perspective, why is it important to develop effective interviewing skills and competencies? Set a goal for yourself, and indicate the extent to which you would like this course to improve your interviewing effectiveness rating.

NOTES

1. Paul Watzlawick, Janet Beavin, and Don Jackson, *Pragmatics of Human Communication* (New York: W. W. Norton, 1967), 54.

2. C. E. Wilson, "The New Generation of Selection Interviews: Structured, Behavior-Based, Valid" (paper presented at the annual meeting of the Speech Communication Association, Chicago, Ill., 1990.

3. A. H. Locher and K. S. Teel, "Performance Appraisal—A Survey of Current Practices," *Personnel Journal* 56 (1977): 245–47.

4. G. P. Latham and K. N. Wexley, *Increasing Productivity Through Performance Appraisal* (Reading, Mass.: Addison-Wesley, 1981).

5. Roger B. Madsen and Barbara Knudsen-Fields, "Productive Progressive Discipline Procedures," *Management Solutions* (May 1987): 18–25.

6. John Quay, "The Art and Science of Effective Interviewing," *Journal of Management Consulting* 2 (1985): 14–17.

7. Wallace V. Schmidt, "Letting Go With Results," *Business Review* (April 1993): 23.

8. Elaine B. Kerr and Starr Roxanne Hiltz, *Computer-Mediated Communication Systems* (New York: Academic Press, 1982), ix.

9. Hugh Sherwood, *The Journalistic Interview* (New York: Harper and Row Publishers, 1972), 19.

10. Shirley Biagi, *Interviews That Work: A Practical Guide for Journalists* (Belmont, Calif.: Wadsworth Publishing, 1986), 2.

11. Felix M. Lopez, *Personnel Interviewing* (New York: McGraw-Hill, 1975), 1.

12. John M. Wieman, "An Explication and Test of a Model of Communicative Competence," *Human Communication Research* 3 (1977): 211.

13. John Stewart and Gary D'Angelo, *Together: Communicating Interpersonally* (Reading, Mass.: Addison–Wesley, 1975), 191.

14. Roderick Hart and Don M. Burks, "Rhetorical Sensitivity and Social Interaction," *Communication Monographs,* 39, (1972), 75–91. Used by permission of the National Communication Association.

15. Excerpts from *Leadership and Interpersonal Behavior* by Luigi Petrullo and Bernard M. Bass, copyright © 1961 by Holt, Rinehart and Winston and renewed 1989 by Luigi Petrullo and Bernard M. Bass, reprinted by permission of the publisher.

CHAPTER

2   The Interview Process

Every interview has a basic framework. The exact structure will depend upon the situation, the type of interview, and the planning. Planning means visualizing possible interview situations, deciding which is the most desirable, and then determining how to move toward that situation and away from paths leading to less desirable situations. No time is more crucial to the success of an interview than that spent on the planning process.

Chapter 2 explores the strategies and techniques pertaining to the interview process. Structuring interviews and the asking of questions are examined in relation to the purpose and agenda for conducting interviews. This chapter is designed to accomplish three objectives:

1. *Awareness.* You will learn strategies and approaches that will elicit the maximum amount of information.

2. *Assessment.* You will be able to identify different types of listening and determine the purposes and intents for which you choose to listen to others.

3. *Application.* You will be able to control and focus the flow of communication during an interview.

*   *   *   *   *

Bill Bradley's Interviewing Dilemma

Following his campus interviews with UniCon, Inc., a large pharmaceutical company, Bill Bradley was pleased to be invited to the corporate headquarters to interview for jobs in two departments. UniCon was known to select only those college graduates who were talented and who had potential. Bill, with a major in communication and a minor in business, was to interview in marketing and human resources. He was given the names of two contacts at UniCon and told to establish his schedule by telephone prior to arriving in Baltimore.

Bill was surprised when he talked with Connie Corbet, the director of marketing. She encouraged him to come to Baltimore for an interview but suggested that he apply only for the marketing position. She considered the human resources position a dead-end job and suggested that the director of human resources, Ed Miller, was a difficult individual. Connie said that once an employee went into human resources there were no other opportunities in the company. Because he did not know how to react to Connie's comments, Bill chose not to respond. Connie did indicate that she was impressed with Bill's resume and looked forward to meeting him.

Ed Miller seemed nothing but professional during Bill's telephone conversation with him. Ed indicated that he wanted someone who was committed to human resources and would not immediately use the job as a stepping stone to other opportunities. He, too, was impressed with Bill's resume. Bill chose to keep both appointments.

The interview in marketing came first. Connie Corbet was enthusiastic when meeting Bill and eagerly provided information about working at UniCon describing the many opportunities in marketing. She concluded her introductory remarks by asking, "Wouldn't you agree that marketing contributes most to the bottom line of any organization?" Bill nodded his head and Connie proceeded to ask him some specific questions about marketing courses taken and his business experience. She was particularly interested in his hobbies and outside activities, and what he did to relax. When Bill inquired about the specific type of position he might fill, Connie was evasive and said she would have to design one to best utilize his talents. At the conclusion of the interview, Connie asked, "Well, what do you think? Wouldn't you like to work in marketing?" She then asked if he was scheduled to meet with Ed Miller. Connie looked displeased when Bill said yes.

Bill left the interview feeling pleased yet uncertain regarding the exact nature of the job and his ability to work with Connie. She was pleasant enough, but the job seemed vague, and he hadn't had an opportunity to ask questions about their working relationship.

Bill's next interview was with Ed Miller. The interview was very different given the discussion with Connie. Ed had specific job requirements, and he "grilled" Bill about the match between his background and the position in human resources. Ed began the interview by asking Bill, "What are you looking for in a job?" After exploring Bill's general career interests, the questions began to focus on the particular vacancy. Bill was presented with several hypothetical situations and asked to respond. His answers were further probed, with Ed asking for more details. Bill answered most of the questions with ease and felt he knew exactly what would be expected of him in the human resources position, Ed closed the interview by asking Bill if he had any questions concerning UniCon and/or the human resources department. When he left, Ed said he hoped to make a final decision regarding the position soon.

Bill felt exhausted but confident with how the interview had progressed. He could not determine from the interview why Connie was so negative about the human resources job or Ed Miller. Bill could not find fault with the position but was still worried based on Connie's warnings. He could not discount the fact that Connie might be trying to help him avoid a big mistake.

Bill believed he would receive offers from both Connie and Ed. He was confused about how to make an informed decision. Bill considered what he should do next.

Discussion Questions

1. How would you describe the interviewing dilemma facing Bill Bradley?
2. Are the two interviews appropriately structured given the purpose and intent of the interview? Why? Why not?
3. What different questioning techniques do Connie Corbet and Ed Miller employ during their respective interviews? Are they equally effective?
4. Do the two interviewers effectively control the interview? What noticeable problems and barriers can be detected? Are the parties in these two interviews engaged in active listening?
5. How would you advise Bill?

Purpose and Agenda

Interviews are purposeful, focusing on certain kinds of information. Interviews differ from other conversations because the participants have a specific reason for taking part. Although it may seem obvious that determining a purpose and an agenda benefits interviews, deciding on the purpose and agenda is often the part of the planning process to which the least attention is paid. As a result, both the interviewer and the interviewee may experience frustration and encounter problems in the interview itself as a result of discovering certain purposes for the interview that may not have been apparent when it was planned.

The overriding purpose of any interview is the acquisition of information. We interview because (1) as the interviewer, we may obtain information that is otherwise unavailable, (2) as the interviewee, we have an opportunity to send a message in a way that might otherwise be impossible, and (3) the typical face-to-face setting allows ways of assessing the other person or the information being communicated that would not be available otherwise.

The interview purpose and agenda, however, need to be more specifically identified. Typically, one's purpose is stated in terms of the reasons for the interview—selection interview, appraisal interview, discipline interview, counseling interview, exit interview, journalistic interview, broadcast interview, or the many types of research interviews. Still, there can be many specific purposes associated with each of these interview types that need to be carefully determined. Certainly, what one wants in terms of the content and the relationship with the other person must be considered. Here some common goals for interviewers include (1) establishing rapport and credibility with the interviewee, (2) establishing a climate in which information will be disclosed freely, and (3) determining what is appropriate information. The purpose and agenda need to be both generally and specifically identified.

The key to determining the purpose and agenda lies in precisely phrasing the purpose/goal statements. To do so requires not just the ability to write clean, clear sentences but to make them reflect the desired substance of the interview. The results of any interview will ultimately be tested by how well it achieves the purpose and objectives. Here are some guidelines to follow:

1. Develop a brief statement that tells why this interview is being conducted.
2. Make a list of the components of information required.
3. Specifically identify how the information will be used.
4. Prepare a list of goals or objectives, taking all of these factors into account.
5. Determine what data is needed from interviewees in order to achieve each goal or objective.
6. Draft questions that, when answered, will provide the necessary information to satisfy the purpose and goals.

The lack of a clear purpose and specific agenda can turn an interview into a jumbled nonconversation that confuses both parties.

*   *   *   *   *

Bill Bradley was anxious to find a challenging job with limitless opportunities. He was understandably excited about the two prospects offered by UniCon Inc., a prestigious pharmaceutical firm. Connie Corbet, director of marketing, and Ed Miller, director of human resources, each had a position to fill. Consequently, the dilemma that confronted Bill was determining which position provided the greatest career potential. This dilemma was further compounded by Connie Corbet's prejudicial comments and attitude regarding human resources and Ed Miller. Moreover, the two interviews failed to completely quell Bill's doubts. Connie Corbet, while enthusiastic, was unclear regarding the specific position in marketing, and the interview revealed little about how Bill would fit into the department. Ed Miller, on the other hand,

clearly outlined the human resources position and followed an interview agenda that rigorously assessed Bill's capabilities. While Bill was
impressed with Ed's professional demeanor, he remained cautiously
nervous given the importance of this decision. Clearly, Connie Corbet
needed to better define her purpose and agenda. Ed Miller demonstrated a keen understanding of the situation and a sensitivity to Bill's
concerns. Still, Bill feared making a mistake.

Structuring the Interview

Not only must there be a clear purpose, but there must also be a suitable approach
to communicate it to the other party. The interview must be carefully structured.
Communication researchers have identified certain basic interview approaches or
structural frameworks—funnel, inverted funnel, quintamensional design, tunnel,
chain-link, and freeform.[1] The exact structure selected will depend on the particular situation and the type of interview. The best interviews often combine more
than one interview approach.

Funnel Sequence

The **funnel sequence** employs a questioning approach that moves from the
general to the specific. It begins with a broad, open-ended question at the top
of the funnel, with each subsequent question becoming more closed and restrictive to the available responses. This sequence of questioning permits the
interviewer to discover the interviewee's frame of reference, encourages the
interviewee to communicate opinions, and avoids possible conditioning or
biasing of responses. An example of the funnel sequence is seen in the following exchange:

MARY: If you could have an ideal job, what would it be like?

JOHN: I enjoy working with people, so I would want a people-oriented position which is personally challenging and permits room for growth and
development. It would also allow me to contribute to problem solving
and reward individual and collaborative accomplishments.

MARY: Well, that's fine. Why are you interested in this job?

JOHN: I'm interested in this job because I want to learn and become an ad
executive. This is a medium-sized agency where I think I'll be exposed to
a wider range of responsibilities than I would at a larger agency. Considering the accounts you have, I think I'd learn a great deal here and eventually be able to take on more challenging assignments.

MARY: Given our varied accounts, what educational/work experience
helps qualify you for this position?

JOHN: My college degree in advertising and marketing gave me the training to handle the problems and decisions you'd expect of me. An internship during my senior year was particularly helpful in exposing me to the real-world responsibilities of such a position. Also, I possess excellent office skills for the tremendous amount of routine paperwork I know goes with this kind of position.

MARY: Why should I hire you over other candidates?

The funnel sequence is effective in a variety of interview settings. Since open questions are easier to answer, pose less threat to interviewees, and get interviewees talking, it is a particularly good way to begin an interview and sensitizes the questioner to the need for follow-up probes.

Inverted Funnel Sequence

The **inverted funnel sequence** follows an inductive thinking process, beginning with a specific question and proceeding to more open-ended, general questions. The purpose of an inverted funnel approach is to reach an opinion, based on a foundation of gradual expansion from a specific incident or fact. It forces the interviewee to think through specific attitudes or facts before articulating a general reaction or a conclusion. An example of the inverted funnel sequence is seen in the following exchange:

BETH: I want to verify that this appraisal covers the period from April 1 to March 31.

BRITT: Yes, that's correct. My last appraisal was a year ago.

BETH: Have you completed the refresher course you were taking to qualify for your real estate broker's license?

BRITT: Yes. It kept me up at nights studying, but I've finished it and am scheduled to take the real estate broker's exam next week. I'm confident that I'll do well.

BETH: I'm sure you will. What additional courses do you have to take before receiving your bachelor's degree?

BRITT: I'm enrolled to take three evening courses this fall which will complete my degree requirements in business. However, the commencement ceremonies won't take place until May. At least I'll be finished. The company's tuition reimbursement policy has sure been helpful.

BETH: Congratulations! We like to encourage the development of our employees. What self-development activities do you plan to engage in during the upcoming year?

BRITT: I would like to attend several seminars and perhaps a couple of workshops. They could be valuable in helping me perform my current job and broaden my area of expertise.

BETH: Speaking of performance, how would you evaluate your overall performance over the last twelve months?

BRITT: I've been personally pleased. The immediate, short-term goals we agreed upon last year have been accomplished, and I'm making steady progress on the longer range goals. As I gain experience, I begin to see my career taking shape.

BETH: What do you think of your career progress to date? How can I help you?

The inverted sequence is useful when you need to motivate interviewees to respond. Respondents may be shy or reluctant to share opinions and attitudes or feel they do not know the answers to questions. Beginning with a narrow topic and broadening to a wider subject can prompt general reactions and plans.

Quintamensional Design Sequence

The **quintamensional design sequence** was developed by George Gallup in 1947 to probe the intensity of attitudes or opinions.[2] This approach is built, as the name suggests, on five questions that proceed from an interviewer's awareness of an issue to attitudes uninfluenced by the interviewer, specific attitudes, reasons for those attitudes, and intensity of attitude. For example:

1. *Awareness.* What do you think about our employee retraining program?
2. *Uninfluenced attitudes.* Which type of retraining is likely to be most effective?
3. *Specific attitude.* Do you approve of the money spent on the retraining program?
4. *Reason why.* For what reason?
5. *Intensity of attitude.* On a scale of one to five, how strongly do you feel about this issue—very strongly, strongly, moderately interested, somewhat interested, not concerned at all?

The quintamensional design is similar to the funnel sequence, differing in that it has limited objectives. The last question in the sequence is the determinant, since the objective is to produce quantifiable data. It is particularly useful for surveying employee attitudes or polling public opinion.

Tunnel Sequence

The **tunnel sequence** uses a series of similar questions, either all open or all closed, to quantitatively solicit immediate reactions or attitudes toward people, places, incidents, or issues. The questions always involve a "forced choice," which means that the respondent is given a finite number of possible responses and must select the one that is most satisfactory. Consequently, the tunnel sequence allows for little probing for in-depth information and often consists of a series of bipolar, either/or, agree/disagree, approve/disapprove questions. An example of the tunnel sequence is seen in the following exchange:

HOWARD: Recently, were rotary bars being attached incorrectly at your assembly station?

GRIF: Yes, but I was away from the station at the time—on break.

HOWARD: But, weren't both you and Don away from the station taking a break together?

GRIF: We were, but Don wasn't scheduled for a break at that time and . . .

HOWARD: Still, did you disregard the quality control supervisor's request to return to your station?

GRIF: I did because . . .

HOWARD: Do you understand why I have to write you up for this infraction? Do you agree with this disciplinary report? Will you please sign it.

Besides getting an interpretation of an incident or quick index of someone's attitude toward a particular subject, the tunnel sequence can be useful in psychological profiling. A long series of forced-choice questions containing several reworded questions on the same issue, to check consistency of response, can reveal personality types.

Chain-Link Sequence

The **chain-link sequence** provides a framework that encourages reflective probing and results in more depth across a broader range of responses. This approach begins with an open-ended question followed by several probes that lead to a closed question calling for a specific response. The sequence ends with a mirror or summary question, which ensures accurate understanding by the interviewer and allows the interviewee an opportunity to clarify, confirm, or modify the information. Following the mirror question, a new chain-link sequence is begun with an open question. An example of the chain-link sequence is seen in the following exchange:

STACEY: Pat, why have you decided to leave Faraday Manufacturing?

PAT: Well, my new position at Bannister pays better and is a more challenging position. It offers greater responsibility and more room for personal development—growth.

STACEY: I see. Go on. What about your position here at Faraday?

PAT: Well, it seems to be a dead end. You know, nowhere to go I mean, I like it and all, but I have a career to think about.

STACEY: Why do you feel that way? What do you mean by "dead end"?

PAT: Well, it's the same routine over and over—never anything new. I'm rarely included in decision making, and there doesn't seem to be anywhere to go.

STACEY: Does your supervisor know about this? Did you ever communicate these concerns to your supervisor?

PAT: Yes, sort of. I went to him and asked to be given different kinds of assignments and to be included in more of the decision making. He seemed to care about me, and I thought I could talk to him. He smiled and said he would look into it but nothing happened. I went back again several times, but it was always the same old story—big smile and no change. So, I gave up—but I'm not angry at him.

STACEY: Okay Pat, let me see if I got this straight. What you're saying is you feel underutilized and left out of the loop, and your supervisor hasn't been able to address these concerns? Have I got it right?

The chain-link sequence invariably takes more time and places fewer constraints on the direction of the interview. It is less rigidly structured and produces more dialogue in the interview situation.

Freeform Sequence

The **freeform sequence** is loosely structured and open-ended; however, it is not without direction. A freeform approach is largely controlled by the interviewee and invites open-ended responses. The objective of the interviewer is to test the interviewee's intellect, to understand the interviewee's reasoning, or to judge the intensity of the interviewee's opinions. An example of the freeform sequence is seen in the following exchange:

CHARLENE: We're currently having personnel problems here at Baystate Rubber, Dave, and we would appreciate your helping us locate the source of these problems. What did you think of Baystate when you first came here?

DAVE: I had heard a lot about Baystate and Baystate quality when I first came here three years ago. But, I don't know what that means now. This is just a job to me.

CHARLENE: Why is that, Dave? What has changed?

DAVE: My supervisor only wants me at my machine at 7:15 A.M. He rarely says anything to me unless I goof up. I just sit here all day long and operate this machine. I don't think the president of the company even knows my name.

CHARLENE: Uh-huh. Tell me more . . .

DAVE: I got a kid at home who is five years old. I call in sick every once in a while to take my kid fishing at the beach. He plays in the sand and I fish. I love it. No company can make me give that up.

CHARLENE: Why do you feel this way? Explain further . . .

The freeform sequence is a valuable approach when you have unlimited time to do a profile or counsel an employee. Follow-up questions are essential, and the alert freeform interviewer must avoid digression while working to maintain the interviewee's interest and cultivating the interviewee's confidence.

An interview is a journey of discovery. A clear purpose and structure ensures that interviewer and interviewee will together reach their destination. An unstructured interview is not a guide at all, resulting in the parties taking multiple detours down one side road or another. While they may be more interesting than the highway, the parties can easily become lost and confused—unable to reach their original destination.

*   *   *   *   *

Connie Corbet approached her interview with Bill as though it were a monologue intended to persuade him to accept the marketing position at UniCon. Her introductory remarks describing UniCon and the marketing department did little to solicit necessary information from Bill. The remaining questions focused on Bill's academic preparation and business experience, but they did not seriously assess his attitudes, skills, and abilities. The general discussion regarding hobbies and pastimes might have been interesting, but yielded little job-related information. While essentially unstructured, this interview attempted to be freeform in approach. However, a freeform approach is not without direction and requires the careful use of follow-up questions. Connie wandered and digressed and failed to effectively motivate Bill and gain his confidence. Little wonder why Bill left the interview pleased but uncertain.

Ed Miller clearly employed a funnel approach, moving from general career-related questions to specific job-related questions. While it is difficult to determine, he may also have used a chain-link sequence when "grilling" Bill about his knowledge, skills, and abilities and probing Bill's answers for more details. Ed's purposefully structured interview contributed to his professional demeanor and, though exhausting, left Bill with a clear understanding of the position and its demands. Certainly, the interview with Ed Miller was more informative and satisfying, but Connie Corbet's negative comments still left Bill with lingering doubts. There is a perfectly good rationale for this reaction, since we are more influenced by unfavorable than favorable information.

Questions and Questioning Techniques

Questions are the interviewer's primary tool in gathering information. The ability to use questions effectively is the key to successful interviewing. There is a great difference between merely asking questions and making questions work for you effectively. Anyone can ask questions; it is a relatively easy activity. The skillful interviewer understands the rationale for selecting certain types of questions over others, knows their functions, and is able to phrase questions that produce useful results. Different kinds of information require different types of questions and questioning techniques.

Several factors need to be taken into account when preparing questions. Interviewers need to consider how *broad* they are in scope, how *leading* they are in directing the interviewee toward or away from one or more answers, and how *personal* they are in their potential for creating a supportive or defensive communication climate. We shall weigh each of these considerations when discussing types of questions and their functions. The following categories represent general, basic, recurring types of questions which might comprise an interview agenda and could be asked. It should only be used as a *guide* for interviewing.[3]

Open Questions

Open questions ask for broad or general information and allow the interviewee considerable freedom to respond in an appropriate way. They are often used to obtain information concerning feelings, goals, and perspectives. Answers to open questions can reveal interviewee uncertainty, intensity of feelings, frames of reference, prejudices, or stereotypes. Open questions generally elicit longer responses than other types of questions because they communicate interest in the interviewee and appear to be nonthreatening. This can result in receiving a lot of unnecessary but perhaps interesting information. However, not all people respond to open questions in a comfortable way. If a participant has some conflict or emotional involvement with a particular subject area or is generally suspicious of the interviewer or the purpose of the question, the response will be more defensive and less extensive. Then, greater specificity and increased probing for information will be required.

Closed Questions

Closed questions are very specific and restrictive in nature. They intentionally limit the range of responses available to the interviewee. Closed questions are useful in gaining a large amount of specific information in a relatively short period of time. Answers to closed questions are brief and succinct and can be easily coded, tabulated, and analyzed. There is no doubt that closed questions are more efficient than open questions; however, they *do not* reveal *why* an interviewee has a particular attitude. Consequently, such questioning requires additional probing by the interviewer.

Probing Questions

Probing questions may be open or closed and grow out of a need for more follow-up information, a feeling on the part of the interviewer that the answer received from the initial question is superficial, vague, or inaccurate and not the full or correct response needed. Probes are of two types: directive and nondirective. **Directive probes** are used to focus answers on specific items of information. **Nondirective probes** are used to keep interviewees talking without biasing their responses or interrupting their line of thought. Basic directive probes include elaboration, clarification, repetition, and confrontation, while nondirective varieties include mirror statements, neutral phrases, and silence.

Elaboration is an assertive probe that asks the interviewee to extend, to amplify, or to provide additional details. Some examples are "Could you go into that more?" "What happened then?" "How did you feel about that?"

Clarification is used to obtain a further explanation when words or phrases used to answer a question are unclear. It may also be used to gain a better understanding of the events being described. Some examples are "What do you mean when you use the term *progressive?* "Could you provide examples of what you mean by 'challenging opportunities'?" "How did the event described produce the ensuing conflict?"

Repetition is used when an interviewee doesn't hear or understand a question or when the interviewee tries to evade a question. The original question is repeated as exactly asked or a reasonable facsimile is presented.

(avoid) **Confrontation** probes call attention to an apparent inconsistency, a misrepresentation, or a contradiction among items of information in the answers. The interviewer points out these errors not to trap the interviewee but to provide an opportunity to clarify the situation or misunderstandings. Many interviewers find it difficult to use this type of probe because of a desire to avoid the stress of conflict and a potentially unpleasant situation. However, confrontation need not be emotionally wrecking and may be a useful and constructive questioning technique.

Mirror statements, also called reflective statements or summary statements, repeat to the interviewee an answer or information in order to indicate to what degree their responses have been accurately understood. They should clearly be perceived as probes and invite further clarification or elaboration as needed. Some examples are "In other words, you're saying . . ." "Okay, let me see if I understand . . ." "You think, then, that you can . . ."

Neutral phrases demonstrate listening, indicate interest, and encourage the other person to continue talking. Typical examples include "Oh," "Hmmm," "I see," "Go on," "Un huh," "Wow!" "And then?" and other nonverbal assents. These phrases are generally a natural part of the conversation and are frequently uttered while the interviewee is talking.

Silence can be an extremely powerful probe in an interview, permitting interviewees time for reflection and thinking while prompting them to continue talking. Research indicates that there is a positive correlation between the amount of silence used by the interviewer and the respondent's general level of spontaneity.[4] Most interviewers do not use silence effectively because they become too anxious to participate in the interview, feeling that nothing is happening unless someone is talking. Skilled interviewers, on the other hand, have learned to use silence deliberately and productively. The use of silent probes distinguishes the novice from the skilled interviewer.

In sum, probes are questions that are either open or closed and may be assertive and direct or neutral and indirect—even silent. Effective probes are suited to the situation and allow the interviewer to delve deeper into areas while maintaining control of the interview.

Hypothetical Questions

Hypothetical questions present interviewees with a set of circumstances which require them to make selective choices. They are designed to see how a person might respond in a given low- to high-pressure situation. Hypothetical questions are particularly useful, because the answers are less abstract, and they reveal the closest thing to actual personal behavior that can be observed in an interview. To assess someone's style for handling conflict, a confrontational situation might be presented, or to discover their supervisory orientation, a group of new, inexperienced employees might be described. The use of such questions can both enrich the information obtained and enhance the interview experience.

Leading Questions

Leading questions suggest explicitly or implicitly the expected or desired answer and make it difficult for the interviewee to present his or her own ideas. Robert Kahn and Charles Cannell note that the leading question "makes it easier or more tempting for the respondent to give one answer than another."[5] The leading question telegraphs its expected answer. Interviewers will use such questions to check for assertiveness, to prod reluctant interviewees, to see how respondents cope with stress, or to provoke unguarded replies. When used judiciously and with care, leading questions can be effective tools but become a serious problem when the interviewer fails to realize that he or she is, in fact, leading the interviewee to potentially distort responses.

Loaded Questions

Loaded questions likewise provide strong direction toward a particular answer but differ from leading questions in that they use emotionally charged language and employ higher degrees of entrapment. They are sometimes used by interviewers to check for defensiveness. When interviewers use loaded questions, they are exercising an extraordinary kind of control. Loaded questions should only be used by skillful interviewers with extreme caution, since they can easily create a dysfunctional communication climate, which will have a negative impact upon both parties in the interviewing situation.

The question is the tool with which interviewers, like archaeologists in search of hidden treasures, remove layers of material in order to arrive at the information they seek. Different types of questions perform different functions, and when carefully employed, they significantly influence the validity and reliability of any interview. Validity refers to the extent to which you are observing, receiving, or measuring what you think you are observing or measuring. Are you getting the information you need or want? Reliability is the extent to which you would get the same results if you or another interviewer were to conduct a similar interview with the same individual. Validity and reliability are important criteria when judging the effectiveness of any particular interview. In sum, question asking is an art, one which requires skill, practice, and attention to how people respond.

* * * * *

Connie Corbet primarily used closed questions to assess Bill's academic preparation and business experience. She further used leading and loaded questions that reflected her personal biases. Naturally, Bill was guarded in his responses, which were abbreviated and brief. Since Connie failed to probe his answers for further detail, Bill did not voluntarily offer clarification and elaboration. While Bill left the interview pleased, he experienced the feeling of having only been a passive participant.

Ed Miller used a variety of questions including open questions, closed questions, probing questions, and hypothetical questions. Bill was challenged to relate his knowledge, skills, and abilities to the specific human resources position described. He was forced to carefully examine his background and experience for details and clearly identify his capabilities. While demanding, Bill left the interview with confidence and an understanding of the position. Unlike the ambiguity and uncertainty accompanying his interview with Connie Corbet, Bill's interview with Ed Miller articulated their working relationship and outlined the responsibilities of the job. Still, Bill intuitively experienced anxiety due to the previously unquestioned negative intimations.

Conducting the Interview

Conducting the interview means adapting the various forms of communication to those of the other party and clearly indicating the purpose, agenda, and intent of the interview. Coordination skills and adaptive skills are critical to conducting an interview. **Coordination skills** are the ability to regulate one's behavior so that it fits the behavior of the other party. In so doing, rapport is established, and the flow of conversation becomes smooth and natural. Coordination skills are important throughout the interview, and the ability to pay close attention to the other party is often a sign of coordinated behavior. **Adaptive skills** are the ability to adjust messages so that they take into account those of the other party. These skills are most important when moving from prepared questions to follow-up questions or probes, and they help respondents decide how to phrase their responses so that they provide the needed information. Coordination skills and adaptive skills are intertwined and contribute to controlling the interview, overcoming problems and barriers, and listening analytically.

Controlling the Interview

In nearly all interviewing situations, the locus of control rests with the interviewer. It is part of the interviewer's role, and one of the worst criticisms that can be leveled against an interviewer is that he or she lost control. However, one of the hardest parts of conducting an interview is to decide how much one should control the content of the discussion. This is a difficult task for two reasons. First, different situations will require different amounts of control. Interviews in cooperative situations will require less control than those in situations that tend to produce conflict or confrontation. Second, our habitual ways of controlling a conversation may not work well in some interviewing situations. For most people, controlling means doing most of the talking, and efforts to exercise control may reduce opportunities for the interviewee to provide information.

Although choosing a level of control is a difficult task, the interviewer must select an appropriate balance given the nature of the situation and the type of interview. The purpose and agenda of the interview can help determine the amount of control, and it can be established by setting a positive climate, by probing, and by motivating the interviewee to respond. The greatest source of control, however, is self-control. Effective interviewers are confident, well-disciplined, and analytical enough to exercise options in ways that will accomplish their purposes.

When the interviewer exercises too little or too much control, responsibility for managing the interview shifts to the interviewee. This requires the interviewee to assertively contribute to directing the interview. The interviewee will want to focus on the mutually relevant issues and provide the needed information. Interviewees, likewise, should have a purpose and agenda that they will want to actively pursue.

Overcoming Problems and Barriers

Often, interviews progress smoothly and problems do not occur. This is particularly true when both parties have clearly identified their purpose(s) and are prepared for the interview. However, at other times, problems may arise and one may be confounded because things happen that were not anticipated. Since the kinds of problems encountered in an interview will vary among different kinds of interviews, we will deal with them in each discussion of a particular kind of interview. However, there are some barriers and inhibitors that cut across all kinds of interviews, and these can be treated profitably here. These problems can be grouped in terms of those that stem from the interviewer and those that stem from the interviewee.

Problems stemming from the interviewer include (1) errors in asking questions, (2) not probing analytically and thoroughly, (3) failure to recognize own biases/prejudices, (4) taking notes ineffectively, and (5) failure to listen.

Errors in Asking Questions.   The previous guidelines should be of value in framing good questions. Nevertheless, certain problems can occur when asking questions. Some common questioning pitfalls experienced by novice interviewers are asking (1) double-barreled questions, (2) two-in-one questions, and (3) bipolar questions. The double-barreled question occurs when the interviewer asks two or more questions before the interviewee has had a chance to answer the first question. For example, asking "What do you know about our company, and why do you want to work for us? What can you bring to this position?" confuses the interviewee who does not know where to go with a single answer. Occasionally, the interviewee will see the problem and ask, "Which of these questions do you want me to answer first?" Taken separately, there is nothing wrong with any of the three questions, but it is not wise to ask the three together.

Occasionally, an interviewer will connect two things in one question so that it appears to be one question when it is actually two. For example, asking "How can we increase job satisfaction so our employees will be more productive?" blends two questions that might well be handled separately. The interviewer in this case is making the unwarranted assumption that there is a relationship between worker satisfaction and productivity. While many may personally accept such a connection, it could be misleading to an interviewee.

Finally, bipolar questions limit the interviewee to one of two choices when in actuality more than two choices are available. For example, asking "Do you agree or disagree with the proposed program to clean up the Everglades?" may prompt a general reaction but oversimplifies the issue and neglects to consider the wide range of possible responses. Certainly, there are occasions when closed questions are entirely appropriate, but one must be careful when using polarized alternatives. A good rule to keep in mind is to give interviewees as many options as possible.

To avoid these errors, the interviewer should keep questions as clear as possible and be sensitive to the understanding demonstrated by the interviewee. An interviewer ought to practice confining questions to fifteen or twenty words and depend on follow-up questions if the answer does not yield the appropriate information.

Not Probing Analytically and Thoroughly.   Many inexperienced interviewers think the proper approach to interviewing calls for asking a set of questions and securing some kind of answer to each one. They tend to state agenda topics and then, with no further comment or follow-up questions, simply sit back deadpan and take notes on what is said, like a stenographer. When the monologue has ended, they ask another question, which introduces another topic, and the monologue begins anew. By contrast, effective interviewers know that the best questions in any interview are the ones they didn't know they were going to ask. The answer to question one leads to subsequent probing questions until they arrive at the heart of the topic. They analyze carefully the answers received and assertively pursue needed information, testing for inconsistencies. Probing is an important skill because most answers, particularly to open questions, are inadequate or deficient in some way. They simply do not cover exactly what the interviewer wants to know in exactly the right amount of detail. Remember, the interview is a dialogue—probe and explore answers.

Failure to Recognize Own Biases/Prejudices.   Individual biases and prejudices certainly shape how people react to messages and how people measure information and other people. They stem from fixed attitudes, mental sets for perceiving the world, expectations, motivations, reactions to certain language, or certain patterns of making inferences. Consequently, it is important for an interviewer to *know* himself or herself, otherwise individual likes and dislikes may unduly influence the information received. Ultimately, the analysis of information is jeopardized and the interview rendered less valid and reliable. Effective interviewers guard against personal biases and prejudices by exploring issues from various angles and inviting other points of view. They *really* listen.

Taking Notes Ineffectively. Taking notes during an interview can pose a major problem, since identifying and recording major points is not easy in informal conversations where people just talk. Often, however, the interviewer and/or the respondent will want some sort of record of what is said. Some interviewers like to use portable tape recorders so that they can listen again to the session to refresh their memories. Other interviewers find that the presence of a recorder inhibits some respondents and the conversational tone of the interview, so they take notes on the respondent's answers. Still other interviewers find that taking notes interferes with the flow of the interview, and so they attempt to reconstruct the questions and the responses immediately after the interview, either by talking into a tape recorder or taking notes. How to record and how much to record depend mostly on the interview's purpose, but they also depend to some degree on the interviewer's communication skill. If the interview is expected to produce answers that will be quoted, then those answers should be recorded precisely, either by tape or in writing, and be checked with the respondent to see whether the quotation accurately reflects his or her views. If accurate quotation is not an issue in the interview, it is probably better to record it by taking a few notes or by reconstructing the interview's content immediately afterwards. In any case, the interviewer wants to put the respondent at ease and should always secure permission to record answers. Consequently, backup procedures should be considered if the respondent is uncomfortable with the method for recording proposed by the interviewer. The best advice on note taking is to select the means best suited to your objectives, the situation, the interviewee, and the interview schedule.

Failure to Listen. People are not insensitive or unperceptive. They quickly perceive the level of interest displayed by an interviewer, and when they perceive a lack of interest, they sometimes turn to short, terse answers to avoid the pain of talking to anesthetized ears. Listening is critical to effective interviewing. A listening interviewer is an active participant who offers encouragement and direction and analyzes responses. The problem of listening cannot be dealt with in a single paragraph and is further explored later in this chapter.

Problems stemming from the interviewee include (1) inadequate responses, (2) nervousness and timidity, and (3) defensiveness.

Inadequate Responses. A major problem confronting the interviewee is giving an inadequate response to a question. A response may be inadequate in a number of different ways. Some interviewees choose not to answer a question; they remain silent, and there may be no response. At other times, the response may be incomplete, or an answer may be irrelevant to the question. Some responses are so poorly organized that they are difficult to follow. Sometimes, inaccurate information is given. Interviewers should continue to probe answers until satisfactory responses are received. Inadequate responses or deficient answers are often due to a lack of knowledge or faulty memory or may result from confusion about what the interviewer wants. Careful planning, preparation, and asking for clarification of questions can help remedy this problem.

Nervousness and Timidity.   Nervousness is the most common problem interviewees experience. Most people are inherently uncomfortable in an interview situation because it frequently takes place in strange surroundings, and one is always somewhat uncertain about what questions might be asked. Shy, timid individuals will be more ill at ease and find it difficult to respond easily during an interview. Certainly, the interviewer can help alleviate nervousness by building rapport, arranging an informal setting, and having a friendly manner. Additionally, by choosing to learn about the interviewing process and participating in that process, interviewees can build their self-confidence. This, too, can help curb one's anxiety or nervousness. Remember, however, experiencing some anxiety can sharpen awareness and actually be productive to the interview.

Defensiveness.   Defensiveness is characteristic of many interviewees. They may be uncertain as to what the interviewer wants or what is the best way to answer questions and still protect their self-image. It occurs most often when the interviewer's purpose(s) and those of the interviewee are not entirely consistent. If both parties assume a mutual responsibility for creating a supportive communication climate, this problem can be significantly diminished. This requires a candid give-and-take, an openness to different points of view, and a willingness to get complete information.

Listening Analytically

Listening is one of our most often engaged in activities, yet research suggests that most of us are poor listeners. We misunderstand others and are misunderstood in return. We become bored and feign attention while our minds wander. We challenge, interrupt, and dismiss the ideas of others without attending to them. We engage in a battle of talking. Consequently, we hear but don't listen. Tom Peters notes that "today's effective leader must become a compulsive listener."[6]

Listening is a complex process. When we truly listen we combine what is coming into our brains from our ears with all of our relevant past experiences, so far as we can recall them. Sounds do not of and by themselves have meaning. The meaning is something that we do when our auditory nerves are stimulated by vibrations in the air about us. Without listening there is no speaking; listening and speaking are as closely related as the outside and inside of a cup. The speaker and the listener mutually share the responsibility and are mutually dependent upon each other for the results of every attempted act of communication. Only when genuine cooperation is achieved is communication really effective. Stuart Chase keenly observes that "Listening is the other half of talking. If people stop listening, it is useless to talk—a point not always appreciated by talkers."[7] Communication is a two-way, reciprocal process, and while one party is more obviously active than the other, this should not lead us to conclude that listening is a passive role. The good listener is creatively active.

Listening is hard work; it requires effort as well as desire. Initially, listening involves the physical process of receiving aural and/or visual stimuli (words, voice cues, nonlinguistic sounds, nonverbal cues). At any moment, numerous stimuli in the immediate environment are vying for attention; thus, it is necessary to engage in a process of selection. Messages are then perceived, registered on the sense receptors, and instantaneously transmitted to the brain through a complex biochemical process and decoded. This cognitive structuring process organizes the message and assigns a meaning to it. The cognitive processes involved in listening are maximized or minimized to the extent of one's vocabulary, language facility, language usage, knowledge, personal experiences, and flexibility. Thus far, listening has been discussed in terms of receiving, attending to, and assigning meaning to a message. Listening is also greatly influenced by certain affective processes. A strong purpose to listen and intrinsic motivation create a listening bond that encourages communicative involvement. The situation, the speaker, and the message can all contribute to a high interest level for listening. There must be a desire to listen. Messages "heard" but never really "received" *do not* exist for the listener. Finally, listening involves remembering—the storage of aural stimuli in the mind for later retrieval or immediate action.

We can all improve our listening skills. However, we must each take the initiative for improvement. Here are some suggestions that can contribute to the development of better listening habits.

Come Prepared.   Listening is a deliberative activity and requires that we come to the situation physically and mentally prepared. Too often, we come to the situation with something less than enthusiasm. A less than positive attitude will produce negative results, while being alive and active will result in more effective listening.

Listen for Main Ideas.   Listen for main ideas, principles, or concepts. This may require some work since the organization may not always be apparent. Don't dwell on the interesting story or anecdote but concentrate on the content. Focus attention on what is being said.

Evaluate.   Listen and evaluate the content of the message instead of judging the speaker's appearance or delivery. Unlike a sponge, don't absorb everything—ask questions. Does the speaker have personal interests, biases, prejudices? What are his or her credentials? When was he or she value programmed? Questioning is a valuable tool for increasing understanding.

Be Flexible.   Objectivity is an important key to facilitating listening. There is no doubt that differences in position will occur, but to be an effective listener, one must learn to tolerate diversity and be flexible. Keep an open mind and compensate for ideas contrary to personal convictions.

Get Involved. Listening to others requires getting involved. Consider the full position of the speaker and identify areas of mutual interest. Carl Weaver, in his book *Human Listening,* observes:

> Basic to the listening process is a desire to learn. It is strange that most people do not really want to listen, but to talk. Sometimes someone will ask a question but refuse to listen to the answer, breaking into the first sentence of response with another question or an argument. Sometimes a listener will hear little of what the talker says but will spend his time planning and organizing a response.[8]

React. Listening is an active, *not* a passive process. By reacting to messages, the listener demonstrates concern and understanding. Reacting helps one to communicate more accurately with other people more often and more clearly.

Care. Caring requires being sensitive to the communication needs and cues of others. Why are they communicating? What are they saying? It's important that one avoid interrupting and be careful of arbitrarily offering advice or prematurely judging or analyzing. Listening takes time.

Be Aware. Communication breakdowns will inevitably occur. Perhaps the "miracle" of communication is that we succeed as often as we do. Reflecting on the types of communication behaviors engaged in when breakdowns and faulty listening occurred can be enlightening as well as instructional. One can learn from their mistakes if they view them in light of the communication contexts in which they occurred.

Commit Yourself. Listening is a learned activity. It requires commitment to a personal program of improvement. Developing good listening habits requires work. To become an effective listener, one must recognize the importance of listening, develop positive listening habits, and practice active listening. A concentrated effort to engage in a program of personal listening improvement is essential.

Hearing is not listening. Listening is a higher cognitive process that is under our control. Listening is a combination of what we hear, what we understand, and what we remember. Listening involves the receiving and attending of stimuli, a combination of cognitive and affective processes and memory. Listening is a complex behavior that significantly effects our communication with others.

*   *   *   *   *

Clearly, Connie Corbet took charge of the interview situation by talking more, asking more closed questions, and limiting Bill's answers to areas directly related to her interests. Her controlling manner and personal biases and prejudices contributed to errors in questioning and a failure to probe thoroughly. Connie's entering assumptions further heightened Bill's nervousness, prompting him to be defensive and provide less than adequate responses. While Bill may have been actively listening, Connie was not so engaged. Consequently, much of the dilemma experienced by Bill stemmed from Connie's inability to conduct an effective interview.

Ed Miller also controlled the interview, but more importantly, he exercised self-control. He provided direction without dominating the interview situation. Bill was an active participant, answering questions and asking questions. His responses weren't just heard and recorded but were listened to and probed. Ed and Bill mutually shared and gained information and mutually worked to achieve their respective purposes. Bill leaves the interview pleasantly satisfied and impressed by Ed Miller's professional conduct. While positively reassuring, the interview failed to completely resolve Bill's dilemma, since he was reticent to question Ed about Connie's remarks.

Bill Bradley, like most interviewees, responded to each interview according to the climate established and tone promoted by the respective interviewer. The adequacy or inadequacy of his responses reflected the type of control exerted. This timid posture resulted in Bill's not assertively probing Connie's negative remarks regarding the human resources position or asking Ed Miller to clarify and elaborate on the potential opportunities in human resources. Consequently, being offered either of the two positions presented Bill Bradley with an interviewing dilemma.

How would you advise Bill? Should he seek additional information before making a decision? Who would best be able to provide any additional information? Could interviewing be a tool used to gather the specific information needed?

Critical Focus

The interview with Dr. Barbara W. Huggins illustrates the interview process while focusing on a most important interviewing skill—active listening. Analyze the interview from the perspective of the interviewer and interviewee, determining the purpose and agenda, identifying the sequence and types of questions asked, assessing the degree of control assumed, and evaluating the responses and information given.

Barbara W. Huggins, M.D., has roots that go deep into the heart of Texas. She was raised in the Houston area and then attended Baylor University in Waco, Texas, where she obtained a bachelor of science degree. During her ten-year career in medical technology, she made the decision to attend medical school. She successfully completed requirements for graduation from The University of Texas medical school at Houston and was elected to Alpha Omega Alpha, the medical honor society. After three years of private practice, she accepted a faculty position at the University of Texas Health Center at Tyler where she now serves as Associate Professor of Pediatrics and director of the Ambulatory Pediatric Clinic. Her job responsibilities primarily require her to listen to children and patients during a medical interview and to family practice residents in pediatrics.

To help you analyze the interview, consider the following questions. These questions direct your attention to critical dimensions comprising the interview process.

1. What is the purpose and agenda of the interviewer? The interviewee?
2. How satisfactory is the opening? Could it have been improved?
3. What structural sequence or sequences to questioning does the interviewer employ? How appropriate is this approach given the purpose and intent of the interview?
4. What types of questions are asked? What functions do the questions serve for each party? Does the interviewer thoroughly probe into answers for further information? Did the interviewer commit any errors while asking questions? How well did the interviewee respond to the questions asked?
5. Do both parties in the interview display active listening? In what ways?
6. Whose responsibility is listening according to Dr. Huggins? How can one improve his or her listening skills?

Summary

Interviewing is a dynamic and complicated process. However, a thorough understanding of the interviewing process and the relationship between the parties is a prerequisite for successful interviewing. This requires determining the purpose and agenda of the interview, structuring the interview, asking/answering questions, probing thoroughly, overcoming problems and barriers, and listening analytically. These represent some of the most important decisions that need to be made when conducting an interview, and behind every decision must lie some kind of rationale.

Effective interviewing results from deliberate planning, *not chance*. This requires determining the intent or purpose of the interview and carefully preparing an agenda that will elicit the necessary information. The specific type of interview often dictates the purpose with the situation—when, where, and how the interview takes place—primarily directing the agenda. A clear purpose and agenda sets the interviewer on a definite course and helps guarantee that the interview will not run amok.

Each type of interview requires a somewhat different structure, but many structural principles and techniques are available from which the interviewer may select the ones most appropriate. When preparing the opening, body, and close of the interview, the interviewer may choose a (1) funnel sequence, (2) inverted funnel sequence, (3) quintamensional design sequence, (4) tunnel sequence, (5) chain-link sequence, or (6) freeform sequence of questioning. The variables of the interviewing process should serve as selection guides.

Questions and questioning techniques are basic to interviewing, and an understanding of the types and uses of questions is crucial to success. The interviewer may choose to ask a limitless variety of questions; however, each type of question has unique characteristics, capabilities, and pitfalls. Questions may be categorized as being (1) open, (2) closed, (3) probing, (4) hypothetical, (5) leading, and (6) loaded. Interviewers must select and phrase the kinds of questions best suited for their purposes and objectives.

When conducting the interview, interviewers must use their coordination and adaptive skills to control the interview, to overcome problems and barriers, and to listen analytically. Coordination skills are used to establish the appropriate climate for an interview, and adaptive skills are used to decide how to adapt to the immediate interaction. Together, these communication skills assist in providing the necessary direction for an interview, help prevent potential problems stemming from the interviewer and/or interviewee, and ensure that mutual goals will be met.

Finally, the ability to listen analytically during an interview is often more important than the ability to talk. While listening has been described as an "invisible skill," it is an active process requiring considerable work. One must work to tune out distractions, concentrate attention, maintain emotional control, and create a caring, supportive climate where participants are free to communicate and relationships can develop and grow. Most people have the *ability* to listen; however, more people need the *willingness* to listen.

This chapter concludes our general discussion regarding the nature of effective interviewing and the interview process. The strategies, principles, and techniques examined will be amplified and applied in each of the chapters that deal with specific types of interviews.

SHARPENING YOUR FOCUS

1. What purpose(s) does an interview serve? Identify guidelines that can help interviewers establish an agenda to successfully achieve their purpose.

2. Compare and contrast the varying questioning techniques, noting how effective interviewing requires more than simply asking questions but rather making questions work.

3. What are some barriers or inhibitors that cut across all kinds of interviews? Note problems that stem from the interviewer as well as the interviewee. How might these problems be resolved?

4. How would you rate yourself as a listener on a scale of 0 to 100? How do you think your best friend, boss, or professor would rate you as a listener? Why would they describe your listening effectiveness differently? Can you be a better listener? Outline a five-step program that you believe will make you a more effective listener.

5. Assess your interviewing skills. Include an assessment of the roles you believe you perform effectively, the role you feel you need to work on, and the types of interviews you feel most/least comfortable with. Identify your interviewing goals for this course.

NOTES

1. Shirley Biage, *Interviews That Work* (Belmont, Calif.: Wadsworth, 1986) and Marvin Gottlieb, *Interviewing* (New York: Longman, 1986).
2. George Gallup, "The Quintamensional Plan of Question Design," *Public Opinion Quarterly* 11 (Fall 1947): 385.
3. Stanley L. Payne, *The Art of Asking Questions* (Princeton, N.J.: Princeton University Press, 1980).
4. Gordon Raymond, *Interviewing* (Homewood, Ill.: Dorsey Press, 1969).
5. Robert L. Kahn and Charles F. Cannell, *The Dynamics of Interviewing* (New York: John Wiley, 1957), 127.
6. Tom Peters, *Thriving on Chaos* (New York: Harper and Row, 1987), 524.
7. Stuart Chase, "Are You Listening?" *Reader's Digest,* December 1962, 80.
8. Carl H. Weaver, *Human Listening* (Indianapolis, Ind.: Bobbs-Merrill, 1972), 82.

SECTION TWO

Interviewing:
Business Practices
and Procedures

3 The Selection Interview I

The selection interview provides an opportunity for the interviewer and candidate to exchange important information and mutually explore the "job fit." During the interview process, employers seek to personally verify candidate information, assess an individual's motivation for working, and evaluate his or her experience, skills, values, and knowledge. Applicants likewise seek accurate information about the employer, the job, and available opportunities. An open, realistic, face-to-face exchange can best accomplish these goals.

Chapter 3 approaches the selection interview from the employer's perspective. Legal considerations are fundamental for the interviewer and should pilot decision making throughout the selection process. They influence the job profile, give direction to the recruitment of candidates, guide the conduct of the interview, and steer a course toward ethical evaluation and follow-up. This chapter is designed to accomplish three objectives:

1. *Awareness.* You will learn how to confidently select employees in compliance with legal guidelines and prepare effectively for the selection interview.

2. *Assessment.* You will be able to judge applicant qualifications according to essential characteristics for performing a job throughout the selection process.

3. *Application.* You will be able to follow essential criteria for recruiting employees and develop strategies and approaches for conducting and evaluating the interview.

* * * * *

The Florida Monthly—A Lesson in Hiring

Bob Anderson, Don Drake, and Cole Calvert were in their thirties when they met five years ago. Three men, each successful in his own way, each dissatisfied with his job, and each wanting to do something important while making money. The three had engaged in serious conversation about their personal needs for something more, something beyond daily newspaper reporting with all its pressure and its inability to recognize creative talent. Several months later, they had begun serious plans to publish *The Florida Monthly*, a magazine which would be distinctively different. A major Florida investor was attracted to the magazine's design, and when start-up funding was secured, the three resigned their previous positions and began raiding their former employers for writers.

Bob Anderson, thirty-nine, went to school and worked in Miami, Florida. Educated at Miami University, Bob was the founding CEO of *The Florida Monthly*. Prior to becoming CEO, he had been a reporter and assistant editor for The Florida Business Review. His work attracted favorable attention, and he had received several awards for outstanding reporting. However, the day he was passed over for a promotion to chief editor, Bob decided to leave for more rewarding opportunities.

Don Drake, thirty-seven, also from Miami, graduated from the University of Florida and had worked as a journalist for the Miami Herald covering the local and state government beat. Prior to assuming the founding editorship of *The Florida Monthly*, Don's dissatisfaction stemmed from the increasingly bureaucratic nature of the newspaper business.

Cole Calvert, thirty-five, a Florida State graduate, was a sales and marketing representative. Unlike the other two, Cole's experience was with multiple publishing companies; he had worked for three publishing concerns with increasing levels of marketing responsibility. He did not like being assigned projects from others and had for some time thought about more independence. The founding position of marketing manager for *The Florida Monthly* provided the initiative to begin something on his own.

Bob Anderson does not believe in organization charts, feeling that they just put artificial barriers between talented people who should be working together. Consequently, he encourages people to "talk things over," and most decisions of any significance are made by all involved. The work itself is exhausting, with most employees averaging seventy hours per week. Friday evenings are reserved for beer and pizza parties, which feature talk of the week's events. Excitement is intense, and a sense of energy is evident.

Don Drake attributes the initial success of *The Florida Monthly* to his ability as an editor who runs a "tight ship." Prudence, deliberation, and thoroughness are encouraged among all his writers. These expectations were explicitly stated to all, as well as the level of commitment necessary to be successful at *The Florida Monthly*.

Cole Calvert is aggressive in his marketing program. Marketing *The Florida Monthly* as a magazine concerned about people, he uses television, radio, and print advertising to saturate all segments of the public. As a result, *The Florida Monthly* has begun to make substantial inroads into its competitors' market share.

Bob, Don, and Cole knew where they wanted to go and have gotten a fine start. Now, after five years, they feel it is time to add to their full-time writing staff. Together with the current staff, they begin to develop the "job profile." The person they hire will be responsible for covering what is happening in the arts and entertainment sector. This individual should be able to effectively communicate with diverse constituencies and must possess quality word processing/writing skills. Consequently, when recruiting, a degree in English or journalism is required, as well as some experience.

After listing the position, they begin to screen the applicants. Reference checks are conducted, and writing samples, required of all applicants, are read. Considerable discussion is given to hiring a recent graduate versus a more experienced writer and whether the ideal candidate should be an insider familiar with Florida or from outside the state. Their tireless efforts and search result in five potential candidates—all seemingly qualified for the position. A telephone conference interview with each narrows the list to three candidates for on-site visits.

John Tight, twenty-three, a recent graduate from Stanford University, is the first candidate to be personally interviewed. A journalism major confined to a wheel chair as the result of an automobile accident with a drunk driver, John has been doing some freelance writing since his graduation. While at Stanford, he was a reporter, assistant editor, and editor of the college newspaper. His special area of interest was arts and entertainment. During his senior term, he completed an internship with the San Francisco Chronicle. His professors and those with whom he has worked consider him to be a conscientious, diligent, and highly energetic reporter. Despite his physical disability, John displayed considerable independence and an ability to get the job done. His writing was applauded for its creativity and style.

Bob, Don, and Cole, as the founders of *The Florida Monthly*, jointly interview John Tight. The opening questions focus on his reporting techniques and writing skills. Story angles are discussed and potential writing blocks explored. More probing questions examine John's limited experience and mind-set regarding the arts and entertainment sector. Over a light lunch, John is provided more details regarding the founding of *The Florida Monthly* and its publishing objectives. The long hours and demanding commitment are made clear. Following lunch, John demonstrates his ability to use a word processor and puts forth possible proposals for several serious pieces pertaining to the Florida cultural climate. The interview closes with John being given a tour of the facility and introduced to several of the senior writers. John leaves a portfolio of his writing with Don Drake, the editor, and is told a decision will be made following interviews with the other two candidates. Before the cordial farewells, John expresses a desire to be a member of this creative team.

John leaves the interview confident. The questions were specific and tough, requiring him to draw from personal experiences, but fair. While some questions were raised regarding his disability, they were presented in the context of getting to difficult assignments and meeting deadlines. He realistically understands the expectations of the position and the intense writing climate characterizing *The Florida Monthly.* No one suggested a secure future.

John Tight's responses and performance is evaluated using a prepared matrix based on the job profile and including the screening criteria. Following all of the interviews, the three candidates are compared. While Bob, Don, and Cole experienced differing "gut feelings" during the interview, their final evaluations reveal unanimous agreement—John Tight is the right person for the job.

Discussion Questions

1. To what extent and in what ways are legal considerations observed?
2. What are the interviewing issues embedded in developing a "job profile"?
3. How does recruiting criteria guide the selection of candidates? What are the principal factors shaping the decision-making process in this case?
4. How was this interview conducted? What are the advantages and/or potential problems?
5. To what extent is the process involved here typical of selection interviewing generally? How democratic is this process? How ethical is this process? What do you predict will happen with John Tight? What lesson(s) in hiring can be learned?

The Interviewer's Perspective

We can broadly define the selection interview as involving at least two people with distinct communicative goals, motives, and needs who speak and listen from time to time. The resulting dialogue helps each make informed decisions pertaining to the hiring and acceptance of a position. An applicant's ability to express thoughts and ideas both verbally and nonverbally affects the interviewer's rating score more than any other factor.[1] Therefore, oral communication skills are the most influential factor affecting applicant success in the selection interview.[2] No amount of computerized testing or psychological assessment can take the place of human interaction during the job interview. A trained interviewer using carefully defined question strategies and subtle probes can assess attitudes, feelings, skills, and knowledge, thereby verifying an applicant's ability to do the job. Still, research suggests that although the reliability of interviews may be high in given situations, the validities obtained are usually low.[3] What forces contribute to such opprobrious results—the disheartening prospect of hiring the wrong person for the job?

One such force is the cavalier approach some employers take toward selection interviewing. Selection interviews require careful preparation and attention, they *don't just happen.* They must be structured or essential information may not be covered. Important questions to consider include: When should you meet? Where? Will you need notes? Will you need records? Documents? What is the interview about? What are your objectives? What questions do you plan to ask? What words will you use? What follow-up actions will be taken? Selection interviewing is about information gathering, and an agenda that permits rigorous probing enables the interviewer to more accurately predict the future performance of any candidate who applies for the job.

A second force inhibiting effective selection interviewing is the supercilious attitude on the part of some interviewers to hire the "best" person, rather than the *best person for the job.* In selecting a candidate, you should consider two issues only—capability and personality. What the candidate can do is essential, but equally important is what the candidate is like. More than 87 percent of all people fail not because of capability but because of personality.[4] Hiring may be likened to a jigsaw puzzle with the interviewer seeking to locate and precisely fit the pieces together to complete the total picture.

Finally, many interviewers are simply "sales representatives" for their organizations focusing on "selling" a position by emphasizing only positive characteristics of the company thus providing an unrealistic picture of the job.[5] Obviously, employers want to promote their organizations in areas that positively appeal to candidates, but presenting necessary negative information helps applicants make realistic, informed decisions. Hiring the wrong person costs a company at least two years' salary and that is if the mistake is discovered and corrected within six months, which rarely occurs. Certainly, candidates are entitled to information about the organization and the job, but it should properly profile duties, responsibilities, and required skills.[6]

Open, candid communication with a job candidate is fundamental to results-oriented selection interviewing. It must be the primary consideration guiding the selection process and determining the principles, practices, and procedures to be used. Crossed fingers and trembling over hiring decisions is not uncommon, but this normal, pleonastic fear can be lessened by understanding the dynamics of selection interviewing.

Legal Considerations

Most employers would agree that employment decisions must comply with Equal Employment Opportunity Commission (EEOC) laws and guidelines. Failure to comply with employment guidelines and regulations, either through ignorance or intent, may result in expensive lawsuits. The major federal laws that deal with EEOC legislation are

- *The Equal Pay Act of 1963.* Part of the Fair Labor Standards Act, it forbids pay differentials on the basis of sex.

- *Title VII of the Civil Rights Act of 1964.* Forbids discrimination because of race, color, religion, sex, or national origin. The 1972 Amendments gave the EEOC the power to bring lawsuits against violators and also the right to expand an individual complaint into a class-action suit in federal court if it believes there is a pattern of discrimination within that organization.

- *Executive Order 11246 issued in 1965.* This order requires that every government contract or subcontract involving $10,000 or more contain a clause against discrimination because of race, color, religion, sex, or national origin.

- *Age Discrimination in Employment Act of 1967.* Bans discrimination due to age for anyone at least forty years old but less than sixty-five. Covers the same employees as Title VII.

- *Revised Order Number 4 issued in 1970.* Revision of Executive Order 11246 requiring that a written Affirmative Action Program be developed and implemented by contractors and subcontractors with fifty or more employees and a governmental contract of $50,000 or more.

- *Vietnam Era Veterans' Readjustment Assistance Act of 1972 with Amendments in 1974 and 1980.* Mandates that federal contracts and subcontracts of $10,000 or more include a clause requiring the contractor not to discriminate against and to take affirmative action on behalf of Vietnam era and disabled veterans.

- *Section 503, Rehabilitation Act of 1973.* Requires that an employer with a federal contract of $2,500 or more must take affirmative action to hire and promote handicapped persons.

- *Americans With Disabilities Act of 1990.* Requires that an employer must make every "reasonable" effort to accommodate handicapped persons in the workplace. This recent act extends previous affirmative action measures regarding the hiring of those with disabilities. Specific applications are still open to legal interpretation.

It is also important to be familiar with the fair employment practice laws of the states in which business operations are conducted, since they may be even more stringent than those at the federal level. While there are many complexities in the law, it is fairly clear that an employer can be found guilty of discrimination in at least two ways:

1. *Adverse (or disparate) treatment.* Essentially, this means that the employer can be shown to have *intentionally* refused to hire, promote, or retain someone because of their race, sex, religion, color, or national origin.

2. *Adverse (or disparate) impact.* In this situation, the employer may have no "evil motive" that influenced them, but an adverse impact may occur. For example, an employer may require that all truck drivers have a high school diploma. This may have an adverse impact on minorities, or an employer may require that all plant employees be at least five feet eight inches tall and weigh 160 pounds. This may have an adverse impact on women. If an employer's selection practices have an adverse impact, it must be shown that the practices are job related. Is a high school diploma necessary for one to be a good truck driver? Is a height and weight requirement necessary to be a successful plant employee?

Generally, understanding and knowledge of the laws pose little difficulty for employers who continually update themselves regarding potential violations.

Employers experience more difficulty in the subtle or specific application of EEOC guidelines when selecting employees for their own organizations. The most common error "is in asking questions during the interview that lead the employer into liability under federal or state law."[7] Employers should not ask questions that could be construed to have discriminatory intent or that might give the appearance of having been used to implement selection standards that have an adverse impact on one group or another. Interviewers may not ask questions concerning an applicant's gender, race, religion, marital status, handicaps, or age unless such information is a legitimate requirement for employment. Questions pertaining to these subjects are considered evidence of discrimination by the EEOC unless the interviewer can explain satisfactorily that they are not used with a discriminatory purpose and are, in fact, job related.

To avoid many problems associated with the selection interview, employers must not only be familiar with EEOC laws and guidelines, but must judge each applicant's qualities and attributes according to essential requirements for performing a particular job. These essential characteristics or **bona fide occupational qualifications** (BFOQs) should determine the questions asked and direct the decisions made regarding an applicant. To do otherwise violates the law as illustrated by the Delta Air Lines example.

In one year, Delta Air Lines was "the target of 62 civil complaints filed by the New York City Human Rights Commission, each involving a potential penalty of $100,000."[8] Applicants at Delta claimed they were asked inappropriate questions about sexual preferences, birth control, and abortions during the interview process. The troubles surrounding improper questioning at Delta represent common complaints facing employers today. While many corporate interviewers recognize "inappropriate" questions that stray from legal guidelines, they often find themselves wandering from appropriate lines of inquiry during those informal moments when conversation is less job specific. Although selection interviews are not interrogations, during casual moments the conversation should not intrude into areas that might lead to charges of discrimination under the law. Legal difficulties can best be avoided if interviewers ask only pertinent, job-relevant questions.

Most interviewers do not feel hampered at all by federal or state guidelines. In fact, only about a third consider having to live with hiring laws a nuisance.[9] Still, government regulations are a fact of life, and interviewers are responsible for protecting the civil rights of applicants. Carefully developing a job profile, delineating objective recruitment criteria, and refining interviewing techniques and evaluation procedures can help protect employers from legal action and lead to safer, more reliable selection decisions. Given the growing number of lawsuits concerning discrimination and reverse discrimination, there may be no such thing as a completely "safe" decision.

*   *   *   *   *

Bob Anderson, Don Drake, and Cole Calvert did an excellent job of protecting the legal rights of candidates applying for *The Florida Monthly* position. Their exemplary observation of EEOC guidelines was no accident. They began the selection process by conducting a careful job analysis—determining the technical and nontechnical skills required for job success. Moreover, they engaged in lengthy discussions regarding the attributes of an ideal candidate. The result was a well-defined job profile outlining the success criteria needed to perform the job. This criteria was then used to screen applicants and interview prospective candidates.

Throughout the interview with John Tight, bona fide occupational qualifications determined the questions asked. Rather than emphasizing his handicap, they questioned him about story angles and covering assignments. Even over lunch the conversation remained focused on the company rather than personal qualities. John was informed of the history regarding the founding of *The Florida Monthly* and encouraged to ask questions. While the interview focused on John's fit with the job requirements, it also assessed his ability to adapt to *The Florida Monthly* culture.

Finally, Bob, Don, and Cole objectively compared John with the other candidates and evaluated him using a jointly prepared action plan that contributed to their reaching consistent conclusions. Their selection approach lent itself to making a confident hiring decision.

Deciding What You Need

Deciding what you need begins with creating a **job profile.** The job profile is a specific, detailed description of performance requirements for a particular job and should be written prior to the recruiting process. Beginning the interview with an accurately written profile (according to EEOC guidelines) offers good protection against possible complaints related to the hiring process.

Begin writing the profile by identifying the specific duties and responsibilities of the actual job. The list should be as complete as possible, consequently, it is best to have those familiar with the job participate in writing the job description. Input from management, coworkers, and human resource personnel can be valuable. A job description checklist might include the following:

1. Dependability—attendance/punctuality
2. Overtime flexibility
3. Travel—local/overnight
4. Communication skills—reading, writing, speaking
5. Customer contact/relations
6. Stress point—operate tactfully under pressure
7. Work without supervision/initiate decisions—leadership
8. Ability to work in set environment
9. Physical strength/stamina and coordination/dexterity
10. Problem solving
11. Technical skills/computer literacy
12. Accuracy/work with details
13. Follow detailed instructions
14. Foreign language fluency
15. Education—high school, vocational training, community college, college/ university

A common pitfall occurs when vague or general language is used, so insist upon concrete terms whenever possible. For instance, instead of writing "to conduct training programs," say "to administer *Frontline* customer service programs to exempt and nonexempt employees." Rather than stating a "foreign language is required," indicate the specific language and level of fluency needed. Job specifications should state the knowledge, skills, abilities, and other characteristics (KSAOs) necessary to perform the job.

The KSAOs identified must next be ranked according to their priority—low to critical. "Critical" requirements *must* indeed be mandatory and not simply used as a means for screening out candidates. For instance, before listing a criterion of a minimum of three-to-five years experience, verify that such limits are necessary. A minimalist approach to critical criteria can ensure that such listings are mandatory and clearly relate to performance required on the job without discriminating. Also, list personal attributes that the new employee will need to satisfactorily fulfill the essential duties identified. For example, consider the following partial list of responsibilities and attributes for a training and development position:

Job Responsibilities	*Personal Attributes*
Strong communication skills	Ability to learn technical material, initiate reports, and orally communicate ideas
Travel 15 to 20 percent of the time	Well organized, capable of being prompt and on time, demonstrates flexibility to changing routines
Administer current training programs in customer service	Ability to plan and schedule, willingness to continue education

An actual list of job responsibilities and personal attributes would be much more extensive. To extend this list, an employer might add working with training teams within the organization, evaluation and measurement of customer service programs, and development of future programs. Each job characteristic and attribute must be consistent with the overall objectives and direction of the organization.

The job profile can guide the personal interview. Questions can be uniformly asked and job related. The identified job responsibilities and personal attributes can be explored in relation to the candidate's educational/training background and previous work experience. The candidate's skills, attitudes, working relationship with others, and goals can be assessed according to established measures for the job. Candidates can then be uniformly evaluated during the interview, ensuring that key decisions are based on the same set of standards for the same job (See figure 3.1).

*   *   *   *   *

Florida Monthly position required candidates to possess particular job-related qualifications. A college degree in English or journalism, word processing skills, and strong interpersonal and writing skills were mandatory. Some experience covering the arts and entertainment sector was considered important and expected. Certain candidate attributes were also discussed and included in the job profile. The desirable candidate would be creative, conscientious, and committed. Bob, Don, and Cole wanted someone who would be comfortable with the long hours and stressful environment. Consequently, energy and enthusiasm would be observed during the interview. They were looking for someone who not only could do the job, but wanted to do the job. The job profile developed was specific in its requirements yet flexible enough to generate a diverse pool of applicants with welcome attributes and qualities.

Recruiting Candidates

Once the job profile has been completed, the actual recruitment of candidates can begin. The goal of recruitment is to balance functional areas in the job profile with personal traits and determine a candidate's fit to the job, as well as the values important to the organization's culture. Doing so will ensure efficiency in the recruiting process and lessen turnover.[10]

Therefore, an initial consideration must be whether to recruit candidates from *within* the organization or from the *outside*. Choosing a candidate internally has several advantages. First, internal selection provides for employee advancement and ensures continuity—an understanding of the organization and its culture. Second,

Interviewer Evaluation Record				

Interviewer Evaluation Record

	LAST	FIRST	MI	SOCIAL SECURITY NUMBER
NAME:				

Do you have U.S. citizenship or are you eligible under U.S. Immigration Laws (other than by means of practical training visa) to work for Midwest Oil in the U.S. in the job for which you are applying? ☐ yes ☐ no

FOR APPLICANT FLOW:
OCC CODE ☐☐☐ JOB NO. ☐☐☐ EEO/JOB GP ☐☐☐ AAP EST CODE ☐

Acquisition Type: (Source) Name of School/Event/Agency

POSITION: _____

DATE INTERVIEWED _ _ _ GRADUATION DATE _ _ DATE AVAILABLE _ _ _ MO DAY YR / MO YR / MO DAY YR

HIRING DEPT:_____ LOCATION: _____

Interviewer(s):

Full-time ☐ Special Helper ☐
Co-op/Intern ☐ Student Learner ☐
Call-In ☐

WAGE/HOUR STATUS: (if known)
Exempt ☐ Non-Exempt ☐ Hourly ☐
EMPLOYEE TYPE: POSITION TYPE:
Regular ☐ Casual ☐ Entry ☐ Experienced ☐
REJECT REASON ☐ (if applicable)

RATING (5 = outstanding -- 1 = unacceptable) COMMENTS

INTERPERSONAL SKILLS (Communication, Disposition)

ACADEMIC/TECHNICAL KNOWLEDGE
Education Level _____ Major _____ GPA ____/____
(Degree) _____ ____/____ Major/Overall
COMMENTS:

WORK EXPERIENCE (Accomplishments, Responsibilities)
COMMENTS:
Related Oil Industry Experience: Yes ☐ No ☐ Years: ____
Previous Midwest and/or Affiliate Experience? Yes ☐ No ☐ Years: ____

ACTIVITIES AND INTERESTS (Leadership, involvement)
COMMENTS:

ADDITIONAL COMMENTS (Other Offers, Deadlines, Goals)
COMMENTS:
Hiring Department Preference:
Geographic Preference:

OVERALL EVALUATION: (Circle One)	5 Outstanding	4 Excellent	3 Above Average	2 Average	1 Unacceptable

RECOMMENDED ACTION INVITE ☐ COMMENTS _____ HOLD ☐ COMMENTS _____ REJECT REASON: ☐ _____

Referred to : (initials) _____ (Hiring Department)_____ (Location) _____ (Date)_____

FIGURE 3.1 Interviewer Evaluation Record

an insider is well-known, having established working relationships with others within the organization. Finally, such a candidate will have an established performance record with evident weaknesses already discovered. However, hiring internally limits the candidate pool and may prove stagnating to the organization.

While hiring from the outside presents a greater gamble, it also introduces new personnel and provides the infusion of fresh ideas and different perspectives into the organization. The outsider may challenge established procedures and can be the creative impetus necessary to trigger organizational growth and change. However, hiring externally requires carefully screening applicants, reading resumes, conducting reference checks, administering integrity tests, and reviewing applicant characteristics.

Screening Applicants

The time spent on screening applicants can be cost effective and minimize potential workplace problems. Careful, thorough checks help employers reduce costs, as well as minimize absenteeism, workplace violence, and sexual harassment problems. Most employers would agree that a background search of applicants prevents future workplace difficulties; however, their increasing workloads often prevent them from conducting thorough screenings. Still, the time and energy spent screening applicants should be considered as an investment in the organization. The National Safe Workplace Institute estimates that in 1995 workplace theft cost employers $120 billion annually, while violence and harassment cases cost $4 billion a year.

APOCA Inc., a Cleveland-based company operating parking facilities, verifies the educational background and past employment of all employees, as well as checking their driving records, criminal records, and credit histories. Intuit Corp., a California software company, asks job applicants for nine to twelve references and extensively checks each reference before hiring. Amtel Corp., a manufacturer of highly specialized semiconductors and microprocessors, requires applicants to undergo Social Security and criminal record checks besides verifying normal background information. These organizations have found that proper screening lessens workplace problems and reduces related costs. They have found thorough screening to be a preventative measure and a proactive approach to coping with the uncertainty integral to hiring decisions.

Proper screening can also help selection interviewers read resumes and evaluate credentials by revealing false information. Between 10 and 30 percent of job applicants falsify their qualifications for a position. This is an increase of 100 percent from twenty years ago.[11] The Port Authority of New York and New Jersey tested this finding by advertising for electricians who could work with Sontag connectors, even though the "Sontag connector" didn't exist. They received 170 responses from applicants claiming such familiarity on their resumes. The Society for Human Resource Management (SHRM) reports that 61 percent of interviewers verify educational information and 92 percent speak to an applicant's former employer(s). Careful, thorough background checks can help detect much of the false information received.

Reading the Resume

When reading a resume, focus on valid data and verifiable facts. The majority of valid data—data by which you can predict job success—is associated with the applicant's knowledge, skills, and abilities. Certainly, this information must relate to job requirements, which points to the necessity of a valid job profile. Verifiable facts, such as training or education, positions held, responsibilities, and salary history, are the most reliable data on which to base selection decisions. Still, as previously noted, significant misrepresentation occurs, so verifying facts is the way to uncover any deception.

Seasoned interviewers weigh strengths (which are probably listed), but they also search for seldom indicated weaknesses. For example, if the applicant's salary progression has been strong, it will be revealed on the resume or in the letter of application. If it was weak, this fact may not be presented or may be obscured. Moreover, experienced interviewers are not misled by generalizations. Ambiguous words and phrases or voids may be used to hide weaknesses. For example, the phrase "better opportunity elsewhere" is sometimes used to divert the interviewer's attention from an unsuccessful experience. Consequently, look for details when reading a resume. Carefully reading resumes can reduce time spent with unsuitable persons while helping to pinpoint the right applicant for the job.

Reference Checking

Robert Half wryly observed that "a bad reference is as hard to find as a good employee."[12] Still, references and reference checking are an important and necessary part of recruiting candidates. Letters of reference may be requested, but they take time to receive, and previous employers may be hesitant to provide candid written evaluations. Consequently, telephone references are more commonly employed. They can be conducted in a timely fashion with the interviewer asking job-specific questions of the previous employer. Moreover, the interviewer may detect vocal inflections that can provide clues to a candidate's strengths and/or weaknesses.

A persistent problem is that many employers still give general references only, fearing that specific facts may make them vulnerable to lawsuits. The Society for Human Resource Management found that nearly two-thirds of employers do not give information about former employees for fear of a lawsuit.[13] Therefore, when references are given, they tend to be limited to job title, position responsibilities, and dates of employment, yet a new trend is emerging with state laws changing such that human resource managers are protected when providing specific, detailed, and verifiable information from personnel files. Performance evaluations, reasons for termination or dismissal, and other confidential information is beginning to be shared with employers conducting reference checks.

Approximately twenty-five states have now adopted laws making it more difficult for former employees to win lawsuits over negative job references. California, Colorado, Illinois, Indiana, Florida, and Maine have been given freedom to release sensitive personnel information when requested. These laws were designed to make the workplace safer and more efficient while protecting employers who release truthful information about former employees. For instance, if an employee with a history of workplace violence is let go, future employers would want to know about this individual's propensity toward violence. The lawsuit against an Allstate Insurance Co. in Florida vividly illustrates this point. Paul Calden, an Allstate employee, had been dismissed for bringing a gun into the workplace. He later accepted a position with Fireman's Fund Insurance Co. However, before the hiring, Fireman's Fund received a reference letter from Allstate claiming the reason for Mr. Calden's dismissal was corporate restructuring. Later in January 1993, Mr. Calden entered the Fireman's Fund cafeteria and shot five people, killing three and injuring the others, before fatally shooting himself. The lawsuit filed by the victims claimed that Allstate had been deceptive in their letter of reference and should have disclosed the violent nature of Mr. Calden to Fireman's Fund Insurance Company. While the new state laws do not require employers to disclose past violent behavior, they do make it safer for employers to reveal such information. As one attorney said, "For the first time, we are saying—with great caution—if there is a safety-sensitive issue, you should make a disclosure."[14] However, when sensitive employee information is sent to another organization, employers should keep good documentation showing that the information was sent in good faith. Some companies ask employees to sign waiver forms promising not to sue over references.

When conducting reference checks, only job-related information should be requested. The requested information should be directed to specific requirements of the job for which the applicant is being considered. Ask questions that lend themselves to objective, factual, and quantitative answers, staying away from subjective areas. For example, ask for exact job title, dates of employment, number of days absent from the job in the last year, performance appraisal ratings, and reasons for leaving or letting the person go. An important closing question to ask might be, "Would you re-hire this person?" Finally, consider and evaluate the individual who provides the information for reference material received. Were they in a position to objectively assess the applicant?

Using Integrity Tests

Honesty or ethical conduct is a growing concern for employers in the selection process. As Clive Fletcher states, "When a major bank can be brought to financial collapse by the actions of an employee allegedly acting alone, and money can be embezzled from a police service by one of its accountants, it is not surprising that there has been growing interest in methods of assessing staff honesty."[15] Consequently, integrity tests are becoming a common tool employers use when recruiting candidates. There are five primary methods used for testing employee integrity: (1) the reference check, (2) the polygraph, (3) the written questionnaire, (4) the simulation exercise, and (5) the selection interview.

Reference checking remains the best and most fundamental way to verify the qualifications of a candidate. Letters of reference can confirm a candidate's knowledge, skills, and abilities, with telephone reference checks exposing blatant deception. One company study found errors in nearly one-third of 200 applicants' resumes. Their resume checks revealed that 11 percent of the applicants lied about why they left previous jobs, 4 percent fudged on job titles, 3 percent listed fake employers, 3 percent fabricated jobs, and 3 percent falsified having a college degree. Legally, candidates who falsify information on their resumes may later be dismissed regardless of their performance on the job. Courts have consistently upheld that employers "who can prove that the employee lied on a resume may not have to defend against other charges."[16]

The polygraph or lie detector was a commonly used physiological measure for determining a candidate's honesty. This testing device assumes that physical arousal through skin conductivity, heart rate, and perspiration can indicate a person's degree of truthfulness to questions presented by a trained professional. However, U.S. courts have ruled that polygraph testing is invalid and potentially discriminating; thus, today few companies use it as a preemployment instrument. Many companies do include random polygraph testing as a condition of employment and require it once employees are hired.

The use of validly recognized integrity questionnaires and personality assessments have replaced polygraph testing. These paper and pencil tests have candidates respond to specific questions regarding their attitudes about theft, dishonest behavior, and "organizational delinquency." The London House Personnel Selection Inventory, Reid Survey, Stanton Survey, and Hogan Personnel Selection Scale are commonly used evaluation instruments. Nordstrom Inc., an upscale, Seattle-based department store chain, estimates that by using integrity questionnaires and personality assessments, their probability for hiring desirable candidates has increased from 60 percent to 90 percent.[17] Although integrity questionnaires have weaknesses and sometimes lack preciseness, employers use them as another important part of the selection process.

Used less frequently, simulation exercises require candidates to respond to a series of written messages or memos, each dealing with a difficult integrity-related issue. They are then evaluated on the necessarily tough decisions needed to handle these "in-basket" exercises. Employers assess integrity through the skills demonstrated in responding to the simulated situations describing specific workplace behavior. Valid integrity simulations are difficult to develop and time consuming to administer; consequently, their application is limited.

Finally, the selection interview itself can be used to probe for discrepancies in candidate information. Through detailed questioning, interviewers can check a candidate's work history and test claims of specific training or knowledge. By carefully observing nonverbal cues and behaviors, interviewers can detect deceptive responses. The interview provides an opportunity to obtain information about a candidate that might not be obtained otherwise. It can supplement, expand, and confirm any written materials. Most people will say more about themselves than they will write down.

Reviewing Applicant Characteristics

While interviewers attempt to evaluate the quality of applicants on objective information provided, in reality it is difficult to distinguish between objective and subjective sources of judgment. Therefore, reviewing the influence of selected

applicant characteristics can be useful, since "all applicant qualifications are filtered through the perceptual mechanism of the interviewer."[18] How do such
characteristics as gender, communication patterns, aggressiveness, dress, grooming, and physical attractiveness effect interviewers and their selection decisions?
A content analysis of interview outcomes with Fortune 500 companies revealed
that "communication patterns exhibited by the applicants and interviewers were
not significantly different from one another regardless of the race or gender of
the participants."[19] However, most interviewers prefer moderately aggressive applicants, whether male or female, over passive ones.[20] Conservatively dressed,
well groomed, physically attractive applicants, regardless of gender, are perceived as being more confident, sociable, friendly, competent, and likely to succeed.[21] They are also seen as being better adjusted and having a more appropriate personality for the job; thus, are more likely to be hired.[22] While interviewers
cannot ignore such applicant characteristics, they must weigh them carefully,
since many candidates have learned impression management strategies.

Recruiting candidates is not an easy task. There are no easy shortcuts. Consider the following dialogue based on a story by John Wareham:

> The president of a substantial corporation calls the owner of a well known re-
> cruiting firm. "Phil," the president asks, "would you mind coming over and join-
> ing our board meeting. I want you to meet a fellow I've just hired and tell me what
> you think of him. In other words, give me a quick rundown."
>
> "Well," Phil replies, "it's not quite as easy as that because I'd need some vital
> background information. An opportunity to conduct a reasonable sort of inter-
> view would be helpful, too."
>
> "Oh, that's a shame," said the corporation president, "because I thought he
> was so good that I played my hunch and snapped him up right away as soon as
> I met him—I didn't want to mess around with too many questions and forms
> and things."
>
> "Where did you meet him?" I asked.
>
> "I got to know him quite well when a friend brought him out for a midweek
> race on my yacht. Then we got on so well at the squadron bar afterwards that I
> just snapped him up right away . . ."[23]

Not surprisingly, two months later the man was fired. It has been suggested that
no more than 10 percent of a candidate's evaluation should be based on subjective or personal perceptions, with the resume and reference checks, personality
analysis and integrity tests, and personal interview each accounting for 30 percent of the hiring decision.[24] Interviewers who take the time to seriously recruit
candidates get results.

*   *   *   *   *

Bob, Don, and Cole thoroughly screened applicants read resumes, and
conducted reference checks. They also required applicants to submit
writing samples which could be evaluated (word processing and com-

puter skills would be tested during the interview). Finally, they conducted telephone conference interviews with selected applicants in order to determine those candidates they would invite for on-site interviews. Telephone conference interviews are increasingly being used by interviewers to narrow their list of candidates.

Job-related factors principally influenced the decision making in this case. Objective recruiting criteria required to perform the job guided the selection of candidates. Their discussions of whether to hire a recent graduate versus a more experienced writer or whether the ideal candidate should be an insider or someone from outside the state all revolved around the person's ability to effectively cover the arts and entertainment field. This is not to suggest, however, that candidate "fit" was not a consideration. Certainly, they wanted to hire a candidate consonant with their culture and capable of contributing to their successful writing staff.

John Tight exhibited the qualities they were looking for in a candidate. He held a journalism degree from Stanford University; had outstanding references, which applauded his writing style and creativity; and possessed some experience with the arts and entertainment area. Moreover, reference checks confirmed his ability to "get the job done." It was not surprising then that they would invite John for an on-site visit.

Conducting the Interview

The selection interview is "the single most *useful* tool in the entire hiring process—useful in the sense that it can produce a picture of a candidate that you can't get from a resume, an application, or references."[25] When properly handled, the interview is a powerful technique for acquiring access to information otherwise unavailable. Improperly handled, the interview becomes a source of serious bias and typically results in information restriction and distortion. To gain valid information and make appropriate interpretations, the interviewer must seek to understand, identify with, and accommodate the person being interviewed. Therefore, careful attention must be given to preparing and conducting the selection interview.

The interviewer's role is to maximize the positive forces to communicate while reducing or eliminating the negative forces. Too often, interviewers concern themselves so much with the "content" of the interview (objectives, strategies, questioning techniques) that they neglect the "context" (physical and psychological setting). Although the specific effects of the environment may often be difficult to assess, there are environmental influences that have a significant impact on the interviewing process.

What changes in psychological climate are created as a result of furniture arrangement? Should a desk separate the interviewer and interviewee, or should

The interviewer's role is to maximize the positive forces to communicate while reducing or eliminating the negative forces.

chairs be situated such that both parties are open to one another? The placement of office furniture and chairs can encourage communication or restrict it. The arrangement of furniture seems to be associated with certain kinds of communication behavior. Studies indicate that where interviewers sit in relation to candidates determines whether they are perceived as conversational and cooperative, or competitive and coactive.[26] Moreover, a series of studies investigating the presence or absence of a desk revealed interesting effects upon an interviewer's credibility. Robin Widgery and Cecil Stackpole discovered that student interviewees who expressed high anxiety during an interview perceived the credibility of the interviewer to be higher when there was no desk between them than when a desk was present. Conversely, student interviewees who expressed low anxiety in the interview assigned higher credibility to the interviewer when he or she sat behind a desk.[27] This would suggest that interviewers must be sensitive to ways in which the physical environment can induce or minimize both interviewee anxiety and subsequent perceptions of interviewer credibility. The placement of furniture and seating arrangements can have a dramatic effect on interviewing outcomes.

In addition to furniture arrangement, attention must also be given to two other considerations when preparing the physical environment for the interview: (1) it should be comfortable and private, and (2) it should be as free from distractions and interruptions as possible. Selection interviews are frequently stressful encounters, so anything the interviewer can do to make an interviewee more comfortable is desirable and contributes to a more successful outcome. Their will be plenty of diversions in most interviews without compounding them by failing to provide something as basic as a comfortable setting. Moreover, a premium should be placed on privacy. An environment conducive to effective interviewing is one in which either party can feel free to express himself or herself with confidence and candor. This applies to potential distractions from the environment as well, such as ringing telephones or employee interruptions. These intrusions can increase the anxiety level of a candidate, break the continuity of the conversation, and create lower interview satisfaction. An interviewer who holds all calls and other appointments until after the interview is completed has done more than merely provide privacy, such actions indicate a purposeful interest in the interviewee by not wanting anything to interfere with the selection conference. Privacy, like comfort, implicitly tells the interviewee that you care about him or her.

Finally, every interview should "go somewhere." In other words, you should have some kind of plan or strategy for arriving at your desired "communication destination." This is determined by the objectives of the interview, the available information regarding the interviewee, and the questioning techniques employed. How these factors influence the conduct of the interview will become more apparent by looking in more detail at the three major selection interview strategies: (1) the standard interview, (2) the behavior description interview, and (3) the structured interview.

The Standard Interview

The standard interview is the most widely used and traditionally employed selection strategy. The interviewer approaches the standard interview with two basic challenges: (1) ask the questions that will provide the most accurate information about the applicant, and (2) present an image of the organization that will make the applicant want to accept the position if an offer is made. The standard interview uses a four-part structure to accomplish its objectives—opening, background, discussion, and close.

To a great extent, an effective opening—getting off on the right foot—will set the tone for the remainder of the interview. The initial impressions gained in the first thirty to sixty seconds of the interview can seriously affect its success. Therefore, some time should be spent in establishing a rapport and creating a positive, supportive communication atmosphere. A warm handshake, a smile, the use of the interviewee's name in the greeting, and a word of thanks for coming will all aid in establishing the desired congenial atmosphere and reducing any natural anxiety. Discussing subjects of mutual interest can also help put the candidate at ease. As quickly as possible, but without unduly cutting off opening pleasantries, the interviewer should clearly state what he or she hopes to accomplish and then move into the background phase of the interview.

The background phase is where the interviewer examines the candidate's basic credentials for the job and tries to determine if the candidate meets or exceeds the requirements. Using questions and answers, the interviewer explores the candidate's knowledge, skills, and abilities. It is also a place to further confirm previously acquired information. Once qualifications have been assessed and verified, the interview progresses to the more open and personal discussion phase.

It is during the discussion phase that the interviewer starts helping the candidate match career goals with organizational opportunities and invites the candidate to ask questions. This is a very important part of the interview because it permits the interviewer to assess more subjective candidate characteristics and to personalize the company. A candidate's enthusiasm, motivation, and career goals can be revealed while providing more detailed explanations about the unique aspects of the job, advancement and self-development, and corporate philosophy. Not every candidate will be interested in the same things; consequently, these questions may vary considerably. The most valuable tools during the discussion phase are the open question, the probe, and active listening. By addressing candidate concerns, the discussion phase leads naturally to the close.

Many times, failure to pay attention to closure in the interview can greatly undermine what has been developed earlier. Regardless of how well a selection interview has gone, closing on the "Well, thanks for coming. We'll be in touch" note can all but destroy earlier progress. The psychological tone of the closing of an interview should be appropriate to what has already transpired. Therefore, a good close quickly reviews and summarizes the major points covered in the interview and provides a thorough orientation toward the next step. The interviewer will want to provide information needed to ensure a clear understanding of the actual employment procedures. The candidate should receive an explanation of when to expect to hear from the company, stated arrangements for any testing, or an invitation for a subsequent interview. An effective close to an interview requires that both parties know "where we're going from here."

The standard interview can be an effective selection strategy, but it has its potential drawbacks. Interviewers' decision-making processes may not be systematic or consistent. Interviewers often do not collect enough job-related information during the interview and may permit one subjective aspect of the interview to influence their overall judgment of a candidate. Finally, interviewers of a candidate often ask similar questions, which duplicates information and wastes time.[28]

Pressure to hire qualified candidates, Equal Employment Opportunity legislation, and the need to rely on something more than a "gut" feeling have prompted recruitment managers to explore new strategies to selection interviewing. Two highly desirable alternatives to the standard interview are—the behavioral description interview and the structured interview. Each is situation oriented, placing greater emphasis on performance and behavior rather than personal attitudes.

The Behavior Description Interview

Behavioral description interviewing proceeds from a structured pattern of questioning designed to probe the applicant's past behavior in specific situations and selected for its relevance to critical job events. It is based on the principle that the best predictor of future behavior is past behavior. Two corollaries fundamental to behavior description interviewing follow:

- *Corollary 1.* The more recent the past behavior, the greater its predictive power.
- *Corollary 2.* The more long-lasting the behavior, the greater its predictive power.[29]

Corollary 1 neither denies nor overvalues behavior from earlier stages of a person's career or life, but it does encourage the interviewer to focus most heavily on the most recent past behavior in similar circumstances. Corollary 2 encourages the interviewer to seek more than one sample of past behavior in similar circumstances. It does not permit overreaction to a single example in either a positive or negative direction. Here personal achievements and credentials are most important in making a recruiting or screening decision, not a selection or hiring decision. Achievements and credentials are important information for evaluating a person's motivations, but the interview should be directed toward gathering performance descriptive information—the application of knowledge, skills, abilities, and other characteristics.

At all times, then, the interviewer must be intellectually alert to reasonable extrapolation from the job analysis findings of KSAOs to the individual's background and back again. The interviewer asks the applicant about real-life work situations and from the applicant's answers assesses judgment and analyzes skills according to company criteria. Candidates have a wide latitude to discuss how they successfully solved a problem or dealt with a difficult issue.[30] For example, the following types of questions elicit behavior description information:

- Tell me about the most challenging project you completed in the past year. Were you given the project, or did you ask around to see what needed doing? What specifically was challenging about it? When did you complete the project? What other work were you doing at the time? Did anyone comment on the project? What were the comments?
- Tell me about a time when you needed to make some important decisions quickly? What were they? What happened?
- Tell me about a time when you helped someone else solve a problem with which they were having difficulty. What exactly proved to be the toughest obstacle? How did you tackle this obstacle? How successful were you in solving this problem? How did the other person respond?

The responses to these kinds of questions, when followed up with further behavior description questions, allows the interviewer to "watch" the applicant perform in the workplace. However, it can sometimes be difficult for candidates to come up with specific past examples; consequently, sympathetic persistence may be required. Sometimes candidates haven't had the experience described or are completely blocked for an answer, but even this can be insightful and revealing to the patient interviewer.

Certain principles or guidelines can help an interviewer move through the behavior description pattern more effectively. First and foremost, the interviewer must develop a "game plan" for the interview—decide ahead of time what is to be covered. The interviewer should develop this "game plan" on the basis of job-related information—the critical dimensions identified in the job profile. Second, the interviewer should balance the sequence of questions asked, being certain to elicit both stories of successes or accomplishments, as well as difficulties or problems. The interviewer wants the pattern of questioning to provide a total picture of the candidate. However, the balance of questions should be 60/40 or 70/30, with the majority on the positive side. Third, the interviewer should conduct the interview so that the applicant does most of the talking. Little information is obtained from a candidate who spends most of the interview nodding and smiling appropriately while the interviewer talks. Interviewers are trying to obtain information from candidates, and this can best be done by asking good questions, letting the candidate talk, and appropriately probing for details. Fourth, use tact in pursuing a behavior description answer. Be persistent and willing to use calculated pauses to provide the candidate time to recall a specific situation, but know when to gracefully move on to other issues. Finally, the interviewer should develop active listening skills and record observations about the candidate during the interview. The notes taken during the interview will be helpful when the interviewer attempts to make judgments about the candidate later. Only by carefully listening and recording impressions can an interviewer hope to keep the information about several applicants from becoming a confusing disarray.

The behavior description interview has several definite advantages over the traditional standard interview. First, the interviewer works from a pattern of questions that takes all candidates through roughly the same performance topics. Second, the topics are closely job related and focus on job performance features that have been found to indicate the difference between effective and ineffective performers. Critics, however, would say that it may be too job-specific, omitting many personality characteristics and other candidate attributes that should also be probed. Moreover, it is an involved process requiring considerable time that may not always be available, particularly when filling nonexempt and entry-level jobs. Consequently, its application may be limited.

While such a strategy may be time consuming and have its limitations, the accuracy for behavior description interviewing exceeds standard interviewing accuracy by three to seven times. Scott Paper initiated behavior description interviewing to find applicants whose judgment and sense of teamwork would fit their corporate culture. Hershey Food began similar training in behavior description interviewing so that managers "can judge between a 'fast horse and a champion' who'll fit Hershey's culture."[31]

The Structured Interview

Structured interviewing has also received increased attention from interviewers.[32] The structured interview is similar to the behavior description interview but has several distinguishing characteristics: (1) it contains a structured series of valid, experience-based questions, usually developed by a human resources team and often with the help of outside consultants, (2) interviewers are uniformly trained, and specific steps are taken to ensure that questions are consistently asked of all candidates for a position, and (3) each question is evaluated by a predetermined rating scale or matrix.[33] It is a carefully designed process in which interview questions are created and tailored to meet predetermined on-the-job criteria. The "W" questions asked are Who was responsible? What skills were needed? Where was this applicable? When did you do this kind of work? Why did you make that decision? Was the problem solved?[34]

Interviewers have a road map of questions and structured answers they use to choose the right candidates. Using this approach, interviewers evaluate candidates on experiential data, and therefore, decrease the potential of overrating individuals who are outstanding on one dimension or placing too much emphasis on some singular negative attribute of candidates. Here, candidates are evaluated only on situation-specific dimensions of the job with a standardized evaluation form or matrix permitting interviewers to rate the strengths and weaknesses of answers.

Successfully using a structured strategy requires analyzing the job, the department, and the entire organization to answer the questions, "What does it take to succeed in this job, in this department, and in this company?"

Interviewers using the traditional standard interview often do most of the talking, describing the job and selling candidates on the company. In the end, they are left with a few scribbled notes and confused impressions regarding the candidate's knowledge, experience, and abilities. Structured interviews have higher validity than less structured standard interviews and better address the troubling legal issues arising from asking questions unrelated to the job. When consistently administered among candidates, the structured interview may help employers have stronger cases against legal suits alleging disparate impact and invasion of privacy in hiring practices.[35] As a result, a growing number of interviewers are finding that the structured interview is a more "scientific" process and gives them greater confidence in the selection process.

*   *   *   *   *

A structured interview strategy was used to interview John Tight for *The Florida Monthly* position. Bob, Don, and Cole cordially greeted John, traced his educational background and limited experience, and asked predetermined job-related questions. They explored the nature of the job, as well as John's attitudes and opinions regarding the arts and entertainment field. Their line of questioning prompted John to discuss possible projects thus providing insights into how he would approach assignments, as well as revealing an independent, take-charge quality. Continued probing helped determine John's "fit" with *The Florida Monthly* culture and further confirmed his qualifications.

The joint interview gave Bob, Don, and Cole considerable control and ensured a uniformity in questioning. They were each able to hear and evaluate John's responses to the questions asked. Likewise, they were able to communicate a consistent message regarding the nature of the job and the company. The interview closed with John being given a tour of the company and letting him know exactly what would happen next. John was able to question other members of the writing staff and could anticipate receiving a hiring decision regarding *The Florida Monthly* position within the next couple of weeks.

The structured interview described was focused, specific, and job directed. Certainly, candidates could have found such a joint interview intimidating and stressful. It was a demanding type of interview, leaving little room for casual conversation. No one guaranteed a secure future, instead candid, realistic job expectations were presented. John Tight considered the interview to be tough but fair and left with a confident understanding of the job and the company.

Follow-Up and Evaluation

After the candidate leaves, the interviewer must carefully record the information and impressions received (See figure 3.2). This becomes important when later comparing and contrasting candidates. Additionally, this evaluative process allows interviewers to judge their skills and determine their personal effectiveness. This can be a useful learning experience and helpful when conducting future interviews.

*   *   *   *   *

This selection interview was atypical, representing an alternative hiring strategy that a growing number of employers are finding useful. It has greater validity and reliability, and is seemingly more democratic and ethical in its evaluative procedures. Candidates are compared and evaluated using a standard matrix instrument, which ensures that objective conclusions are reached regarding the fit between interviewees and the job requirements. Potentially discriminatory inquiries are avoided and personal biases curbed. Here, individual impressions were recorded and measured against an objectively prepared action plan, which resulted in a unanimous hiring decision. The final decision was to hire John Tight who will probably prove to be a successful writer and journalist. Certainly, a traditional standard selection interview or behavior description interview could have resulted in the same hiring decision and outcome.

Hiring is a time consuming and involving task. It requires a seriousness of purpose and expenditure of energy. Multiple decisions regarding potential candidates, the job, and the company must be made and communicated throughout the selection process. Therefore, effective interviewers should be particularly concerned with assessing their communicative strengths and weaknesses, including potential background biases and prejudices, personality variables, use of language, effectiveness in listening, and giving and receiving feedback. Interviewers who thoughtfully prepare, plan, and conduct selection interviews should have considerable confidence in their hiring decisions.

Interviewees must also mindfully approach the selection process, but that is the subject of chapter 4.

Candidate Review

Candidate_____ Date _____

Interview Summary (technical knowledge, maturity, ability to communicate, initiative, experience related to position, management style, etc.)

Candidate Strengths (key abilities, and characteristics)

1._____
2._____
3._____
4._____
5._____

Candidate Weaknesses (concerns about the candidate)

1._____
2._____
3._____
4._____
5._____

Summary (all things considered)

No Go		Marginal		Satisfactory		Desirable		Outstanding	
0	1	2	3	4	5	6	7	8	9	10

Interviewer's Signature   Date

FIGURE 3.2   Sample Candidate Review Form

Critical Focus

To better grasp the selection process, analyze the interview between Kevin Klee, founder and president of CompDesign Inc., and Nancy Byll, a twenty-three-year-old computer science major. An entry-level software design/computer programmer position has become available, and Kevin Klee is interviewing the top candidates. Using the interview between Kevin and Nancy, critically focus on Kevin's skill at conducting a selection interview.

CompDesign Inc. was started by Kevin Klee in 1990 as a specialized computer software design company providing creative custom work for a highly selective clientele. Klee prides himself on launching a company that takes innovation and quality seriously, never compromising on necessary details. For Klee, to work at CompDesign is a privilege, because rather than simply offering people jobs, it offers them a unique and challenging experience. Therefore, Klee's approach to potential employees is highly unorthodox. He insists on interviewing all promising recruits to assess their passion for excellence and test their commitment before they become a part of the CompDesign "family." This selection strategy has allowed him to put together in short order a talented and enthusiastic team, which has carved itself a prosperous niche in the software industry.

About three months ago, an entry-level software design/computer programmer resigned after only a year with the firm. The long, demanding hours forced him to choose between his career at CompDesign and his family, so he left the company for another job. A large number of qualified people have applied for the position, but somehow only a select few seem to exactly fit the bill. Some were dismissed because they expressed doubt about working long hours, others were passed over because they didn't seem to be team players, and a number were rejected because they didn't have the right attitude. However, the resumes of three seemingly enthusiastic candidates, among them Nancy Byll's, appear particularly promising, and Kevin Klee is hopeful that the position can be filled.

Kevin Klee and his team of employees have all agreed on the essential behavioral dimensions for the position. The new recruit should meet the following criteria:

1. Demonstrate technical expertise in designing programs and document software clearly, applying the full power of the software and hardware *versus* being sloppy and careless, taking many more operations than necessary and producing software that is difficult for others to follow.
2. Check work and test programs in a meticulous and thorough manner *versus* overlooks errors, doesn't thoroughly debug and verify test programs.
3. Demonstrate the ability to extract what the user really needs, provides advice and assistance to users when necessary *versus* having little or no communication with users.
4. Keep up to date with internal and external research in job-related topics *versus* being out of touch with recent research.
5. Seek stretching assignments, is creative *versus* avoiding challenges or preferring the routine.

Certainly, everyone at CompDesign Inc. agrees that whoever they hire must show an unswerving commitment to perfection and relate pleasantly and professionally with peers. With this preparation and general agreement among his team, Kevin Klee looks forward to interviewing Nancy Byll.

Nancy Byll, a computer science major, just graduated with honors from San Francisco State University. She has spent the last part of her senior year working closely with career counseling, preparing a resume and exploring the job market. Nancy realizes that a college degree alone does not guarantee a good job, so she has spent considerable time identifying career objectives and developing a personal career path.

She was delighted when CompDesign invited her to visit the company for an interview, since it was one of several companies on her preferred list. Her background research indicated that CompDesign does not offer high salaries but does provide extensive training and excellent experience. She is well aware of their superior reputation, as well as their commitment to excellence. Nancy understands that the hours will be long and the work demanding, but working with their creative team should be most rewarding. Moreover, an added benefit would be that Nancy could remain living in California, close to her family, friends, and boyfriend.

Nancy has been dating Carl Zgura, a business major at San Francisco State University, for a year. Carl has been accepted into an MBA program at Berkeley, and they had hoped to continue to see one another. An entry-level position at CompDesign would permit Nancy to establish her career and continue her relationship with Carl. After graduating with his MBA, they might even get married. The variety of work assignments, creative challenges, and desirable location makes this a promising position and CompDesign Inc. an ideal company. Nancy Byll anxiously looks forward to the interview.

The following critical questions can direct and guide your analysis of the ensuing interview between Kevin Klee and Nancy Byll.

1. Why do organizations conduct selection interviews? What are the phases of the selection process? Is Kevin Klee adequately prepared for the interview?
2. Was the interview conducted in an appropriate setting? Did it contribute to a supportive communication climate? Did Kevin act professionally?
3. How was the interview structured? What questions were asked? Were any discriminatory questions asked?
4. Did Kevin actively listen and carefully probe for details? Were all relevant issues discussed? How satisfactory was the closing?
5. Describe the factors influencing CompDesign's decision-making process. What recommendation is Kevin Klee likely to make based on this interview?
6. What lessons can be learned from the interview in the video segment?

Summary

The selection interview is crucial to the hiring process and an essential tool in selecting candidates. The EEOC has provided guidelines for interviewers to ask appropriate questions. Straying from a prepared schedule of job-related questions may open the interviewer to violations of federal and state laws.

Developing a job profile can guide key employment decisions made during the interview. The first step in creating an accurate profile is identifying required job responsibilities and duties. These duties, along with parallel personal attributes, must then be ranked according to job importance. The knowledge, skills, abilities, and other characteristics (KASOs) deemed important to performing the job will serve as the set standard for evaluation and measurement of candidates.

A carefully crafted job profile allows one to approach the recruitment process with confidence. Recruiting requires that applicants be carefully screened, resumes read, references checked, integrity tests administered, and applicant characteristics reviewed. Candidate credentials need to be assessed, verified, and evaluated.

The personal interview itself provides a critical time for making key decisions regarding hiring. However, the interviewer must create a positive interviewing environment and be sensitive to questioning techniques when choosing a selection strategy. While the traditional or standard selection interview can be effective, a growing number of interviewers are finding such alternatives as the behavior description interview and structured interview to be more valid and reliable. Each interviewing strategy has certain advantages and disadvantages which must be weighed and considered.

Finally, candidates must be compared and a hiring decision made. Additionally, effective interviewers should be particularly concerned with assessing their communicative strengths and weaknesses. They should take some time to evaluate their personal interviewing skills and competencies.

Ultimately, no substitute can be made for face-to-face communication during the selection interview and being able to assess an individual's knowledge, skills, and abilities. This important opportunity allows the interviewer and candidate to candidly exchange job-related information and find if the right "fit" exists. When properly conducted, the organization benefits with lower turnover, lower hiring costs, and stronger personnel.

SHARPENING YOUR FOCUS

1. What are some of the common mistakes made in selection interviewing? Discuss also the forces inhibiting effective selection interviewing. How can they be tempered so as to produce a dialogue which can help the interviewer make informed decisions?

2. Compare and contrast the standard interview, behavior description interview, and structured interview. Note strengths and weaknesses of each.

3. Behavioral interviewing is a relatively new style of interviewing developed by industrial psychologists. The key to "getting good responses" is posing a question that elicits a behavioral example of the interviewee's behavior. A behavioral example is a description of a specific life history event which can be used to rate the presence of a job skill. STAR is a simple interview question model used to probe for behavioral information. The interviewee is asked for a Situation or Task performed, what Action was taken, and what Result(s) came of the action. The following is a list of responses collected from interviewees by interviewers. Some of the responses are complete STARs, while others lack one or more of the components. For those that are not complete behavioral examples, indicate which part of the STAR is missing:

a. "Right after I broke the wheel down, I asked for new bearings and then found out we didn't have any. So I just repacked the bearings and put everything back together. The wheel still ran too hot. My boss was furious when I told him what I did."

b. "I overloaded the roaster with coffee beans before the final roasting cycle every day until the machine finally broke down and had to be replaced."

c. "When I first joined the company, the way we handled customer billings was a real mess. There was no system at all."

d. "I was responsible for ensuring that the annual stockholders' report was prepared on time, so I always made sure that I planned it well in advance, and that usually seemed to work."

Answers: (a) Complete STAR, (b) Needs situation/task, (c) Needs action and result, (d) Is a "False STAR" and needs a complete STAR.

4. How would you, as an interviewer/interviewee, prepare for a behavioral interview?

5. What impact are civil rights legislation, EEOC rulings, and court decisions having on selection interviewing? What types of questions would be considered inappropriate or discriminatory?

6. Describe your best-ever job interview. How was the interview planned and conducted? What contributed to its success? How did you feel during and after the interview? Why? Who was responsible for its positive results? The interviewer? The interviewee? Both? Could more selection interviews be conducted as effectively as this "best-ever" experience?

7. Choose a particular job—perhaps your own—and plan an interview. Develop a job profile, and note important legal considerations. Would you test for integrity? How? Provide a rationale for the selection approach chosen and sample interview questions. What are the critical items on which you would make decisions about candidates? How would you evaluate your skills at selection interviewing? Circle the term that best describes your current competency level: superior/ excellent/ above average/ average/ below average/ poor/ terrible. Explain your answer.

NOTES

1. A. Kinicki and C. Lockwood, "The Interview Process: An Examination of Factors Recruiters Use in Evaluating Job Applicants," *Journal of Vocational Behavior* 26 (1985): 117–25.
2. Michele K. Kacmar and Wayne A. Hochwarter, "The Interview as a Communication Event: A Field Examination of Demographic Effects on Interview Outcomes," *Journal of Business Communication* 32 (1995): 207–32.
3. Eugene Mayfield, "The Selection Interview—A Re-evaluation of Published Research," *Personnel Psychology* 17 (1964): 171–180 and Orman R. Wright, Jr., "Summary of Research on the Selection Interview Since 1964," *Personnel Psychology* 22 (1969): 394–401.
4. Dina Ingber, "How Not to Hire a Turkey," *The Dallas Morning News,* 17 September, 1985, 1C–2C.
5. Gillian Flynn, "Closing Time: Master the Art," *Personnel Journal* (August 1995): 23–26.
6. Leyland F. Pitt and B. Ramaseshan, "Realistic Job Information and Salesforce Turnover: An Investigative Study," *Journal of Managerial Psychology* 10 (1995): 29–36.
7. Phillip M. Perry, "Legal Traps in Interviews," *Cellular Business,* September 1995, 24.
8. Junda Woo, "Job Interviews Pose Rising Risk to Employers," *The Wall Street Journal,* 11 March, 1995, B5.

9. Cal W. Downs, G. Paul Smeyak, and Ernest Martin. *Professional Interviewing* (New York: Harper and Row Publishers, 1980), 134.
10. Francesca Spilelli Souza and Jay J. Zajas, "Recruiting Executives in Business: An Organizational and Conceptual Perspective," *Executive Development* 8 (1995): 23–27.
11. Samuel Greengard, "Are You Well Armed to Screen Applicants?" *Personnel Journal* 74 (December 1995): 84–95.
12. Robert Half, *On Hiring* (New York: Penguin, 1985), 126.
13. Frances A. McMorris, "Ex-bosses Face Less Peril Giving Honest Job References," *The Wall Street Journal,* 8 July, 1996, B1, B6.
14. Ibid, B1.
15. Clive Fletcher, "What Means to Assess Integrity?" *Personnel Management* 1 (August 1995): 30–31.
16. Joan E. Rigdon, "Deceptive Resumes Can Be Door-Openers but can Become an Employee's Undoing," *The Wall Street Journal,* 17 June, 1992, B1.
17. Fletcher, "What Means to Assess Integrity?" pp. 30–31.
18. Kim J. Wade and Angelo J. Kinicki, "Examining Objective and Subjective Applicant Qualifications within a Process Model of Interview Selection Decisions," *Academy of Management Journal* (1995): 155.
19. Kacmar and Hochwarter, "The Interview as a Communication Event, p. 221.
20. Fredrick M. Jablin and Karen B. McComb, "The Empolyment Screening Interview: An Organizational Assimilation and Communication Perspective," in *Communication Yearbook* 8 ed. Robert N. Bostrom (Beverly Hills, Calif.: Sage, 1984) 137–63.
21. Richard J. Ilkaa, "Applicant Appearance and Selection Decision Making: Revitalizing Employment Interview Education," *Business Communication Quarterly* 58 (1995): 11–18.
22. T. F. Cash and R. N. Kilcullen, "The Eye of the Beholder: Susceptibility to Sexism and "Beautyism" in the Evaluation of Managerial Applicants," *Journal of Applied Social Psychology* 15 (1985): 591–605.
23. John Wareham, "How to Judge an Executive Candidate," *Across the Board* 22 (1980): 29.
24. "Learning to Read Job Applicants Like a Book," *National Petroleum News,* 87 (May 1995): 44.
25. Half, *On Hiring,* 76.
26. Mark L. Hickson and Don W. Stacks. *NVC Nonverbal Communication: Studies and Applications.* 3d ed. (Dubuque, Iowa: Brown and Benchmark, 1993).
27. Robin Widgery and Cecil Stackpole, "Desk Position, Interviewee Anxiety, and Interviewer Credibility: An Example of Cognitive Balance in a Dyad," *Journal of Counseling Psychology* 19 (1972): 173 77.
28. Erica Gordon Sorohan, "Haphazard Hiring," *Training and Development* 49 (July 1995): 14.
29. Tom Janz, Lowell Hellervik, and David Gilmore. *Behavior Description Interviewing* (Boston: Allyn and Bacon, 1986), 33.
30. Robert L. Desatnick, "Behaviorally Oriented Interviews Find the Right Hires," *Human Resources Professional* 8 (May/June 1995): 6–9.
31. "Creative Interviewing Takes Firmer Hold as the Job Pinch Worsens," *The Wall Street Journal,* 8 May, 1990, A1.
32. See S. D. Maurer and C. Fay, "Effect of Situational Interviews, Conventional Structured Interviews, and Training on Interview Rating or Agreement: An Experimental Analysis," *Personnel Psychology* 41 (1988): 329–44; W. L. Tuller, "Relational Control in the Employment Interview," *Journal of Applied Psychology* 74 (1989): 971–77; and P. M. Wright, P. A. Lichtenfels, and E. D. Pursell, "The Structured Interview: Additional Studies and a Meta-Analysis," *Journal of Occupational Psychology* 62 (1989): 191–199.
33. Elaine D. Palakos and Neal Schmitt, "Experience-based and Situational Interview Questions: Studies of Validity," *Personnel Psychology* 48 (1995): 289–308.
34. C. E. Wilson, "The New Generation of Selection Interviews: Structural, Behavior-Based, Valid." (paper presented at the annual meeting of the Speech Communication Association, Chicago, Ill., 1990).
35. J. Hollwitz, "Legal and Ethical Implications of Structural Interviewing" (paper presented at the annual meeting of the Speech Communication Association, Chicago, Ill., 1990).

4 The Selection Interview II

When we think of job hunting, the selection interview immediately comes to mind, and for good reason. It is the most common form of interviewing in organizations. Often an employee's first contact with an organization is through the selection interview. The principles, practices, and procedures you will learn from this chapter are key for a successful employment interview.

Chapter 4 approaches the selection interview as only one of several important written and verbal communication variables in the selection process. Hiring and selection decisions are based not only on oral communication factors during the actual interview, but also on written communication factors, such as the resume and letter of application. The actual interview must be viewed only as part of the total selection interview process. Within an ethical framework, we discuss career planning, resume preparation, writing the letter of application, and participating in the interview itself. This chapter is designed to accomplish three objectives:

1. *Awareness.* You will learn how to prepare for the selection interview through career planning, as well as resume and application letter strategies.

2. *Assessment.* You will be able to determine what is important in a resume and application letter and assess your interviewing effectiveness within an ethical framework.

3. *Application.* You will be able to approach a selection interview with confidence and understanding, applying techniques of effective interviewing.

* * * * *

It Was Just Chit-Chat

Don Bollin has worked as a Human Resource manager for Midwest Manufacturing Oil for twelve years. Considered as one of the top managers at the company, he is experienced with policy, as well as current on EEO laws and guidelines. He takes pride in his department and staff, especially in his track record of hiring and keeping employees, and maintaining high ethical standards in hiring. In fact, nearly all the employees he has personally interviewed and hired since 1992 have remained with the company and become top performers. As Human Resource manager, Don makes hiring decisions and reports directly to Fred Myrick, president of operations.

Midwest has added fifteen new employees over the past three years, increasing Don's workload and pressuring his department. A growing company, Midwest manufactures synthetic oil, a highly specialized lubricant needed for electric motors and engines requiring a high grade of machine oil. Most of the company's fifty-two employees work in a manufacturing plant on company property. Turnover has been low. The sales staff have increased to ten full-time staff, increasing annual gross sales to $10 million in 1997 from $8 million in 1996. One reason Don attributes to low turnover and increased growth is that the managers and owners function as a close-knit group. Several of the owner's family members have been hired as staff and sales representatives. In this close family atmosphere, morale is high, and Don keeps a keen sense of responsibility when hiring.

The Friday Don was scheduled to interview Sue Fling had been a particularly hectic one. He had been out of the office since 8:30 A.M., and the 3:00 P.M. interview caught him by surprise. He remembered the interview during the day but was unable to prepare as he would have liked. A few minutes before, he hurriedly reviewed Sue's file and headed to the conference room.

As Sue waited patiently in the conference room, she quietly reviewed her research about Midwest and prepared for the interview. She had researched Midwest's background and found a high-growth company with excellent salary and benefits. The company was also located near her home and would not require a move for her and her family. She definitely wanted the job and hoped to convince the interviewer of her worth, but she was slightly nervous about omissions and slight exaggerations on her resume. She had not indicated that several of her previous jobs were only part time and had perhaps overstated her computer compatibility and program fluency. At the time, she had dismissed this since "everybody enhances their qualifications somewhat." Now, she's fearful of coming on too strong.

When Sue applied for the accounting position, Don had briefly checked her credentials. He called her background references and verified college transcripts, but he did not thoroughly check the work experience listed on her resume. Otherwise, her credentials were in order, and he purposed in the selection interview to check for "fit" with the close family culture at Midwest Manufacturing.

The interview began well. After the initial greeting, Don made inquiries about Sue's home and family, hoping to "break the ice" and make her feel comfortable. Sue seemed happy to discuss how close she was to her children and family. The interview was conversational, with each "chatting" away. Subsequently, Don proceeded to discuss the more technical aspects of the accounting position. As the interview progressed, Don realized Sue's accounting experience was limited and incomplete. Two of her previous jobs had been only part time. Furthermore, she was not familiar with the software systems Midwest used. When asked if she had any questions, Sue said, "No, you've clearly described the duties required for the position and answered questions about salary and benefits." Don ended the thirty-minute interview cordially but knew he would not hire her.

Within two weeks following the interview, Don sent Sue a letter thanking her for her application but turning her down for the job. He attributed his decision to her limited experience and inadequate software skills, but the rejection left nagging questions in Sue's mind. Midwest eventually hired Bob Maxwell for the position. He was a certified public accountant and familiar with a variety of computer applications ideally suited to Midwest Manufacturing. Incredibly, a few months afterwards, Don receives a surprise notice that Sue Fling has filed a complaint against Midwest alleging sexual discrimination. She claims that the informal inquiry during the interview regarding her family and children would not have been asked of a male candidate and that she lost the job as a result. Don sits at his desk, pondering his fate, his department's excellent track record shattered by the notice.

Discussion Questions

1. Did Don Bollin and Sue Fling approach the interview with a similar ethical understanding?
2. Had Sue adequately considered her career objectives and prepared a career plan?
3. Did Sue's resume and letter of application appropriately outline her qualifications and strengths for the accounting position?
4. Was Sue adequately prepared for the interview? How might she have responded to the technical inquiries? How important were the inquiries about Sue's family and children?
5. What kind of follow-up and evaluation should Sue pursue?

The Interviewee's Perspective

Because most organizations use the selection interview, we encounter it at some point during our lives. Over 99 percent of organizations rely on the selection interview as part of their hiring procedures.[1] Thus, unless we work in a family-owned business or pursue a career not requiring an interview, the selection interview emerges as a major step in obtaining employment. No two interviews are the same, individual personalities and philosophies influence the conduct of any interview. However, the purposes of selection interviews, generally, are to give information and to seek information. In this sense, they are informational conversations in which the interviewer seeks information from you, the job applicant, but there are also times at which you, the applicant, seek information from the interviewer.

Although the selection interview is the most commonly used tool of the selection process, most hiring managers do not rate it positively.[2] *The Wall Street Journal* further reports that one in four entry-level hires fails to make it through the first year, and this can be costly to any company or organization.[3] With this rather gloomy but accurate perspective in hiring, it is little wonder why John Lafevre observes that "interviewers are merely professional gamblers who have been provided a thirty-minute tip sheet analysis to help them decide on which candidate to place the bet."[4] However, through knowledge and understanding of the selection interview, we will see how this formidable process can be a positive, beneficial experience for both the interviewer and interviewee.

Ethics and Selection Interviewing

Someone once said, "No one is more ethical than someone who has just become ethical."[5] A proper understanding of the selection interview first requires relating the purpose of the employment interview with certain basic ethical principles. Most of us would state categorically that the interview's only purpose is to get a job; William Kirkwood and Steve Ralston would disagree. They perceive the selection interview as "a collaborative dialogue that acknowledges and supports the needs of employers and applicants to make informed decisions about whom to hire and which offers to accept."[6] They emphasize that the interview's ethical purpose is to discover whether you are right for the company and the company is right for you. The purpose is not to get a job, but to get the *right job*. The needs of both applicant and employer must be addressed. The interview achieves its purpose through the exchange of relevant, honest, and candid information by both employer and applicant. All too often, they assert, "students are sometimes taught that the aim is not sharing useful information, but rather creating favorable impressions."[7]

Two ethical principles should guide the selection interview process. First, interviewees should not conceal or distort information about their abilities or motives with respect to a given job. Second, interviewees should not use irrelevant appeals to influence the hiring process. Emphasizing the positive and glossing over the negative means giving an ethically questionable or "best" answer to an employer which may place expediency over honesty and relevance. Although interviewees want to show "their best face" in an interview, the goal of a selection interview is the candid, genuine exchange of information so that an informed decision can be made by both employer and applicant. To "manage your impressions" otherwise would be unethical.

*   *   *   *   *

Don Bollin and Sue Fling approached the interview with differing ethical principles, which became apparent during the interview. Don was particularly interested in hiring a qualified candidate who could "fit" into the distinct "family atmosphere" characterizing Midwest Manufacturing. He saw the interview as an opportunity to not only explore technical skills but to also probe attitudes and opinions, which would reveal the personality of a job applicant. For him, the task was hiring the right person for the right job. Don's previously successful hiring experiences instilled in him a sense of confidence and pride in his ability to match people and positions to Midwest's close-knit partnership.

Sue Fling was certainly a decent, upright, moral person of worthy character—and probably, basically honest. She expressed a genuine closeness to her family and community. However, her immediate concern to get a job has created an ethical dilemma, whereby she distorted and exaggerated her qualifications. While some applicants may enhance their credentials, this *does not* give one license to do so. Hyperbole and overstatement can only jeopardize the effectiveness of the interview. Here, her omissions and embellishments were revealed during careful questioning by Don Bollin. Sue needed to take a look at herself in the mirror and have a talk with herself about who she is, what her skills are, what she wants, and what value she has to offer a company. Until she does this, she will be wasting her time and the interviewer's. The interview should not be a battle of wits, but rather a meeting of minds. Sue's goal should not be a job, but the right job.

The Uniqueness of the Selection Interview

The selection interview possesses no common content, and no single interview procedure exists. Because the content varies widely, each selection interview is unique and may vary widely in several respects. This uniqueness of the selection interview is both an asset and a challenge to the employer and applicant.

Selection interviews are distinctive in at least five respects.[8] First, some organizations use a simple, single-step process when selecting applicants. **Single-step selection** means that an organization usually makes a final selection decision based on a single phase, such as one interview. In contrast, when using a **multi-step process,** the organization requires candidates to pass several steps or phases before making a final employment decision. These additional steps may include multiple interviews, physical skills testing, or psychological assessments, or drug tests. For example, a large grocery company in the Southwest requires each applicant for a position in its warehouse division to take a physical skills test. One part of this test, a computerized physical exam that measures an applicant's muscle and back strength, helps the company reduce unnecessary medical costs and lessen employee time away from the job due to physical injuries. The grocer also requires drug tests as part of its employment process. Other companies, however, may not require physical examinations and drug tests, but rather psychological or honesty tests.

Second, selection interviews vary greatly in the breadth and depth of what is discussed. Some interviewers may only cover in depth one or two of your personality attributes related to the job. For instance, a bank employer may look for such attributes as honesty and accuracy in a teller position and spend most of the time discussing these characteristics. Similarly, a physician may look for such attributes as warmth and openness in an office receptionist who frequently greets patients. In contrast, other interviewers may try to "learn a little about a lot of things," broadly covering a number of topics but not discussing any of them in depth.

Third, different structures also make each selection interview unique. While some interviewers use a highly standardized question format, restricting the interview to an elaborate scoring procedure, others use a moderate schedule, allowing open-ended questions and unstructured evaluations. In a moderately scheduled interview, the candidate has more room to talk freely and may choose which topics to discuss. A more open schedule may allow employers to assess your communication skills by asking you to clearly explain a solution to a hypothetical problem.

Fourth, the role of the interviewer also varies widely. For instance, you may encounter a decision maker whose sole purpose is to evaluate the interview and render judgment on your application. In contrast, another interviewer may only seek to gather information about you and make a recommendation to a supervisor concerning your application. In fact, many interviewers who serve as recruiters function only in a public relations capacity for the company.

Fifth, some selection interviews emphasize behaviors on the job, while other interviews focus only on personality traits of the applicant, such as motivation, honesty, or dependability. These five unique characteristics of the selection interview demonstrate why each situation you encounter is dynamic, requiring knowledge and skill to adapt to the process. Some information about a candidate can *only* be obtained through the interview. Written materials don't reveal certain characteristics.

Getting a job at Carrier Corp., a major air conditioning manufacturing company, illustrates the uniqueness and variety of the selection process. For them, the interview is an invitation to do the job, and successful candidates will win the job by doing it. Being hired by this manufacturer has been likened to a multistep approach of a college application. Carrier uses a variety of interviewing approaches, but its worker involvement in the interview is noteworthy. An Arkansas plant first requires applicants to hold a high school diploma or general equivalency degree and to pass a standard state skills test, choosing only those who score in the top third. Next, interviews with assembly line workers or other peers occurs, and their impressions often determine whether candidates are hired. Those who do well in the interviews advance to the next step, enrolling in a six-week training course to learn mathematics, statistics, problem solving, and computer skills. The applicants, who are not paid for their time in the course and typically hold other jobs, are discretely observed by the instructors regarding how well they work with others. This elaborate, time-consuming selection process at Carrier virtually guarantees employment if applicants make it through the course. As a result, many benefits follow, giving new employees greater say-so in company decisions and more authority over decisions which affect their work. While it is an involved process and not suited for all companies, it works for Carrier.[9]

Remember, you can best prepare for elaborate selection interviews by not assuming an interview formula exists. Each interview in which you participate will be unique, varying in its content, structure, question format, interviewer role, and focus on job behaviors and/or traits. Despite these wide variations, certain interview principles are common to each selection interview. The remainder of this chapter focuses on these principles. How well you learn them will determine your success in the interview.

*   *   *   *   *

Don Bollin experienced many of the common pressures human resource professionals face today. Growth at Midwest Manufacturing Oil had greatly increased Don's workload. Because fifteen employees were added in three years, Don's responsibilities included more travel, increased paperwork, and supervision of more staff. He enjoyed the hard work and kept long hours. Conducting interviews within this growth climate, however, occasionally distracted Don from fully concentrating on the interview. Like many interviewers, he sometimes was unable to prepare fully for the interview. When he found himself unprepared, he relied on his background, experience, and knowledge to guide his actions during the interview.

The interview between Don Bollin and Sue Fling was a single-step process, with Don empowered to make the final selection decision. He followed a moderate interviewing schedule, focusing on technical skills and selected personality traits. Sue was encouraged to elaborate on open-ended questions. While this interview appeared conversational and "chatty," it was purposeful and directed. Clearly, Don was assessing Sue's abilities and evaluating her corporate suitability. Sue should not have been lulled into dismissing this interview as mere chit-chat.

Career Planning and Preparation

Preparing for a selection interview begins long before you actually begin writing your resume or participating in the interview. Early preparation involves planning—setting career goals and determining your job objective. Remember, employers are not in the business of career planning and quickly lose patience with undirected job seekers.

Career planning requires knowing yourself and giving serious thought to your needs, interests, skills, and goals. Whether you are about to graduate, are a recent graduate, fast-tracker, workforce reentrant, career-changer, or what have you, pause and take stock. If you don't do the work necessary to identify *where you want to go,* you'll never get there. Respond to the following checklist (See figure 4.1) before reading on and then score yourself.

Scoring these questions and developing thoughtful answers can serve as a useful self-inventory before writing your resume. Such a personal inventory will

---

Where Are You in Your Career Planning/Job Search?

This checklist is designed to help you determine if you are on target in your career planning and job search. The way you answer the following questions may yield some important clues. Answer each question "Yes" or "No", then tally you "Yes" answers at the end of the form.

What You Know About Yourself

_____ 1. Can you articulate what you have gained from your education?
_____ 2. Can you explain why you chose your major?
_____ 3. Can you name the work activities you do well and most enjoy? How about nonwork activities?
_____ 4. Can you list at least five marketable skills and abilities you possess?
_____ 5. For each of you most important job-related experiences, can you list:
    _____a. Five things you did?
    _____b. Five things you learned?
    _____c. Several contributions you made or things you accomplished?
_____ 6. Can you describe your greatest strength? Your greatest weakness?
_____ 7. Have you clearly defined your geographical preferences and limitations?
_____ 8. Have you determined the salary range you will consider?

What You Know About The World Of Work

_____ 9. Can you name at least three fields of employment in which you are interested?
_____10. Do you know the type of organization for which you would like to work?
_____11. Can you describe the characteristics of the work environment in which you feel you would be happiest and most productive?
_____12. Can you name at least five kinds of employers that might hire a person with your background?

FIGURE 4.1   Career Checklist

_____13. Do you know at least four or five resources to help you find answers to questions 9, 11, and 12?
_____14. Can you name at least four sources of information that could help you discover potential employers in a particular geographical area?
_____15. Have you recently talked to at least three people who are employed in your field of interest with the purpose of learning more about what they do?

Goal Setting

_____16. Can you clearly and confidently state your career goals?
_____17. Can you distinguish your more immediate job objectives from your long-range career goals?

Job Hunting

_____18. Can you name at least five employers whom you plan to contact regarding employment in the near future?
_____19. Are you familiar with the organizational structures, services, programs, or products of the employers whom you are planning to contact?
_____20. Can you clearly state why you are interested in working for each employer whom you contact?
_____21. Have you prepared a resume with which you are satisfied?
_____22. Do you know the questions employers are likely to ask you in an interview?
_____23. Have you used any of the following methods to prepare for interviews?
_____a. Career Placement Services interview workshops/seminars?
_____b. Role playing with a friend or relative?
_____c. Writing out answers to common interview questions?
_____d. Role playing by yourself in front of a mirror?
_____24. Have you considered ways of developing job leads other than advertised listings?
_____25. Have you consulted the schedule of employers who will be conducting on-campus recruiting visits to determine the organizations with which you might like to interview?

Now What?

Add up your "Yes" answers for each section and enter them below:

What You Know about Yourself _____
What You Know about The World of Work _____
Goal Setting _____
Job Hunting _____

                          Total _____

Total Score 25 35   On the right track
Total Score 15 24   Close
Total Score 14 or below Need help and advisement

*Taken from the University of California-Berkeley and University Communications

FIGURE 4.1   Continued

save you from making some job-selection errors, such as accepting a job that is incompatible with your needs, aspirations, or temperament.

Making an informed decision about your career also demands that you "rule some things in and rule some things out."[10] Therefore, your personal career assessment must include and integrate five interrelated conditions. First, it must be something you genuinely like to do. This choice requires you to identify your own strengths, weaknesses, and interests. Some excellent psychometric tests are available to help with this need. Second, it must be something you have the ability to do. You must have the necessary academic background, talent, and aptitude. Third, it must be something you can earn a living by doing. Being successful may be one thing, but maintaining a desired standard of living may be another. Fourth, it must be something you are permitted to do. Any profession or occupation selected must be socially acceptable. Finally, it must be something that brings cultural affirmation. In other words, most people need to feel some measure of respect from their contemporaries for what they do.

It may be better to think of a career less as a ladder and more like a web; webs have a center but no top and a lot of paths that connect. Moving along webs, you earn from the skills developed rather than simply seniority. Today, the notion of a career ladder is somewhat antiquated. Most people find that they spiral from job to job, sometimes in the same company, sometimes between companies. They stay within a general field of competence, but generally, that field has no sharply defined borders.

Once you've set career goals, analyzed what you have to offer, and determined what you want, the next step involves matching your qualifications with an employer. When you walk into an interview, it has to be for a job you carefully selected; a job that you are ready and able to do. Here, you are seeking to relate your skills and abilities directly to the needs of a potential employer.

Develop and use a network of contacts. When you talk with people working in the career field or make important contacts with friends or former colleagues in your field, you are networking. *The Wall Street Journal* reported that of 351 job-seeking clients surveyed over an eighteen month period, 60 percent found employment through networking, with only 15 percent responding to newspaper listings.[11] Similarly, Cheryl Hamilton and Cordell Parker report "of those looking for a job, 5 percent were found through newspaper ads, 10 percent were found through job agencies, 85 percent were found through networking or direct employee contact."[12] Recently, Labor Secretary Robert Reich also advised graduates and job candidates to "network" with others in their professions if they had a sincere desire to locate employment opportunities.[13]

Regularly visit the career counseling center at your school and take advantage of their services. Moreover, according to Tony Lee, 83 percent of college placement offices also offer alumni individual career counseling.[14] College centers offer free (or for a nominal fee) personal inventories, seminars, mock interviews, and placement advice. Furthermore, most career counseling centers host or sponsor job fairs, which attract employment recruiters.

Research and contact those organizations you consider particularly desirable as a potential employer. You might consult organizational directories appropriate to your field of interest, such as *Thomas' Register of American Manufacturers, Standard and Poor's Register, Moody's Industrial Manual, Macmillan Job Guide to American Corporations, 25,000 Leading American Corporations,* or the *United States Government Manual.* Your research should include products or services, history, corporate culture, organizational goals, advancement paths, and industry ranking with competitors. Read articles about the organization published in newspapers, magazines, or professional/trade journals, as well as study the organizational literature and annual reports. Also, online databases are available to aid your search for a particular position. For instance, the Dow Jones/Retrieval offers internet access to the on-line version of *The Wall Street Journal* and to the Dow Jones news wire (internet address: http://wsj.com) for a fee. This on-line service allows key word searches of articles and companies, helping the user to conduct searches by name. Furthermore, calling or visiting an office can assist in gaining useful information and may open up an opportunity. Investigating a potential employer not only demonstrates your knowledge and seriousness, but it can also help determine if the company is right for you. Students would be wise to engage in shadowing programs or enroll for an internship with an organizational sponsor. This can provide excellent exposure to potential employers, as well as practical career experience.

Check the help wanted ads, and contact employment agencies and contractors for possible job vacancies in your area. Newspaper listings can be a readily accessible resource, however their published listings usually constitute only 20 percent of the market.[15] Public and private hiring agencies also have current, dependable information and can be found in any telephone directory. However, be sure to inquire about employment fees in advance. Public agencies don't charge or require small fees, while the higher fees of private agencies may be charged to you or the employer if the listing is fee paid. Interestingly, some employers notify these agencies first about a job. One major oil company headquartered in Texas notifies the Texas Employment Agency (TEC) one week before advertising the position in company ads or other bulletin boards. The worldwide net can also be a useful resource for job listings and available positions.

Finally, make contacts through active membership in professional organizations. Membership in national, regional, and state associations demonstrates a keen interest in your career field. It also keeps you on the cutting edge, alert to current developments and changes. Once you have decided on a prospective employer or position, you are ready to write your resume.

*   *   *   *   *

> Sue Fling explored her career choices and defined the type of job she wanted. Additionally, she gave some time to researching Midwest's background, discovering that it was a "high growth" company. Company reports and brochures, as well as articles in business and trade journals, were probably helpful in this regard. However, despite this laudable beginning, her homework was incomplete and superficial.

Rather than focusing on the job to be performed and the software systems employed, she was diverted by salary, benefits, and geographical location. While these are not unimportant considerations, the job and her value to the company should have commanded her attention. Talking with people in the field and available Midwest employees could have revealed job-specific information. This would have permitted an opportunity to familiarize herself with the requisite accounting procedures and computer applications. Questions requiring technical expertise regarding specific projects might then have been more adequately answered. Moreover, a plan to remedy any background deficiencies could have been prepared and presented. The investment made in finding important information can pay off during the interview.

The Resume

The purpose of a resume is to sell yourself and get an interview. It is an opportunity to organize the relevant facts about yourself in a concise written presentation and to communicate your value as a potential employee. Moreover, by identifying your strengths, you will also better understand those areas in which you are weak. As a biographical summary or career portrait of one's professional and educational background, the resume is one of the most important documents that a person creates.

Resumes are likely to play an increasingly important role in the selection process during the next decade. A marked decrease in on-campus recruiting during the past several years has forced applicants and employers to rely increasingly on resumes for preliminary screening. Moreover, over 75 percent of those newly jobless are managers, professionals, or administrative or technical staff, and this influx of white-collar workers is affecting the job market.[16] Under these circumstances, the traditional one-page resume is likely to be an inadequate hiring tool. Harold Hellwig notes that "the one-page resume, though still the norm, is fading fast."[17] A one-page resume may not allow an applicant to present him- or herself well nor provide employers with enough information for adequate evaluations and comparisons of applicants. Authorities note that student applicants more often err on the side of making resumes too short rather than too long.[18]

Because the hiring manager who looks at your resume will spend less than a minute reading it, your resume should clearly and concisely state important points.[19] When considering your application with literally hundreds of others, an employer looks for "knock-out factors" or those errors or missing information which cause your resume to be rejected. Most knockout factors can be avoided by screening your finished resume carefully for typographical errors, missing information, or poor formatting and presentation. Remember, the resume is a written document that provides a basis for judgment about your capabilities.

Content and Structure

There are no panaceas or absolutes for writing the resume; however, there is certain standard information that should appear on every resume. This includes your name; address; telephone number(s); qualifications including education, training, and work experience; and references. Remember that your content should relate to your knowledge, skills, abilities, and other characteristics (KSAOs) that relate to the job. *Do not* include personal information regarding height, weight, health, marital status, or children.

Frequent questions arise over resume content and should be addressed. Answers to the following questions must also be based on your research of the company, analysis of the job, and network contacts with others in the field.

Do I include a job objective or summary statement of career goals? Many writers consider this material optional since it can appropriately be included in your letter of application. This also permits you to tailor your job objective and career goals to the particular position. Others consider it standard, particularly in technically specific fields. When included, objectives and goals must be precisely stated rather than the customarily ambiguous "challenging position where I can apply my education and work experience."

Should I include my grade point average (GPA)? If your GPA reflects academic excellence, a B average or above, it should be included. Also note if you graduated with honors. Otherwise, to place your GPA on the resume may not be the best guideline to follow. If you worked full time while attending school, your GPA may reflect time management difficulties more than educational ability. Obviously, your GPA should be included if the employer requests it.

Should I place the category "Education" before "Work Experience" or after? Some argue that "Education" should precede "Work Experience," since many positions require a college degree. This permits an employer to immediately qualify you as a potential candidate. Moreover, it attests to your having the necessary academic training. However, if you wish to emphasize relevant work experience, place it first. Place the category first that you wish to receive the most attention.

How far back do I include work experience? Whether you include five, ten, or more years of work experience, your decision should be guided by the relationship of the experience to the job description. Omitting work experience and creating gaps in your resume may raise questions, since employers are assessing your work ethic, as well as job relevance. A recent student debated over listing his twelve years full-time experience on off-shore oil rigs in the Gulf of Mexico, since he was pursuing an accounting degree and hoped to become a certified public accountant (CPA). However, after graduation, he accepted a position with a firm specializing in oil and gas accounting, and his unique off-shore experience actually helped him obtain the job. It is generally advisable to include at least the last ten years of work experience, but *all* work experience must be listed on the official application form prior to employment. Any omissions on the official job application could be grounds for later dismissal.

How long should I make my resume? The length should fit your individual needs and the position for which you have applied. Burdette Bostwick, a foremost career consultant, observes that "there is no standard resume length . . . a six-page resume can be concise, a three-page resume verbose."[20] The resume should answer the question: Who are you? What do you know? What have you done? What are your special assets or attributes? and What you can do? Many managers consider a two-page limit a conservative and safe guideline.

Should I include community service? Community service can be important as corporations come to accept the idea that community activities are good public relations. A seat on the city/village council, work with the Boy Scouts/Girl Scouts, voluntary service, charitable cause involvement, or fund-raising work are all activities that show a willingness to involve oneself and can often demonstrate organizational abilities. Omit references to any religious, political, or otherwise potentially controversial affiliations.

Are personal hobbies and interests important? Hobbies and activities can be worth noting if they fit into certain broad categories. These would include team sports (baseball, basketball), individual determination activities (tennis, golf, jogging, swimming, skiing, bicycling), and "brain activities" (bridge, chess, backgammon, reading). They reveal how you use your leisure time. In an age when "burnout" has become a recognized phenomenon, they suggest stress-reducing outlets. Omit listing any high-risk or dangerous activities, such as hang gliding, sky diving, or auto racing.

Should I use a computerized resume program to construct my resume? Although several good programs exist, a resume arranged by a software program may take on a "cookie cutter" look." Dwight Foster, a New York based executive recruiter, says, "The best resume is a homemade resume . . . Everyone recognizes the store-bought resume."[21] Your resume should reflect originality and creativity to avoid a "canned" appearance. However, computerized resume programs can help you get started. Any software program used should be flexible, allowing you to add unique areas that might not normally fit in a standard resume.

Finally, do I need more than one type of resume? It depends. Some people have a background that qualifies them for more than one job. If this applies to you, be certain that each resume relates to the desired position. The process can be as simple as changing your objective for various employers and rewriting along appropriate guidelines, while at other times it may require choosing an entirely different format. Your resume is a fluid document that requires constant updating to keep it current, and changing circumstances may require different formats.

"Give me a moment of your time! Listen to me! I have something to say!" That's what your resume must scream—in a suitably professional manner, of course. You may be the subject of the resume, but the employer is its object. Be certain that your resume accurately represents you and clearly demonstrates your ability to produce valuable results in an area of concern to potential employers.

The organizational structure of a resume and how you arrange, detail, and label specific areas is an important initial decision. Resume experts acknowledge two essential styles for presenting your credentials to a potential employer—the chronological plan and the functional plan. Each of these plans differ in their approach and meet different applicant needs.

The Chronological Plan

The **chronological resume** (See figure 4.2) is the most common and readily accepted form of presentation. It starts with your educational background, then lists your most recent employment; working backwards, it notes job titles as well as responsibilities, and it finally includes other relevant information. A chronological resume usually incorporates contact information, a job/career objective, education, a description of work experience, and optional categories determined by the unique aspects of your background.

This traditional pattern is easy to read, and information is easy to find. Those who choose a chronological structure seek to make their information readable and readily available to the busy employer. It is "especially effective for applicants who have progressed up a clearly defined career ladder and want to move up another rung."[22] You would choose a chronological plan if you have a stable career, are following a continuous track of employment, and are progressing up a clearly defined career ladder.

The Functional Plan

The **functional resume** (See figure 4.3) de-emphasizes dates, job titles, and specific employers, focusing instead on the professional skills you have developed over the years. Attention is directed more to *what* you did rather than where or when you did it. Order of importance takes precedence over order of time. Important skills and knowledge are emphasized over the number of years on the job. When using a functional plan, the applicant highlights job successes and accomplishments rather than the chronology of events.

This less orthodox format is suited to a number of different personal circumstances. The functional plan works well for mature professionals with a storehouse of expertise, entry-level types or career-changers with limited job-specific experience, and people whose careers have become stagnant or who are returning to the workplace after a long absence. The functional resume can "help those who have frequently switched jobs or have gaps in their resume . . . that they may want to gloss over."[23] Supporters of the functional resume believe there is no correlation between a person's time on the job, position title, and that person's skills and abilities.

Critics of the functional resume claim it is difficult to read since successes and accomplishments are typically described in categories and not linked to specific jobs. Thus, employers have to engage in more time-consuming background research of applicants, which they may simply choose not to do. Moreover, the functional resume is more free-form; thus, it presents a major challenge for the writer. Because it focuses so strongly on skills and the ability to contribute in a particular direction, you must have an employment objective clearly in mind. Without such a focus, this format loses its direction and tends to drift without purpose. However, when appropriately applied and carefully crafted, such a resume can be very effective.

Marguerite P. Salines

Present Address:
4320 Sweetwater Lane
Dallas, TX 75227
(214)327–3984

Permanent Address:
8120 Adirondack Trail
Austin, TX 78759
(512)345–8400

OBJECTIVE

A position in corporate consulting or training using oral and written communication skills.

EDUCATION

Baylor University, Waco, Texas 76798 Bachelor of Arts Degree, Organizational Behavior, May 1997 Graduated *Magna Cum Laud*

ELECTIVE COURSES:

• Business Computer Applications
• Human Resources Management
• Corporate Communications

Internship: Chamber of Commerce, Waco, TX 1996 Directed community public relations project for chamber.

Honors and Awards: *Included in Who' who in American Colleges and Universities,* 1997; Phi Beta Kappa; Outstanding Student Intern, Waco Chamber of Commerce, 1996

EXPERIENCE

Assistant Manager of Human Resources, 1990–1993 Nordstrom's Department Stores, Austin, TX 75760
• Administered and directed customer service programs
• Directed department in manager's absence

Sales Representative, ComTel, Monterey, Mexico 1988–1990
• Maintained top 10% sales in communications products
• conducted on-going sales training
• Developed databases system for sales department

PROFESSIONAL MEMBERSHIPS

Society for Human Resources Management (SHRM) American Society for Training and Development (ASTD) Business and Professional Women's Club (BPW)

OTHER SKILLS AND ACTIVITIES

Bilingual skills (fluent in Spanish); Pi Kappa Delta Nationals Tournament, First place in Persuasive Speaking, 1995; Secretary, Speech and Debate Club; President, Spanish Club

HOBBIES

Tennis, jogging, and reading

REFERENCES

Available upon request

FIGURE 4.2   The Chronological Plan

Marguerite P. Salines

Present Address:
4320 Sweetwater Lane
Dallas, TX 75227
(214)327–3984

Permanent Address:
8120 Adirondack Trail
Austin, TX 78759
(512)345–8400

OBJECTIVE

A position in corporate consulting or training using oral and written communication skills.

SUMMARY

Training and experience in Human Resources and Corporate Communications. Responsible for administrating, training, and directing customer service programs.

ADMINISTRATION

Administered a variety of staff development programs and developed a database system for sales department. Involved with national customer service training programs.

MANAGEMENT

Managed a team of sales representatives and maintained top 10% sales in communications products.

TRAINING AND DEVELOPMENT

Designed and implemented employee training programs in management and supervisory skills, oral and written communication, and computer skills. Used a variety of training techniques and multimedia applications.

PERSONAL SKILLS/ATTRIBUTES

Possess business computer skills and word processing. Award winning platform and presentational skills. Can speak fluent Spanish. I am creative, conscientious, punctual, energetic, and ambitious.

EDUCATION

B.A., 1997, Baylor University, Waco, TX 76798

REFERENCES   Available upon request

FIGURE 4.3   The Functional Plan

In view of the criticism, some have proposed a **combination resume** that describes skills, achievements, and personal traits while outlining your educational preparation and providing a brief chronological history with names of companies, dates, and titles.[24] It spotlights a past with solid contributions and projects a clear focus on future career growth. It has all the flexibility and strength that comes from combining both the chronological and functional formats.

Electronic Resumes

Technology is increasingly playing a more dominate role in the job search, and the novice and veteran job hunter may soon encounter computerization of the job search process. Recently, when Walt Disney World Co. advertised in the *Orlando Sentinel* for legal positions, its ad specifically required resumes to be formatted chronologically on white or light colored 8.5 x 11 inch paper. Disney required the standard, chronological formal so information could be electronically scanned into their computer tracking system. An **electronic resume** simply means that information is obtained and analyzed electronically by an employer. While the basic content remains essentially the same, electronic resumes differ from traditional or functional resumes in several important respects, including wording, format, and focus.[25]

Ignore the urge to be creative and original. Electronic resumes require standard formats and blocklike letters. Use a sans serif font ("sans serif" means "without added strokes" in typeface) that is plain and simple. Avoid using underlining, bold, italics, or other special effects, such as bullets or other stylistic techniques. These special effects only confuse computerized word searches or interfere with the scanning process.

Focus on nouns instead of the traditional action verbs. For example, list "oral and written communication skills" instead of "communicates well" or "organization skills" instead of "managed 20 employees." Because your resume will be selected based on key words, care must be taken in which words are chosen.

Center your address on the first lines of the resume, and list a paragraph block of key words immediately following your name and address. These key words should appear in the first section because some databases limit the amount of information they search. Consequently, key words scattered throughout the resume or only appearing at the end may not be recognized by the database. To determine which key words to use, consult a recent job-vacancy notice, making certain the words are appropriate for your situation. Remember, the applicant with the greatest number of key words better produces a "hit" for the employer.

Electronic resumes offer a number of advantages for job seekers as well as employers. Job seekers are relieved of having to send resumes and letters of application to a large number of prospective employers; the initial screening is done by a bias-free computer rather than a potentially biased employee; and resumes of job seekers are potentially available to a large number of employers nationwide. Employers can conduct a highly focused job search, selecting a particular qualification or characteristic for a job, and the computer easily sifts through literally hundreds of applicant resumes to produce an unbiased list of qualified applicants in a matter of seconds. This can, of course, save the employer time and money.

Whether writing a traditional or electronic resume, format, design, and careful planning are important. While changing technology and differing company guidelines can pose a challenge for today's job seeker, the preceding resume guidelines should equip you with the necessary tools to succeed. Having completed your resume, you should be ready to write the letter of application.

The Letter of Application

Your letter of application, or cover letter, is the personalizing factor in the presentation of an otherwise essentially impersonal document—your resume. Some European companies may even require that it be handwritten, since they often request graphologists to analyze your personality from your handwriting. A good letter of application may take time and be difficult to write, but it sets the stage for the reader to accept your resume as something special.

Letter Content

The letter of application should follow accepted business letter protocol and be concise and to the point, rarely exceeding one page. As we discuss letter content, consider the case of Marguerite Salines, a recent organizational behavior graduate who responded to the following position advertisement listed in a trade publication.

> CONSULTANT/TRAINING SPECIALISTS NEEDED. Career opportunity with prestigious firm to direct training/development programs for exempt/nonexempt associates in retail customer service. Bachelor's degree in organizational behavior, communications, or related area required. Fluency in Spanish desirable. The chosen candidate will direct some of the best human resource development programs available today. Qualified candidates must have strong written, conceptual, and platform skills for this southwestern region position. Warsaw Communications and Training, Inc. offers a 401(K) plan and comprehensive health benefit package.

> Warsaw Communications and Training, Inc. is an emerging national leader in organizational consulting and training. We are a growing national company with a seventeen-year history of helping Fortune 500-type clients improve their leadership/management skills, and organizational communication. Send resume to: Ms. Taressa Brice, Human Resources Manager, Warsaw Communications and Training, Inc., 1695 Corporate Drive, Los Colinas, TX 74112-1000.

Marguerite has set her career goals and determined what she wants in a position. She believes her qualifications for the consultant/trainer listing are an excellent match and drafts the following letter of application (See figure 4.4) to Ms. Brice.

Although a cover letter was not requested in the advertisement, a letter appropriately accompanies the resume. Moreover, the letter is personalized and sent to a specific individual. It is imperative that letters be sent to a specific "decision maker" and never generically addressed "To Whom it May Concern," "Dear Sir," "Dear Madam," or "Dear Gentlemen. When you don't know the name of the manager

4320 Sweetwater Lane
Dallas, TX 75227
October 20, 1997

Ms. Taressa Brice
Human Resources Manager
Warsaw Communications, Inc.
1695 Corporate Drive
Los Colinas, TX 74112-1000

Dear Ms. Brice:
I would appreciate your considering me for the position of Consultant/Training Specialist which you advertised in the September 1997 issue of Communications World. My formal education in organizational behavior, related work experience, and an internship in public relations qualify me to direct your training and development programs in retail customer service.

Earning a bachelor's degree in organizational behavior has provided me with an in-depth understanding of organizations while developing the skills required in training employees. Travel and participation with the speech and debate club gave me opportunities to practice my presentation skills. I especially enjoyed Corporate Communications. Designing training programs and learning to adapt platform skills to diverse audiences in corporate settings were my favorite assignments.

Working as Assistant Human Resources Manager at Nordstrom's gave me valuable opportunities to work with customer service programs in a retailing setting. My experience with Frontline Service, a national customer service training program, involved administering, training, and directing employees for ComTel. I learned to appreciate the long hours and hard work to achieve program goals.

After you have reviewed the enclosed resume, I would enjoy an opportunity to discuss the consultant/trainer position in customer service with you. When a date or time can be arranged, I would like to talk with you about joining Warsaw Communications, Inc. If there is any other information needed to act on my application, you can reach me at 9214)327 3984.

Thank you for your consideration. I look forward to hearing form you.

Sincerely,

Marguerite P. Salines
Marguerite P. Salines

Enclosure

FIGURE 4.4   Sample Cover Letter

of the department you want, call the main company number and ask who is in charge of the department. Nicholas Corcodilos, a successful headhunter, emphasizes that you "find the guy who needs you, he's the person who has a vested interest in hiring you."[25] Of course, if you're responding to a post office box in a newspaper ad, you may have to use "Dear Manager," "Dear Director," or "Dear Department Head."

The opening paragraph of the letter of application is without a doubt the most difficult for most applicants to compose, yet it is the most important paragraph to write. Specifically, this paragraph should (1) state the purpose of the letter, (2) identify the exact position for which you are applying, and (3) provide an initial summary of accomplishments and qualifications linking you to the job. All of this needs to be accomplished in no more than two or three sentences. Marguerite's letter starts concisely, stating her intent, identifying the position, and drawing attention to her qualifications. If someone had recommended the position, she might also have referred to that individual, thereby using a contact to establish initial rapport.

The middle paragraphs represent a one-two punch within your letter. The goal is to *selectively tailor your strengths* to the needs and interests of the potential employer. This section should provide a general summary of your education, experience, and other areas of significance without simply restating material detailed in your resume. It should emphasize two or three primary qualifications, as well as personal characteristics and attributes related to the job. Avoid clichés such as, "I'm looking for a challenging opportunity" or superficial statements, such as "I'm a people person." These paragraphs should address the specific criteria listed in the job advertisement and include a sufficiently detailed description of your educational training and related work experience. Marguerite notes her bachelor's degree in organizational behavior and calls attention to her platform skills. Furthermore, by noting her experience at Nordstrom's and with *Frontline Service,* she focuses on customer service training and the requisite skills of working with others. Finally, she acknowledges an understanding of administrative planning and setting program goals.

The closing serves as a summary statement of your cover letter. It contains essential information that an employer will want for an oral interview or prior to employing you. It should note that a resume is enclosed, express a willingness to provide any other materials that might be needed, and state that you are available for an interview. Be certain to include your telephone number for easy access even though it will also be on the resume. Marguerite mentions the enclosed resume, includes her telephone number, and cordially expresses a desire to talk with Ms. Brice about joining Warsaw Communications, Inc. Marguerite's cover letter is succinct, yet it speaks to her abilities.

Style, Mechanics, and Length

A person's distinctive way of writing is called **style.** It is the choice and selection of words that go in the application letter. You should try to keep your sentences short—an average of fourteen words per sentence is about right—and use short words rather than business jargon. Another important element of style is called "you emphasis," or writing the application letter with the company's needs, expectations, and wants in mind. Coutland Bovee and John Thill note that "it isn't just a matter of using one pronoun as opposed to another; it's a matter of genuine empathy."[27] In other words, "you emphasis" is more than using the second pronoun "you" in place of "I"; it means showing how your qualifications will help the employer. The letter's wording becomes stronger and less self-centered when you take this approach; it becomes receiver centered rather than writer centered. The employer may not consciously notice this subtle shift, but the letter will unconsciously carry more impact and interest. Consider the following examples from Marguerite's letter to illustrate this difference:

"I Emphasis"
Standard Letter

I wish to apply for the position of consultant/trainer that I saw advertised in the September 1997 issue of *Communication World.* I believe my qualifications are right for the opening.

I carefully chose electives in human resources management and corporate communication that prepared me to work with training programs.

I have vast experience in platform skills, and was the best in directing training programs at Nordstrom's. I also offer you experience as a customer service representative while working for ComTel.

As an outstanding company and leader in the communications industry, I would like to interview with Warsaw Communications at your earliest convenience. Enclosed please find a resume for your consideration with reference to your vacancy.

"You Emphasis"
From Marguerite's Letter

I would appreciate your considering me for the position of Consultant/Training Specialist which you advertised in the September 1997 issue of *Communication World.* My formal education in organizational behavior, related work experience, and an internship in public relations quality me to direct your training and development programs in retial customer service.

I especially enjoyed corporate communications. Designing training programs and learning to adapt platform skills to diverse audiences in corporate settings were my favorite assignments.

Working as Assistant Human Resources Manager at Nordstrom's gave me valuable opportunities to work with customer service programs in a retail customer service programs in a retail setting. My experience with *Frontline Service,* a national customer service training program, involved administering, training, and directing employees for ComTel.

After you have reviewed the enclosed resume, I would enjoy an opportunity to discuss the consultant/trainer position in customer service with you. When adate or time can be arranged, I would like to talk with you about joining Warsaw Communications, Inc.

While the standard letter addresses the essentials, Marguerite's letter suggests a "you" attitude in accomplishing these ends. The "you" attitude places emphasis on the reader of the letter. Successful job candidates will focus on the company's needs before focusing on their own.

When the envelope is opened, your letter of application is usually the first thing read and can make an indelible first impression. Be sure to take the same care with neatness and accuracy in writing it as you do with a resume. Select quality paper and use a good typewriter/word processor with a quality ribbon or printer. It is particularly important to review the letter for proper spelling, typographical errors, and correct English. A careless error in an application letter communicates much about you and may cost you a job interview. See if you can spot the typos and blunders in this not-so-humorous cover letter. (Hint: each sentence contains at least one error.)

Dear Mr. Rowe:

Please find me resume inclosed. As you may not, my education and work exprience quantifies me for the position that is open at you're firm.

For the past 9 yrs., I've worked in a managerial capacity, so I have plenty of written english experience; organization; and time-management skells; and am specially experienced with comminations with employees.

My previous work hysterical is also in this field, through I started at the bottom of the ladder and worked my way upword. I guess its a kind of "risen through the rungs" story. All of these positions at the varous companies listed in my resume have given me the skills and experience to make me the professinal I am today.

While handling my responsibilities at the firm, I've held positions with the local city counsel on the Wet Coast as will as various volunter positions in the surounding area. Leadership skills as well as good language skills have served my well both at work and in the communitie.

Obvously, my back ground is vary strong in this field. Please call me for an intreview at you're earliest convenience. I look foreword to meeting with you and giving you a more in-depth picture of my qualifications.

(no signature)

P.S. Call me for an interview soone.

Remember, the letter of application precedes you and initially represents *you;* you are judged by it. Therefore, it shouldn't be slighted or hastily written. It is carefully read, not scanned like most resumes.

*   *   *   *   *

Sue Fling used the traditional chronological plan to outline her educational background and work experience. Don Bollin briefly confirmed references and verified her date of graduation and college degree. However, his reference check did not reveal her "part-time" employment status or enhanced credentials. Consequently, while it contained commonly included information, it failed to accurately represent her— the primary purpose of the resume.

The case told us little about her letter of application. We could assume it presented her well, since Sue was invited for an interview. Certainly, she must have stated the position sought and made a clear case for her being hired. However, based upon a less than accurate resume, its authenticity in accurately presenting Sue should also be questioned.

The resume and letter of application both directed the interview; therefore, the delinquencies jeopardized its effectiveness and endangered Sue's chances of being hired. These personal portraits must be realistic rather than impressionistic.

Preparing for the Interview

Interviewing requires careful preparation and attention. Companies invite people to interviews because they need to get a job done, not because they are handing out jobs to those who will sit through an interview. You will have to clearly convey that you *understand* the work the employer needs to have done. If, during the interview, the employer is not convinced that you understand the work to be done, you will not be hired. Learn all you can about the company, the manager(s), and the job. Read company reports, brochures, press releases, and biographies of key managers. Also review business publications, trade journals, and articles pertaining to the company. Finally, talk to people about the job and the company. You can sit in an interview and talk all you want about yourself, your experience, your accomplishments, your skills, your strengths, and your past jobs, but you will be sabotaging yourself if you can't talk about the one thing that makes a manager automatically start thinking about hiring you—the job.

Every employer who interviews you has a problem—a job that needs doing. You will have to convey your *ability to do the job*. That is, that you possess the knowledge and skills necessary to do the job the way the employer wants the job to be done. While it may benefit the company to know your career plans, or job objectives, or attitude about working with others, these are all secondary considerations in hiring a good worker. This is not to say these aren't important items. You have to be compatible with the employer, you have to be motivated, you have to indicate you're going to stick around, and you must fit with the rest of the team. If you say all the right things on theses topics and can't convince the employer that you can *do the job*, the other "stuff" won't matter. The interviewer and the candidate must confirm that the candidate can do the job. This requires carefully reviewing your educational background, training, and work experience, selectively identifying specific, job-related examples to be cited during the interview. You should be prepared to present detailed instances as evidence of your ability to perform. This behavioral exchange must be thorough, and it must be complete. It is ultimately up to you to guide the interview toward its critical purpose—proof that you can do the job. If a poor interviewer doesn't know how to accomplish this, you must seize the interview. Show the interviewer how to turn the interview into a demonstration of your abilities and into proof that you can do the job. Let the interviewer benefit from all the research and homework you did in preparation for this job.

Finally, a positive self-image is absolutely necessary if you are to perform well in the interview. Keep in mind that no one is perfect. The interviewer knows this and will discount the applicant who admits to no faults. Employers seek *human beings,* and productive employees are most often those who have positive and constructive attitudes concerning their strengths and weaknesses. In the interview, you need to capitalize on your strengths yet not gloss over or deny your weaknesses. Action plans to remedy them can usefully portray you as being realistic and self-confident. With a knowledge of what to expect and preparation, you can keep things in perspective and prevent the interview from becoming "The Great Confrontation." Anticipating interview questions and participating in mock interviews can significantly strengthen your interview performance while helping you to relax and enjoy the experience. Practice makes perfect, so practice answering potential questions, including difficult questions.

Even if you are completely prepared, an interview can be terrifying. Will I say the wrong thing? What if I forget what I know? What if I just clam up and can't talk? What if I screw up everything I planned and rehearsed? If you feel nervous, it's because you are concerned about your performance. Your body is adjusting by providing essential energy. Channel that energy into listening and responding to the best of your ability. Keep in mind that you were invited in for a talk—the company is interested in *you.* Understand one thing about employers before you walk into an interview: they want to hire you. They have a vested interest in your being the right candidate. If you are, they will save time, money, and anxiety; and the workplace will function more smoothly.

Doing the Interview

An employer has very little time to get to know you in an interview. Therefore, it's critical to project a professional image. From the moment you arrive for the interview—between five and ten minutes early—you must sell yourself as a capable, together person. Your attire should reflect the standards of the industry and job you are seeking. Men should always wear a tie to an interview and at least a sport coat if not a suit. Women should wear their most professional business attire. Hair should be combed or fixed in a style appropriate to the job you're seeking, and shoes must be polished. It's the little things interviewer's notice first and remember longest, so attend to them. Put your best foot forward. Finally, even though the meeting might be relaxed and friendly, take care not to slip into a slouching, at-home informality. Rather, lean slightly forward from the middle of your chair with your arms free from your sides, and be prepared with paper and pen to take notes. Speak up, speak clearly, and give answers that are right to the point.

Companies interview people because they want to find a specific person. Every other candidate is a waste of their time. The candidate who proves that he or she can do a specific job better than anyone else will likely be the one hired. Therefore, you have three major objectives during the selection interview: (1) to provide accurate information while articulating your abilities, (2) to effectively communicate interest and enthusiasm for the job, and (3) to clearly indicate that you want the job.

Interviews can be an exciting engagement between two people who share a common goal: to take a fresh look at a job that has to be done. Employers can, for a change, stop and look at exactly what has to be done and possibly find a worker who can bring new vitality and talent to doing the job. Candidates have an opportunity to demonstrate their abilities for an employer who really needs help. Fundamental to this process, however, is honesty. Your effectiveness in interviews depends in large part on how honest you are with yourself and the interviewer about the particular job for which you are interviewing. If you are honest and candid during the interview, you will relax and talk about the things that matter. You will hear the interviewer better, and you will have a professional dialogue. If you are not honest, you're wasting your time.

Interviews can be an exciting engagement between two people who share a common goal.

Questions asked during the interview are intended to probe your abilities, to determine your "fit" for the job, and to assesses your compatibility with other team members and the company's culture.[28] The *Endicott Survey,* published by the Placement Center of Northwestern University, periodically lists the most commonly asked questions during an interview. The following questions are adapted from their list:

- What do you see yourself doing five years from now?
- What are your long-range career objectives?
- What are the most important rewards you expect in your career?
- What do you expect to be earning in five years?
- Why did you choose the career for which you are preparing?
- What do you consider to be your greatest strengths and weaknesses?
- How would you describe yourself?
- How do you think a friend or a professor who knows you well would describe you?
- How has your education prepared you for a career?
- In what ways do you think you can make a contribution to our company?
- What qualities should a successful manager possess?
- If you were hiring someone for this position, what qualities would you look for?
- What do you know about our company?
- What two or three things are most important to you in your job?
- Why should I hire you?

Thoughtfully preparing answers to these commonly asked questions can build your confidence and give you more control over the interview. The "best" answers will focus on the job at hand and the company's needs. For example, consider that first question which can prove problematic for someone with little or no related work experience: "What do you see yourself doing five years from now?"[29] A truthful answer might be, "I want a job like yours," but it probably is too strong and may be threatening to the interviewer. Responding by saying, "I hope that I'm settled in my career and a productive employee in your company" is weak and superficial, showing more concern with security and a regular paycheck than with personal growth and challenge. An honest, personally realistic, and company-oriented reply might be, "A lot will depend on the work that I'm doing five years from now, the skills and abilities that I will have developed, and the opportunities that will exist. I'd like to discuss that question with you from time to time. In the meantime, I'll learn all I can about the company and continue my personal growth so that I can complement the company's future plans." We're *not* asking you to memorize answers to certain questions, but to carefully listen to the questions and to think through your responses.

The WinWay Corporation of Sacramento, California, has also produced a helpful interactive software program containing examples of over 200 of the most commonly asked questions for prospective job interviewees. It provides hints on how to answer each question and gives sample answers. Pictures of animated male and female interviewers appear on the screen while users hear each question as it is asked.[30]

When the interview turns to questions about your interests, past jobs, hobbies, and so on, the interviewer is trying to get a feel for your personality. Can you get along with others and will you comfortably fit into the company? The interviewer wants to learn about you, so talk about yourself when asked to, but don't go on and on about yourself. It's also important to show an interest in the interviewer as well, so turn the discussion around to the interviewer, without being presumptuous or asking personal questions. You might ask, What led you to work in this industry? What do you find most challenging about it? What do you find most exciting about your current project(s)? This can assist in establishing a comfortable relationship with the interviewer and demonstrates your interest in others. The successful formation of this relationship will make you stand apart from all other candidates for the job.

Aside from your skills, expertise, and ability to work with others, perhaps the most important qualities you can demonstrate are an interest in the work itself, personal motivation, and genuine enthusiasm. You want to indicate that you find the work exciting and show an eagerness to involve yourself with whatever you're working on. This requires assuming the role of the interviewer and asking appropriate questions. Avoid asking questions that should have been researched in advance, but do ask thoughtful questions that reflect your knowledge of the organization. You can indicate your interest by asking: In what areas does the company excel? What are some of the major objectives of the company? In what directions would you like to see your department go? What qualities are most important to you, in the people who work for you? How are your employees evaluated? What type of training program do you have, and how long will it last? What opportunities do you see for a person with my background? In addition to providing necessary information, such questioning communicates a professional image. Notice that these questions focus on the work you would be doing and the company's goals. You are *acting* like an employee.

During the interview, you can also demonstrate your motivation and enthusiasm in different ways: Ask to tour the company. Identify things you've done that prove you are self-motivated, such as projects where you went "the extra mile," new ideas you had that benefited your past employers, or awards and recognition you received for doing a good job. Finally, discuss your possible contributions, and explain why doing this kind of work is important to you. If you go into an interview with simply the intent of answering an interviewer's questions, you put the interviewer in total control. This permits you to assert yourself and prevents the meeting from turning into a dull, unproductive question-and-answer interview. Make it your responsibility that the needs of the employer are met while revealing that you can satisfy those needs.

As soon as you have shown the interviewer that you are the person best suited for the job, the power in the interview has tipped in your direction. However, you must make it clear that you want the job. The interviewer knows you want the job only if you indicate you want the job. You must take care of this at the end of an interview by making a commitment. Looking the interviewer directly in the eye and maintaining eye contact, you might say, "I want this job, and hope I have convinced you that I can do it, and do it well. I would enjoy working on your team and would seriously consider an offer from you." Likewise, use this opportunity to obtain a commitment from the interviewer by asking, "Do you think I would fit on your team?" or "Are you as interested in me as I am in working for you?" It's up to you to make a commitment and to win a commitment. This doesn't mean you have to accept an offer if made. The offer still must be attractive, and it is legitimate to turn down an offer for a job you really want if the offer isn't acceptable or if you can't negotiate a mutually acceptable deal.

Interviewing, therefore, is not about sitting and answering a bunch of questions correctly. It is about *proving* to the interviewer that you understand the job to be done, *showing* that you can do the job, *demonstrating* that you can do it the way the company wants it done, and *indicating* how your contributions will benefit the company. These action tasks permit you to reveal your interest, motivation, and enthusiasm in the work to be done. Consequently, they will help you avoid the pitfalls which may lead to rejection (See figure 4.5) and take you to where you want to go—to the job. More importantly, they will let you take the interviewer with you.

*   *   *   *   *

Don Bollin's track record of matching candidates with job listings was excellent. Acting consistently with his past record, he followed good procedure again in Sue Fling's interview by writing a detailed job profile for the accounting position. Specific computer skills, for example, were listed. Detailed knowledge was required of two major software systems, and the ideal candidate was required to have at least two years full-time accounting experience in an oil manufacturing or related environment. Don made sure that his job profile gave him a clear picture of the individual needed for the job.

By asking Sue Fling on-site for an interview, Don Bollin felt sure she was the right candidate. Her academic references were excellent. Her college transcript showed an accounting degree and an outstanding grade point average. Moreover, two previous employers praised Sue's work, complimenting her accuracy, dependability, and conscientious work. However, Don failed in his background checking in one important respect—he didn't confirm with Sue's previous employers whether she was employed full-time. Thorough reference checking would have revealed this weakness and despite her strong academic qualifications, Don would not have invited her for an interview.

With the profile in hand, Don began the interview with Sue Fling. Fortunately, as she described her work experience, he quickly detected the missing full-time work experience required for the accounting position. Through in-depth, probing questions, he verified this weakness and learned that she was not the right candidate for the job.

Why Applicants Are Rejected

The results of a survey conducted by Northwestern University of 153 companies shows in rank order the factors that most often lead to a rejection of applicants.

1. Poor personal appearance.
2. Overbearing, overaggressive, conceited, "superiority complex," "know-it-all."
3. Inability to express her-or himself clearly   poor voice, diction, grammar.
4. Lack of planning for career   nor purpose and goals.
5. Lack of interest and enthusiasm   passive, indifferent.
6. Lack of confidence and poise   nervousness, ill-at-ease.
7. Failure to participate in activities.
8. Overemphasis on money   interset only in the best dollar offer.
9. Poor scholastic record   just got by.
10. Unwilling to start at the bottom   expects too much too soon.
11. Makes excuses   evasiveness   hedges on unfavorable factors in record.
12. Lack of tact.
13. Lack of maturity.
14. Lack of courtesy   ill mannered.
15. Condemnation of past employers.
16. Lack of social understanding.
17. Marked dislike for school work.
18. Lack of vitality.
19. Fails to look interviewer in the eye.
20. Limp, fishy handshake.
21. Indecision.
22. Loafs during vacations   lakeside pleasure.
23. Unhappy married life.
24. Friction with parents.
25. Sloppy application blank.
26. Merely shopping around.
27. Wants job only for short time.
28. Little sense of humor.
29. Lack of knowledge of field of specialization.
30. Parents make decisions for her or him.
31. No interest in company or in industry.
32. Emphasis on whom he or she knows.
33. Unwillingness to go where we send him or her.
34. Cynical.
35. Low moral standards.
36. Lazy.
37. Intolerant   stong prejudices.
38. Narrow interests.
39. Spends much time in movies.
40. Poor handling of personal finances.
41. No interest in community activities.
42. Inability to take criticism.
43. Lack of appreciation of the value of experience.
44. Radical ideas.
45. Late to interview without good reason.
46. Never heard of company.

FIGURE 4.5   Why Applicants Are Rejected

47. Failure to express appreciation for interviewer's time.
48. Asks no questions about the job.
49. High-pressure type.
50. Indefinite response to questions.

FIGURE 4.5 Continued

Sue Fling had good reason to be nervous about the interview. She was inadequately prepared to answer the tough technical questions Don Bollin asked during the interview. She was unable to discuss the particulars of the job and attempted to gloss over or hide her weaknesses. Sue undermined her efforts by not being able to talk about the one thing that would have automatically made Don Bollin start thinking about hiring her—the specific job. She couldn't seriously discuss the position because she was unfamiliar with their accounting procedures and software systems. Being knowledgeable about the job would have allowed her to talk about particular projects and about how Midwest would benefit by hiring her. She would have been aware of her shortcomings and could have developed action plans to remedy them. Then the technical inquiries could have been more directly addressed.

The initial possession of control gave the interviewer huge power in the interview. However, Sue could have derived power during the interview when Don asked if she had any further questions. Here was an opportunity to put forward the action plans that might have remedied her weaknesses and convinced Don that she could be a profitable and contributing employee to Midwest. Instead, Sue declined this offer to show her energy and motivation to learn Midwest's practices and procedures while demonstrating her interest in the work to be done. Rather than seizing the interview, she expressed satisfaction with the salary range and benefit package.

Sue communicated a pleasing personality and concern for others, but these were secondary to her ability to perform. Don Bollin's goal was to confirm whether Sue could do the job; thus, he knew all he had to know about hiring her for the position.

Sue Fling failed to understand that the interview is not the job.

Discriminatory Questions

The inexperienced interviewer may occasionally ask discriminatory questions because they lack the skills to seek necessary information in a non-discriminatory way. This is no excuse, of course, yet it places you, the interviewee, in an uneasy situation—the prospect of responding to a discriminatory question without providing inappropriately requested information. Discriminatory questions disregard equal employment opportunity (EEO) laws related to race, color, sex, religion, national origin, or physical disability. Any question that has the potential to discriminate among groups of people may be considered discriminatory. Questions on the subjects of marital status, pregnancy, and future plans to have children; garnishment of records; arrest records; height; weight; age; credit references; child care arrangements; or physical and mental handicaps may lead to charges of discrimination. The U.S. Supreme Court has said that "the touchstone is business necessity."

While discriminatory questions are difficult to answer and there is no comfortable, easy way to respond, you do have a number of options. First, you can answer directly. If an employer, out of a concern for your availability and career commitment, tactlessly asks about plans for having children, you can briefly answer, "Yes, we plan to have children within two years." However, this response violates your rights as a job candidate and may be regarded as a personal infringement. Second, you can answer the inquiry, but take advantage of the question to support your candidacy. You might say, "Yes we do, but you'll find that a benefit. Statistics show employees with families have lower turnover, higher morale, and are more involved in the community." However, this is often difficult to do on the spot since the necessary supporting information may not be readily available. Third, you might give a "tongue and cheek" response hoping to avoid the issue and defuse the situation, "Is this a test to see if I can recognize a discriminatory question?" This is a personally risky approach, since the interviewer may fail to recognize your intent and rather perceive an unwarranted aggressiveness. Fourth, when asked about children, your reply might be a courteous refusal, "I fail to see how our plans for having children relate to the training position," or "My plans for having children will not interfere with my time on the job or commitment to the company." While such responses protect your rights, the interviewer may feel embarrassed or experience a loss of face. Fifth, you can "neutralize" the interviewer's apparent concern by responding to the legally appropriate question which should have been asked. To offset an interviewer's concern, your reply when asked about children might be, "If what you are concerned with is my availability or career commitment, I can assure you that I am quite aware of the job's responsibilities and am serious about pursuing my career. There are no outside commitments which should interfere with my employment." Such a response permits you to retain your legal rights and still address the interviewer's legitimate *fear* of training an employee who may leave due to family commitments or whose family commitments may pose a problem due to excessive time away from the workplace. Both the interviewer and interviewee save face. Your goal should be to protect your rights yet not place your candidacy in jeopardy. As you become knowledgeable and skilled at interviewing, and thoroughly prepare, the threat of difficult questions will lessen and your confidence will increase. However, as an applicant, you would want to consider carefully whether to work for an employer who persists in asking discriminatory questions.

*   *   *   *   *

Don Bollin was rightly concerned about the "fit" of any candidate with Midwest's close, family culture. However, this does not permit disregarding equal employment opportunity laws and violating the rights of candidates. Questions regarding Sue Fling's family were personally infringing and could be viewed as discriminatory. Job-related questions which targeted her experiences with project and quality teams would have more effectively revealed Sue's ability to work well with others. Assessing her collaborative skills and team attitude would have answered his concerns. It was surprising, given Don's experience and tenure as an interviewer, that he pursued such a line of questioning. Even if his partial intent was to put Sue at ease, rapport could have been established through a different line of questioning. However, Don fell into the trap of breaking-the-ice in an informal, friendly manner and strayed from his prepared structured questions. While the incident may have seemed minor at the time, Don discovered after the notice of complaint arrived how "chit-chat" unrelated to the job could cause a major problem.

Sue Fling answered the questions regarding her family rather than attempting to neutralize them and redirect the interview. Admittedly, she was nervous and uncomfortable and probably felt obligated to answer Don's inquiries. Still, a more desirable response would have been to reframe the questions and address the legitimate "company interest" prompting them. This would have reflected positively on her professional savvy and contributed to a more balanced relationship during the interview. Instead, Sue perceived this as part of the "chit-chat" characterizing the interview. Only later, after being rejected for the position, does she have "nagging" thoughts about possible discrimination, which prompted her to file a claim.

Certainly, the apparent basis for a sexual discrimination claim existed. However, actual discrimination would be proved during an EEOC hearing or in court. Since the rejection letter cited a lack of necessary technical skills, Sue would have a difficult time proving discrimination. However, if the hiring of Bob Maxwell showed a gender bias on the part of Midwest's employment practices, then discrimination charges would be warranted and sustained. However, the case provided little information regarding this possibility. Don Bollin's record of unchallenged interviews had been shattered, and he needed to review his approach. While not guilty of illegal practices, he certainly was guilty of poor judgment and apparent discrimination. Asking a single discriminating question could be costly and quite significant. In the future, Don would only ask questions that were pertinent to the bona fide occupational qualifications of the position.

Thank You and Follow-Up Activities

When the interviewer concludes the interview, shake his or her hand warmly, smile as though you have just been given the job, and thank him or her. The interview does not end when you leave the employer's office. Send a thank you letter to the interviewer within twenty-four hours. The thank you letter is an important detail that many interviewees overlook. This is particularly unfortunate in light of the fact that thank you letters correlate positively with job offers. A recent survey revealed that 80 percent of the employers questioned strongly believed that applicants should send a letter shortly after the interview expressing appreciation for being considered for the job.[31]

Each thank you letter (See figure 4.6) should be highly individualized and tailored to the company, the industry, and the person with whom you inter-

---

7320 Sweetwater Lane
Dallas, TX 75227
November 18, 1997

Ms. Taressa Brice
Human Resources Manager
Warsaw Communications, Inc.
1695 Corporate Drive
Los Colinas, TX 74112-1000

Dear Ms. Brice:

Thank you for meeting with me today to discuss the Consultant/Training Specialist position with Warsaw Communications, Inc. I was very interested to hear about he company and its services.

With my administrative and training background, I feel that I could perform the duties you described very competently. As I mentioned in our conversation, I have experience in customer service training and can deal with a variety of situations. I possess excellent communication skills and my adaptability and flexibility would be useful traits during the current transition period being experienced by the company. Having an opportunity to apply my skills to the sales field is also very appealing given my previous sales background.

Thank you for the time you spent with me during the interview. I would like to put my training and experience to use in a company of your caliber. Please feel free to call me at (214)327 3984 concerning the status of my credentials. I look forward to hearing from you soon.

Sincerely,

Marguerite P. Salines
Marguerite P. Salines

FIGURE 4.6   Sample Thank You Letter

viewed. A typed letter is preferred, but if that is not possible within 24 hours, a handwritten letter is acceptable. Using a standard business letter format, thank the interviewer and demonstrate your enthusiasm and continued interest in the position. Refer to specific points discussed during the interview, and highlight again facts about your background that are pertinent to the position you are seeking. Be specific. The close should state your continued interest in maintaining contact with the interviewer.

The thank you letter is your chance to add something you might have neglected. It will also bring you to mind again. Most importantly, the interviewer will be impressed with your thoughtfulness.

Moreover, after leaving the interview, carefully record the information and impressions received. This evaluative process provides you an opportunity to assess your skills and determine the effectiveness of the interview. It can also be helpful when preparing for future interviews.

*   *   *   *   *

Don Bollin's strength in the interview was clear in the preparation he did on the job profile. His weakness was evident when he didn't concentrate fully on the interview and made a discriminatory inquiry of Sue Fling that wasn't part of the job profile. However, Sue Fling would do better by learning from this interview and being better prepared for future interviews. Just because an interview does not lead to a job does not mean it has to be a waste of time. Any interview can add something valuable to your understanding about yourself, your work, and your profession. Sue should acknowledge that the interview is over, she is not getting the job, and shift her point of view.

Critical Focus

Review the Critical Focus presented in chapter 3 involving Kevin Klee of CompDesign Inc. and Nancy Byll, a computer science major seeking an entry-level software design/computer programmer position. Replay the videotape segment, and analyze the selection interview from the interviewee's perspective. The following critical questions can direct and guide your analysis.

1. Is Nancy Byll adequately prepared for the interview? Does she demonstrate an understanding of the position and the company?
2. What questions were asked? How would you evaluate Nancy's answers? Did she adequately present her knowledge, skills, attitudes, and unique attributes which might significantly contribute to the company? During the interview, did Nancy raise questions indicating her interest and enthusiasm for the position? At the close of the interview, did Nancy make it clear that she wanted the job?

3. Were any discriminatory questions asked? How would you evaluate Nancy's responses?
4. How would you evaluate the amount of participation by the interviewee? Did Nancy demonstrate active listening throughout the interview?
5. Did Nancy act professionally? Ethically? What should Nancy emphasize in her thank you letter?
6. What lessons can be learned from the interview in the video segment? What interviewer/interviewee issues were raised? What career issues? Will Nancy be offered the position? What recommendation would you make?

Summary

The selection interview is an integral part of any career search and necessary when hiring the right person for the right job. The resume, the letter of application, the interview, and follow-up/evaluation activities are critical components to this selection process. When carefully addressed, they can give you the winning edge.

The resume must speak loudly and clearly of your value as a potential employee. The value must be spoken in a few seconds, because in the business world, that's all the attention a resume will get. Creating an effective resume requires that you carefully select an appropriate plan—the chronological plan, the functional plan, or the electronic resume. Regardless of format, however, the resume must reflect your knowledge, skills, abilities, and other unique characteristics.

The letter of application introduces you to the organization and permits you to tailor your qualifications to its organizational needs. Following standard business letter guidelines, it should briefly set the stage for the employer to accept your resume. Taken together, the letter of application and resume let you get your foot in the door for an interview.

The selection interview is where decisions regarding hiring will be made. You must plan and prepare for the selection interview if it is to be successful. Read, study, do research. Learn everything you can about the company, the job, and the people. During the interview communicate an understanding of the job and your ability to do the job. The interviewer wants to learn about you, and being a good communicator means answering questions appropriately. It also means *asking* appropriate questions, *offering* your ideas without always being asked, and *showing* enthusiasm for what you can do. Remember, however, interviews are not jobs, and the goal is getting the right job, not more interviews. Therefore, after the interview, pursue follow-up and evaluation activities. Review your impressions of the interview, and within twenty-four hours, send a thank you letter demonstrating your interest in the work and the company. Quite simply, the most important thing to do, after interviewing well, is to make a commitment—tell the employer you want the job.

Companies are always looking for good employees. Even a company with no growth rate can still be expected (according to national averages) to experience a 14 percent turnover in staff over the course of a year. The selection interviewing process discussed remains the most viable means of filling these vacancies. Consequently, selection interviewing is a vital part of organizational life and equally important in career development and growth. The higher up the professional or occupational ladder you climb, the more important this process becomes.

SHARPENING YOUR FOCUS

1. Visit the Career Services Center and discuss potential career opportunities. List the advantages and disadvantages of selected career paths. What "first steps" should you take toward reaching your desired career objective?

2. Discuss the nature and function of the letter of application and resume. Note the "should's" and "should not's" of each. Compare and contrast chronological and functional resumes.

3. Create a personal selection interview agenda. What is your specific purpose during a selection interview? Recall positive past work situations and list tasks performed, actions taken and the results. What skills and competencies emerge? Can this list support your job objective? How else might you support your purpose?

4. How can you demonstrate your motivation and enthusiasm during a selection interview? Discuss the extent to which what you have done in the past is the best predictor of what you will do in the future.

5. Discuss the extent to which you would be willing to reveal negative information about yourself to an interviewer. Make a list of those items that you feel are negative. How would you treat each? How would you respond to discriminatory questions?

6. Identify three or more job interview episodes in which you have been involved as the interviewee. Is there a common thread that runs through these episodes that can explain the results? What steps could you take to make yourself a better job candidate? Note the difference between getting *a job* and getting the *right job*.

NOTES

1. Charmaine E. Wilson, "The New Generation of Selection Interviews: Structured, Behavior-Based, Valid" (paper presented at the 1990 annual meeting of the Speech Communication Association, Chicago, Ill., 1990).
2. Richard L. Dipboye, *Selection Interviews: Process Perspectives*. South-Western Series in Human Resources Management (Cincinnati, Ohio: South-Western Publishing, 1992).
3. Selwyn Feinstein, "The Checkoff," *The Wall Street Journal*, 6 November, 1990, A1.
4. Jack Gratus, *Successful Interviewing: How to Find and Keep the Best People* (New York: Penguin Books, 1988), 36.
5. Robert Half, *How to Get a Better Job in This Crazy World* (New York: Penguin Books, 1990), 6.
6. William G. Kirkwood and Steve M. Ralston, "Ethics and Teaching Employment Interviewing," *Communication Education* 45 (April 1996): 175.
7. Ibid, 169.
8. Dipboye, *Selection Interviews*.

9. Erle Norton, "Small, Flexible Plants May Play Crucial Role in U. S. Manufacturing: Carrier Facility in Arkansas Picks Workers Carefully, Gives Them Autonomy," *The Wall Street Journal,* 13 January, 1993, A1.

10. James C. Dobson, *Life on the Edge: A Young Adult's Guide to a Meaningful Future* (Dallas: Word Publishers, 1995), 11.

11. Albert R. Karr, "It's Who You Know," *The Wall Street Journal,* 16 October, 1990, A1.

12. Cheryl Hamilton and Cordell Parker, *Communicating for Results: A Guide for Business and the Professions* (Belmont, Calof.: Wadsworth Publishing, 1993), 231.

13. Glenn Burkins, "Reich's Rules: Labor Secretary Gives Career Advice," *The Wall Street Journal,* 4 June, 1996, A1.

14. Tony Lee, "Alumni Go Back to School to Hunt for Jobs," *The Wall Street Journal,* 11 June, 1991, B1.

15. Daryl L. Kerr, "Employment Interviewing: A Job Search Course," *The Bulletin of the Association for Business Communication* 55 (June 1992): 5–7.

16. T. F. Boyle and C. Mymowitz, "White-Collar Blues," *The Wall Street Journal,* 4 October, 1990. A1.

17. Harold H. Hellwig, "Job Interviewing: Process and Practice," *The Bulletin of the Association for Business Communication* 55 (June 1992): 8.

18. B. S. Moskal, "Caps, Gowns, and Jobs," *Industry Week* 22 January, 1990, 62; and Martin J. Yate, *Resumes that Knock'Em Dead* (Boston: Bob Adams, 1990).

19. Pat Brett, *Resume Writing for Results: A Workbook,* 2d ed. (Belmont, Calif.: Wadsworth Publishing, 1993).

20. Burdette E. Bostwick, *Resume Writing: A Comprehensive Guide to How to Do It* 2d ed. (New York: John Wiley and Sons, 1980), 155.

21. William M. Bulkeley, "Job Hunters Turn to Software and Databases to Get an Edge," *The Wall Street Journal,* 16 June, 1992, B13.

22. Carol L. Lehman, William C. Himstreet, and Wayne M. Baty, *Business Communications,* 11th ed. (Cincinnati, Ohio: South-Western Publishing, 1996), 416.

23. Lane M. Sixel, "Resumes Remain a Matter of Debate: Traditionalists Want Chronology; New-Agers Back Function," *The Orlando Sentinel,* 15 October, 1995, D1.

24. Yate, *Resumes that Knock'Em Dead,* 12.

25. Zane K. Quible, "Electronic Resumes: Their Time Is Coming," *Business Communication Quarterly* 58 (September 1995): 5–9.

26. Nicholas A. Corcodilos, *The New Interview* (Lebanon, N.J.: North Bridge Press, 1994), 110.

27. Courtland Bovee and John V. Thill, *Business Communication Today* 4th ed. (St. Louis, Mo.: McGraw Hill, 1995), 145.

28. See Jeffrey G. Allen, *The Five Hundred Interview Questions and How to Answer Them* (New York: John Wiley and Sons, 1988); John T. Hopkins, The Top Twelve Questions for Employment Agency Interviews," *Personnel Journal* (1980): 379–404; and John Martin Yate, *Knock'Em Dead: With Great Answers to Tough Interview Questions* 3d ed. (Boston: Bob Adams, 1988).

29. "How to Handle, 'Where Do You Want To Be?'" *Tyler Courier Times Telegraph,* 27 October, 1991, sec. 4, p. 1.

30. *WinWay Job Interview for Windows: Interview with Confidence . . . and Win the Job!* WinWay Corporation, 5431 Auburn Blvd., Suite 398, Sacramento, CA, 1994.

31. Barron Wells and Nlda Spinks, "Interview: What Small Companies Say," *The Bulletin of the Association for Business Communication* 55 (June 1992): 18–22.

5 The Appraisal Interview

Organizations are becoming increasingly aware of the critical importance of performance appraisals for the effective management of human resources. Performance appraisals can be described as an evaluation process to determine how an employee performs over a specified period of time. The goal of this evaluation process is to develop and train employees and improve performance. Communication is central to effective appraisals, and feedback is a key component of the appraisal process.

Chapter 5 defines the appraisal process, examines the purposes for conducting appraisals, and presents guidelines for effective performance appraisals. It outlines the necessary communication competencies for appraisal interviewing and further explores the need for evaluation, feedback, and analysis. This chapter is designed to accomplish three objectives:

1. *Awareness.* You will learn the functions performed by appraisal interviews, as well as how to prepare, conduct, and participate in appraisal interviews.

2. *Assessment.* You will assess methods for adapting the knowledge and skills of performance analysis and interviewing to the work situation.

3. *Application.* You will be able to identify the essential features of the appraisal process and employ the necessary communication competencies to effectively participate in a performance appraisal interview.

* * * * *

Susan Whitefield's Appraisal—Reappraising Performance Appraisals

Susan Whitefield, a five-year, middle-level manager for Metropolitan Savings and Loan Company, entered the conference room fifteen minutes before her scheduled appointment. Though she was knowledgeable of her company's new performance appraisal system, she needed a few minutes alone to gather her thoughts before her supervisor arrived and the feedback interview began. Metropolitan Savings and Loan had changed its formal appraisal system last year after a lawsuit was filed by an employee claiming sexual discrimination. The suit was dropped, but the appraisal process was changed. Now, many employees were apprehensive of these appraisals. In a memo Susan received last week, she was informed her future pay increases and bonuses were based on these evaluations. In addition, her promotion and advancement within Metropolitan would be largely determined by the performance appraisal process. A lot was riding on this interview.

Susan recognized the weaknesses of the past performance appraisal system and welcomed the changes. The old system had its faults. She remembered informal and spontaneous interviews with her supervisor in the hallway, which her supervisor called a feedback interview. When her supervisor made a suggestion in the hallway, she barely had time to process it and think about it. Nothing was ever written down, except a yearly essay in October by her supervisor, which was usually short, ambiguous, and difficult to interpret. Now, she hoped these formal interviews would remedy some of the old problems. What her supervisor called an interview, an informal and spontaneous chat in the hallway, was not her idea of an interview. She was glad to see the formal interviews added. She hoped the written feedback would be specific and clear.

Susan's supervisor, Johnnie Burke, arrived on time and took a seat at the side of the rectangular table to Susan's left. After an initial handshake and greeting, the interview began smoothly. Johnnie and Susan easily established rapport and an understanding of purpose. Johnnie produced Susan's self-evaluation, and the two went over it together. During the course of the hour-long interview, specific strengths and weaknesses were mentioned, expectations were communicated, and a developmental plan for Susan's future work performance was created. When Susan left the interview, she sensed for the first time that Johnnie had really listened to her. She felt like she was involved in mutual goal setting and establishing objectives. Susan was clear on what was expected of her and knew some specific ways to improve her performance. The appraisal interview seemed positive.

Susan said to herself, "Maybe the appraisal process doesn't have to be so difficult after all. I'll have to reappraise appraisals."

Discussion Questions

1. How would you describe the performance appraisal strategies adopted by Metropolitan Savings and Loan?
2. Identify the critical issues appraisal interviews must address and the questions involved parties must ask/answer.

3. What communication competencies and skills are needed for effective performance appraisals?
4. How democratic is the appraisal process? Is it a complementary or symmetrical exchange?
5. Was Susan correct to be concerned about her performance appraisal? What did she mean by the need to reappraise appraisals?

The Purposes of the Appraisal Interview

Today, most organizations follow some type of formal performance appraisal process. Nine out of ten American corporations require their managers to complete an annual appraisal of their employees.[1] Appraisal systems vary from organization to organization, but the almost universal acceptance of performance appraisals reflects their value and importance to organizations.

Performance appraisals have become a means of documenting hiring and termination information. This attention has specific implications for the conduct of appraisal systems—they must meet legal standards. F. Cascio and H. F. Bernardin have identified eight characteristics of legal appraisal systems:

1. Appraisal of job performance must be based on an analysis of job requirements as reflected in performance standards.
2. Appraisal of job performance only becomes reasonable when performance standards have been communicated and understood by employees.
3. Clearly defined individual components or dimensions of job performance should be rated, rather than undefined global measures of job performance.
4. Performance dimensions should be behaviorally based, so that all ratings can be supported by objective, observable evidence.
5. When using graphic rating scales, avoid abstract trait names (e.g., loyalty, honesty) unless they can be defined in terms of observable behaviors.
6. Keep graphic rating scale anchors brief and logically consistent.
7. As with anything else used as a basis for employment decisions, appraisal systems must be validated and be psychometrically sound, as well as the ratings given by *individual* raters.
8. Provide a mechanism for appeal if an employee disagrees with a supervisor's appraisal.[2]

The performance appraisal process and interview almost always involves the employee and supervisor and may also involve other members of the organization. As a general guideline, anyone completing an appraisal of another must have the opportunity to observe a representative sample of that employee's performance. Further, to the extent that appraisers lack the technical knowledge to make reasonable judgments, they would be poorly advised to rely solely on their own assessment of performance.

Communicating clear expectations is central to this ongoing process.[3] Fully informing all employees of appraisal policy and purposes minimizes uncertainty and potential resistance. Employee understanding will increase the potential for positive results from appraisals. The supervisor and employee have opportunities to communicate with one another, provide feedback about expectations and performance, and establish mutual goals and objectives. The performance appraisal may be viewed as "the process by which an organization measures and evaluates an individual employee's behavior and accomplishments for a finite time period."[4] The process doesn't have to be a difficult one because it involves those who have common purposes. Properly conducted appraisal interviews reduce the emphasis on evaluation that creates conflict and substitutes a concern for common interests.

Performance appraisals serve multiple functions but should be principally perceived as a tool for management development, that is, to be a means for preparing the organization's future by answering the question: who among today's workers will be tomorrow's managers? When appropriately designed and conducted, appraisals can serve as a strategy for (1) meeting the needs of employees by helping them understand how well they are performing in the organization, (2) meeting the needs of supervisors and managers by providing a tool to evaluate the performance of employees and to create developmental plans for improving performance, including future training and specific action plans, and (3) meeting the needs of the organization by fulfilling legal requirements and providing *prima facia* evidence of "good faith" and equal treatment. Robert Johnson observes that inherent in the employer-employee relationship is the need for performance appraisal and summarizes the effective use of appraisal interviews:

> The employee has a legitimate need to know how his performance compares with his supervisor's expectations. It is not merely a matter of idle curiosity, but a true need, an essential link of communication between employer and employee. . . . In the absence of specific feedback on performance, some serious problems may develop. The employee may be forming undesirable work habits, but he may assume quite erroneously that the supervisor's silence means approval. . . . The employer—specifically, the supervisor—needs to carry out the essential process of communication between employer and employee. If the employee is doing less than satisfactory work and his performance is correctable, the supervisor needs to convey this in the appraisal interview and arrange for improvement. If the employee's work is satisfactory, the supervisor has a stake in that person's future and will use the appraisal interview to promote continued satisfactory performance.[5]

When approached constructively by both parties, the appraisal interview can be a significant doorway to better morale and productivity.

Typically, employees are evaluated after a probationary period and then periodically on an annual or semiannual basis. Assuming an annual time frame, the appraisal process would progress through the following phases:

1. During the first month, the supervisor shares expectations with the employee.

2. During the next nine or ten months, the supervisor observes and evaluates the employee's performance.
3. After evaluating the employee's performance, the supervisor documents the performance in predetermined ways.
4. In the final month, the supervisor shares the evaluations with the employee, recommends administrative actions, and announces administrative decisions.

Thus, before you are actually involved in an appraisal interview, your supervisor may have already communicated expectations about your performance. Additionally, you may have completed a self-evaluation form and returned it to your supervisor. Your supervisor reviews the evaluations, identifying similarities and differences, and then schedules an interview. The actual appraisal interview or feedback interview occurs during this fourth phase when you and the supervisor engage in a mutual exchange of ideas.

In spite of the importance accorded performance appraisals, the prevailing attitude of many supervisors toward conducting an appraisal interview ranges from reluctance to pure disdain. This disdain for conducting appraisal interviews can be explained in several ways. Supervisors are not comfortable in openly discussing performance analysis with their subordinates. Many feel that the process serves no constructive purpose. Others realize that they lack the necessary communicative skills. According to surveys of more than 400 companies by Drake-Beam-Morin and Opinion Research Corporation, the major failure of these evaluations is an inability of managers to communicate with their subordinates about their strengths and weaknesses. Stephen Morriss, Executive Vice President of Drake-Beam-Morin, observes that "it's just something that people really dislike because they have to sit down one-on-one with another individual and tell him what he is doing right or wrong."[6] Roy Serpa adds that if superiors (1) do not define objectives, (2) establish vague personal goals, (3) reward arbitrarily, (4) promote on the basis of personal relationships, and (5) do not develop their subordinates, then the prevailing belief will be that performance appraisals are useless and unnecessary.[7] However, research indicates that employees at every level like to know where they stand, and when left in the dark, they feel cheated and become angry, resulting in attitude and morale problems.[8]

*   *   *   *   *

When Susan Whitefield entered the conference room for her feedback interview, she was nearing the end of the performance review process. Still, her concerns and anxiety were justified, since her performance was on the line and the outcomes would be significant. The performance appraisal interview can be one of the most important and most difficult interviews in which one participates. Susan could recall past appraisals that had proven to be disappointing and unproductive.

Rather than perceiving appraisals as an opportunity for a meaningful exchange, past experience led many to judge the whole process as a waste of time and energy. However, Metropolitan Savings and Loan listened to the legitimate complaints of employees and managers and instituted a new, more responsive appraisal system, which encouraged open communication and participation. The new performance appraisal strategies at Metropolitan Savings and Loan are clear. They want to meet the needs of employees, supervisors, and the organization while fairly and objectively evaluating performance. This requires developing quantitative standards for measuring job performance and qualitative standards for measuring behavioral performance. The ultimate goal is to develop as many people as possible to realize their potentials and rewarding them accordingly. Formal interviews that engaged the concerned parties in mutual dialogue and action planning were an integral part of this new system. The interview helped Susan understand the strengths and weaknesses of her job performance. Her supervisor gave clear and positive feedback, and Susan left the interview knowing how well she was doing and in what areas she needed to improve. Johnnie Burke also discussed a developmental plan with Susan and communicated future performance expectations. Susan left the interview understanding her supervisor's expectations and feeling positive about herself, Metropolitan Savings and Loan, and the appraisal process.

Preparing for the Appraisal Interview

There are no shortcuts to successful performance appraisals, and there are a number of options as to the form that actual evaluations can take. Preparation for the appraisal interview is a crucial step that is often overlooked. Many supervisors dread this confrontation with their employees and try to "get it over with" as quickly as possible. Employees might display a variety of reactions, the majority of which are going to be negative if they are not also prepared. The goal of preparation should be to do everything possible to pave the way for a well-informed, productive discussion of employee performance.[9] Laws do not require performance appraisal by organizations; however, civil rights EEO guidelines state that those that are conducted must be standardized in form and administration, measure actual work performance, and be applied to all classes of employees. Employees with equal experience or seniority in jobs requiring the same skills, effort, responsibility, and working conditions should receive equal compensation.

Today, the most commonly used appraisal methods are of a behavioral type. Instead of measuring personality traits, scales related closely to the employee's job description are employed. There are seven categories of performance measurement systems: (1) global essays and ratings, (2) trait-rating scales, (3) ranking procedures, (4) critical incident methods, (5) behaviorally anchored rating scales, (6) objective and goal-setting procedures, and (7) organizational records.[10]

Global Essays and Ratings

Using this method, the rater describes in narrative form the strengths and weaknesses of the employee and assigns an overall performance rating of "Outstanding," "Excellent," "Satisfactory," or "Poor." The rater usually omits specifics in the evaluation, indicating only if the employee is "above expectation," "at expectation," or "below expectation." No set form is used, and no particular items are prescribed. It has the advantage of flexibility and the disadvantage that the essays for several different subordinates may be very hard to compare. This method has been seriously criticized for legal reasons because of the lack of specific performance criteria.

Trait-Rating Scales

It has been estimated that approximately 75 percent of the formal appraisal systems in use today are derivations of what are generally known as trait rating systems.[11] This traditional approach assesses an employee's performance by rating certain personality traits on a scale of one to five, where one is low and five is high. These scales usually include such factors as oral communication, cooperation, problem solving, accepting responsibility, and getting along with people. There is no doubt that factors, such as initiative, enthusiasm, loyalty, cooperation, leadership ability, dependability and adaptability are important. However, they are also exceedingly difficult to define and measure, and it is difficult to demonstrate a direct relationship between levels of such performance. If no convincing case can be made for the job relatedness of such personal characteristics, then use of such criteria would be open to challenge. Since these scales relate to personality traits and often lack specific job-related definitions or behavior correlates, they have been severely criticized and are legally untenable.

Ranking Procedures

This method distinguishes itself from the previous methods by including percentage rankings. Just as students are ranked in a percent of their class, such as the top 10 percent, employees are ranked according to an overall evaluation by a rater. Raters rank employees in categories which include top 1 percent, top 3 percent, top 5 percent, top 10 percent, top 30 percent, top 50 percent, bottom 30 percent, marginal, and unsatisfactory. Often, managers are directed to use a "forced fit" distribution. That is, only 5 percent of a manager's subordinates can receive a top rating and 20 percent the second highest rating. Everyone else, regardless of their performance, can receive only an average rating or worse. This is not likely to help morale and may foster competition instead of the cooperation needed to work as a unit. These scales, too, have been criticized and have little legal validity.

Critical Incident Methods

This method represents a transition from assessments of personality traits toward more behavioral measures. Raters assess employees according to certain important positive or negative events in an employee's performance. These events, or critical incidents, combine to form an overall evaluation. Often, other techniques are used in combination with this method. While focusing more on actual performance, this method is still highly subjective and possesses many of the disadvantages associated with global essays, trait-rating scales, and ranking procedures.

Behaviorally Anchored Rating Scales (BARS)

Behaviorally anchored rating scales are potentially more reliable and therefore more defensible. Managers using this method evaluate an employee's performance on clearly observable behaviors. For example, "initiative" reflects a willingness to pursue responsibilities with little or no urging or direction. A BARS method of rating measures an employee's performance against an established standard. When based on the employee's job description, the BARS method is more objective and legally defensible. Much of the criticism focuses on who establishes the standard for performance. Moreover, established performance standards may be difficult to establish for certain types of jobs.

Objective and Goal-Setting Procedures

This category of methods include management by objectives (MBO), goal setting or work planning, and review. It focuses on what the employee produces as a result of his or her work performance. The MBO method is the most commonly used method of performance appraisal in business and industry. The management by objectives technique is a format whereby the manager and the employee interact to set goals that become the criteria used for appraisal purposes. The supervisor and employee mutually set these goals, thus *together* establishing the measure for effective performance. If the employee meets these goals, then performance standards have been met. This participative approach relies heavily on effective communication skills and produces more positive outcomes. If appraisers adopt a coaching approach to supervision and performance planning, then appraisals are more likely to serve the personnel development and motivation functions for which they are often touted.

Organizational Records

Using this method, organizations apply general information from their database to the performance appraisal. Information ranging from production rates or cost variances to personnel information, such as turnover rates, absenteeism, and accident rates, are used to evaluate employees. This objective information requires little interpretation from the raters; and thus, it suits performance appraisals well.

The method(s) of appraisal selected should provide believable information about performance—so believable, in fact, that during the discussion no time at all is spent asking who (did this to me), where (did these data come from), why (do we have to do this at all), how (were the results calculated), or when (can I talk to my lawyer). The only question ought to be, "How do those who know me on the job view my performance in all the different areas of my responsibility?" What is needed is a clear and credible statement of strengths and areas for needed improvement, not a single number or a bunch of numbers. If the appraisal interview meets these conditions, the discussion will smoothly lead to the critical question, "Where do we go from here?"[12]

Organizations vary according to the degree of complexity and structure of their appraisals. Some organizations have elaborate appraisal techniques and forms, while others may be much less formal. However, most appraisals cover similar topics: (1) work quality, (2) employee potential, and (3) personal attributes and qualities. Most organizations attempt to measure an employee's performance against some standard, usually an objective one. However, whether or not objective standards exist, the appraisal must make a statement about the work quality of the person being evaluated. Of all types of information contained in appraisals, the work quality statement is the most important and should take up the bulk of the evaluation. As a normal practice, many organizations will assess the potential of the person being evaluated. Statements regarding the employee's long-term service in the organization or possibilities for advancement indicate what the organization thinks about an employee's future. Finally, personal attributes and qualities may be discussed. Such attributes as motivation, ability to get along with peers, ability to follow direction, initiative, and communication skills may be included in such comments. The danger here is that as the appraisal moves from a concern about performance to a concern about personality, it becomes a much less effective communication vehicle. Personality judgments are more subjective than are assessments based on work performance. These topics account for most of the comments made during the appraisal process and lead to decisions concerning the employee's status in the organization.

*   *   *   *   *

The appraisal instrument used by Metropolitan Savings and Loan probably used a variety of scales, rankings, and open-ended responses. This quantitative and qualitative information should provide Susan a means to compare and contrast her present and past performance. It should indicate areas of improvement, strengths and weaknesses, and smoothly lead to the critical question, "Where do I go from here?" The performance appraisal should serve as a useful guide for Susan as she works toward organizational goals and charts her career with Metropolitan Savings and Loan Company. However, if performance appraisals are to be effective, employees must clearly understand what is expected of them. The formal appraisal system designed by Johnnie Burke to replace the previous appraisal chats clearly alerts Susan to performance expectations and standards. The appraisal process can lead to decisions concerning her status in the organization, as well as her future development with Metropolitan Savings and Loan.

Conducting the Appraisal Interview

The appraisal interview is a part of a broader, organizationally sanctioned yet individually focused performance review process. That process usually incorporates assessment and evaluation of performance; problem solving that requires analytical, facilitating, and counseling behaviors; and career planning. A successful performance review is characterized by (1) candor, trust, and openness in the discussion between supervisor and subordinate about performance and career planning; (2) clarification for the employee of his or her performance measurement, career alternatives, and career planning; and (3) employee feedback regarding supervision and organizational goals and objectives. The purpose is not to prove a point but to seek solutions beneficial to both parties and the organization alike.

Effective performance appraisal depends on open and honest communication between supervisors and employees. Such openness and honesty are encouraged by skilled supervision, mutual respect and trust, and a perception of fairness on the part of employees. If distrust, suspicion, or strong uncertainty exist in the minds of employees—about the appraisal policy, the appraisal process, or use of the appraisal

When approached constructively, the appraisal interview can be a significant doorway to better morale and productivity.

results—openness will be discouraged. To the extent that employees understand the system and its uses and see it as a fair and objective system, most employees will welcome a chance to participate.

Supervisors should initiate the performance appraisal. When supervisors initiate and conduct appraisals, employees should receive no surprises. This requires creating a supportive communication climate and not arousing defensiveness during the appraisal interview. Initial rapport and orientation can set a supportive tone, but it is also important to continue a supportive climate throughout the interview. When we feel that the other person is supportive of us, our anxieties are reduced and message distortion is less likely to occur; consequently, clearer communication and a more candid dialogue result. Critical to building a supportive climate is creating a confidential environment, selecting a neutral setting, using an appraisal plan that is both fair and productive, and asking the right questions.

Creating a Confidential Environment

A confidential, distraction-free environment creates the best atmosphere for good communication between supervisor and employee. Imagine for a moment that you are in an appraisal interview discussing a sensitive point regarding your performance when another manager suddenly interrupts the discussion to request a signature on an important document. Your supervisor signs the document, talks to the other manager for a moment, and then turns to you and says, "Now, where were we?" Your concentration has been disrupted, and the emotional tone of the interview has changed. You wonder how much the other manager overheard about your work performance before entering the room. You experience frustration at the disruption. Appraisal interviews should be conducted in a confidential environment where both parties are free to communicate without interruptions.

Selecting a Neutral Setting

A neutral setting works best for an appraisal. Research indicates that an appraisal interview conducted in the "boss's territory" or another non-neutral area may inhibit open communication.[13]

Environmental structuring refers to the way we express ourselves in our environment. The seating and arrangement of furniture exert an influence on the parties involved and determine whether they will cooperate, converse, compete, or coact with one another. For example, corner or adjacent seating preferences are normally found in cooperative task situations, while opposite seating arrangements are found in competitive situations. It is important for both interviewer and interviewee to be active participants in the appraisal interview.

Using an Appraisal Plan

It seems no more than reasonable that a supervisor or manager should be able to define what is expected of employees. What results are required? What conditions will exist when a job has been done well? The work plan sets the standards by which the employee is measured during the appraisal process. More than a simple measure of performance, the work plan takes into account the employee's development as well. Marion S. Kellogg observes that "ultimately what an employee and his manager agree to do represents a psychological contract between them. If the work package requires the employee to add to his knowledge, develop his skills, fill an experience gap or undertake a desired modification, the groundwork for the employee's development is established. And the manager's guidance will contribute not only to organization results but to employee growth as well."[14]

A six step process for performance appraisals can help ensure the effectiveness of these evaluations:

Step 1: Schedule the performance appraisal in advance and be prepared. The employee should prepare a report on his/her performance and submit it to the supervisor a week ahead of the interview and be prepared to discuss it. You can then compare ratings. This increases the employee's involvement in the process. The appraisal interview is at its worst when it comes as a surprise to the employee.

Step 2: Create the proper atmosphere for two-way communication. To create a co-equal atmosphere, the appraiser would (a) state the purpose of the interview, (b) use the employee's first name or nickname if appropriate, (c) position the furniture so that both parties have an unimpeded view of each other, and (d) provide a comfortable physical interview setting in which both parties can relax. Often, the employee will feel more at ease if the interview is conducted in a conference room rather than the supervisor's office.

Step 3: Begin with a statement of purpose. The employee will probably be anxious, so a clear statement of the purpose of the interview, its format, its uses, its expected outcome, as well as thoughtful responses to the employee's questions will help put him or her at ease. If the employee knows what the interviewer is trying to accomplish, he or she will avoid false expectations and be properly prepared. The employee should feel that the supervisor has a sincere desire to help improve his or her performance and overall productivity; therefore, the following points should be addressed at the beginning of the interview:

- Why this discussion is taking place;
- How the interview will be handled and what role each party will play;
- The importance of two-way communication throughout the course of the interview.

Step 4: Encourage the employee to participate. The skillful manager will indicate from the outset an interest in the employee's opinions and concerns. An effective method for conducting appraisals is to follow a nondirective approach. A nondirective approach encourages the employee to identify strengths and weaknesses and to investigate means for working out solutions to strengthen the weak areas. In this approach, the interviewer refrains from telling the employee what the problem is, or what the solution is. Instead, the interviewer provides a sounding board for the employee to investigate problems and solutions. When the employee provides insightful responses, the interviewer reinforces those responses through verbal or nonverbal agreement. Allowing the employee an opportunity to provide a verbal self-appraisal can be a good starting point. Studies have revealed that when employees are actively involved in the appraisal interview, they are more likely to react positively to the entire evaluation process.[15]

Step 5: Discuss total performance, setting future performance goals, and formulate a development plan. This is perhaps the most important part of the appraisal interview, and each major area of responsibility and results achieved should be reviewed, allowing time for adequate discussion of how well targets were met. Do not dwell primarily on negative aspects of performance, and do not allow the employee to do so. Discuss strengths and identify specific opportunities for growth and improvement, outlining methods for achieving agreed upon goals. The **20/80 rule** specifies that one should concentrate on the 20 percent of the problems that will yield an 80 percent improvement in performance.[16] It may not be possible to reach total agreement on all points, but it is essential that both parties reach an understanding of the other person's views. Above all, base your appraisal on performance, not the individual. It is useful if you can separate salary issues from performance evaluation.

Step 6. Summarize the interview and provide documentation. Summarize the discussion and clarify any disagreements. At this point, the supervisor and employee can also work together on a action plan agreement for the next review period. This agreement will outline major objectives for the employee in the coming year, target dates for achievement, and document employee development commitments from the supervisor. Obviously, the employee will be more willing to work toward specific goals if he or she has had an opportunity to have vital input into the decision-making process; thus, both the employee and supervisor should equally contribute to this effort. Both should initial established goals for the coming year. The wrap-up should include assurances for the employee that his or her future is a matter of priority and that together his or her talents and skills will be developed for the good of both the employee and the improved condition of the job. Build an image of potential rather than an image of doom. Appraisals offer one of the best means of documenting why organizational decisions have been made and serve as a form of management protection.[17]

The assessment of the employee's overall performance and potential will determine the basic approach that should be taken in the appraisal interview. The less satisfactory the overall performance, the more one will have to focus on here-and-now issues. The employee's improvement program will be of much shorter range and will be of greater urgency. However, when overall performance is good, the discussion and its preparation can concentrate on different objectives. For example, one may focus attention on working with the employee on changes to increase satisfaction on the current job or helping him or her to acquire the experience and skills needed for success on the next job. The success of any appraisal interview ultimately rests on the positive attitudes and constructive approach assumed by the participants. The appraisal interview is a collaborative effort.

Asking the Right Questions

Supervisors must be careful of the *paper tiger,* that is, overemphasizing the importance of the form and thereby allowing the "paper" rather than the "people" to determine the outcome of the interview process.[18] This necessitates asking the right questions. The key to asking the right questions is to encourage as much participation as possible. This will make the appraisal a joint effort and gain increased commitment from the employee. Talk in terms of "we" rather than "I." "*We've* discussed this a number of times; how do you think *we* can improve it?" This is more than a communication trick. It signifies a willingness to share responsibility for unacceptable performance. It suggests that the supervisor and employee are together. In interdependency there is strength.

If the aim is to open up discussion, ask open questions. Questions should be designed to (1) discover what employees think and what they like and dislike; (2) test for resistance, attitudes, opinions, and controversy; and (3) get employees to express their frustrations as well as their aspirations. Therefore, avoid the following:

- Questions that require a "Yes" or "No" answer—that's probably all you'll get.
- Questions that are overly ambiguous and too general. For example, "Tell me about the year; what's your assessment of it?"
- Questions that are threatening and defensive in nature. For example, "Why in the world didn't you meet that deadline?" or "You couldn't possibly consider that a good approach, could you?"

Some good questions to stimulate discussion about performance include:

- What accomplishment do you feel best about? Why was that project so satisfying to you?
- What project excited you most?
- What current project is most challenging to you? What project is most boring?
- What was your biggest disappointment in the job? Why were you disappointed?
- How would you change the job to produce more effective results? Could you expand on it?
- How would you change the department to obtain more effective results? How would you carry it out?
- How would you change the organization to gain more effective results?
- What are the key behaviors that lead to success in this job?
- Which behaviors would lead to failure?
- Are there any parts of your job for which you would like more experience or training?

- What do you see as your competitive advantages for promotion? Your disadvantages? What can be done to overcome the disadvantages?
- What do you consider to be primary goals for the next year? Why?
- How do you feel about your career progress to date?

There is no one type of question that should be used to the exclusion of all others. The most effective appraisal interviewer uses a wide range of question types, mixing them skillfully to achieve his or her objectives: to get the employee to open up, to provide the requested information, and to do as much of the talking as possible.

Listening is an essential skill to building trust between the supervisor and employee. Good listening paves the way for good two-way communication. There are four key skills that will provide the employee with the feeling that the supervisor is not only listening, but cares about what is being said:

1. *Listening to the whole message.* Evaluate the employee's tone of voice, rate of speech, expression, gestures, and posture. Try to understand his or her goals and what is being conveyed between the lines. Practice being silent, and take notes if necessary.
2. *Attending.* This is the art of making a person feel that every word he or she utters really counts. Practice physical attending by removing all physical barriers and outside distractions. Psychological attending can be achieved by facing the person directly, leaning forward, nodding your head, smiling, and making eye contact.
3. *Reflection.* This is the skill of acknowledging the employee's message both in terms of content and feeling. It is not judgmental or questioning and opens the way to further communication. This technique of paraphrasing is particularly powerful because it shows the employee that you are seriously trying to understand his or her point of view. You are restating what the other person said but doing so in a very special way. You are concise, focusing on the essential parts of the other person's statement, and using many of the speaker's own words.
4. *Stroking.* This can be either conditional or unconditional. It lets the employee know that they are appreciated and play an important role in the organization.

Listen to the employee being appraised. This is one of the best ways of encouraging participation.

* * * * *

Johnnie Burke created a supportive climate for the appraisal interview by selecting a neutral site. Physical and psychological barriers were removed, and every effort was made to put Susan at ease. The positive value of the interview was emphasized, thus reassuring Susan that this was not an inquisition. Together, they discussed her strengths and weaknesses but always with the emphasis on progress. Negatives were stated in terms of the job and translated into agreed upon action plans to remedy the problem. Susan was able to respond to open questions which probed her immediate performance and challenged her to consider her future career development. Throughout the discussion, Johnnie listened and expressed understanding. The shared responsibility of the appraisal interview provided each with essential feedback and the necessary information to establish goals consistent with the objectives of the department and the mission of Metropolitan Savings and Loan.

Participating in the Appraisal Interview

The job performance review provides a unique opportunity for two-way communication. Employees can make the session a profitable one by developing a constructive attitude of cooperation with the interviewer. They should approach the interview by first completing a self-evaluation. Here, they identify their strengths and weaknesses, their points of high performance and low performance over the time period in question. They should be able to identify the areas in which they have shown improvement and be able to offer solutions for their problem areas. The appraisal interview provides them with the opportunity to create a positive image and participate in goal setting.

The manner in which employees respond makes a great deal of difference in the interview climate and influences the overall effectiveness of the appraisal process. Employees can react in ways that can make conducting the appraisal interview comfortable or very uncomfortable for the superior. Consciously or not, subordinates often slip into one of several patterns, which range from an aggressive attitude to open cooperation.

Some employees may become angry and persist in disagreement. They are prepared to argue about everything and refuse to accept even well-intoned advice. These employees try to avoid criticism by taking the offensive. They often shift the blame to another worker, a company policy, or even to the supervisor. The supervisor should try to calm the employee by explaining the purpose of the appraisal interview. It is important that the supervisor not become defensive with the employee. The objective is to hear another point of view. This is an opportunity to evaluate the reasonableness of the employee's position and attempt to reconcile it with your own. If the emotional level remains intense, reschedule the review.

Other employees may withdraw from the interview and become apathetic. They assume a "sit-and-listen" attitude, saying "yes" to everything to avoid unpleasantness. These employees are not accepting the interview and plan to do things their own way no matter what is said during the appraisal. The supervisor will want to go back over the purpose of the interview and stress the need for open, honest dialogue on performance. Under these circumstances, the supervisor will want to make certain the employee understands the improvements needed and get them to indicate how they intend to fulfill the expectations agreed upon. A written plan of action with a schedule for reviewing progress is critical.

Constructive participation is the alternative to the previous patterns and involves active cooperation in conducting the appraisal. This means helping to maintain a productive climate; working actively to understand comments, criticisms, and suggestions; and contributing to the development of ideas. Unless the employee assists by asking questions, seeking clarification of unclear points, and introducing topics, the supervisor's effectiveness will be limited and the full value of the appraisal interview reduced. Certainly, a positive approach to the appraisal interview makes it a more comfortable and productive activity for both parties and facilitates the overall process.

Adopting a positive attitude is easy when the performance evaluation is positive. It is more difficult when the supervisor has to give negative feedback. However, the appraisal should be a frank and open discussion with the employee, and the supervisor should not hesitate to give negative feedback when necessary. Some helpful guidelines for discussing deficient performance follow:

- Target one negative at a time. Don't overload employees so that they feel inadequate.
- State the negative in terms of the job, rather than the employee. For instance, describe a job that was not accomplished rather than the accusation: "Why are you so lazy?"
- Express understanding. This doesn't mean agreement with employee perceptions, but it does mean seeing "where they are coming from." Check the employee's perception of the problem.
- Discuss possible causes. Probe employees' views. If they rationalize or point the finger at outside sources, point out factors that are in their control.
- Agree on remedial actions. Together, work out a solution that employees will commit themselves to and will correct the problem.
- Share responsibility for translating the negative into a positive. It is difficult to turn performance around without the manager's encouragement. Commit to some specific action in support of the employee.

The roles of the participants in the appraisal process are usually well defined by the organization's structure, and the appraisal's success will be determined by the interviewer's and respondent's success in fulfilling these respective roles. Each participant in the interview needs to be aware of the other participant's role and interpret the interview with this in mind.

*   *   *   *   *

Susan Whitehead understood how her performance was being measured, so there were no surprises for her during the appraisal interview. Using management by objectives techniques, Johnnie Burke and
Susan together arrived at a clear understanding of expectations and
necessary career development. Working from the same criteria, each
had taken time to carefully prepare for the appraisal interview, and
this formal meeting served as a vehicle for sharing their thinking. The
issues central to Susan's performance were discussed and priorities established. She left knowing what was expected of her.

Evaluation, Feedback, and Analysis

To ensure that the review produces results, record impressions and suggestions
for improvement. Whatever commitments are made must be acted upon. Successful employee evaluations depend on regular, prompt feedback throughout
the evaluation period. Supervisors need to evaluate the results of any appraisal
interview and develop a plan for following up on their commitments to the employee. This plan should include the following:

- Supplying informal coaching and information on a continuous basis;
- Providing the employee with assignments and other types of opportunities
  to practice what he or she is learning—and develop experience; and
- Providing timely and useful feedback on the employee's progress.

Feedback is essential to effective communication and especially to performance appraisal interviews. Feedback is the only way a person can know
whether messages sent are interpreted as intended. Without feedback, all one can
do is assume that the messages have been received correctly.

Perhaps the most sophisticated work on feedback and performance was
done by Robert Pritchard in a study of Air Force personnel. He examined productivity and feedback among 133 employees engaged in a task of completing
purchase requisitions. His results indicated that: (1) *absolute* (how the individual
is doing) and *comparative* (how the individual is doing compared with the group)
feedback produced statistically significant increases in productivity, (2) group goal
setting (individuals participating in establishing goals) and feedback was more effective then goal setting alone, and (3) satisfaction levels under feedback conditions were better after than before the treatment. Pritchard found that feedback
caused both improved performance and satisfaction.[19] Thus, it is important to involve the employee in the process at every stage—planning, follow-up, and
appraisal—get the employee to contribute ideas, discuss pros and cons, even do

self-appraisal. This involvement will result in greater employee enthusiasm. People like to have a say in decisions that affect their lives.

The time spent in appraisal can only be useful if there is some follow-up. This means that periodic checks need to be made to determine how well an employee is accomplishing the goals established; the difficulties, if any, that are being encountered; and whether the goals need to be restated.

*   *   *   *   *

Susan Whitefield realized that she was being evaluated but found the process to be democratic in that she was permitted to voice her opinions. The exchange was symmetrical in that both she and her supervisor equally contributed to the discussion. Certainly, Johnnie Burke had more formal authority, but rather than a "tell-and-listen" or complementary exchange, they jointly examined her performance, explored goals, and developed future action plans. Rather than a strictly superior-subordinate interaction, he served as a counselor, coach, and mentor. He outlined their agreed upon commitments and noted specific follow-up procedures. They set deadlines for accomplishing the goals and for meeting again to discuss progress and potential problems. Susan had a clearer understanding of her accomplishments and where she fit in the scheme of Metropolitan Savings and Loan. She also had areas where she needed improvement, and the discussion produced corrective measures. Susan Whitefield left the interview with confidence and encouraged about her future with the company. She now realized that properly executed appraisals can lead to improved performance, increased employee motivation, and greater productivity. Appraisals are intended to reduce uncertainty and clarify one's position with the company. Was Susan correct to be concerned about her performance appraisal? How would you reappraise appraisals?

Critical Focus

To understand how an appraisal functions, analyze the interview between Marilyn Hart, a sales representative for Affirmative Financial Services Group, and her supervisor, Sandy Dodler. The interview is part of Marilyn's annual review. Using the interview between Marilyn and Sandy, critically focus on Sandy's skill at conducting an appraisal interview and Marilyn's participation.

Marilyn Hart has been a sales representative for Affirmative Financial Services Group since graduating from the University of Southern California. Affirmative Financial Services Group is involved in investment management, estate planning, property management, life and health insurance, and the whole financial services scene. Currently, Affirmative is exploring cross-selling, networking, and integrating its service lines. For the past three years, Marilyn has noticed these changes, as well as the increasingly competitive nature of the financial services market. She realizes that the companies that will do well in this new climate will be the ones that are quickest to grab new opportunities and capitalize on them.

Marilyn realizes that life at Affirmative Financial Services Group is going to be tougher but also more exciting. It'll be tougher because they'll expect more from everyone—thinking through things and questioning practices rather than just following directions. She looks forward to these changes with enthusiasm, but also with some uncertainty and anxiety. She will have to broaden her understanding of the financial services market and develop new skills in order to productively address the upcoming challenges.

Sandy Dodler has supervised sales representatives at Affirmative Financial Services for the past seven years. Her keen understanding of the financial services market and background in psychology and organizational development have been assets to the company. She prides herself on being tough minded, decisive, and quick to act. However, she is open, willing to discuss things and to listen to what others have to say. She is willing to accept a failure now and again so long as the sales representative learns from it.

Sandy sees a bright future for Affirmative Financial Services Group but has some concerns regarding Marilyn's professional development. In the future, Affirmative will want everyone to be on their toes asking if this is the best thing to be doing, is this the best way to do it? Marilyn's past performance reviews have shown her to be a reliable employee who does a satisfactory job servicing traditional lines. She follows directions well, is detail oriented, and interested in the needs of her clients. However, her knowledge base is limited, she rarely displays assertiveness, and she hesitates when asked to assume a leadership role. In the past, these qualities were less critical, but they will become increasingly important given the future direction of Affirmative Financial Services Group. Sales representatives with a positive career trajectory will have to possess knowledge and skills commensurate with the new emerging opportunities.

Marilyn and Sandy have prepared in advance for this appraisal review, and both understand its value to the employee as well as the company.

To help you apply your understanding of the appraisal interview, consider the following questions. These questions can direct your attention to the critical features of appraisal interviews and guide your analysis.

1. Was the interview conducted in an appropriate setting? Did it contribute to a supportive communication climate? Who conducted the interview? Should other people have been involved?
2. What issues must a supervisor/employee consider during an appraisal interview? Should these issues be discussed in any particular order? What are the characteristics of goals that should be set in an appraisal interview?

3. How was the appraisal interview structured? What are the advantages of using a highly structured format in an appraisal interview? What are the advantages of using a relatively unstructured format in an appraisal interview? What questions were asked?
4. How would you evaluate the amount of participation by the interviewee? How did the interviewer generate this participation? What are the most useful communication skills for an interviewer in an appraisal interview? What techniques does Sandy use to facilitate communication?
5. To what extent did the interviewer act as a counselor, coach, and mentor?
6. What follow-up plans were made regarding the commitments made during the interview?

Summary

The performance appraisal interview fits into the context of the larger appraisal process in an organization. The appraisal interview is widely used, but it is sometimes a difficult process, since it is often called on to do more than it is capable of delivering. Organizations rely on the appraisal process to evaluate employees, make administrative decisions, provide legal protection, and create action plans.

A variety of performance appraisal methods exist. Each has its own strengths and weaknesses, but the most widely used is management by objectives. In this method, the supervisor and employee set mutual goals, and the employee is involved in the process. Participating effectively in performance appraisal interviews involves a number of factors, but perhaps the most important is effective feedback. The interviewer and interviewee should both be active participants in appraisal interviews. They share responsibility for avoiding verbal and nonverbal behaviors that can create defensive situations and for maintaining a supportive climate. A good interview means that both participants have tried to understand and identify with the other's message.

Certainly, there are major differences between "good" and "bad" appraisals just as there are differences between effective and less effective supervisors. Research demonstrates that the more effective supervisors do some things differently, which makes their relationships with their employees much more effective:

- More effective supervisors are more "communication-minded." They enjoy talking and speak up; they enjoy conversations with subordinates; and they are able to give instructions well.
- They tend to be willing to listen and to respond with empathy and understanding to employees' questions. They are approachable.
- They tend to be sensitive to the feelings and ego-defense needs of employees. These defensive needs are especially likely to occur in any kind of evaluative situation, and the effective supervisor handles them carefully.

- They tend to be more open to passing information to employees. They give notice of impending changes and explain the reasons behind their actions and regulations.
- They are more adept at setting realistic goals with employees.
- They see the appraisal as not just an isolated event but as part of an integrated personnel system that is related to recruitment, placement, and development of employees.[20]

In the final analysis, the integrity, effectiveness, and legal defensibility of a performance appraisal system will depend on its legitimacy as a tool for making employment decisions.

S H A R P E N I N G   Y O U R   F O C U S

1. For what purposes are appraisals used? In what ways has equal employment opportunity legislation and rulings affected performance appraisals?

2. Members of organizations quite often treat performance appraisal as an almost meaningless process where a supervisor sits down with a subordinate, rates him or her on an appraisal chart, makes a few general comments, and terminates the interview. Often, the interaction lasts no longer than ten or fifteen minutes. Why do you suppose this practice occurs? Outline and discuss the six-step process for appraisals which can help ensure the effectiveness of performance evaluations.

3. Differentiate between (a) trait rating scales, (b) ranking procedures, (c) critical incident methods, (d) behaviorally anchored rating scales, and (e) management by objectives. What procedures of appraisal produce the greatest reliability? What should be the optimum amount of participation by the interviewee during an appraisal interview? How can this participation be generated?

4. What are the major differences between effective and less effective supervisors during an appraisal interview? Identify and discuss what effective supervisors do differently. Also discuss the ethical considerations that should guide a supervisor in appraising someone's performance.

5. Describe the performance appraisal process used by your organization or an organization with which you are familiar. What performance standards or objectives does the organization use? How often does it measure each person's performance? How is the appraisal interview structured? What kind of communication climate is established between the interviewer and interviewee? How well does it deal with personnel who are not performing satisfactorily?

6. Develop a teacher/course evaluation form. What criteria should be used? Should closed questions with a rating scale be employed or open-ended questions? Both? What are the advantages/disadvantages to a quantitative/qualitative instrument? How does your teacher/course evaluation form compare to that used at your college or university? Why might differences exist?

NOTES

1. Patricia King, "Rats, It's Performance Appraisal Time!" *Bottomline* (December 1984): 45–47.
2. W. F. Cascio and H. J. Bernadin, "Implications of Performance Appraisal Litigation for Personnel Decisions," *Personnel Psychology* 34 (1981): 211–12. Used by permission.
3. Gary Kreps, *Organizational Communication* 2d ed. (New York: Longman Press, 1990).
4. D. L. DeVries, A. M. Morrison, S. L. Shullman, and M. L. Gerlach. *Performance Appraisal on the Line.* (Greensboro, NC: Center for Creative Leadership, 1986).
5. Robert G. Johnson, *The Appraisal Interview Guide* (New York: AMACOM, 1979), 3–5.
6. "Performance Reviews: Waste of Time?" *Duns Business Monthly,* October 1984, p. 57.
7. Roy Serpa, "Why Many Organizations—Despite Good Intentions—Often Fail to Give Employees Fair and Useful Performance Reviews," *Management Review* (July 1984): 43–44.
8. Wallace V. Schmidt, "Communication and Job Satisfaction," *Proceedings of the Association for Business Communication-SW* (1989): 77–83.
9. Robert L. Brady, *The Supervisors' Guide to Hiring, Firing, Motivating, and Disciplining . . . Without Violating the Law* (Stamford, Conn.: Bureau of Law and Business, 1982).
10. DeVries, Morrison, Shullman, and Gerlach, *Performance Appraisal on the Line.*
11. Ronald G. Wells, "Guidelines for Effective and Defensible Performance Appraisal Systems," *Personnel Journal* (October 1982): 776–82.
12. J. Peter Graves, "Let's Put Appraisal Back in Performance," *Personnel Journal* (December 1982): 918–23.
13. M. L. Hickson and D. W. Stacks. *Nonverbal Communication: Studies and Applications* 3d ed. (Dubuque, Iowa: Wm. C. Brown and Benchmark, 1993).
14. Marion S. Kellogg, *What to Do About Performance Appraisal,* rev. ed. (New York: AMACOM, 1975), 169–70.
15. Richard F. Olson, *Performance Appraisal, A Guide to Greater Productivity* (New York: John Wiley and Sons, 1981).
16. Cal W. Downs and David Spohn, "A Case Study of an Appraisal System" (paper presented to the Academy of Management, Kansas City, Mo., 1976).
17. H. Kent Baker, "Two Goals in Every Performance Appraisal," *Personnel Journal* (September 1984): 75–81.
18. Michael Smilowitz and Kay Holden, "Conducting an Appraisal Interview Workshop" (paper presented to the Organizational Communication Interest Group, Western Speech Communication Association, Albuquerque, N Mex, 1983).
19. R. Pritchard, "Enhancing Productivity Through Feedback and Goal setting," *USAFHRL Technical Report,* TR 81–7, July, 1981.
20. Fredric Jablin, "Superior-Subordinate Communication: The State of the Art" (paper presented to the International Communication Association, Chicago, Ill., 1978).

6 The Workplace Counseling Interview

Most of us will be involved in a counseling interview in our career as a supervisor, coworker, or simply as a friend of someone who needs help. Counseling in the workplace places a unique focus on interpersonal communication, specifically on foundational areas, such as listening, responding, paraphrasing, and reflecting skills. Effective listening is a thread that weaves the fabric of the counseling interview together. It combines the behaviors of attending, empathizing, verbal tracking, and feedback with a mosaic of effective counseling interviewing.

Chapter 6 defines workplace counseling and explains the need for it. Typical activities included in employee counseling and the skills necessary for effective counseling are identified and described. Workplace counseling can be used to remedy behavioral problems, as well as maintain effective performance and encourage superior performance. This chapter is designed to accomplish three objectives:

1. *Awareness.* You will learn when and how to help others in the workplace through counseling and coaching by becoming alert to the special role and techniques of workplace counseling.

2. *Assessment.* You will be able to assess employee problems, determine your counseling role, and accurately respond using the workplace counseling interview.

3. *Application.* You will be able to identify and describe the steps and essential skills necessary for effective workplace counseling, using them within a legal and ethical framework.

* * * * *

Downsizing, Right-Sizing, and Employee Capsizing

Ellen Betz has been employed at a university in the California state system for over twelve years. Her work as an Accountant II has been enriching for her. She immensely enjoys working with financial statements and numbers. Known for her accuracy and thoroughness, Ellen has progressed steadily through her years at the university from an entry-level position in bookkeeping to positions of increasing responsibility and pay. She began working at the university with a bachelor's degree in business administration and planned to further her education while she worked. That goal was met two years ago when she completed her MBA degree at the university under a tuition reimbursement plan for university employees. Promoted to Accountant II after receiving her degree, she moved to a larger office with a window, which was located down the hall from the general accounting department, and was given her own personal assistant. She receives excellent health and retirement benefits and enjoys her job.

Recently, the university financial environment has been changing. Budget tightening across the campus has stressed both faculty and staff. State revenues to the university's local funds have declined over several years to less than 45 percent, causing the university to drastically reduce operation costs. These costs have been cut as much as possible, and now personnel are being laid off, including staff in Ellen's department. Along with decreasing revenues from the state, student enrollments have slightly dropped, forcing budgets to shrink even more. Morale on campus is at the lowest point Ellen has seen in her twelve years at the university. Ellen's job seems secure, but other staff on campus feel they may receive a termination notice any day. Many feel the university has violated the psychological contract with them.

On another part of the campus, Stacey Ross, a new employee in the public information office, sits staring at her computer. This morning her morale is especially low. She does not feel positive about anything. Her daughter was sick, and she has been late again to work. Taking nine semester hours of classes, working full-time as a single mother, and starting a new job have been overwhelming. Now she can not figure out how to make a simple software program work. The news of the staff reductions at the university are the last straw. She wants to quit.

Hired as an employee communications representative, Stacey is responsible for print and electronic newsletters, state and national publications, and internet web pages. She is comfortable with the print side of her job, but the software is unfamiliar. While working on her major in journalism, she has gained experience in electronic publications and layout. Her current job also requires, however, proficiency in computer software, such as Quark Express (a document layout program), Windows, and E-mail/network applications. She had gained limited experience with Quark when she worked as editor on the university student newspaper. Today, she cannot make the program work. She wonders if her lack of experience may make her a candidate for a layoff. All this downsizing and right-sizing has all but capsized previous plans, causing her to seriously think about attending school full time. She has called Ellen to see if they could meet for lunch.

Ellen knows Stacey is under pressure and fears losing her job. She willingly agrees to meet for lunch. After Stacey called, she remembers how they had first met eight months earlier in September at a new employee luncheon. A good friendship began right away. Since that luncheon, they had met at least once a week for lunch, enjoying their time together laughing and talking about supervisors, discussing problems at the university, and sharing experiences of parenting small children. Ellen always encouraged Stacey. Ellen was not overtly religious, but her genuine faith seemed to carry over into her job and family and influenced Stacey positively. During their lunches, Ellen freely disclosed about her own family. She talked about her relationship with her husband, which was good, but often worried aloud about fear of pregnancy with her teenage daughter. Her openness and candor created an environment for Stacey to easily talk about her own concerns.

Because of their strong relationship, Stacey knows she can tell Ellen how she really feels about her job. Ellen knows the layoffs at the university have unsettled Stacey, and she is also aware of Stacey's financial problems. Ellen wants to help Stacey, so they meet in the lunchroom, and Stacey begins to confide in Ellen.

Discussion Questions

1. What is Ellen's role in this interview? What is Stacey's role?
2. How important is relationship to the workplace counseling interview? How does relationship determine the degree of openness and candidness between the interview participants?
3. What workplace counseling skills are required in this situation? Because of their previous relationship, how much should Ellen "just listen" to Stacey and how much advice should she try to offer?
4. Is this a workplace counseling situation? Coaching situation? Both?
5. Should Ellen refer Stacey to the human resource department for further help? What legal or ethical issues, if any, pertain to this situation?

An Orientation to Workplace Counseling

Many initially picture counseling as involving a trained professional asking solemn questions in a sterile, clinical voice to a disturbed patient on a couch. This image of the thoughtful professional listening to a troubled patient lying on a couch usually portrays the counselor as someone who occasionally utters an "uh-huh" or stereotypically asks, "Why do you think that way?" Obviously, workplace counseling differs from this Hollywood version. It is important to note that this chapter focuses on the workplace counseling interview and not the clinical interview or professional consultation. Certainly, trained psychologists and professional consultants do help employees in the workplace, working with those who experience substance abuse problems, marital or personal problems, as well as medical or legal problems. However, we will be discussing more common workplace counseling situations intended to help another individual by promoting emotional and intellectual growth.[1] We will discuss those situations in which you are most likely to participate at some point in your career as either an interviewer or interviewee.

Workplace counseling is essentially a "helping" relationship with the main objective being to change the counselee's behavior or the attitudes that motivate the behavior. For either of these objectives to be reached, the counselee must want to change and must seek help. Moreover, the counselor must want to help, demonstrating excellent listening and probing skills and expressing empathy toward the counselee. The effective counselor will also be optimistic about people's abilities to improve, change, and grow, viewing workplace counseling as an investment in the individual. The counselee should approach workplace counseling as a learning process, realizing that change takes time and may be difficult. Therefore, workplace counseling is more than just giving a little friendly advice, having a heart-to-heart talk, or even helping someone simply make up his or her mind regarding a solution to an immediate problem. The object of workplace counseling is to change the attitude and behavior of counselees by changing the thinking which has contributed to the existing attitudes and behaviors.[2]

Many have only a restricted, reactive, and remedial view of workplace counseling. This perception limits workplace counseling to problem intervention. Consequently, performance management often becomes an aversive activity. Such a narrow view often means that the only time managers or supervisors discuss performance with employees is when there is a problem or need for improvement. Consequently, they miss opportunities to encourage effective performance and prevent problems. Effective managers and supervisors realize that they must take an active and positive role in employee performance to ensure that goals are met. They intervene not only to correct problems or increase production but also to empower employees. In short, coaching becomes an integral part of workplace counseling for them. Coaching creates a partnership with employees who are dedicated to helping them get the job done.[3] Consequently, performance discussions become positive opportunities and are less likely to be seen as confrontation and avoided. Therefore, we believe coaching is also an important function of workplace counseling.

Workplace counseling takes place in many forms, and many people act as counselors aside from their professional role. Examples include managers and supervisors whose subordinates ask for help with family problems or need direction, teachers who advise students on questions outside their area of expertise, and anyone other than a psychologist, psychiatrist, or social worker who helps friends deal with personal problems. You may be in a counseling situation without

Workplace counseling is essentially a "helping" relationship.

recognizing it. When someone needs help they will often begin by speaking to friends or relatives. If the help from these sources is inadequate, they may turn to coworkers, professional associates, or members of the clergy. Once these sources are exhausted, they may seek out truly professional help. An important point to remember is that the techniques used in workplace counseling are common to all types of counseling interviews. However, the more complex the issues are, the greater will be the necessity for competent professional assistance. Therefore, recognizing your own limitations is essential.

At a minimum, workplace counseling involves a person with whom employees can discuss difficulties and/or seek help. The counseling approach can vary from a candid talk with a coworker about a personal problem to a frank discussion with a manager or supervisor about a work-related or performance problem to meeting with a mental health professional skilled in diagnosing and treating such problems as depression or substance abuse. In large organizations, workplace counseling often occurs within the structure of formal Employee Assistance Programs (EAPs), Stress Management Interventions (SMIs), and Health Promotion Programs (HPPs). These organization-based counseling systems constitute part of an employee's benefits and help workers solve personal problems.[4]

Employee assistance programs (EAPs) are defined as "job-based programs operating within a work organization for the purposes of identifying troubled employees, motivating them to resolve their troubles, and providing access to counseling or treatment for those employees who need these services."[5] EAPs are based on the notion that work is very important to people and that the workplace should help employees identify personal problems and motivate them to seek help. Originally developed to deal with alcohol abuse, today many EAPs also help employees with drug and mental health problems that may be affecting their work.[6] According to this approach to workplace counseling, managers or supervisors monitor their employee's job performance and constructively confront them when performance is unsatisfactory by coaching them to improve and urging them to use the EAPs if they have personal problems. However, employees with personal problems may contact the EAP directly and receive counseling without the manager's or supervisor's knowledge. The effectiveness of EAPs is widely accepted, with studies indicating reductions in absenteeism, sick leave usage, and turnover. Moreover, those experiencing substance abuse improved work performance as a result of constructive confrontation and workplace counseling.[7] EAPs are not medical programs; they concentrate on personal issues and job performance.

Stress management interventions (SMIs) are defined as "any activity, program, or opportunity initiated by an organization, which focuses on reducing the presence of work-related stressors or on assisting individuals to minimize the negative outcomes of exposure to these stressors."[8] Stress costs the U.S. economy between $50 and $90 billion a year, so it is little wonder why SMIs are among the most widely offered employee counseling programs.[9] SMIs can be categorized as either educational or skill-acquisition oriented. Educational interventions are designed to inform the employee about the sources of stress, what stress feels like, how stressors can be avoided, and how the individual can better cope with stress. Skill-acquisition interventions, such as time management or assertiveness training, are designed to provide employees with new ways to cope with stressors affecting their lives and performance, and help keep the effects of stress in check. A number of research studies and many anecdotal reports documenting the use of such SMI tactics as meditation and biofeedback give rise to optimism that SMIs are effective in helping employees manage stress and saving organizations money.[10]

Health promotion programs (HPPs) are comprised of activities that promote behavior and company practices that ensure employee health and fitness. These programs attempt to encourage individuals to adopt lifestyles that maximize overall well-being. Common counseling components of HPPs are exercise and fitness, smoking cessation, nutrition and weight control, and hypertension control.[11] Ultimately, these programs try to create an organizational environment that helps employees maintain healthy lifestyles.[12] Interest in health promotion and fitness is very strong; and organizations stand to gain significant benefits from taking steps to improve employee mental and physical health.

While many organizations have seen fit to implement formal intervention programs, all employees, managers, and supervisors have a role to play in workplace counseling. Much more common to workplace counseling are the face-to-face discussions between coworkers and between managers and subordinates. Coworkers can play an important role by using their relationship to encourage troubled employees to seek formal assistance. Managers and supervisors certainly play a key role in the effectiveness of any workplace counseling effort, since they are in regular contact with employees, responsible for their development and evaluation, and ultimately held responsible for their performance. Managerial and supervisory counseling should focus on being aware of employee performance problems that might be the result of personal problems, supporting troubled employees by helping them obtain the care they need to improve performance, motivating the employee to improve, and monitoring performance to ensure that it does improve. Workplace counseling is a challenging task for all concerned.

*   *   *   *   *

In studying the university situation, we see Ellen Betz and Stacey Ross brought together by a common set of events. The downsizing and right-sizing has created a confusing, jumbled work environment where morale is low, and employees are questioning their psychological contract with the university. Not surprisingly, such conditions foster workplace counseling where friends, coworkers, managers, and supervisors are all trying to discover some sort of pattern in a snarled milieu. The fundamental question asked by all is "What should I do?"

Ellen Betz is a trusted coworker and compassionate friend. Her primary job at the university is performing the tasks of an Accountant II employee. Counseling is a secondary activity she willingly accepts because of a genuine interest in Stacey Ross. Ellen realizes she is not professionally trained to handle complex personal problems but feels she can help Stacey through these troubled times and, if necessary, recommend other assistance programs or available resources. For example, the university's stress management intervention program may be a desirable referral, or perhaps Stacey should request coaching from her immediate supervisor. Ellen, however, will want to carefully define the counseling relationship and actively listen to Stacey, trying to understand her feelings, thoughts, and experiences.

Stacey Ross needs help, and it is natural that she should turn to a friend and coworker. Stacey believes Ellen will kindly listen to her problems and help her explore options and alternatives. Moreover, given Ellen's twelve years with the university, she may be able to recommend other outlets for assistance. Certainly, something needs to be done, and Ellen is the best person to turn to right now.

The Workplace Counseling Interview

The workplace counseling situation is defined by the fact that one person turns to another for help in dealing with a personal or work-related problem. There are two commonly advanced schools of thought about workplace counseling that significantly influence interviewer/interviewee roles. At one extreme, some theorists emphasize the use of very **directive** counseling strategies in which the counselor assumes complete control of the interview. At the other extreme, theorists suggest using **nondirective** methods in which the counselor lets the interviewee take control of the interview.

Directive counseling is advisory in nature, with the counselor telling the interviewee how to deal with a problem. The directive counselor follows a problem-solution format in conducting the interview by gathering data from the interviewee, defining and analyzing the problem, and providing a solution. Use of a directive approach assumes that the counselor (1) is better able to solve the problem than the interviewee, (2) can understand and evaluate the problem on the basis of information presented by the interviewee, (3) can make the interviewee understand and accept the solution recommended by the interviewer, and (4) can motivate the interviewee to act. While directive methods may be appropriate when expert professional advice is needed, they do not help interviewees deal with the emotions that often accompany a problem, and they often make interviewees dependent upon the counselor because they do not nurture or develop the ability to independently solve problems.

Nondirective counseling centers on the interviewee's motivations, perceptions, and feelings. It assumes that by creating the proper emotional environment and interpersonal trust levels, the counselor can help the interviewee resolve the problem. When using a nondirective approach, the counselor acts more like a facilitator than an advisor. Control and content structure of the interview is given to the interviewee, and the interviewer uses active listening and other techniques to help the interviewee explore factors underlying the problems. This nondirective method aims to help the interviewee understand the problems and assumes that the interviewee is best able to solve the problems once they are recognized. The primary value of this approach is that it helps the interviewee develop problem-solving skills and reduces reliance upon the counselor. However, when the interviewee cannot analyze a problem or refuses to admit that there is a problem, little progress can be made using the nondirective approach.

In addition to the directive and nondirective approaches, there is also the **controlled nondirective** approach. The controlled nondirective approach requires that the counselor maintain control over the major topic(s) to be discussed, but once they are raised, nondirective techniques are used.[13] The counselor is more involved in the *process* of reaching a solution than in the actual *content* of the decision itself. Here the direction involves probing and asking questions to ensure that all options and alternatives are explored.

The techniques of each of these approaches can be quite complementary, with the ultimate choice of which to use depending upon your own personality, objectives, relationship with the counselee, and mutual expectations. Help is often appreciated regardless of approach, depending on the manner in which it is given. Therefore, the best counselor will not get locked into any particular style but will develop the ability to determine when each approach is needed and the necessary skills to conduct each type well.

Planning the Counseling Interview

Unlike the other types of interviews we have discussed, workplace counseling is often spontaneous. The problems that cause interviewees to seek help are often matters of immediate concern, and interviewers may not have much time to prepare for the interview. Even when someone has made an appointment, interviewers often will not know enough about what is bothering the person to begin conducting research. The skills required in these circumstances include patience, probing, and listening in order to discover exactly what the other party wants or expects. Skilled interviewers know when to ask the right questions and have the ability to go beyond "canned" or programmed answers to questions. Moreover, they know how to give appropriate verbal and nonverbal feedback, which allows them to individualize the interview, making appropriate judgments in a unique situation with a unique individual.[14] Frequently, initial sessions can be used to gather preliminary facts and set up a later meeting when interviewers can better plan how to approach the specific workplace counseling situation.

When interviewers initiate the counseling session, it is essential that they give sufficient time to planning and preparation. Planning and preparation involves (1) determining the objective(s) of the interview, (2) creating an appropriate physical setting, and (3) selecting the best approach or interview style. This permits interviewers to focus on their purpose and the outcomes they expect from the interview.

Whether initiated by the interviewer or interviewee, a very objective decision must be made as to whether or not you can actually be of help to the individual and what the consequences will be to the relationship. Many personal and workplace problems can be profitably reconciled through your intervention, but whenever problems with drugs, alcohol, debts, or personality disorders are encountered, the best help you can give a person is to refer them elsewhere. The desire to help, for all its altruistic motives, may not be enough. Having decided to help, a good counselor collects the facts and specifically determines the purpose of the interview. Sometimes the focus may be on transforming attitudes or behaviors, and at other times, workplace counseling involves helping individuals cope with situations that are unlikely to change. The purpose may be to sharpen awareness, increase understanding, or explore specific changes. Additionally, it is wise to restrict the number of problems to be addressed during any single session. An interviewee can become overwhelmed if too many problems are covered in one interview. For example, a manager or supervisor may constructively confront absences due to alcoholism by discussing how they are jeopardizing the subordinate's job without trying to work directly on the alcoholism problem itself, preferring instead to refer the employee to someone else for such counseling. Later follow-up sessions may explore the employee's efforts to resolve the root of the problem. Remember, counseling takes place over time.

Certainly, too, the purpose of workplace counseling should be congruent with the interviewee's purposes. Understanding the participant's motive for coming to the interview is important in determining objectives, as well as establishing trust and commitment.[15] For example, interviewees who seek assurance may simply want someone to listen to them. Those requesting advice may want to hear your ideas or get additional information. Still others may merely want to "bounce" an idea off of you. Thus, it is important to distinguish between a request for understanding, a request for information, and a request for responsible involvement and action.

Planning the interview also involves choosing an appropriate physical setting and creating an open, interactive psychological climate. The physical environment establishes the tone for the counseling interview; therefore, the interviewer should choose a setting where the interviewee feels comfortable and secure. The location should be private with no distractions and no chance for interruptions. It is foremost, however, that any physical setting promote confidentiality. Confidentiality plays a more important role for the counseling interview than other types of interviews. Professionalism, openness, and supportiveness are enhanced when both parties believe the conversation will not be overheard or inappropriately disclosed to other third parties. Absolute confidentiality is a prerequisite to creating an open, interactive psychological climate. At the beginning of the interview, the interviewer may even want to acknowledge the confidentiality of the setting, thus reassuring the interviewee that whatever is said will be kept private. Thus, the setting is an important determinant of the kind of interaction that will occur.

Skilled interviewers should create an open, interactive psychological climate that supports a candid discussion with the troubled interviewee. Openness is characterized by self-disclosure and trust. Therefore, the interviewer's manner of listening should encourage the interviewee to talk, and the interviewer's postural, facial, and verbal cues should draw out the interviewee. The greatest contributor to an open, interactive climate comes when interviewees are convinced that "you have a genuine interest in them as a person, if they sense you understand them, even when you are expressing dislike for an idea or their behavior."[16]

Conducting the Counseling Interview

When conducting the counseling interview, emphasis should be on getting the interviewee to verbally accept responsibility for confronting the problem and to involve the interviewee in developing the courses of action needed to solve the problem. A five-step approach to conducting workplace counseling involves: (1) confronting/presenting, (2) using reactions to develop information, (3) setting specific goals, (4) resolving, and (5) follow-up.[17] The distinct tasks comprising each stage of this counseling process provide convenient points for organizing our discussion.

The goals of the **confronting/presenting stage** are to establish rapport with the interviewee, identify the individual's problem, limit any negative emotion the person might feel toward the problem situation, and establish that the goal is to help them assume ownership of the problem by committing themselves to solving it. These vital introductory tasks can be accomplished by making the interviewee comfortable enough and trusting enough to want to disclose his or her problem, express feelings about the situation, and willing to explore solutions. By being honest, showing acceptance, and listening from the start, the interviewer demonstrates a commitment to being helpful. Actions that tend to inhibit a clear presentation of the problem are voicing negative comments, assigning blame, relying on presumption and supposition, and displaying a condescending attitude. Getting a person to describe the problem is essential, since an interviewer cannot get at the root of a problem if the person avoids discussing it. If the interviewer has a strong personal relationship with the interviewee or the interviewee has voluntarily sought help, this can serve as a useful basis for initially establishing goodwill. Other situations may be more complicated, especially when the interviewee is compelled to participate or feels helpless and believes that there is no other alternative. In these instances, interviewers must carefully show by their words and deeds that they support the interviewee and that they empathize with—and are sensitive to—the interviewee's needs. Failure in getting the interviewee to confront and present the problem should lead the interviewer to reschedule the counseling session or suggest a referral to someone else, perhaps a professional counselor.

After the interviewee has confronted/presented the problem, the interviewer must offer assistance in examining the causes of the problem. This is done during the second stage of the interview process, **using reactions to develop information.** The interviewer acquires information by attending to the interviewee's explanations, acknowledging important points, probing for information, and periodically summarizing what is discussed. In probing reactions, the interviewer should ask evocative questions and not allow the interviewee to avoid topics just because they are unpleasant. Indeed, the fact that a topic is unpleasant may indicate the importance of it to the general problem area. People often describe their problems in the abstract without indicating how their behavior contributes to them. The goal here is to candidly explore perceptions and get interviewees to personalize their problems and identify with them. At the end of this second stage of the counseling discussion, the interviewer and interviewee should be in a position to agree on the nature of the problem and its causes.

The third stage has the interviewer and interviewee agreeing on what needs to be done, **setting specific goals.** This is a crucial part of the interview process where the interviewer explains what is meant by setting goals and making certain that the interviewee selects only attainable goals. Implicit here is a realistic examination of the ramifications of the problem and the consequences of failing to set specific goals. Establishing clearly stated goals can provide a focus for exploring alternatives and developing an action plan, as well as follow-up activities.

The fourth stage is called **resolving.** Here, the interviewee takes ownership of the problem and agrees to positively seek a best solution. Responsibility for decision making rests with the interviewee who now understands the problem and can find ways to solve it. This is done by examining alternative courses of action, reviewing key points of the session, and affirming that the problem can be successfully managed. Both parties at this point express commitment to the agreed upon plan of action and to maintaining a positive relationship.

Far too frequently, counseling interviews end without either party knowing what is going to happen next; thus, the final stage involves some provision for **follow-up.** Closing arrangements should be made regarding when the interviewee will report back in order to monitor counseling progress and goal accomplishments. Moreover, this reaffirms the interviewer's role as a helper and interest in the interviewee's well-being.

It is unrealistic to expect an interviewee to work through all five steps in a single session; therefore, interviewers should expect to spend several sessions with each interviewee. Predicting the pace at which interviewee's will progress is very difficult, since some will respond positively and rapidly move from one step to the next, while others will encounter difficulties and may even regress between visits. Workplace counseling is a concerted effort, requiring time, energy, and patience.

Interviewee Responses to Workplace Counseling

The workplace counseling situation creates unique concerns for the interviewee. Many people find it difficult to analyze their own problems because they are just too close to the problems. Moreover, the personal and sensitive nature of counseling problems can create an emotional tension which may cause the interviewee to avoid or deny help. Consequently, interviewees should keep five points in mind as they approach the workplace counseling interview.

First, the interviewee should know when to seek help. In general, individuals should seek help whenever a problem interferes with important parts of their lives. Difficulty functioning at work or in social situations accompanied by feelings of desperation, inadequacy, and vulnerability certainly signal the need for some counseling. In addition, friends, co-workers, managers, and supervisors may notice attitudinal or behavioral changes, which might prompt them to offer or recommend counseling assistance. Any denial that a problem exists or avoidance of the need for help must be overcome in order for progress to be made.

Second, solving problems often requires discussion of potentially sensitive matters; therefore, the counselor selected should be someone with whom you are comfortable and you can trust. You will accomplish little if you don't think you can be open with the counselor. Friends, relatives, clergy, co-workers, managers, supervisors, and trained professionals are all resources you can draw upon. In addition, you should be prepared to change counselors if you do not believe you are making progress. If you don't feel that you are moving in a productive direction after several sessions, you may be wise to seek help elsewhere.

Third, approach counseling with a realistic attitude. The counselor can help identify troubling areas and even suggest possible reactions, but the responsibility for overcoming the difficulties remains with you. Counseling should be an empowering experience where you overcome feelings of powerlessness by taking control of your problems. Moreover, counseling is rarely a short and easy process. Some problems with which you will need to deal have developed over a lifetime, and you cannot expect to solve them in a single session. Because finding a solution will require a substantial commitment of time and energy, you must be willing to invest in yourself.

Fourth, you need to view counseling as a positive learning experience. Today, much attention is given to the notion of lifelong learning, and counseling should be perceived as a natural extension of this self-discovery process. Whether you voluntarily seek help or are requested to participate in counseling, opportunities for enhanced self-awareness, understanding, and growth exist. Workplace counseling should not be considered disciplinary or reprimanding even though it may involve correcting behavior.

Finally, adopt a transformative orientation to counseling. From a transformative orientation, counseling is first and foremost a potential occasion for personal change and self-improvement. The essence of counseling involves strengthening the self. This occurs through realizing and strengthening one's inherent human capacity for dealing with difficulties of all kinds by engaging in conscious and deliberate reflection, choice, and action. Counseling challenges you to grapple with your problems and in so doing, clarify your needs and values, as well as discover and improve upon your own resources for addressing both substantive concerns and relational issues. In short, workplace counseling problems should be viewed *not* as problems, but as opportunities for change and transformation.

*   *   *   *   *

Ellen Betz is a good counselor for Stacey Ross. Obviously, Stacey is feeling the stress of working full time, going to school, and parenting a child. She is overwhelmed and needs someone with whom she can talk. As someone who works at the university with Stacey, Ellen is in a position to help her. They mutually understand and accept their role expectations.

The spontaneous appointment for lunch does not allow Ellen much time for preparation. However, given the current climate at the university, Ellen can anticipate Stacey's concerns and need to meet. Ellen should approach the interview in a nondirective way, encouraging Stacey to take the lead in willingly disclosing her fears and worries. The discussion and interaction over lunch exhibits all the elements of a counseling interview. Stacey voluntarily confronts and presents her troubles, using Ellen's reactions to gather useful information for setting specific goals and developing an action plan. Follow-up discussions after the luncheon meeting will be useful in evaluating the appropriateness of the agreed upon actions. Stacey faces a critical job-related decision, and Ellen is a key person at an important time for her.

Their established relationship provides a solid basis for straight talk. The luncheon setting is a neutral place where Stacey and Ellen can candidly discuss the direction Stacey should take with her job. Since the relationship is based on equality, Stacey realistically understands that ultimate responsibility for solving her problems rests with her. Ellen may offer advice or make recommendations, but any decisions regarding what to do will be made by Stacey alone. From this perspective, their meeting is an occasion for exploring personal change and self-improvement. Time, energy, and patience will be required of both Stacey and Ellen.

Skills Necessary for Effective Workplace Counseling

Of all the types of interviews discussed, workplace counseling situations are the most like casual conversations. A properly conducted counseling interview uses this similarity to produce an informal atmosphere that promotes free and open discussion of the topics proposed. Interviewers will normally take the lead in counseling interviews, and the manner in which they respond makes a great deal of difference in the interview climate and eventual outcomes. Achieving mutually desired ends while maintaining a comfortable exchange is one of the most demanding tasks interviewers may face when counseling. However, certain identifiable skills can be useful in creating a carefully defined interview structure which purposefully promotes dialogue and positively solicits responses from the interviewee. Here, we will specifically examine (1) listening behaviors, (2) attending behaviors, (3) using language responsibly, (4) feedback skills, and (5) being empathetic or mindful of others.

Listening Behaviors

Listening behaviors underlie all that a counseling interview involves. When we truly listen, we understand and retain information about the other person, enabling us to function in a helping role. Listening further enables us to evaluate and respond appropriately to messages, which helps to build and maintain relationships, an important component of the counseling interview.

Listening goes beyond the mere reception of sound, it requires us to attend, understand, and remember. There are two basic types of listeners—the passive listener and the active listener. The **passive listener** exerts a minimal level of physical energy and attention to the communication process. In other words, the passive listener may attend to the speaker, but minimal effort is made toward understanding the speaker's message, and the responsibility for communicating is placed on the speaker. The passive listener merely wants to *receive* the message, not take part in it. In contrast, the **active listener** responsibly participates in the communication process. The heart rate increases, blood circulates faster, and the body temperature rises as the active listener concentrates on the message and uses extra mental time to review and interpret the content rather than allowing the mind to wander.

In the counseling interview, the counselor must have the intellectual capacity and the emotional willingness to actively listen and must exhibit good listening practices, such as those discussed earlier in chapter 2. The counselor must want to become a sounding board for one who is troubled. Ralph Nichols, who first popularized listening as a subject for discussion and a topic for study, offers a number of useful suggestions regarding active, nondirective listening:

1. Take the time to listen whenever you sense that someone is disturbed, is ready to "explode," or just needs to talk.
2. Be attentive and make every effort you can to understand what is being said.

3. Employ guggles ["eloquent and encouraging grunts"], use silence, and use mirrors and restatement.
4. Probe to help the counselee understand rather than to meet your own needs for inquisitiveness.
5. Withhold evaluations until the whole story has been heard.
6. Strive to provide the environment that allows the counselee to work things out for himself [or herself].*,18

Clearly, listening is the best avenue for counseling, and the counselor who actively listens absorbs what is being said and attends to all the messages being sent by the interviewee.

Attending Behaviors

Attending effectively is a first step in active listening. More than in other types of interviews, the building blocks of attending behaviors are needed to create the foundation for an effective counseling interview. Without effective attending behaviors, the interviewer will miss what an interviewee has said and not fully understand what is happening in the interview. Basic attending behaviors can be defined as "the facility to identify and interpret verbal and nonverbal messages through careful observation."[19] When the interviewer attends skillfully, the interviewee will be encouraged to talk, to self-disclose on personal topics, and to be open with feelings. Attending means the interviewer will demonstrate interest in the person and the message. We can identify four basic dimensions of attending behaviors: (1) eye contact, (2) body language, (3) vocal qualities, and (4) verbal tracking.[20]

The first attending behavior concerns use of the eyes, or **eye contact.** In our American culture, direct eye contact is desired more than in other countries. Though the preference for eye contact differs among cultures, we universally use our eyes to express interest and meaning. During the interview, eye contact and facial expressions tend to be most influential in revealing power and status in the relationship. If the interviewer and interviewee look directly at each other while speaking and listening, a message of equality is conveyed. Credibility and trust are enhanced between participants. When one person looks at another with a steady, direct gaze and the other does not return the eye contact, inequality is established. The speaker directing the gaze may have more power and or influence. Moreover, if one person intentionally avoids eye contact with the other or displays "gaze aversion," an impression of lack of power and credibility is evidenced.[21] Finally, certain eye behaviors usually convey negative messages in the interview. An interviewee who has shifty eyes or displays increased blinking may be indicating psychological, physical, or emotional stress.[22]

A second attending behavior, **body language,** or kinesics, refers to accurately observing physical movements of the feet and legs, shoulders and head, hands and arms, and the trunk of the body. These movements can convey impor-

*Ralph G. Nichols and Leonard A. Stevens, *Are You Listening?* (New York: McGraw-Hill, 1957), 53–54. Copyright © 1957 by Leonard A. Stevens. Reprinted by permission of Curtis Brown, Ltd.

tant meaning about attitudes, perceptions, liking or disliking of the other person, and acceptance of verbal statements during the interview. When people like each other, they generally face each other more directly than with those whom they dislike. Direct body orientation is also considered more empathic and communicates equal status. Men tend to be more relaxed and expansive in their movements than women. They use more personal space when talking, sprawling out on chairs and using wide, sweeping gestures. Women are generally more restricted in their postures and gestures.[23]

Accurately attending to body language and nonverbal communication may also yield clues to detecting hidden or deceptive messages. Deception serves as a blocking function in the counseling interview when an interviewee is not telling the whole truth. Deception means the interviewee will try to distort or cover up the truth or hide feelings that are being felt at the moment. Body language rather than facial expression best reveals to an interviewer information about deception. For instance, fidgeting feet, frequent changes in crossing of legs, and unnaturally still leg positions may suggest deception. Also, unnatural or stilted hand movements can signal possible deception. Excessive self-touching, such as stroking of the chin, scratching the head, clasping and unclasping of the hands, and grooming of the hair may demonstrate an uneasiness that reveals hidden information. Moreover, deceptive or nervous participants may sit on their hands, hold their knees with their hands, and use frequent hand-to-hand actions. Understanding the meaning of this "nonverbal leakage" is a complex task, but the interviewer may also attend to verbal signals, which may indicate deception. Speech rate, speech errors, pitch variation, and pauses are major predictors of deception. Mark Hickson and Don Stacks reported interesting differences between prepared and spontaneous liars. Prepared liars tend to take a shorter time to answer, exhibit less leg and foot movement, less hand movement, and fewer head nods than spontaneous liars. Spontaneous liars show more leg and foot movements, hand movements, head nods, and laughing and smiling than prepared liars. They also exhibit longer and more frequent pauses and greater numbers of speech errors.[24] However, the skilled interviewer must still look at the context of the interview and carefully learn to distinguish between normal anxiety or a lack of communication competence, and possible deception.

A third dimension of attending behaviors are **vocal qualities.** By listening carefully, the interviewer will notice how emphasis is placed on particular words or phrases and will look for meaningful patterns in the interviewee's vocal behavior. The vocal qualities of pitch (the highness and lowness of our voice), rate (how fast or slow we speak), inflection (the degree of emphasis we place on various syllables or words), volume (loudness or softness of voice), and quality (clarity, pronunciation, and ease of understanding) are the most revealing categories of vocal cues. Men tend to speak louder than women, though with less expression, while women tend to speak with more expressive intonation patterns. Women also tend to use better pronunciation than men. Skilled participants in an interview will detect subtle changes in vocal qualities. Understanding these qualities can give clues to a participant's mood, honesty, feelings, and attitude. Accurately discerning them further aids the counselor in conducting the interview and in sharing meaning.

The final attending behavior is **verbal tracking.** Certain nonverbal regulatory cues enable the participants in the interaction to follow or "track" the flow of conversation. Missing the flow of the interaction may create confusion in the dialogue, resulting in the interviewer or interviewee wandering from the topic of concern. From the handshake at the beginning, a smile at a seemingly innocent question, crossing and uncrossing legs, the observant counselor notices nonverbal cues that regulate the conversational exchange. Turn-taking skills are an important aspect of interpreting regulatory cues and function like traffic signals that allow the conversation to flow smoothly. Turn-taking skills may be divided into four categories: (1) turn requesting, (2) turn maintaining, (3) turn yielding, and (4) turn denying.[25] Interviewers or interviewees signal **turn requesting** any time they wish to speak. Suddenly sitting upright, leaning forward, or raising a hand or finger may indicate a desire to speak. **Turn maintaining** behaviors indicate that one party wishes to continue speaking even though the other may be displaying a turn request. Speaking more loudly or at a faster rate, or raising a hand or finger as if to say "just a minute" all signal turn maintenance. Sipping coffee or drawing on a pipe in the middle of a sentence can also indicate a desire to maintain a speaking turn. **Turn yielding** behaviors acknowledge a willingness to give up the speaking turn and yield to the other participant. Relaxing, pausing at the end of a statement, or using tag questions may indicate a request for the other party to respond. Finally, **turn denying** communicates a wish to not want to respond. Silence, head nods, eye contact, and smiling can indicate attentiveness without accepting the turn-taking offer. Turn-taking behaviors help the counseling interview to move smoothly and easily without creating discomfort. The observant counselor understands and positively responds to regulatory cues and turn-taking behaviors that control the back and forth process of speaking and listening and regulate conversation flow. An interviewer's knowledge and skill in applying these cues and skills will enhance success in a counseling interview.

Empathy and Mindfulness

Besides listening and actively attending, the interviewer who empathizes with and is mindful of the interviewee will better succeed in developing a helping relationship. Empathy can be described as "experiencing the world as if *you* were the other person."[26] Empathic understanding is the caring skill of temporarily laying aside our views and values and of entering into another's world without prejudice. It is an active process of seeking to hear the other's thoughts, feelings, tones, and meanings as if they were our own.[27] Mindfulness suggests that the interviewer consciously monitors the ongoing communication process, making necessary changes in order to more effectively address the needs of the interviewee.[28] Counselors must be willing to acknowledge the seriousness of another person's problem and work to draw the other person out so that he or she is able to discuss the problem and come to terms with it. Empathy and mindfulness doesn't happen by accident but are deliberately nurtured and developed. Indifference and neutrality are dialectically opposite forces that can sabotage the establishment of a helping relationship in the counseling situation.

Using Language Responsibly

Effective counselors are skilled in using language responsibly. They understand that words by their very nature are abstract and imprecise, yet language is integral to the counseling situation. Language structures our perception of reality. Several aspects of responsible language are particularly relevant to the counseling interview and can help us better understand the word game in which we all are players.

Understanding **"I" versus "You" language** indicates the degree of responsibility parties assume for their statements. "I" statements make ownership of a message clear and are a way of accepting responsibility for a message. These messages are honest, clear, and confessional. "I" statements describe (1) the other person's behavior, (2) your feelings, and (3) the consequences the other's behavior has for you.[29] For example, consider this encounter where a supervisor counseling an insubordinate and trenchant employee says, "I was angry yesterday (descriptive of personal feelings) when you engaged in carping and faultfinding with me in front of coworkers (descriptive of the other person's behavior). They now have less respect for me and are seemingly expressing open disapproval (descriptive of the consequences of the other's behavior for the supervisor)." The supervisor is assuming personal responsibility for anger and indicating ownership for his or her feelings while making clear the consequences of the employee's actions. In contrast, "you messages" using the second-person pronoun "you" imply evaluative statements, which are criticisms, labels, or ways of fixing blame. As a "you" statement, our counseling example would take the form, "You made me angry when you ridiculed me in front of other employees in the workroom. They don't look up to me at all now and are openly critical of me." Here, the supervisor sounds judgmental and accusing, characteristics that will inhibit the counseling encounter. Avoiding judgmental speech is difficult for even a trained counselor. To ask, "Who did that?" is difficult without being seen as accusing.[30] However, we are not suggesting using only "I" statements and shunning "you" statements. An abundance of "I" statements can make the counselor appear self-centered and egotistical, and "you" statements can emphasize another's needs and wants. What is critical to any case is being aware of the responsibility inherent in our language.

Another aspect of using language responsibly relates to the use of "it" statements. Parties to counseling who show responsibility for their messages use "I" statements rather than "it" statements. "It" messages subtly dodge ownership of feelings and are imprecise. For example, interviewers often open with "It's good to see you again today," when a more direct and personal approach would be to say, "I'm glad to see you again." An interviewee might say during the course of counseling, "It's necessary to stretch the rules in this organization in order to get the job done," rather than more responsibly saying, "I had to stretch the rules to get the job done." At other times, an interviewee might avoid personal responsibility by making an impersonal reference to "people" in general. Saying, "People are stressed out these days," is a way of avoiding "I'm stressed out these days." The subtle shift to the personal pronoun "I" is difficult for most of us. Once again, however, when judiciously used, our language can be more direct and concrete. Skilled interviewers will listen carefully to the language of interviewees to assess their position or stand and their degree of ownership for feelings.

"But" messages are a third way to avoid taking direct responsibility for a statement. Interviewers often avoid taking direct responsibility for negative statements by beginning with a soft, positive buffer and then using *but* to communicate the real negative message. When a supervisor says, "You are doing a fine job, *but* more attention needs to be given to accurately recording details," the use of "but" weakens the admonition. When a teacher says, "I liked your paper very much, *but* the introduction fails to get the reader's attention," the critical suggestion is masked by faint praise. Certainly, *but* is an effective transitional devise; however, responsibility is avoided when it is used to diminish or hide a negative message. This is not to suggest that counselors should be harshly insensitive, rather to say that understanding comes through responsibly expressing considerate constructive criticism.

Using language responsibly also implies an awareness of "powerful" and "powerless" speech, or the ability of a person to influence another. An individual's choice of words determines whether he or she sounds apologetic and uncertain or confident and competent. Generally, people who use powerful speech appear to be more competent and credible, have higher status, and have greater influence on others. Powerless speech, on the other hand, creates a perception of diminished authority, less credibility, and inadequacy.[31] Powerful and powerless speech can significantly influence the tone and tenor of a counseling session. Consider the following two possible openings to a counseling exchange between a supervisor and employee.

Opening 1

Well, hello, Gene. I'm not really sure we needed a meeting today, but uh, I figured we could accomplish at least something. Sorry for the lack of notice. I guess, maybe, we should begin with, you know, your last evaluation. You've been working here ten years, haven't you? It seems to me that your past evaluations were very good, but you seem to have slacked off somewhat, don't you think? I probably shouldn't say that I am very surprised by your less than excellent performance lately. If you want to, tell me about it?

This opening reveals several linguistic features of powerless speech. **Hesitation forms,** commonly known as "verbal fillers" appear in the opening as, "Well, hello, Gene," "but uh," and "you know." When a speaker is unsure or tentative, hesitant speech mannerisms occur. Uncertainty is further revealed when the supervisor uses such **hedges,** or softening statements, as "I guess," "maybe," and "somewhat." The supervisor also uses **intensifiers** when saying, "I'm not really sure we needed a meeting today" and "I am very surprised." Furthermore, **questioning forms** are tacked on as queries permitting a quick retreat in the event of disapproval when the supervisor says, "You've been working here ten years, haven't you?" and "If you want to, tell me about it?" This is a way to avoid taking a definite stand and tends to weaken the supervisor's position. Finally, the use of such **disclaimers** as "I'm not really sure we needed a meeting today," and "I probably shouldn't say this," further weakens the supervisor's credibility, authority, and position.[32] Certainly, such an opening jeopardizes the latent potential of the counseling session.

Opening 2

Hello, Gene. I'm pleased that you were able to come in on such short notice. During the ten years you've been with us, you've maintained an excellent work record. Your last performance evaluation revealed a downward change I'd like to discuss with you. Tell me why you think this change in your evaluation occurred.

Here, Gene's supervisor sets a positive tone while powerfully communicating the intent of the counseling session. The language focuses on Gene instead of the supervisor, and apologetic language is noticeably missing. Position, authority, credibility, and competence are established from the outset and will contribute to a fruitful counseling exchange. Still, achieving the right balance between "powerful" and "powerless" speech requires knowledge and awareness of both participants.

At an empirical level, language is a tool, perhaps the most powerful and adaptable tool we have devised. It provides a "handle" by which we can manage and work with the important aspects of our social and physical world. Still, while the most obvious function of language is its ability to refer or represent, its most important misuse is misrepresentation and inaccuracy. Counselors have an obligation to use language accurately and responsibly.

Feedback Skills

Carl Rogers wrote, "In our daily lives there are a thousand and one reasons for not letting ourselves experience our attitudes fully, reasons from our past and from the present, reasons that reside within the social situation. It seems too dangerous, too potentially damaging, to experience them freely and fully."[33] The workplace counseling situation is no exception. Feelings of anger, fear, or insecurity can build and if not constructively dealt with may reach a boiling point and explode. Therefore, feedback skills are essential to effective workplace counseling. Paul Pedersen and Allen Ivey suggest six guidelines for providing feedback in the counseling interview.[34]

First, *focus on a person's behavior, rather than on the person himself or herself.* By carefully using language, the interviewer can subtly shift from placing evaluation on the person and focus instead on his or her behavior. Rather than saying, "You're not a good worker," the interviewer can say, "You did not achieve the goals you set." Keeping the focus on behavior creates a supportive environment that helps the individual change.

Second, *focus on observations rather than on inferences.* Separating fact from inference is not an easy task and is often a source of frustration. Interviewers who fail to distinguish between what is actually said and what is inferred or assumed may jump to hasty and incorrect conclusions. When an interviewer asks, "Why are you angry with me?" an inference is being made with an implicit assumption regarding the other person's emotions. To rephrase the question as an observation, the interviewer might ask, "When you did not speak to me the other day (an observation), I got the idea you were angry with me (an inference)." Now, the inference is linked to an observation, and the interviewer subtly assumes responsibility for the conclusion—be it right or wrong. Though most of us make inferences when communicating with others, problems arise when we are unaware of these inferences and believe them to be facts.

Third, *focus on description rather than evaluation*. Description means being non-judgmental toward another. When an interviewer asks questions, the questions are perceived to be genuine requests for information. No implication is made toward the interviewee that he or she must change. Evaluation, on the other hand, means to pass judgment on an individual's actions. The interviewer who evaluates tends to make moral assessments, blaming or praising the standards, values, and motives of the interviewee. Use of descriptive statements places the ownership of feelings, attitudes, and beliefs on the speaker, while evaluation places this ownership on the other person.

Fourth, *focus on the here and now, rather than on the past or future*. Focusing on what the interviewee is saying and doing at the present time enables the interviewer to fully understand what is happening. Looking to the past can distort feedback through selective memory and interpretation. Accurate feedback relates to how closely the feedback is to the present. Distance and time from the present increases the potential for distortion.

Fifth, *focus on sharing information rather than on giving advice*. Too many counselors tend to give advice when another expresses an emotion. They reply to "I'm mad!" with "It'll be okay!" or "Go talk with her about it." Advising, moralizing, criticizing, or ridiculing serve little to advance the counseling interview. Inappropriate or self-referenced preaching and advice can only move the interview away from information sharing. Workplace counseling requires listening and accurately reflecting objective information rather than reacting.

Sixth, *focus on what is said rather than on why it is said*. Speculating on an interviewee's reasons for making a statement may result in arguments. Better feedback results when the interviewer focuses on expressed statements only. Interpreting another's motives is risky at best. These guidelines can help interviewers create an appropriate counseling environment and constructively approach the counseling situation.

*　　*　　*　　*　　*

While no information is provided regarding the actual conduct of the counseling luncheon, we can infer from their relationship that Ellen carefully attended to Stacey's presentation of the bothersome problems plaguing her and displayed empathy and mindfulness. She probably provided honest, focused feedback rather than dismissing Stacey's concerns by simply saying, "Don't worry, everything will be okay."

Ellen will help Stacey by responsibly using language and accurately reflecting Stacey's feelings about her job. When Stacey says, "I don't know whether I should continue working at the university since everybody else seems to learn the software faster that I do," Ellen might respond with a paraphrasing statement, "You feel like giving up because you see yourself not doing as well as others." This will avoid shifting responsibility and being judgmental while focusing on what Stacey said. If Stacey says, "I'm an incompetent person," Ellen will want to provide confidence in Stacey's abilities and help her concentrate on what can be done here and now. Ellen can best help Stacey by accurately reflecting Stacey's feelings about her job and encouraging her to constructively explore solutions. Ellen's attention to the flow of communication and practical optimism may prompt Stacey to engage in reality testing and gain a better perspective about her job. By helping Stacey feel understood, appreciated, and valued as a person, Ellen can cheer her spirit and brighten her outlook.

Helpful advances have been made, but a single luncheon will not resolve all of Stacey's problems. Therefore, Ellen and Stacey will want to make arrangements to meet again. Ellen will be able to better prepare for later sessions and may assume a more directive approach depending upon Stacey's progress. This also permits Stacey time to explore other available programs and resources.

Coaching and Workplace Counseling

While most employees perform as expected, there will always be those employees who fail to meet expectations. J. F. Viega observes that "if there is one universal truth about managers, it is that all of them have problem subordinates."[35] It is a manager's job to confront and deal with poor performance, and to create conditions that minimize the chances that it will occur again. Coaching is an aspect of workplace counseling which can do this.

Coaching is a face-to-face discussion between a manager and a subordinate to get the subordinate to stop performing an undesirable behavior and begin performing desirable behaviors. Consequently, coaching may be defined as a "mutual conversation between a manager and an employee that follows a predictable process and leads to superior performance, commitment to sustained improvement, and positive relationships."[36] Because of the similarities, many draw an analogy between organizational managers and athletic coaches. Both sports coaches and managers must orient individuals to the team, develop potential skills, motivate, and ensure results. Likewise, many of the characteristics of an effective athletic coach are shared by a manager-coach. These characteristics include optimism, a strong sense of moral values, honesty, trust, humility, warmth, and self-confidence. Ultimately, however, it is the "context of committed partnership" in which athletic coaching occurs that is the key to defining management coaching.[37] To coach effectively, managers must bring individuals together and "encourage them to step up to responsibility and continued achievement, treating them as full-scale partners and contributors."[38] Acting as a coach makes the manager or supervisor a partner with employees and a facilitator of their performance.

Coaching is a mutual conversation which makes both parties partners in productivity.

Don Shula, one of professional football's most successful coaches and Ken Blanchard, author and consultant, describe the needed abilities for effective coaching by using the acronym COACH which stands for Conviction-driven, Overlearning, Audible-ready, Consistency, and Honesty-based. *Conviction-driven* coaches are clear in their vision and have a plan on how to achieve it. *Overlearning* is perceived as preparing team members for future opportunities by helping them achieve practice perfection. *Audible-ready* is the ability to be adaptable and ready to change the game plan when the situation demands it. *Consistency* means coaches are predictable in their response to performance, and coaching is conducted on a regular basis, correcting and redirecting when necessary, as well as praising and recognizing a job well done. Finally, *honesty-based* coaching refers to a coach's integrity and ability to walk-the-talk.[39] Today, organizations must have managers or supervisors who are able to coach peak performance from their direct reports. Employees must work smarter, not harder.

The Role of Manager or Supervisor in Coaching

Clearly, the employee's direct manager or supervisor bears the responsibility for coaching. While other managers or even coworkers can provide workplace counseling to help overcome personal problems or serve as mentors to teach new skills and improve an employee's opportunities for success on the job, coaching occurs within the context of an ongoing relationship between employee and manager or supervisor. It is the manager or supervisor who must ensure that his or her unit meets its goals, and this means ensuring that employees perform their tasks effectively. The manager or supervisor delegates assignments, establishes standards, and monitors performance and, therefore, is the only one uniquely equipped with sufficient information, opportunity, and authority to carry out coaching effectively.[40]

Conducting the Coaching Discussion

Employees often show early warning signs of a difficulty which may indicate the necessity for coaching. These signs may include "overreacting emotionally, blaming others for mistakes and not leading a balanced life, with deteriorating relationships outside of work or poor health."[41] This should prompt a manager or supervisor to immediately analyze factors that may be contributing to unsatisfactory performance and to choose an appropriate response to improve performance. When conducting such a coaching analysis, certain questions should be asked: What specifically is the employee doing wrong or failing to do? Does the employee know that their performance is not satisfactory? Does the employee know how to perform effectively? Are there obstacles beyond the employee's control contributing to the performance problem? Could the employee perform more effectively if he or she wanted to? Can the task or job be modified?[42] Answers to these questions can help identify the causes of poor performance and suggest possible solutions. More importantly, this information can be helpful when conducting the coaching discussion and exploring appropriate action plans to improve performance.

The coaching discussion is designed to help the employee perform effectively. The goal of the discussion is to get the employee to agree that a problem exists and commit to a course of action to resolve it. Ferdinand Fournies suggests a five-step approach to the coaching discussion that assumes the manager or supervisor has conducted a thorough coaching analysis and has determined that the employee can improve his or her performance.[43]

> *Step 1: Get the employee's agreement that a problem exists.* Unless the employee believes there is a performance problem, he or she will have no reason to change. Thus, getting an agreement that a problem exists is critical for the coaching process to work. Gaining agreement involves describing the problem behavior and its consequences for the manager or supervisor, co-workers, and the employee.
>
> *Step 2: Mutually discuss alternative solutions to the problem.* During this part of the discussion, the manager or supervisor asks the employee for alternatives to solving the problem. Their role is only to help the employee come up with and clarify alternatives, since employees will more likely be committed to alternatives they suggest themselves. Moreover, this is in keeping with the principle of empowering the employee to solve his or her own problems.
>
> *Step 3: Mutually agree on action to be taken to solve the problem.* After sufficient alternatives have been discussed, the manager or supervisor and employee can agree on which alternatives to pursue to solve the problem. At this point,

both should clearly understand what will be done and when it will happen. They should also agree on a specific time to followup on the coaching discussion to determine whether the agreed-upon action(s) have been successful in resolving the problem.

Step 4: Followup to measure results. It is imperative that the manager or supervisor followup to determine whether the agreed-upon actions have been taken and the problem resolved. Without follow-up the employee may conclude that the manager or supervisor doesn't really care about the problem.

Step 5: Recognize any achievement when it occurs. Many performance problems will not disappear overnight. Even if a problem is not completely eliminated, the employee should be recognized for any effort and improvement made. The idea is to motivate him or her to further improvement. When necessary, further discussions should be held to determine any additional steps needed to resolve the problem. Follow-up, recognition of improvement, and updated improvement planning should continue until the employee is performing effectively.

Coaching, indeed, can be an effective way to manage employee performance. Having the employee participate in the discussion, setting goals for improvement, offering specific behavioral feedback, and being supportive and helpful are all related to positive coaching outcomes. Understanding the coaching process and the skills necessary to conduct it well can prepare managers or supervisors for this challenging and rewarding responsibility.

*   *   *   *   *

Ellen Betz and Stacey Ross are involved in a common workplace counseling situation. Ellen principally responds to Stacey's personal problems by listening, paraphrasing, and reflecting, without specifically exploring ways to reduce her stress or resolve performance problems. However, Stacey's performance difficulties with Quark Express, Windows, and E-mail/network applications should prompt Ellen to suggest seeking coaching. Stacey's immediate manager or supervisor is in the best position to assess the nature of her performance problems and conduct a coaching discussion. Since Stacey already agrees that a problem exists, the discussion could quickly move to exploring alternative solutions and mutually agreeing upon an action plan and follow-up activities. Besides improving performance, coaching could also strengthen the work relationship between Stacey and her manager or supervisor. This might further help to alleviate the stress and concerns regarding job security. Coaching has become a popular part of managing employee performance, so Stacey's manager or supervisor would probably welcome such a request.

Legal and Ethical Considerations

Federal and state legislation has had a significant impact on the growth of workplace counseling programs, especially in the area of alcohol and drug abuse. Federal laws, such as the Federal Rehabilitation Act of 1973 and the Drug-Free Workplace Act of 1988, have encouraged the adoption of EAPs. Also, many state laws require drug-testing programs to be accompanied by EAPs or some other form of rehabilitation counseling. Moreover, the Americans with Disabilities Act of 1990 may serve as an impetus for further development of SMIs and HPPs.

These laws prohibit employers from discriminating against individuals with disabilities and require that employers make "reasonable accommodations" to help such employees perform their jobs. Included in this legal definition of disability are individuals who experience alcohol and drug problems. Employees with disabilities may be discharged only for job-performance reasons. Consequently, an alcoholic employee may not be fired because of alcoholism, but only for the negative effects the alcoholism has on job performance. In addition, it is unlawful to simply permit the employee's performance to deteriorate to a level that would justify termination. According to the law, the employer must make reasonable accommodations that help the employee resolve the problem and improve performance.[44] In the case of substance abuse, "reasonable accommodation" has been interpreted to mean the employee must be offered the opportunity for treatment and permitted the time necessary for the treatment to take effect before terminating for poor performance is justified.[45] Clearly, the impact of future legislation may be to broaden counseling assistance programs aimed at employee well-being.

Legal and professional constraints also govern the conduct of professional counselors, specifying the conditions under which they may grant or withhold treatment, the kinds of treatment appropriate for different problems, and the release of confidential information. Professional counselors may be held legally responsible for unprofessional conduct, just as physicians are accountable for malpractice. However, individuals outside the helping professions who might engage in workplace counseling are not formally bound by these codes of conduct.

Still, confidentiality is a key concern for all involved in workplace counseling. One must hold in strictest confidence any information shared, and organizations must guarantee confidentiality of all employee counseling records. Simply put, counseling is an intensely personal and private affair, requiring the sensitive handling of information.

*   *   *   *   *

Ellen Betz is not legally or professionally bound to any code of conduct, but her own moral values and sense of ethics governs her counseling behavior. Ellen clearly understands the limits of her abilities and displays a genuine interest in helping Stacey while not assuming responsibility for Stacey's actions. Moreover, Ellen is keenly aware of the confidential nature of counseling and deliberately works to preserve that confidentiality.

Certainly, Ellen should recommend that Stacey take advantage of the programs offered through the Human Resource department. The university may provide technical training seminars, which could assist Stacey in upgrading her computer skills. Also, the human resource department might offer stress management interventions or health promotion programs, which could help build self-confidence and well-being. Finally, their familiarity with community outreach programs may be useful in addressing Stacey's child care needs. Downsizing, right-sizing, and layoffs can cause employees to feel as though they are capsizing, and workplace counseling is a lifeboat. However, workplace counseling is not any one person's responsibility; therefore, Stacey should be encouraged to take advantage of all available counseling services. Counseling can only be beneficial if it is used.

Critical Focus

To understand the multiple purposes of the counseling interview, consider the workplace grief confronting Ron Ortega, the newly appointed quality assurance (QA) manager for Winter Springs Hospital. Winter Springs Hospital is located in Florida and has just initiated an aggressive marketing and community outreach project after having been purchased by The Cambridge Group, a health care conglomerate with a network of hospitals. Ron Ortega was personally asked by the chief executive officer of the hospital to take the QA job.

Ron has experienced success in his six-year career at Winter Springs Hospital, and his achievements have not gone unnoticed. He began as a trainer in customer service, and under his guidance, a new mission statement was developed, the training department expanded, and customer approval increased. The working relationships among the medical staff became more productive, and patients evaluated highly the care and consideration displayed by the hospital. His abilities were recognized by The Cambridge Group when they assumed ownership, and he was the natural choice for the QA position.

The Cambridge Group is efficiency minded and bottom-line oriented. This has resulted in a number of layoffs, with those remaining having to assume increased responsibilities. The downsizing increased the anxiety level throughout the hospital, as well as created an uncertain climate detrimental to the QA department. The hospital's QA department and QA processes were in trouble when Ron assumed leadership, and the difficulties have only been exacerbated by the changes. The former head, while popular among the staff, was let go because of numerous errors in the pharmacy and on medical records which had created concern among the medical quality boards. Ron's mission was to change the processes, reduce the overall error rate, and improve efficiency. He has not been welcomed as manager of the QA department, and for the first time in his career, he has found a group resistant to him personally, as well as resistant to change.

Ron Ortega knows he is not performing up to his standards and is experiencing considerable frustration. His senior staff members are making minimal efforts to change, since they believe the problems are beyond the QA department's control. They can establish processes, train, and monitor, but they do not do the actual work or make the mistakes for which they are being held accountable. Moreover, they are discouraged with the layoffs and fear they may lose their jobs. Therefore, Ron has begun to rethink the situation and has scheduled a counseling session with Beth Croft, the Human Resource director for the hospital.

Beth Croft has been Human Resource (HR) director for Winter Springs Hospital for the past ten years. She participated in hiring Ron and has been delighted with his career development, taking pleasure in observing his achievements. Beth has also noticed a decline in his performance since taking the QA position, which she attributes to the increased stress. Everyone has undergone changes that have effected their work since being taken over by The Cambridge Group. Hopefully, the downsizing will not result in a downswing, and this will only be temporary until things settle down and people adjust to the new program. However, Beth is pleased that Ron has requested a meeting where they might discuss the situation. She has confidence in his abilities and believes a counseling session could be beneficial for both of them.

Critically focus on Beth Croft's skill at conducting a counseling interview and Ron Ortega's participation. The following questions can direct and guide your analysis.

1. Why do organizations conduct counseling interviews? Would you classify this as remedial counseling or coaching? What is the purpose and agenda of the interviewer? The interviewee?
2. Who controlled the interview? Did the parties actively listen and probe for solutions? Were solutions objectively explored and alternatives impartially considered? Is the counseling approach appropriate given the purpose and intent of the interview?
3. Did any special problems or obstacles arise? Were there any constraints?
4. How satisfactory was the closing? Were the interests of both parties achieved?
5. What recommendations would you make regarding the role of the interviewer? The interviewee?

Summary

Employee well-being affects the ability, availability, and readiness of employees to perform their jobs. The effects of problems with alcohol and drug abuse, stress, and health are widespread and are estimated to cost organizations billions of dollars in lost productivity. Both the organization and the individual stand to gain from employer attempts to provide information and programs that help employees deal with these problems. Therefore, workplace counseling is critical to promoting the intellectual and emotional growth of employees.

The workplace counseling interview, whether directive, nondirective, or controlled nondirective, provides an essential means for helping employees confront and present a problem, use reactions to develop information about possible causes and solutions, set goals, determine what should be done to solve the problem, and follow-up to ascertain success. Active listening underlies all that takes place in this interview. By improving listening and developing good attending behaviors, the interviewer easily develops a caring, supportive environment. Moreover, the interviewer must pay attention to eye contact, body language, and the vocal qualities of the interviewee. These regulatory cues yield important information to the watchful eye. Responding appropriately to these messages facilitates the conversation and interaction. When responding appropriately, the interviewer changes topics at the right time, develops and discusses subjects at an appropriate length, and promotes the quality of interaction that the interview requires. Finally, the interviewer must offer responsive feedback. Good feedback concentrates on the interviewee's behavior, not on the person. It keeps the focus on observations, description, and the "here and now." Workplace counseling is a challenging, dynamic experience but one that can afford significant personal rewards.

Coaching focuses on helping employees improve their job performance. It is a five-step process whereby managers or supervisors encourage employees to accept responsibility for performance, enable them to achieve and sustain superior performance, and treat them as partners in working toward organizational goals. Coaching involves both analyzing performance and conducting a discussion with employees to solve performance problems and determine ways to enhance performance. Drawing upon effective communication and interpersonal skills, managers or supervisors help employees acquire a sense of ownership for their performance.

Legal and ethical issues also affect workplace counseling programs. Laws and regulations have both fueled the growth of counseling programs and raised questions about the role of workplace counseling. The nature of participation and confidentiality are ethical considerations which must be dealt with when conducting workplace counseling. Still, there is general agreement that effective workplace counseling benefits the individual's well-being, as well as the organization's bottom line.

SHARPENING YOUR FOCUS

1. Outline and describe the five-step approach to workplace counseling. Explain why it is necessary, during workplace counseling, to get the other person to assume responsibility for the session. When would you recommend using such formal counseling services as employee assistance programs, stress management interventions, and health promotion programs?

2. Counseling requires a depth of self-disclosure, which involves great potential cost. When will people take that risk? What is the workplace counselor's responsibility for maintaining confidentiality?

3. Describe a relationship you shared that you believe was based on trust. Identify the trusting and trustworthy behaviors exhibited by you, as well as the other party and attempt to determine the factors in your relationship that permitted a climate of trust to develop.

   Next, describe a second relationship you shared that you mistakenly believed was based on trust. Identify the trusting and trustworthy behaviors that were missing, and describe the negative consequences that resulted from the situation. Attempt to determine the factors in your relationship that prevented or inhibited the development of a climate of trust.

4. Carmen Berry and Tamara Traeder in *Girlfriends* describe the importance of friendship. Through personal stories, they note the importance of honesty and trust as friends are there as a counselor. If you do not feel you can trust a friend enough to discuss your personal history with them, then it would be difficult to go to them for counseling or strength. Compile a list of behaviors you believe will help build trust in a counseling relationship. Recall a time when you were there as a counselor for a friend. How did you act—respond? Did this experience help build "enduring ties" and develop "invisible bonds?"

5. Talk to a coach about what they do. How is the role of manager-coach similar to that of the sports or athletic coach? Outline and describe Fournie's five-step approach to coaching. Many managers or supervisors find coaching difficult to do or are reluctant to do it. What do you believe are two important reasons for this? How do you think the obstacles you identify can be overcome?

6. Distinguish between workplace counseling and coaching. Explain why it is important to counsel/coach both employees with performance problems and employees who are performing well. Describe a personal coaching experience, and identify the behaviors exhibited that permitted a supportive climate to develop.

NOTES

1. Lester N. Downing, *Counseling Theories and Techniques* (Chicago: Nelson-Hall, 1975).
2. Walter R. Mahler, *How Effective Executives Interview* (Homewood, Ill.: Dow Jones-Richard D. Irwin, 1976).
3. R. D. Evered and J. C. Selman, "Coaching and the Art of Management," *Organizational Dynamics* 18 (1990): 16–32.
4. J. Spicer, *The EAP Solution: Current Trends and Future Issues* (Center City, Minn.: Hazelden Educational Materials, 1987).
5. William J. Sonnenstuhl and Harrison M. Trice, *Strategies for Employee Assistance Programs: The Crucial Balance*, 2d ed. (Ithaca, N.Y.: ILR Press, Cornell University, 1990), 1.
6. William F. Casscio, *Applied Psychology in Personnel Management*, 4th ed. (Englewood Cliffs, N.J.: Prentice-Hall, 1991).
7. See J. T. Wrich, *The Employee Assistance Program* (Center City, Minn.: Hazelden Educational Foundation, 1984); H. M. Trice and J. M. Beyer, "Work-Related Outcomes of the Constructive-Confrontation Strategy in a Job-Based Alcoholism Program," *Journal of Studies*

on Alcohol 45 (1984): 393–404; and William F. Cascio, *Costing Human Resources: The Financial Impact of Behavior in Organizations,* 3d ed. (Boston: PWS-Kent, 1991).

8. J. M. Ivancevich, M. T. Matteson, S. M. Freedman, and J. S. Phillips, "Worksite Stress Management Interventions," *American Psychologist* 45 (1990): 252.

9. J. M. Ivancevich and M. T. Matteson, "Organizational Level Stress Management Interventions: Review and Recommendations," *Journal of Occupational Behavior Management* 8 (1986): 229–48.

10. See L. R. Murphy, "A Review of Occupational Stress Management Research: Methodological Considerations," *Journal of Occupational Behavior Management,* 8 (1986): 215–28; R. S. DeFrank and C. L. Cooper, "Worksite Stress Management Interventions: Their Effectiveness and Conceptualization," *Journal of Managerial Psychology* 2 (1987): 4–10; and J. M. Ivancevich, M. T. Matteson, S. M. Freedman, and J. S. Phillips, "Worksite Stress Management Interventions," *American Psychologist* 45 (1990): 252–61.

11. D. L. Gebhard and C. E. Crump, "Employee Fitness and Wellness Programs in the Workplace," *American Psychologist* 45 (1990): 262–72.

12. M. P. O'Donnell. *Design of Workplace Health Promotion Programs* (Royal Oak, Mich.: American Journal of Health Promotion, 1986).

13. Michael Z. Sincoff and Robert S. Goyer, *Interviewing* (New York: Macmillan Publishing, 1984).

14. Paul B. Pedersen and Allen Ivey, *Culture-Centered Counseling and Interviewing Skills: A Practical Guide* (Westport, Conn.: Praeger, 1993).

15. Robert J. Craig, *Clinical and Diagnostic Interviewing* (Northvale, N.J.: Jason Aronson, Inc., 1989).

16. Mahler, *How Effective Executives Interview,* 136.

17. See Wayne W. Dyer and John Vriend, *Counseling Techniques that Work* (New York: American Association for Counseling and Development, 1988); D. Kinlaw, *Coaching for Commitment: Managerial Strategies for Obtaining Superior Performance* (San Diego, Calif.: University Associates, 1989); and Alfred Kadushin, *The Social Work Interview* (New York: Columbia University Press, 1990).

18. Ralph G. Nichols and Leonard A. Stevens, *Are You Listening?* (New York: McGraw-Hill, 1957), 53–54. Copyright © 1957 by Leonard A. Stevens. Reprinted by permission of Curtis Brown, Ltd.

19. Pedersen and Ivey, *Culture-Centered Counseling and Interviewing Skills,* 103.

20. Allen E. Ivey, *Intentional Interviewing and Counseling: Facilitating Client Development* (Pacific Grove, Calif.: Brooks Cole, 1993).

21. Mark L. Hickson, III and Don W. Stacks, *Nonverbal Communication: Studies and Applications,* 3d ed. (Brown and Benchmark, 1993).

22. Andrew Wolvin and Carolyn G. Coakley, *Listening,* 5th ed. (Dubuque, Iowa: Wm. C. Brown and Benchmark, 1995).

23. Hickson and Stacks, *Nonverbal Communication*

24. Ibid.

25. Mark L. Knapp and J. A. Hall, *Nonverbal Communication in Human Interaction,* 3d ed. (New York: Holt, Rinehart and Winston, 1992).

26. Pedersen and Ivey, *Culture-Centered Counseling and Interviewing Skills,* 160.

27. Carl Rogers. *On Becoming a Person* (Boston: Houghton Mifflin, 1961).

28. Ellen J. Langer, *Mindfulness* (Reading, Mass.: Addison-Wesley, 1989).

29. Ronald B. Adler, L. B. Rosenfield, and N. Towne. *Interplay: The Process of Interpersonal Communication,* 6th ed. (Fort Worth, Tex.: Harcourt Brace College Publishers, 1995).

30. Jack R. Gibb, "Defense Level and Influence Potential in Small Groups," in *Leadership and Interpersonal Behavior,* ed. L. Petrullo and B. M. Bass, (New York: Holt, Rinehart and Winston, 1961), 66–81.

31. S. H. Ng and J. J. Bradac. *Power in Language: Verbal Communication and Social Influence* (Newbury Park, Calif.: Sage Publications, 1993).

32. B. Erickson, E. A. Lind, B. C. Johnson, and W. M. O'Barr, "Speech Style and Impression Formation in a Court Setting: The Effects of Powerful and Powerless Speech," *Journal of Experimental and Social Psychology* 14 (1978): 266–79.

33. Rogers, *On Becoming a Person,* 111.

34. Pedersen and Ivey, *Culture-Centered Counseling and Interviewing Skills,* 89.

35. J. F. Viega, "Face Your Problem Subordinates Now!" *Academy of Management Executive* 2 (1988): 145.

36. D. Kinlaw, *Coaching for Commitment: Managerial Strategies for Obtaining Superior Performance* (San Diego, Calif.: University Associates, Inc., 1989), 31.

37. R. D. Evered and J. C. Selman, "Coaching and the Art of Management," *Organizational Dynamics* 18 (1990): 16–32.

38. T. Peters and N. Austin, *A Passion for Excellence: The Leadership Difference* (New York: Random House, 1985), 325.

39. Don Shula and Ken Blanchard, *Everyone's a Coach* (New York: Harper-Collins, 1996).

40. B. Geber, "From Manager into Coach," *Training* 29 (1992): 25–31.

41. Perri Capell, "Salvaging the Careers of Talented Managers Who Behave Badly," *Wall Street Journal,* 24 December, 1996, B1.

42. R. F. Mager and P. Pipe, *Analyzing Performance Problems* (Belmont, Calif.: Fearon Publishers, 1970).

43. Ferdinand F. Fournies, *Coaching For Improved Work Performance* (New York: Van Nostrand Reinhold, 1978).

44. R. K. Good, "Employee Assistance," *Personnel Journal* 65 (1986): 96–101.

45. H. Axel, *Corporate Experiences with Drug Testing Programs* (New York: The Conference Board, 1990).

CHAPTER

7 The Discipline Interview

In confronting an employee about a performance problem, there are two important goals. The first goal is to solve the problem, and the second is to maintain or enhance a good working relationship. In any organization, these outcomes are desirable. The discipline interview and a clearly stated disciplinary policy are critical to achieving these ends.

Chapter 7 examines the most effective way to solve performance problems and maintain good working relationships with employees. It explores strategies and techniques for administering discipline and addresses common problems and constraints to discipline. This chapter is designed to accomplish three objectives:

1. *Awareness.* You will learn to discipline without punishment, correcting employee performance problems in a non-threatening, problem-solving manner that results in a lasting solution.

2. *Assessment.* You will be able to assess the do's and don'ts of performance management, identifying those factors contributing to a positive discipline interview orientation and a renewed employee commitment.

3. *Application.* You will be able to identify, analyze, discuss, and document performance problems while concentrating on gaining the individual's agreement to change and perform properly in the future.

* * * * *

What Time Is It Anyway?

The Madison County Health Department is located in a small midwestern town with a population of 25,000. Dr. Raymond Smith officially oversees the various divisions comprising the Health Department, but Steve Jones directs the day-to-day operations. Service to the county has been outstanding, with the administration receiving a number of regional and state awards for excellence.

The physicians and staff generally get along fine, and Steve respects their loyalty and sense of commitment. He has promoted a team climate, encouraging participative decision making and problem solving. Recognition is readily forthcoming for both individual and team accomplishments, thus creating a jointly supportive environment. Admittedly, from time to time, tensions produce difficulties, which Steve manages in what he perceives to be a firm but fair manner.

Recently, Gail and Pat, two staff secretaries with over five years employment with the Madison County Health Department, have noticed a disturbing personnel problem. They are hardworking and expect peer staff members to be similarly responsible for assigned duties. However, Cindy Crawford, a coworker with a little over a year's employment with the department, seems to receive preferential treatment from Steve. Cindy has been late to work on several occasions and has twice taken the afternoon off without saying anything to anyone. Gail and Pat also see Cindy sitting around not doing what she should be doing when at her desk. This behavior and the apparent leniency on the part of Steve have become a point of contention in the department. At an appropriate moment and in private, Gail and Pat raise these issues with Steve who listens attentively, asks a few questions, and thanks them for sharing their concerns with him.

Steve is disturbed by these reports and realizes that he must confront Cindy, but only after he has ascertained all the facts. He determines that Cindy has been late to work three times in the last month and absent during the afternoons twice in the past week. When at her desk, Cindy has been making and accepting a number of personal telephone calls. With this information, Steve proceeds to draft a specific description of desired performance versus actual performance and outlines the impact of the problem, describing how it adversely affects the quality and quantity of work, professional standards, other staff, and the department itself.

DESIRED PERFORMANCE: Be at work every day on time, performing assigned duties and not engaging in personal business. Any time off must be arranged and approved by the director.

ACTUAL PERFORMANCE: Cindy Crawford has been late three times in the last month, absent during the afternoons twice in the past week, and has frequently engaged in personal telephone conversations.

IMPACT:
- throws staffing and scheduling off
- standby or backup may not be available
- disrupts the department causing delays

- jeopardizes good working relationships
- adversely affects morale of other team members

Steve schedules the discipline discussion for a Friday afternoon. When Cindy enters his office, he closes the door and quietly begins by saying, "I have a problem." Standing and pacing the room while Cindy sits in front of his desk, Steve clearly discloses the behavioral improprieties. He closes by sitting behind his desk and asking Cindy, "What do you have to say?"

Cindy sits quietly on the other side of his desk refusing to respond. Steve calmly says to her, "Tell me about it." Pausing, he explains the need to understand the problem from her perspective. After convincing Cindy that his purpose is not to punish but to correct the problem, she begins to discuss the difficulties outlined.

Cindy agrees that she has been late and absent, and that personal telephone calls have interfered with her job performance. However, she lives with her widowed mother who recently became ill and has had to be hospitalized. This has interfered with her personal life, and she now realizes has disrupted the department. Cindy, then, breaks into tears.

Steve hands Cindy a tissue and waits while she composes herself. After asking about her mother's current condition, they discuss solutions to the problem. It is agreed that Cindy will be to work on time and arrange with Steve any release time should her mother's condition worsen. Furthermore, she will instruct the hospital to call her at work only if there is an emergency warranting her attention. Steve assures Cindy that such changes should resolve the problem, but if it persists, the consequences may be suspension or even termination.

Steve documents the discussion on paper which they both sign:

9/9/98

REASON FOR DISCUSSION: Cindy Crawford has been observed being late to work three (3) times in the past month and absent from her assigned work area on two (2) separate occasions during the past week. She has also made and received an undue number of personal telephone calls, which have interfered with performance of duties. I want to make clear that my expectations are for Cindy to be at her work area performing her duties. She will notify me if she needs to be gone from her work area for any length of time.

ACTION TAKEN: I am giving Cindy notice that should this occur again in the future it could result in suspension or termination.

EMPLOYEE COMMENTS: My mother's illness and hospitalization prompted the problem. I failed to go through proper channels to arrange release time and allowed personal telephone calls to interfere with my duties. I agree to the solution discussed and accept personal responsibility for changing my behavior.

Steve Jones   Cindy Crawford
Supervisor   Employee

During the next month, Steve monitor's Cindy's performance, asks about her mother, and offers support and encouragement. Cindy continues to perform well, receiving a positive appraisal at the end of the year.

Discussion Questions

1. How would you describe this discipline interview situation? Was it positive or punishing?
2. Was the problem specifically identified and analyzed? How was the discussion structured? Were all pertinent topics explored? Were the results adequately documented? Did follow-up occur?
3. Describe Cindy's participation in the discipline discussion. Did Steve appropriately respond to the problems and situational constraints raised?
4. Does Steve provide the needed encouragement to positively restore the work relationship? Is a preventive orientation fostered?
5. How can discipline be an educational process contributing to the overall health of the organization?

A Positive Approach to Discipline

Ask any group of managers or supervisors "What part of your job do you hate the most?" and 95 percent will agree that firing an employee ranks number one, while having to reprimand or discipline an employee comes in a close second. It is handling the less severe or less obvious behavioral breaches that managers and supervisors find particularly difficult and unpleasant.[1] Regardless of how distasteful a task it may be, discipline is necessary and should be approached as a constructive interaction designed to personally benefit the employee and the organization. Today, more and more organizations are proactively including a discipline process as an integral part of their personnel policies and procedures in an effort to avoid potential litigation.[2]

The word *discipline* shares the same root origin as *to teach* or *to mold,* but discipline as defined by the behavior and policies of many American organizations means punishment. Often paralleling the criminal justice system, the discipline process these organizations use provides for increasingly serious sanctions as misbehavior mounts. Warnings and reprimands are followed by suspensions and probations, all in the hope that the individual will come to his or her senses and start performing properly.

Under traditional "progressive discipline," when an employee breaks a rule or fails to meet expectations, management sees its responsibility as determining the appropriate amount of punishment, based on the nature and severity of the employee's offense. The organization's primary objective then becomes the enforcement of compliance. Instead of concentrating on common goals, the supervisor and subordinate often become locked in an adversarial "we/they" battle. Only the past is discussed; action plans for the future are not requested or created. Thus, employees who do not meet organizational standards are absolved of personal responsibility simply by accepting their punishment, and the organization loses the benefits of individual commitment and acceptance of personal responsibility.[3]

Rather than looking at "discipline" as something that a manager or supervisor *does to* a poor performer when he or she misbehaves, forward thinking organizations are approaching discipline as something that must be *created*. They are discarding the traditional punitive measures and in their place are developing systems that require acceptance of personal responsibility, individual decision making, and true self-discipline. They are making a transition from the concept of *doing discipline* to the more constructive perspective of *being disciplined*.[4]

Instead of using warnings and reprimands, the managers or supervisors concentrate on identifying the specific discrepancy between actual and expected performance and the reasons why the performance expectations must be met. They describe why meeting the standards are important and concentrate on gaining the employee's agreement to change and perform properly in the future. The emphasis in these discussions is not on warning employees of the future negative consequences that will follow other violations, but on reminding them that they are responsible for proper performance and behavior. Such an approach to performance management recognizes that commitment cannot be mandated—it must be built. James Black observes that "discipline should be a constructive, positive force that enables people to work together harmoniously."[5]

The organizations that have abandoned punishment and moved to a commitment orientation for their discipline system have realized a number of benefits.[6] For managers and supervisors, one of the biggest benefits is the formal transfer of responsibility to the employee. Through the training they receive, supervisors discover that their responsibility is no longer to "write up bad guys," but to reinforce good performance and let problem performers know the consequences of their decision not to meet the organization's expectations. In dealing with disciplinary lapses, they no longer have to "play the heavy" and can deal with difficult situations with skill and confidence. Another major benefit to managers is faster resolution of problem situations. Since they are no longer required to be punitive and judgmental, managers tend to confront problems earlier. With the change in emphasis from punishment to commitment, the tone and tenor of performance discussions also change. Immature, emotional, and inappropriate behaviors diminish when managers confront employees as mature adults. Apologies and guilt disappear. By treating employees as responsible adults, managers and supervisors earn the right to expect a reciprocal response.

For employees, the emphasis on commitment to the future rather than punishment for the past builds relationships of mutual respect between the individual and his or her supervisor. Rather than "preparing stories that explain why past efforts went awry," disciplined employees are empowered to succeed through commitment and hard work.[7] The majority of employees also benefit by knowing that others who may not share their level of commitment will be confronted with the need to improve. They will find far fewer instances of having to shoulder more than their fair share of the workload because someone else isn't pulling his or her weight. Perhaps the greatest benefit is the increased managerial attention that can be given to those individuals who already are performing well. Rather than having to focus solely on getting the poor performers through punishment, managers and supervisors can devote more attention to motivating the good workers.

Finally, an approach to discipline that concentrates on commitment makes the organization's actions easier to defend. Exposure to Equal Employment Opportunity and wrongful termination suits is reduced, since employees now commit to good performance and create their own action plans. All disciplinary action is fully and properly documented. With the goal of solving problems rather than punishing offenders, less conflict is experienced.

In sum, the most effective way to solve performance problems and maintain good working relationships with employees is to gain an agreement that there is a problem and get the employee to commit to change and improvement. This more positive approach to performance management treats discipline as a very necessary educational process, the aim of which is to let a person know through concrete experience what is expected. However, gaining the employee's agreement and commitment requires careful preparation and planning.

*   *   *   *   *

Steve Jones, as director of operations at Madison County Health Department, should have noticed the problem regarding Cindy Crawford before it was brought to his attention by other staff members. However, to his credit, he thanked Gail and Pat for identifying the problem, and he promptly began to analyze the situation. His analysis reflected an objective, nonvindictive perspective. The aim was to correct the problem, improve Cindy's job performance, and restore morale to the department. It was not his intent to punish Cindy, but to solve a problem that had temporarily disrupted an otherwise productive environment. He hoped that Cindy would accept personal responsibility for the problem and commit to a satisfactory solution. He knew that discipline was never easy but was necessary for both the betterment of the employee, as well as the organization.

Administering Discipline

Core task proficiency, demonstrated effort, and maintenance of personal discipline are major performance components of *every* job. A discipline interview occurs when the employer perceives an ongoing problem which is in clear violation of organizational policy, rules, or regulations.[8] Some of the most common problems that warrant disciplinary actions are nonperformance of duties, chronic absenteeism, disobedience or insubordination, disruptive relationships, the damaging of property, carelessness, violations of safety regulations, and poor workmanship. In short, discipline becomes necessary when there are disruptive problems that must be curtailed.[9] The causes for disciplinary problems vary but usually include the following factors:

- The rules and regulations are viewed by employees as meaningless.
- Employees believe they are underpaid or that management discriminates against them.
- Employees have lost a sense of commitment and no longer feel personally responsible.
- Creating discipline problems is viewed as a way to retaliate against one's supervisor.
- The violation of the rules is unintentional, reflecting an ambiguity or a lapse in memory.[10]

Obviously, every performance or behavioral problem has a unique set of circumstances that requires an employee's work history, past experience, and merit needs to be considered. Every case is somewhat different because every individual is different. Thus, the better managers or supervisors know their employees, the better they will be able to effectively handle disciplinary action.

Still, organizations must have consistent procedures for correcting behavior and performance of employees. These procedures must incorporate the guidelines issued by the Equal Employment Opportunity Commission and should include the following key steps: (1) *identify* the performance problem, (2) *analyze* why it's important to solve the problem, (3) *discuss* the problem with the employee, (4) *document* the results of the discussion, and (5) *followup* to ensure that the problem has been solved.[11]

Identify

Identify the performance problem by establishing what the performance expectation is and specifically how the employee is failing to meet it. Do the necessary homework and investigation by acquiring the facts, reviewing similar situations, examining previous documentation in the employee's file, and assessing the employment record. Determine why the organization established this policy or procedure. Gather specific examples of how the problem is affecting the department and/or the organization. Clearly outline what needs to be changed. Finally, don't procrastinate. Putting off a confrontation hardly ever makes it easier. While there may be times when a mistake can be overlooked or a situation can be corrected with a casual remark, discipline is necessary when the infraction is serious or a bad habit has become chronic. If a supervisor reacts promptly and in a deliberate manner, the employee will take note of their concern rather than viewing the supervisor as "having a bad day" or "getting up on the wrong side of the bed." Kenneth Blanchard and Spencer Johnson, in *The One Minute Manager,* suggest four key steps when reprimanding employees: (1) reprimand them immediately, (2) be specific about what they did wrong, (3) remind them how much you value them, and (4) realize that when the reprimand is over, it's over.[12]

Analyze

Analyze why it's important to solve the problem. The most common approach taken by managers and supervisors in discussing a performance problem with an employee is one of power and authority. "I'm in charge" and "It's a rule" are indications of this approach. While it is true that the manager or supervisor has power and authority and a rule has been violated, this approach tends to be counterproductive in a professional discussion designed to bring about a positive change.

Employees tend to be defensive and resentful when a supervisor bases a discussion about the need for a performance change on power and authority. While this orientation may correct a problem, it rarely maintains or enhances a good working relationship with the employee. Concentrating on performance impact and consequences is a more successful approach.

It is necessary to ascertain the accuracy of the behavior that the employee is charged with and also to analyze the consequences, considering what might happen if the problem is not solved. Most of the time, an employee will agree to solve a problem when the discrepancy between desired and actual performance is shown and the reasons why a change must be made are clearly stated. If an employee does not agree that what he or she is doing is a problem and refuses to take steps toward improvement, then the manager or supervisor must be able to discuss what further actions may result by presenting the available options. These might include (1) closer supervision, (2) suspension, (3) postponement of a merit increase, (4) denial of a promotion, (5) reassignment, (6) demotion, (7) voluntary resignation, and (8) termination.

Managers or supervisors are ready for a face-to-face discussion with an employee only after they have determined the impact of the problem, the consequences the employee will face if there is no change, and the appropriate action step. They should be able to answer the following questions: (1) Do I know all the facts? (2) Is there a reasonable excuse for the violation? (3) Did the employee know the rule? If not, should he or she have known it? (4) Is the employee getting the same treatment others have gotten for the same offense? Am I being fair? Are the available options clearly outlined? (5) Is the rule being applied appropriately in this case? Being objective is critical and requires separating emotions and feelings from the situation—looking at the circumstances factually *before taking any action.*[13]

Discuss

Discuss the problem with the employee. The discipline interview may assume a direct approach, but it is still a two-way interaction with the primary purpose being to gain the employee's agreement to solve the problem. This is important for two reasons. First, the employee is more likely to actually solve the problem if there is agreement rather than being commanded to do so by the manager or supervisor. Then, if the employee fails to correct the situation after agreeing to do so, the next conversation will focus not only on the continuation of the original problem, but also on the employee's failure to live up to the agreement—a far more serious situation.[14]

Preparations for the meeting with the employee should include selecting an appropriate place to conduct the interview. Always hold the meeting in private, and make sure there will not be any interruptions. The employee's performance should be kept private. There *never* is an excuse for disciplining an employee in front of others. Employees fear public embarrassment more than discipline itself. It is appropriate, however, to consider having a witness or a union representative present. Their presence ensures procedural integrity and guards against any false charges or claims being raised at a later date.

Still another planning consideration is scheduling the interview. Many managers and supervisors prefer to schedule discipline interviews at the end of a day or late on a Friday afternoon. The reasons for this are that (1) the manager or supervisor has more flexibility at the end of the day with fewer potentially interrupting commitments; (2) the employee has finished work, which prevents him or her from returning to the work station and stirring up support or disrupting other people's work; and (3) the employee has time to think about what happened, reassess the situation, and consider his or her future, deciding whether he or she is willing and able to meet the standards. Regardless of any particular time schedule, adequate time must be provided to present the problem, fully discuss options and consequences, and allow the employee to respond.

The first few seconds of the interview can determine its success, so it is important to gear the tone of the discussion to the seriousness of the problem. If it is a minor problem that has not been talked about previously, a firm yet informal posture might be most appropriate. However, if it is a serious problem or a minor problem that has been previously reviewed with the individual without any change occurring, the interviewer will want to be firm and formal. Above all, remain calm and objective, keeping emotions under control. Remember, the goal is to attack the problem, not the employee.

When the problem is discussed in a candid, straightforward way, real agreement and a commitment to change are more likely. An effective way to open the interview is by saying, "I have a problem." Then, describe the desired and actual performance, and finally, invite the employee to discuss the situation and the reasons for the problem. Saying "I have a problem" instead of "You have a problem" tends to reduce defensiveness. Also, getting right to the point and describing the problem in terms of specific behavior and performance as opposed to making judgmental statements helps put the person at ease. By using prefacing phrases,

Discipline concentrates on a commitment to change and the first few seconds of the interview can determine its success.

such as "From what I know," "As I understand it," and "I have observed," the manager or supervisor maintains a factual focus and creates an information seeking rather than accusatory climate. Finally, by actively listening with an open mind to the employee's perspective, resentment can be reduced, and the manager or supervisor can better answer the following questions: (1) What actually happened from the employee's point of view? (2) Why did it happen? (3) What was his or her perceptions of the rules, regulations, or circumstances? (4) What is the employee's response to the discipline? Answers to the first three questions help in determining how completely the situation was assessed. The last question gauges whether or not the manager or supervisor is likely to have future problems with this individual. Most of the time, the employee will agree that a problem exists and agree to solve it after the actual and desired performance are reviewed.

Once the employee agrees to solve the problem, discuss possible solutions. Keep in mind that the employee is ultimately responsible for changing behavior and correcting the problem. Then, agree on the action the person will take to make sure that the problem is solved. Be specific about the plan. At this juncture, the manager or supervisor should discuss what further consequences will occur if the standards are not met. Do this in an information-presenting tone of voice, not a threat-making one. Whatever disciplinary actions are proposed, they should be consistent and appropriate to the gravity of the error.

Final comments should be directed toward building positive expectations for improvement and reminding the employee that they must accept personal responsibility for meeting the performance and behavior standards. A good final statement is "Thanks for your help in getting this problem solved. I'm sure we won't need to talk about it again."

Document

All formal disciplinary actions must be documented. It is also wise to record informal sessions in case the problem arises again. For legal purposes, the documentation should describe the problem, review the history of the problem, and summarize the interview with the employee. It should specifically state the deficiencies observed in the employee's performance, the improvement needed, and what further action may result if the employee fails to show satisfactory improvement. Lee Paterson and Michael Deblieux, management/employee professionals, recommend a four-step system called FOSA to help properly document the behavior of employees. The acronym FOSA stands for Facts, Objectives, Solution, Action. *Facts* are specific observations, not conclusions, assumptions, or probabilities, and when objectively written, allow the reader to draw the same conclusion regarding the disciplinary action taken against the employee. *Objectives* describe the behavior expected of the employee and can be written in behavioral terms or results terms. *Solutions* are suggestions to help the employee reach the described objectives and demonstrate a willingness to help the employee succeed on the job. *Action* describes the consequences of the employee failing to meet the established objectives. It warns the employee that if the objectives are not met, progressive disciplinary action will continue up to and including termination if the employee does not correct his or her behavior. FOSA is designed to focus attention on the behavior of the employee as objectively reviewed by the supervisor and to clearly document the actions taken by a supervisor in dealing with employee problems.[15]

Typically, the discipline report is signed by both the employee and the manager or supervisor. If the employee refuses to sign, the manager or supervisor should have a witness sign, indicating that a discipline interview occurred and that the employee was made aware of the identified problem. With an increasing amount of litigation over work relations, organizations need documented proof to protect themselves in case they become involved in a legal action.

Follow-Up

Follow-up is often overlooked, particularly if an employee corrects a problem after a discipline interview.[16] Follow-up, however, involves more than simply confirming that a problem has been solved. It is also an opportunity to develop a stronger relationship with the employee and gain a higher level of commitment. A follow-up conversation demonstrates that while the situation was serious, the manager or supervisor recognizes performance improvement as well as performance deficiency. Also, if improvement is occurring but the problem has not yet been completely solved, follow-up is the best way to assure that improvement will continue. Here, it is not meant to humiliate but to provide any help the employee may need to succeed. Following-up assures that the employee will honor his or her commitment so the problem will not occur again.

While specific techniques may differ with interviewers and guidelines may vary among organizations, the following characteristics are common to discipline interviewing and the proper implementation of disciplinary actions: (1) discipline should be immediate, (2) discipline should have prior warning, (3) discipline should be consistent, (4) discipline should be impersonal, (5) discipline should be documented, (6) the reprimand should be appropriate, and (7) the interviewer should maintain cordial and sincere seriousness throughout the interaction as well as the follow-up.[17] Discipline is a serious business designed to *correct* behavior and contribute to a more productive employee, *not to punish behavior*. It is never easy.

While the employee is in trouble and really not in any position to bargain or negotiate, he or she is still an active participant in the discipline interview. The employee should be candid and forthright when discussing the problem, explaining the circumstances and acknowledging any violation of policy, rules, or standards. This is not the time to launch into an emotional harangue or debate the philosophical merits of the policy, rule, or standard. By agreeing that a problem exists, the employee is in a better position to discuss with the manager or supervisor possible solutions and to explore the options or alternatives. Furthermore, the employee displays a willingness to accept personal responsibility and a desired commitment to the organization. Thus, the discipline interview becomes a creative conversation about how the employee can become a more productive organizational member whose talents and potential can be more fully tapped. This positive, non-threatening approach toward the manager or supervisor permits the employee to exert some control regarding the consequences of the disciplinary action. Moreover, since the record of a discipline interview is initialed by both parties and becomes a part of the employee's file, a constructive attitude can do much to soften a discipline report.

However, if the employee is being unjustly disciplined, then procedures within the organization should be pursued. The Affirmative Action Officer or Union Steward would be appropriate sources for further information.[18]

*   *   *   *   *

Steve approached the discipline discussion by specifically comparing job expectations with job performance and clearly noting the impact of the problem on the department. He did the necessary homework ahead of time and scheduled a discipline discussion with Cindy only after documenting the facts and careful preparation. It was conducted in his private office at the end of the day when there would be no interruptions.

He opened the discussion by saying, "I have a problem," hoping to reduce any natural defensiveness and put Cindy at ease. However, by standing and pacing about the room while disclosing the problem to Cindy who sat in front of his desk, Steve accentuated his power and authority. Any attempt to curb defensiveness and put Cindy at ease was mitigated by his body language. His calm, objective description of the problem and its impact seemed accusatory when he sat behind his desk and asked, "What do you have to say?" Cindy, wanting to respond, felt both threatened and challenged. She felt embarrassed and personally diminished for creating a problem, even though she considered it to be unintentional. Sitting across the desk and looking at Steve, Cindy chose not to respond and remained silent.

Problems and Constraints to Discipline

If used wisely and well implemented, the discipline interview can have a positive impact on the health of the organization. However, there are a number of problems or obstacles that can constrain and inhibit constructive disciplinary outcomes. These problems may result from the manager or supervisor falling prey to certain pitfalls or from the likely frustration and anger experienced by the disciplined employee. Circumstances themselves might present a potential difficulty. Therefore, the following special problems and constraints deserve consideration: (1) generalizing about performance, (2) identifying problems in terms of attitude or personality, (3) failure to examine situational constraints (4) hostility, (5) tears, and (6) disciplining more than one person at a time.

Generalizing about Performance

Managers and supervisors all too frequently generalize about a person's performance instead of clearly and specifically describing what they see. An accurate, objective assessment of employee behavior is critical to effective employee discipline. What, when, where, and how an employee behaves on the job are important facts which must be objectively documented to demonstrate why the employee has not lived up to the expectations of the organization or supervisor.[19] One way to avoid generalizing or being judgmental about problems is to ask the question, "What do I know for sure?" The more "black and white" the problem statement, the easier it will be to discuss the problem. Talking in generalities or making judgments about the person's performance opens the door to excuses and defensiveness. More specific statements make it easier to get the employee to agree to change. For example, instead of saying, "Your work has been unacceptable," one might say, "You have made fifteen billing errors in the past three weeks."

Identifying Problems in Terms of Attitude or Personality

Problems are often identified in terms of poor attitude or personality flaws instead of a specific undesired behavior. Managers or supervisors can avoid this tendency by focusing specifically on what their concerns are. For example, if the initial diagnosis of a performance problem is "bad attitude," ask these questions: (1) What is it about this person's attitude that adversely affects the work to be done? (2) What are the things I see and hear that make me think this individual has a bad attitude? (3) What should this person do or stop doing to convince me that the "attitude problem" is solved? The answers to these questions can help in clarifying the difficulty and drafting a specific problem statement.

Use the SAM test on your problem statement. SAM is an acronym for the three characteristics of a good problem statement. First, it is *specific;* second, it is *attainable;* and third, it is *measurable.* When writing statements of desired and actual performance, test them against these principles. This will ensure that the employee will know what the problem is and leave the interview with a clear understanding of what, if anything, he or she is expected to do. If the statement of desired and actual performance is specific, attainable, and measurable, the discipline discussion with the employee will be productive in bringing about a change.[20]

Failure to Examine Situational Constraints

Managers and supervisors often view all error as human error. However, there are times when people are put in situations in which the situations themselves contribute to a failure. There is merit in examining the situation to determine to what extent it is a causal factor.

We frequently make causal inferences from the perceived behavior of others. The process involves (1) perception of action, (2) judgment of intention, and (3) attribution of disposition.[21]

Fritz Heider defined attribution as an effort to "predict and control the world by assigning transient behavior to relatively unchanging dispositions."[22] We constantly assess how much an action is due to personality as opposed to environmental pressures.

Attributions depend on perceived freedom of choice. If we see others as compelled to act as a result of circumstances beyond their control, we won't assign their behavior to enduring traits of character. However, we more frequently assume that people are responsible for the things that happen to them. Stanford psychologist Lee Ross labels this tendency for observers to underestimate situational influences and overestimate dispositional influences upon behavior the "fundamental attribution error."[23] Managers and supervisors, when disciplining employees, must be careful not to err by holding people more responsible for their actions than the situation warrants.

Hostility

The discipline interview is a stressful, tense, and potentially ego diminishing situation for the employee. Thus, allowing the employee some latitude to vent feelings can help preserve one's sense of self-worth, relieve tension, and reduce anxiety. However, the display of open or silent hostility reduces the prospects for positively solving the problem. Open hostility becomes readily apparent when the employee refuses to rationally discuss the problem, exaggerates viewpoints, and polarizes the situation. The manager or supervisor should respond by calmly focusing on facts and, if necessary, employing the legitimate use of power and authority to maintain control. Do not resonate the employee's hostility, but do establish an objective and impartial climate. Keeping your voice down, quietly say something like "I'm willing to discuss this matter further with you, but I must insist that you not speak to me in this manner; you must treat me with the same civility and respect that I'm according you." If this doesn't work and the employee continues to be disrespectful or abusive, stand up and say, "This meeting is over. I cannot allow you to continue to talk to me in this manner. I will reschedule the interview for a later date when the problem can be more coolly discussed."[24]

Equally disconcerting, silent hostility occurs when an employee seemingly understands the disciplinary action but refuses to respond verbally or participate in the discussion. Often, he or she will not respond to any invitation to speak. Silent hostility, in contrast to open hostility, is less easily resolved. However, Lawrence Steinmetz lists four ways of handling such situations:

1. Recognize when an employee is disaffected or alienated.
2. Encourage the employee to open up, to express his [or her] point of view. . . . You may have to ask him [or her] a point blank question, such as "Bill, I sense you don't agree with what I'm saying. Would you mind telling me why?"
3. Try to summarize the points of disagreement.
4. Build patiently an atmosphere which will convey to him [or her] a feeling of being a member of the team. If the subordinate does not want to talk, he [or she] should not be forced to. However, the point should be made that by remaining silent he [or she] is not contributing to the problem-solving situation.[25]

Remember, if two people can exchange views and talk openly, there is a greater likelihood that problems can be solved.

Tears

People differ in how they respond to criticism and vary in their reactions to discipline. Having an employee begin to cry is a traumatic moment for many managers and supervisors. The natural inclination is to try to console the person and to stop the tears. Often, managers and supervisors respond by making concessions that they later regret. The proper reaction to tears is to give the person time to regain control and to offer the person a tissue. Don't become apologetic or timid; this is the time and place for fairness, clarity, objectivity, and professionalism.

Disciplining More than One Person at a Time

Sometimes two or more people are involved in breaching policy, rules, or standards. The question then arises as to what is the best way to handle the discipline procedure? Certainly, to talk to all the involved parties at the same time would save time and energy. However, the benefits of such an approach are offset by the following problems: (1) there is something intimidating about being outnumbered, particularly in highly emotional situations; (2) research indicates that it is more difficult to change a person's mind if there is someone else in the group who supports his or her position; and (3) it is more difficult to tailor the discipline interview to the particular individual if someone else is present. Consequently, it is advisable to have separate interviews that result in consistent remedies.[26]

No matter how effective a discipline policy seems to be on paper, if it is not implemented fairly and efficiently, it is worthless. Joseph Seltzer notes that "if employees feel that a supervisor is unfair or weak, there is a tendency to lose respect for the rules—and for the supervisor."[27]

* * * * *

Certainly, Cindy's silence and refusal to participate in the disciplinary discussion does not contribute to a satisfactory solution. However, following mindful probing and encouragement, Cindy finally opens up when Steve quietly says, "Tell me about it." She agrees that a problem exists and displays professionalism by accepting personal responsibility rather than debating or arguing the issue. Her mother's illness and hospitalization are situational constraints to consider, but they don't relieve Cindy of her work obligations and commitments to the department. When the stress and tension produce tears, Steve appropriately hands Cindy a tissue and waits until she composes herself.

Then, keeping in mind the emotional circumstances contributing to the problem, Steve and Cindy jointly explore solutions and examine the consequences should change not occur. They agree she will report to work on time, curtail personal telephone calls that interfere with her duties, and may request release time should her mother's condition worsen. The disciplinary discussion is duly dated, documented, and signed by both parties.

Final Considerations

Discipline requires deliberate preparation, firm execution, and concerned follow-up. Active listening, cautious probing, and consideration of the employee's circumstances are needed in order to avoid potential problems. Still, there are some important closing thoughts regarding discipline that must be addressed. Skillfully employed, discipline can be a learning experience resulting in an improved and perhaps even enhanced working relationship. These constructive outcomes occur only if managers or supervisors are willing to forgive and forget and assume a proactive, preventive posture that recognizes good behavior.

Forgive and Forget

What is going to happen after the discipline? The relationship should return to normal. Once a person has paid for a mistake, forget it. Managers or supervisors should not freeze their evaluations of the employee or constantly refer to the incident. It is a poor manager or supervisor who makes the subordinate pay continually for past mistakes. In such cases, discipline becomes vindictive rather than educational.

The principle objective of any disciplinary policy is to make the employee a valuable member of the organization again by insisting on changed behavior. To forgive and forget once the employee has demonstrated a commitment to change makes the disciplinary action an educational experience and leaves the employee with the hope of being recognized for improvement in the future. The test of a good manager or supervisor is the ability to restore the work relationship and retain the trust and loyalty of the employee. Remember, the commitment that employees willingly make to their jobs is a function of priorities, requirements, expectations, and relative value of the rewards of work compared to the costs.[28]

Prevention Is the Best Policy

Prevention is the key to reducing disciplinary action. Effective discipline is not just reprimanding. It's an entire program of teaching and guiding employees to become loyal, devoted, and responsible members of the organization. Thus, managers and supervisors must be constructive and recognize employees for their contributions. A significant part of being an effective manager or supervisor includes being able to demonstrate efforts to assist employees in succeeding on the job. This means showing good coaching before disciplining employees.[29]

Just as important as the formal levels of disciplinary action is the system's formal provision for recognizing good performance. Most individuals in an organization are never involved with the formal discipline process. Too often, though, their self-discipline and commitment go unrecognized. Therefore, a system whose goal is commitment rather than punishment must provide specific means to recognize the fully acceptable performance of the majority of the organization's members. The premise of this approach is the belief that the organization and its managers have the right to set reasonable and appropriate standards, that managers have the responsibility to point out performance discrepancies when they arise, and that only the individual can decide whether or not to perform properly and meet those standards and expectations. The burden of responsibility for appropriate performance is placed squarely on the shoulders of the employee and not the organization and its managers. Therefore, managers and supervisors must be proactive in acknowledging employee efforts and abilities. Mark Twain once said, "When a man has credit due him, now is the time to give it to him, for he cannot read his tombstone when he's dead."

* * * * *

Steve closely monitored Cindy's performance for the next month, showing sensitivity to the circumstances that prompted the problem and providing any necessary support and encouragement. Cindy had accepted personal responsibility for change and displayed a renewed commitment to the department. Her excellent performance was rewarded by a positive appraisal at the end of the year. By forgiving and forgetting, Steve provided Cindy with hope for the future.

As Steve sits in his office reflecting on this incident, he realizes that not all disciplinary interviews proceed as smoothly or conclude as successfully. There will be times when more severe consequences may have to be imposed and resentment cannot be avoided. However, by recognizing good behavior, rewarding accomplishments, and assuming a positive approach when discipline is necessary, he hopes to prevent the frequency of such unpleasant occurrences.

The question, then, is How can discipline be an educational process contributing to the overall health of the organization?

Critical Focus

To illustrate the importance of discipline interviewing, consider the case of Logoprint Advertising, a small agency located in Pensacola, Florida, specializing in promoting marine, sailing, and fishing products. A relatively new agency, it consists of a thirty-person staff divided into three teams of ten, each supervised by a project director. Frank Simon directs the team responsible for fishing products, working with clients to promote Logoprint's designs and advertisements.

Frank was recently perusing a trade magazine when he came across a particularly fine promotional piece for the "Destin Fishing Rodeo" in nearby Destin, Florida. Curious to know who created the advertisement, he called the magazine's editor and was surprised to discover it was done freelance by Paul Brandon, a Logoprint employee and member of his team. Disturbed by what he considers to be a conflict of interest, Frank decides to confront Paul.

Paul Brandon is new to Logoprint, having freelanced in advertising for several years. While he enjoys the supportive and creative atmosphere promoted at Logoprint, he occasionally accepts freelance assignments from previous clients to help make ends meet. These are selectively chosen so as not to conflict with the primary interests of Logoprint and are always done in his own free time—evenings and weekends. Some of the other staff members have similarly freelanced or taken second jobs until becoming more fully established and better compensated. Paul suspects that Frank's request for a meeting is to discuss this freelancing.

The following critical questions can direct and guide your analysis.

1. Was the interview properly planned and administered? Who controlled the interview? Was Paul given an opportunity to respond to the charges? Did Frank actively listen and mindfully probe for further details?

2. Did any problems or obstacles arise? Was Frank cognizant of any situational constraints? Were solutions objectively explored and alternatives impartially considered? Did Frank and Paul act professionally?

3. How satisfactory was the closing? Was the discipline consistent and were subsequent consequences uniformly presented? Did the disciplinary action contribute to restoring the work relationship and improving performance? What recommendations would you make?

Summary

Discipline is the arena in which the organization displays its most fundamental beliefs about people and professionalism. It is through the discipline system that the organization's culture is revealed most directly to the individual. A positive approach to discipline reduces the gap between the organization's publicly stated beliefs and values and the day-to-day behavior of its managers and supervisors. Organizations taking such a perspective are redefining discipline—changing from a traditional punishment orientation to a new orientation of building commitment. Accepting a commitment orientation to discipline generates a discipline system that applies to all employees. Discipline, then, becomes a means to solve specific performance or behavioral problems, educate, and maintain or enhance a good working relationship with employees.

This chapter outlined the benefits of abandoning punishment and moving toward a disciplinary policy emphasizing individual responsibility. It reviewed the administration of such a policy that requires managers and supervisors to (1) clearly *identify* performance problems, (2) *analyze* them, (3) *discuss* the problems with the employee, (4) *document* the results, and (5) *follow-up* to ensure that the problems are corrected. Specific strategies and techniques pertaining to these five key steps were presented. The why, when, where, and how to discipline an employee was discussed.

Administering discipline is not easy, and potential obstacles and pitfalls must be considered. These include (1) generalizing about performance, (2) identifying problems in terms of attitude or personality, (3) failure to examine situational constraints, (4) hostility, (5) tears, and (6) disciplining more than one person at a time. Managers and supervisors must develop a specific problem statement, being vigilant to situational constraints and anticipate open or silent hostility, even tears. At times, they must decide how to discipline two or more individuals jointly involved in a breach of policy, rules, or standards.

The end of the discipline interview is a time to forgive and forget, building on the experience to improve and enhance the future work relationship. Ideally, managers and supervisors will openly recognize and reward good behavior, thus reinforcing responsible adherence to policy, rules, or standards and preventing the need for disciplinary actions. In the long view, proactive prevention is the best disciplinary policy.

SHARPENING YOUR FOCUS

1. Outline and discuss the five-step disciplinary process. What is the role of the interviewer? What is the role of the interviewee? Besides falsely accusing some subordinate of wrongdoing, what is the worst mistake a manager or supervisor can do when conducting a discipline interview? How can this be avoided?

2. What should happen if you observe an action but decide that the other person had not intended to do it?

3. Discipline puts managers or supervisors in a dilemma. How can they expect their subordinates to continue to regard them as a source of help when discipline is by nature painful? Discuss interviewer skills and competencies which may be applied to disciplining without generating resentment.

4. What steps should you take to make certain that you don't commit the fundamental attribution error?

5. What disciplinary strategies would you use to handle each of the following situations? Be explicit in giving the rationale behind what you would do. What considerations would you take into account?
   a. Employees are consistently not wearing their safety goggles in areas where they are required to be worn.
   b. Two receptionists spend too much time talking to one another and are not very friendly with clients.
   c. A worker refuses to comply with one of your orders in front of other workers.

   Why is documentation of disciplinary actions necessary?

6. Describe a situation where you were disciplined. During the course of your description, identify the nature of the disciplinary action, the behaviors of the person conducting the disciplinary action, and your strategies during the disciplinary action. What were the results? How satisfied were you with the outcome? Next, describe a situation where you had to discipline someone. Again, identify the nature of the disciplinary action, your behaviors during the disciplinary action, and the strategies used by the other person during the disciplinary action. What were the results? How satisfied were you—the other person?

NOTES

1. Rodney P. Beary, "Office Discipline: Getting the Lead Out," *Modern Office Technology* (May 1986): 96–99.
2. Roger B. Madsen and Barbara Knudsen-Fields, "Productive Progressive Discipline Procedures," *Management Solutions* (May 1987): 18–25.

3. Richard D. Arvey and Allan P. Jones, "The Use of Discipline in Organizational Settings: A Framework for Future Research," *Research in Organizational Behavior* 7 (1985): 367–408.

4. Wade Humphreys and Neil J. Humphreys, "The Proper Use of Discipline," *Management Solutions* (May 1988): 6–10.

5. James Black, *Positive Discipline* (New York: American Management Association, 1970), 27.

6. Eric L. Harvey, "Discipline vs. Punishment," *Management Review* (March 1987): 21–25.

7. Roger Connors, Tom Smith, and Craig Hickman. *The Oz Principle* (Englewood Cliffs, N.J.: Prentice-Hall, 1994), 14.

8. Marvin D. Dunnette and Leaetta M. Hough, *Handbook of Industrial and Organizational Psychology* vol. 1, (Palo Alto, CA: Consulting Psychologists Press, 1990).

9. Louis V. Imundo. *Employee Discipline, How to Do It Right* (Belmont, Calif.: Wadsworth, 1985).

10. Thomas W. Zimmerer, *Management for Supervisors* (Englewood-Cliffs, N.J.: Prentice Hall, 1978).

11. Peter A. Veglahn, "The Five Steps in Practicing Effective Disscipline," *Management Solutions* (November 1987): 24–30.

12. Kenneth Blanchard and Spencer Johnson, *The One Minute Manager* (New York: William Morrow and Company, 1982), 101.

13. Robert N. Lussier, "A Discipline Model for Increasing Performance," *Supervisory Management* 35 (1990): 6–7.

14. Joseph T. Straub, "Disciplinary Interviews: The Buck Stops with You," *Supervisory Management* 36 (1991): 1–3.

15. Lee Paterson and Michael Deblieux, *Supervisor's Guide to Documenting Employee Discipline* (Los Angeles, Calif.: Parker and Son Publications, 1988).

16. John M. Ivancevich, *Human Resource Management: Foundations of Personnel,* 5th ed. (Homewood, Ill.: Irwin, 1992).

17. James M. Black, *How to Get Results from Interviewing* (New York: McGraw-Hill, 1970).

18. James R. Redeker. *Employee Discipline: Policies and Practices* (Washington, D.C.: Bureau of National Affairs, 1989).

19. Lloyd L. Byars and Leslie W. Rue, *Human Resource Management,* 4th ed. (Homewood, Ill.: Irwin, 1993).

20. Eric L. Harvey and Sharon E. Middaugh, "Discipline Without Punishment," *AORN Journal* 37 (April 1983): 914–24.

21. Kelly G. Shaver, *An Introduction to Attribution Processes* (Hillsdale, N.J.: Lawrence Erlbaum Associates, 1983).

22. Fritz Heider, *The Psychology of Interpersonal Relations* (New York: John Wiley and Sons, 1958), 79.

23. Lee Ross, "The Intuitive Psychologist and His Shortcomings: Distortions in the Attribution Process," in *Advances in Experimental Social Psychology,* ed. Leonard Berkowitz (New York: Academic Press, 1977), 184.

24. Niki Scott, "Right Way to Reprimand Employees," *The Orlando Sentinel,* 6 June, 1994, E–15.

25. Lawrence Steinmetz, *Interviewing Skills for Supervisory Personnel* (Reading, Mass.: Addison-Wesley Publishing, 1971), 70.

26. Dan Cameron, "The When, Why, and How of Discipline," *Personnel Journal* (July 1984): 37–39.

27. Joseph Seltzer, "Discipline with a Clear Sense of Purpose," *Management Solutions* (February 1987): 32–38.

28. Martin Broadwell, *Supervising Technical and Professional People* (Canada: John Wiley and Sons, 1986).

29. K. E. Kram. *Mentoring at Work* (Glenview, Ill.: Scott, Foresman, and Company, 1984).

CHAPTER

8 The Exit Interview

The formal exit interview is one of the best ways to find out where personnel, operation, and employee relations problems exist, as well as what attitudes employees hold about their jobs, management, and the organization. Each termination provides an opportunity to conduct a mini opinion poll at a time when the exiting employee feels free to say what is on his or her mind without fear of reprisal. By analyzing the information gained from such an interview, management can take remedial action to improve working conditions as needed. Management can also eliminate factors adversely affecting morale and treat the symptoms causing unwanted turnover.

Chapter 8 examines the benefits of the exit interview and explores strategies and techniques for conducting the exit interview. Listening and probing thoughtfully, feedback, and evaluation are critical to the exit interviewing process. This chapter is designed to accomplish three objectives:

1. *Awareness.* You will learn strategies and approaches that will elicit the maximum amount of information.

2. *Assessment.* You will be able to identify and assess those factors contributing to a positive exit interview orientation.

3. *Application.* You will be able to listen attentively, probe thoughtfully, provide feedback, and be mindful of others.

* * * * *

Enough's Enough

LightWaves is a national chain of camera retailer/photo labs. Privately owned, there are over 400 stores located primarily in shopping and strip malls across the country. The primary business of LightWaves at its inception over twenty years ago was retailing video and still cameras and accessories. Since then, LightWaves has expanded rapidly and added one-hour photo processing labs in 95 percent of its locations.

The stores are grouped into geographic regions. Headquarters for LightWaves is South Orange, New Jersey, a community of 50,000 white- and blue-collar workers. The owner and president, vice presidents, and the inventory and human resources departments are all centered at this LightWaves complex. In addition, there are five regions and forty districts, each with their own managers.

District managers are responsible for the stores in their area and visit most of them four or five times a month. However, it is not unusual for stores on the outskirts of districts to be visited with less regularity. The district manager's time is primarily spent arranging the monthly display changes mandated by headquarters and assisting stores experiencing problems. District managers are also charged with supervising each store's quarterly inventory and conducting biannual inspections. Their salary is supplemented with bonuses based on districtwide performance.

Each store has a store manager responsible for supervision of salespeople, total sales, and the photo lab. Store managers have little authority to make decisions other than scheduling, as all paperwork, inventory, pricing, displays, and store goals are determined by headquarters. Their principle function is to handle customer complaints and maintain superior sales figures.

In stores where the lab volume is high, there is a lab manager responsible for lab inventory, supervision of technicians, lab scheduling, and quality control. The lab manager also serves as the assistant store manager, taking over store duties when the manager is absent. If the lab volume is low, control of the lab is turned over to a key technician. The position of key technician differs from that of lab manager in salary, responsibility for scheduling, and store managerial duties.

The photo labs in LightWaves stores are somewhat separated from the retail sales both physically and operationally. Due to the time constraints of a one-hour operation, responsibility for taking customer orders and handling the completed orders falls on the sales staff. There is always more coverage available on the sales floor, and once an order is written up and bagged, it is delivered to the lab technicians for processing. Lab technicians are paid hourly and receive no commission. Although on certain occasions when the lab work is light, they will help with customers in the retail area.

Tim Wirth, a paraplegic since a skiing accident five years ago, is the key lab technician at the Country Roads LightWaves store in Omaha, Nebraska. The staff consists of three full-time and two part-time salespeople, the key lab technician, and two part-time lab technicians. A new store manager took over eighteen months ago. His managerial style coupled with a more aggressive sales approach has significantly increased the volume of sales, as well as one-hour photo lab processing. This has placed increased responsibility on Tim Wirth and created a number of problems. Scheduling complaints are frequent, and on numerous occasions, the lab experiences inadequate coverage or no coverage at all. When lab coverage is inadequate or missing, the sales staff must attempt to take care of lab duties, which affects lab quality. Moreover, it is not unusual for salespeople to promise one-hour photo service for more rolls of film than can actually be processed. Tim and his part-time assistants have returned from lunch breaks to find ten to twenty rolls of film due in thirty to forty minutes. Consequently, failing to deliver film at the promised time is no longer an uncommon occurrence.

Moreover, the new manager is often out of the store monitoring the competition, leaving Tim to act as assistant store manager. This further disrupts photo processing schedules. Increasingly, Tim is putting in longer hours with little additional compensation. Upset and frustrated, Tim resigns—enough's enough. On Tim's last day with LightWaves, John Calendar, the store manager, hurriedly conducted an exit interview.

John cordially greeted Tim, and after informing him when he would receive his last paycheck with accrued vacation pay, John asked, "Why are you leaving us after three years of excellent service?"

Tim carefully thought about the question, and answered, "Well, I just got this terrific opportunity to work at Johnson's Video and Photo Studio." He went on to say that it paid more money.

John accepted Tim's answer and proceeded to tell him that money shouldn't be the primary consideration for selecting a career. However, he understood Tim's situation and asked if a salary increase would cause him to change his mind about leaving. Surprised, Tim said that he had made up his mind and now looked forward to working at Johnson's as a lab manager.

John closed the interview by expressing his regrets at Tim's leaving. He noted that it would temporarily put him in a bind. Tim thanked John for the opportunities that LightWaves had provided and, before leaving, asked about future references. John simply said, "Sure, no problem."

Later, John Calendar wondered how such a good employee as Tim could just walk out like that.

Discussion Questions

1. How would you describe this exit interview situation? What are the potentially conflicting issues?
2. Who controlled the interview? How was the interview structured? Would an alternate structure or approach have resulted in more information being gathered?
3. Were all pertinent topics explored? Did John listen and thoughtfully probe for information? Describe Tim's participation in the exit interview.

4. Is encouragement provided and positive feedback given? What noticeable problems and barriers can be detected? Does John usefully report the information gained from this exit interview?

5. What can this exit interview tell LightWaves about potential problems? How would you advise LightWaves?

The Benefits of the Exit Interview

The exit interview as used by eight out of ten firms in the United States can help control attrition and identify areas where changes need to be instituted.[1] However, with the critical importance of the skills of the interviewer, exit interviews have been consistently criticized for their lack of reliability and validity of procedure. Furthermore, there is limited data on the extent to which information obtained in interviews has been useful. One pioneering study concluded that for many organizations the exit interview is only a symbolic gesture, because no use is made of the information obtained. Still, many organizations are securing information on a variety of factors affecting the quality of work life and using it as a basis for turnover reduction programs.[2] The primary purposes for conducting the exit interview are to process the removal of an employee in an orderly way and to collect information relative to the employee's reasons for leaving, which later can serve as a means of organizational diagnosis. Basically, the interview is intended to draw out the departing employee's opinions about the employment experience and to obtain through discussion an informed understanding of the reasons for termination. Regardless of the structure of the exit interview, it always serves four functions: (1) diagnosis, (2) therapy/improvement, (3) separation assistance, and (4) determination of reasons for leaving function.[3] Thus, the exit interview is both an administrative and fact-finding endeavor.

Administratively, persons leaving need to be informed about severance pay, insurance, pensions, vacation pay, personal references, and other topics. If all necessary records are assembled at the outset of the interview, this administrative function can be handled swiftly and easily.

The information-gathering function of the exit interview is considerably more difficult. Most people who are leaving one job for another tend to keep their real reasons to themselves. When a 1991 survey by the Society for Human Resource Management and the Bureau of National Affairs asked 672 human resources professionals whether they conducted exit interviews with departing employees, 96 percent said yes, but only 60 percent of the respondents thought the information they got was "somewhat accurate and truthful."[4] Only moderate correlations exist between the reasons for leaving as recorded during exit interviews and as reported on subsequent follow-up questionnaires. Interviewees most frequently cite higher earnings as the reason for leaving than conflict with management, dissatisfaction with advancement, or dissatisfaction with the content of the job.[5] Studies reveal big differences by employees between the reasons for leaving an organization at the time of departure and a year later.[6] It is estimated that less than one out of four times can an interviewer get a complete and factual statement from an employee regarding reasons for terminating.[7]

Numerous discrepancies have been found between reasons for termination offered by employees during exit interviews and reasons cited in a questionnaire administered at a later date. The reasons accounting for this phenomena are varied. Perhaps the employee has had an opportunity to reevaluate and develop a clearer perspective on leaving, or the employee may be initially hesitant to present valid information at the time of the exit interview fearing a poor reference, which might affect future employment. Finally, they may simply want to avoid an involved, face-to-face confrontation. Therefore, it is essential that the interviewer not introduce personal biases or take a value stand on the accuracy of statements presented.

American Telephone and Telegraph Company supports information gained from exit interviews by conducting further investigation. In order to identify why employees are not satisfied with their jobs, a sample of current employees are interviewed whenever a management problem is suspected. The ideas expressed in the interviews are presented to management and, in turn, are shared with the groups on the job. William E. Luthle, Jr., personnel administrator for AT&T, claims that this method is more effective than just the exit interview.[8]

Still, at a very basic level, the exit interview can benefit an organization and provide it with some immensely rich information. First, data from exit interviews provide organizations with a means of monitoring attrition. Organizations lose many valuable employees each year due to turnover. One study indicates that large organizations may lose up to 50 percent of their college graduates during the first four or five years of post college employment.[9] The costs incurred by organizations due to turnover are fringe benefits, severance pay, overtime costs, underuse of facilities, administrative expenses, training costs, and productivity losses.[10] It is estimated that a rank-and-file employee who quits can cost an organization at least $3,000, and the costs are significantly greater for managers and professional employees. Thus, if 10 percent of a rank-and-file workforce of 1,000 workers quits each year, then turnover costs will amount to at least $300,000.[11] This is not to argue that all attrition is harmful. In fact, there is some indication that moderate attrition can actually be positive.[12] The key to effective management is selective control of attrition. To be productive, an organization needs to be able to recognize those employees who are high performers and would be a real loss to the organization in comparison to those marginal employees that the organization can afford to lose.[13] It is part of a general personnel function to know who is leaving, why, and whether the loss will be a plus or minus. It is in this regard that exit interviews can be useful instruments.

Second, data from exit interviews is helpful in identifying problem areas in the organization which may be corrected. For example, exit interviews can improve the hiring process by providing a realistic view of job requirements and hints regarding problems to be considered in the hiring process. They can also alert management to such specific problems as poor supervision, low pay in comparison to similar work in other organization, or lack of opportunities for advancement. To be most effective at all levels of employment, all employees should be exit interviewed, including hourly, nonexempt, and exempt employees when they retire, resign, or are released due to poor performance. Exit interviews, of course, are not a magic cure for all employee relations problems, but they can help improve hiring efforts, maintain morale, and correct unsatisfactory work conditions. In a recent survey of 150 executives conducted by Robert Half International, over 40 percent said that exit interviews provided valuable information on departmental matters, and more than a third claimed to have learned how aspects of corporate policy could be refined.[14]

Finally, exit interviews document employees' reasons for leaving, which could later prove legally beneficial. The documentation provides a permanent record for management, which has legal implications if the termination is ever questioned. Since research shows that employees who are leaving an organization often skew their answers or change their minds about why they are leaving, it is useful to have a record of what they said at the time of departure. Exit interviews complete the file on any employee.

While exit interviews can benefit the organization, they also perform functions beneficial to employees leaving the organization.[15] First, data from exit interviews provide departing employees with a status assessment. They can determine what, if any, severance pay, vacation pay, and benefits will be forthcoming and what information the organization will release to prospective new employers. In addition, arrangements can be made for receipt of the last paycheck, and all expense reimbursement forms for money owed can be processed. This can assist employees in bringing closure to their employment, assessing short-term and long-term options, and planning their future.

Second, exit interviews permit employees an opportunity to share their perceptions of the organization and voice their specific reasons for leaving. Typically, the areas covered include salary, benefits, management style, supervision, coworkers, work relationships, on-the-job challenges, organizational climate, and growth and advancement opportunities. In an open and supportive environment, employees can clarify their position, provide personal insights and observations, and document for the record their reasons for leaving.

Finally, exit interviews can contribute to positive image building by allowing employees to reestablish rapport. Departing employees can conclude their organizational relationship on a positive note and wish the organization well. Likewise, the organization can express its appreciation for their contributions and offer help, if applicable, in the future. Both parties can separate with a positive image, knowing that they were respected.

*   *   *   *   *

Exit interviews are always somewhat stressful. Besides bringing closure to an employee's file, the interviewer wants to determine the reasons for leaving. The departing employee hopes to gain information regarding the separation and, at the same time, maintain goodwill.

Candid rather than cautious answers may jeopardize this objective. Here, John Calendar, the store manager, hurriedly conducted the exit interview. His presence heightened the uneasiness felt by Tim Wirth and probably prompted the wary responses. This, combined with the hurried routine nature of the interview, explains Tim's reluctance to mention managerial and workload problems. After all, Tim hoped to maintain a positive future reference. LightWaves should have had someone in human resources from headquarters or the district manager conduct the exit interview. The full organizational benefits of the exit interview might not then have been compromised, and Tim may have felt more comfortable exploring the real reasons for his leaving.

Conducting the Exit Interview

It is important to distinguish between voluntary and involuntary exits, as well as avoidable and unavoidable separations. Avoidable separations relate to conditions the employer has some control over, such as wages, benefits, and working conditions. Unavoidable separations generally are not controllable by management and include retirement, death, and maternity leave. Voluntary exits, frequently referred to as quits or resignations, are initiated by the employee, while involuntary terminations, such as dismissals or layoffs, are initiated by the employer. Consequently, there are two types of exit interviews, the interview when an employee leaves an organization voluntarily and the interview when the employee is dismissed. Most research on exit interviewing focuses on voluntary and avoidable separations. Because they are more subject to control by management, they usually occur in a more open communication climate, and they may assist in identifying organizational problems. Thus informed, the organization can then take steps to eliminate them.[16]

The unavoidable separation and involuntary exit interview presents obvious difficulties. It is usually conducted in a defensive communication climate with an employee who probably believes he or she has been unjustifiably discharged. Still, it is administratively useful and can contribute to employee relations. Moreover, the involuntary exit interview, if properly conducted, can produce excellent results and can even provide useful information about employee attitudes.

Persuading an employee to tell the truth about why he or she is leaving is a difficult and complex task. By being perceptive, however, one can detect signs that may provide information that, taken with data furnished by other exit interviews, forms a storytelling pattern. From this, an organization can learn much about operational situations and make necessary changes, which can improve the circumstances and result in the retention of valuable employees.

The exit interview includes both information gathering and information giving. It is usually conducted as a controlled nondirective interview in which the interviewer controls the general categories to be discussed, but the departing employee provides specific information within the categories in whatever fashion it

Exit interviews allow departing employees to conclude their organizational relationship on a positive note and permit organizations an opportunity to express appreciation.

comes to mind. A basic outline for conducting the exit interview should include the following elements: statement of purpose, relevant background information, positive aspects of the job, negative aspects of the job, critical incidents, reasons for leaving, suggested changes, and separation agreements.[17] Information is elicited by each party from the other in an open and supportive environment. Essentially, the exit interview is composed of discovery and communication. However, neither the discovery of an employee's motivation for vacating a position nor the sharing of this information with management are easy tasks. The following represent important factors to consider when conducting effective exit interviews.

Prepare Carefully

The exit interview does not create a mutually beneficial condition and, with little to gain from the experience, an employee may be unwilling to provide detailed and accurate information. If the interview is scheduled hastily and conducted haphazardly, it will be even more difficult to identify reasons for leaving. The time to exit interview an employee is a day or two before the employee actually leaves. The interview should be conducted at the place of employment in the privacy and relaxed atmosphere of an office or a conference room.

In the event that it is not possible to interview the employee before he or she leaves, an effort should be made to conduct the interview by phone. As a last resort, an exit interview form and a self-addressed stamped envelope should be sent to the individual's home with a request that it be completed and returned.

The immediate supervisor or manager should not conduct the interview, since he or she will not be objective when asking the questions and might be inclined to censor and slant the replies for self-protection. Exit interviews should be conducted by members of the personnel department who have more objectivity and more experience and finesse in interviewing. If this is not possible, a supervisor or manager who doesn't directly supervise the individual should conduct the interview.

The key to successful exit interviewing is thorough preparation. The interviewer should previously review the employee's file and have it available during the interview. An examination of the file may offer clues as to why the employee is leaving and lead to suggested policy changes.

It is essential that the interviewer prepare an agenda and structure the interview. The agenda items should reflect the two basic purposes of an exit interview: (1) necessary administrative items needed to bring closure to the employee's file, and (2) pertinent organizational/job-related items used to review the employee's perspective and solicit personal opinions.

Research indicates that structured exit interviews are generally more effective than unstructured ones.[18] Care must be taken in selecting a structure that gives the respondent maximum flexibility in how to answer questions. Beginning with routine administrative items can break down pre-interview tension and enable the interviewer to establish a satisfactory climate before addressing the other more difficult organizational/job-related items.

Put the Employee at Ease

The attitude of the interviewer sets the tone of the interview and creates the climate for discussion. Therefore, it is important to initially outline the reasons for the interview, how it will progress, and what the psychological contact will be between the interviewer and the interviewee. The interviewer's voice must not sound threatening or hard, and the interviewer's speech must be free from sarcasm or prejudice. If the employee detects a lack of interest or senses that this is simply a routine matter, the response will be in kind, and the answers will not be very informative. However, if the interviewer expresses empathy for and understanding of what the interviewee is feeling, the departing employee will be inclined to open up and candidly share opinions. Research indicates that feelings toward a topic and status have an interactive effect on a person's willingness to discuss an issue.[19] Once the interviewee begins to talk, the interviewer probably will be able to accomplish most, if not all, of the purposes of the exit interview.

Seek Information

Keep in mind that the exit interview is an information-giving and information-receiving interview. This is not a time to attempt to convince the employee to stay. He or she has made a decision, and the interviewer's task is to determine why that choice was made. Do not ask questions that can be answered with a "yes" or "no," but employ an open-ended questioning technique. After preliminary niceties—"We really hate to lose good people like you"—an adroit interviewer will start asking open-ended questions beginning with the least threatening queries. Beware the standard beginning, "Can you tell me why you're leaving?" since asking the reasons for departure at the outset may only bring out a sense of defensiveness. Once someone has decided to move on, it is hard for him or her to square this with a belief that the job being vacated is the best in the world. Consequently, there is a tendency to deprecate it, subtly or not so subtly. What the interviewer wants are questions that encourage the exiting employee to share information, not to justify decisions. After some rapport develops, the interviewer can zero in a bit, tailoring the inquiries to the employee's job experience and position within the company. The exit interview results will generally target several key areas: management practices, employee placement, training and development, compensation and benefits, health and safety, job security, and supervisor/employee relations.[20] The comments, opinions, and suggestions provided by a departing employee can be helpful in assessing policies and procedures and in implementing changes. These employees are familiar with their departments and understand the attitudes of employees working in them; consequently, their experience can be profitable.

Use Tact

The departing employee is likely to be on guard and will probably want to avoid saying anything that can be used against him or her either now or later. The individual may want references later; thus, she or he does not want to jeopardize a good reference by citing criticism of individuals or the organization. One cannot force an employee to reveal his or her thoughts; however, an open, encouraging climate can cause the respondent to answer honestly rather than safely. If the employee avoids answering a specific question or is reluctant to discuss a subject, drop it. Persistence could place the employee on edge. Moreover, in an interview where the interviewee is openly hostile, venting his or her anger and frustration, do not become involved in the personal diatribe. Tact is necessary if the interviewer hopes to prompt participation, glean useful information, and maintain goodwill.

Be Honest

Credibility and confidentiality are crucial to effective exit interviewing. The departing employee is under no obligation to give information and will share confidences only with someone he or she trusts. A major threat to the value of exit information has always been the omnipresent threat of interviewee lying or distortion. On the part of the interviewee, be it conscious or unconscious, distortion is mostly aimed at creating a favorable image in the eyes of the interviewer. Thus, falsification of interview data may be used to posture the interviewee's image in the eyes of the company. Such posturing often results in the employee misleading the company into a favorable image of itself so that the former employee gets further rewards in the form of positive recommendations or an improved reputation. Any communication between the interviewer and interviewee is subject to distortion; however, credibility and confidentiality can reduce the risk of invalid or unreliable results.[21] Do not attempt to trick or mislead the employee. The interviewer should not lead the interviewee or help the interviewee solve problems. Rather, the interviewer should honestly probe for information and record it for later analysis. Finally, since an employee's reasons for leaving are often intensely personal, it is necessary that no one overhears or interrupts the discussion and that provisions be made to keep the information confidential.

Conclude the Interview

When it is obvious that the interview is over and all willingly provided information has been supplied, work toward a mutually satisfying close. The close of the exit interview should reaffirm the positive tone established at the outset and reassure the interviewee that responses and comments will be kept confidential. If the interviewer wants to administer a written questionnaire, give it at the end of the interview, after the organization has demonstrated its interest and concern by talking with the employee and listening carefully. As the session concludes, wish the employee well, and thank him or her for the time spent in the interview and for the service given to the organization.

Complete the Exit Interview Report

As quickly as possible following the interview, write down the reasons given for leaving, information given on how operations could be improved, and personal "impressions" of the discussion. Completing the exit interview report assures an accurate record of the proceedings. The exit interview report should include the employee's name; address; telephone number; status as hourly, nonexempt, or exempt; date of birth; EEOC code; job title; grade, if applicable; date hired; division and department; final base salary; effective date of termination; time in present job; and total time with the organization. There should also be a section to record the type of termination: resignation with or without notice, layoff, discharge, early retirement, release, and "other." A spot should be included to check off whether the termination was voluntary or involuntary. The balance of the report should consist of questions designed to obtain the employee's opinions and the responses.

These guidelines and procedures can result in a more effective exit interview. However, even when carefully observed, employees may prefer to give "safe" rather than "real" reasons for their leaving. The traditional exit interview format using mutual dialogue cannot always bridge this barrier. However, Martin Hilb, of Schering-Plough International, has developed an interesting alternative procedure for conducting the exit interview. It includes built-in control mechanisms that make it more accurate than the typical exit interview, which consists of (1) meeting with the terminating employee, (2) asking certain selected questions, and (3) completing a written exit interview report. *The Standardized Exit Interview* developed by Hilb is characterized by (1) the standardized interview situation, (2) the use of "image cards" to aid in managing the interview, and (3) the "profile" method for evaluating the results.[22]

This procedure employs the standardized techniques and guidelines previously discussed. However, by using a "special incident technique," the interviewer can direct questions that result in more specific responses. For example, the interviewer might ask, "If you think back, what did you like most during the years you stayed with us?" and then follow with, "What was it you disliked during your time with us?" This makes the comparing of results easier while improving validity, reliability, and efficiency.

Following the asking of standard questions, the departing employee is handed numbered cards, each with an internal organizational "image" factor written on it. Image factors might include (1) good external image of the organization, (2) job security, (3) good relationship with superior, (4) good relationship with colleagues, (5) interesting, challenging job, (6) fair salary, (7) fair performance review, (8) good, clear departmental organization, (9) clear, cooperative objectives, and (10) good career possibilities. The exiting employee is asked to group the cards according to (1) those characteristics realized, (2) partially realized, and (3) not yet realized. The interviewer then discusses with the employee the categorization of these factors beginning with those "not yet realized" areas and progressing through the "realized" areas. During the discussion, the interviewer talks candidly with the employee about the particular arrangement of the cards, prompting suggestions as to how unsatisfactory situations might be improved.

As a normal control factor, some of the internal image items are an obvious part of the organization. This aids in detecting whether a departing employee is falsifying information. For example, if the organization has a particularly good salary schedule or fringe benefits and the employee ranks them negatively, it is possible that either the employee is naive or falsifying information.

Annually, a "profile" of the arrangement of image factors can be made, representing the final outcome of all exit interviews done in that year. These annual results can reveal the organization's strengths and weaknesses, thus assisting managers in formalizing departmental objectives and making necessary changes. This profile method can depict organizational progress from year to year so that ongoing progress can be accurately assessed.

This standardized interview procedure offers a number of advantages. The interviewer can accumulate a good deal of feedback information, which can later be factor analyzed, cross tabulated, and correlated. The image cards stimulate interest in the exit interview process and motivate departing employees to reveal "real" rather than "safe" reasons for leaving. This method also permits the interviewer to be more objective, so the exit interview becomes a less defensive communication situation. Finally, the interviewer is better able to evaluate and assess policies and procedures, which in turn, can prompt necessary changes.

The standardized interview procedure also has its shortcomings. It is a more time-consuming process, occupying the activities of the personnel staff or private interviewers. Moreover, nonexempt employees can offer attitudinal comments but little in the way of operational suggestions, so it is essentially limited to management-level employees who have elected to leave the organization. Finally, it requires a considerable amount of sophistication on the part of both the interviewer and the interviewee to be effective. Still, it represents an alternative procedure for conducting the exit interview with the possibility of overcoming the difficulties encountered when using traditional exit interview techniques.

* * * * *

John Calendar arranged the exit interview with Tim and ostensibly controlled it. However, Tim was in actual control of the information shared. Since John failed to carefully prepare for the interview, his unstructured approach permitted Tim considerable freedom to choose areas to discuss and weigh his responses. While John covered some of the administrative details, such as receipt of the last paycheck with accrued vacation time, he neglected to explore important organizational/job-related items. Rather than pursue Tim's reasons for leaving, John simply accepted his answer regarding a better position as lab manager with Johnson's Video and Photo Studio. Moreover, John attempted to tactlessly persuade Tim to stay with LightWaves by suggesting a salary increase. This less than professional approach surprised Tim and increased his uneasiness. The time to resolve employee differences and perhaps persuade them to remain is during a counseling interview well before they choose to separate from the organization. Consequently, John's failure to structure the exit interview and deliberately seek information resulted in less than honest responses from Tim.

In this case, the standardized exit interview proposed by Martin Hilb might have been a more appropriate alternative, even with John conducting the interview. It would have imposed a structure on the interview, guaranteeing that John would cover all pertinent administrative and organizational/job-related items. Moreover, the use of image cards might have put Tim at ease. Since Tim was functioning as lab manager, although holding the position of lab technician, he had considerable knowledge and experience that could have been shared. The standardized exit interview approach could have been more information rewarding, offsetting the increased time needed to conduct such an interview.

Listening and Probing Thoughtfully

The categories to be covered during an exit interview may be framed as questions that restrict the general parameters of the answer but that then are followed by questions that allow more wide-ranging responses. This requires attentive listening and probing thoughtfully.

The interviewer is essentially a data-collector, a recorder, and a listener. This necessitates keen skills at sensing, interpreting, evaluating, and reacting. Sensing, getting the information with all your senses, is the foundation of effective listening. A breakdown at this first step destroys the entire listening process. Interpreting requires the interviewer to identify the interviewee's purpose and intended message. Do the words mean the same thing to both of them? It can be helpful for the interviewer to ask such non-threatening clarifying questions as, "What do you mean by that . . .?" or "Would you clarify your point concerning . . .?" or "Would you mind repeating . . .?" Evaluating asks the interviewer to draw conclusions and decide if the message is fact or opinion. Reacting lets the interviewee know their message was sensed, interpreted, and evaluated. The interviewer needs to continually encourage and invite the interviewee to continue talking, as well as show that he or she is listening and understanding what is being said. The conch shell is believed to hold a mysterious ability to reflect the sounds of the ocean. By placing the shell to your ear, you can hear the roar of the waves pounding in the surf. It is said that the conch shell's unique power to mirror the sound of the ocean comes from its willingness to listen to its surroundings, completely and undisturbed. By absorbing so perfectly what it hears, the conch is then able to share with the listener the secrets of the sea. Similarly, by talking less and listening more, the exit interviewer can hear the reasons why departing employees are leaving and use that information to strengthen the organizational environment. Lee Iacocca, former CEO of Chrysler Corporation, has observed: "Listening can make the difference between a mediocre company and a great company." Listening is the *silent success skill* that makes all the difference in effective exit interviewing.

The questions asked and areas probed during an exit interview will depend on what one wishes to find out and the particular needs of the organization. However, there are areas that every interviewer will want to explore (see figure 8.1).[23] One should ask if the employee's compensation level was about right or less than expected or desired. Does the employee believe that company salaries are competitive? Were salary increases fair, adequate, or frequent enough? Does the employee's new position represent a promotion or salary increase? Remember, departing employees often prefer not to reveal data about their new positions.

A similar tack should be taken with benefits. Was the employee benefit program satisfactory? Did it fill the employee's needs? If not, why not? Was it comparable in relation to similar companies? Again, if the person is going to a new company, are the benefits better there? If so, how? What benefit program changes or improvements would the employee recommend? Explore and probe specific programs—medical and dental insurance, pensions, vacations, and holidays.

Questions about working conditions should focus on the physical environment, workload, and career planning. Is the workplace clean, comfortable, and pleasant? Are conditions safe and healthy? Do employees need better tools or equipment? If not, why not? Ask for suggestions for improvement. How can work conditions be improved—more space, better air quality, less pressure, more social and recreational programs, or better eating facilities? Next, ask about the employee's workload. Was the employee overworked, underworked, or given the proper workload? Was the work challenging and interesting? If not, why not? Was the employee under stress, and if so, why and how? Was the job

---

Sample Exit Interview Questions

- What did you like most about your job?
- What did you like least about your job?
- Describe the amount of variety in your job.
- How would you evaluate the quality of job training?
- What could be done to make your job easier/more challenging/more interesting?
- What improvements in communication would make this a better place to work?
- What resources might be made available to make this position better for your successor?
- If you were in charge here, what would you change?
- What contributed to making your employment here enjoyable?
- What do you feel good about having accomplished?
- do you feel that performance expectations were reasonable and clearly explained?
- Did you receive clear and adequate directions regarding the specific duties to your position?
- How would you characterize the support you got from your supervisor?
- Was the feedback you received about your performance timely, helpful, and specific?
- What best helped you achieve your goals?
- What makes your new position more attractive than the present job?
- What factors contributed to your decision to leave?

FIGURE 8.1   Sample Exit Interview Questions

properly defined? Finally, ask about career development. Was progress through the ranks satisfactory? Were promotions or job upgrading frequent enough? Does there appear to be opportunity to advance? Does the employee believe that the organization and its supervisors were concerned about individual growth and progress? Was there sufficient training? How would the employee improve this aspect of employment?

It's helpful to determine the employee's relationship with coworkers and probe the issue of morale in order to later interpret answers and comments. Did the employee like the coworkers? Did he or she get along well with others? Did a theme of teamwork exist? Was there a friendly, helpful atmosphere? If not, why not? Was the employee reasonably happy at work? Was there pride in the job and the company and faith in management? Was the company a good place to work? If not, why not? Was the organization properly people-minded? Did you and your fellow employees receive proper job satisfaction? If not, list the major complaints and the reasons for low morale. Depending on the answers, further probing may be desirable and valuable.

Questions should also probe the employee's relationship with his or her supervisor or manager. Was the supervisor or manager friendly, helpful, and concerned about the employee and coworkers? Was the supervisor or manager communicative, fair, and supportive—a good boss? If not, what were his or her shortcomings? Most departing employees are reluctant to be completely frank in their answers even though they are leaving. Whatever is learned here, however, will be most useful in solving problems on the job and helping to determine long-term supervisory training needs. Last, there should be a candid exploration of organizational policies and procedures that affect all employees. Are current policies and procedures communicated and understood? Are they applied fairly across the board? Do they improve or hamper productivity, and how? What improvements in policies and procedures would the employee suggest?

It is important to get the departing employee during the exit interview to "open up" as much as possible by listening attentively and encouraging suggestions and comments. An even temperament, courtesy, good listening skills, and open-ended questioning techniques are the interviewer's strongest allies. In all cases, listening and probing thoughtfully contribute to a meaningful dialogue and useful information.

*   *   *   *   *

John may have heard Tim, but he wasn't listening and failed to thoughtfully probe responses. Rather than directly asking, "Why are you leaving us after three years of excellent service?", John might have phrased this opening inquiry with greater tact and rapport building. For example, he could have expressed the purpose for the interview and provided encouragement by saying, "Tim, we're sorry that you're going to be leaving us. It's important to us to know why people leave. Sometimes where we have been at fault, we can do something to prevent it from happening in the future. Could you tell me why you're leaving?" Then, following Tim's response, "Well, I just got this terrific opportunity to work at Johnson's Video and Photo Studio," John should have thoughtfully probed for further detail and clarification. Possible probes could have been: "What makes Johnson's better than your opportunities here?" or "What made you apply there in the first place?" or "We're particularly interested in why you were willing to leave here and move there. Could you tell me something about that? Is it a promotion? Are you getting more money there?" If this approach had been followed throughout the interview, exploring the various relevant topics, it would have yielded more beneficial information.

Tim's participation during the exit interview reflected John's uncaring attitude and the defensive communication climate created. Tim was naturally cautious and chose to provide safe reasons for leaving, only hinting at other more immediate considerations that prompted his resignation. He was able to determine his status with LightWaves, gain assurance from John Calendar for positive future references, and maintain goodwill.

Feedback and Evaluation

Feedback and evaluation are critical for effective exit interviewing. Feedback communicates that the parties understand what each is saying. It should contribute to establishing an open atmosphere for people to share their feelings without being judged. The following guidelines can be helpful to both the interviewer and interviewee in providing positive feedback and avoiding common feedback pitfalls.

Maintain focus. The objective of the exit interview is to discuss the departure and the available options. It is a fact-finding mission intended to provide the interviewer with the reasons for leaving and the interviewee with information regarding the separation. Both parties need to take care not to wander or lose focus.

Separate the problem from the person. Emotions can run high on both sides during an exit interview. The departing employee may feel self-pity, ego damage, and anger leading to personal accusations against a supervisor or the organization. For the organizational representative conducting the exit interview, there may be feelings of guilt and a desire to avoid confrontation leading to a desire to help and a counseling mode. A problem-solving orientation contributes to calmly exploring the reasons for leaving, separating individual personalities from the immediate circumstances.

Act professionally. The interviewer's primary purpose is to gather information, even from the most reluctant interviewee, and nothing will be gained if the interviewee walks out. Thus, the interviewer should introspectively ask him or herself: Does my voice sound threatening or hard, which would place the departing employee on edge? Is my speech free of sarcasm and prejudice? Am I being encouraging rather than confrontational? Likewise, the departing employee should ask her or himself: Are my answers candid or cautious? Is the information I'm sharing helpful to the organization or simply self-serving and personally gratifying? Don't whine, launch into ad homonym attacks, or take this as the opportunity to finally let out years of bottled-up rage or frustration. Acting professionally helps both parties succeed and ensures a positive posture of goodwill. This is not a time to burn bridges or taint relationships.

One individual interview is not very helpful as a data-gathering device. The information is only truly helpful when it is analyzed and periodically evaluated along with data from other exit interviews to determine whether or not there is some pattern developing in terms of why people leave. Consequently, many organizations employ a postinterview survey as a complement to the conventional exit interview. Several advantages are cited for the use of questionnaires. The lapse of time will encourage former employees to make more rational and honest assessments of the employer and supervisor, particularly if offering opinions from the security of a new position. If surveys are conducted anonymously, both the employer and the employee are relieved of the pressure of a face-to-face confrontation. The use of questionnaires enables the organization to sample consistently rather than depend on evidence produced by the sporadic statements of individual employees. However, the questionnaire results should not digress into a record-keeping device, for if they do not prompt corrective measures such surveys quickly become viewed as another futile personnel gimmick.[24]

The exit interview report cannot be filled out and then simply filed away. To get maximum benefit from the process, the completed exit interview report should be circulated to local management and then to the human resources department at headquarters. Information gathered through exit interviews and surveys is invaluable management data. No exit interview program can proceed successfully without a clear organizational commitment to communicate and act upon the findings.

The person in charge of the exit interview process at headquarters should analyze the reports on a regular basis and issue a summary report to company officers and division or department heads so all can see what's happening in each area of responsibility. This evaluation should show total departures by division or department and a break-down of the total according to quits, layoffs, discharges, releases, and other. It should indicate whether departures were involuntary and voluntary, giving name, grade, job title, supervisor, division or department, location, time with organization, and reason(s) for leaving.

The human resources department can then follow-up and work with those groups that need help to reduce turnover and implement change.

*   *   *   *   *

John's lack of focus during this interview resulted in his counseling Tim and attempting to change Tim's decision to leave. Rather than acting professionally and exploring the problems that prompted the resignation, John perceived Tim's leaving as a good employee creating a temporary inconvenience. Tim responded by withdrawing, providing "safe" responses, and expressing appreciation for the opportunities that Light-Waves had provided. He had already decided that enough's enough, so why jeopardize his positive image as a respected, hardworking employee?

It is easy to understand why John Calendar later wondered how such a good employee could just walk out, since the exit interview yielded little real information. His report will be useful only in that it brought Tim Wirth's file to closure. However, this exit interview should alert LightWaves management to the critical need for a structured and systematic exiting process. Such a process would contribute to providing a profile or pattern for leaving that could prompt changes and lead to organizational improvement. How would you advise LightWaves?

Critical Focus

To illustrate the importance of exit interviewing, consider the case of Allnet Paging Company (APC) involving Walter Hogan and Harold Ives. Walter Hogan opened his own business in the wireless communication industry in 1984, receiving a license to operate a paging network. Harold Ives, a respected branch manager of APC for ten years, has just resigned to take a position with a competing firm. Walter was shocked and dismayed, since he was unaware of any problems.

Allnet Paging Company opened in South Florida selling pagers and providing all the customer service support for their product. APC rapidly expanded from a paging service in a single county with 4,200 subscribers to a network servicing sixty-six counties with 258,000 subscribers. The customer operations department, based in the main office in Miami, Florida, had initially handled all facets of customer service. Services included approving credit, issuing bills, resolving billing problems, technical problems, and handling customer complaints and questions. However, the rapid expansion required Walter Hogan to decentralize his customer operations base and establish four regional offices. The Miami office would handle the area from Vero Beach to Key West. The Central Florida office would include Brevard county, Orlando, Daytona, and Jacksonville. The West Coast office would encompass Ft. Myers, Tampa, and Gainesville. Finally, the Tallahassee office would service the panhandle and any unincorporated zones. This decentralization of customer operations gave APC an edge on its competition.

Implementation of the decentralization plan went smoothly, and customers responded positively to dealing with customer service representatives from their own vicinity. However, changing circumstances in 1994 necessitated further reorganization. The Central Florida office was growing faster than any other APC office and had outgrown its physical surroundings. Originally opening with one manager, thirteen customer service representatives, and a customer base of 24,000, it now had thirty-two customer service representatives and a customer base of 87,800. Further complicating matters, the Federal Communications Commission (FCC) increased the number of paging channels available from two per county to six. The FCC decision created a very competitive atmosphere, and four new paging companies began vying for APC's current customer base.

This recent reorganization provided advancement opportunities for the current employees. Walter Hogan decided to add an executive vice president and an additional manager to direct the Central Florida customer service team. Terry Francis, a customer service representative who had assisted with the opening of the Central Florida office, was selected as the new manager. She was respected by her colleagues and was praised for her willingness to help others and work extra hours when needed by her supervisors. It was a good choice.

Filling the executive vice president position proved more difficult. Harold Ives, the current branch manager with ten years of service and a reputation for fairness and effectiveness, applied for the position, as well as Judy Lewis from the South Florida office. Walter considered Harold a loyal and trusted employee, but Judy had an extensive technical background, as well as several years of direct customer service experience. The diversity of her background was the deciding factor in promoting her to the new position.

Judy Lewis immediately began to exert her own leadership style. She did not approve of the "lackadaisical" practices she believed characterized the current management team. The installation of a time clock was the first change she made. Prior to this, the customer service representatives had kept their own hours and only turned in time sheets when they worked overtime. Judy felt that the employees were taking advantage of the "trust" method and needed closer monitoring. A second change, quickly instituted, was the installation of a new phone system that monitored all inbound and outbound calls. Daily monitors registered idle time, the amount of time a phone is on hold, and the number and duration of all calls handled by each customer service representative. Further changes included limiting the interoffice electronic mail for office discussions, restricting customer service representatives from phoning one another on interoffice lines, and prohibiting any type of solicitations. The result was a decline in morale, an increase in absenteeism, and the dismissal, as well as resignation, of several customer service representatives. Judy perceived this to be the price for efficiency and dismissed the unrest as a temporary condition.

Three months after Judy Lewis's promotion, Harold Ives resigned—disappointed, angry, and frustrated.

The following critical questions can direct and guide your analysis:

1. Why do organizations conduct exit interviews? Are those purposes achieved in this exit interview?
2. Was the interview conducted in an appropriate setting? Did it contribute to a supportive communication climate? What challenges confronted Walter as he interviewed Harold? How did Walter try to defuse the situation and create goodwill for the company?
3. How was the exit interview structured? What questions were asked? Did Walter listen and thoughtfully probe into answers for further information? Was Harold open and candid, providing "honest" rather than "safe" answers?
4. Who controlled the interview? Was positive feedback provided? Did any feedback pitfalls occur during the interview? Did Walter and Harold act professionally?
5. Would the standardized exit interview proposed by Martin Hilb have been a preferable alternative? Why, why not?
6. How satisfactory was the closing?
7. How should the information obtained be used? What steps can Walter take to turn this situation around? What policies and procedures should be changed? How can morale be improved? What would you recommend for improvement?

Summary

Despite performance appraisals, counseling, and career planning interviews, it is common for an employee's resignation to come as a surprise to the supervisor. The inability to predict an employee's voluntary separation from an organization can often be traced to a poor organizational structure, communication barriers between worker and supervisor, and a host of other factors. Whenever an employee leaves, however, the organization is liable to loose something of value. His or her knowledge, views, and experience walk out of the door. One way of capturing that knowledge is via an exit interview.

Still, the exit interview has probably been the least reviewed or studied interview type. It is often overlooked because of its highly confidential nature and its difficulty to study and replicate. However, the exit interview, if done well, benefits both the organization and the employee by providing useful information. The hiring, retention, promotion, and exiting process affects employees and influences organizational activity.

This chapter reviewed the purposes of the exit interview, strategies and techniques for gathering and giving information, the importance of listening and probing thoughtfully, and the necessity for providing feedback and evaluation. Still, important research questions remain unanswered. Is the exit interview organizationally specific, or can it be uniformly employed? How can the trust and confidence of departing employees be gained so that "real" rather than "safe" reasons for leaving are given? What verbal and nonverbal factors exhibited by interviewers most significantly influence departing employees? What about the communication situation? Who is best suited to conduct the exit interview? What techniques, methods, and procedures are most effective? Time efficient? These questions will not be easily answered, but the results can make the exit interview a more effective strategy for organizational change.[25] James Black observes that:

> The exit interview is very much like a jig-saw puzzle. The experienced interviewer realizes that his [her] search for information is similar to a treasure hunt; a small clue here or a sign there turn up unexpectedly . . . may be explored . . . and if the exploration is successful highly valuable information can be discovered.[26]

Managers are beginning to consider the exit interview an opportunity to run a reference check on their entire company.

SHARPENING YOUR FOCUS

1. How might exit interviews be most constructively used? List and discuss the benefits that can be accrued from effective exit interviewing. What are the immediate and long-term benefits to the organization? How does the employee benefit from the exit interview?

2. When employees are laid-off or terminated, is it necessary to conduct an exit interview? Why? How should employees in such situation behave?

3. What questions should be asked during exit interviews? Why do you think many interviewers do not probe as well as they ought to? Given the following exchange, what direct/indirect probing techniques would you use?

   Interviewer: Sarah, we regret your leaving us because you've been such a fine employee. It's important to us to know why someone chooses to leave. The information you can share will help us improve in the future. Let me assure you that whatever we discuss will be held in the strictest confidence. Could you tell me why you're leaving?

   Sarah: Well, I just got this better opportunity to work at Republic Engineering.

4. Some employees choose to vent their emotions during an exit interview. How should the interviewer handle anger and hostility? Discuss the extent to which you would be willing to reveal/not reveal negative information. Why? How could negative information be appropriately conveyed?

5. Outline and discuss the standardized exit interview procedure as an alternative to the traditional exit interview. What advantages does it offer? What are its shortcomings?

6. No exit interview program can proceed successfully without a clear organizational commitment to communicate and act upon the findings. How should exit interview information be circulated to get maximum benefit from the process? How can the information gained during exit interviews and surveys be used by the organization?

NOTES

1. F. M. Lopez, *Personnel Interviewing* (New York: McGraw-Hill, 1975).

2. Garretson and K. S. Teel, "The Exit Interview: Effective Tool or Meaningless Gesture?" *Personnel* 59 (1982): 70–77.

3. S. M. Klein and R. R. Ritti, *Understanding Organizational Behavior* (Boston: Kent, 1984).

4. Jayne Pearl, "Exit Interviews: Getting the Truth," *Working Woman* (June 1993): 16.

5. J. Lefkowitz and M. L. Katz, "Validity of Exit Interviews," *Personnel Psychology* 22 (1969): 445–56.

6. W. L. McNaughton, "Attitudes of Ex-employees at Intervals after Quitting," *Personnel Journal* 35 (1956): 61–63.

7. James M. Black, *How to Get Results from Interviewing* (New York: McGraw-Hill, 1970), 10.

8. H. Wilke, "Making Use of the Exit Interview," *International Management* 26 (1971): 32–34.

9. M. D. Dunnette, R. D. Avery, and P. A. Banas, "Why Do They Leave?" *Personnel* 50 (1973): 25–39.

10. T. A. Jeswald, "The Costs of Absenteeism and Turnover in a Large Organization," in *Contemporary Problems in Personnel*, ed. W. C. Hammer and F. L. Schmidt (New York: St. Claire Press, 1974).

11. S. S. Fader, "Answers to Tough Interview Questions," *Working Woman* 6 (1981): 24, 26.

12. J. R. Hinrichs, "Employees Going and Coming: The Exit Interview," *Personnel* 48 (1977): 346–51.

13. S. B. Wehrenberg, "The Exit Interview: Why Bother?" *Supervisory Management* 25 (1980): 20–25.

14. "The Feedback Factor," *Management Today* (January 1995): 10–11.

15. Laurel Allison Touby, "Career Control: How to Leave Without Burning Your Bridges," *Working Woman* (April 1991): 30.

16. Robert A. Giacalone and Paul Rosenfeld, *Impression Management in the Organization* (Hillsdale, N.J.: Erlbaum, 1989).

17. Robert A. Giacalone and Stephen B. Knouse, "Farewell to Fruitless Exit Interviews," *Personnel* 66 (September 1989): 60–62.

18. C. Bahn, "Expanded Use of the Exit Interview," *Personnel Journal* 44 (December 1965): 620.

19. Robert A. Giacalone and David Duhon, "Assessing Intended Employee Behavior in Exit Interviews," *Journal of Psychology* 125 (January 1991): 83–90.

20. Walter Kiechel III, "The Art of the Exit Interview," *Fortune*, 13 August, 1990, 114–15.

21. Wehrenberg, "The Exit Interview," 20–25.

22. Martin Hilb, "The Standardized Exit Interview," *Personnel Journal* 57 (1978): 327–29.

23. Jill Werman, "What You Should Learn from Every Employee Who Quits," *Working Woman* (January 1990): 14.

24. James G. Neal, "Employee Turnover and the Exit Interview," *Library Trends* 38 (Summer 1989): 32–39.

25. Wallace V. Schmidt, "The Exit Interview as Monitor for Change: A Review of Literature," *Proceedings of the Southwest ABCA Spring Conference*, ed. Sam Bruno (Houston, Tex.: University of Houston-Clear Lake, 1984).

26. Black, *How to Get Results from Interviewing*, 10.

9 The Negotiation/Sales Interview

Negotiation is a common, everyday activity that most people use to influence others and to achieve personal objectives. We all need things: resources, information, cooperation, support from others. At the same time that we have these needs, others from whom we expect these things have needs of their own. Negotiation is basic to satisfying our needs through others while at the same time taking the other party's needs into account. It is a fundamental skill essential to living an effective and satisfying life.

Chapter 9 treats negotiation as a process, not an event. It emphasizes the importance of building relationships based on trust which can facilitate the exchange of information. Available sources of personal power are explored, styles of negotiation analyzed, and specific persuasive strategies and techniques explored. This chapter is designed to accomplish three objectives:

1. *Awareness.* You will learn when and how to use information, collaborative action, hard work, commitment, time, and patience to satisfy the negotiation needs of all concerned.

2. *Assessment.* You will be able to assess the needs of others, using power and tactics to move a negotiation from competitive to collaborative and ultimately resolving deadlocks and impasses.

3. *Application.* You will be able to transfer to a broader view of influence the principles of negotiation, particularly as they apply to sales situations.

* * * * *

Let's Make a Deal!

Teresa Trainer is a sales representative for D.C. DeGroot Inc., a 110-year-old established, quality manufacturing organization that produces parts for a variety of heavy and light industrial manufacturers. She has been with the organization for one year after spending several years in office supervision with another firm. The regional sales supervisor considers Teresa to be an above average sales representative despite the fact that she is light on product knowledge. She is learning fast, and most situations encountered are within her realm of competence. Thus, the regional sales supervisor perceives Teresa to be a promising young sales representative for DeGroot Inc.

Teresa is preparing to meet with a purchasing agent at Perfectrol Corporation, a manufacturer of liquid level and pressure controls for the power industry. DeGroot Inc. has been supplying Perfectrol with parts for six years and considers the company a good customer. However, the regional sales supervisor has made the point on several occasions that "They certainly don't give anything away," a comment on their reputation for being tight and tough in negotiations. Teresa's only experience with Perfectrol occurred shortly after joining DeGroot Inc., and at that time, she left feeling that she had been had, which her supervisor verified when he stated, "Well, at least we'll break even on the deal."

Perfectrol has asked for a quote on 500,000 Mod-2Xs, a part used in their basic control. The current catalog price is $550 per thousand for this item. In looking through the Perfectrol file, Teresa notes that the regional sales supervisor sold the first Mod-2X order to Perfectrol five years ago. This Mod-2X order was for 400,000, and the price was $450 per thousand when the catalog price at that time was $498 per thousand. This original arrangement stated that Perfectrol was to supply the dies for the Mod-2X part produced for them by DeGroot Inc. In addition, there was a note in the file that said, "Thompson given verbal assurances by purchasing agent that they would supply new dies when old needed replacing." Further investigation reveals that approximately 20,000 Mod-2X's were rejected by Perfectrol's quality control department. The DeGroot production people explained, "We are using old dies, and they are the root of the problem." Teresa discovers that new dies will cost approximately $24,000 to make.

The regional sales supervisor has given Teresa the authority to discount the catalog price up to 8 percent, depending upon volume and the "quality" of the customer. However, at the monthly meeting of the entire sales force, he stated that it was necessary to try to hold the line on discounts this year because of the financial needs of the organization.

D. C. DeGroot's earnings dropped during the past year, and dividends were reduced by 10 percent, however, they are currently at full capacity after a one-year slump due to a recession. Moreover, delivery schedules are now being pegged at 120 days after order date by Production Control. Still, all exempt personnel, including sales representatives, have had a freeze imposed on their salaries during the slump. The two major competitors are near full capacity and actively selling.

Teresa is keenly aware of the importance of the Perfectrol contract but has also developed several promising contacts with other firms. While nervous, she feels a little better having established alternative plans.

Ted Tredwell is a purchasing agent for the Perfectrol Corporation, a medium-sized manufacturing company. The company builds a quality line of liquid level and pressure controls, 25 percent of which include some custom features. The balance is stock items. Ted has been working for Perfectrol for ten years in this capacity and has gained a reputation, deserved or undeserved, for being a no-nonsense purchasing agent.

Ted has received a requisition for 500,000 Mod-2Xs, which are used in quantity by the factory to build the basic control. Customized features may be added, but this does not change the design of the basic unit. Currently, there are 80,000 orders to be filled, and it is estimated that 475,000 controls will be built this year. Presently, there are 150,000 Mod-2Xs in the stock room.

Profectrol Corporation is coming out of a recession; however, the customers in the power industry have not been affected as much as others. Still, in the control industry, the price of parts purchased has risen faster than the price on completed controls. Profits of Perfectrol have leveled off, with dividends being maintained at the same level. Expense controls are on internally.

Ted reviews the pricing information, noticing that the current DeGroot catalog price for the Mod-2X is $550 per thousand, with the two major competitors showing catalog prices only 1 percent to 2 percent higher or lower on most items. The file further reflects that 5 percent of DeGroot's Mod-2Xs were returned for not meeting specifications. He is also aware that Perfectrol is facing a critical space problem and is considering leasing additional space for storage.

Ted has called D. C. DeGroot Inc. and asked them to prepare a quote on 500,00 Mod-2Xs and has also established a date to meet with Teresa Trainer, whom he knows to be relatively inexperienced. When he last transacted business with Teresa, he was able to reach a quick agreement that saved Perfectrol $5,000. The scheduled meeting with Perfectrol Corporation will be in Ted's office.

After opening pleasantries are exchanged, Teresa quotes $550 per thousand for the Mod-2X, with Ted protesting that no discount is reflected in the price. He offers $450 per thousand given the recession, the past rejection rate, and the previous arrangement negotiated by Teresa and accepted by D. C. DeGroot Inc. He further notes the increased quantity reflected in this order. Teresa acknowledges the limited influence of the recession and the increase of 100,000 Mod-2Xs. However, the rejection rate will be reduced with new dies provided by

Perfectrol and a newly initiated Total Quality Control program at D. C. DeGroot Inc. Therefore, recognizing Perfectrol to be a "quality" customer, she would be willing to accept $533 per thousand, which places the DeGroot Mod-2X well within the range of the two major competitors who are near full capacity. Teresa notes that while the previous agreement may have been advantageous to Perfectrol, it represented only a "break-even" arrangement for D. C. DeGroot Inc.

Ted and Teresa continue to negotiate and "jockey for position" by exploiting personal sources of power and developing their own special tactics. The quantity, the rejection rate, the cost of new dies, and the delivery schedule dominate this reconnoitering period. Finally, after exchanging empirical data, arguing statistics, and questioning one another, Ted says, "Now, let's be *honest* with each other. You *certainly* don't expect us to pay that price for the Mod-2Xs when *everybody* knows DeGroot needs this contract." Teresa angrily replies, "Let me tell you this much, this quote was developed by highly qualified people. And of course, you know that DeGroot Inc. would *never* accept your offer!" The exchanging seemingly concludes when Ted says, "*Obviously* an agreement is not possible."

After several tense moments, Teresa breaks the silence by saying, "Ted, hear me out, we have made some progress, and it would be a shame to lose the momentum now. You always listen to both sides before you make up your mind, and that's why you are a good negotiator." Ted sits back in his chair and asks, "Well, how can we meet our needs and reach a mutually satisfactory agreement?" Teresa and Ted reexamine their respective interests and with renewed energy explore the barriers to obtaining their goals. Perfectrol's need for additional storage space helps open the door for an action plan leading to an agreement. Teresa offers $512 per thousand for the Mod-2X and proposes a just-in-time delivery schedule with limited storage at D. C. DeGroot Inc., which should offset the production of new dies by Perfectrol and resolve their storage difficulties. Ted agrees that the plan seems workable and is pleased to continue purchasing the Mod-2X from DeGroot Inc.—a company with a proven record. Standing, Ted extends his arm to shake hands and smiling says, "Let's make a deal."

Discussion Questions

1. How would you describe this negotiation/sales interview situation? Was there adequate planning? Were personal power resources used?
2. Which style(s) of negotiation characterize this encounter? Did each party carefully articulate their arguments? What specific strategies or tactics were used?

3. What agreements were arrived at? To what degree were the interests of each party satisfied? How were deadlocks/impasses overcome?
4. How do you think this negotiation result will affect the career of Teresa Trainer? Of Ted Tredwell?
5. Would you categorize this as essentially a negotiation interview or a sales interview?

The Nature of Negotiation

What exactly is negotiation? **Negotiations** represent a special form of social interaction or decision making that (a) involves more than one party: (b) who hold some potentially conflicting interests, as well as common interests or interdependence to motivate each to remain within the relationship or complete the exchange; and (c) requires a reciprocal exchange of information.[1] It is a process where two (or more) individuals combine their respective points of view into a single decision. Both have reasons to agree and to disagree, to cooperate and to compete, to concede and to compel. Herb Cohen, nationally recognized negotiator, more succinctly observes that negotiation "is the use of information and power to affect behavior within a web of tension."[2]

A Dyadic Model of Negotiation

Any definition can be a bit cold, sometimes hard to visualize, and usually not easy to apply to the "real" world. What we need is a more in-depth way to treat the term, *negotiation*. We need to consider the comprehensive meaning of the word and identify the factors comprising the arena in which it takes place. The following **dyadic model** (see figure 9.1) of negotiation provides an integrated framework to explore the nature of negotiation and uncover the complex and highly variable relationships present. It consists of three phases: background, process, and outcome.[3]

The **background phase** comprises the personality mix of the negotiators, as well as their perceptions and expectations, and role definition. Personal traits, such as level of self-esteem, sense of fairness, anxiety, tendency to be conciliatory, ambition, assertiveness, likes, hates, seriousness, ruthlessness, humor, and others have mixed influence on negotiating behavior and actions taken.[4] Each negotiator may serve as a catalyst, facilitator, or impediment to the other. Complementary personalities are likely to communicate with each other in a cooperative and nondefensive way. Highly dissimilar personalities, on the other hand, may be more rigid and defensive in their dealings, with a higher probability of failing to reach a satisfactory outcome.

Jeffrey Rubin and Bert Brown, in an effort to deal with the mercurial nature of personality variables, propose a single dimension to explain the relationship between personality predispositions and negotiation outcomes—interpersonal orientation (IO).[5] They classify individuals as either high or low in their interpersonal

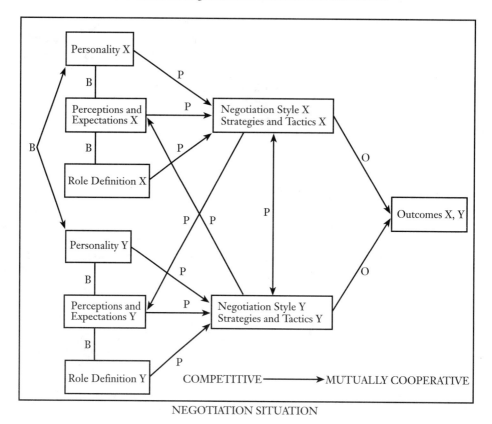

Key: B = Background phase, P = Process phase, O = Outcome phase

FIGURE 9.1   Communication and Information Sharing

Based on a model developed by Bertram I. Spector, a Senior Research Associate in the Policy Sciences Division of the research firm CACI, Inc. located in Arlington, Virginia. See I. William Zartman, ed., *The Negotiation Process: Theories and Applications* (Beverly Hills, Calif.: Sage, 1978), 55–66. See also M. Holmes, "Phase Models of Negotiation," in *Communication Perspectives On Negotiations*, ed. L. Putnam and M. Roloff, (Beverly Hills, Calif.: Sage, 1992), 83–108. Reprinted by Permission of Sage Publications, Inc.

orientation. Those with a high interpersonal orientation are responsive to the interpersonal aspects of their relationships with others and determine their own behavior in a conflict setting by "tuning in" to the behavior of others—the degree of cooperativeness or competitiveness, relative amount of power and use of power, and adherence to negotiating norms. In contrast, those with a low interpersonal orientation are nonresponsive to the interpersonal aspects of their relationships with others and through cooperation or competition seek to maximize their own gain. In short, in order to achieve their goals and preferred outcomes, they are less concerned with the behavior of others.

Perception and expectations, as background factors, represent the ways individuals select, organize, and interpret information from their environment. Perception is "the process of screening, selecting, and interpreting stimuli so that they have meaning to the individual."[6] It is a "sense-making" process that shapes our expectations and contributes to our accurate or inaccurate communication with others. Perceptions and expectations are shaped by the manifest positions and actions taken by others, as well as our own personality structure.

Stereotyping and halo/pitchfork effects are examples of perceptual distortion by generalization. **Stereotyping** occurs when attributes are assigned to people solely on the basis of their membership in a particular social or demographic group. This simplistic process of dividing people into groups prompts group members to define themselves as "we" and "they," and then to make evaluative comparisons and judgments. **Halo and pitchfork effects** in perception are similar to stereotypes, but rather than using group membership as a basis for classification, one attribute of an individual is generalized to include a wide variety of other attributes. Halo effects are positive while pitchfork effects are negative. A good attribute can be generalized so that one sees others in a very positive light, and a negative attribute has the reverse effect. Stereotypes and halo/pitchfork effects are equally common in negotiation; we often form rapid impressions of others based on very limited initial information.

Selective perception, projection, and perceptual defense are examples of perceptual distortion by the anticipation of encountering another whom we believe to have certain attributes and qualities. **Selective perception** occurs when we single out certain information that supports or reinforces a prior belief and filter out contrary information. Thus, selective perception has the effect of perpetuating stereotypes or halo effects—quick judgments are formed about others on the basis of limited information, while any further evidence that might disconfirm the judgment is "filtered out" by attending only to the confirming information. **Projection** involves ascribing to others characteristics or feelings we possess. It arises out of a need to protect our own self-concept; therefore, perceived negative attributes are ascribed to others rather than to oneself. In negotiation, for example, it is common for negotiators to mask their own deceptiveness by claiming that they want to be cooperative and to develop a positive relationship, but the other party is behaving uncooperatively. **Perceptual defense** is the result of the same instinct for self-projection and helps our perceptual apparatus defend us by screening out, distorting, or ignoring information that is threatening or unacceptable to us. Information about ourselves or others that doesn't "fit" our self-image, or the image of others, is likely to be denied, modified, distorted, or redefined to bring it into line with our earlier judgments. Each of these errors adds a source of noise, distraction, or distortion to the perceptual process and the information being received, which influences our expectations during the negotiation process.

A final important background factor is the negotiator's role. Negotiators may come with minimal role obligations, empowered to obtain the best compromise possible, or with formal role functions as delegates of a group, committed to certain positions and bound by rigid instructions. The more highly defined the role obligations of negotiators, the greater are the constraints on concession-making and the greater the probability of deadlocked outcomes.

The **process phase** contains the complex relationships derived from each negotiator's background, which contribute to their choice of negotiation style and selection of negotiation strategies and tactics. It is during this phase that individuals interact to maximize their own interests. They test the feasibility of possible demands, evaluate the strength of the positions, and assess the power of each side. Ultimately, the negotiation styles of the parties and selected tactics or actions will shape and determine the outcome. During the process phase, negotiations usually proceed from an individually competitive position to a more mutually cooperative orientation.

A field of forces comprise the negotiation situation driving the negotiation process, and styles and tactics are parties' attempts to navigate this field.[7] They represent the orientation or approach parties assume during negotiation, but what each does can change initial attitudes and intentions. Thus, it is not uncommon for parties to change styles as the negotiation unfolds.[8]

The **outcome phase** is the culmination of power plays between the participants leading to a joint solution or helpless deadlock. The outcome of any negotiation results from a gradual search process to identify self-interests, likely areas for accommodation and compromise, sensitive issues, limits of acceptability, strengths of commitments, and optimal use of persuasion to reach convergence and ensure agreement. The negotiation process as a whole may best be considered a series of reciprocal bargains in which (a) the parties discover that two issues afford possible exchanges, (b) terms of trade are settled on, and (c) an agreement is struck before the next pair of tradable issues has even been discovered.[9] Of course, agreement is not always assured.

Communication and **information sharing** bridge the three phases and are critical to the effectiveness of the entire negotiation process. Communication is at the heart of the negotiating process. While planning, evaluating the parties within the situation, and strategizing are all key elements to the diagnosis and understanding of negotiation, communication is the central instrumental process. Negotiator's must be able to clearly present their case, using language that encourages the exploration of alternatives and search for a solution. It is through communication and active listening that trust is established and information is shared.

Information is basic to the negotiation process and the basis for agreement. The more dependable information available, the more options which can be developed and the better the decisions. In any situation, the parties are able to make quality decisions only if they are based on quality information. Decisions, no matter how well thought out, are poor decisions if they are based on poor information.

Asking questions, listening, and observing can yield the quality information necessary for effective negotiation. The skillful use of questions can secure attention, maintain interest in the matter under discussion, and give direction to the negotiation effort. When used with discretion and judgment, questions not only provide information, but also start people thinking. Gerard Nierenberg emphasizes that questions can secure a great deal of information about the other party's position, supporting arguments, and needs.[10] He suggests that questions can be divided into two basic classifications: those that are manageable and those that cause difficulty. Manageable questions positively promote dialogue between the parties. They cannot be answered with a simple "yes" or "no," focus on specific points, and provide insights into the other party's thinking and feelings. Unmanageable questions, or ones that cause difficulty, coerce, intimidate, trigger emotional responses, and trick the other party. While they may yield information, they are likely to produce defensiveness and anger, which can jeopardize an otherwise trusting climate.

Effective negotiators also observe the behavioral cues from the other party to acquire added information. The inquiring look, the shake of the head that suggests a lack of understanding, the pondering look that communicates uncertainty, and the slight nod that might mean partial acceptance can all be revealing. Thus, through adroit questioning, active listening, and carefully observing behavioral cues, the amount of known information can be substantially increased and mutually achieving an ultimate agreement improved.

The **negotiation situation** encompasses and influences the entire process. Failure to accurately recognize which type of negotiation is necessary in a particular situation can lead to the wrong approach and to failure. For example, we would negotiate personal or family affairs differently than business matters. Moreover, the negotiation situation may be subject to economic or time constraints, as well as other restrictions.

Persuasion and the Negotiation/Sales Interview

In a broad sense, persuasion plays a role in all interview situations. For example, a job applicant must persuade an employer to recommend him or her for employment; a manager when counseling or coaching must persuade the employee to act on the recommendations; and a journalist must persuade a news source or public figure to reveal information. However, during the negotiation/sales interview, the interviewer deliberately tries to persuade someone to accept a proposal or follow a course of action. The roles are well structured and defined, with the interviewer arguing for the proposal with enthusiasm and motivation, and the other party evaluating the claims and making judgments regarding the proposal. In comparison with that of other interview types, persuasion is a dominating feature characterizing the situation.

However, the negotiation/sales interview *is not* a debate, and unlike other persuasive settings, it should encourage mutual dialogue, the exploration of alternatives, and freedom of choice. This reciprocal "side-by-side" focus on working together to advance their substantive interests may be labeled **responsive persuasion.** The parties size up each other, posture themselves, center the challenging issues posed, and then make their choices freely. Responsive persuasion permits the parties to define their problems, change them, stretch them, and squeeze them until reconciled. The word *reconcile* aptly frames this use of persuasion, because it literally means to "unite again." Scholars at the Harvard Negotiation Project have proposed the need to be "unconditionally constructive" in the process of getting people together.

*   *   *   *   *

Teresa Trainer and Ted Tredwell's meeting represented a typical negotiation/sales interview situation. Teresa had a product to sell, and Ted was an interested and potential customer. Each has interests and objectives they will promote to the advantage of D. C. DeGroot and Perfectrol, respectively. Their individual personalities, perceptions, experiences, and definitions of role influenced the negotiation styles, strategies, and tactics selected and, in turn, affected the eventual outcome(s).

Teresa had limited experience as a sales representative and was under some pressure to secure a more advantageous agreement for D. C. DeGroot than occurred during the last negotiation with Perfectrol. At that time, Perfectrol "didn't give anything away," and D. C. DeGroot only "broke even" on the deal. Thus, she rightfully perceived Ted Tredwell as a "tough" negotiator who would challenge her skills of persuasion. However, her increased product knowledge and understanding of Perfectrol would prove helpful in working within her limited authority to offer any discounts. Moreover, Ted displayed a willingness to take her seriously and to make concessions when well argued and warranted. Increased competence and assertiveness combined with careful planning and preparation did produce a mutually satisfactory agreement.

Ted Tredwell was an experienced purchasing agent who took pride in his "tough" reputation as a negotiator. He has enjoyed the working relationship with D. C. DeGroot and respected the maturing negotiation skills of Teresa Trainer. Ted was cognizant of the advantageous agreement he secured last time and anticipated that Teresa would be more assertive during their upcoming negotiations. Still, he firmly believed that any "fair" agreement was one that was in the best interests of Perfectrol, and any concessions must be well articulated and supported. Negotiation was not a game or exercise in debate, but a necessary process for conducting business. His meeting with Teresa was a cordial, focused dialogue between two actively interested parties seeking to discover a mutually satisfactory working relationship.

This negotiation situation was also characterized by the prevailing economic climate. D. C. DeGroot was coming out of a recession that had affected earnings. While currently operating at full capacity, they were still in a state of recovery. The recession had affected Perfectrol to a lesser degree, but dividends were still a very real concern. Thus, both companies were experiencing economic constraints that influenced the negotiating activities of their representatives.

Planning and Preparation

On the surface, the drama and theatrics of face-to-face confrontation can easily create the impression that success lies in persuasiveness, eloquence, clever maneuvers, and occasional histrionics. While these tactics make the process interesting and at times even entertaining, the foundations for success are the preparation and planning that take place prior to actual negotiation. Planning and preparation are critical in achieving negotiation objectives. With effective planning and goal setting, most negotiators can achieve their objectives; without it, results occur more by chance than by what the negotiator does.

Regrettably, systematic planning is often neglected because of time constraints and work pressures. Moreover, planning is a little boring and tedious, and therefore, easily put off in favor of "getting into the action" quickly.[11] The objective of planning and preparation is to establish long-range and short-range goals, and to position oneself in order to achieve those goals. It is the process by which information is marshaled to make the negotiation proceed smoothly. Good planning and preparation helps negotiators accomplish what they set out to do, and they can achieve their goals because they have also organized themselves to ensure success.

Defining the Negotiation Situation

Being thoroughly prepared requires understanding the negotiation situation. What kind of situation is this going to be? Does it appear possible for all parties to achieve their goals? What has been the relationship with the other party in the past, and how will that affect the current negotiations? The dyadic negotiation model presented earlier in the chapter can be helpful in assessing orientation and useful in defining a particular negotiation situation.

There are times when individuals meet once, negotiate, reach a settlement, and then go their own ways, never to meet again. However, a great deal of our negotiating is in the context of a continuing relationship with people we know. The way that these negotiations evolved in the past, and the settlements that were made or not made, can greatly affect the approach taken during current negotiations. The history of the relationship between the parties "sets the tone" for current relations. Moreover, when defining the situation, consideration must be given to the immediate setting. Selecting a mutually convenient time and a setting free from interruptions will provide the negotiators the best opportunity to explore one another's thinking in detail. Meeting on one's own turf may be psychologically intimidating to the other party; however, meeting away can be used deliberately to provide a built-in excuse for delay. Meeting in a neutral setting may help reduce the pressures, giving the appearance of bargaining from good faith. Negotiators do not always have the luxury of making decisions about the setting, but whenever possible, they should make the setting work for them.

Goal Setting and Identifying the Issues

When entering negotiation, the parties usually have some idea of what they would like the outcome to be. They often say, "I'd be happy if . . ." and then state something they wish to achieve in a settlement. However, goals are not wishes, especially in negotiation. In negotiation, the goals of the parties are linked, and this linking relationship between the two parties' goals defines the issues to be settled. Moreover, there are boundaries, or limits, to what the goals can be. Therefore, the parties must define targets that are attainable. Generally speaking, then, it is preferable to set specific goals that one can realistically expect the other person to accept. The less concrete the goals are, the more difficult it is to communicate mutual needs and determine the satisfaction of particular outcomes. For this reason, negotiators must carefully differentiate between what they really hope to achieve and what they are willing to accept. In short, negotiators must engage in reality testing.

The **target point** is the point of highest settlement satisfaction for a party and "aimed for" outcome in a negotiation. However, since the other party wants a different outcome, negotiators recognize that they are not going to be able to get this preferred outcome. Therefore, they must determine their **resistance point,** or point beyond which they will *not* go and beyond which there is no further point in negotiating. The target and resistance points define a range of acceptable outcomes for a negotiation. The target point defines success; the resistance point defines minimum acceptability. The area between these points is the **settlement range.** It is within this range that negotiation will occur and agreements will be made. However, each party can be expected to try to reach a settlement as close to the other party's resistance point as possible. Consequently, a major paradox for most negotiators to unravel is establishing the bargaining range. To establish this range, negotiators tend to adopt one of four basic approaches: (1) a tough initial offer, (2) a moderately tough offer, (3) a soft initial offer, and (4) a fair offer.[12]

A tough general offer and bargaining approach is characterized by an initial high demand and an unyielding stance. This approach can reduce the other party's expectations and, if maintained, produce a favorable settlement for the negotiator who chooses to be inflexible. However, this approach does run the risk of prolonging the negotiations and also of leading to a situation in which agreement or compromise cannot be reached. The rewards may be greater, but the risk of failure is also greater.

A moderately tough general offer and bargaining approach is characterized by a willingness to make concessions and consider alternatives. This approach can induce the other party to make concessions and create a mutual dialogue permitting an exploration of priorities. Since concessions pull parties together, the chances for a successful settlement increase.

A soft general offer and bargaining approach is characterized by an initial low demand and low minimum expectations. While made in good faith, this approach can be dangerous, since it may raise the other party's expectations and demands. This could make concessions difficult, prolong negotiations, and endanger any settlement.

A fair offer and bargaining approach is characterized by an attempt from the outset to find a solution that is advantageous to both parties. This is an integrative approach where the parties display a willingness to work together toward mutually beneficial ends. The fair initial offer is the ultimate attempt to translate the two positions into win-win situations.

The various characteristics of the negotiators and the negotiation situation itself will play a large part in determining whether a particular bargaining approach will be effective. There is no magical bargaining formula, rather negotiators must analyze each new situation and carefully frame offers and evaluate counteroffers. By defining their goals and determining a bargaining approach, negotiators become more aware of the possible outcomes.

Once goals are set, negotiators must identify the salient and related issues to be deliberated. These issues will form the **negotiating agenda** with the combination of agendas from each side in the negotiation comprising the **bargaining mix.** There is usually one major issue and several minor issues in any negotiation; hence, there is a need to determine which of the issues are "primary" or most important versus those lower in importance. Moreover, it is important to determine whether the issues are linked or separate. If they are separate, they can be easily added or subtracted; if connected, then settlement on one will be related to settlement on the others. Being clear which issues are most important and least important, which are connected or separate can accelerate the negotiating process and lead to a more satisfactory settlement. Once negotiation begins, parties can easily be swept up in the rush of information, arguments, offers, counteroffers, trade-off, and concessions. Negotiators who are unclear about the issues and do not know what they want can easily lose perspective or get hung up on points that are relatively unimportant and be left unsatisfied in the final agreement. Identifying and prioritizing issues permits negotiators to be more flexible in what they will accept and creates better conditions for arriving at a mutually satisfactory outcome.

Developing Arguments and Building a Case

The single most powerful aspect of any negotiation is the ability to marshal ample supporting facts and arguments, and clearly argue a case. People are persuaded in a variety of ways—by the credibility of the source, through emotional appeals with which they can identify, and by logical or rational facts that support a given point of view. In general, information should be presented that highlights the attractive features it offers to the other, or appeals to the other's sense of what is fair, right, and principled. Arguments that contain fear appeals and threats or try to distract the other may have limited effectiveness and are only likely to work when used selectively. Either one-sided or two-sided messages may be used, depending on the circumstances. For example, one-sided arguments are more effective when the other party is already in agreement with a negotiator's point of view, while two-sided messages are preferable when the other party initially disagrees or will be exposed to arguments and points of view different from the one being advocated. Finally, arguments are likely to be more effective if the other party is intellectually involved and permitted to actively participate rather than passively respond—so present facts and *ask questions.*

Since negotiation involves persuasion and problemsolving, negotiators can find Alan Monroe's motivated sequence useful for both casebuilding and case presentation.[13] The conventional divisions of a presentation—introduction, body, and conclusion—are discarded in favor of a "motivated sequence" of five steps:

> *Step 1: Attention.* Gain attention, adapt to the other party, and build personal credibility. Here it is important to motivate and compel the other party to listen to the presentation by introducing the problem in an interesting way.

Step 2: Need. Describe the problem and support it with the necessary evidence and reasoning to prove its significance. Present the other party with a problem, and give them a strong need for solving it. Why is it necessary to consider a change?

Step 3: Satisfaction. Provide a desirable solution for the outlined problem. Support is provided here to prove that the solution satisfies the need—that it is workable and remedies the problem. Remember, there is an advantage in having more than one way to support a point. Arguments are more convincing when supported from several different directions. Negotiator's may want to consider Claude Bernard's observation when he said, "[A fact is] nothing. It is valuable only for the idea attached to it, or for the proof which it furnishes."

Step 4: Visualization. Paint a picture of—or visualize—the outcomes of the proposed solution. Make the solution attractive and arouse a strong desire in the other party for its adoption. How will change or lack of action directly affect them?

Step 5: Action. Specify action to be taken, and make that behavior convenient. Call for a clear response from the other party, inviting them to act on the presentation.

The very essence of persuasion is casebuilding and the ability to explain the case to someone else in an effective manner. Monroe's motivated sequence provides a proven and workable approach. However, its effectiveness depends on the negotiator's ability to analyze and adapt to the other party, and their willingness to listen analytically during the interview to assess how the other party is reacting to specific points.

Analyzing the Other Party

Gathering information about the other party is a critical step in preparing for negotiation. A negotiator will learn much about the other party at the negotiating table. However, as much information as possible should be gathered in advance through research and homework. That data that is most relevant will depend on the negotiation and who the other party is. A surface analysis of the situation and the other party's orientation toward the subject matter can reveal their potential objectives and possible opposition or support of an alternative point of view. Probing beneath the surface, the other party's mental capacity and socioeconomic and cultural backgrounds can offer insights into their perception of self. The other person's intellectual ability and thinking patterns will influence the negotiator's use of vocabulary, depth of explanation, strategy selected, and kinds of appeals. Finally, at a deeper level, negotiators will want to explore the other party's needs and associate them with the different motivational strategies. This deeper understanding of the other party can be useful in not only satisfying needs, but also creating them, causing the other party to favorably accept a new point of view.

Developing the Best Alternative to a Negotiated Agreement (BATNA)

Earlier, we noted that a key part of the planning process is establishing target and resistance points, since these points define the feasible settlement range, which allows negotiators to determine whether any particular offer or proposed settlement should be accepted or rejected. However, this alone can lead to "bottom line" thinking, which inhibits imagination and reduces the incentive to invent alternatives that might reconcile differing interests in a mutually advantageous way for both parties. Roger Fisher and William Ury strongly suggest that negotiators devote sufficient time and attention to developing their best alternative to a negotiated agreement (BATNA).[14] *This* should be the standard against which any proposed agreement will be measured. A vigorous exploration of what one will do if an agreement is not reached can greatly strengthen a negotiator's posture with the other party.

Discovering and developing the best possible alternative to a negotiated agreement requires negotiators to (1) create a list of actions they might conceivably take if no agreement is reached, (2) improve some of the more promising ideas and convert them into practical alternatives, and (3) select the alternative that seems best. Knowing the best alternative to a negotiated agreement makes it easier to break off negotiations if they begin to move in an unsatisfactory direction. Moreover, the more easily and happily negotiators can walk away from a negotiation, the greater their capacity to affect its outcome.

*　　*　　*　　*　　*

Teresa was aware of the economic constraints affecting D. C. DeGroot and clearly understood the limits of her authority to negotiate an agreement. She also realized an ideal agreement would be under the 8 percent discount limit authorized. This information regarding the negotiation situation further helped her plan and prepare for the meeting with Ted Tredwell. Her goal, or target point, would be $550 per thousand for the Mod-2X, but the settlement range would probably be between $550 per thousand and $506 per thousand. Certainly, an important issue influencing the price would be the number of Mod-2X's purchased by Perfectrol. A review of the previous contract had also revealed quality to be a salient issue. Ted Tredwell would undoubtedly be concerned with the past rejection rate. Finally, Teresa was alert to the importance of Perfectrol as a preferred customer and the desire to maintain an ongoing relationship with them. With this information in mind, along with her perceptions of Ted Tredwell as a negotiator, she drafted her arguments and built her case. She was able to competitively posture D. C. DeGroot with other potential suppliers and support improved quality based on the newly initiated Total Quality Control program and new dies to be provided by Profectrol. While her research warranted positive action and agreement within the settlement range on the part of Perfectrol, she realistically knew that there were no guarantees to reaching a negotiated agreement. Consequently, Teresa had developed several promising contacts with other firms as a best alternative to a negotiated agreement. These contacts made her less nervous about the upcoming negotiations with Perfectrol and could be fruitfully developed even if a satisfactory agreement was achieved.

Ted had also done his homework. He knew that Perfectrol paid $450 per thousand for the Mod-2X order last time and was aware of the rejection problem. Certainly, the two most important issues would be quantity and quality. Profectrol was ordering an additional 100,000 Mod-2Xs and must be assured of quality—that the rejection rate would decrease. Moreover, unknown to Teresa, Ted was concerned about the storage problem affecting Profectrol. While he hoped to maintain a working relationship with D. C. DeGroot, Ted realized that current economic constraints and the possible leasing of storage space placed the catalogue price of $550 per thousand for the Mod-2X beyond his resistance point. If a satisfactory cost discount would not be offered, his best alternative to a negotiated agreement would be to explore the options provided by other more competitive suppliers. However, he looked forward to the meeting with Teresa and hoped their past negotiated agreement would not be a barrier to their current negotiations.

Their communication and information sharing was the key to achieving any agreement(s). Each had information commonly known to both and each had information known only to themselves. Their ability to question, probe, and share information significantly influenced the outcome, unknown to both.

The Role of Power

Power is an important factor in negotiations. In a broad sense, negotiators have power when they have the ability to bring about outcomes they desire or the ability to get things done the way they want them to be done. As such, it isn't good or bad. It isn't moral or immoral. It isn't ethical or unethical. Power is the capacity anyone has to make an impact on a situation.[15] Warren Bennis and Burt Nanus observe that "power is . . . the capacity to translate intention into reality and sustain it."[16]

Understanding the different ways that power can be exercised is best accomplished by a description of the various sources or bases of power. John French and Bertram Raven describe five different bases of power: reward power, coercive power, legitimate power, expert power, and referent power.[17] **Reward power** rests on the ability to control and distribute something of value to others. Although rewards are often tangible, like money, they might also be intangible, like verbal approval, praise, or supportiveness. Regardless of type, rewards must be desirable to serve as sufficient motivators. The use of reward power in negotiation is an effort to exert more direct control over the opposing negotiator than may be achieved by simple presentation of information. **Coercive power** is based on the ability to withhold something or to administer punishment or to give negative reinforcement. Coercive power is more likely to be used as an instrument for material gain—to coerce a particular concession or settlement—when the good will of the other party is less important, or the influence attempts are directed at changing some behavior rather than maintaining it. **Legitimate power** resides in the position, title, or role a person occupies. People holding legitimate power have the right to prescribe our behavior within specified parameters. Since negotiations occur within a social structure, that structure may impose obligations to respond to others in an appropriate way. The need for social ordering and social structure creates the basis for legitimate power. **Expert power** is accorded to those who are perceived as having mastered and organized a great wealth of information in a particular field or who possess particular skills. Their credentials and experience confirm their expertise. Expert power is based on the person not the position, in contrast to legitimate power, and can be used to considerable advantage over the nonexpert. Finally, **referent power** is derived from the personal qualities of the powerholder and the personal relationship created with the other party. It is role model power, assigned by others and arising when one person admires another. Referent power through identification is an uncertain tool in negotiation because its basis is "in the eyes of the beholder." Still, through identification and imitation or through the cultivation of commonality and friendships, referent power can be used to develop a relationship between negotiators.

In addition to the five power bases identified by French and Raven, we would add information power, connection power, risk-taking power, and the power of commitment. **Information power** refers to the accumulation and presentation of relevant information that will change the other's point of view or position on an issue. Fortunately, most negotiators can develop their information base even if their credentials are not expert. Within the context of negotiation, informational power is at the heart of the process. **Connection power** results from the people negotiators know and their networking with others. Its strength is derived from the "connections" or links with others. These connections may enhance the other elements of one's power base, as well as make available potential options or alternatives. **Risk-taking power** involves mixing courage with common sense and the willingness to take calculated chances. Risk taking is useful because it creates incentives to aspire to a higher goal. Finally, the **power of commitment** can be an overwhelming source of influence. People support what they help create, and negotiators who can gain the commitment of others possess considerable power to shape the eventual agreements.

Power is a negotiator's currency. In every negotiation, it is vitally important for negotiators to take great care to fully analyze the elements of their own negotiating power, as well as the potential power of the other party. Then, they must use that power with care and caution to ensure that their goals are obtained and that long-term relationships are preserved for future interactions.

*   *   *   *   *

Teresa and Ted each possessed personal power resources that influenced their negotiation together. Their personalities, perceptions, and experiences determined how these resources were used.

Teresa was the legitimate sales representative for D. C. DeGroot. She possessed product knowledge and information about the competition that assisted her in presenting a persuasive case and negotiating an agreement. Furthermore, her connections with other firms provided a best alternative to a negotiated agreement. Finally, her desire to achieve a favorable agreement and maintain a working relationship with Profectrol prompted her to risk exploring new possibilities with Ted. This risk taking led to an agreement that neither party had considered.

Ted was the legitimate purchasing agent for Profectrol. He had the power to reward Teresa with the contract or to reject any effort at a negotiated agreement. He, too, had information that shaped the outcome, and his connections with competitive suppliers influenced his decisions. Moreover, his enviable image as a "tough" negotiator affected the interaction between himself and Teresa. She perceived him as a role model to emulate and fashioned her negotiation style accordingly. Certainly, there was some pressure for her to exhibit a "tougher" and more assertive posture. Finally, Ted's potential willingness to risk exploring new possibilities contributed to a greater likelihood of reaching an agreement.

Styles of Negotiating

At the beginning of negotiations, each party is faced with the perplexing problem of what style, stance, or attitude to adopt. Is one going to be competitive—fighting to get the best on every point—or collaborative—willing to be flexible in making concessions and compromises? Most people see their choice of negotiating strategies as between these two styles.

Competitive/Positional Negotiation

Competitive or positional negotiators seek to meet their own needs at the expense of the other party. Their basic strategy is to manipulate the final settlement to their own advantage—in part, through concealing information, attempting to mislead, or applying pressure. The tactics used involve getting information about the other party and their positions; convincing the other party to change their mind about their ability to achieve their goals; and promoting one's own objectives as desirable, necessary, or even inevitable. Thus, negotiators choosing this style start with an extreme position characterized by tough demands and stubbornly hold to it, making limited concessions only as necessary to keep negotiations going. Competitive or positional negotiation often becomes a contest of will where negotiators assert what they will and won't do.

Negotiators are advised to use a competitive or positional style with caution since it strains and often shatters the relationship between the parties. Still, many negotiators constantly employ this style without making a distinction between an associate and a true adversary, being concerned only with their winning and the defeat of the other side, resulting in a legacy that will affect the future relations of the parties.[18] The moral may be that the competitive or positional negotiator had better make the best possible deal the first time, because there won't be a second chance.

Collaborative/Principled Negotiation

Collaborative or principled negotiation is an attempt to identify a common, shared, or joint goal and developing a process to achieve it. It is an integrative process in which the parties define their "common problem" and pursue strategies to solve it.[19] Collaborative or principled negotiators seek to find a solution or reach an agreement that satisfies the mutual interests of all concerned. Here, negotiators are seeking those creative solutions that only arise after a dialogue occurs, creating an atmosphere of trust and exploring nontraditional approaches to the problem, conflict, or situation. It is a pragmatic choice where helping the other party advances the best interests of the negotiators themselves.[20] Successful collaborative negotiation lies in finding out what the other side really wants and showing them a way to get it, while you get what you want.

In order for this integrative process to succeed, negotiators must share a motivation and commitment to work together, to make their relationship a productive one. They must be able to trust one another and to work hard to establish and maintain that trust. There must be clear and accurate communication about what each one wants and a genuine concern about the other's interests. Collaborative or principled negotiation is a *way* of acting and behaving that can develop understanding, belief, acceptance, respect, and trust. It is an all-purpose strategy that *anyone* can use and where *everyone* can win. The parties to negotiation sink or swim together.

There are several avenues whereby a party to negotiation can attempt to transform a face-to-face verbal confrontation into a side-by-side dialogue.[21] Charles Osgood's Graduated Reciprocation and Tension Reduction (GRIT) strategy is a method designed to overcome lack of trust between parties and produce a more cooperative relationship.[22] The key is to make a conciliatory or cooperative move yet not let one's guard down so that the other can take advantage. If the other party responds in a positive fashion, then subsequent integrative moves can be made until a collaborative negotiating relationship exists. It is a deliberate effort to change an otherwise hostile situation into a positive, productive climate for negotiation. Also, an attempt can be made to reframe issues in an effort to discover superordinate goals that might unite and move both parties toward a common objective and productive outcome.[23]

*   *   *   *   *

Initially, Teresa and Ted assumed "hard" bargaining positions, which seemingly characterize a competitive style of negotiating. However, these rigid offers yielded when collaboratively exploring the issues. They discussed their mutual concerns regarding quantity and quality, as well as their desire to maintain a working relationship. Arguing from their legitimate positions of sales representative and purchasing agent, each became keenly aware of the other's interests and sought to discover a mutually satisfactory negotiating range. Still, their back-and-forth communication on the merits of each case yielded few concessions and culminated in an apparent deadlock or impasse until they began to invent options for mutual gain.

Each was prepared and articulated their case well, supporting arguments and persuasively appealing for compliance. From the outset, they chose strategies and tactics that reinforced a competitive orientation, but eventually, they used strategies and tactics consonant with a collaborative or integrative approach. Their positional postures gave way to principled negotiation, which productively led to a mutual agreement. This was understandable, since negotiators frequently consider a competitive style desirable for achieving their own ends, but when open to considering the other party's interests, discover that by working collaboratively both can win.

Negotiation Strategies and Tactics

A **strategy** is the overall game plan, while the short-term moves designed to implement a strategy are called **tactics.** Negotiation strategies and tactics are the methods for carrying out a plan of operation designed to favorably motivate the other party toward specific objectives. They are the real instruments of negotiating power, and their use can spell the difference between success and near-success for a negotiator. Thus, it is important for negotiators to know how to use particular strategies or tactics effectively. It is also valuable to be able to realize when a strategy or tactic is being used in order to react appropriately.

There are a number of strategies or tactics commonly used, and effective negotiators create new ones as warranted by the situations in which they find themselves. Here, we will selectively describe some common strategies or tactics, and consider how they might affect negotiations.[24] Some represent persuasion at its bluntest, while others reveal the subtle art of persuasion.

• *The "paper stack" tactic.* Negotiators may proceed to stack their data and files in front of them at the outset of a negotiation to emphasize the full impact of their preparation and intimidate the other party. To be effective, it is important that all of the visible data be relevant to the negotiation and that negotiators actually use the data during the negotiation. Otherwise, the other party will become suspicious that the data is for "show" only and credibility will be lost.

- *The "inundation" tactic.* Negotiators may attempt to overwhelm the other party with information at the beginning to intimidate them and circumvent their arguments. This tactic can be effective if carefully planned.

- *The "building block" tactic.* Negotiators may choose to parcel out the facts supporting their case over the length of the negotiating session, thus incrementally revealing their objectives. The cumulative "building" effect can transform a mediocre or otherwise weak case into one that seems much stronger.

- *The "timely disclosure" tactic.* This is a calculated tactic whereby negotiators suddenly reveal information that can have an impact on the direction of the negotiation. To be effective, the disclosed information must be carefully and skillfully woven into the proposals and then specifically directed toward the negotiating objectives. Moreover, the other party must be genuinely surprised.

- *The "vinegar and honey" tactic.* Negotiators may initially impart bad news and then gradually relieve the bad news with doses of good news in order to gain acceptance. Here, a decidedly unfavorable outcome is contrasted with more acceptable options yet less than originally desired. To be effective, it is important that the unfavorable news not be too sour, or the other party may merely walk away from the negotiations.

- *The "nibble" tactic.* Here, an agreement has seemingly been arranged, when unexpected extras are added to the agenda and asked to be included in the settlement. Creative negotiators can enhance their objectives by presenting minor items and persistently requesting that they be simply added on. The danger is perceived "bad faith," which could breakoff negotiations.

- *The "silence" tactic.* Often, silence prompts the other party to draw false conclusions and to further concede on issues. Effective negotiators *do not* negotiate by ceaselessly talking, but by actively listening and analyzing the information shared.

- *The "appeal to an authority" tactic.* Negotiators may use a respected authority or expert to support their case. To be effective, the other party must recognize, willingly acknowledge, and accept the authority or expert. Often, they have authorities or experts of their own.

- *The "greater fear" tactic.* Negotiators often attempt to play upon the other party's fears in an attempt to promote action. To be effective, the other party must be cognizant of the negotiator's capabilities and acknowledge the likelihood of the consequences.

- *The "war and peace" tactic.* Using two negotiators, the first literally wages "war" with the other party, while the second quietly and tactfully conducts the negotiation in a peaceful manner but with the always present threat of the first negotiator. This tactic is often transparent, and the risk of complete break off of the negotiation is very real.

- *The "rainy day" tactic.* The apocryphal story goes that twelve jurors, all active farmers except one who was retired, were diligently deliberating a case in a rural community during haying season. Due to the resistance of the retired farmer, they were unable to reach a unanimous verdict until the first clap of thunder, threatening their harvest, caused them to acquiesce in favor of his vote. The story illustrates the power of deadlines—here set by circumstances. Negotiators may also set deadlines and play upon the anxiety produced as those deadlines near to affect progress. It is a statistical fact that most negotiations, particularly those that are highly controversial, are settled at or near a set deadline. However, for this technique to be effective, negotiators must be fully prepared to live with the consequences of any time limits set.

- *The "exhausting your opponent" tactic.* Negotiators may consciously decide to extend negotiations with the hope of exhausting the other party. Unlike the "rainy day" tactic, deadlines are not set, and negotiators deliberately allow the other party to proceed without paying any particular attention to them until they exhibit a willingness to be conciliatory. This is an excellent method to defeat an otherwise aggressive opponent; however, there is the danger that negotiations may simply breakoff out of frustration.

- *The "bland withdrawal" tactic.* Negotiators interrupt the negotiation process by suddenly leaving. The resulting confusion might make the other party more conciliatory, but it risks promoting anger and rupturing the negotiation climate.

- *The "apparent withdrawal" tactic.* Less risky is to withdraw from the scene but leave a representative behind to heal the rift, argue the case, and suggest amends for reinitiating negotiation.

- *The "conduit" tactic.* When a negotiator's principle opponent proves difficult to work with, appeals might be directed toward the other representatives. The more supporting associates there are to work on, the better the tactic usually works.

- *The "fait accompli" tactic.* This is a unilateral action taken to expedite an agreement with the hope that the other party will accept it. It is, however, a risky tactic and negotiators must carefully consider the consequences if it should fail.

Strategies and tactics are the tools negotiators employ in the process of influencing decisions and behavior. They are designed to test the commitment of the parties to their goals, force the revelation of backup positions and options, and stimulate the sharing of additional information. When used in a timely manner, and within a framework of trust and mutual respect, they can be instrumental in the achievement of agreements that all parties can be committed to.

Negotiations, however, are never the same, and some parties may be able to reach agreements quite easily, while at other times, the parties may constantly appear on the brink of disaster or impasse. The following strategies can be useful in breaking deadlocks or impasses and creating an important turning point in the discussions, allowing the parties to see more clearly the nature of their dispute and what must be done to achieve an agreement.

- *The "gearshifting" tactic.* Experienced negotiators know that sometimes an issue will not settle because the time is not right for it to settle. This tactic permits them to smoothly shift from one issue to another with the unresolved issue being settled later.

- *The "it's-a-shame-to" tactic.* Whenever there is more than one issue and some of the issues have been resolved, negotiators can use the agreed-upon issues as a basis for motivating the other party to continue negotiations. The basic appeal is, "It's a shame to quit now, after having already made so much progress."

- *The "you-say-you-don't, but-you-do" tactic.* This tactic permits negotiators to broach delicate or sensitive issues that could create an impasse to the negotiation. By saying, "I don't want to get into, but . . . ," effective negotiators can skillfully motivate the other party to discuss an otherwise touchy issue important to their negotiation objectives.

Most deadlocks or impasses occur because of failure to identify and work actively for the needs of the other party. Actively working for the needs of others can provide the key to unlock dilemmas and stimulate creative solutions. However, deadlocks or impasses are not always unjustified and may, in fact, be preferable to an otherwise unsatisfactory agreement.

Still, another perspective for understanding the use of negotiation strategies and tactics is provided by contemporary communication researchers studying what people say when they are trying to influence others. Often, persuasive messages are not fully developed expositions or narratives but are short conversations or even single sentences that influence us in one way or another. These short units of discourse, representing a personal repertoire of self-contained persuasive strategies, are labeled "compliance-gaining messages."[25]

Lawrence Wheeless, Robert Barraclough, and Robert Stewart provide one of the most comprehensive analyses of the compliance-gaining literature and believe that compliance-gaining messages are best classified according to the kinds of power employed by communicators when attempting to gain the compliance of others.[26] Compliance-seekers choose strategies or tactics permitting them to manipulate the consequences of a situation, exploit a relational position, or define the values and/or obligations for another. Individuals tend to use their power and appropriate compliance-gaining techniques to get what they want. Thus strategies and tactics should be regarded as just tools to be used and managed along with other aspects of the negotiation interview.

*   *   *   *   *

Information power was used by both Teresa and Ted, and each attempted to inundate the other with facts and statistics. They selectively disclosed information in the building of their respective cases and each hoped to intimidate the other into accepting their positions. Moreover, Teresa reminded Ted of his "debt" to her, given their last agreement, which favored Profectrol. Ted, in turn, used fear of rejection and implied threats of going to competitive suppliers to gain compliance. Each chose persuasive strategies and tactics designed to produce a win-lose or lose-lose outcome until they openly explored the issues and began to acknowledge one another's interests. As they displayed a willingness to be flexible, Teresa and Ted engaged in actively listening to and reflecting on the mutually shared information. They questioned one another and probed responses, hoping to find an acceptable settlement range. Still, their efforts were frustrated, and Ted's "talking down" to Teresa almost stopped negotiation altogether. She angrily responded to Ted's superior attitude, and the negotiation process became deadlocked. However, after several tense moments of silence, they were able to redirect their attention to the problem. Praising Ted's open-mindedness and very real intent to negotiate in "good faith," Teresa noted that "it's a shame to" stop now after expelling so much positive energy to find a workable agreement. This got them through the impasse, allowing them to brainstorm other options. Their goal became agreement rather than victory. Profectrol's need for storage space became a critical piece of information, which permitted Teresa and Ted to reframe the issues and reach an agreement. Adversarial strategies and tactics, and communication "stoppers" could have thwarted the negotiation process, but their dedicated and sincere efforts led them to search for a single solution they both could accept. Rather than pursuing a haggling contest of wills, Teresa and Ted were able to "make a deal" that promoted the best interests of both D. C. DeGroot and Profectrol.

Managing the Interview

Planning, building a case, assessing personal bases of power, choosing a negotiation style, and selecting strategies and tactics are all important and provide the necessary framework needed to effectively negotiate with another party. Ultimate success however, depends on how well the negotiator can manage the interview. Managing the negotiation/sales interview requires skillfully using communication to (a) build rapport, (b) establish trust, (c) present the case, (d) reframe issues, and (e) actively listen and reflect.

Building Rapport

Rapport is necessary in achieving a basis for negotiation. **Rapport** refers to a feeling of harmony between the parties and a resulting relationship where the parties feel comfortable working together. The most positive negotiation relationships begin because the parties discover similarities that draw them toward one another.[27] One way to achieve this is by establishing some common ground with

The negotiation/sales interview is not a debate—establishing rapport and building trust are essential for reaching a satisfactory agreement.

the other party. For instance, attention can be focused on mutually shared experiences, beliefs, values, attitudes, opinions, or goals. Such similarities can be a potent force in building common identification and facilitating persuasion.[28]

However, it must also be noted that the efforts given to building rapport can be easily sabotaged by insensitive, condescending, and otherwise hostile actions. Interrupting the other party, calling them derogatory names, talking down to them, or challenging their integrity all betray an attitude of superiority, and most people resist being thought of as inferior. Also, laughing off new ideas or brushing-off the other party's arguments reveals a hostility to change, and people are reluctant to negotiate with or be persuaded by anyone who is inflexible. Therefore, negotiators need to carefully monitor their communication behaviors to maintain the valuable rapport developed.

Establishing Trust

While **trust** is of obvious advantage to the negotiating climate, it is not easily established. Generating trust is a complex, uncertain process, depending in part on what the parties do to one another and also on the personal characteristics of the parties. When people trust one another, they are more likely to communicate accurately their needs, positions, and the facts of the situation. In contrast, when people do not trust one another, they are more likely to engage in positional bargaining, use threats, and commit themselves to tough demands.

Given that trust has to be established during the negotiation, opening initiatives are crucial. They not only set the tone for negotiation but also the momentum. The more cooperative, open, and nonthreatening the opening statements and actions of a party are, the more trust and cooperation is engendered in the other party. Once a cooperative position is established, it is more likely to persist. However, trust is the result of many interactions in a developing process. Thus, negotiators must continuously consider how the use of a strategy or tactic will affect the climate of trust between the parties and whether it is worth the risk of damaging that climate. Establishing and maintaining a climate of trust is a test of a negotiator's skill, but negotiators who are trusted by the other side discover many more opportunities for agreement.

Presenting the Case

Negotiators must present their case with confidence. This requires an understanding of the arguments, a familiarity with the supporting material, and the ability to articulate their ideas. Moreover, negotiators must constantly analyze, adjust, and adapt as they "realize" their ideas in the presence of the other party. Negotiation is a structured and purposeful process, and those who participate in it must be stringent in their adherence to the requirements.

Presenting the case is a challenging and demanding task. It is not a speech that can be thoroughly rehearsed in advance, but practice is possible. Many negotiators find role playing, with a colleague or friend acting as the other party, useful. This can simulate the actual negotiation, forcing them to clearly advance their ideas and consider the other party's responses. In this way, they can discover any gaps or potential weakness in their case, be better prepared to respond to the other party's arguments, and ensure to some degree that there will be no surprises. However, there are no absolute guarantees, and negotiators must always anticipate the unexpected.

Reframing Issues

Negotiation occurs within a dynamic, give-and-take forum, and successful negotiators must be able to effectively frame and reframe the issues.[29] **Reframing** is an effort to redefine the issues in a way that the two opposing parties are no longer regarded as opposites. It requires that negotiators try to present information in a way that leads the parties to see what they have to gain from a risk-free settlement. Negotiators who view possible outcomes in terms of gains rather than losses are more likely to attain better overall outcomes.[30] Through reframing the issues or interaction, the parties can move the negotiation in new and more productive directions.

Reframing is the sudden "ah-hah" of looking at things in a new light. With this type of thinking, participants focus on "what is to be gained" rather than "what is to be lost." The gentle art of reframing can help negotiators effectively manage negotiation and "build bridges not walls."

Active Listening/Reflecting

When negotiators fail to actively listen and provide feedback while the other party explores ideas, the negotiation process suffers. Active listening and reflecting takes time and requires that negotiators be nonjudgmental. However, it can reveal what the other party is thinking, accepting, or rejecting at the moment. This can assist negotiators in understanding the nature of the other party's position, the factors and information that support it, and the ways that it might be compromised, reconciled, or negotiated in accordance with their own preferences and priorities. In addition, **active listening** and **reflecting** contributes to building rapport, establishing trust, and effectively reframing issues. It is a skill that can encourage productive outcomes.

* * * * *

Teresa and Ted achieved a final agreement because both effectively participated in managing the negotiation interview. The time spent building rapport and establishing trust during the early part of the interview helped them through the frustrating cycle of offers and counteroffers. Their recognized competence and credibility permitted them to "try on" each other's views and eventually to engage in a side-by-side search for a fair agreement advantageous to each. Negotiating from firmness and openness, they welcomed new inputs and fresh ideas, and slowly constructed a satisfactory settlement. Using questions instead of statements of demands, they developed a productive negotiating relationship that contributed to their mutual commitments. It wasn't an easy task, but negotiation isn't a simple process.

The final agreement had Perfectrol purchasing 500,000 Mod-2Xs and paying $512 per thousand. In addition, they would provide new dies to help ensure quality. D. C. DeGroot would subject the Mod-2Xs to further quality testing and develop a just-in-time delivery schedule for Profectrol, which could offset otherwise potential storage problems. The final agreement reflected the salient issues identified by Teresa and Ted, and addressed the primary concerns of D. C. DeGroot, Inc. and Profectrol Corporation.

Teresa and Ted should be complimented on successfully negotiating an agreement that satisfied the interests of their respective organizations and can only advance their careers. Teresa increased the previous Mod-2X order by 100,000, remained within her authorized discount limits, and maintained the preferred working relationship with Profectrol. Ted, assured of a quality product, was able to purchase the necessary 500,000 Mod-2Xs at a realistically discounted price well below that offered by competitive suppliers and, at the same time, resolved Profectrol's storage problem with a just-in-time

delivery schedule. Equally important to Teresa and Ted was the learning experience resulting from the negotiation process. Each emerged
a more competent and skilled negotiator.

How would you have negotiated in this situation?

Sales and Negotiation

The **sales interview** represents a typical application of the negotiation principles
discussed and is a situation common to anyone who has ever purchased a product or service. Unfortunately, many do not perceive that a sales transaction is a
negotiation, because skilled salespeople frequently appear to work by instinct,
and the casual observer often dismisses their successful efforts as the result of a
"natural talent to sell" or "just luck." However, closer examination reveals the use
of negotiation skills essential to sales—determining purpose or objective, identifying customer needs or interests, delivering the sales presentation, and managing the sale through to a close.

Presale planning is critical if salespeople hope to be successful. This initial
analysis should focus on the proposal and product, on potential customers, and
on the professional image to be conveyed. Al Ries and Jack Trout observe that "if
you want to be successful, you'd better have a good strategy."[31] Salespeople must
clearly know what they want and how they hope to achieve it. They must also
have a thorough understanding of the product or service they are selling and how
it compares with the competition—product knowledge. Product knowledge helps
to maintain a professional image and makes it possible to answer questions potential customers may ask. Developing and maintaining product knowledge is an
ongoing process. Scott Parker, Western Area Sales Manager for National Semi-
conductor, says that the most important information in his "sales kit" is "knowing how our solution will help our clients achieve their goals."[32]

Identifying potential customers and understanding their needs must also be
given serious consideration when engaged in presale planning. Finding potential
customers is often referred to as "prospecting," and anyone who may need the
product or service is a potential customer. Consequently, special attention must be
given to the "how, why, and what" of a customer.[33] This means understanding the
personality, motivation, and background factors of potential customers. Automa-
tion has increased data availability, and current technology and computer software is making it easier for salespeople to access information about corporations
and potential customers. Thus, the laptop has proven to be a valuable tool for the
successfully prepared, professional salesperson who wants to remain updated on
potential customers.[34] Since a salesperson's livelihood depends on sales, understanding customer needs and establishing a customer base is vitally important.

Like all interviews, the sales interview is a distinct communication event, and
salespeople must adapt their presentation to the immediate situation. Presale

preparation and being aware of the events that have preceded the interview can all be helpful, but "success is possible only when salespeople recognize each sale as a distinctively different situation."[35] Consequently, salespeople must devote sufficient time to building rapport, establishing trust, and qualifying the customer before presenting their proposal. Skilled salespeople use the phrase "qualifying the customer" in a very specific way. To qualify a prospect means determining what the customer thinks he or she needs, what the customer wants to accomplish, how soon the customer is prepared to buy, and the customer's authority to commit. This information can influence the direction of the interview and sales presentation.[36]

The sales presentation itself should maintain the customer's interest and attention, and provide convincing arguments supporting the purchase of the product or service. The salesperson must also be alert to customer objections and be prepared to answer them. Most objections should be regarded as an expression of a customer's need for more information. Tom Hopkins positively notes that "objections aren't sales-killers, they're sales-makers," and selling has not really begun until the customer voices objections.[37] The challenge for the salesperson is to listen carefully, evaluate the objection correctly, and satisfy the customer's concerns, fears, misunderstandings, or misinformation regarding the product or service. Salespeople can no longer depend on fast talking, a pleasing personality, and a bag of tricks to produce volume and profitable sales.

Once the customer responds favorably, the skilled salesperson moves quickly to secure final commitment by working out details of the agreement. Jack Royhl, Sales Consultant for Liberty Promotions, Inc., notes that "if I have listened to what my clients goals are, and give them a solution that fills those needs, that solution will be my sales clincher."[38] Clinching the sale, however, does not end one's relationship with the customer. Successful salespeople maintain customer contact and continuously develop customer relationships with an eye toward future sales.

Today, professional salespeople who want to be set apart from the competition use a laptop computer presentation that incorporates three-dimensional computerized graphics and actual videotape clips. The computer-assisted sales pitch helps keep them on course and eliminates omissions while prompting the prospective client to lean forward in the buying position from the first five seconds. It answers prospective questions before they are asked and never fails to make its impact even after 1,000 repetitions of the same pitch. Moreover, it can be used to ask a closing question or a series of closing questions, which the prospect interactively answers with ordering information or information that confirms the sale. This is the cutting edge of sales technology. The prospect is mesmerized by a state-of-the-art presentation, has all questions and objections answered, and is led to a positive close.[39]

Customer's are an integral part of the sales interview, and they should approach it with as much care and preparation as salespeople. Prior to the interview, they should examine their needs and do systematic research. During the interview, they should ask questions, probe responses, weigh alternatives, record important information, and avoid making snap decisions. Finally, it is essential that they read and understand any agreement, being certain it reflects their interests. The sale should satisfy both parties.

* * * * *

> Would you categorize Teresa and Ted's situation as essentially a nego-
> tiation interview or a sales interview? The question is unfair, since all
> sales transactions are negotiations. Teresa and Ted were using negoti-
> ation principles to achieve a favorable sales outcome. They were con-
> sciously engaged in promoting a positive climate conducive to a long
> association. They mutually valued a win-win philosophy, which was a
> barometer of their success.

Critical Focus

To demonstrate the application of negotiation principles to the sales setting, analyze the interview between Heather Kidwell, a twenty-seven-year-old commercial real-estate associate, and Bob Cheatum, a used car sales representative for
World Motors. Critically focus on the interaction between the parties, noticing
their orientation to the situation and identifying their objectives and use of persuasive strategies or tactics.

Heather's car was stolen and wrecked two weeks ago. Since her real-estate
position requires her to do a lot of driving and the Ford Mustang she is renting is
costing a great deal, she would like to buy another car as quickly as possible. However, it must be economical and easy to drive. The insurance company gave
Heather $3,500 for her old car, and she does have another $2,000 in savings, which
she has intended to spend on a cruise with an extremely attractive companion—a
chance she really doesn't want to pass up. Since her credit is currently stretched to
the limit, she is reluctant to borrow money. She has found a used 1989 Yugo for
$3,200 that gets good mileage, but she is attracted to a Nissan recently listed by
World Motors. The Nissan would be economical and a fun car to drive.

Bob Cheatum placed the listing for the Nissan in the newspaper only a couple of days ago and has already received several calls regarding it. The car is in
particularly good condition and should bring a good price. He could probably re-
sell it to the local Nissan dealer for a modest profit. However, his sales record has
been down this month, and the Nissan represents an opportunity to not only improve this record but to help offset his commissions.

Bob shows Heather the car, letting her test drive it, before they meet in his
office at Dance Motors to continue negotiating.

The following critical questions can direct and guide your analysis:

1. Did the parties take time to build rapport and establish trust? Does Bob
   qualify Heather as a potential customer? Are the goals and objectives of the
   two parties clearly stated? How are questions used to establish the negotiation climate and gather information? Was the interview properly planned
   and conducted?

2. What strategies and tactics are employed? Did compliance-gaining messages surface within the exchange? How did the parties use their respective power bases? Who controlled the interview?
3. What problems or obstacles arose? Was Bob prepared to answer potential objections? Did Heather probe his responses and weigh her alternatives? Were mutual solutions objectively explored and considered?
4. How satisfactory was the closing? Did the final agreement reflect the interests of both parties? Would Heather buy another used car from Bob at a later date?
5. How would you have negotiated in this situation? What would you have done differently?

Summary

Once upon a time a hunter named Noneck had in his cave more rabbit meat than he needed; however, he had lost his hunting club. His neighbor, Twelvetoes, happened to have two clubs but no meat. Twelvetoes could have bopped the unarmed Noneck and taken his food. Or both could have ignored the opportunity for an exchange. Instead, they squatted by the fire (for in those days the three-martini lunch was unknown) and haggled until they agreed on exactly how many rabbits were worth one club. That's how negotiation began.[40]

Negotiation, occurring in a variety of contexts and regularly influencing our work and personal lives, is a basic social process for peacefully resolving differences. The dyadic negotiation model presented identifies the critical elements comprising this process and outlines the background, process, and outcome phases that contribute to its drama and tension. Essentially, interdependent parties engage in a dialogue regarding their personal goals and interests which will hopefully lead them to discover a mutually satisfactory solution.

Planning and preparation are paramount if negotiation is to succeed. Planning requires that negotiators understand the situation and clearly formulate their goals and frame the salient issues for discussion. This requires homework and research: putting together the information and arguments to support and defend the desired goals, analyzing the other party to determine the potential settlement range, and finally, assessing the best alternatives to a negotiated agreement.

The planning and preparation should further lead negotiators to evaluate their personal power bases and select an appropriate negotiating style. A competitive or positional style is characterized by the exercise of power in a win-lose manner, with negotiators making rigid demands and remaining adamantly inflexible. By contrast, collaborative or principled negotiation is an open, integrative style where each party exerts power and the best possible solution for both parties is the intended outcome. While negotiators frequently choose a competitive style concerned only with their own ends, we propose that a collaborative style can better produce "winning" agreements because the settlements most satisfactory and durable are the ones that address the needs of both parties. Moreover, such settlements help to maintain a positive and continuous relationship between the parties.

Successful persuasion is an important key to effective negotiation. Consequently, the parties engage in all manner of strategies and tactics to persuade the other. We identified some of the commonly used strategies or tactics and further noted the influence of compliance-gaining messages. All of these strategies or tactics are methods for achieving personal aspirations and motivating the other party toward specific objectives.

Ultimately, the negotiation interview must be effectively managed. The parties must initially build rapport and establish trust if agreements are to be achieved. Their arguments must be tactically advanced and evaluated, requiring the parties to actively listen and reflect. Questions will be raised and objections voiced, necessitating the reframing of issues and a mutual exploration of alternatives until a mutually satisfying solution surfaces.

Negotiation is an uncertain and complex process. It involves a dynamic interpersonal event. It involves both behavioral and analytical skills. It involves the values and beliefs of people. It is also a skill that can be learned and when used well can bring people together.

The last part of the chapter focused on the sales interview as a typical application of the negotiation principles previously discussed. Both sales-people and customers must clearly identify their objectives and carefully plan for the sales interview. Each must be able to articulate their goals and effectively use questions to gather information, probe responses, and discover a mutually satisfying solution. The sales interview should meet the needs of both the salesperson and customer, with each perceiving the ultimate sale as being beneficial; thus, negotiating skills are integral to the sales interview.

S H A R P E N I N G   Y O U R   F O C U S

1. Planning and preparation are critical in achieving negotiation objectives. Why do negotiators frequently fail in their planning process? How can these weaknesses be corrected?

2. Describe the dyadic process of negotiation.

3. List and define five negotiation strategies. Discuss the ethical considerations that ought to guide a person's negotiation.

4. How does the sales interview represent a typical application of the negotiation principles discussed? Discuss each phase of the sales interview—presale planning, sales presentation, and close. Why can salespeople no longer depend on fast talking, a pleasing personality, and a bag of tricks to produce volume and profitable sales?

5. What kind of negotiation style do most sales representatives employ? Why might they choose this style? What kind of style do you *think* they should employ? Why?

6. Describe how you handle negotiation/sales situations. Use the following chart to record your observations.

My Personal Negotiation/Sales Inventory

The Negotiation/ Sale Situation	*How It Was Handled*	*The Outcomes*
Who was involved? What was it about?	What did I do? What did the other party do?	How did I feel? How did I think the other party felt?

Use your chart to help you answer the following questions: How often are you involved in negotiation/sales situations? Over what issues? How often are you involved in negotiations/sales with the same party? What negotiation/sales strategies do you use? Do you think they are effective? Why? How does the other person (or people) react to them? What negotiation/sales strategies does the other person use? Do you think they are effective? Why? To what extent do you think the issues were resolved satisfactorily? Why? What did you learn about yourself in this experience? What did you learn about the people with whom you negotiate/sell? What did you learn about the negotiation/selling process?

NOTES

1. L. Putnam and M. S. Poole, "Conflict and Negotiation," in *Handbook of Organizational Communication*, ed. F. Jablin, L. Putnam, K. Roberts, and L. Porter (Beverly Hills, Calif.: Sage, 1987), 549–99.
2. Herb Cohen, *You Can Negotiate Anything* (New York: Bantam Books, 1980), 16.
3. Based on a model developed by Bertram I. Spector, a Senior Research Associate in the Policy Sciences Division of the research firm CACI, Inc. located in Arlington, Virginia. See I. William Zartman, ed., *The Negotiation Process: Theories and Applications* (Beverly Hills, Calif.: Sage, 1978), 55–66. See also M. Holmes, "Phase Models of Negotiation," in *Communication Perspectives On Negotiations*, ed. L. Putnam and M. Roloff, (Beverly Hills, Calif.: Sage, 1992), 83–108. Reprinted by Permission of Sage Publications, Inc.
4. M. G. Hermann and N. Kogan, "Effects of Negotiators' Personalities on Negotiating Behavior," in *Negotiations: Social-Psychological Perspectives*, ed. D. Druckman, (Beverly Hills, Calif.: Sage, 1977), 91–113.
5. Jeffrey Rubin and Bert Brown, *The Social Psychology of Bargaining and Negotiation* (New York: Academic Press, 1975).
6. R. M. Steers, *Introduction to Organizational Behavior*, 2d ed. (Glenview, Ill.: Scott Foresman and Company, 1984), 98.
7. L. R. Singer, *Settling Disputes* (Boulder, Colo.: Westview Press, 1990).
8. C. Conrad, "Communication in Conflict: Style-Strategy Relationships," *Communication Monographs* 58 (1991): 135–55.
9. L. Putnam and T. Jones, "Reciprocity in Negotiations: An Analysis of Bargaining Interactions," *Communication Monographs* 49 (1982): 171–91.
10. Gerard Nierenberg. *Fundamentals of Negotiating* (New York: Hawthorn Books, 1973), 125–26.
11. H. H. Calero and B. Oskam, *Negotiate the Deal You Want* (New York: Dodd, Mead and Company, 1983).
12. W. Clay Hamner and Gary A. Yukl, "The Effectiveness of Different Offer Strategies in Bargaining," in *Negotiations*, ed. Daniel Druckman (Beverly Hills, Calif.: Sage, 1977), 141–57.
13. This discussion of the motivated sequence is based in part on information in Bruce E. Gronbeck, Raymie E. McKerrow, Douglas Ehninger, and Alan H. Monroe, *Principles and Types of Speech Communication*, 11th ed. (Glenview, Ill.: Scott, Foresman/Little Brown, 1990).

14. Roger Fisher and William Ury, *Getting to Yes,* 2d ed. (New York: Penguin Books, 1991).
15. Cuming, *The Power Handbook* (Boston: CBI Publishing, 1981).
16. Warren Bennis and Burt Nanus, *Leaders: The Strategies for Taking Charge* (New York: Harper and Row, 1985), 17.
17. John French and Bertram Raven, "The Bases of Social Power," in *Group Dynamics,* ed. D. Cartwright and A. Zander (New York: Harper and Row, 1968), 259–68.
18. G. T. Savage, J. D. Blair, and R. L. Sorenson, "Consider Both Relationships and Substance when Negotiating Strategically," *The Academy of Management Executive* 3 (1989): 37–48.
19. Linda Putnam, "Reframing Integrative and Distributive Bargaining: A Process Perspective," in *Research on Negotiation in Organizations,* vol. 2, ed. R. J. Lewicki, B. H. Sheppard, and M. H. Brazerman (Greenwich, Conn.: JAI Press, 1990), 3–30.
20. Alfred Kohn, *No Contest: The Case Against Competition* (Boston: Houghton Mifflin, 1986).
21. S. Lindskold and S. Walters, "Transforming Competitive or Cooperative Climates," *Journal of Conflict Resolution* 30 (1986): 99–114.
22. Charles E. Osgood, *An Alternative to War or Surrender* (Urbana, Ill.: University of Illinois Press, 1962).
23. L. Putnam and M. Holmer, Framing, Reframing and Issue Development," in ed. L. L. Putnam and M. E. Roloff *Communication Perspectives on Negotiations,* (Beverly Hills, Calif.: Sage, 1992). 128–55.
24. See Gerard I. Nierenberg. *Fundamentals of Negotiating* (New York: Hawthorne, 1973); John Ilich, *Power Negotiating* (Reading, Mass.: Addison-Wesley, 1980); and Calero and Oskam, *Negotiate the Deal You Want.*
25. For a comprehensive review of this line of research, see Daniel J. O'Keefe, *Persuasion: Theory and Research.* Newbury Park, Calif.: Sage, 1990; Michael G. Garko, "Perspectives on and Conceptualizations of Compliance and Compliance-Gaining," *Communication Quarterly* 38 (1990): 138–57; David R. Siebold, James G. Cantrill and Renee A. Meyers, "Communication and Interpersonal Influence," in *Handbook of Interpersonal Communication,* ed. Mark L. Knapp and Gerald R. Miller (Beverly Hills, Calif.: Sage, 1985), 551–611; and Gerald Miller, Frank Boster, Michael Roloff, and David Siebold, "Compliance-Gaining Message Strategies: A Typology and Some Findings Concerning Effects of Situational Differences," *Communication Monographs* 44 (1977): 37–51.
26. Lawrence R. Wheeless, Robert Barraclough, and Robert Stewart, "Compliance-Gaining and Power in Persuasion," in *Communication Yearbook 7,* ed. Robert N. Bostrom (Beverly Hills, Calif.: Sage, 1983), 105–45.
27. Robert Shuter, "The Centrality of Culture," *The Southern Communication Journal* 55 (1990): 237–49.
28. Ellen Berscheid, "Opinion Change and Communicator-Communicatee Similarity and Dissimilarity," *Journal of Personality and Social Psychology* 4 (1966): 670–80.
29. R. Axelrod, *The Evolution of Cooperation* (New York: Basic Books, 1984).
30. M. H. Bazerman, T. Magliozzi, and M. A. Neale, "Integrative Bargaining in a Competitive Market," *Organizational Behavior and Human Decision Processes* 35 (1985): 294–313.
31. William Keenan, Jr., "Drawing the Line," *Sales and Marketing Management* (August 1993): 36.
32. Gener Trumfio, "Ready! Set! Sell!" *Sales and Marketing Management,* (February 1994): 82.
33. Gary M. Grikscheit, Harold C. Cash, and W. J. Crissy. *Handbook of Selling* (New York: Ronald Press, 1981).
34. Melissa Campanelli and Thayer C. Taylor, "Meeting of the Minds," *Sales and Marketing Management* (December 1993): 80–85.
35. John J. McCarthy, *Secrets of Super Selling* (New York: Boardroom Books, Inc., 1982), 52.
36. Tom Hopkins, *How to Master the Art of Selling* (New York: Warner Books, 1982).
37. Ibid, 187.
38. Trumfio, "Ready! Set! Sell!", 84.
39. Jeffrey Gitomer, "Computer-Assisted Sales Pitch the Way of the Future," *Orlando Business Journal,* 5–11 April, 1996, 33.
40. Max Ways, "The Virtues, Dangers, and Limits of Negotiation," *Fortune,* 15 January, 1979. Copyright ©1979 Time, Inc. All rights reserved.

Interviewing:
Research Practices
and Procedures

10 The Survey Interview and Telephone Interview

The survey interview is a ubiquitous part of our lives. We are stopped on the street and asked our opinions. When we exit a polling booth, we are asked about our vote. We're asked to complete grocery store surveys, participate in marketing surveys in a mall, or answer questions about our household over the telephone. Most of us, or at least a member of our family, has answered census taker questions at our front door. The goal of each of these survey interviews is to provide valid and reliable data for the interested organization. Each survey is intended to better our lives and keep us informed. Survey interviews are an important part of any discussion about research interviewing.

Chapter 10 discusses how to prepare and plan for the survey interview, as well as how to design and conduct surveys to obtain the best results. Also, it closely explores the interviewer characteristics important for such an interview. Finally, it examines the uses of telephone interviews as applied to survey interviewing. This chapter is designed to accomplish three objectives:

1. *Awareness.* You will understand the nature of surveys and polls and will gain fundamental knowledge of how surveys are conducted via pencil-and-paper, as well as by telephone.

2. *Assessment.* You will be able to construct appropriate questions and scales and accurately analyze the results, thus being able to evaluate whether you've successfully conducted a survey/telephone interview.

3. *Application.* You will be able to apply your understanding of survey/telephone approaches and participate effectively as an interviewer or interviewee.

*   *   *   *   *

Busy Work or Necessary Detail: Surveying Opinions in the Business Community

Dawn Rooth had just sat down at her desk when the phone rang again. She answered the call, although she expressed irritation aloud at the continuing interruptions to her morning. She had an important project due at 11:00 a.m. and needed some time to polish her presentation. Her staff assistant hadn't arrived yet, and the phone had rung continuously since 8:00 a.m. Her position as president of Rooth Realty Group challenged her, and it was truly energizing, but recently she seemed barely able to stay ahead of her company's rapid growth. Her company currently employed thirty realtors and was establishing itself in the community as a solid residential properties group.

The voice on the phone was Jennifer Hudnall, director of the local Chamber of Commerce. She greeted Dawn warmly and began explaining the purpose of her call. Jennifer and Dawn were longtime friends, so Dawn smiled and relaxed in her chair. For Jennifer this was the first of twenty-five scheduled phone interviews today. A team of other interviewers she trained were assisting her with other calls. The Chamber of Commerce had mailed questionnaires to all its members two months earlier to assess the business community's attitudes toward the economic impact of Loop 49, a proposed new outer loop on the city's south side. Jennifer's follow-up calls were designed to verify the questionnaire's results.

Surprisingly, the Chamber's survey had revealed what Jennifer thought to be conflicting results. Apparently, the questionnaire indicated local business leaders were negatively inclined toward the construction of the new loop because they believed it would have a significant environmental impact. The survey had also indicated that the business leaders were neutral and even negative toward relocating their businesses near the new loop. However, from Jennifer's own conversations, she had learned most were positive toward the new loop and thought it would have little effect on the environment. The Chamber had approved telephone interviews to followup on the questionnaires' results. Jennifer was seeking to gain objective community opinions about the project. She hoped her efforts would settle the issue for good.

Dawn quickly granted Jennifer's request for a ten-minute telephone interview. As their conversation began, Jennifer oriented Dawn to the topic, although Dawn was already familiar with some of the controversy surrounding the questionnaire's results. Dawn had heard critics on television oppose the project because of the anticipated environmental impact and its closeness to an elementary school. They also believed that the city's traffic problems would not be helped by the new loop. Despite these objections, Dawn also knew business leaders were favorable and that the city would benefit as a whole with the additional east/west traffic flow. For her company, she felt the proposed roadway would open prime real estate opportunities over the next ten years. She eagerly participated in the interview.

Discussion Questions

1. What ethical issues surround Jennifer Hudnall's telephone interviews? In believing that the survey results are incorrect, can she be objective when asking questions?
2. How would you describe the purpose of Jennifer Hudnall's telephone interview? Write a simple, standardized introduction to begin the interview.
3. What is the best approach Jennifer can take in designing and structuring her telephone interviews?
4. When selecting interviewers to help her, how will Jennifer ensure that the telephone interviews will be standardized? How will she make certain that her interviewers do not bias results?
5. Write five sample demographic questions that Jennifer Hudnall can use in her survey. Include nominal and interval type question formats.

Preparing for the Survey Interview

In 1887, English writer Sir Arthur Conan Doyle created a fictional character, Sherlock Holmes, as a legendary mastermind detective. Mr. Holmes was characterized as one who used purely scientific reasoning to solve crimes and make startling deductions from seemingly trivial, insignificant details. He had the uncanny ability to observe tiny bits of physical evidence overlooked by others and draw amazing conclusions. Similarly, survey research may be likened to the good detective work done by Mr. Holmes. The researcher must understand how to conduct the survey interview, know the right questions to ask, wisely interpret answers, and draw accurate conclusions from data results and analysis. As a type of detective, the researcher must look beyond the obvious to discover true answers. As some have noted, survey methods may be viewed "as the strategies researchers use to solve puzzling mysteries about the world. Like any good detective, researchers want to make sense of what's unknown."[1]

The survey interview is an ideal tool for discovering "tiny bits" of information important to a research topic. Audible and visual communication with the respondent permits the researcher to observe feelings or attitudes, or probe unclear areas. The way the respondent answers a question yields key nonverbal information for the researcher. The interviewer, talking to the respondent personally, can win cooperation and hold it throughout the interview. By establishing a relationship with the respondent, the interviewer can put puzzle pieces together that aid the researcher in validating information.

As two parties interact during the traditional interview, most of the information takes the form of words rather than numbers. Although the statements made by the respondent can be put into numerical form, standard interviews yield **qualitative** information for the researcher to use. In contrast, paper-and-pencil methods or telephone surveys yield **quantitative** data, information that takes the form of numbers rather than words. Words are rich in content and may contain stories, illustrations, or personal examples. They give breadth and depth of information to the researcher, a depth that cannot be obtained from mail or telephone surveys. However, "quantitative methods are appropriate (1) when measurement can offer a useful description of whatever you are studying, (2) when you may wish to make certain descriptive generalizations about the measures, and (3) when you wish to calculate probabilities that are beyond simple, chance occurrences."[2] Steinar Kvale sums up this qualitative/quantitative distinction nicely when he observes that *"quality* refers to what kind, to the essential character of something . . . *quantity* refers to how much, how large, the amount of something."[3] Quantitative research is just one among many methods of research. The main distinguishing characteristic is that measurement is used, and various mathematical formulas and procedures, called statistics, are used to assist in making generalizations or in testing hypotheses. Quantitative research methods are seen as no better (or worse) than qualitative counterparts; mainly, the criterion for determining which to use is appropriateness to the subject or phenomena under study. Therefore, like any good detective, the interviewer's ability to probe with words and numbers makes the survey interview a valuable tool to gather quantitative and qualitative information.

Determining Survey Purpose and Goals

The goal of the survey interview is to obtain reliable and valid information about a particular research question. The survey interview is a tool that aids the researcher in investigating factual details about topics; verifies existing research information, such as personal interviews; and explains a topic by quantitatively examining attitudes and feelings. Questionnaires are widely used to obtain facts about past, present, and anticipated events, conditions, and practices. Through survey interviews, you can "investigate (1) where you have been by analyzing and interpreting the past, (2) where you are now by examining present services or markets, (3) where you might go in the future by investigating desires for new directions, and (4) what you have to do to accomplish your goals."[4] This unique type of interview gives the researcher insight into the human condition and allows subjects to convey to others their situation.

The survey interview is widely used today and has become a common tool in data gathering. For some studies or certain phases of them, presenting respondents with carefully selected and ordered questions is the only practical way to elicit the data required to confirm or disconfirm a hypothesis. Marketing researchers investigate customers wants and needs through survey interviews, learning specifically how to target new products and services. Politicians verify their constituents' feelings about proposing specific legislation through mail and telephone survey interviews. Community leaders may verify a consultant's report through survey interviews before adopting an expensive recommendation for the city. City planners may use survey interviews to explain why the population in the city's north side has dropped dramatically. The purpose and goals of a survey interview can vary greatly, and each researcher will want to choose the specific purpose that obtains reliable and valid knowledge of the topic or question.

Time constraints, limited financial resources, and the availability of trained interviewers are also factors that must be taken into account before undertaking a series of survey interviews. These factors grow out of the research purpose and goals, and they, in turn, shape the kinds and types of interviews conducted. The length of the interview, for instance, would be an important factor if patrons of a retail business were surveyed as they exit a store. Grocery shoppers may give five minutes to answer a store manager's questions, but requesting fifteen or twenty minutes of their time may be unrealistic. A member of a focus group interview, on the other hand, willingly gives between one and two hours to discuss a topic in detail. Moreover, the number of interviewers who can conduct surveys will be determined by budget and financial resources. Conducting survey interviews can be a costly and time-consuming process. The number and kind of interviews you consider will ultimately be based on the purpose and goals of the research project.

Ethical Issues

Ethical issues must also be considered when planning to use survey interviews. Because the knowledge gained from surveys direct policy decisions that affect peoples' lives, ethical guidelines should be applied throughout the interview process. These guidelines pertain to such issues as confidentiality, the nature of sensitive questions, and consent to participate in the survey.

At least three factors should be considered when thinking about ethics in the survey interview: (1) informed consent, (2) confidentiality, and (3) outcomes. Informed consent means keeping the interviewees informed about the overall purpose and goals of the research, making sure their participation is voluntary, and explaining how the information will be used. Who should give the informed consent must also be considered. If a researcher is surveying young children, for example, must consent be given by the children themselves, their parents, or a designated authority, such as a teacher, camp leader, or pastor.

Deciding *how much* information should be given and *when* is another aspect of informed consent. For example, when conducting a survey, the researcher will want to initially inform group participants of the general purpose of the research. However, only after the discussion has concluded will the researcher fully debrief participants about specific details of the research purpose, telling them how the information will be used. Otherwise, full disclosure of the purpose may bias the direction of the survey interview. Full disclosure in informed consent also rules out deception and manipulation of the interviewees. Manipulation may be keeping information from the interviewee for the purposes of obtaining a certain outcome in the survey. To prevent deception is essential to review a survey's design and peruse interview questions prior to beginning the actual interviews.

Confidentiality is a second factor to consider when establishing ethical guidelines. Confidentiality means that an individual's responses will not be identified or that answers will not be reported individually. Results are confidential when all interviewees' data are reported together in aggregate form, not individually. Although the interviewer may ask for personal information, confidentiality is maintained by keeping that information private. In contrast, answers are anonymous when individuals are not identified in the research. Mail surveys, for instance, usually maintain anonymous answers because the researcher does not know who completed the survey.

A third ethical factor that should guide the research purpose is the consequence or outcome of the interview. The researcher will want to assess how the benefits of the interviews outweigh the potential harm for the interviewees. If results are made public, the researcher will want to ask how the outcomes will affect the participants and the groups they represent. Thus, both benefits and harms of the interviews should be considered. The interviewer and interviewee should fully understand what outcomes the research study will have on the parties involved. The moral implications potentially affecting a survey interview project must be determined and seriously reviewed.

*   *   *   *   *

Jennifer Hudnall works as director of a neutral community organization and will most likely be perceived as neutral toward the Loop 49 issue by business leaders. Personally, she can maintain her own objectivity as she asks questions and probes for answers during the telephone interviews. If a business leader is not informed about the controversy, she will want to be prepared to respond to questions about the Loop. Jennifer will need to determine prior to the interviews how much information she will discuss. She will also want to express confidentiality about the interview by including a statement such as, "Your opinions today will be kept confidential. We will combine results from all our interviews before reporting results." Finally, Jennifer may want to state how the results will be reported to the community.

Jennifer must constantly be cognizant of the Loop controversy and take into consideration the potential biases of respondents. Certainly, Dawn Rooth has a personal business interest in the proposed Loop and also being a friend of Jennifer may influence her responses. Consequently, Jennifer will want to carefully design and structure the survey questions before conducting the interview.

Design and Structure of the Survey Interview

Good research requires one to clearly define the problem and determine the specific information needed. It is only when you know the specific problem areas that you want to investigate that you will begin to design and structure the survey interview. The initial design and structure of the survey interview will include making a brief guide that outlines the general points and adapts to the survey length. The moderate structure of the guide should be clear and allow for flexibility, adapting the topic to the interviewees interests, personality, and knowledge level. A university administrator, for example, interviewed key alumni about why they gave money to the university. After the interviews began, the administrator realized that his questions were not on target. Alumni were not giving financially to programs in the way he thought. They were designating most of their funds toward specific academic programs in which their own children were enrolled, not toward the general university fund. After a few preliminary interviews, the administrator developed key questions about family and children and their future education. By planning flexibility into the guide, the interviewer can adapt to the interviewees interests, personality, and knowledge level. However, while some flexibility is desirable, it is also essential to treat everyone alike. In order to be rigorous about obtaining information, the researcher must not vary the questions and must not vary the style.

Establishing Rapport and Eliciting Honest Replies

To establish rapport and elicit honest replies, the interviewer must first ask several important questions about the design and structure. Does the survey explain clearly the purpose of the study, indicate that the investigation is sponsored by a reputable institution, arouse interest in contributing accurate information, and offer to provide respondents with a summary of the findings? Are directions and questions worded and ordered to allay any fears, suspicions, embarrassment, or hostility on the part of the respondent? If personal questions are asked, is a guarantee of anonymity given, or is there assurance that the responses will be held in strict confidence? Are respondents asked for information concerning subjects about which they have sufficient knowledge? Are specific questions asked in order to check the truthfulness of answers to general questions? Is the study of sufficient importance to warrant asking busy people to answer the questions? The answers to these questions can nurture cooperation, build rapport, and ensure valid, reliable responses.

Unique to the survey interview, you will want to create **natural involvement** with the interviewee. The interviewer creates this environment through introductory comments that "convey an interest in and a supportive attitude toward the interviewee's life and work."[5] This helps to establish some commonalty with the interviewee and garner support. Creating natural involvement provides a smooth transition into the formal interview, lessens anxiety and tension, and encourages openness on the topic.

Similarly, the conclusion should maintain this natural involvement as the interview draws to an end. This is a good time to introduce additional information or explanation about the research. If the respondent wants to discuss the topic or project, allow time for answering questions. Participants will be most responsive and candid if you can demonstrate that the project is worth their time and that they will receive some intrinsic or extrinsic reward for participating. You want to make it a pleasant and beneficial communication experience for the interviewee.

Preparing the Questionnaire

Preparing the questionnaire involves consistency in approach among interviews, finding the appropriate structure of the questionnaire, and developing question strategies that fit the survey interview. Perhaps the most important consideration of these tasks is achieving consistency from interview to interview. Clearly, the survey interview differs from other types of interviews. The selection interview, appraisal interview, and counseling interview require you to be flexible in your approach, adapting questions to the interviewee's style and personality. Questions may be worded differently in each interview as the interviewer adapts to the interviewee. In contrast, you want to ask survey questions in a like manner from respondent to respondent. Otherwise, you may influence or bias the survey information you receive. To obtain accurate and reliable information from the survey, set a goal of asking questions uniformly in each interview.

The structure of the questionnaire is another important factor in conducting an effective survey interview. Recall from chapter 2 that the interview structure can follow a funnel, inverted funnel, tunnel sequence, or several other formats. You may want to review these formats before developing your questionnaire. Similar to an actual interview, the survey questionnaire should adopt a structure that best meets the research purpose and the sample being studied.

Finally, question strategies and questionnaire structures will vary depending on the objectives and goals of the research project. When developing strategy and structure, researchers suggest three general guidelines to follow when preparing the questionnaire: (1) demographic questions should come first, (2) questions about the same topic should be linked together, and (3) the format of scales used should be varied (that is, reverse the polarities throughout a questionnaire) to minimize the tendency for respondents to get into a question/response set.[6]

Types and Uses of Questions

Ultimately, the value of survey interviews rests on the kinds and quality of questions the interviewer asks. Questions are essential tools integral to the survey's results. They determine whether valid and reliable information are obtained. The question types also determine the kinds of responses given, affecting the outcome of the survey. However, asking questions that will obtain the precise data required is no easy task. When making important decisions about survey design, several factors must be considered when constructing the questionnaire: (1) the question format, (2) the question content or type, and (3) the way questions are ordered.

A researcher may cast questions in a closed, an open, or a pictorial form, using one type exclusively or a combination of them when structuring the questionnaire. The nature of the problem and the character of the respondents determine which form or forms will most likely supply the desired data. Robert Kahn and Charles Cannell suggest five factors to consider when making this decision: (1) the purposes and objectives of the interview, (2) the respondent's knowledge level about the topic, (3) the degree to which the respondent has thought through the topic, (4) the ability and willingness of the respondent to freely answer, and (5) the degree to which the previous factors are known to the interviewer.[7]

Closed-form or **structured questionnaires** usually consist of a prepared list of specific, concrete questions and a choice of possible answers. To indicate their reply, respondents mark "yes" or "no;" check, circle, or underscore one or more items from a list of answers; or rank a series of statements in the order of their importance (1, 2, 3, . . .). Closed-form questionnaires keep the respondent's mind riveted on the subject, facilitate the process of tabulation and analysis, and are useful in gaining large amounts of information in a short time. Also, because most researchers want statistical information from surveys, closed questions are preferable. If the researcher needs to present statistical trends to a board or supervisor, answers from closed questions can be easily quantified, yielding reliable and valid results.[8]

However, closed questions often fail to reveal the respondent's motives, do not always yield information of sufficient scope or depth, and may not discriminate between fine shades of meaning. Fixed alternative responses may make respondents take a stand on issues about which they have no crystallized opinion or may force them to give answers that do not accurately express their ideas. Moreover, the listed alternative answers may be placed in an order that encourages the respondent to rely in accordance with the researcher's wishes. If proper precautions are taken in constructing the questionnaire, however, these potential weaknesses can be overcome. To avoid biasing the results by placing the desired answers in the most conspicuous place, for example, items in a checklist may be randomized. Yes/no, true/false, and agree/disagree questions may be improved upon by inserting a third choice, such as "undecided" or "no opinion." Also, researchers may leave a blank for comments where the respondent may clarify, amplify, or qualify their answers.

Rather than forcing respondents to choose between rigidly limited responses, the **open-form questionnaire** permits them to answer freely and fully in their own words and from their own frame of reference. This method of collecting data gives the subjects an opportunity to reveal their motives or attitudes and to specify the background or provisional conditions upon which their answers are based. Generally, open questions provide a better format for a survey when a researcher initially begins the investigation, since they work well when the respondent knows little about the topic or has had little experience with it, and the interviewer wants to find out how much the respondent knows.

However, there are some disadvantages associated with the open-form questionnaire. When subjects have no clues to guide their thinking, they may unintentionally omit important information or fail to note sufficient details. Moreover, if subjects are not highly literate and willing to give considerable time and critical thought to questions, they cannot provide useful data. Also, open questions tend to be more difficult to code and tabulate for the researcher. If someone were asked, "How do you feel about President Clinton's administration?" the investigator may be presented with a broad array of possible answers. Opinions may be directed personally toward the president, the U.S. economy, foreign policy, defense spend-ing, education, or taxes, all reflecting on how the respondent feels about the current administration. The researcher is then required to categorize the respondent's com-plex answer, allowing interpretation and possible interviewer bias to influence the answer. These drawbacks must be taken into consideration during question design.

Some questionnaires present respondents with drawings or photographs rather than written statements from which to choose answers. This form of ques-tionnaire is a particularly suitable tool for gathering data from children and adults with limited reading ability. Pictures often capture the attention of respondents more readily than printed words, lessen subjects' resistance to responding, and stimulate their interest in the questions. Also, pictures may depict clearly some situations that do not lend themselves readily to verbal descriptions or may en-able one to detect attitudes or to gather information that could not be tapped by other procedures. However, a pictorial format can be used only in limited situa-tions involving distinguishable and understandable visual characteristics and is particularly difficult to standardize.

Questions should be stated in clear, simple language and be focused sharply on specific points. All questions should be framed to elicit unambiguous answers. This requires that the question as understood by the researcher be the same as the ques-tion as understood by the respondent; it also requires that the answer as understood by the respondent be the same as the answer as understood by the researcher. Cer-tain structured questioning types and scaling techniques can assist the researcher in this regard. **Paired comparisons** ask the respondent to make a choice between two alternatives. The **semantic differential** exposes respondents to a series of bipolar adjectives, such as warm/cold, competent/incompetent, or active/passive for which they indicate their relative degree of feeling or attitude toward the subject or topic. **Rank order** assesses people's priorities and the degree of importance given a list of items. Finally, **rating scales** can provide direct information about respon-dents' degree of preference by indicating on a continuum the strength of their feel-ings. Questionnaires are often subject to severe criticism, but many common weak-nesses can be avoided if they are structured carefully and categories, format, and directions are designed to elicit accurate, unambiguous answers facilitating the tab-ulation and interpretation of data, which permits the quantification of results.

Last, the sequencing or ordering of questions can assist participants in re-sponding appropriately and contribute to the analysis and interpretation of the survey. Questions should be arranged in a logical sequence with simple, interest-ing, neutral questions preceding more difficult, crucial, or personal ones and those that establish a frame of reference or provide keys to recall before those ask-ing for details. The funnel, inverted funnel, and tunnel structures are commonly used when sequencing questions.

Piloting the Questionnaire

Once we have determined the questionnaire items and the scales, it should be pi-loted. We pilot questionnaires to make sure that they are providing reliable in-formation. The instructions should be understandable to the population receiving the questionnaire. We also want to make sure that each item on the questionnaire is correctly understood by the respondent. In addition, we want to ensure that respondents correctly understand each point on the rating scales.[9]

Select a sample from each group that will be receiving a questionnaire, and arrange for each of the groups to meet with you in a room where you can observe them completing the questionnaire. Distribute the questionnaire with its instruction sheet to the participants, but do not answer any questions unless they are totally unable to complete the questionnaire. Note the time when each person begins to complete the questionnaire and the time when each person has concluded it. As the questionnaire is being completed, observe any particular questions or pages that appear to cause difficulty. It can be helpful to ask participants to make a check mark next to any question they find unclear; this helps them locate those questions during the debriefing. Once all of the individuals have completed the questionnaire, go through it page by page, asking participants to indicate any questions they found confusing or difficult to answer. Look for patterns of feedback from the respondents. When someone indicates a difficulty, ask whether anyone else experienced the same difficulty. Be certain to ask participants what needs to be done to improve the questionnaire. What suggestions can they offer you? Also, be certain to take notes on the information being given to you and be prepared to answer questions from the participants about the study. People often want to know why the study is being done and how they were selected to be a part of the pilot. This provides you with an opportunity to build interest in the assessment before it is distributed to a larger population. Based upon the results of the pilot, the questionnaire is revised. If major revisions are required, it is wise to pilot the questionnaire again. If small revisions are required, then the questionnaire is ready to be distributed.

In sum, when designing and structuring the survey interview, we recommend the following procedures: (1) clarify the purpose of the data collection, (2) determine the questions and rating scales to be used, (3) design and pilot the questionnaires, (4) revise the questionnaire, and (5) distribute the questionnaires to selected participants. To ensure a good response, it is important to include a cover letter describing the purpose of the questionnaire, the sponsors of the project, its importance to the person completing the questionnaire, the length of time it takes to complete the questionnaire, where and how to return the questionnaire, and what information the respondent will receive about the results of the study.

* * * * *

Jennifer Hudnell was in one sense a detective who was trying to unravel conflicting information about the business community's attitudes toward the new Loop. Her main purpose was to obtain valid and reliable information from business leaders about their attitudes and feelings. Because of the in-depth, probing nature of the telephone interviews, she hoped to ascertain how business leaders truly felt about relocating their businesses on the new Loop and learn about their perceptions of the

Loop's environmental impact. With these goals in mind, she could begin her interview in the following manner: "Hello, my name is Jennifer Hudnell. I'm director of the area Chamber of Commerce. We are interviewing selected local business leaders throughout the city who have responded to our recent questionnaire. We want to briefly ask some follow-up questions about your attitudes and feelings toward the new Loop. (NOTE: Because the survey requires an interview with business leaders, the first question may be about who answers the phone. If someone besides the manager or owner answers, Jennifer will want her call to be directed to the right person.)

Jennifer can best prepare for the survey interview by developing a series of well-designed questions to ask over the telephone. The questions should be specifically worded and concern business leaders' feelings about the environmental impact of the proposed Loop. The tunnel sequence, a string of similar type questions organized topically, may fit her purpose. Jennifer Hudnall might ask the following questions about the new loop: As a business leader, do you approve or disapprove of the new Loop 49 bypass? Do you think Loop 49 will help or hurt traffic congestion in the southern part of the city? Do you think the economic impact of the project will be positive or negative on the city's economy? Are you interested in remaining in your current location or relocating near the new bypass? Certainly, she will want to read questions exactly as they are written to avoid bias in the results. She also can prepare possible probing questions and anticipate potential questions. Because respondent's knowledge about the topic will be high, she will want to use closed questions that target specific attitudes. Open questions could be used if business leaders had not heard about the Loop and she needed to discover their level of knowledge.

Conducting the Survey Interview

No matter how well you prepare for the survey interview, not conducting it properly will prevent you from achieving your purpose. Conducting a successful survey interview poses a difficult challenge for the interviewer. It is not an easy task to obtain valid and reliable information, but good results can be achieved through cautiously choosing respondents, carefully selecting and training interviewers and properly administering the interview.

Selecting Respondents

Selecting appropriately relevant respondents is one of the most important considerations you will have to make. When considering possible respondents, you will want to target those who can most directly relate to the topic or problem of investigation. These are the people who can provide the most valid and reliable information. If the total targeted population is small, the entire group might be surveyed. However, when the potential population is large, a representative sample must be chosen for the survey. A stratified, random procedure can yield statistically significant results and be cost effective. A **stratified sample** means you try to cover people in all sex, race, age, or income levels that are important to the study. A **random selection** means that theoretically each person within the targeted group has just as much probability of being selected for an interview as any other person in the potential population. Taken together, this approach can help reduce research error. Moreover, mailed questionnaires to selected respondents may reach many people in widely scattered areas quickly and at a relatively low cost. Unfortunately, however, returns do not always bound back with equal celerity, and partial returns may introduce a bias that will render the obtained data useless. Therefore, if you expect a return rate of 80 percent, you need to increase the number of questionnaires sent by 25 percent. In this manner, you will have some certainty that whatever results you obtain are, in fact, generalizable.[10] The ultimate objective is to survey the relevant population, and this may involve using a statistically appropriate sampling procedure.

Choosing and Training Interviewers

A well-designed survey will still produce poor results if interviewers do not have the right characteristics, experience, and training to properly ask questions and record answers. Not all interviewers conduct the interview in the same way. Some communicate well with people, relating and adapting to individual respondents. Other interviewers fail to establish rapport, ask questions in a leading manner, or make numerous errors in recording answers. Others may skip questions or leave portions of the survey incomplete. To avoid these problems, what characteristics should a researcher look for in an interviewer? What types of interviewer ensure the best results?

Of all the factors a researcher may want to consider, education is one of the most important interviewer characteristics. Most national polling organizations require a college education when hiring interviewers. A researcher will also want to require strong interpersonal skills. A good interviewer is cognizant of nonverbal communication and adapts to a respondent. Age is another characteristic to consider. Young interviewers tend to be informal, lack interviewing experience, and make more errors when conducting a survey. Older interviewers tend to commit fewer errors and follow the script. Reading questions and writing answers are minimal competencies for interviewers. However, the researcher will want to train and direct interviewers to ask questions in a neutral manner and record answers in an unbiased way. Specifically, individuals who can conduct successful survey interviews will be able to complete the interviews, handle refusals professionally, and keep terminations to a minimum.[11] Finding individuals who can meet these requirements and training them is time consuming, but in the end, it will enhance survey results.

Administering the Survey

Floyd Fowler and Thomas Mangione have suggested four basic steps involved in administering the survey interview. Following these steps will help ensure that the interviewer obtains accurate and reliable results: (1) reading questions as they are designed on the survey, (2) probing incomplete questions in a neutral manner, (3) recording answers without error, and (4) communicating nonevaluatively about the topic.[12]

It is critical for the interviewer to *read questions as written.* This is seemingly a simple and easy rule to follow, but studies have found that about one-third (20 to 40 percent) of interviewers modify questions from the written, standard format, and most change a question at least once and many ten times or more.[13] Interviewers alter questions for a variety of reasons. They may not understand the question and want to paraphrase it in their own words to make it more understandable, or a question may be difficult to read for the interviewer and it is restated in simpler terms. Interviewers may also emphasize certain words or phrases, which can change the question. What effect do these word changes or "personal touches" have on the results of a survey? Howard Schuman and Stanley Presser reported significant differences from respondents in these two questions: (1) Should Communists be forbidden to speak in public places in the United States? and (2) Should Communists not be allowed to speak in public places in the United States? In responding to these questions, approximately 20 percent of the respondents said the United States should "forbid Communists to speak," while nearly 50 percent said the United States should "not allow Communists to speak." Clearly the substitution of "not allowed" for "forbid" significantly influenced the survey results.[14] Whenever questions are not read exactly as written, the researcher cannot be sure of the validity of the results. Generally, interviewers who have been trained to read questions exactly as written and who have good interviewing skills will obtain unbiased results.

Although questions may be read exactly as written, respondents may not answer a question adequately. If a question is answered unsatisfactorily or incompletely, the interviewer must *probe incomplete questions in a neutral manner.* A variety of questionnaire problems may create difficulties for respondents. Respondents may not understand the intent of a question or its applicability to them, or they may not understand the meaning of a word in the question. Also, during telephone surveys, respondents may not actively listen to the question when its being read. Often, these difficulties can be resolved by rereading the question or providing appropriate clarification. As long as interviewers consistently answer questions about terms, they will obtain reliable results. However, design and wording problems are best worked out ahead of time during the piloting phase.

Not only must interviewers read questions as written and effectively probe incomplete answers, they must *record answers neutrally* (without error) in a descriptive, nonjudgmental manner. This is critical for successfully conducting the survey interview and obtaining valid information. For closed questions, "recording without bias" may simply mean circling a "yes/no" or checking an appropriate box. When asking open questions in a survey, the interviewer must record the respondent's answers verbatim. Any interpretation or editing may prejudice the answer. If the questions tend to be objective and factual, the interviewer may choose to record key words only without affecting survey results. For example, when responding to "Tell me about your sports activities," the interviewer may want to write down names of sports only as key words.

Finally, the interviewer will want to remain *nonevaluative about the topic* throughout the interview. Interviewers do not want to disclose personal predispositions that might influence a respondent's answer during the survey interview. Certainly, some factors that might influence the respondent's answer the interviewer cannot control. An individual's perception of another's social status, age, gender, appearance, and culture tend to effect the outcome of research results but are beyond the control of the interviewer.[15] Other factors the interviewer can control. An interviewer's positive view toward a survey topic may result in communicating positive expectations about an answer. The popular concept of "self-fulfilling prophecy," well documented in psychological literature, occurs when an interviewer's expectation of an answer influences the respondent's answer. It is usually subtle, nonverbal expectations, such as vocal inflection or a smile that influence respondents. Therefore, researchers should instruct interviewers not to express feelings about the topic or volunteer personal information of any kind. This can be controlled through well-designed surveys and by training the interviewers.

*   *   *   *   *

To ensure that the telephone interviews will be standardized, Jennifer Hudnall will want to produce written training materials for interviewers to read. The materials can be detailed and extensive, such as a training manual. However, she may also want to draft several sets of guidelines that explain how to administer the interviews. The materials should include explanations on recording data neutrally, how to handle refusals properly, and explain how to ask probing questions in a neutral manner.

To lessen interviewer bias, Jennifer will want to monitor each interviewer on a regular basis. She will need to listen to a complete conversation on about every tenth telephone interview. With her knowledge of interviewing, she can evaluate the interviewer's performance and, if necessary, correct errors or techniques that may bias information. A written checklist would be helpful. Having written criteria set before hand will help interviewers understand what is expected and keep the focus positive. After a call has been monitored, Jennifer will want to give immediate feedback. Going over the form with the interviewer will provide objective feedback.

Analyzing the Results

To obtain valid and reliable results from the survey interview, the researcher must accurately code, tabulate, and analyze the results. If a survey has been properly planned and the questionnaire well designed, the analysis stage will be easy. It will seem to naturally flow from the interviews themselves. However, if questions were poorly designed, the analysis stage will pose difficulties for the researcher no matter how well it is done. Good questions must be written prior to the interviews. Understanding how to write good questions, code, and tabulate their answers will aid the researcher in obtaining accurate data.

To understand the concepts of reliability and validity in survey research, picture an outdoor thermometer hanging on a tree near your window. Assume the thermometer is round, about twelve to fourteen inches in diameter, and can easily be read from your window. You know from experience, however, that the thermometer is not accurate; it consistently shows four degrees warmer than the actual air temperature. Whether the temperature is warm or cold, the thermometer consistently reads high, and you arrive at the actual temperature by subtracting four degrees. Although it is inaccurate, the reading on the thermometer is reliable because it is consistently high. Reliability implies dependability and stability, although the measurement may be inaccurate. On the other hand, the thermometer is invalid in its measure of the outside air temperature because of the instrument's inaccuracy. Therefore, a thermometer is both reliable and accurate only when it shows correctly the actual air temperature and does so reliably.

Survey interviewers who are consistent in their approach with each respondent, who establish objective question strategies, and who carefully prepare the questionnaire will more easily obtain accurate and reliable research results. Surveys can have internal and external validity. When a survey's conclusions are accurate, it is considered to have internal validity. In other words, we can depend on the survey's findings to be true. When these findings can be generalized to outside people and contexts, the survey's findings have external validity.

The personal computer has made tabulation of questionnaires relatively simple and inexpensive. Because computer hardware and software are changing at such a rapid rate, we will not describe either the hardware or software required for data tabulation. Instead, we will focus on how the format of questions affects the analysis stage, as well as the data required for the output report and suggest that you use a local resource for more information about computer hardware and software. Constructing questions and answers properly best aids the researcher's analysis. Remember, the goal of the survey interview is to obtain the most valid and reliable data possible. Each step in the survey interview is essential to reaching this goal, but the analysis step is critical to getting accurate results for the eventual report. Coding questions in various ways will result in different types or levels of information. To show how questions can be coded and analyzed, consider the following illustration.

Assume as a researcher, you want to examine current viewer preferences of customers who rent movies at a local video store, which is part of a nationwide chain, and relate that information to customer age, gender, location of residence, and income level. You have obtained permission to use mail surveys and personal interviews to contact the customers about what they like and dislike in movies. The store has over thirty-five categories of movies, ranging from Alfred Hitchcock mysteries to science fiction, but nine categories seem to be chosen more often. To obtain information on a simple level about customers' viewing habits, you could draft a question such as the following:

> Check the three most frequent movie categories you have rented during the last month.
>
> ___ Action ___ Children's ___ Classics ___ Comedy ___ Drama
>
> ___ Family ___ Horror ___ New Releases ___ Science Fiction ___ Other

You can easily count and tally the results, getting a basic idea of customers' preferences in renting movies. The results could be reported to the store management with the outcome possibly influencing the stocking and availability of certain types of films. Listing categories in this manner is called **nominal measurement,** and it is the simplest type of measurement that can be used in your analysis. Nominal categories are descriptive and do not rank order the responses. In the video store example, the customer was asked to check the three most frequent rental categories and not to rank them in any way.

To accurately code and tabulate a nominal scale, several rules or qualities apply to their construction. First, the categories must not overlap, otherwise the results will be misleading. In the video store survey, the rental categories are designated by a standard label, and movies whose content fits that primary classification are placed into that category by the store management. Comedies, for example, may have dramatic content and some action but receive a classification as a comedy because of their primary content. Second, nominal categories must be similar in their type and content, otherwise the results will be confusing. Thus, in our example, Nintendo or Sega game rentals would not be considered "video rentals," since they cannot be compared in the same category as movies. Third, categories must cover all possibilities, otherwise the results will be incomplete. What if a customer had rented a "mystery" but found no category in which to reply? By listing the "other" category, you ensure that all possibilities are covered.

The use of nominal categories is common in most surveys and provides rich descriptive information. Designing good categories initially will help during coding, tabulation, and analysis. Analyzing nominal data statistically is limited to percentages, frequency counts, or other simple statistical procedures. Other types of scales allow for more sophisticated analysis.

To understand the second level of measurement, assume you changed the question about customers' preferences in the following way:

> Rank the top three categories in which you have rented the most movies during the last month, where 1 = highest and 3 = lowest.
>
> _1_ Action ___ Children's ___ Classics ___ Comedy _3_ Drama
>
> ___ Family ___ Horror _2_ New Releases ___ Science Fiction ___ Other

Now, not only do customers indicate their preferences for movies by categories, their responses are ranked from "highest" to "lowest." Again, you can easily tabulate the responses, however, you have obtained a different level of information and can report which category of movies customers prefer the most, which category is second, and which is third. This second level of measurement is an **ordinal response** and requests respondents to rank categories and place responses in order.

Finally, **interval scales** not only rank and categorize information, but they also indicate *how strong* the degree of preference. Interval scales can measure the range of attitudes and feelings by giving the respondent a number of choices from which to choose. Using a three-point scale, you might ask:

> Do you usually find the video selection you want?
>
> _____ Yes _____ Sometimes _____ No

To code and tabulate this question, you would record "1" if the person checked "yes", "2" if "sometimes" was checked, and "3" if "no" was the response. Thus, you could easily determine what percent of the sample was generally satisfied with the service they received. However, the three-point scale would be improved by rewording the question(s) and giving it a five-point scale:

> Indicate how strongly you agree or disagree with each statement using the following key: 1 = strongly agree, 2 = agree, 3 = neutral, 4 = disagree, and 5 = strongly disagree.
>
> 1. _____ The video store has a good variety of rentals available.
> 2. _____ Store personnel are courteous to me when I have a question.
> 3. _____ Videos are always rewound when I rent them.
> 4. _____ Rental prices here are competitive with other video rental stories.
> 5. _____ The video store always has the selection I want.

The expanded scale permits a more discrete measurement of customer attitudes and feelings. Results from interval scales can be analyzed with powerful statistical tools and provide a wealth of information for the researcher.

Survey data lends itself to reporting, with the possible use of graphs and charts to make the results clear. The quantitative analysis precisely describes the situation and with the use of more sophisticated procedures can reveal the strength of attitudes and feelings. The main objective of the investigator is to present findings and note relationships.

*   *   *   *   *

To gather demographic information during her telephone interviews, Jennifer Hudnall will want to ask questions about local businesses. She will also want to gather personal information about the respondents. Sample questions might include:

1. Check the type of business that most closely applies to you:
   ( ) Manufacturing   ( ) Education/Training
   ( ) Finance/Insurance   ( ) Hospitality/Food Service
   ( ) Hospitals/Medical   ( ) Accounting
   ( ) Retail   ( ) Construction
                              ( ) Other _____

2. Circle your gender: Male Female

3. What is the size of your business?
   ( ) 1–15 employees
   ( ) 16–50 employees
   ( ) 51–100 employees
   ( ) 101–500 employees
   ( ) 500+ employees

4. Check your age category:
   ( ) under 25   ( ) 25–34   ( ) 35–44   ( ) 45–55   ( ) over 55

5. Number of years you've worked full time:
   ( ) less than 1   ( ) 1–5   ( ) 6–10   ( ) 11–20   ( ) more than 20

Jennifer will also want to use ordinal responses and interval scales to assess community leader's preferences and attitudes toward the proposed Loop. Taken together, this data should provide a clear picture regarding the potential environmental impact of Loop 49.

Telephone Interviewing

Telephone interviewing is one of the most common methods of conducting survey research. Almost everyone has a telephone, and conducting telephone interviews means reaching nearly every household in the United States. Random digit dialing bypasses the barrier of unlisted numbers and makes it easier to reach people in remote locations. Telephone interviewing has become widespread because of its costefficiency and speed of data collection.

Basically, researchers have three primary methods for collecting data: by mail, over the telephone, and through face-to-face interviews. Each of these methods must be considered when designing the survey interview, since each can positively or negatively affect the results of the survey. It has been suggested that the primary difference between these data collection methods "is the intensity of contact between the researcher and the respondents."[16] Mail surveys have the least intensity of contact with the respondent but give the researcher greater control over results. In personal interviews, the interviewer has the most complete contact with the respondent, receiving both audible and visual communication. The telephone interview permits moderate contact with the respondent and still retains considerable control of the situation. In this section, we will discuss the advantages and limitations of telephone interviews, as well as present some guidelines for conducting telephone interviews (also see chapter 14).

The deciding factor when choosing any data collection method should be the information needs of the survey. Telephone interviews can be inexpensively conducted over a short period of time and yield considerable information that possesses high validity and reliability. No other data collection technique allows for as quick a turnaround time as the telephone interview, and this savings in time has a monetary value. Cost is a primary consideration when deciding whether to choose telephone interviews as a method of data collection. Telephone interviews cost as little as one-fifth of the cost of face-to-face interviews in business-to-business research.[17] Moreover, unlike personal interviewing where respondents are often reluctant to participate, telephone interviewing has a lower refusal rate, allowing respondents anonymity and protection. This feeling of privacy further encourages respondents to answer frankly and candidly rather than in a socially desirable way.[18] Telephone interviews also permit easy follow up on questions and probing of answers if necessary. Finally, interviewers can be easily trained and supervised, ensuring a consistency in data collection and greater accuracy in results.

Besides reducing costs, technology is further changing the nature of the telephone interview. A company called PinPoint Research in California has developed a totally automated telephone interview system, eliminating the need for a live interviewer.[19] Totally automated telephone interviewing works by first inviting respondents to call a toll-free number. Invitations may be mailed or given to customers while in a store. A pleasant computer voice answers the toll-free call and asks respondents to punch numbers on the phone in response to questions. Typically, verbal data is recorded on audiotape. PinPoint claims that their system has conducted more than 750,000 telephone interviews, and apparently, the trend is catching on.

Still, there are some limitations to conducting interviews by telephone that must be recognized. One of the main limitations is that the interview agenda or questionnaire must be shorter for telephone use than for either personal interviews or mail surveys. In general, it is recommended that telephone interviews be kept under twenty minutes, with most averaging about ten minutes. This requires that the questionnaire be simple, focused, straight forward, and well written, since complicated instructions or explanations cannot be used over the telephone. Telephone interviewing is further criticized for not being able to collect highly personal information. Respondents may be cautious or defensive when asked to provide highly sensitive information, making such data difficult to obtain. Of course, a great deal depends on the interviewer's ability to establish rapport with respondents, and novel approaches can reduce refusals on sensitive topics in telephone surveys.[20] Finally, telephone interviewers must confront the problem of inconveniently interrupting individuals. However, courtesy and tact can often overcome this difficulty.

When designing and conducting telephone surveys, particular attention should be given to the introduction, since 80 percent of refusals occur between the introductory remarks and the first question. While you must introduce yourself and describe the "survey project" in general, your introduction needs to be brief in order to ask the first question as soon as possible and minimize the respondent's opportunities to refuse. Remember, never ask the respondent, "May I ask your opinion on a few questions?" since this opens the door for the interviewee to say, "No." The questions themselves should be simple, clear, and unambiguous, with special care being given to limiting rating scales and structuring lists of items. Again, brevity should be the goal, since the longer the interview, the greater the likelihood of a sudden termination. Finally, telephone interviews should be administered by trained interviewers following the practices we discussed earlier in the chapter. Being thoroughly prepared and thoroughly familiar with the interview guide should help guarantee success with any telephone interview.

* * * * *

Jennifer Hudnall should have a relatively easy time gaining the cooperation of community leaders to respond to her telephone interviews since the proposed Loop directly influences them. However, she will still want to keep the questionnaire brief and focused on the topic, since people like Dawn Rooth are busy, and their time is valuable. The telephone interviews should be cost efficient and will help clarify the results of the earlier mail questionnaire. Telephone interviewing is often used in conjunction with other forms of data collection. Jennifer's positive attitude and advance preparation promises rewarding results and should help ensure success.

Critical Focus

To illustrate the use of interviewing as a research tool, consider the innovation and reengineering occurring at Scholar Educational Products. Scholar Educational Products was started in 1946 by Olaf Erickson, a former teacher, who firmly believed there was a market for good, low-cost reference materials. He and his academic friends managed to assemble a variety of products, including illustrated state almanacs, a modern English dictionary, and an easy-to-read encyclopedia with yearly updates. A hard-driving door-to-door sales network, easy credit terms, and low prices combined to make the company's products well known among families with school-age children. The postwar baby boom and growing American families soon made Scholar Educational Products a prosperous company.

Scholar eventually branched out into related educational products, targeting elementary and secondary school students. Although these new products contributed to the company's profits, the almanacs, dictionaries, and encyclopedias remained the financial mainstay. Olaf Erickson retired as the CEO of Scholar

Educational Products in 1989, content with the regular and unchanging market share enjoyed by the company. However, when stepping down, he voiced a warning with board members and raised a question of critical concern, which gave direction to the executive search: "The whole educational products industry is going to get turned upside down by computers, electronic generated imagery, and interactive formats over the next few years. How long can Scholar keep on turning a profit if the educational industry changes and we don't change with it?"

Andrea Anderson was hired as the new CEO in 1990 and was specifically charged to prepare Scholar Educational Products for the future and lead it into the twenty-first century. Her early efforts to introduce tape cassette programs and a line of educational software met with success and have prompted her to not only investigate new product areas but to also rethink the organizational structure of Scholar Educational Products. For this innovative resurgence and reengineering to be accepted, Andrea realizes she must work closely with all department heads.

Andrea enters the meeting with department heads prepared to provide a few general remarks and then brainstorm possible information-gathering methods. Previous meetings to discuss up and coming technologies in education and restructuring options have prepared department heads for this brainstorming session. All agree that quality decision making depends upon quality information. Consequently, identifying a research methodology and selecting appropriate research tools will be an important first step in their arduous task. This meeting gives them a chance to do just that.

Critically focus on the research and information gathering proposals generated during the meeting, particularly noting the advantages and disadvantages, as well as the appropriateness, of survey and telephone interviews. The following questions can direct and guide your analysis:

1. What is the purpose and agenda of the meeting? Why do organizations conduct research? How can interviewing be used as a research tool?
2. When is it appropriate to conduct a survey? Who should be surveyed? What types of questions should be included on a survey? How should a survey be administered?
3. What are the advantages and disadvantages of a telephone interview? When designing and conducting a telephone interview, what obstacles or constraints must be considered? How can these problems be resolved?
4. In what sense is a telephone interview different from a survey questionnaire? Which provides the best results?
5. Interview a professional researcher to discover some of the individual's guidelines for doing research and the techniques employed.

Summary

The survey interview has become increasingly popular and is widely used. Politicians are concerned about how people are thinking; businesses are concerned about trends that may affect them economically; and researchers want to test their hypothesis. The result has been an extensive use of questionnaires and telephone interviews designed to gather accurate quantitative data.

The survey interview requires careful preparation with attention being given to determining your purpose and goals, as well as considering certain ethical issues. The design and structure of the survey interview necessitates using a variety of questions and scales to elicit honest replies. Piloting the questionnaire helps tremendously to ensure its success in achieving desired results. When conducting the survey interview, you will want to randomly select a stratified sample representative of the target population, choose and train your interviewers, and consistently administer the survey. Ultimately, the effectiveness of any survey interview rests with the analysis of data and reporting of results.

Quick results, cost effectiveness, low refusal rates, probing and efficient follow-up, as well as ease of training and supervision, make telephone interviews advantageous when conducting survey projects. Still, the narrow scope of questioning and potential difficulties in obtaining sensitive information are limitations that must be weighed. However, current technological changes are making the telephone interview a more popular option.

No matter how intricate the research project might be, it is still important that the study and methods "makes sense" to you. A common failing is that researchers often leap to the use of a particular method without carefully considering its underlying assumptions. They get carried away with their methods and lose sight of their object of study. M. Trow cautiously observes, "Every cobbler thinks leather is the only thing. Most social scientists . . . have their favorite research methods with which they are familiar and have some skill in using. And I suspect we mostly choose to investigate problems that seem vulnerable to attack through these methods. But we should at least try to be less parochial than cobblers."[21]

SHARPENING YOUR FOCUS

1. Outline and discuss the steps in preparing a successful survey.

2. Compare and contrast the advantages and disadvantages of conducting a pencil-and-paper survey versus a telephone survey.

3. Select an area of interest, and develop it into a problem for research. Write your problem either as a question or as a statement of purpose. Next, develop a survey questionnaire by which you intend to gather some or all of your data. Finally, analyze each question: What is the basic assumption underlying the reason for this question? How does the question relate to the research problem? What type of question (multiple choice, yes/no, completion, ranking, rating) is being used? How do you expect to relate this question to the research effort? With this guide for the construction of a questionnaire, there will be much less chance that you will produce a questionnaire that may be grossly faulty or that may have in it major defects that might impair your study.

4. List the advantages of conducting a pilot study. Why do some researchers avoid administering a pilot study? Are there circumstances when not administering a pilot study would be appropriate? Explain.

5. Recall a situation when you were the subject of a survey. Was it a mail survey or telephone survey? How did you respond? Were you cooperative? Did you refuse to participate? Why? What prompted your behavior? What can you learn from this experience that will assist you in conducting a survey?

6. Develop a survey of alumni to gather their impressions of your college or university. Would a telephone survey be better suited for this project?

NOTES

1. Lawrence R. Frey, Carl H. Botan, Paul G. Friedman, and Gary L. Kreps, *Investigating Communication: An Introduction to Research Methods* (Englewood Cliffs, N.J.: Prentice-Hall, 1991), 11.
2. Frederick Williams, *Reasoning with Statistics* 4th ed. (New York: Harcourt Brace Jovanovich, 1992), 5.
3. Steinar Kvale, *Interviews: An Introduction to Qualitative Research Interviewing* (Thousand Oaks, Calif.: Sage, 1996), 67.
4. Cal W. Downs, G. Paul Smeyak, and Ernest Martin, *Professional Interviewing* (New York: Harper and Row Publishers, 1980), 353.
5. Herbert J. Rubin and Irene S. Rubin, *Qualitative Interviewing: The Art of Hearing Data* (Thousand Oaks, Calif.: Sage, 1995), 128.
6. Frey, Botan, Friedman, and Kreps, *Investigating Communication,* 193.
7. Robert Kahn and Charles Cannell, *The Dynamics of Interviewing* (New York: John Wiley and Sons, 1957).
8. Barbara Dohrenwend, "Some Effects of Open and Closed Questions on Respondents' Answers," *Human Organization* 24 (Summer 1965): 175–84.
9. Dana Gaines Robinson and James C. Robinson, *Performance Consulting* (San Francisco: Berrett-Koehler Publishers, 1996).
10. Ibid.
11. James H. Frey and Sabine Mertens Oishi, *How to Conduct Interviews by Telephone and in Person* (Thousand Oaks, Calif.: Sage, 1995).
12. Floyd J. Fowler, Jr. and Thomas W. Mangione, *Standardized Survey Interviewing: Minimizing Interviewer-Related Error* (Thousand Oaks, Calif.: Sage, 1990), 35.
13. Pamela Kiecker and James E. Nelson, "Do Interviewers Follow Telephone Survey Instructions?" *Journal of the Market Research Society* 38 (April 1996): 161–76.
14. Howard Schuman and Stanley Presser, *Questions and Answers in Attitude Surveys* (New York: Academic Press, 1981).
15. Robert Rosenthal, "Interpersonal Expectations: Effects of the Experimenter's Hypothesis," in *Artifact in Behavioral Research,* ed. Robert Rosenthal and Ralph Rosnow (New York: Academic Press, 1969), 181–277.
16. Pamela L. Alreck and Robert B. Settle, "Planning Your Survey," *American Demographics* (August 1995): 12.
17. Nick Watkins, "Losing Face to Phones," *Marketing,* 8 September, 1994.
18. Frederick Wiseman, "Methodologial Bias in Public Opinion Surveys," *Public Opinion Quarterly* (Spring 1972): 105–8.
19. Tim Triplett, "Survey System Has Human Touch without the Human," *Marketing News,* 24 October, 1994, 16.
20. Jacob Hornik, Tamar Zaig, and Dori Shadmon, "Reducing Refusals in Telephone Surveys on Sensitive Topics," *Journal of Advertising Research* (June/July 1991): 49–56.
21. M. Trow, "Comment on 'Participant Observation and Interviewing: A Comparison,'" *Human Organizations* 16 (1957): 35. Used with permission.

11 The Focus Group Interview

The focus group interview is a qualitative research technique used to reveal patterns of viewpoints, attitudes, and feelings. The method can be used to complement other quantitative methods, such as the survey or questionnaire, or it can be used informally to generate ideas or reactions. The focus group interview is reemerging as a popular data-gathering method because it lends itself to many different areas—marketing, advertising, management, politics, and communication research.

Chapter 11 will consider a rationale for focus group interviewing, examine the functions and benefits of focus groups, and outline how to effectively conduct such groups and analyze the data acquired. Particular attention will be given to the important roles played by the moderator and participants in this unique type of research interview. This chapter is designed to accomplish three objectives:

1. *Awareness.* You will understand the nature of focus group interviewing and its diverse functions.

2. *Assessment.* You will be able to appraise the value of using focus groups as a "stand alone" data-gathering tool or in combination with other research methods and learn how to analyze the qualitative information gained.

3. *Application.* You will be able to effectively conduct and participate in a focus group interview.

* * * * *

Litter in City Streets—A Community Problem

Vicki LaFollett hung up the phone and quickly began jotting notes to herself about the call. She chuckled, muttering aloud, "If I don't write it down, I'll forget it." She had just finished an interesting discussion with Andre Biddulph, a university professor who teaches marketing at a large city in Minnesota forty-five minutes away from Vicki's smaller locale. She had contacted Professor Biddulph about his conducting several focus groups with selected citizens in her community. As an assistant municipal manager, Vicki was charged with developing and directing a new campaign against littering city streets and neighborhoods. She wanted to discover creative ways to launch the "Don't Mess With Us" campaign and combat the litter problem, so she had contacted Professor Biddulph to discuss the use of focus groups.

Vicki knew that outside the municipality, an antilitter program called "Adopt-a-Highway" had worked successfully in her state for a number of years. The Minnesota Department of Transportation started a program involving civic service groups, nonprofit organizations, and businesses, who adopted a two-mile stretch of highway and volunteered to keep it litter-free. "Adopting" meant the organization agreed to send volunteers every few months to pick up trash along the selected stretch of highway. The trash was bagged in sacks provided by the state and left for pickup at a designated location along the roadway. In return, the state provided a large colorful sign with the organization's name on the section of highway as recognition or advertising.

Vicki was charged with developing a similar antilitter program within the municipality, since trash was becoming an increasing problem, especially in the business district. Citizen complaints about litter had skyrocketed, resulting in part from reduced city budgets and cutbacks in maintenance crews. With awareness and education as goals, Vicki believed that involving citizen volunteers would be an excellent way to control municipal litter without additional cost to the city. However, she needed accurate information and ideas for her planned "Don't Mess With Us" campaign to succeed. Focus group interviews would reveal solid, creative approaches to the problem and immediately involve businesses and concerned citizens.

Fortunately, Professor Biddulph agreed to conduct the sessions. As a noted expert in research and focus group interviews, his $200 fee per group interview did not seem exorbitant and was not prohibitive given Vicki's allowed budget. Three group sessions would be conducted involving eight to ten participants per group and lasting about two hours. Also, each citizen who agreed to participate would be given $35 for their time and assistance. Professor Biddulph agreed to conduct pre-interviews to discover what areas to address during the focus groups and helped Vicki select the community members and set up the groups. He suggested that the sessions be audiotaped for later analysis.

According to schedule, the first focus group interview met on a Tuesday afternoon at 4:00 p.m. and was facilitated by Professor Biddulph while Vicki sat quietly in the room and observed the discussion. An interviewing/conference room at city hall provided an excellent setting free of distractions. The room included a large, oval table with comfortable chairs, and a pleasant atmosphere. All ten participants who were preregistered arrived, and Professor Biddulph began the interview by stating its purpose, noting that the discussion would be audiotaped, and explaining how the results would be analyzed and interpreted for the city council. The first session started on time and proceeded smoothly with a lively exchange of ideas. The few problems that did arise had been anticipated by Professor Biddulph and were easily resolved. Vicki LaFollett was confident that the subsequent sessions would likewise yield valuable information that could contribute to the success of her "Don't Mess With Us" campaign. She was optimistic that the litter in city streets, a community problem, just might be "cleaned up."

Discussion Questions

1. How could focus group interviews be used? What was the purpose of the city's focus group research?
2. What functions can focus group interviews serve? What results did Vicki hope to find after the sessions were completed?
3. What benefits does the focus group interview have over other survey techniques? Can the city's focus group research "stand alone" as a data collection method?
4. How were the focus group sessions conducted? Was a productive climate for discussion created? What constituted the interview guide? How should participants be chosen? What should be the role and function of the moderator? How should the data be analyzed?
5. What responsibilities do the participants have in the focus group?

The Nature of the Focus Group Interview

The **focus group interview** is a unique type of group interview facilitated by a trained moderator who keeps the group "focused" on a particular research topic, product, or subject area.[1] This distinguishes the focus group from other types of group activities that are not primarily a part of data collection or research. The focus group interview places a unique perspective on research and data gathering through its interactive processes.

Richard Krueger defines a focus group as "people assembled in a series of groups who possess certain characteristics, and provide data of a qualitative nature in a focused discussion."[2] Krueger's characteristics stress the qualitative nature of focus groups. Typically, a series of groups are conducted to detect important patterns and trends in data collection. Research based on only one group is risky because focus groups can vary greatly in their nature and composition. A "cold" or "flat" group, for example, may have participants who are quiet and have limited information to share. The results will be reflected in the discussion and may be skewed by the particular group of participants. Therefore, conducting several focus group sessions with different participants can provide a more accurate assessment.

Focus groups can stand alone as a research technique and may be the sole means for information gathering. Some researchers believe the focus group is superior to the individual personal interview for attaining quality information because it often reveals an interviewee's attitudes, feelings, and behaviors that cannot be obtained through the traditional interview.[3] Although individual personal interviews also provide in-depth information, many researchers feel the group "process" generates more information in one meeting than the one-to-one interview. Also, while a series of focus groups can be "self-contained" or stand alone as a research technique, they can also be used to complement other research/survey methods.

The nature of the interview format distinguishes the focus group from other structured small-group activities. The interviewer in a focus group encourages active participation throughout the process and strives to create an atmosphere that will contribute to a lively interchange among group members. Ideally, during the focus group discussion, the concept of "synergy" takes affect, and ideas are generated that would not have otherwise occurred to a single individual. One participant's ideas may build on another's and will often serve as an impetus for further suggestions. Such focused interaction allows the group to work creatively and freely. This interactive format makes the focus group a unique research tool.

Another distinguishing characteristic of the focus group is that of the central interviewer or facilitator/moderator. While other group activities have leaders, the focus group has an interviewer who leads the group through a question-and-answer format. The interviewer's probing questions elicit in-depth information about participants' attitudes and behaviors; thus, a focus group is not merely a public forum where prepared remarks are made and questions are asked and answered. A focus group comprises two parties (the interviewer and the group itself) who purposefully interact with one another in an effort to gain and share information about a specific topic. In a sense, the focus group interview is a small, task-oriented group that gives respondents a chance to express their opinions and talk openly and freely about their beliefs, attitudes, and experiences. Thus, it is an excellent means of securing subjective information that has rich explanatory value.

*   *   *   *   *

Vicki LaFollett and Professor Biddulph used focus group research in a municipal government. They recognized its unique value in gathering accurate qualitative information while actively involving the citizens of the community. Their purpose was to garner citizen participation in their efforts to combat the city's litter problem. The findings should help the city initiate a successful, low-cost litter control program.

The Functions of the Focus Group Interview

Traditionally, the most popular uses of focus groups were seen in advertising, marketing and sales, and politics. Advertisers would use focus groups to pretest the effectiveness of commercials, and marketing/sales managers would use them in an attempt to gain qualitative insights into potential customers. In politics, focus groups became an "obsession" with American candidates running for political office during the 1980s. Today, American political candidates continue to seek information about voters' interests and ideas through focus groups. On an international level, Russian Prime Minister Boris Yeltsin gained office in 1996 by adopting the American political strategy of widespread use of focus groups to obtain in-depth information from Russian citizens. Ivor Gaber, a professor of broadcast journalism in London, also points out how integral focus groups have been to British elections.[4] Now, focus groups as a method of information gathering are used for many other purposes, and their potential is unlimited.

During the last several years, technology has begun to change the traditional uses of focus groups. Utility companies, to discover new ways to market products and services to customers, have combined technology with focus groups to gain immediate feedback and reach a greater number of customers. In 1996, Oklahoma Gas and Electric (OGE) decided to introduce fifteen new products and services and used focus groups consisting of thirty to fifty people to determine which to initially introduce. The utility company combined focus groups with a new computer marketing tool called a Rapid Analysis Measurement system (RAM). RAM consists of a wireless, electronic feedback system that allows respondents (while participating in the focus groups) to register immediately their opinions on a product or service. The technology has the advantage of promoting honest responses and allowing shy or more quiet participants to register their opinions without intimidation. The facilitator of the group can see immediate reactions to questions, and a computer immediately tallies statistical data for the group, providing a breakdown by age, gender, or other variables. Although OGE paid a consulting group $120,000 for three to four hours of interviews involving 400 participants, the expense proved beneficial when OGE determined that a targeted marketing approach with its products and services was better than a mass market approach.[5] Before spending millions of dollars to launch a new product, they had gleaned essential data from focus groups to make its marketing decisions.

Focus groups have also gone on-line in other ways. Cyber Dialogue of New York City, specializing in on-line market research, uses focus groups in "chat rooms" and reports that participants tend to be more honest on-line than in face-to-face group meetings.[6] The company's software allows a researcher to interrupt the focus group facilitator with a "flash e-mail" without the participants' knowledge, which permits interjecting spontaneous questions into the discussion through the facilitator's computer. This allows for customized probing of targeted participants. While a lack of body language, facial expressions, and other nonverbal communication are important drawbacks, on-line focus groups provide accuracy, low cost, and immediate results for researchers. Computer networks can enhance the focus group methodology, and computer interviews permit reaching large numbers of individuals efficiently and quickly (see chapter 13).

Focus groups can also be used to complement and verify other research methods. Sociologist David Morgan found that focus group interviews were most frequently paired with either in-depth, individual interviews or with surveys.[7] Personal interviews often follow focus group interviews in an effort to gain more in-depth information from individuals. In individual interviews, a person tends to give narratives explaining his or her comments and opinions. When researchers use the focus group interview with individual interviews, each method complements the other and helps to confirm findings.

Focus groups also complement paper-and-pencil questionnaires and mail survey research. After surveys have been administered, returned, and analyzed, researchers may form focus groups to discuss the survey findings. The information from the survey can be used as a basis for the focus group sessions and allow the interviewer to explore in-depth certain areas of the questionnaire. While surveys often limit how much a respondent can say about a topic, the focus group provides a broader forum for discussion. Moreover, it can help clarify contradictory results from a survey.

Focus groups can additionally be used as exploratory research for surveys. For example, focus groups have been used to design a needs assessment for recreation[8] and to prepare questions for health surveys.[9] Before the actual surveys were constructed and administered, focus groups were used in an exploratory way to identify specific topics and subject areas that assisted in questionnaire preparation. Certain themes or issues that might not otherwise have been included were covered in the questionnaire. Here, focus group interviews are an ideal way of bringing together qualitative and quantitative methods of research.

Finally, focus groups can complement large-scale systems research projects (see chapter 12). The intensive moderated discussion with key people can provide unique personal information or identify flaws or serious problems with a program that may necessitate redesign. It can guide the design and use of other data-gathering methods, as well as confirm or clarify their findings. In sum, it can be easily integrated into a methodological package and research plan.[10]

*   *   *   *   *

The city has a litter problem and needs community support for the "Don't Mess With Us" campaign. The focus group sessions can generate new ideas regarding the problem and function to measure the concern and interest of the citizenry. The results of the focus group sessions should reveal in-depth, insightful ideas on involving citizen volunteers with the city's anti-litter efforts. The suggested monetary incentive along with the relevancy of the problem should encourage focus group participation.

Advantages and Disadvantages of Focus Groups

Focus group interviews have both advantages and disadvantages; consequently, researchers must weigh each carefully when making methodological choices. The benefits derived from using focus groups are that they give respondents a chance to talk openly and freely, provide a depth and breadth of information, reveal unique insights, confer a satisfactory return on investment of time, and it can be useful for clients to observe the groups.

The focus group interview *provides a forum for free and open expression of ideas.* When a facilitator moderates well, the focus group interview creates a safe atmosphere for participants to candidly comment without the strictures of systematic questioning. Because focus groups are typically homogeneous (a group composed of members with similar backgrounds, attitudes, or behaviors on an issue), highly apprehensive members feel more comfortable "to speak, even for those who are characteristically less apt to do so."[11] In other words, people of like-kind are often more likely to voice what is truly on their minds. Moreover, a group of people chatting together is more natural and relaxed than a single individual being interviewed. For this reason, focus groups have sometimes been likened to "self-help" groups or "support" groups because of the social dynamics and interpersonal reactions of participants.

A particular advantage of focus group interviews lies in the *depth and breadth of information* researchers can obtain. Although an individual participating in a focus group produces only two-thirds as many ideas as an individual in a personal interview, the sheer number of interviewees present generate more ideas.[12] Moreover, the interaction in a focus group is multiplicative, with each participant becoming a richer source of information than he or she would be alone. One person's ideas may trigger comments from another, which in turn, may serve as a springboard for further discussion. The resulting group interaction can crystallize ideas and reveal useful connections. Members respond to one another, and this give-and-take reveals insights into their thinking. Called "the group effect," the focus group process develops synergy, resulting in an improvement over the sum of information gained from individual interviews.[13]

The small-group process and the dynamic interactions that take place within focus groups can also *reveal unique insights into human motivations and behaviors.* In a focus group of ten people, for example, a good facilitator will encourage participants to question each other and explain their opinions and feelings. This spontaneous challenge-response format gives valuable clues to the minds and actions of participants. A good researcher will observe how group members defend their ideas and "link" them with others to reach a consensus.

Focus groups also provide a *satisfactory return-on-investment through quick results and an efficient use of time.* Peggy Byers and James Wilcox note that "eliciting responses from eight to twelve respondents in a focus group lasting one to two hours is more time effective than interviewing the same number individually."[14] The group interview means a number of respondents are interviewed simultaneously, and data is collected at one time. Thus, focus group interviews can be a comparatively economical and efficient tool for researchers.

Finally, *clients can observe groups* expressing their opinions, which may be a genuinely eye-opening experience. The focus group can be conducted in a room with a one-way mirror, or clients can quietly sit in with the group itself. Seeing and hearing respondents as they give their ideas lends credibility to their statements and permits clients to perceive them as real persons rather than tabular inputs. Clients can witness the personal conviction of participants and experience the stimulating exchange of ideas, which helps to validate the methodology. However, if group members feel they're being observed, it may inhibit their participation, and they may become more self-conscious. Still, a skilled moderator can diffuse the observing presence of a client and develop an open, supportive climate within the group.

Beside these advantages of focus groups, there are several limitations or disadvantages in using focus group interviews. First and foremost, focus group interviews *limit the ability to explore and probe each person's opinions and experience extensively.* Unlike individual interviews, focus group sessions consist of several people being interviewed simultaneously; thus, a single individual's attitudes and beliefs are visible only in bits and pieces. However, computer interviews permit tailoring questions to individual participants as well as the entire group.

The limited size of focus group interviews requires that researchers be careful in *generalizing results of focus groups.* The small number of participants limits how results can be applied to an extended population. Moreover, because group members are similar, they may not adequately represent the larger population. While the intensive discussions might add insightful explanations to statistical data, focus group sessions produce no information that can be considered quantitatively or statistically significant. Consequently, data is often difficult to analyze and interpret. Furthermore, analysis of focus group sessions can be hampered by problems of identifying who said what, and due to the noise or members talking simultaneously, a participant's statements can easily be taken out of context. Therefore, it is useful to audiotape the proceedings. Computer networks have permitted expanding the size of focus groups, and computer technology can greatly assist in the analysis and subsequent interpretation.

A *participant's tendency toward conformity* is another limitation of focus groups. During the discussion, the group itself will have an impact on an individual's responses. A dominant member, for example, may inadvertently bias another's decisions. A strong member may overly influence the other participants' opinions. Group members may conform in other ways, too. Most of us are motivated to some degree to make "socially desirable" responses when in public settings. If we are socially motivated, we tend to state what others like to hear rather than expressing our true feelings or opinions. Consequently, divergent individual opinions may be repressed or silenced by the more popular group opinion. Individual interviews and anonymous surveys offer considerably more control. Currently available computer software programs, however, are also allowing for more control and anonymity when using focus groups.

A *potential disposition toward biased results* can also be a disadvantage of focus groups. Poor moderators may slant the discussion in desired directions, skew opinions, or twist ideas, leading the group toward biased results. A poorly trained moderator who allows interruptions and changes in topic may allow others to corrupt the results. The role of the moderator is crucial in overcoming this limitation and in producing accurate, quality data. A good moderator keeps the group interview on its topic and remains "focused."

Finally, there is an *inclination to overuse focus groups*. With their increasing popularity, some researchers are substituting this methodology for other types of information gathering and data collection. Often, little attention is given to the appropriateness of other types of survey research. Moreover, current computer software programs have helped to rectify a number of the disadvantages listed, thereby further contributing to the use of focus groups for almost every project. Still, focus groups are only one tool whereby researchers can collect information. The value of both qualitative and quantitative data must be carefully considered when designing a research project.

*   *   *   *   *

Vicki LaFollett knows that focus groups are a dynamic and unique research tool, and she wants to gather as much data as possible. Questionnaires and telephone surveys could elicit information given specific questions but would not generate new ideas or permit the active involvement produced in focus groups. Consequently, focus groups will be the principal research method the city uses in developing the campaign, with other survey techniques possibly being used as follow-up measures for evaluation purposes. Vicki LaFollett plans to quietly observe participants while Professor Biddulph moderates the discussion. Her record of participants' ideas and her observations of the motivations of group members will complement the audiotaped data. She understands that free and open expression is an advantage of focus groups and that her presence in the room may inhibit that expression. Therefore, she will be careful not to sit at the oval table with the members of the group but will sit unobtrusively to one side, listening and taking notes. Her training and experience along with the expertise of Professor Biddulph should help counter potential liabilities and make the focus groups a quick and timely information-gathering vehicle.

Conducting Focus Groups

The primary objective for using focus group research is to obtain accurate, qualitative information. To reach this goal, the researcher and facilitator must first create an open environment where group members feel free to discuss their beliefs and opinions. The physical environment is key to achieving this end and making the experience a rewarding one. Focus group interviews are typically held in such "safe" settings as public buildings, community halls, hotels/motels, colleges/universities, or business/professional conference rooms. In selecting a location, one should give consideration to geographical location, comfort, and informality. Serving light refreshments will also contribute to a warmer atmosphere.

To stimulate open discussion, the seating of the group should be set so that participants can see each other when talking. An open arrangement of chairs in a room allows face-to-face interaction, but participants often feel more comfortable seated around a table where they can take notes and feel less conspicuous during the discussion. The researcher may also want to give each participant a name tag or "name T" (a folded triangle shaped card ten to twelve inches long) with their first name only for easy identification. The facilitator's seat at the table should be equal with other members, not at the "head" of the table or as one "in charge" of the discussion. The facilitator or moderator should maintain a neutral presence.

The physical presence of the client or researcher in the room can often influence the outcome of the group discussion. Most clients or researchers want to record the data and information from the focus group, whether its audio recorded, video recorded, or simply observed by an inconspicuous researcher. When specially designed facilities are available, one-way mirrors can be used to observe the discussion. If the group is observed, the facilitator should acknowledge the presence of the observer at the beginning of the discussion to put participants at ease. The facilitator should introduce the observer by name only, with other information such as company name, how the data will be used, why the observer is present,

The primary objective of focus group interviewing is the free and open expression of ideas.

and what decisions will be made based on the group discussion being omitted until the debriefing at the end. It may then serve as a springboard for further discussion.

Videotaping the focus group discussion has advantages and disadvantages. Video recordings can give important information about the nonverbal communication of participants. The participant's facial expression, smile, or crossed legs can contain important meaning, and the videotape proves helpful when interpreting a participant's statement(s). Despite this advantage, some participants may feel uncomfortable with the presence of a videotape camera and may not be as free with their comments. An obtrusive camera can prove distracting and may bias results for the researcher. Videotaping is difficult and, unless a special room is available, should be considered carefully by the researcher.

Developing an Interview Guide

Before the actual focus group discussion begins, it is essential to develop an interview guide. This guide is a logical outline of topics that set the agenda for the focus group session. Written in outline form, it provides structure to the discussion and ensures that the interviewer covers all important topics. Unlike other interview agendas, it may not list actual questions for the focus group session, rather, it will indicate specific areas and subareas for discussion, helping the interviewer avoid "rabbit trails" during the interactive discussion. Based on the research question, the guide helps the interviewer distinguish between relevant and irrelevant material.

When developing the interview guide, two important principles should be followed. First, *establish the order of the topics.* A good rule to follow is the "general-to-specific" rule where the facilitator or moderator begins with general topics that can be turned into open questions during the session. Toward the end of the guide, the focus should be on specific areas that need to be addressed. This funnel approach allows the facilitator to ask open questions at the beginning of the group discussion and gradually focus on specific questions toward the end of the session. Remember, the guide should be a flexible game plan that sets the direction of play, but it may require modification as the dynamics of the discussion evolve. A plan is necessary, but the facilitator may need to change or adapt the interview guide as the process proceeds.

A second important principle when developing the interview guide is *ordering the topics according to their importance to the research agenda.* Following the "primacy rule," the most important topics should be discussed first, with topics of lesser importance being discussed toward the end of the session. When the "primacy rule" conflicts with the "general-to-specific" rule, the researcher and facilitator should mutually determine which topics are initially discussed and modify the guide as needed.

Finally, the researcher will want to outline or structure the interview guide. This outline gives direction to the session and should include four general phases or steps: (1) the introduction, (2) warm-up questions, (3) a series of exploratory questions, and (4) the closing.[15] The introduction should permit everyone to greet one another, as well as state the purpose and ground rules of the group. In addition, stating the approximate length of time the group will meet and encouraging each person to openly express their thoughts and opinions sets a positive tone for the discussion. After the introductions, the interaction should flow smoothly into a warm-up period and orientation. The facilitator may want to suggest a "round robin" question for each person to help orient the group to the topic and begin interactions among group members. Once rapport has been established, the facilitator will introduce a series of exploratory questions that address the primary topic area to be covered. The number of questions will vary depending upon the complexity of the topic and how emotionally "charged" the subject is to the group. If a group is similar in background and interests, the moderator may quickly lead members through a number of questions. However, if the group is diverse in its background and interests, the discussion may take more time, and fewer topics can be covered. Typically, most interview guides will "consist of fewer than a dozen questions, though the moderator frequently is given considerable latitude to probe responses and add new questions as the actual interview progresses."[16] Finally, the facilitator will want to end the focus group on time. The interviewer should signal the close of discussion and allow for a clearinghouse question, such as "Is there anything else you would like to add that we have not touched upon?"

Choosing Participants

The composition of focus groups vary, of course, with the purpose of the research project. However, to obtain the most valuable qualitative information, the researcher will want to ask several important questions: Who should be invited? How should they be selected? What should be the size of each group?

Who should be invited? Because the focus group composition determines the outcome of the discussion, the researcher will want to take great care when choosing participants. The characteristics of the people in the group should be identified as accurately as possible. Depending on the goals of the researcher, choosing a group with homogeneous or heterogeneous characteristics is an important decision. When a group is "homogeneous," participants have significant similarities in one or more attributes, such as occupation, education, background, experience in a program, age, gender, social status, or family characteristics. A "heterogeneous" group, on the other hand, has significant differences. Most focus group researchers prefer groups with similar characteristics, believing that participants should have some unifying elements out of which true discussion can grow. In short, it is possible to select a group that has too much diversity where the interplay among participants jeopardizes the objectives of the focus group by directing attention to the differing personal viewpoints rather than the immediate topic. Furthermore, even when composing groups based on similar characteristics, other factors should be considered. For example, when both husband and wife are included, one spouse tends to speak, while the other remains silent; or mixing young, working women with women aged fifty or more who work at home may produce a wide disparity of viewpoints. Some researchers even recommend against mixing men and women in focus groups, especially if the topic is experienced differently by each sex.[17]

Besides involving total strangers in focus groups, the researcher may also want to consider using already existing groups in the organization. Using pre-formed groups or teams can save time and resources. Naturally formed groups "approximate naturally occurring data."[18] In other words, participants who are familiar with each other tend to be more open with their opinions and feelings, while pressures to conform may exist in a group of strangers. However, a potential disadvantage of preformed groups is that they may have an established hierarchy of relationships, which can inhibit equality of interaction. Consequently, the moderator must be particularly skilled in group dynamics, helping participants give true opinions and feelings regardless of composition.

Finally, when selecting participants, the researcher may want to provide an incentive. A study by Rodgers Marketing Research in Canton, Ohio, revealed that two-thirds of those surveyed indicated money was their main motivator for participating.[19] Choosing an appropriate amount to pay participants, of course, depends on the research project budget. Paying members too little may inhibit an individual's willingness to participate, while paying too much will quickly drain research funds. On the average, focus group members are generally compensated from $35 to $50 each for participating, although higher amounts are paid for "experts," such as health care providers, attorneys, or other trained professionals. Certainly, the researcher should suggest to participants the value of their contributing data to an important topic and emphasize the enjoyable benefits of participating in the group discussion. This can be a particularly strong incentive if the individuals have previously participated in focus groups and have had positive experiences.

How should participants be selected? Participants may be randomly chosen from telephone surveys, picked from prepared lists of potential participants, solicited through newspaper advertisements, or obtained from recommendations of others who have participated in previous focus groups. Members can be contacted in person, by similar telephone exchanges, or by mail according to zip codes. Whatever method the researcher chooses should meet the goals of the project.

One of the most common approaches to choosing participants is through convenience sampling or nonrandom "purposive" sampling.[20] Participants are selected because they possess a particular characteristic critically related to the focus group agenda. A university evaluating its academic programs may choose alumni who have recently graduated from the university, or auto manufacturers wishing to evaluate customer satisfaction may select focus group participants from new car buyers only. Also, a nonprofit organization wanting to assess the effectiveness of a public information campaign may choose group members from that segment of the community who have heard the message. The objective in every instance is to get the best possible sample.

How many participants should be included in a focus group? The size of the traditional focus group ranges from six to twelve participants. Groups larger than this tend to limit individual participation and prevent individuals from having an opportunity to comment or share observations. Also, private conversations, frequent murmuring, and distractions become all too prevalent. Smaller, "mini-focus groups," are vulnerable to individual personalities or biases and decrease the benefits of a group interview by concentrating discussion and limiting the total number of ideas and observations.[21] However, when choosing the number of participants, the researcher should include one or two members more than necessary as alternates. Typically, there are several "no shows," and having at least two alternates will give the researcher some leeway in keeping a complete group. If all members who were recruited arrive on time, including the alternates, the last two people should be thanked, given any monetary incentive, and allowed to leave.

Determining the exact number of participants in a focus group depends on the research goals and objectives. While larger groups tend to give researchers a variety of opinions and experiences, smaller groups are preferable for obtaining in-depth information. Moreover, smaller groups of five, six, or seven participants are easier to manage and better fitted for controversial or emotional topics. Consequently, moderating three focus groups comprised of eight participants may benefit the researcher more than two groups of twelve participants. While this will be more time consuming, the quality of the data can be significantly increased.

The Moderator

The moderator plays a pivotal role in focus group interviewing, and effective facilitation requires careful thought and attention. Each interviewer must learn how to moderate a focus group interview that will be consistent with his or her own personality, as well as consonant with the composition of the group and appropriate to the situation. Successful moderators seem to have a natural ability to talk with people, lead the discussion, and make decisions. They appear to be assertive, cooperative, decisive, adaptable to situations, energetic, and willing to assume responsibility.[22] However, the moderator's knowledge of the topic, leadership style, and understanding of group dynamics directly influence the productive outcome of the group.

The moderator must possess a basic knowledge of the topic and be able to demonstrate a familiarity with the issues being discussed. A successful moderator will serve as a catalyst for generating different viewpoints and prompt participants to explain their comments or amplify their thoughts. A moderator who has inadequate knowledge of the topic or incomplete background information is unable to responsibly direct the focus group and usually assumes a hands-off approach. As a result, the participants often view such a moderator as lazy, uninvolved, or naive and become frustrated with the process. Remember, the objective is to go beyond mere surface reactions, and the key for unlocking this information is sufficient knowledge to thoughtfully probe for the reasons behind expressed opinions.

An effective moderator must exert leadership and control without stifling the free flow of ideas. Leadership and control means keeping on top of the discussion and gently nudging it in the direction that is most beneficial. Commonly recognized authoritarian, democratic, and laissez-faire leadership styles or behaviors may be appropriately employed given the task, need for social maintenance, and maturity or experience of the group. The **authoritarian moderator** acts like an authority figure in the focus group and maintains a high degree of control over the questioning. In essence, this type of moderator determines all policy for the focus group, is subjective in praise and criticism, stays impersonal and aloof, and accepts no suggestion uncritically. It may be appropriate when the task is foremost, decisions must be made quickly, and the group has little or no previous focus group experience. Such conditions require more control to ensure that all members are involved in the discussion and all of the topics are covered. The **democratic moderator** outlines the steps to reach the group's goal, allows the participants to determine how the group will operate, responds personally with group members, maintains objectivity in praise and criticism, and reaches decisions jointly with the participants. This style is more time consuming, but it is highly rewarding when spontaneity and interaction are important. It can be very effective when sensitive or controversial topics are being discussed. Finally, the **laissez-faire moderator** takes a hands-off, freeform approach and participates as little as possible. Here, the moderator serves merely as a group guide, supplying little information during the discussion. This style works best with a group of highly trained experts or professionals who can effectively monitor themselves and provide self-direction. Leadership and control of the group is essentially a function of influencing the group processes, but this does not mean stifling responses or particular points of view. Each group develops its own tone and mood, which determines the need for direction and encouragement. Consequently, the moderator must constantly be aware of what is going on and what participants are doing and feeling. The moderator in a focus group setting may be likened to a conductor orchestrating an improvisation or a jazz bandleader. The leader of a jazz band must "choose the music, find the right musicians, and perform . . . but the effect of the performance depends on so many things—the environment, the volunteers playing in the band, the need for everybody to perform as individuals and as a group, the absolute dependence of the leader on the members of the band, the need of the leader for the followers to play well."[23]

Inevitably, moderators will have to deal with difficult people from time to time and ensure that problem respondents do not deter the group from its task. Some participants may become overly talkative, dominating the conversation, while others may remain quiet and subdued. Still other participants may use the focus group to vent their anger or demonstrate their knowledge. These are all difficult people who frustrate others and jeopardize the focus group process. Some of the most frequently encountered "problem people" are group hogs, wallflowers, eager beavers, ax bearers, whiners, know-it-alls, think-they-know-it-alls, compromisers, maybe people, yes people, and no people.[24]

Group Hogs try to dominate and control the group discussion. They are often pushy and aggressive, and their loud, forceful manner tends to intimidate others. Dealing with them requires assertively maintaining control and perhaps interrupting or stifling their excessive remarks. The best way to interrupt someone is to evenly say their name over and over again until they halt and then tactfully note the importance of hearing everyone's opinion. Aggressive people require assertive responses.

Wallflowers may be shy, thoughtful individuals who are reticent to express their opinions or nonperformers who offer no verbal feedback or nonverbal feedback—nothing. The goal is to persuade the wallflower or "nothing person" to talk. One method of getting these individuals to participate is to ask them direct questions that invite their opinions. The best kind of question to ask them is an open-ended question. One that can't be answered with a yes, a no, or a grunt.

Eager beavers are anxious to participate and fervently express ideas before anyone else has an opportunity to speak. They are not trying to dominate the discussion but are really trying to be open and cooperative. In fact, such individuals often perceive themselves as being helpful in consistently getting things started. Consequently, a great deal of tact is needed to circumvent this problem. To effectively handle eager beavers, the moderator might simply intervene by asking someone else in the group to begin the discussion on a particular issue. This allows others in the group to initiate discussion and share in starting the conversation.

Ax bearers have a one-track mind and one point to make regardless of the issue being discussed. They have a personal, private agenda or grievance that is repeated again, and again, and again, resulting in a loss of task orientation for the entire group. When confronting ax bearers, the moderator must firmly hold his or her ground and ask questions to expose the disruptive behavior. Asking, "When you say that, what are you really trying to say?" or "What does that have to do with this?" can expose the Ax Bearer's singular purpose or grievance while demanding relevance to the present situation. By asking for the true meaning behind the ax bearer's comments and inquiring about the relevancy of remarks, the moderator can assume control and refocus the attention of the group, thus getting them back on track.

Whiners see only what's wrong and never offer constructive solutions. These individuals go on and on about how things should be different, but their complaints are not geared toward change of any kind. Such behavior creates a feeling of helplessness and frustrates the efforts of those members trying to generate new ideas. The best way to handle someone who is constantly complaining, and for everyone around them, is to help them identify solutions. We recommend actively listening for the main points and then taking command of the conversation by tactfully asking clarification questions to get the specifics of the whiner's complaints.

Know-it-alls are knowledgeable and extremely competent people. They are highly assertive and outspoken in their viewpoints. They are also very controlling, with a low tolerance for correction and contradiction, since to be wrong is to be humiliated. New ideas, alternative approaches, or differing viewpoints are frequently perceived as a challenge to their authority and knowledge, regardless of the merit of the idea, approach, or viewpoint. Their behavior can be extremely intimidating and can seriously diminish the participation and involvement of other group members. Know-it-alls must be approached indirectly and in a nonthreatening way. Using softening words like "maybe," "perhaps," or "suppose," indirectly invites consideration without presenting a challenge. Also, using plural pronouns like "we" or "us," rather than singular pronouns like "I" or "you" promotes joint ownership over ideas as they are considered. The strategy is to capitalize on their recognized expertise while opening their minds to new information, ideas, and viewpoints.

Think-they-know-it-alls are abrasive, pushy, insecure individuals who know just enough about a subject to sound conversant in it. They try to take charge by boldly proclaiming, "I know exactly what we need. Trust me!" While they can't fool all the people all of the time, they can fool some of the people enough of the time to produce disastrous consequences for any focus group interview. Their conviction can potentially sway other group members and lead them down illusory paths. The moderator must reveal their misinformation and catch them in their act. This requires tactfully asking clarification questions for specifics and then telling it like it is.

Compromisers want to get along, which evidences itself in a strong desire for peer approval; consequently, they tend to change their opinions to accommodate others. This can prove confusing to the moderator, as well as other group members and raise questions regarding the substance of their opinions. Compromisers require reassurance and appreciation; therefore, the moderator will want to be alert to subtle and overt shifts in position and sensitively question them for an explanation. Reassuring compromisers that their ideas are valuable helps promote honest, candid participation.

Maybe people are unable to make a decision and procrastinate in the hope that a better choice will present itself. Their problem is a simple one—they don't have a system or method for choosing between imperfect choices. The moderator must patiently probe and explore issues and give them a strategy for decision making.

Yes people don't want to offend anyone, particularly the moderator and researcher. Because they are nice people and out of a desire to get along, they will say whatever they think will placate the facilitator and please the researcher. Their strong people focus and desire to fit prevents them from being open and candid or expressing unpleasant opinions. The moderator must carefully take the time to make the communication environment a safe one in which to be honest and forthright. The key to safety is providing verbal and nonverbal reassurance from the outset.

No people find the negatives in every idea and everyone. They focus on what did, is, or will inevitably go wrong, as well as the short comings, weaknesses, and failings of others in the group. Unlike the whiner who merely complains, the no person can see what could and should be and presents targeted, negative attacks. No people have the ability to extinguish any creativity while alienating and frustrating the other group members. Of all the difficult people, the behavior of negative people has the most insidious effect on others. Their negativity can undermine and stifle the focus group interview. The key to dealing with no people is to recognize their negativity, channel it, and use them as a resource. By acknowledging and accepting their negative outlook, the moderator and other group members can use no people to identify and point out any problems. The strategy is to defuse their emotional impact so that their analytic perfectionism can be expressed in a more useful way.

To gain control over problem people requires maintaining a positive attitude and strategically dealing with their difficult behaviors. Understanding what needs to be done and doing it can help you take charge of an unpleasant situation and redirect it to a worthwhile result. Effective moderators will insist that every group member can be a valuable participant, and difficult people are simply more challenging contributors.

Analyzing the Data

The most significant and consequential step in focus group interviewing is analysis and interpretation. The data from focus groups may be recorded by discretely taking notes, audiotaping, or videotaping the interviews. An observer can sit quietly in the room, recording information in the form of penciled notes on a legal pad, as well as ratings and/or rankings. Audiotaping is the most common method for recording data and is relatively unobtrusive while capturing detailed comments of the participants, as well as their intonation and paralanguage. Finally, the focus group interview may be videotaped. Unless the focus group is conducted in a special room suited for camera use, however, videotaping is rarely used. Although a videotape records essential nonverbal information about participant responses, the presence of a camera poses special problems of space and influence. If a camera is used, the room should be large enough for cameras to be easily moved about so as to get close-up facial shots of all participants. When a video camera is visibly present in the room, it can cause "camera shyness" and distract participants, inhibiting an open expression of their opinions. The use of specially designed rooms with one-way mirrors can help to overcome this potential obstacle when videotaping.

Collected data can be analyzed in a number of ways, depending upon the purpose of the focus group interviews and why the research was conducted. If general results only are desired, the researcher will reread and edit handwritten notes for wording and clarity or listen to the audiotape of the discussion summarizing main points, or view the videotape and categorize and sort the data. Common themes and consensus opinion are identified and reported in a narrative format for others to read.

The researcher can transcribe an audiotape word for word and organize the content of the focus group around each question in the interviewer guide. By organizing participant's comments according to content, their opinions become more clearly revealed in relation to the topical categories of interest to the researcher or client. Since transcription services are inexpensive and readily available, this type of analysis is common and satisfies the objectives of most research projects.

If further detailed analysis is needed, the researcher can content analyze the transcript of the audiotape. Content analysis means the data is quantified and submitted to mathematical analysis. Specific units of the transcript are analyzed, such as words, phrases, or sentences that relate to a topic. The time and effort of examining a full transcript yields a truer understanding of the participant's opinions.[25] This approach is used when the research requires quantitative/qualitative analysis beyond a descriptive summary.

Computer programs are readily available for a more detailed content analysis. Many of these programs have been applied to focus group data and give the researcher measurable information about the transcript. Use of computers enables the researcher to conduct fast, efficient analyses. The Key-Word-In-Context (KWIC) technique, for example, searches for key words and lists each key word along with the text that surrounds it.[26] Although such programs provide numerical information about the transcript, the researcher must still exercise human judgment in discovering overall themes and pivotal ideas within the transcript. A computer counts frequency of comments; the researcher decides what the frequency means. A computer estimates intensity of data by words in context and related adjectives; the researcher determines whether the intensity is important and interprets its significance. Besides time and efficiency, computer programs benefit researchers through reducing large amounts of data into a manageable form; however, the researcher makes final judgments and interprets the results of the research.

During the analytical phase, the researcher acts like a detective searching for clues. When analyzing data, sometimes the obvious, surface clues seem confusing and even contradictory. However, by digging deeper into the data, these clues begin to take on new meaning, and the researcher finds greater insights into the research question. As a detective, the researcher must patiently analyze and interpret the data. Which method the researcher chooses depends on the goals and objectives of the research.

Reporting the Results

Ultimately, the results must be reported. The final report is a means of presenting results clearly and effectively to managers, supervisors, or others who requested the focus group research. The report is perhaps the most important part of the focus group process. In its final form, the report represents an overview of the entire focus group process. It summarizes key results and presents them in readable form. It represents a written record or "history" to which researchers can refer at a later time. In its final form, the report must have a professional look and be an example of good communication. A well-written, colorful document free from grammatical errors conveys a high degree of professionalism to all involved. Without communicating results in an effective way, the coding, interpretation, and analysis of data will have little benefit for researchers.

The focus group report can be presented in oral or written form. Most likely, it will be a combination of both. Each part of the report is important, and a missing element will cause it to be incomplete. The writer must decide how long or short the report is to be and whether it will be formal or informal. A short report containing only a few pages tends to be informal and may be written in memorandum format, depending on the needs and objectives of the research.

Longer reports tend to be more formal and contain preliminary parts and addenda missing in shorter reports. Preliminary pages that introduce the text itself preface the results and help the reader locate information in the main report. Examples of preliminary pages would include a title page, an authorization page, a table of contents, a figures or tables page, and an executive summary. These pages are numbered with small roman numerals (i, ii, iii, etc.) and are necessary only when an organization requires these formalities. Addenda may consist of attachments or technical data. If the focus group session was transcribed, for instance, a copy of the word-for-word manuscript would be included as an addendum to the report. Descriptions and examples of these pages can be found in most business communication textbooks.[27] On the other end of the report continuum, the researcher may need only produce a short, informal report. Short reports omit preliminary parts and addenda, presenting only primary parts, such as the statement of the problem, results, conclusions, and recommendations.

Most focus group reports tend to have moderate length and formality. Richard Krueger recommended eight parts to a focus group written report: (1) cover page, (2) executive summary, (3) table of contents, (4) statement of the problem, (5) results, (6) limitations and alternative explanations, (7) conclusions and recommendations, and (8) appendix.[28] One of the most frequently read parts of a focus group report is the executive summary, a smaller-scale version of the larger report. Busy executives tend to read the executive summary first to get an overview of the reports findings. The executive summary includes all the major elements of the report itself, such as a clear statement of the problem, results, explanations, conclusions, and recommendations. It is a miniature version of the longer report. The summary's length should rarely be more than two pages and must be concisely worded when presenting an overview of the entire report.

The backbone of the report is the body. The body contains the essential elements the reader is expecting, including an introduction, data discussion, summary of research findings, and recommendations. These elements address the primary concerns that prompted the focus group project and interested the participating parties.[29]

The introduction orients the readers. In the introduction, the writer introduces the project to the reader(s) and previews the report. The introduction usually contains a purpose statement, topics that will be covered in the report, and background information (such as the history or a description of the problem). Sometimes it is helpful to the reader to mention what the report is *not* covering, especially if it could be confused with other projects or problem areas. It is important here to focus the attention of your reader(s).

The discussion of the report is the complete, detailed account of the problem. The research purpose, methodology, and results are specifically defined. The discussion also includes the analysis of the data collected, as well as an interpretation of the results. The discussion of the report should be enhanced with charts, graphics, and visual aids for comprehension, interest, or summarization.

A summary provides a synopsis of the main points from the introduction and discussion. It is an overview of the research report. A conclusion is a response to the research purpose. Normally, the conclusions are prioritized and stated in order of importance.

Recommendations proceed from the conclusions. Recommendations are suggestions for action to be taken based on the conclusions. In some reports, the recommendations are included in the conclusion section. Recommendations should be stated in specific terms, guiding the reader to a clear plan of action. Recommendations are generally used when the writer considers them beneficial or when they are expected by the sponsoring parties.

Finally, focus group reports often include an oral presentation of the results. The oral presentation parallels the executive summary format with more elaboration on results, conclusions, and recommendations. The oral presentation is intended for the principle parties involved, who may then discuss with the researchers their findings.

In sum, final reports represent the last stage of focus group research. Whether the report is written or oral, it will meet research needs and objectives and will bring closure to the process (see chapter 12). The format and presentation often reflect not only on the researchers but also on the quality of the research itself.

*   *   *   *   *

Vicki LaFollett and Professor Biddulph have thoroughly discussed and planned how the focus group interviews will be conducted. A comfortably appointed conference room, free of distractions, will be used. Moreover, coffee, soft drinks, and light refreshments will be provided.

Vicki understands that the preparation of an interview guide, a written outline of topics that sets the discussion agenda, is critical to the success of conducting focus groups. The topics covered during the discussion must be thorough and complete. Therefore, she will work closely with Professor Biddulph, as well as with the city manager and members of the city council. Because the city is funding the research, city council members may have specific topics they want covered in the focus groups. By involving all parties, Vicki will ensure efficient use of time and money, and will receive necessary and accurate data about the litter problem. Each person involved in the research project will contribute important items to the guide's content and assist in structuring the focus groups. A sample interview guide might take the following form:

Introduction. Welcome to our session today. Litter within our city has been a concern of the city council over the past six months. Our discussion today will help us determine the significance of the problem and generate ways to better control the litter problem. We have invited residents who live in the city to share their perceptions and ideas. You were selected because of the things you have in common and what you might be able to contribute regarding our "Don't Mess With Us" campaign. Before we begin our discussion, let's get better acquainted.

Here are a few ground rules for our group. We will spend the next two hours trying to discover inexpensive, creative ways to combat the litter problem by using citizen volunteers. Feel free to openly express your opinions and ideas on each topic we discuss. There are no right or wrong answers. We simply want to know what you honestly think. Second, we will audiotape today's session. The information will be used confidentially by the city to derive solutions to the litter problem. All results will be reported anonymously. If anyone is uncomfortable with the tape recorder, please say so now. Third, as a matter of courtesy, when someone is speaking allow them to finish before you begin speaking. In this way, only one person is talking at one time.

Warm-Up Question. As we get started, let's talk about how you see litter as a problem in our city. Where are some places you have observed the litter problem to be serious?

Questions. (This section includes open questions, in a funnel sequence, that cover the primary topics for discussion.)

- How serious is litter in the city? Distinguish between industrial pollution, garbage, and common litter.
- How well does the city sanitation department aid in preventing litter?
- How successful do you feel the "Adopt-a-Highway" program has worked outside the city?
- What types of litter appear to be most common?
- Who do you perceive to be the source of the litter problem? Visitors and tourists? Business and industry? Private residents?
- In what specific areas of the city have you observed litter to be most prevalent? Downtown area? Streets and sidewalks? Specific suburbs or neighborhoods? Business districts, restaurants, or shopping malls? Around schools? City parks?
- How willing are private citizens, civic service groups, and other nonprofit groups or businesses willing to volunteer in combating the city's litter problem? Will they support the "Don't Mess With Us" campaign? Will you?
- What creative ideas and approaches to controlling litter can be identified from our discussion?

Closing. (In summary fashion, the moderator will identify the main topics discussed. The session can be concluded by reviewing the main ideas discussed. A clearinghouse question can then be used as the final comment.) Is there anything else about the litter problem you would like to add that we have not touched upon? Thank you for your time and thoughtful comments.

The moderator may want to turn the meeting over to the observing researcher, who can debrief the group on the purpose of the research, how the data will be used, and what decisions will be made based on the group discussions.

Professor Biddulph knows that participants in a focus group are typically chosen on the basis of a common purpose, interest, or location. Participants are not necessarily chosen randomly from the larger population. Therefore, selected citizens for these focus groups should be representative of the different community constituencies and have similar concerns and interests. Such participants will provide the best information about the litter problem in specific areas of the city.

The role of the moderator is critical; therefore, Vicki has hired Professor Biddulph to facilitate the group sessions. He is knowledgeable and well trained in providing the necessary leadership, as well as handling difficult people. As the moderator for the focus group, Professor Biddulph observed the participants beforehand standing informally around the room. One gregarious member was loudly speaking to others and dominating conversations. Believing this individual may also talk excessively during the actual discussion or inhibit free interaction, Professor Biddulph elected to take a seat immediately beside the individual at the beginning of the focus group. This arrangement would allow him to better control the interaction through nonverbal communication to other group members. In the event that subtle body language doesn't work to reduce this potentially problematic participant, he may want to interrupt by saying, "Judy, your comments have been helpful, and does anyone else want to add to what she said?" or "Thank you, Judy—are there other viewpoints?" Seating is often a simple solution to controlling overly talkative members, but most importantly, tact and courtesy must be observed. Professor Biddulph will also want to be alert to other problem participants and difficulties that might arise.

Finally, the data must be analyzed and interpreted. Organizing content around each question in the interview guide would appear to be the best approach, given the objectives of this research project. By organizing participant's comments according to content, the researcher places all participant comments about a topic together in one section. This level of analysis is the most common, and further detailed analysis would be unnecessary.

Participating in the Focus Group Interview

Thus far, our approach has been from the perspective of the researcher. This section addresses the participant's point of view and provides several guidelines for effectively participating in the focus group interview.

Potential group members are usually contacted at least two weeks prior to the actual focus discussion. The invitation is normally personalized through a letter, telephone call, or face-to-face meeting. This advance notice allows participants to adjust their schedules and avoid other conflicts. Moreover, it allows the researcher to outline the general nature of the research topic, as well as note the approximate size of the group, starting and ending times, date, and location of the focus group. Most researchers will followup with a reminder the day before the focus group meets. Remember, once you've confirmed your willingness to participate in the focus group, your attendance is critical.

When participating in a focus group interview, come alone and plan to arrive at the location at least fifteen minutes prior to the starting time. Guests, other family members, friends, or children will most likely distract the other participants in the group. Arriving ahead of time allows you to register, get your name tag, meet the moderator, and find a comfortable seat. It's a good idea to spend informal conversational time with the other participants prior to the beginning of the focus group. Finally, and most important, when the focus group actually begins, *get actively involved in the discussion.* This may seem obvious as a participant, but your comments and opinions, no matter how small or seemingly insignificant, will add to the group. Not participating lessens the benefits of the research.

Participating in a focus group is a time-consuming activity. So why participate in a focus group interview? Often, there is a monetary incentive or other premium provided. However, these are nominal at best and used only to encourage cooperation. The experience itself can be very enjoyable—a stimulating discussion with others can be rewarding. Finally, you will be contributing to an important research project, which may ultimately benefit you, the organization, and the community. A group as a whole has more information than any one member, and groups are better at catching errors than are the individuals who proposed ideas. Viewed as a spontaneous and dynamic process, focus group discussions are a useful and powerful tool for participants and researchers.

*   *   *   *   *

The effectiveness of any focus group interview depends upon the active involvement of participants. Prior to the beginning of this discussion, Professor Biddulph observed one participant, Patricia Freeman, who had arrived fifteen minutes early, gotten her name tag and found a comfortable seat in the conference room. Despite having two young children, she had arranged day care and gotten specific directions to city hall. When she arrived, Patricia promptly registered and introduced herself to Professor Biddulph. She appeared organized and willing to participate in the discussion. In his later analysis of the data, Professor Biddulph commented on how Ms. Freeman contributed significantly to the group. Her opinions and ideas were thoughtful and insightful.

Critical Focus

Review the Critical Focus presented in chapter 10 describing the meeting of Andrea Anderson with the department heads at Scholar Educational Products, and replay the videotape segment, analyzing the proposal regarding focus group interviews. The following critical questions can direct and guide your analysis of the discussion.

1. What is the rationale for focus group interviewing? What is the confidence level of the information obtained?
2. Who should lead a focus group interview? How should participants be selected? Where should a focus group interview be conducted?
3. What are the most useful communication skills for an interviewer when conducting a focus group interview? What problems or obstacles might arise during a focus group interview?
4. What problems arise when analyzing the data and writing the report based on a focus group interview?

Summary

A focus group interview typically represents a small group of people brought to a central location where a skilled moderator leads an intensive discussion on a predetermined topic, issue, or problem. Through delicate probing and a lively interaction, qualitative data and new ideas may be generated.

The use of the focus group interview as a valid research technique has increased in recent years across a broad spectrum of organizations and fields. Previously limited to advertising, marketing, and politics, the focus group is used widely today by health organizations, colleges and universities, government agencies, and business organizations. This broad acceptance and use demonstrates its usefulness as a qualitative research tool. Whether we conduct research ourselves or serve as a participant in a discussion, the focus group has a significant role in many of the decisions that affect our lives.

Computer technology has enhanced the focus group interview, with computer networks extending its use. Moreover, the focus group is often used to complement other research techniques, such as the questionnaire, individual interview, or telephone survey. Consequently, the focus group interview is a versatile and comparatively advantageous research tool.

The focus group interview has a number of advantages that contribute to its growing popularity. By providing a casual, conversational forum for free and open expression, group members provide unique qualitative insights and often build on another's ideas, producing a synergistic effect resulting in a depth and breadth of information. Moreover, researchers find focus groups offering a satisfactory return-on-investment of time and energy given the quick results. Still, certain limitations or potential liabilities must be considered before using the focus group interview as a data collection technique. Focus groups do not provide for in-depth individual probing, and researchers must be careful in generalizing their results. Moreover, tendencies toward conformity and biased results exist. Finally, the subjective data obtained can be difficult to analyze and interpret. Therefore, care should be taken not to overuse the focus group interview as an information-gathering tool but thoughtfully consider its benefits given the particular research project.

When conducting the focus group interview, attention must be given to creating a safe, open environment for discussion. Participants must be carefully chosen, and an interview guide must be developed to ensure that all pertinent topics are covered. The researcher should outline or structure the interview guide to assist the moderator in his or her role. The quality of the data gained and the success of any focus group interview largely depends on the leadership provided by the moderator, as well as role functions assumed and ability to handle difficult people. A trained, professional moderator will appropriately address these challenges by flexibly adapting to the group. Finally, the data must be analyzed and interpreted. The extent and detail of the analysis depends on the goals of the research project.

The use of focus groups as a research method is growing in popularity. Ultimately, their success depends on the active involvement of the participants. Effective participation can make focus group interviews an excellent means of securing subjective information that has rich explanatory value.

SHARPENING YOUR FOCUS

1. List and discuss the advantages and disadvantages of the focus group interview as a stand-alone research method.

2. Explain and discuss the following general phases for structuring the interview guide: (a) introduction, (b) warm-up questions, (c) exploratory questions, (d) closing.

3. Define the role/function of the moderator and participants. How do they contribute to the effectiveness of focus group interviews?

4. Report on a group experience where you had to deal with a "difficult" person. Indicate the type of person you were dealing with, the reason for the difficulty, and your reactions to the person. How did this effect the relationship you were developing with the group?

5. How might one analyze the data collected from focus groups? What should the final written report contain? How important is the issue of confidentiality?

6. Design and conduct a series of focus groups involving freshmen or first-year students at your college/university to assess their attitudes and gather impressions of the orientation program and first-year experience.

NOTES

1. David L. Morgan, "Focus Groups," *Annual Review of Sociology* 22 (1996): 129–52.
2. Richard A. Krueger, *Focus Groups: A Practical Guide for Applied Research* 2d ed. (Thousand Oaks, Calif.: Sage Publications, 1994), 16.
3. Linda C. Lederman, "Assessing Educational Effectiveness: The Focus Group Interview as a Technique for Data Collection," *Communication Education* 38 (April 1990): 117–27.
4. Ivor Gaber, "Hocus-pocus Polling," *New Statesman and Society,* 16 August, 1996, 20–21.
5. Brian Silverman, "Get'em While They're Hot," *Sales and Marketing Management* 149 (February 1997): 47–52.

6. Sarah Schafer, "Communications: Getting a Line on Customers," *Inc.* 18 (1996): 102.
7. Morgan, "Focus Groups."
8. A. Mitra, "Use of Focus Groups in the Design of Recreation Needs Assessment," *Evaluation and Program Planning* 17 (1994): 133–40.
9. K. O'Brian, "Using Focus Groups to Develop Health Surveys: An Example from Research on Social Relationships and AIDS-Preventive Behavior," *Health Education Quarterly.* 20 (1993): 361–72.
10. David W. Stewart and Prem N. Shamdasani, *Focus Groups: Theory and Practice* (Thousand Oaks, Calif.: Sage Publications, 1990).
11. Lederman, "Assessing Educational Effectiveness," 20.
12. E. F. Fern, "The Use of Focus Groups for Idea Generation: The Effects of Group Size, Acquaintanceship, and Moderator on Response Quantity and Quality," *Journal of Marketing Research* 19 (1982): 1–13.
13. Morgan, "Focus Groups."
14. Peggy Y. Byers and James R. Wilcox, "Focus Groups: A Qualitative Opportunity for Researchers," *Journal of Business Communication* 28 (Winter 1991): 66.
15. Lederman, "Assessing Educational Effectiveness."
16. Stewart and Shamdasani, *Focus Groups: Theory and Practice,* 62.
17. Krueger, *Focus Groups: A Practical Guide.*
18. J. Kitzinger, "Introducing Focus Groups," *British Medical Journal* 311 (1995): 300.
19. Krueger, *Focus Groups: A Practical Guide,* 93.
20. Lawrence R. Frey, Carl H. Botan, Paul G. Friedman, and Gary L. Kreps, *Investigating Communication: An Introduction to Research Methods* (Englewood Cliffs, N.J.: Prentice-Hall, 1991).
21. Krueger, *Focus Groups: A Practical Guide.*
22. R. M. Stogdill, *Handbook of Leadership: A Survey of Theory and Research* (New York: Free Press, 1974).
23. Max DePree, *Leadership Jazz* (New York: Dell Publishing, 1992), 8–9.
24. See Cal W. Downs, G. Paul Smeyak, and Ernest Martin, *Professional Interviewing* (New York: Harper and Row, 1980), 405–7; Rick Brinkman and Rick Kirschner, *Dealing with People You Can't Stand* (New York: McGraw-Hill, 1994).
25. See L. A. Gottschalk, *The Content Analysis of Verbal Behavior* (Jamaica, N.Y.: Spectrum, 1979); Krippendorf, *Content Analysis: An Introduction to Its Methodology* (Beverly Hills, Calif.: Sage, 1980).
26. Krueger, *Focus Groups: A Practical Guide.*
27. Carol Lehman, William Himstreet, and Wayne Baty, *Business Communications,* 11th ed. (Cincinnati, Ohio: South-Western College Publishing, 1996).
28. Krueger, *Focus Groups: A Practical Guide,* 126–27.
29. Richard Dodge, "What to Report," in *Strategies for Business and Technical Writing,* 2d ed. ed. K. J. Harty (San Diego: HBJ, 1985).

12 The Organizational Audit

Effective communication is the lifeblood of any organization. Few people would deny the importance of effective communication in maintaining a healthy organization—we know it intuitively, we experience its importance daily, and we have faith in what it can accomplish. Still, our tendency is to take effective communication for granted until there is some breakdown or problem, and this can lead to serious difficulties. The organizational audit can provide the periodic monitoring critical to maintaining effective communication, diagnosing problems, and providing systematic feedback.

Chapter 12 examines the rationale and benefits of interviews involved in organizational audits; outlines the planning and administration of the organizational audit; and describes the data-gathering, data-analyzing, and reporting techniques used in the organizational audit. This chapter is designed to accomplish three objectives:

1. *Awareness.* You will understand the purpose and benefits of an interview used in organizational assessments.

2. *Assessment.* You will be able to assess the value of specific data-gathering and analysis tools used in an organizational audit.

3. *Application.* You will be able to effectively plan and administer an interview within an organizational audit, as well as report the results of audits.

*   *   *   *   *

The Merger: Grumbles at Gumble's Merchandising

Gumble and Quiver are both department store chains thriving in Portland, Maine, during a period of low inflation and low unemployment. Gumble's is the larger of the two merchandising companies, with a chain of stores targeting middle-income shoppers in Portland and along the southern coast of Maine. Quiver's is a smaller concentration of up-scale department stores in the Portland area. Fred Daley, the CEO at Gumble's, and his executive committee decided seven months ago to expand into the up-scale merchandising market. Their choice was either to go it alone, which would require a sizable investment of funds, or to acquire the resources through a merger. They approached Quiver's and agreed that it made sense financially to merge the two chains of stores into GQ Ltd.

While the two chains share a common interest in merchandising, they are very different in their approach and supervisory areas, such as management philosophy and employee relations. Gumble's emphasizes efficiency and cost reductions through standardized, centralized operations, whereas Quiver's places priority on store autonomy to facilitate customized, personal service adapted to each neighborhood served. Gumble's managers use a controlling, authoritative style with uniform employee training, while Quiver's builds commitment through delegating responsibility and initiative, as well as Christmas parties, employee picnics, and retirement ceremonies. Moreover, Gumble's stores are typically decorated in a more functional and standardized manner than the beautifully furnished Quiver stores, which reflect the taste and values of their up-scale clientele.

For almost seven months prior to the merger, managers and employees of both chains were kept in the dark concerning personnel decisions. During discussions and the actual application to merge, no information was shared regarding its implications except for top executive ranks. Rumors are running rampant and undermining morale and productivity. Quiver's employees feel particularly threatened because Gumble's management will clearly be in control. The secrecy has prompted negative comments concerning the conservative, autocratic, and nonparticipative management style practiced by Gumble's. These concerns have resulted in a number of very good middle managers from Quiver's accepting offers from other department stores who are pleased to acquire such fine talent. Faced with further resignations and the dilemma of converting two groups of employees into one coordinated, productive, and cohesive work body, Fred Daley appoints a committee with representatives from both Gumble's and Quiver's to conduct a company-wide audit and assessment to focus on management communication and employee relations. When making this decision, he told the committee, "I don't want to get caught behind the eight ball and snookered on this opportunity to successfully launch GQ Ltd." He indicated he wanted to provide a "fair break" for everyone, and the committee's efforts would provide him a "clear shot" at accomplishing this goal and implementing needed changes and programs.

Jim Beard, vice president for Resource Management at Gumble's, and Suzanne Land, vice president for Human Resources at Quiver's, are to jointly chair the audit and assessment task force. When making their joint appointment, Daley said, "You two are my best shot at positioning managers and employees to positively accept the challenges and possibilities created by the merger." Jim learned the business in "the school of hard knocks" and is widely respected by Gumble's employees for his tough-but-fair approach to handling the operations parts of the retail merchandising business. Suzanne also worked her way up but earned an MBA on the way to becoming Quiver's first female executive and a role model for many female employees. Doing what you're told, working hard, and producing is Jim's definition of a "good" employee. He feels recent college graduates are long on theory and self-interest, and short on practical experience and commitment. Suzanne looks for initiative, creativity, and flexibility in an employee, believing education and life-long learning are essential to remaining current and competitive. Despite their personal differences, Jim and Suzanne meet and agree on a memo to be sent to all personnel, urging them to be patient during these turbulent times and informing them about the audit. Furthermore, they gain an agreement to withhold any personnel actions until the audit is completed and recommendations are reviewed.

During the first team-building session, they define the purpose of the audit and explore various approaches. Jim insists on cost efficiency and an emphasis on performance data, with Suzanne being systems oriented and concerned with reliability, validity, and thoroughness in data gathering. Subsequent sessions involve discussing methodologies, developing an agenda, and scheduling audit activities. After collecting the data, considerable time is spent interpreting results, drawing conclusions, and making recommendations. While there is much debate over the far-reaching changes proposed, eventually a consensus is reached and a three-pronged approach to the problems agreed upon. The report will advocate (1) reorganization to reduce duplication and waste, (2) implementation of a participatory management philosophy at all levels to maintain and increase productivity, and (3) gaining management/employee support and commitment through building work relationships.

However, on the way to her office Suzanne Land overhears Jim Beard saying to a member of the audit team, "I'll never believe in this one-company fantasy." She is determined to candidly speak to Jim and the audit team about this grumbling.

Discussion Questions

1. What purposes would an organizational audit serve? Discuss some strategies that might be used. What are some of the practical implications of a communication audit?

2. How would GQ Ltd. benefit from a communication audit? What rationale should guide the audit? What kind of data should be generated?
3. What are the important planning considerations? How can the trust of the organization be gained? What practical problems could be confronted in administering the audit? How might they be overcome?
4. What data-gathering techniques should be used? List specific instruments. What kinds of information might be derived from interviews that could supplement other methods?
5. What major considerations should guide feedback to the organization? How should the findings be presented? How inclusive should it be? Who should receive the report?

The Nature of Organizational Audits

In recent years, top executives in large organizations have begun to realize the need to help ensure that the total organization is well managed. Consequently, organizational audits are now being used to promote a well-managed organization. Organizational audits have been adopted for various purposes and have proved themselves in numerous organizations. For example, climate surveys gather information on attitudes or opinions; organizational characteristics surveys aim at getting data about teamwork, team play, and relationships; and decision-flow analysis is an attempt to look at the flow of work in terms of the decisions or actions to be taken by individuals. Other applications explore coaching practices, delegating responsibility, employee performance, intergroup conflict problems, and time pressures.[1] And, the ICA communication audit uniquely examines the communication system within organizations and will be our focus when discussing organizational audits. It is representative of the organizational audit approach and uses interviewing as a principal data-gathering method. Moreover, it reflects Chester Barnard's classic dictum: "The first function of the executive is to establish and maintain a system of communication."[2]

* * * * *

Fred Daley, CEO of Gumble's and now the newly created GQ Ltd. prudently arranges for a companywide audit to determine potential problem areas and assess the influences of the merger. He clearly understood differences existed between the two chains before the merger and realized that significant changes would be required to make GQ Ltd. one company. Jointly appointing Jim Beard and Suzanne Land to lead the audit task force comprised of representatives from both

Gumble's and Quiver's ensures a balance of interests and tests their team-building capabilities.

Jim and Suzanne are both capable human resource specialists but do have obvious differences of opinion regarding management and promoting employee performance. These differences will have to be reconciled or set aside if they are to objectively direct the audit team, interpret data, and make productively solid recommendations. Their initial decision to issue a memo announcing a freeze on personnel actions and the formation of an audit/assessment team necessitating companywide participation displayed an ability to work together. They realized the importance of decreasing employee uncertainty, stemming damaging rumors, and gaining widespread support. Any organizational audit requires energy, time, and patience; consequently, gaining a commitment to the auditing process is important.

The singular purpose of the audit is to advance recommendations which will make Gumble's and Quiver's one company with one group of dedicated employees working toward a common vision and goal—the success of GQ Ltd. This will require defining the mission statement; identifying core values; understanding job functions, duties, and responsibilities; and gaining an awareness of employee attitudes, perceptions, and opinions. Strategies could include an organizational culture survey, values appraisal, climate survey, decision-flow analysis, and needs/task assessment. The comprehensive nature of a communication audit would certainly include it as a strategic choice. Jim and Suzanne would find a communication audit highly beneficial in providing factual information regarding company structure, value information pertaining to performance and effectiveness, and descriptive data leading to a consideration of policy/procedural options and actions. The lack of communication has contributed to the current situation, characterized by high anxiety, and improved communication will be essential in creating trust and encouraging employees to work together in a concerted effort to make GQ Ltd. succeed. A companywide communication audit is a practical and pragmatic choice at this juncture. The snapshot taken will significantly assist Fred Daley and top management in their action planning.

The Rationale and Benefits for Audits

The value of conducting an organizational communication audit seems obvious, if "good communication makes a difference—then an understanding of what is good communication and its correlates should increase our knowledge of organizational behavior."[3] More importantly, however, a communication audit prioritizes the need for effective communication and implicitly says to everyone in the organization, "Don't take communication for granted." Consequently, it sensitizes people to how they are communicating and motivates them to improve their communication performance.

The primary objective of a communication audit is to evaluate an organization's communication system, furnishing information that will help an organization improve both its communication practices and its overall effectiveness as an organization. Data collection is central to evaluation, and the communication audit provides a plan for conducting this effort. It spells out the types of information to be collected, how it will be collected, and the data analysis techniques to be used.

The communication audit is also a process by which an organization's communication needs are identified and articulated. With this information, an organization learns where and what kinds of training programs are needed and who needs to be included in those programs. Auditing forecasts problems by pinpointing those communication areas where some repair is needed before they actually break down. Here, audit information can be used to identify performance deficiencies and developmental needs. In this sense, an audit becomes an important component in a feedback loop, which can assist in designing and implementing necessary communication training programs.

The systematic collection of information permitted by the use of a communication audit also can guide future decision making and assist in developing ongoing action plans. A communication audit focuses on the organization's goals and its effectiveness in accomplishing those goals. The information derived can help an organization understand what it is trying to accomplish, what potential roadblocks to success exist, and what training may be needed to enhance effectiveness. The recommendations suggested can be used in decision making and strategy planning. Although the communication audit often reviews the entire organization, it may also be used to examine only specific departments or programs of interest to management.

Finally, the communication audit can serve as a starting point for an organization's communication training process. By determining the necessary knowledge, skills, and abilities required for maintaining an effective communication system, the communication audit can help identify those areas that can benefit from training and prioritize those areas. This information can further serve to identify which employees should participate in such training programs. Finally, it can assist in selecting the most appropriate training method—on-the-job training, classroom workshops or seminars, or computer-based training. This principal educational benefit should not be overlooked. Ultimately, the goal of an audit is to improve the organization's communication effectiveness by solving current problems, preventing anticipated problems, and including as participants in training those individuals and units that can benefit the most. The communication audit provides an opportunity to gain critical insights into the whole communication process and become sensitized to the human element comprising the organization. A cautionary, yet noteworthy, observation is expressed by Cal Downs when he stresses that "communication is not the only process in an organization that needs auditing, and communication audits certainly do not solve all problems and create the perfect organization; nevertheless, audits offer important means of improving organizational life."[4]

*   *   *   *   *

Jim Beard and Suzanne Land need to use as their guide for planning the audit the needs and interests of GQ Ltd. A communication audit can help sensitize them to the needs, focus on critical relational links, and help them see ways of adapting to new technologies, markets, and challenges created by the merger. Reliable, valid information about the communication system can assist in answering questions about who receives/needs what information from whom and by what means. Problem areas and bottlenecks can be determined, leading to recommendations for improving the quality of information and the effectiveness of the communication system. The strengths, weaknesses, and needs can be identified and used as a basis for decision making and strategy planning by top management.

Jim's concern for performance data is reasonable, but Suzanne's systems orientation more appropriately addresses the situation. Performance data along with other information will have to be generated given Fred Daley's charge. Reliable, valid data from all segments of the company will need to be collected. Quantitative and qualitative information from key people in all departments, as well as a random sampling of employees, will be essential for drawing conclusions and making recommendations. Admittedly, some data will be more difficult and time consuming to gather and analyze, but thoroughness is key to this project. The communication audit can serve as a beginning point for integrating, building, and developing the newly merged managers/supervisors and employees. Jim and Suzanne may also wish to audit other processes, but the communication audit can significantly improve morale and work conditions at GQ Ltd. It will affect future growth and development.

Planning and Administering the Organizational Audit

Despite the challenge and the opportunity for growth, however, the planning and administration of an organizational or communication audit is hard work, taking as long as six months to complete. Its planning and administration requires earnest attention, patience, and enormous energy. The audit directors, as well as team members, must have a genuine eagerness to learn, a sense of curiosity, and a zeal for inquiry.

Planning the Audit

Managers and researchers have consistently recognized the necessity for and importance of planning in the execution of long-term projects. Planning requires (1) defining the purpose and scope of the audit, (2) identifying focal areas and selecting audit instruments, (3) determining and committing available resources, (4) developing an audit schedule and formalizing audit arrangements, and (5) deciding on the nature of the final report.

An essential first step in planning is to gain consensus regarding the purpose and scope of the audit. A communication audit is one way of gathering valid information, focusing the organization's attention, and creating effects, but it is not the only way. Consequently, a key question to initially answer is "What do we want/need to know?" This requires deciding what kinds of information will be most useful to the particular organization and whether a communication audit is most appropriate. Planning necessitates comparing the alternatives available in light of the objectives desired. Criteria for evaluating alternatives might include organizational expectations, information utility, instrument reliability and validity, efficiency, and return on investment. If the purpose is to gather useful information pertaining to an organization's communication system or to improve an organization's communication performance, a communication audit would be appropriate. The purpose further determines the scope of the audit. The macroaspect of communication system appraisals studies the entire organization, while the microaspect of communication system appraisals concentrates on specific units in the organization or individual communication activities. There can be an advantage in considering the overall communication system first and studying specific communication activities later in that the broader analysis can lay the necessary groundwork for a more specific and targeted examination. Ultimately, however, the scope will be determined by what the organization values most at the time and by where management thinks problems can be uncovered.[5]

Every communication audit must be focused and use appropriately reliable data-gathering techniques. In choosing focal areas for auditing and selecting specific instruments, auditors are setting the parameters for their study and determining the information to be gained. Basically, the data to be collected should focus on the most important elements in the organization: the explicit and implicit communication policies, the organizational structure, the task processes, the flow of communication, the communication channels used, the types of information exchanged, the people in their relational networks, and the specific communication activities. This requires understanding the communication and organizational processes, examining the tasks and functions performed by communication, assessing the mediums used, determining the adequacy of information exchanged, and being sensitive to the quality of communication relationships. The focus should give direction to the audit, and the data-gathering instruments selected should provide the best information possible regarding those areas. Usually, a variety of data-gathering techniques are employed, with each possessing special qualities and unique features. These will be identified and discussed in more detail later in the chapter. Finally, the focal choices and information-gathering tools needed should be made in collaboration with management, since these decisions will affect the resources needed to administer the audit.

The organization must carefully determine and commit the resources necessary for conducting a communication audit. This determination entails answering the question: "What resources are necessary for administering the intended communication audit?" Obviously, if the organization is unwilling to commit necessary resources, there is no point in trying to conduct an audit, regardless of its scope or focus. The essential resources to consider are time, money, personnel, and space. A communication audit may take from three to six months to complete and will periodically take people away from their routine work. Financially, the commitment involves personnel salaries, supply outlays, computer charges, communications costs, and possibly travel expenses. Probably the most important resource commitment is in people. There must be a small central task force of selected individuals responsible for directing the audit, as well as people available to administer surveys, conduct interviews, lead discussions, input the data, interpret the results, write the reports, and answer any questions about the audit. While audit teams may vary in size depending upon the desired involvement of the organization, a commitment to human resources is indispensable for the success of an audit. Finally, rooms will be needed for meetings, interviews, data collection, and feedback sessions. The rooms allocated must ensure privacy and freedom from disruptions. The specific space needed will depend upon the audit instruments chosen, sample size, and administration procedures. While uncontrollable events can occur, organizations must anticipate any other decisions, plans, programs, or projects that may have an impact upon resources and affect or be affected by an audit. Ultimately, an organization must thoughtfully analyze its resources and seriously commit to the audit before developing an audit schedule and formalizing audit arrangements.

Once resources have been committed to an audit project, the central task force must develop an audit schedule and formalize audit arrangements. These administrative planning decisions address the question: "What has to be done to conduct and complete the communication audit?" Operating without a plan creates a lack of definition while increasing anxiety and promoting uncertainty. Therefore, a checklist of procedures and audit agenda with target dates should be established. Schedules must allow enough time for participation to be meaningful, and all arrangements must accommodate space requirements, workloads, and other key events. Moreover, decisions to sample a cross section of the organization or canvass employees must be made, as well as how to let employees know about the project. While the choice of employees to be audited will be most affected by how the organization wants to use the audit data, all key people should be included, and it is better to have too many people included than too few. Since an audit is a major undertaking, every effort should be made to publicize it in advance by providing a simple overview of some of the procedures and why it is being done. This helps legitimize the project and gain necessary organizational support.

Finally, planning decisions must be made regarding the nature of the final report. From the outset, it must be clear to everyone involved what information is going to be provided to whom and by what means. Normally, data is reported in written and oral form. A brief written report summarizing findings may be circulated to all members of the organization. This report confirms the importance of the audit and demonstrates to those participating that their time and effort was not wasted. A lengthier, more detailed written report is submitted to top management for limited circulation. This report focuses on the conclusions, recommendations, and findings of the audit, with supporting charts, tables, and figures provided in a series of appendices. Last, a comprehensive oral presentation of the audit is often provided to top decision makers and action planners, as well as selected managers or supervisors. When reporting information, it is important to remember that an audit is intended to help solve problems, not to create them.

Administering the Audit

Four basic activities constitute the administration of a communication audit: (1) data collection, (2) data evaluation and interpretation, (3) data reporting, and (4) action planning and implementation. The effectiveness of each of these activities contributes to the overall effectiveness of the communication audit. Although the activities are closely related, they each require unique skills for effective performance.

Commonly employed techniques for data collection include survey questionnaires, observations, personal interviews, focus groups, critical incidents, ECCO analysis (a specialized questionnaire specifically oriented toward individual messages), network analysis, content analysis, communication diaries, and cost analysis. Each technique can yield valid, reliable, useful information, and the techniques often are combined to provide a more comprehensive understanding of potential problems and issues. It is advisable to use multiple techniques when possible, since each can supplement one another and provide consistency to audit findings. The ultimate goal of data collection is to obtain a realistic picture of the organization.

Once data is collected, evaluation and interpretation begins. To interpret means to try to make sense of or to understand something in a particular way; as understanding increases, the auditing process becomes worthwhile and valuable. However, different auditors may occasionally interpret the data differently. What separates better interpretations from poorer ones is the "degree to which the interpreter has knowledge or imagination to provide a plausible rendering of events that might have generated the present display."[6] Consequently, evaluation and interpretation is the art and science of constructing answers that make practical sense. From this frame of reference, evaluation and interpretation requires mental leaps from data to conclusions and going beyond mere descriptive statements.

Decisions concerning the importance of data can only be made after collating and thoroughly examining it. Quantitative information must be tabulated and statistically analyzed to develop a numerical description of the issues or problems under consideration. The use of appropriate statistical tests, an understanding of the limits of particular tests, and an ability to translate the numerical data into the essence of the problem are important during this phase of the evaluation/

interpretation process. Qualitative information must be coded to discover recurring themes or identify unique problems or issues. Quantitative and qualitative data can then be examined for convergence, that is, whether the two forms of data yield essentially the same understanding of the problem. When they do, there is added confidence in the accuracy of the findings. When findings are dissimilar, the discrepancies must be reconciled. Contradictions may sometimes be accounted for by the differences among the methodologies employed, while at other times the audit team must spend time discussing the differing results and what they mean. There will be disagreements, and much time can be consumed, but the time is not necessarily wasted. Remember, all the information needs to be digested and integrated, and interpretation cannot be hurried.

The evaluation and interpretation process should lead to some basic conclusions about the organization. The final conclusions should be general statements addressing only the most important items and reflecting strengths as well as weaknesses. The conclusions and recommendations should always address the practical realities of the organization. Are they practical or workable? Are they desirable? Are they cost efficient?

After the data from an audit has been collected, evaluated, and interpreted, it must be reported. The report lets the organization learn what it is doing right; gives it a sense of where, what, and why problems exist; and allows it to focus its resources on its greatest needs. The value of the report lies in that it heightens the awareness of communication processes, problems, and behaviors within the organization, increasing an understanding of the affects of communication changes on effectiveness and encouraging acceptance of organizational interventions.

A concise, simple, objective, or analytic report should be circulated to all employees, informing them of the audit results. This report should be limited to the major findings and general conclusions. The final written report for the top management of the organization should reveal all areas studied, recite the findings of the audit, enumerate conclusions, and specify recommendations. While providing the organization with something tangible to work with at its own pace, the report should give readers enough information to be useful yet not so much that they will be overwhelmed. This report should be written in a personalized, plain English style rather than an academic, research report style. Finally, an oral briefing for the CEO and/or key members of the organization should also be provided, again summarizing conclusions, recommendations, and findings. It is helpful if the presenter prepares charts, graphs, or diagrams to illustrate major points. This oral presentation should allay fears, reduce defensiveness, ease anxiety, and hopefully lead to a constructive discussion for action planning and intervention strategies.

The principal payoff to an organization from studying its communication system, however, comes through action planning and implementation of changes in the system to improve communication. The responsibility for generating priorities, developing action plans, and implementing recommendations is upon the members of the organization, not upon the facilitators of the audit. The organization must take the data from its communication audit and integrate it with implementation theory to enhance its own development and growth.

Implementation theory focuses on specific intervention strategies designed to induce changes and includes human processual, technostructural, sociotechnical systems design, and large systems. **Human processual intervention** concentrates on changing behaviors by modifying individual attitudes, values, problem-solving approaches, and interpersonal styles. In order to facilitate this planned change, a person must have useful information with which to diagnose the situation and to act. "Free choice" further implies that the person(s) involved in the change process has the autonomy, control, and motivation to implement the intervention activity—possesses internal commitment and has assumed "ownership" of the strategy. The implicit belief is that the person(s) "have processed valid information and made an informed free choice."[7] The retraining of certain management personnel in communication skills, such as writing, listening, public speaking, and open discussion, is a result of actual recommendations implemented by some organizations audited which portrays processual intervention.

Technostructural intervention focuses on improving work content, work method, work flow, performance factors, and relationships among workers.[8] One of the key concepts here is job design. A job has several distinguishing characteristics, including individual tasks or duties, responsibilities, authority, relationships, and skill requirements. These job characteristics affect employee psychological states, which in turn affects work outcomes and satisfaction. Therefore, changing one or more of a job's characteristics—a strategy called job enrichment—can induce positive psychological changes, resulting in improved performance and satisfaction.[9] The broader implications include a more supportive organizational climate.[10] Real recommendations implemented by audited organizations illustrating technostructural interventions are improving the quality of quarterly officers' meetings by adding question-and-answer periods and open discussion or improving informal communication through luncheons with key executives, social events, rap sessions, and open-door policies.

Sociotechnical systems interventions are "directed at the fit between the technological configuration and the social structure of work units . . . [which] results in the rearrangement of relationships among roles or tasks or a sequence of activities to produce self-maintaining, semiautonomous groups."[11] This research explores the quality of worklife interventions, including such areas as organizational democratization, participative management, job enrichment, and work rescheduling. The underlying theme is the efficacy of interventions on empowerment, worker satisfaction, and productivity. Sociotechnical systems interventions may be depicted by audited organizations implementing such recommendations as adding liaison personnel to facilitate horizontal communication between computer users and computer personnel to propitiate understanding and reduce costly programming mistakes or adding new formal channels of communication, such as newsletters, videotape playback of key memoranda, news bulletin boards, new meeting structures, and new telephone systems.

Finally, **large systems interventions** approach an organization as a complex, human system with a unique character, its own culture and value system, and "information and work procedures that must be continually examined, analyzed, and improved if optimum productivity and motivation are to result."[12] It is based on an understanding that there are numerous challenges facing managers of complex organizations, including changes in the culture of the organization, the structure or shape of the organization, and the mission or "reason for being." Consequently, in order to meet these challenges, organizational leaders must be able to develop a vision guided by beliefs and principles that can be translated into a mission and goal that will form the basis for managing the organization. Examples of limited large system interventions by audited organizations include the development of communication goals, objectives, and policies and the disclosure of these to employees, or hiring and shifting personnel to improve the communication function in the company.

Depending upon the purpose, scope, and focus of an audit, selected interventions may modify worker behaviors, improve work content, create a more suitable relationship between technology and workers, or affect organizationwide change by altering the existing paradigm and the multiple dimensions comprising an organization. However, while the planning and implementing of needed change can come about in diverse ways, ultimately the resulting change itself must be studied, measured, and evaluated. Consequently, the organizational audit *should not* be perceived as a *program* with a beginning and end, but as a *process* that must be ongoing in order to sustain maximum effectiveness.

*   *   *   *   *

The first planning session helps to define the purpose and scope of the audit while contributing to building a unified team effort. The latter is essential if the audit is to succeed. Jim and Suzanne both agree to committing available resources to the project, but Jim insists on carefully monitoring costs in relation to the return on investment. Cost is important but must be considered in relation to the value of needed information generated. It is initially understood that a final oral and written report will be submitted to Fred Daley and top management at GQ Ltd. It would also be advisable to prepare a brief report of general findings and conclusions for managers, supervisors, and employees. This would help calm their fears while acknowledging their participation. Later sessions are given to selecting audit instruments, developing an audit schedule, and formalizing audit arrangements.

Given the situation at GQ Ltd. establishing trust will be crucial in garnering support and gathering needed information. Confidentiality of information will have to be emphasized, with the protection of sources maintained. This will require carefully interpreting data and reporting results. Any repercussions would jeopardize the integrity of the auditors and damage efforts to unify employees into one company.

Several practical problems may confront the auditing team, but they can be anticipated and overcome. It is important that team members be familiar with field study procedures and trained in the auditing techniques selected. Skill in analysis and interpretation is necessary, and the auditors must be able to detect issues, identify recurring themes, and determine problems. When differences arise, they will have to work together to reconcile the data. Ultimately, a consensus must be reached regarding conclusions, with unbiased recommendations addressing the practical realities at GQ Ltd.

Data-Gathering and Data-Analyzing Techniques

The importance of information in today's ever changing and more complex world cannot be overstated. Understanding the various available methodologies or techniques is a necessary step in acquiring needed information. The audit uses a variety of data-gathering and data-analyzing techniques. These may include performance analysis, questionnaires, personal interviews, focus groups, trained observations, critical incident reports, communication diaries or duty studies, content analysis, ECCO (Episodic Communication Channels in Organizations) analysis, network analysis, and cost analysis.

Performance Analysis. Performance data exist as a result of the daily operations of the organization. It comes from mission statements, annual reports, quarterly profit statements, turnover rates, employee absenteeism, and policy and procedure manuals. This data can reveal an organization's routine operations. Such performance data can be useful to substantiate or expand understanding of problems identified with questionnaire and interview techniques. Performance data familiarizes auditors with the organization and the situation.

Questionnaires. The mainstay of most audits is some type of questionnaire, because questionnaires are inexpensive, expedient, and efficient instruments for acquiring information on a range of topics from a sizable sample population while assuring a certain amount of anonymity (see Chapter 10) A questionnaire may provide auditors with a permanent written record about people's attitudes, emotions, beliefs, intentions, and behaviors. Questionnaires portray how people think and feel about issues and begin to address questions of causation, allowing auditors to begin to understand how variables may relate to each other and, in particular, describe their identity with real-life settings. The questionnaire is a useful self-report data-gathering technique from which to generalize results and build a comprehensive assessment of the organization.

Personal Interviews. The interview is a *live* exchange between a questioner and a respondent, allowing for a personal interaction (see chapter 1). Collecting data through in-depth personal interviews has several advantages: (1) auditors can develop a firsthand familiarity with the people and their work processes, (2) auditors may take more time to explore in detail the selected topic areas, and (3) auditors might discover through their discussions new issues requiring examination.[13] The major advantage of interviews over other methods is that they can grow, be refined, and change in light of the information received. However, interviews are time consuming, and since information acquired is limited to perceptual reports, it can be difficult to code, analyze, and interpret. Moreover, interviews are only as good as the interviewers make them. Therefore, interviewers should clearly determine their purpose or objectives and identify the issues to be uncovered (see chapter 2). The questions should be well thought out to reveal the kind of information needed. Questions should be adapted to the specific people being interviewed and should draw the interviewee out. Personal interviews are an invaluable part of any auditing process.

Focus Groups. Focus group interviews bring a cross section of people together for an intensive discussion of various topics (see chapter 11). The intent is to probe intensively for qualitative data related to specific problem areas. Focus group interviews can supply auditors with quick results of subjective experiences from a random sampling of employees across the organization.

Trained Observations. If real-world behavior is of major concern for auditors, then the use of trained observers is an appropriate methodology. Trained observation allows auditors to get close to the organization and "shadow" the actions and behaviors of a specific group of people in a natural setting. This technique provides a convenient method for describing the communication of key personnel and identifying networks and directions of communication. Clearly, training is important, and any training program must include an understanding of communication roles, rules, and routines, as well as careful note taking. Trained observation is used in organizations to determine the answers to general questions concerning different levels of communication, and skilled observation can uncover information not previously known to the organization and, therefore, difficult to collect in formal questionnaires or interviews. It can benefit the auditing process by providing an empirical model representing the organization as it was when the observations were collected.

Critical Incident Reports. The critical incident technique is intended to identify and determine the most vital communication behavior(s) on which success or failure depends. Respondents are asked to describe and evaluate specific communication behaviors critical to their job performance. They are asked to think of an experience in which communication was particularly effective or ineffective and describe the communicative experience, the circumstances leading up to it, what they did that made them an effective or ineffective communicator, and the results or outcome. The technique is open ended and unstructured, allowing respondents complete freedom in choosing and assessing incidents that have high priority to them. They are particularly useful in pinpointing or localizing specific problems and balancing the perceptual data obtained from standardized questionnaires or personal interviews. Since the critical incident reporting can be adapted to any specific observable situation or context, it can be of value in auditing an organization. The results can enhance awareness and enrich an auditors' understanding of the organization.

Diaries/Duty Studies. Diaries or duty studies are other self-recording techniques that allow respondents an opportunity to record their own communication behavior, either continuously or periodically. While the specific categories for observation will be developed by the auditing team, such techniques can provide descriptive information about the amount of communication, the channel(s) employed, the network(s) used, and the direction followed. Auditors can learn who communicates what to whom and how. If real-world behavior is a major concern of auditors, then diaries and duty studies are an appropriate methodology. They permit auditors to understand and feel how the participants felt as they were involved in an ongoing event since such techniques deal with real behavior as it occurs in a natural setting.

Content Analysis. Bernard Berelson defines content analysis as "a technique for the objective, systematic, and quantitative description of the manifest content of communication."[14] Content analysis techniques, then, seek to systematically analyze "message content and message handling."[15] Any message of which there is an obtainable record can be content analyzed. Speeches, conversations, memos, letters, e-mail, manuals, and newspaper articles are potential sources for content analysis. It involves selecting the communication to be examined, developing categories for

Diaries or duty studies allow respondents to record their own communication behavior.

measurement, measuring the frequency of the categories, applying appropriate statistical tests to the data, and drawing conclusions.[16] Conclusions can be drawn regarding readability levels of material, types of words used in messages, and specific themes communicated. Its advantages lie in an ability to describe the messages under study and to make inferences about the creator(s) of the messages. Content analysis is another measure auditors can use in conjunction with other methods.

ECCO Analysis. ECCO (Episodic Communication Channels in Organizations) analysis was developed by Keith Davis to trace a particular message through an organization measuring rate of flow, distortion, and redundancy.[17] It deals with concrete messages rather than with perceptions or attitudes. Judgments can then be made about the length of time information takes to circulate, the media usage for this message, and the ways that different types of information are processed. Respondents are asked to complete an ECCO log, which focuses on whether or not they know a very specific message. They are further asked from whom they first received the information, where, when, and by what method. The ECCO log is then coded, tabulated, and analyzed by means of appropriate statistical techniques.[18] Auditors may choose to develop several different ECCO logs for different kinds of messages or different channels of communication. ECCO analysis is a convenient, fast, reliable, and relatively inexpensive field instrument. ECCO analysis's ability to monitor formal and informal channels, pinpoint information blockages, assess channel adequacy, examine roles and network structures, and determine how information is processed makes it a valuable audit tool.

Network Analysis. The goal of communication network analyses is to better understand the structure of an organization's communication flow in order to identify where it is blocked or overloaded, who is responsible, and what new constructs might improve communication. The flow of information is vital to a healthy organization, and when the communication system is blocked or overloaded, resources are wasted, and decisions are made prematurely, inaccurately, or not at all. Such an analysis provides an empirically derived pictorial map of all operational communication networks comprising the organization and permits a computer-generated comparison of actual with expected networks and member roles. Network analysis can be a complicated task, and creating a geometric map and giving meaning to numbers can be difficult without sophisticated computer programs.[19] Still, network analysis provides auditors with a logical and pragmatic means for collecting essential data that may be integrated into an overall plan for organizational communication change and development.

Cost Analysis. Cost analysis assumes that communication behavior has both human and financial consequences. Although cost analysis can be used to determine the cost efficiency of particular types of communication, the primary purpose of collecting cost data is to understand the financial effects of the event, task, or behavior within the broader context of what the organization needs. Cost analysis requires describing the task to be costed in terms of behaviors and computing the total cost of communication for the task by identifying those behaviors and determining the value of the time each person spends involved with the task.[20] Gathering data about the cost of a problem can prompt the organization into reality testing and contribute to directing action toward solutions.

The effectiveness of any organizational audit, including a communication audit, depends on the data-gathering and data-analyzing techniques selected. When choosing techniques, certain variables must be considered, such as the type of data provided, the quality of data, the ease of use, and the cost. This permits a comparison of techniques that can assist in determining appropriate methodologies.

All organizations are different and there is no cookie-cutter way to facilitate change. Tools and techniques need to be adapted to fit an organization's unique needs and culture.

*   *   *   *   *

What do we want/need to know? What resources are necessary for administering the audit and their cost? What has to be done to conduct and complete the audit? These are the questions that will guide the selection of data-gathering techniques. Jim Beard would probably prefer to rely on cost analysis, performance analysis, and questionnaires, which would include critical incidents. These techniques are relatively inexpensive, easy to administer, require little to moderate time to complete, and yield largely reliable, valid, quantifiable data. They reveal the quality of past performance; identify vital tasks or functions; examine knowledge, skills, and competencies; and explore attitudes, beliefs, and perceptions. Obtrusive and unobtrusive measures provide data that requires only moderate skills to analyze and may be uniformly interpreted.

Suzanne Land, being cost conscious and mindful of available resources, would still probably want to include more subjective, qualitative measures, such as personal interviews and trained observations, as well as network analysis in order to more completely assess the total system. These measures are more costly and time consuming but yield rich data regarding personal insights and structural/relational links. Members of the auditing team would have to be carefully trained in field procedure and instrument use, and an outside consultant with computer expertise would probably have to assist with the network analysis. While information obtained could still retain high reliability and validity, greater skills would be needed for analysis and interpretation, with the likelihood of discrepancies arising. These would have to be further discussed and resolved before drawing conclusions and advancing recommendations. Fred Daley's charge to the audit committee and the benefits of such information would warrant the inclusion of these techniques, including hiring an external network programming specialist.

> Multiple techniques, which include personal interviews, permit describing actual behaviors and tapping into the cross section of employee perceptions. Quantitative measures can provide important statistical/numerical information, while qualitative measures offer valuable data in terms of in-depth explanations of responses. Issues can be probed and problems more completely examined. The situation at GQ Ltd. requires that an accurate picture be taken, not a hurried instant snapshot or filtered glamor portrait.

Writing the Report

Once the data have been collected and analyzed, a critical phase begins—writing the report. The final report is the reason the audit was conducted and must justify all the hard work; thus, it may well represent the most important step in the audit process. Cal Downs emphasizes *"the* report" when he observes that this is "the one opportunity that the auditor has to discuss the issues and make important points. . . . The final report must be a superb form of communication about communication."[21] Consequently, this final phase should be accorded great care and attention.

When conducting a communication audit and writing the final feedback report, auditors must clearly understand the differences between the roles of change manager and change agent. The **change manager,** CEO and top management, oversees the design of intervention strategies and has overall responsibility for determining the appropriate intervention activities and implementing the strategies. The **change agent** assists the change manager in designing and implementing change strategies. As change agents, auditors have primary responsibility for facilitating all of the activities surrounding the design and implementation of strategies. In this capacity, they serve as advocates, technical specialists, trainers/educators, fact finders, collaborators in problem solving, process specialists, and reflectors.[22] Auditors advocate certain approaches, provide specific technical knowledge on special problems, and educate the CEO and top management on different intervention strategies. They further serve as fact finders and provide assistance in problem analysis by identifying solutions and action steps. Finally, they help facilitate meetings and group processes, and they aid the CEO and top management in understanding the situation by reflecting or reacting to information. Ultimately, the auditor must document the results of these duties by reacting to the information gained and clarifying the situation. The written report permits the auditor and team members an opportunity to reflect on the data and explain the findings. The CEO and management can then make the tough decisions necessary for action planning and implementation.

Choosing what to include in the final report and how to present it will take a great deal of consideration, since most audits generate more information than it is possible to report. Still, the report should be thorough, well organized, and visually attractive. The report should convey an overall estimate of the state of the organization, noting problems as well as organizational strengths. It is critical not to overwhelm the CEO and management "with negative findings that leave them with disproportionate feelings of helplessness and, therefore, unable to act."[23] Auditors should be neutral and objective in portraying the total reality by including the variability in responses. Averages alone can be misleading, so it is important to represent the range of responses. The information in the report should be logically arranged, using headings and subheadings as well as summaries for quick review. Cal Downs suggests the following outline which can serve as a useful guide in preparing the written report:

1. Statements of purpose.
    a. Identifies major thrusts of the diagnosis.
    b. States the limitations of the audit.
    c. Describes the particular client system for the study.
    d. Provides historical background for the study.
2. Review of the procedures for the data collection.
    a. Includes copies of all instruments used.
    b. Describes the sampling techniques for collecting responses.
    c. Indicates the formats used in collecting data.
3. Summary of raw data obtained for each question.
    a. Includes separate sections for each kind of data. For example, summaries from interviews and questionnaires may be written separately.
    b. Reports information in a descriptive, nonevaluative way.
    c. Pinpoints any problems with data, such as absences of responses.
4. Description of analytic procedures.
    a. Describes statistical manipulation of raw data.
    b. Summarizes results of the analysis.
    c. Provides narrative descriptions of tables.
    d. Amplifies results with relevant examples or details to make them meaningful to the client.
5. Conclusions about strengths in, and obstacles to, communication.
6. Recommendations for future development.[24]

Like any professional document, the audit report should be bound and written on quality bond paper with appropriate margins, white space, and section dividers. Remember, visual appearance can be powerfully appealing and influential.

The conclusions reported should be limited to the purpose of the audit and relate to the goals of the organization. Choose only the most important findings, emphasizing problem areas where realistic intervention is possible. These conclusions should be adequately supported by the data collected. Charts and graphs can certainly add explanatory power, but it is imperative to go beyond statistics and numbers. Descriptive examples drawn from personal interviews, critical incident reports, and diaries or duty logs can add a human dimension to the "story" not evident in a strictly quantitative presentation.

It is up to auditors to pinpoint needed changes and make recommendations that may benefit the organization. Ultimately, this is the payoff for organizational leaders whose responsibility it will be to implement an action plan. This requires making realistic, short-term, cost-efficient recommendations, as well as long-term recommendations that may direct future growth and development. Recommendations should address critical priorities, be consistent with the organization's core values, and have a high probability of success. A rationale must be provided for each recommendation made and the consequences of the recommendation explored. Recommendations must never be made nonchalantly or with indifference, nor should they simply reflect the personal biases of auditors. Throughout the audit process, auditors must continually consider the well-being of the particular organization and heed its selected goals and objectives when writing the report.

*   *   *   *   *

The needs and demands of GQ Ltd. should guide audit feedback. Undoubtedly, not all of the information gathered will be reported, only the critical findings and conclusions reflecting the realities of the situation and providing direction. Certainly, too, the auditors must carefully balance the presentation of strengths and deficiencies. The recommendations should be a hopeful impetus for change and improvement. Probably the final written report should be discussed with Fred Daley prior to the oral presentation and release to top management. This can be helpful in resolving potential differences and gaining CEO support.

The final oral and written report to the CEO and top management should be inclusive, with specific recommendations prescribing short-term actions, as well as projecting a long-term view. It is vital to protect the confidentiality of sources when reporting information and rationally supporting recommendations. A more general, less inclusive report should be circulated to all managers, supervisors, and employees, and may also be prepared as a press release for interested external constituencies.

Certainly, Suzanne Land must candidly speak to Jim and the audit team about his overheard cynical remark. The team must be unified and reinforcing when advocating reorganization, participatory management, and team building. Any differences of opinion or doubts must be resolved before submitting the final written report and open discussion with top management. The responsibility for implementing needed interventions will rest with Fred Daley and his executive committee, and they must have confidence in the audit results submitted. Based on the auditing teams report, they will decide upon the human processual, technostructural, sociotechnical, and large systems interventions needed to effectively manage the growth and development of GQ Ltd.

At this point, Suzanne may wonder whether Jim's expressed attitude also reflects Fred Daley's and Gumble's views. She might question Daley's initial remarks when appointing the assessment committee. A cursory content analysis of such pool metaphors as "caught behind the eight ball," "snookered," and "positioning employees" could cause her to doubt the genuineness of his concerns and the sincerity of his motives. After all, pool is an individual rather than team activity, as well as being highly competitive and requiring skillful manipulation and placement. Still, he did indicate a desire to provide everyone a "fair break" and perceived the auditing team as being his "best shot" at gaining the necessary support and commitment for change. Hard work, a commitment to principles, and optimism has gotten Suzanne Land this far and should serve as her guide in dealing with Jim Beard's grumbling and rallying the auditing team, as well as when submitting the final report.

Critical Focus

Review again the Critical Focus presented in chapter 10 describing the meeting between Andrea Anderson and the department heads at Scholar Educational Products. Replay the videotape segment analyzing the recommendation to conduct an organizational audit. The following critical questions can direct and guide your analysis of the discussion.

1. What purposes are achieved by conducting an organizational audit? What are the assumptions on which a good diagnostic system should be based? What planning needs to precede an organizational audit?
2. What are the phases for conducting an organizational audit? What are some of the interview guidelines that should be used in organizational audits? What are the major considerations when analyzing the data and feeding back the results?
3. Locate an organizational consulting agency in your city and interview some of the consultants. Discuss the strategies they use when conducting an organizational audit.

Summary

Top executives, managers, and supervisors have progressively become concerned with monitoring how their organization's work. They have learned that in order to accomplish their mission and goals, the organization needs to be healthy, to operate efficiently, and to fulfill employee's needs. Consequently, organizational audits have become a vital means whereby action planners and decision makers can acquire a comprehensive portrait of the organization and its potential problems.

These analyses can examine the total organization or focus on a specific area, such as the communication system. The ICA communication audit is designed to diagnose the communication effectiveness of an organization. The ICA audit process, like other organizational audits, uses a variety of data-gathering techniques and analytical instruments. These may include performance analysis, questionnaires, personal interviews, focus groups, trained observations, critical incident reports, communication diaries or duty studies, content analysis, ECCO analysis, network analysis, and cost analysis. Taken together, the package can provide useful, timely, and practical information. It should be remembered, however, that these methods can stand alone and still provide tangible results of benefit to the organization.

Performance, content and cost analysis can provide a historical context and situationally locate the organization. Questionnaires may offer insights regarding employee attitudes and perceptions. Personal interviews and focus groups can help identify problem areas and determine issues for examination and follow-up. Trained observations, critical incident reports, and diaries or duty studies can reveal employee actions and behaviors. Finally, ECCO and network analysis assists the CEO and top management in gaining an understanding of the organization's structure and its relational links.

In most audits, interviews play a supplementary role and are used in conjunction with other data-gathering techniques, most notably participant observations and survey questionnaires. Nevertheless, they allow auditors to probe answers in depth and get information not permitted by any other method, thus making them worthwhile. Interview data can expand understanding of complex problems and identify resistance to organizational change. Felix Lopez perceptively observes that the interview "mines the richest desposits of employee feelings."[25]

While any organizational audit, including the ICA communication audit, is subject to some vulnerabilities, it remains a viable resource that merits our attention. Many objections can be overcome with careful design, attention to goals, and refined practice, making derived data and conclusions more applicable. Seasoned practitioners still find the organizational audit a valuable proactive approach to organizational development and growth. It can be "one of the most exciting forms of research, because you are not only collecting data, you are also discovering the processes inherent in a living organization. . . . You can see how your information is going to relate to making the organization function better."[26]

S H A R P E N I N G   Y O U R   F O C U S

1. Discuss the value of conducting an organizational communication audit. What characteristics distinguish a communication audit from other organizational audits? How can a communication audit benefit an organization?

2. Attend a local chapter meeting of the Society for Human Resource Management or American Society for Training and Development, and ask attending members how they use organizational audits. This can also be a valuable networking experience.

3. Read Noel M. Tichy's *Control Your Own Destiny or Someone Else Will* to discover how a change agent boldly acts to start a revolution with one central idea: GE would be number one or number two in any business it was in or that business would be fixed, closed, or sold. It reveals how Jack Welch, CEO of General Electric, created a transformation as a coach, teacher, and shaper of GE's destiny.

4. Define and explain the use of questionnaires, personal interviews, trained observations, diaries/duty studies, network analysis, and cost analysis. Discuss the advantages and disadvantages of each.

5. Outline what should go into the final report. How should data be reported to the different organizational constituencies?

6. Using selected information-gathering instruments, design and administer an abbreviated audit of professors and students to identify the "best" teaching practices or techniques.

NOTES

1. Walter R. Mahler, *Diagnostic Studies* (Menlo Park, Calif.: Addison-Wesley, 1974).
2. Chester Barnard, *The Functions of the Executive* (Cambridge: Harvard University Press, 1938), 226.
3. K. Roberts and C. O'Reilly, "Measuring Organizational Communication," *Journal of Applied Psychology* 59 (1974): 321.
4. Cal W. Downs, *Communication Audits* (Boston: Scott, Foresman and Company, 1988), 9. Reprinted by permission of Addison Wesley Educational Publishers Inc.
5. See Howard Greenbaum, "Organizational Communication Systems: Identification and Appraisal," (paper presented at a meeting of the International Communication Association, Phoenix, Ariz., 1971) and "The Appraisal of Organizational Communication Systems," (paper presented at a meeting of the International Communication Association, Atlanta, Ga., 1972).
6. Karl Weick and Richard Daft, "The Effectiveness of Interpretation Systems," in *Organizational Effectiveness,* ed. Kim Cameron and David Whetten. (New York: Academic Press, 1983), 75.
7. Chris Argyris, *Intervention Theory and Method: A Behavioral Science View* (Reading, Mass.: Addison-Wesley Publishers, 1970), 20.
8. F. Friedlander and L. D. Brown, "Organization Development," *Annual Review of Psychology* 25 (1974): 313–41.
9. J. R. Hackman and G. R. Oldham., *Work Redesign* (Reading, Mass.: Addison-Wesley Publishers, 1980).
10. W. W. Burke, *Organization Development* (Reading, Mass.: Addison-Wesley Publishers, 1987).
11. J. M. Nicholas, "The Comparative Impact of Organization Development Interventions on Hard Criteria Measures," *Academy of Management Review* 7 (1982): 532.
12. R. Beckhard, *Organizational Development: Strategies and Models* (Reading, Mass.: Addison-Wesley Publishers, 1969), 3.
13. Downs, *Communication Audits..*
14. Bernard Berelson, *Content Analysis in Communication Research* (New York: Free Press, 1952), 18.
15. R. W. Budd, R. K. Thorp, and L. Donohew, *Content Analysis of Communications* (New York: Macmillan, 1967).
16. K. Krippendorff, *Content Analysis: An Introduction to Its Methodology* (Beverly Hills, Calif., 1980).

17. Keith Davis, "A Method of Studying Communication Patterns in Organizations," *Personnel Psychology* 6 (1953): 301–12.

18. Norman Nie, C. H. Hull, J. G. Jenkins, Karen Steinbrenner, and Dale H. Bent, *SPSS: Statistical Package for the Social Sciences,* 2d ed. (New York: McGraw-Hill, 1975).

19. J. D. Johnson, "Approaches to Organizational Communication Structure," *Journal of Business Research* 22 (1991): 28–40. A lack of computer software or familiarization with computer programs may require organizations to contract with external auditors.

20. Gerald Wilson, H. Lloyd Goodall, and Christopher Waagen, *Organizational Communication* (New York: Harper and Row, 1986).

21. Downs, *Communication Audits,* 204.

22. Burke, *Organization Development.*

23. Harry Levinson, *Organizational Diagnosis* (Cambridge, Mass.: Harvard University Press, 1972), 496.

24. Downs, *Communication Audits,* 205–6. A partial final audit report is also provided on pages 213–27.

25. Felix M. Lopez, *Personnel Interviewing* (New York: McGaw-Hill, 1975), 294.

26. Cal Downs, G. Paul Smeyak, and Ernest Martin, *Professional Interviewing* (New York: Harper and Row, 1980), 425.

CHAPTER

13 The Computer-Assisted Interview

When survey research interviews began in earnest in the 1930s, data collection was done via face-to-face, paper-and-pencil methods. To collect data, researchers contacted respondents personally. Interviews were conducted in living rooms, on doorsteps, on the streets, and in offices or conference rooms. Beginning in the 1980s, the computer-assisted interview entered the scene and has fundamentally altered not only the survey research interview, but the broad spectrum of face-to-face interviews. For example, health care organizations gather information through computer-assisted interviews and offer support for patients in remote locations. Businesses conduct marketing research, use customer satisfaction surveys, and employ new product information polls through a computer terminal, gaining information about customer preferences overnight. Most national surveys today conducted by governmental and private organizations use the computer in a significant way in the interview process, changing the speed and accuracy through which data is obtained. The transformations of the face-to-face interview are increasing rapidly, and exciting new challenges await the interview as technology integrates with the communication process from beginning to end.

Chapter 13 considers the impact of technological changes in the traditional face-to-face interview. It defines the nature and function of the computer-assisted interview, compares it with the face-to-face interviewing process, discusses insights on the social presence of technology, and looks ahead to important trends and developments in interview technology, such as electronic mail and computer networks. This chapter is designed to accomplish three objectives:

1. *Awareness.* You will understand how computer-assisted technology has influenced the face-to-face interview process and changed traditional interviewing formats.

2. *Assessment.* You will be able to judge the effectiveness of a computer-assisted interview and assess your own abilities for participating in employment, research, sales, or marketing computer-assisted interviews.

3. *Application.* You will be able to participate effectively as an interviewer or interviewee in a computer-assisted interview.

*   *   *   *   *

Home-Based Health Care: Telemedicine for Rural America

Kathryn Colby has seen a lot of technological changes in her lifetime, but none was as fascinating to her as what she observed now. She watched with amazement the computer's small screen on her kitchen table that still showed activity at the nurse's station in the hospital. Through a live, direct video link she observed nurses working forty-five miles away. Sitting at the table, the nurse finished setting up the computer and began the interview, typing in medical information and sending it directly to the hospital. The results of her temperature, blood pressure, pulse, and heart rate were also relayed to the hospital. The nurse also readied information from a portable blood analysis machine to send to the hospital.

Much to Kathryn's delight, the hospital had decided to include her in the in-home visits program. She was pleased with the prospect of cutting in half the number of trips to her doctor's office. Living in rural Kansas forty-five miles from health care, Kathryn felt increasingly isolated from the medical attention she needed. She had close friends and neighbors who took good care of her, and daily she talked with her daughter, Jeanie Baldwin, who lived less than a half mile away. However, as Kathryn passed seventy years of age, the trips to the city were increasingly difficult. She lived alone and could no longer drive safely at night. The hospital's new home-based health care program was the right thing at the right time for her.

The interview proceeded smoothly as Kathryn listened carefully to the nurse's questions. Participating in an in-home interview was positively changing Kathryn's attitudes about health care. When she had traveled to the hospital in the past, Kathryn always had a long wait before an appointment. At home, there was no waiting time, and the nurse immediately gave her attention. Moreover, the nurse was in Kathryn's "territory," making Kathryn feel comfortable and relaxed, while the nurse gathered information about her medical condition.

As the interview continued, the nurse asked Kathryn detailed questions about her medications. When Kathryn could not answer, the nurse asked if she could look at medicines on the shelf for specific information about dosages and amounts. When Kathryn said her back hurt her, the nurse looked at her sleeping conditions, including the type of mattress on her bed. The nurse also offered suggestions on the steep steps coming into her house. As the interview ended, the nurse explained that her diabetes and high blood pressure were not serious problems but could become serious without close monitoring.

The computer link was a new way of keeping in-touch with the hospital. Using the computer, she could contact her nurse directly. The telephone was handy, but sometimes calls got lost in the hospital's switchboard or were not answered. With the computer, she felt in-touch with her nurse and close to needed health care. Whenever Kathryn had a question during the week, the nurse suggested sending the question via electronic mail to her mail box. She would get an answer quickly. The "buttons, scrolls, and bars" on the computer screen took a little getting used to, but Kathryn believed the quality of her care was improved, and she seemed in closer contact now with the nurses than when she made regular visits to the hospital.

Discussion Questions

1. What role did the computer have in the home-based health care interview between Kathryn Colby and her nurse?
2. In what kind of computer-assisted interview were Kathryn and the nurse participating?
3. What were the advantages of a computer-assisted interview in a home-based health care program?
4. As Kathryn's medical information was transmitted to the hospital, how did she benefit by having direct access to the hospital data-base?
5. Although Kathryn had no prior experience with a computer, how did she feel about using the new technology?

The Nature and Function of the Computer-Assisted Interview

"Technology is changing our lives" appears to be the cliché of the 1990s, but as we are well aware, computers and business communication technologies in general have dramatically affected every aspect of our lives. Electronic mail, fax machines, voice mail, the internet, computer databases, computer billboards, and interactive videoconferencing have shifted and changed the workplace as never before. The way we conduct business, access information, and communicate with one another is rapidly changing, requiring knowledge and skills that adapts to the changes. In this environment, the traditional face-to-face interview has not been exempt from change. Computer-assisted interviews (CAIs) are becoming a fact of life, and most of us will participate in a CAI in the future. Elaine B. Kerr and Starr Roxanne Hiltz describe the prospects for computer-assisted communication in the following way:

> More than a replacement for the telephone, mails, or face-to-face meetings, computer communication is a new medium for building and maintaining human

relationships. It is faster and cheaper than alternative methods for linking geographically dispersed people in working groups. But more importantly, it tends to expand greatly the human and information resources to which one has constant and convenient access.[1]

Computer-assisted technology is now an integral part of many face-to-face interviews. The computer-assisted interview entails more than number crunching and analysis of scanner-fed data. In many cases, the computer substitutes for a person and actually does the interviewing. Computer-assisted interviewing is an interview technique, not merely a way of entering data into a machine. It is not a substitute for face-to-face interviewing, it complements and assists.

The **computer-assisted interview** may be defined as the presence of computer technology in face-to-face interviews. In this broad definition, the computer's presence may function in minor or major ways. Picture a continuum where on one end the computer has a small, incidental role in an interview, yet its use is critical to the interview's success. As an integral part of the interviewing process, the computer may simply be used to display interviewing questions. The interviewer asks the questions as they are shown and follows the computer's lead during the interview, branching to different areas of the interview guide as needed. Answers are recorded instantly in a database that can be continuously updated. On the other end of the continuum, the computer actually substitutes for the interviewer. An interviewee interacts with the computer with no one else present. This new technology is particularly felt in research where it can be used effectively.

The impact of technology on survey research alone has been dramatic. Two major trends have transformed data collection in the United States over the past two decades. First, computerized tools for surveys have been introduced and adopted widely, automating many routine tasks and changing the speed and quality of data collection. As much as 40 percent of computing costs may be saved with computer-assisted interviews when data is entered directly into the computer.[2] Technological innovations include "optical scanning of self-administered forms, word processing software for producing questionnaires, computer-assisted telephone interviewing, computer-assisted data entry, and computer-assisted personal interviewing (CAPI)."[3] Moreover, Touch-Tone data entry and voice recognition data collection demonstrate how developing technologies have made computerized survey research more "user friendly." In fact, the computer-assisted personal interview is perhaps the most common method of data collection in survey interviewing today, especially with large federal agencies that conduct national surveys.

A second trend, paralleling the introduction of new computerized tools, has transformed survey research. Survey questions increasingly address more sensitive areas of information, such as drug use, abortion, AIDS transmission, and other sensitive health issues. These sensitive questions require a more private interview format. In the past two decades, the AIDS epidemic and increases in teen pregnancy have driven researchers' desire for specific information about an individual's sexual contact and practices. Asking sensitive questions poses problems for researchers in obtaining accurate and reliable information while maintaining confidentiality. Respondents are more reluctant to answer questions about their behavior with an interviewer than with self-administered questionnaires.[4] On the computer, respondents appear to have more privacy when answering sensitive questions, increasing the candor of answers. Computer-assisted interviews increase respondents' willingness to answer potentially embarrassing questions in survey research. These two trends have significantly altered survey research and data collection, changing the nature of the face-to-face survey interview.

Commercial uses of computer-assisted interviews in business have also become commonplace. When businesses conduct computer-assisted customer surveys, they are able to gain customer demographic reports instantly and respond immediately to customer preferences. As a result, companies target niche markets for their products, reducing marketing and advertising costs. Business can compare customer information obtained from computer-assisted interviews with information from other databases in short periods of time. Besides commercial uses, political organizations integrate computers with telephone pools and surveys to conduct research with constituents and compile statistical information overnight. Similarly, government agencies incorporate computers with national surveys, saving weeks of normal research time when compiling information.

A national retailer can use computer-assisted survey interviews commercially. Along with direct mail questionnaires, focus groups, and individual interviews, Spiegel began using computer-assisted interviews in 1991 to meet customer requests. When a shopper answers a survey over the telephone, for instance, the information is tallied in a computer and merged with an existing customer database. The resulting information enables Spiegel to closely monitor the needs and motivations of patrons. It identifies "market niches," or specific customer groups, and produces specialty catalogs targeting those groups. The company's president, John Shea, observes that while the "catalog is one of our significant channels, we are first and foremost in the retailing business, and success will be dictated by responding to what the customer wants, regardless of the channel we use to deliver it."[5]

Futhermore, the selection interview has been fundamentally transformed by the computer-assisted interview. Job applicants who face computer-assisted selection interviews must not only have traditional knowledge, skills, and abilities about job hunting, but they must also adapt to the new technologies. Answering questions on a computer, overcoming computer anxiety, and adjusting to new software programs will be part of the new portfolio of job skills in the future. According to the *Wall Street Journal,* future job applicants may be surprised when they carry their resumes into the next job interview and are asked to be seated at a computer. Becoming increasingly common with more organizations, staff assistants will instruct applicants when they arrive on how to use a computer program for the job interview—"you punch a few buttons and are greeted by a mechanical voice: 'Welcome to the interactive assessment aid.' Your job interview has begun."[6] Those who can acquire the necessary skills and adjust to these changes will be competitive in the job market.

New skills are required with computer-assisted interviews, and those who gain those skills will be competitive as computer-assisted interviewing becomes an established format in the 21ˢᵗ century.

Pic 'n Pay Stores, a national chain of approximately 1,000 self-service shoe stores, illustrates how a national company uses computer-assisted selection interviewing. In 1992 when Pic 'n Pay initiated computer-assisted interviewing, the company was attempting to reduce high employee turnover rates and improve customer service. Because their employee turnover rate had reached 247 percent per year, customer service was hard to improve when customers met new employees each time shopped at the store. Once computer-assisted interviewing was implemented, Pic 'n Pay reduced turnover by one-half, and customer service improved substantially. An additional benefit from the computerized interview was an increase in minority hiring by 7.9 percent. At Pic 'n Pay, the job interview process began when an applicant first talked with a store manager and completed an application form. After the manager initially screened the potential employee, the applicant was instructed to call an 800 telephone number and take a computerized survey originating at Pic 'n Pay headquarters. The 100-question survey lasted about ten minutes, playing a recorded message that instructed applicants to press "1" for "yes" and "0" for "no." Questions were stated only once and occurred at five-second intervals. A computer not only recorded answers but also measured how long an applicant paused to answer. Once the interview was completed, a follow-up telephone call was made within a few minutes by a "live" interviewer who probed unusual or questionable responses. Some questions concerned honesty or previous drug use. Depending on the applicant's answer or delay in answering, the live interviewer asked additional probing questions in these sensitive areas. Afterward, the interviewer faxed results to the store manager recommending or not recommending the applicant for hiring; however, the store manager made the final decision. Background information and references were checked by the central office. The software program used was "HR Easy," developed by MCI Communications, who worked with Pic 'n Pay in implementing their successful computer-assisted employment program.[7]

In the health care industry, telemedicine has integrated with and changed the traditional interview between physician and patient. Health care organizations use computer-aided technology when gathering medical information and assisting patients long distance. Besides simply gathering information on-site, doctors in remote locations, viewing results of a diagnostic test on a computer screen, can consult with specialists in another city or country and receive immediate help in a patient's diagnosis. These computer-assisted programs offer cost-effective alternatives to patient care. Frequent in-home visits, for example, feature tabletop telephone units with pop-up screens at the patient's home and a central nursing station to allow the nurse and patient to interact with each other electronically. Such technological advancements in health care have transformed the health care interview.[8]

In counseling interviews, interactive computer programs appear to be as effective as a human therapist in relieving mild psychological problems.[9] Computer-assisted interviews can be helpful to psychiatrists and psychologists because of the computer's ability to integrate large amounts of information. Computer consultation programs (CCPs), for example, complement the clinician and even substitute for one when the clinician is unavailable.[10] Computer administration of psychological assessments has also gained widespread acceptance in the last decade. Tests administered on the computer are at least as reliable as the pencil-and-paper-administered test with examinees being much faster in the computer mode. Correlations between paper-and-pencil and computer modes are high, except when task differences are introduced by computer implementation.[11] Furthermore, the computerized interview is being used as an assessment tool in marital and family therapy, finding acceptance by patients and providing low-cost routine interviewing. Such technology provides a balance of structure and reliability with flexibility and individualized question flow.[12]

As these examples show, the computer-assisted interview has integrated with the face-to-face interview across a broad spectrum of organizations for a variety of purposes. Over the last two decades, fundamental transformations have occurred with technology that dramatically influence the traditional interview. The integration of computer technology with the interviewing process appeals to organizations because of increased speed and access of information. The computer-assisted interview has enabled these organizations to cut costs and save time with recruitment, data collection, and information gathering. New skills are required with computer-assisted interviews, and those who gain those skills will be competitive as the computer-assisted interview becomes an established format for the next century.

*   *   *   *   *

The computer had an important role in the home-based health care interview between Kathryn Colby and her nurse. In many ways, the interview was a traditional one, much like a standard information-gaining medical interview. Kathryn sat face-to-face at a table with the nurse, answering questions related to her illnesses and drug prescriptions. In addition, the questions the nurse asked were familiar to Kathryn. However, the way the information was recorded was different. Using the computer to enter data improved the speed of the process greatly. Previously, when information was recorded using pencil-and-paper, the nurse's duties demanded returning to the hospital and transcribing the patient's data into other medical records at the nurse's station. The delay sometimes slowed the health care process and lessened the quality of care. Computer-assisted interviewing saved time for the nurse and improved the speed of updating Kathryn's medical records. As the nurse's time was reduced, costs of health care were reduced, and the speed of health care was improved.

Types of Computer-Assisted Interviews

The computer-assisted interview integrates computer technology with traditional interview formats. The computer may have a small, incidental role in an interview, such as assisting a "live" interviewer in information gathering and record keeping, or it may have a larger role, becoming the primary vehicle through which the interview takes place. An interviewee may even interact with a computer without the presence of a "live" interviewer. When the computer is the other party, the interviewee may use a keyboard terminal to interact with the computer by simply touching the screen to indicate responses or using other interactive devices to respond to questions from the computer. This technological integration is better illustrated when we look at various types and functions of the computer-assisted interview.

Computer-assisted interviews have been classified into at least three forms or types.[13] First, when the computer supplements face-to-face interviews, or **computer-assisted personal interviewing (CAPI).** This type of interview includes an actual face-to-face interview where one of the participants uses a computer terminal to record information. Instead of taking paper-and-pencil notes, the interviewer records the interviewee's answers to questions at a computer terminal. The results can be edited, stored, and distributed electronically, thus saving paper and storage space. A common variation of this type of computer-assisted interview occurs when the interviewee records the answers to questions. For example, after a brief face-to-face interview the interviewer may instruct the interviewee to sit at the computer screen, which displays questions and answer categories. As the interviewee responds to the displayed questions, his or her answers are recorded in the computer's database, and the computer branches to the next question. Interviewers have discovered that questionnaires displayed on a computer can easily replace paper-and-pencil questionnaires.

A second type of computer-assisted interview is the **computer-assisted self interview (CASI).** In this type of interview, the interviewee responds to questions on a fully-automated computer without the presence of a "live" interviewer. Marketers or data collectors in shopping malls, for instance, will place a computer terminal in a small, open booth or kiosk for research purposes to access customers. Without an interviewer present, the interviewee responds to survey questions on the screen. However, the CASI places limitations on the researcher. Customers or shoppers who answer the survey must be computer literate and have time in a busy schedule to complete a survey. They must also be willing to participate without incentive or reward. Based on a convenience sample, this type of research limits the population to be sampled. Finally, this type of interview prohibits probing for clarification.

Finally, a third type of computer-assisted interview is the **computer-assisted telephone interview (CATI).** Conducted over the telephone, the interviewer sits at a computer terminal and calls the respondent. As the respondent answers, the interviewer keys answers directly into the computer, with the computer branching and skipping to questions. During the survey, the computer performs consistency checks and prompts the interviewer to fill in missing data. Commercial uses of the CATI began in the 1970s and is now widely used by marketing organizations, as well as educational and government agencies. Its popularity has grown because of low cost compared to the individual interview, speed and efficiency of survey administration, close interviewer supervision, ease of data coding, and ability to use elaborate branching patterns, explain questions, or reconnect the respondent from a central location.

In each of these types of computer-assisted interviews, the computer assumes responsibilities and tasks normally performed by a face-to-face interviewer. To what degree is technology able to assume interviewer activities? Can the computer-assisted interview replace interviewer tasks?

While obtaining cooperation and motivating are interviewer tasks done better by a person, the computer-assisted interview can assume many of the tasks and responsibilities of the interviewer, particularly administrative tasks. Checking for appropriate answers, helping the respondent if the question is not correctly understood, coding answers, and recording the answers can easily be done by the computer. For example, the computer can explore a range of appropriate answers quickly, check the answer against an existing body of knowledge, and immediately code and record the electronic data. Moreover, the computer-assisted interview can better overcome such interviewing obstacles or problems as lack of interviewer preparation, experience, and negative bias. Also, when used appropriately, the computer-assisted interview can complement the face-to-face interview in unique ways. The degree to which interviewer tasks are integrated with technology should be determined by each organization.

*   *   *   *   *

Kathryn Colby participated in a computer-assisted personal interview (CAPI) with the nurse. Appropriately, the computer was positioned on the table in front of the nurse, and as Kathryn answered questions about her illnesses, the nurse entered the information for Kathryn. The nurse would not want to use a computer-assisted self-interview (CASI). Having the patient sit at the keyboard and enter medical information herself may prove to be time consuming and error prone. Although the computer was involved in a minor way, it was extremely important to the interview process and assisted the overall purpose and goals of the exchange.

Advantages and Disadvantages of the Computer-Assisted Interview

The computer-assisted interview provides a significant increase in speed, improvement in data accuracy, and decrease in cost when compared to a face-to-face or paper-and-pencil interview. A personal interview requires considerable preparation, as well as time to conduct and evaluate the results. Similarly, mail surveys require considerable preparation time in validating the questionnaire design, as well as length time schedules for typing, printing, and distribution. Moreover, once mailed, several weeks normally pass before questionnaires are returned and then data must be tabulated, coded, and entered into a computer database before analysis can begin. The computer-assisted interview reduces or eliminates a number of these steps, and at the close of the interview, the data is already entered into a database. A further advantage of the computer-assisted interview concerns the use of branching questions in surveys. The computer can prevent unnecessary questions from showing on the screen. When questions are not appropriate or applicable to a respondent, a "chain or contingency strategy" can be used, whereby questions are subdivided in the survey to skip over certain areas. When using a highly standardized format, these surveys allow for preplanned secondary questions. Scott Dacko observes in *Marketing News* that "computer-based surveys can easily accommodate vast and complex arrays of branching questions, greatly increasing the capacity of data collection and substantially reducing confusion and errors by interviewer and respondents."[14] Finally, data quality is improved, since computer-assisted interviewing reduces errors in coding and tabulation. Research has shown that 77 percent of data errors in a standard survey could have been avoided using a computer-assisted interview format.[15] Most data entry errors are avoided in a computer-assisted interview because the computer can check for inconsistencies and ask for corrections during the interview.

A unique advantage of computer-assisted interviewing concerns the computer's ability to measure response time to key questions. If a respondent delays in answering a question, no matter how slight the delay, the computer measures the exact time taken to respond and compares it with an expected time. If the computer expects a five-second response to a question about honesty, previous history with theft, or drug abuse in the workplace, a small delay in responding to the question may send up a "flag" for the employer. Delays might also indicate the degree of difficulty of a question. This data can provide the interviewer with a distinctive measurement for analysis.

Although the computer-assisted interview can benefit researchers in a number of ways, certain disadvantages must be considered before undertaking computerized interviewing. Willem Saris cautions researchers to consider at least three disadvantages:

- The cost-effectiveness of the extra equipment and extra employees needed to maintain the computer systems.
- The extra skills required of interviewers and respondents, and the consequences of training time and/or nonresponse.
- The increased and decreased flexibility of the process.[16]

While the purchase of computer hardware/software involves considerable resources for an organization, additional disadvantages include potential computer anxiety, lack of computer skills, and an inability to adapt to computer requirements. Despite these advantages, the integration of the computer-assisted interview with face-to-face interviewing has significantly changed the nature of research and data collection.

* * * * *

The computer-assisted interview benefited both Kathryn Colby and the hospital. By using the computer to enter information, the nurse kept data entry errors to a minimum and was able to immediately update Kathryn's medical records. The technology saved time in coding and transcription. The information was also available to other personnel at the hospital if necessary. Branching options further benefited both parties. As the nurse read questions on the screen, the computer selected questions that specifically related to Kathryn's condition. Finally, and most importantly, Kathryn was able to receive the same quality of health care as she would have at the hospital.

Computer-Assisted Interviews within Networks

Traditionally, communication "networks" has referred to how people communicate face-to-face within organizations, including the study of day-to-day relationships among employees. In contrast, computer-based communication today has expanded our terminology to include electronic issues and an emphasis on electronic networks. Computer networks add enormous flexibility and power to the communication channels available to people. Although many aspects of computer networks are very technical, you don't need to know a great deal about how they work to use them. In fact, a brief, nontechnical description of a common system is probably all you need to appreciate the opportunities that computer networks provide.

Most common computer networks require participants to communicate with one another by using personal computers or terminals to create messages. Messages are created by typing at a keyboard that looks very much like that of a standard typewriter. As users type a message, their computer converts typed characters into electrical impulses that are stored in the machine. When the user or a program instructs the computer to send the message, the electrical impulses are sent over telephone lines to a central computer. The central computer stores the message until someone else instructs the computer to send the message to his or her computer. When the electrical impulses are sent, the reader's computer converts them back into a message that it prints or displays on a screen. The receiver can either read the message as it is reproduced on the computer, save the message for reading at a later time, or both. While the actual process of creating, saving, transmitting, storing, and recreating a message is somewhat more complicated than this description indicates, the beauty of a well-designed computer system is that the users don't need to worry about how the system works. All they need to know are a few instructions that tell their computer to create a message and send it to the central computer. As computer networks become more sophisticated, they become even easier to use. Data collection through computer networks is becoming a more routine research tool, and surveys conducted over computer networks increase self-disclosure and improve response rates.[17]

Currently, the most common and least expensive format of a computer-assisted interview involves the "stand-alone" computer, one that is not connected to a centralized server or network. In most computer-assisted interviews, the interviewer sits at a computer and enters responses directly into it. In a survey interview, for example, the interviewee may go to a central location for the interview, or the interviewer may carry a laptop or notebook computer to the individual or place of business to conduct the interview. Information or data received is stored on a disk or in the computer and brought back to a central location for analysis. When conducting a computer-assisted self-interview, the interviewee reads questions on the screen and responds directly to the computer. If interviewers are present, their role is to provide general guidelines and clarify instructions. These "stand-alone" formats are an elementary but inexpensive form of computer-assisted interviewing.

Today, the trend in computer-assisted interviews is toward linked computers in **local area networks (LAN).** When individual computers connect over cables or telephone lines to other computers within the organization, they form a communication system through which information is shared. When these networks are used for computer-assisted interviews, interviewers create a more efficient flow of information and see significant improvements in task efficiency. By increasing information sharing, interviewers have greater access to decision makers and can make faster decisions. As the term *local* implies, computer-based networks are a mainstay of schools and universities, business and industry, and nonprofit or government organizations.

Wide area networks (WANs) expand the LAN concept beyond organizational boundaries to include the nation and the world. The internet is the most popular WAN and has been described as "a loose collection of millions of computers at thousands of sites around the world (universities, government offices, and businesses) whose users can pass along information and share files."[18] Communication over wide area computer networks, including the internet, is quickly becoming the popular communication media of the 1990s. The "net" or "web" is widely available, with new computer networks evolving rapidly to provide users with helpful communication options. Options include electronic mail, computer databases, computer billboards, and interactive computer videoconferencing. When using a computer network, it is important to select the appropriate system.

Electronic Mail

Electronic mail (e-mail) is a unique media type defined as "person-to-person(s) communication that takes place between computers . . . it is a paperless written communication transmitted and received by computer."[19] The name is well chosen because electronic mail systems allow users to create and deliver messages to other people who read them at their own convenience. The system works just like regular mail but with a very, very fast computerized letter carrier handling deliveries. Whether e-mail is sent locally over an organization's network or externally through the internet across continents, it is inexpensive and fast, enabling individuals to send and receive messages at any time of the day in a matter of seconds. In addition, e-mail enables multiple messages to be sent simultaneously, thus expanding the communication process.

The growing popularity of electronic mail has enhanced personal communication within networks. In 1997, an estimated 55 million Americans, which is more than one-fifth of the population, live in homes wired for electronic mail. That's a significant increase from 5 million users in 1992. According to the *Wall Street Journal,* e-mail has boomed among consumers of the internet, and projected consumer use of electronic mail is only expected to increase, with 135 million users sending 500 million messages per day by the year 2001.[20] Many people feel freer and more adept at using technologies, becoming familiar with sending and receiving information on the "web" and using e-mail to correspond with others. The speed and technology of e-mail is quickly being adapted to the interview. As more individuals turn to their computer for information and communication, the segue to computer-assisted interviewing seems apparent.

The increase in popularity of electronic mail has paralleled the increase in computer-assisted interviews. Computer-assisted interviews conducted through interactive e-mail, especially survey or research interviews, combine the advantages of a letter written on paper with a telephone call. According to many e-mail users, using the U.S. postal service or "snail mail" is slow and the conversational "train of thought" is lost by the time a letter is mailed and delivered. When using e-mail, results can be achieved with short turnaround time, and messages still can be printed, saved, and read by others. E-mail users also find the internet more convenient than the telephone, noting that "staying in touch by phone often means one person is getting in touch when the other doesn't have the time to talk, or isn't in the mood." In contrast, e-mail messages can be read at the receivers convenience. Moreover, e-mail helps eliminate "telephone tag." Most of us have experienced calling someone by telephone and, after leaving a message, have missed the return call of the other individual, who in turn has left us a message. Missed messages and back-and-forth "tagging" cost organizations and researchers valuable time, which is avoided with e-mail. Finally, having correspondence and text electronically stored also allows for electronic searches.

Electronic mail has not replaced business letters, memos, written reports, or telephone calls, but it is a unique medium growing in popularity because of its special properties. The normal lag time that letters and telephone messages take is greatly reduced or eliminated by electronic communication. Distributing electronic messages simultaneously to a number of people eliminates duplication of messages and photocopying paper, as well as changing decision-making time. Moreover, interviews that do not require interactive conferences can usually be conducted through electronic mail. JoAnne Yates of the Massachusetts Institute of Technology observes that "while e-mail does not displace face-to-face communication, it may enrich face-to-face interactions by providing a channel through which minor details can be handled, thereby leaving more substantive issues for direct discussion."[21]

Computer Databases

Databases are organized collections of information designed for rapid search and retrieval, and they are an integral part of most computer-assisted interviewing programs. They are usually a set of computer files that have been cross-referenced and contain information arranged in a meaningful way. A retailer's database, for example, might contain information about a customer's preferences and previous purchases, which can be compiled in a few minutes and help direct an upcoming sales interview. A college/university advisor may want to access a student's academic records through a database prior to a counseling interview. In a job search, databases serve an invaluable function prior to the actual employment interview. Certainly, research databases are essential to effective survey interviewing. Once survey information has been coded and entered into a database, statistical information can be quickly obtained for analysis and interpretation. Good databases are periodically updated and permanently maintained for later reference.

Computer Billboards

Using a **computer billboard** is much like placing an advertisement in the want ads of a newspaper. A user creates a message and sends it to the central computer. The central computer stores the message in a file with other messages on the same subject, and anyone who is interested can read all the messages. For example, users who are looking for a new job can create an electronic resume. The resume is nothing more than a message indicating what kind of job they want, describing their qualifications, and identifying their electronic mailbox. They instruct the central computer to save their message in a file where anyone looking for a new employee can read it. The computer sorts the resumes in its files according to job types, applicants' credentials and experiences, and other factors that might be of interest to potential employers. Then, potential employers can read all the resumes or just those that match particular characteristics. When the employer identifies a person who has the necessary qualifications, he or she can respond by sending a message to the applicant's mailbox. If the applicant is interested in the job, he or she can respond by scheduling a time for an interview. Most interviews still take place in face-to-face settings, but more and more companies use interactive computer videoconferences for initial screening interviews. The ideal use of computer billboards is to contact strangers who may share your interests or who can provide information that you need.

Interactive Computer Videoconferencing

Interactive computer videoconferencing refers to the transfer of audio and video between remote sites. If a camera, microphone, and software are added to a computer, an interviewer can conduct an interview with anyone in the world who has similar equipment. To engage in an interactive conference, both participants use their computers at the same time, with a central computer receiving messages from one and passing them to the other as rapidly as possible. Interactive computer videoconferencing comes closest to normal conversation, and the relatively inexpensive additions to a computer that allow videoconferencing have popularized distant face-to-face communication in remarkable ways. More than half of the largest corporations in the United States have adopted state-of-the-art systems using videoconferencing.[22] Advancing technology, access to individuals in remote locations, and reduced costs appeal to interviewers in business, education, and government organizations. This trend will be the most significant advancement for interviewing in the next decade, revolutionizing the interview. It allows participants to exchange ideas as they develop, and it is best used for situations in which you want to respond to the other person immediately. Despite its benefits, there are some good reasons to avoid interactive videoconferencing. It is usually the most expensive form of networking, with the combined cost for the participants being double or triple the cost of using other systems even at prime times. Other drawbacks to videoconferencing technology include poor audio quality and unsatisfactory video image. The poor audio quality results when the signal moves from one site to another through a long-distance telephone line or satellite link, and the signal is delayed by a half-second or more. Poor video quality results when cameras focus on only the participant speaking, and viewers miss responses from other members participating in the conference, as well as screens being too small and a jerky image at best. In addition, use of interactive videoconferencing reduces some of the advantages of other computer networks. Interactive conferences require both participants to be "on-line" at the same time; thus, the benefits of time and pacing are lost. However, as technology advances, many of these concerns will disappear. However, not even the most ardent advocates of the office of the future claim that electronic meetings will replace face-to-face meetings for all purposes.[23] John Sherblom pragmatically observes that "even when all participants remain constantly on the screen and are large enough to be seen, a spatial relationship may be felt to be missing, eye contact may be difficult, and facial expressions may be hard to interpret. When these nonverbal communication channels are critical to the purposes of the meeting or the groups, videoconferencing may not be the appropriate medium. A face-to-face meeting is the better choice."[24]

Experienced professionals have learned to use computer networks for particular kinds of communication and to avoid the use of computer networks for other kinds of communication. Computer networks are as good as, or better than, face-to-face conversations when participants are (1) exchanging technical information, (2) asking questions, (3) exchanging opinions or orders, (4) staying in touch, or (5) generating ideas. However, computer networks do not appear to work as well as face-to-face communication when participants are (1) bargaining, (2) resolving disagreements, (3) getting to know each other, (4) establishing personal relationships, or (5) working on tasks that require constant focused attention. Still, computer networks have created important new opportunities for communication. These networks provide relatively complete control over the amount and kinds of information transmitted, the people to whom the information is addressed, and the times at which messages will be exchanged. As a result, they represent a significant new dimension that will undoubtedly have a far reaching impact on the interviewing process.

*   *   *   *   *

As Kathryn Colby's medical information was transmitted to the hospital, she benefited as a patient by having direct access to the hospital database. As the hospital received the records through a direct link from the computer, Kathryn's current medical information was compared with previous information. The nurse would have been notified immediately if abnormalities appeared or certain data were out of range. If blood pressure readings changed significantly, the computer would "flag" the measurement. Furthermore, the nurse also had instant access to other hospital personnel via a video connection if additional consultation was required.

The "Social Presence" of the Computer

Is participating in a computer-assisted interview truly an impersonal experience with a machine, devoid of emotional feeling or content? Interviewees who assume that the computer-assisted interview is impersonal may "become self-centered, and relatively unconcerned with social norms and with the impression they give others."[25] In contrast to a nonhuman experience, interviewees find that there is a social dimension to interacting with a computer. The psychological aspects of using telecommunications and technologies has been termed **social presence,** or the degree to which that technology feels sociable, warm, sensitive, and personal. Social presence can be practically described as "the difference between a friendly conversation and a business letter, a pleasant telephone conversation and a complex computer printout, or a warm conversation between two lovers and the proverbial 'Dear John' letter."[26] The greater the degree to which an interviewee feels personal with the computer, the more "social presence" exists. Technologies may not be inherently personal or impersonal; the challenge for the user is to adapt his or her stylistic and persuasive strategies for their most effective use."[27]

However, for those having a first-time experience, the emotions surrounding the interview can be negative. If high levels of fear or anxiety are present, labeled "technophobia," the negative emotions may be a barrier to participating effectively. Other interviewees, who cannot functionally read, write, or type well will be "handicapped" when being interviewed by a computer. Still others may feel their age is a barrier to the technology, believing that "high-tech stuff" is for younger minds and a younger generation. On the other hand, typing responses affords the interviewee more time to think of a response and to choose the right words than in a face-to-face interview, thus providing a degree of emotional satisfaction for the interviewee, and confidence with technology can transcend age barriers. Still, a national Adult Literacy Survey revealed nearly one-fourth of U.S. adults perform at the lowest level of literacy, and any computer-assisted interview will present difficulties for this significant portion of the general population.[28]

An important social factor in a computer-assisted interview concerns the effects of "aloneness" or the absence of a real person. Interviewees may feel estranged with the computer, viewing it as unable to promote interpersonal communication. Lack of face-to-face contact may lead to undue criticism of the interview, organization, or process. In contrast, other interviewees feel "at home" with the computer because they are knowledgeable of technology, have experience with computers, and possess a high level of task-related commitment to participate in the interview. Comfortable with the technology, these interviewees believe they are communicating with another person and have a greater chance of succeeding during the interview. Amy Friedman Phillips expresses this paradox of human/computer interaction when she observes that "people can be totally alone and yet feel that they are part of a currently communicating group or entity."[29]

Besides these factors, the actual content of messages represents a social dimension. Through the typed message and its content, emotional messages are conveyed through word choice and tone. What would be good-natured humor in a face-to-face interview is done overtly in a typed message. Certain symbols have been created to convey feeling. "Smileys" or "emoticons" have been created to personalize messages. James Bach defines an emoticon as "a figure created with the symbols on a key board that is read with the head tilted to the left and used to convey the spirit in which a line of text was typed."[30] Variations on the symbol :) for a smiley face include :-# meaning "My lips are sealed," :-& meaning "I'm tongue-tied," or :-0 meaning "I'm bored." Even though there is no direct interpersonal contact, interviewees understand the emotional tone of the writer. It seems a smile, so wondrous and complex off-line, has multiple meanings even on-line.

Frederick Williams and Ronald Rice, in summarizing the literature, identify four qualities that play an important role in drawing distinctions between face-to-face interviewing and the computer-assisted interview.[31] First, and perhaps most important is the restricted nonverbal communication. The more a medium can transfer personal information through nonverbal communication, the more personal the medium will become. Obviously missing in the computer-assisted interview are nonverbal cues; still, it may benefit from such restricted nonverbal communication. Absent are evaluation anxiety or other interpersonal pressures that exist when sitting face-to-face with someone in an interview. When interviewing face-to-face, participants may become inordinately conscious of their nonverbal communication and distracted by concerns regarding body posture, eye contact, placement of arms and legs, and voice quality. When interviewing at the computer, the interviewee is free to concentrate solely on answering the questions posed.

A second important differentiating quality is channel redundancy. The "information-rich environment" of multiple channels in face-to-face interviews reduces uncertainty to a sufficient degree to enable highly personal relationships to form. For communication through a computer to become personal, the message must overtly convey personal qualities. The writer must learn to substitute written cues to personalize the message. The more these personal qualities can be added to the message, the greater social presence the computer-assisted interview will assume.

A third quality that enhances the "social presence" of the computer-assisted interview is the potential for interactivity meaning an immediate, two-way exchange among interviewer and interviewee. The greater the degree of interactivity between participants, the more personal the medium will become and the higher the social presence. Obviously, high interactivity exists in face-to-face interviews during question-and-answer sessions. In the computer-assisted interview, interactivity depends on how well the interviewee receives instantaneous feedback, immediate answers to questions, or spontaneous results of the interview. As computer systems allow for video and audio interactivity in addition to text interactivity, the computer-assisted interview will increase in its social presence.

Finally, a fourth issue concerns privacy versus public qualities of the interview. The more confidentiality is missing from the interaction, the more the interview becomes public and the communication less personal. If someone outside the interview can eavesdrop on the interaction, participants will experience less privacy, and the interview will take on a less personal tone. Consequently, if an individual participating in a computer-assisted interview can feel free from public pressure, the medium takes on a personal presence. Lack of nonverbal feedback and being alone at a computer may lessen social desirability issues and allow the interviewee to relax and "let down" his or her public image. Those participants in computer-assisted interviews who understand these qualities and overcome the inherent differences will more likely succeed.

*   *   *   *   *

Although Kathryn Colby had no prior experience with a computer, she felt positive about using the new technology. In a secure environment at home, Kathryn could take her time and learn to use the "buttons, scrolls, and bars" on the computer screen. Before the nurse left her house, she encouraged Kathryn to send one e-mail message successfully. Kathryn was elated at learning how to directly contact the nurse. She acknowledged that she typed slowly but could take her time and practice. The nurse also showed Kathryn how to play "Free Cell," one of the card games that came with the computer. Kathryn was having "fun" and wanted to learn more about her amazing new gadget.

Critical Focus

Finally, review once more the Critical Focus presented in chapter 10 describing the meeting between Andrea Anderson, CEO of Scholar Educational Products, and the department heads. This time replay the videotape segment examining the discussion regarding interviews on computer networks. The following critical questions can direct and guide your analysis.

1. When is computer network interviewing appropriate? What functions do the different types of computer networks serve?
2. What guidelines should be used for choosing the most suitable system? What procedures should be established to ensure quality information?
3. What are the significant differences between face-to-face and computer-assisted interviews? Which do you prefer?
4. What recommendations would you make to Andrea Anderson and the department heads regarding the research options available as Scholar Educational Products strives to seek a new direction and competitive future?

Summary

Computer-assisted interviews integrate computer technology with traditional interview formats. They are used widely in business, health, education, and government fields. Computer networks add enormous flexibility and power to the communication channels available to professionals through such options as electronic mail, computer databases, billboards, and interactive videoconferencing.

The integration of technology with interviews has reduced cost, increased speed, and given interviewers greater access to information. However, users must understand the technology and realize that organizational resources are required to take advantage of computer-assisted interviews.

Computer-assisted interviews have a bright future. Advancing technology, familiarity with e-mail, and communication over the internet will drive acceptance of computer-assisted interviewing. As inexpensive hardware/software becomes available for an interviewer's desktop computer, face-to-face computer-assisted interviews will be conducted over the internet. Interviewers will have access to interviewees in remote locations, reducing travel costs and other expenses related to traditional research or employment interviews.

If you think CD Rom is a country and western singer and the internet is a headdress worn during food preparation or by servers in a buffet line, the bridge to the twenty-first century lies over "troubled waters," because what we know as the internet today will seem boring and quaint in the next century. Education, medicine, the workplace, travel, entertainment, and how we eat, socialize, consume, and—produce—everything human beings do or benefit from will be transformed. In the end, the world of computers as we know it today will metamorphose into one enormous interactive global link of limitless potential. The knowledge of thousands of libraries, the sum of the world's greatest minds, all will be readily accessible by anyone, and everyone will be one keystroke away.

S H A R P E N I N G   Y O U R   F O C U S

1. Today, computer literacy is essential for job effectiveness. Describe your comfort level with computer technology. Discuss your ability to use computer technology on the job. What are your strengths? Your problem areas? Identify your communication goals for the coming year.

2. Compare and contrast the advantages and disadvantages of face-to-face interviewing with computer-assisted interviewing.

3. Define and discuss the following computer network options: (a) electronic mail, (b) computer databases, (c) computer billboards, and (d) interactive computer videoconferencing.

4. Select an interview type discussed in the text and surf the Web for "hits." Select five or more sources to download. How does this information compare/add to your awareness of the principles, practices, and procedures covered in the text?

5. List and explain four qualities needed to establish the "social presence" of the computer for interviewing purposes.

6. We all have excuses for not fully using the new computer technology. Compile a list of excuses that either you or others you know use to avoid dealing with computer technology. Explain how change makes the validity of each of these excuses doubtful. Identify data that could be used to expose the fallacies in these evaluations.

7. As authors of the text, we are interested in your feedback and personal interviewing experiences. E-mail us at rconaway@mail.uttyl.edu or wschmidt@rollins.edu

NOTES

1. Elaine B. Kerr and Starr Roxanne Hiltz, *Computer-Mediated Communication Systems* (New York: Academic Press, 1982), ix. Reprinted with permission.
2. Sara Kiesler and Lee S. Sproull, "Response Effects in the Electronic Survey," *Public Opinion Quarterly* 50 (1986): 402–13.
3. Roger Tourangeau and Tom W. Smith, "Asking Sensitive Questions: The Impact of Data Collection Mode, Question Format, and Question Context," *Public Opinion Quarterly* 60 (1996): 276.
4. William S. Aquilino and Leonard A. Lo Sciuto, "Effects of Interview Mode on Self-Reported Drug Use," *Public Opinion Quarterly* 54 (Fall 1990): 362–95.
5. "Spiegel Keeps in Touch," *Stores* 75 (October 1993): 78.
6. William M. Bulkeley, "Replaced by Technology: Job Interviews," *The Wall Street Journal*, 22 August, 1994, B1.
7. "Recruitment Goes High Tech," *Personnel Journal* (August 1994): 6–10 and Gary Robins, "Dial-An-Interview," *Stores* 76 (June 1994): 34–35.
8. C. C. Lindberg, "Implementation of In-Home Telemedicine in Rural Kansas: Answering an Elderly Patient's Needs," *Journal of the American Medical Informatics Association* 4 (January/February 1997): 14–17.
9. Paulette M. Selmi, Marjorie H. Klein, John H. Geist, Steven P. Sorrell, and Harold P. Erdman, "Computer-Administered Cognitive-Behavioral Therapy for Depression," *American Journal of Psychiatry* 147 (January 1990): 51–56.
10. Harold P. Erdman, "Computer Consultation in Psychiatry," *Psychiatric Annals* 18 (April 1988): 209–16.
11. Valerie A. Greaud and Bert F. Green, "Equivalence of Conventional and Computer Presentation of Speed Tests," *Applied Psychological Measurement* 10 (March 1986): 23–34.
12. Harold Erdman and Sharon W. Foster, "Computer-Assisted Assessment with Couples and Families," *Family Therapy* 13 (1986): 23–40.
13. Scott G. Dacko, "Data Collection Should Not Be Manual Labor," *Marketing News* 29 (August 28, 1995): 31.
14. Dacko, "Data Collection Should Not Be Manual Labor," 31.
15. Willem E. Saris, *Computer-Assisted Interviewing* (Newbury Park, CA: Sage Publications, 1991), p. 7.
16. Willem E. Saris, *Computer-Assisted Interviewing* (Newbury Park, CA: Sage Publications, 1991), p. 7. Reprinted by Permission of Sage Publications, Inc.
17. Lee Sproull and Sara Kiesler, "Reducing Social Context Cues: Electronic Mail in Organizational Communication," *Management Science* 32 (1986): 1492–1512.
18. Carol M. Lehman, William C. Mimstreet, and Wayne M. Baty. *Business Communications*, 11th ed. (Cincinnati, Ohio: South-western College Publishing, 1996), 111.
19. William Galle, Jr., Beverly H. Nelson, Donna W. Luse, and Maurice F. Villere, *Business Communication: A Technology-Based Approach* (Chicago: Richard D. Irwin, 1996), 76.
20. Jon G. Auerbach, "Getting the Message: As E-mail Booms, It Is Changing the Frequency—and Texture—of the Way We Communicate," *The Wall Street Journal*, 16 June, 1997, R22.
21. JoAnne Yates, "Electronic Mail," in *Communication and Technology: Today and Tomorrow*, ed. Al Williams (New York: Association for Business Communication Publication, 1994), 122.
22. Joyce Lain Kennedy, *Job Interviews for Dummies* (Foster City, Calif.: IDG Books Worldwide, Inc., 1996).

23. Thomas V. Dock and James C. Wetherbe, *Computer Information Systems for Business* (St. Paul, Minn.: West Publishing, 1988).

24. John Sherblom, "Teleconferencing," in *Communication and Technology: Today and Tomorrow,* ed. Al Williams (New York: Association for Business Communication Publication, 1994), 170.

25. Kiesler and Sproull, "Response Effects in the Electronic Survey," 405.

26. Frederick Williams and Ronald E. Rice, "Communication Research and the New Media Technologies," in *Communication Yearbook 7,* ed. R. Bostrom (Beverly Hills, Calif.: Sage, 1983), 202.

27. Ibid. 204.

28. Mick P. Couper and Benjamin Rowe, "Evaluation of a Computer-Assisted Self-Interview Component in a Computer-Assisted Personal Interview Survey," *Public Opinion Quarterly* 60 (1996): 89–105.

29. Amy Friedman Phillips, "Computer Conferences: Success or Failure?" in *Communication Yearbook 7,* ed. R. Bostrom (Beverly Hills, Calif.: Sage, 1983), 841.

30. Bernard Blackman and Theodore Clevenger, Jr., "Use of Computer Symbols as Nonverbal Communication in Computer Bulletin Boards," (paper presented at a meeting of the Florida Communication Association, Tallahassee, Fla., 1990).

31. Williams and Rice, "Communication Research and the New Media Technologies."

SECTION FOUR

Interviewing: Media Practices and Procedures

14 The Journalistic Interview and Investigative Reporting

James Reston observed that where "the nineteenth century was the era of the novelist, the twentieth is the era of the journalist." The journalistic interview, as a means of gathering information, has emerged as an invaluable tool for the journalist of today. For journalists, interviewing is a craft and a profession; rarely a science, sometimes an art. Regardless of how fine a writer they might be, they are crippled if they are not effective interviewers.

Chapter 14 defines journalistic interviewing and the investigative report, outlines the stages of the journalistic interview, explores questioning strategies and techniques, and discusses the role of telephoning, note taking, and taping. Ultimately, the journalist must write the news or investigative report—arranging the pieces of the interview and taping sections together so that one subject leads inexorably to the next. This chapter is designed to accomplish three objectives:

1. *Awareness.* You will understand the essential stages of journalistic interviewing, learn the fundamentals of news gathering, and acquire an appreciation for the practice of journalism.

2. *Assessment.* You will be able to assess the factors comprising a situation and, using thoughtful, probing questions, insightfully report the news.

3. *Application.* You will be able to gather the news, write the news, and responsibly evaluate the news.

*   *   *   *   *

On the Record—Off the Record

The Northern Michigan Power Company (NMP) is an old, established utility. Five years ago, NMP officials approved and began construction of a state-of-the-art nuclear power plant. Residents of the communities of Big Rapids and Mt. Pleasant had mixed opinions about building the local nuclear power plant. However, unemployment was high, and Northern Michigan Power Company provided hope for an upturn in the economy. A new reservoir was built, the fishing was excellent, and the company and its contractors employed a sizable number of new workers. Now, with construction still incomplete, there are rumors of rate increases and construction overruns. Presently, Northern Michigan Power is preparing to present a rate case before the Michigan Commerce Commission. The case is a request for money, only part of which would be used to help complete the nuclear facility. A negative decision would seriously damage company plans.

Charles Creamer is a reporter for the local *Journal Star.* Nine years ago, he graduated with honors from the University of Central Michigan and went to work for the *Journal Star,* where he has acquired respect and recognition as a writer. His journalism degree has served him well as a general assignment or investigative reporter. Charles realizes that this special investigative assignment regarding Northern Michigan Power will be the most controversial thing he has ever done.

Charles spent several months examining the nuclear power industry, scrutinizing a Presidential commission report on the hazards of nuclear power plants, and researching the background of Northern Michigan Power Company. As this stage of the story developed, he arranged interviews with NMP officials and several former employees from the plant construction site. The issues were complex, so he carefully considered the questions to ask, as well as how to ask them.

An interview with Howard Nottingham, NMP executive vice president, was conducted at the offices of Northern Michigan Power Company. After a series of questions confirming background information and the decision to build the nuclear power facility, Mr. Nottingham was asked about the cost overruns and delay in construction. He showed Charles a list of all nuclear power plants being built in the United States, noting that the NMP plant had the lowest cost increase. Moreover, he emphasized that only part of the proposed 14 percent rate increase being requested was for the nuclear plant, with the balance going for general revenue purposes. When challenged by Charles, the NMP vice president did say that "unquestionably, the driving force for the requested electric rate increase is the Company's need to generate revenue to support the construction of the nuclear facility." While reticent to speculate on a final date of construction, Howard Nottingham did acknowledge that "construction is two-and-a-half years behind schedule" and off-the-record "will probably take four or five more years to complete." Still off-the-record, he observed that "further rate increases will probably be necessary to provide the kind of service our customers expect."

Beverly Brinkley, NMP public affairs director, also agreed to meet with Charles. She began the interview by reiterating to Charles that, "In line with our policy of providing all news media with the facts about our operations, Northern Michigan Power is pleased to cooperate fully with you." However, she refused to comment on schedule delays or a projected completion date, noting only that "full-system testing takes a considerable amount of time." She then showed him a milestone chart indicating the approximate time during which the tests would be made. Beverly did emphasize that once on line the new nuclear power facility would provide Northern Michigan Power customers with long-term, inexpensive electricity. Charles thanked Beverly for her time, and when she requested an advance copy of the story, he refused, saying, "It's Journal Star policy," but he would send her a copy of the article when published.

The interviews at *Charles's Journal Star* office with three former employees were more revealing. Two of the men had been fired for cause and the third had resigned, so all were eager to disclose information regarding the nuclear facility. All were critical of the project and provided examples of expenditures without incentives for cost controls. One stated, "They've got themselves committed. They went into it and all of a sudden they've got a bear by the tail, and they don't know how to let go." Another questioned the limited experience of the contractor building the facility and speculated on the possible dangers to the local community. Charles didn't take out a notebook or use a tape recorder as he had during previous interviews with NMP representatives but rather "chatted" with the former employees about the circulating "rumors."

A number of follow-up phone calls finalized the research. Charles took several days to review his notes, listen to tapes with NMP officials, and write the story. He worked on it at the office in between his general assignment duties. Finally, he edited and rearranged things and filed the story.

The headline read: "NMP Nuclear Power Project in Trouble!" The story documented the troubles experienced by nuclear power plants generally, including the potential hazards to the environment. It then went on to discuss the problems confronting the facility under construction by Northern Michigan Power Company. Limited construction experience, costly schedule delays, and proposed rate increases were vividly presented as "a China Syndrome of cost." The story concluded by stating: "If the charts are correct, it will take NMP five more years to complete the project and costs will continue to rise. The thing is, someone has to pay for all that. That someone, of course, will be, one way or another, sooner or later, the customers of Northern Michigan Power."

Northern Michigan Power was appalled by the story and received an immediate barrage of calls from stockholders, customers, and the general public. Moreover, the story potentially jeopardized their rate case before the Michigan Commerce Commission. The NMP rebuttal was immediate.

Beverly Brinkley, as public affairs director, challenged the credentials and accusations of the former employees, criticized inaccuracies and misleading comments, and refuted the allegations made in the story. She pointed out that the construction firm was part of a consortium that had worked on fourteen nuclear projects and that only a portion of the proposed rate increase would go toward completing the nuclear facility. Emphasizing that NMP was doing a "good job," Beverly described the story as "yet another example of sensationalism in journalism at the expense of the facts of the matter."

Charles "personally" regretted the way NMP officials felt about the story but strongly believed that he was "fair" and "reasonable" in his treatment of the "horrendous and endemic cost overruns" by Northern Michigan Power Company.[1]

Discussion Questions

1. Was the *Journal Star* acting as a ferocious "watch dog" or perpetuating "yellow journalism?" Did Charles' story document the news or create the news? Were Beverly Brinkley's efforts to "defuse" the impact of the story effective?

2. Was there adequate background research and planning prior to conducting the interviews? How were questions used to gather information and probe for facts? Did the parties reveal noticeable agendas?

3. Did Charles actively listen and accurately observe? How was telephoning, note taking, and taping used to report and write the story?

4. Was the story thoughtfully and insightfully written? Did it conform to fundamental journalistic structure and style? Would you label this an investigative report?

5. Did Charles violate the ethics of "good" investigative journalism? Is the *Star Journal* subject to libel charges by Northern Michigan Power Company?

A Short History of the American Press

Although the book is the oldest medium in use today, the newspaper is the oldest *mass* medium, for it was the first form of communication to reach a mass audience. The newspaper's early identification with the masses made it a powerful medium for democracy. Thomas Carlyle observed that the printing press was "creating a whole new democratic world," because it could take formless thoughts from the mind of one person and pass them on to the minds of a billion others.[2] This often placed the press in opposition to those with power and authority, and the history of the newspaper is a story of a continuing struggle to be free to publish news, facts, information, and opinion. Thomas Jefferson summed up the political philosophy of the role of newspapers in a free society when he said, "Our liberty depends on the freedom of the press and that cannot be limited without being lost."[3]

The most important journalistic tradition of all, the right of a free press to criticize the government, was established in 1735 at the libel trial of John Peter Zenger. Zenger, printer of the *New York Weekly Journal,* was defended by a shrewd Philadelphia lawyer named Andrew Hamilton who argued that one should be able to print the truth, even if libelous. In a decision that shocked the Royal Governor of New York, a colonial jury held that the press has the right to expose arbitrary governmental power by "speaking and writing the truth."[4] This ability to print attacks on the follies and abuses of the government has given journalists unprecedented power in the modern world.

Just forty years following the end of the Revolutionary War, America stood on the brink of the Industrial Revolution. New York City had replaced colonial Boston and Philadelphia as America's financial and intellectual center, and it was here that the press would reach its greatest power ruled by "newspaper barons" and men who would truly become known as "lords of the press." Men like Benjamin Day, James Gordon Bennett, Horace Greeley, Henry Jarvis Raymond, Adolph Ochs, Joseph Pulitzer, and William Randolph Hearst would indelibly influence and shape American journalism.[5]

Benjamin Day was an almost bankrupt printer whose only real asset was an idea, but it was an idea that would change the face of journalism. In 1833, Day started the *New York Sun* and, using the new, fast cylinder press, sold it for one penny rather than the usual six cents. Moreover, by hiring men and boys to hawk the newspapers on the streets, he succeeded in making up in volume what he lost in individual sales. The *New York Sun* became a major publishing success and started the era of the "penny press," the first mass circulation medium.[6]

James Gordon Bennett started the *New York Herald* in 1835, two years after Day had started the *Sun,* and it would soon become the prototype of the newspaper as we know it today. Day and Bennett both realized that to sell penny papers on a mass basis the newspaper had to contain material of interest to many people. This simple economic factor led to the development of the profession of news gathering. The *New York Herald* was the first paper to have men assigned to cover various city departments on a regular basis and to go out and find the stories. These men were called "reporters," and when the telegraph became a possibility in the 1840s, Bennett was the first to station a Washington correspondent in the nation's capital to send back to New York City telegraphed stories about Congress and the government. However, James Gordon Bennett gained his greatest notoriety by using the columns of his *Herald* as a weapon, attacking anyone and anything that disturbed him. In return, he was at various times vilified as a "half-crazy, uneducated wretch," "an immoral and blasphemous monstrosity," and "a stigma on the city filled with ignorance and bloated conceit."[7] The public loved it and the *Herald* prospered. Only fifteen months after Bennett's *Herald* was born, it had a circulation of more than 40,000, and the numbers of readers grew steadily.

Horace Greeley would stride onto the scene in 1841, and his new penny paper, the *New York Tribune,* would make him a giant of journalism. Less concerned with crime and corruption than Bennett's *Herald,* Greeley's highly successful *Tribune* crusaded vigorously for social reform and equal justice. Greeley soon became widely known as "Uncle Horace," and he liked to think of his *Tribune* as the "conscience of the nation." For example, in 1846, while the United States was fighting its war with Mexico, Horace Greeley led the opposition by printing words of protest in his strictly establishment *New York Tribune.*[8]

Henry Jarvis Raymond, believing that people had tired of reading stories of violent crimes, reports of tragedies and calamities, and editorials advancing social crusades, started the *New York Times*—a paper that wouldn't take sides and would report the news without being sensational. This concern for responsible journalism was continued when, in 1896, a thirty-eight-year-old publisher named Adolph Ochs bought the *Times* for the bargain price of $75,000 and set out to print a newspaper that would "not soil the breakfast linen." In an obvious slap at "sensationalist" papers, Ochs coined the slogan, "All the news that's fit to print," which remains to this day on the *Times* front page.[9] Over a century later, many observers believe that the *New York Times* sets the standard by which all other papers should be measured.

By 1861, with the nation enthralled in the Civil War, there were 387 daily newspapers in the United States, but none were more powerful than the *Herald,* the *Tribune,* or the *Times.* A number of characteristics of modern newspapers emerged during the Civil War. For example, the byline resulted when Union army generals, distressed at the publication of information about troop movements before they happened, ordered that all stories about the Union army carry the name of the reporter who wrote them. The inverted pyramid style of journalism in which the writer tries to summarize all the important elements of the story in the first paragraph stemmed from problems with faulty telegraph transmission. To insure that at least the most important elements of the story got through on the wire, correspondents would give those items first, in the initial paragraph, creating the summary lead.[10] As the Civil War began to fade into history, so did Greeley and Bennett. It was time for new giants who would build newspaper empires through aggressive promotion.

Joseph Pulitzer was a penniless, chronically ill immigrant from Hungary who had come to America to fight in the Civil War and later drifted to St. Louis where he became a reporter. In little more than a decade, the brilliant Pulitzer would make a fortune as owner of the *St. Louis Post-Dispatch,* which he built into what was then and still is one of America's most respected newspapers. By 1893, Pulitzer was ready to take on New York. He bought a dying newspaper called the *New York World,* which he turned into a thriving success. The *World* had a circulation of

20,000 when Pulitzer took it over, and less than a decade later, by 1892, he had raised its readership to 374,000. Pulitzer's secret was to give the *World* a split personality, which shouldn't have worked but somehow did. The front page contained stories of crime, sex, and sensational exposés, and the editorial pages putting forth Pulitzer's ideas for social reform were a haven for thoughtful idealism appealing to the intellectual.

William Randolph Hearst entered journalism as the student business manager of the *Harvard Lampoon* and then received the *San Francisco Examiner* as a gift from his immensely wealthy father, who was also the Senator from California. In 1895, Hearst moved to New York, purchased a floundering paper called the *New York Journal,* and declared journalistic war on Pulitzer and the *World.* With tales of corruption and lurid sex and violent crime, the *Journal* was soon out sensationalizing anything ever dreamed up by Bennett, Greeley, or even Pulitzer himself. The classic film, *Citizen Cain,* was the thinly disguised story of Hearst's life and his flare for sensationalism.[11]

Pulitzer's *World* was the first newspaper to feature a regular comic section printed in full color. The most popular cartoon was a strip drawn by Richard Outcult called *The Yellow Kid.* When Hearst purchased a color press and hired Outcult away to draw *The Yellow Kid* in his bright yellow nightshirt, the *World* and the *Journal* engaged in a battle, which critics of both papers soon labeled "yellow journalism." The name has lived on as a description of journalism that is irresponsible or sensational.[12] While the era of sensationalism was not journalism's finest hour, the yellow press did exercise great influence on public opinion. By exposing graft and corruption in society, newspapers found they not only could sell more papers, but they could also perform a social service. A new breed of reporter began to develop who was interested in investigating the sins of society and the hidden perversions of power. These new investigative journalists, to use Theodore Roosevelt's expression, "raked the muck of society," and as so-called "muckrakers" did considerable social good.[13] By the beginning of the twentieth century, the daily newspaper had become the first and most influential mass medium, with circulation reaching the hundreds of thousands.

Sensational journalism did not die completely in the twentieth century despite a growing maturity and more responsible phase. By the 1920s, the brawling city of Chicago, dominated by gangsters and corruption, began to steal some of the journalistic spotlight from New York. For the first time, the competition between papers was fought not from the offices of the editors and publishers but by the reporters on the "beat." It was called "jazz age" journalism, and the hard-drinking, do-anything-for-a-story reporters it produced became models for a stereotype that still persists decades after the reality has disappeared. The classic play, *The Front Page,* captures the insanity of these wild days. This period marked the rise of tabloid newspapers, which made extensive use of photographs and concentrated coverage on one or two major headline stories.[14]

In the twentieth century, magazines also became a vital political and social force challenging newspapers. Innovation in the magazine field came particularly from individual genius, often the vision of the young with new ideas and fresh talent. Henry Luce was one such editorial genius whose contributions included bringing the world a kind of journalism never before seen. In 1921, when he was only twenty-three, Luce and fellow Yale classmate Briton Hadden began developing a weekly news magazine. They raised $86,000, hired a staff of young writers, and on March 3, 1923 the first issue of *Time* was on the newsstands. The format, revolutionary for its time, was to condense the week's news and divide it into various subjects or departments, so busy readers could easily pick and choose their areas of interest. However, its bright, breezy, and literate style soon made every department one of interest. By the mid-1930s, *Time*'s format was a familiar part of American life. However, Luce had an instinct for what would work and later started *Fortune*, which became an immediate success. A quarter century later, Luce would start another magazine, against the advice of experts, which would become the most successful sports magazine ever published—*Sports Illustrated*. Perhaps the greatest Luce success was *Life* magazine. *Life* first appeared in November 1936 offering ninety-six pages of news and feature photographs. Luce insisted on using the world's greatest photographers, and he printed their pictures on expensive, glossy paper. *Life* magazine carried very few words; the pictures themselves were meant to tell the story, and today, by looking back at *Life*'s great pictures, one can see the unfolding of an entire era of American history.[15] Henry Luce had turned the weekly news magazine into a viable journalistic medium that persists today.

The number of daily newspapers reached its high point in the United States immediately before World War I, in 1914, with 2,250 individual papers.[16] By the 1950s and 1960s, the rising costs and competition by television set off the beginning of a decline in the number of American newspapers that has never been reversed. New York City, which once boasted fifteen major daily papers, would be reduced to having only three, and the story would be much the same in other cities across the nation. To offset rising costs and growing competition, a number of papers consolidated, and newspaper chains owned by "media moguls," such as Rubert Murdoch, surfaced to take advantage of management efficiency.[17] Still, a number of great newspapers have emerged in America as economically sound, politically independent, and socially responsible organs, despite competition and high costs. The *New York Times* has maintained a position for nearly a century as the newspaper of record. The *Washington Post* has risen rapidly to challenge the premier position of the *New York Times,* as has the *Los Angeles Times* on the West Coast, under the dynamic leadership of Otis Chandler. Other great newspapers, such as the *Manchester Union Leader, Boston Globe, The Wall Street Journal, Kansas City Star, Charlottee Observer, Louisville Courier-Journal, Christian Science Monitor, Minneapolis Star-Tribune, Rocky Mountain News,* and *Miami Herald* to name a few, have won wide respect for their coverage of important news and their penetrating analysis of events.

However, there is increasing criticism of the American press. According to Larry Sabato, author of *Feeding Frenzy: How Attack Journalism Has Transformed American Politics,* the media, and particularly the press, have become "junkyard dogs," instead of "watch dogs."[18] There is also concern within the media industry that a widening gulf may exist between journalists and their public. Journalists, by choice, circumstance, or tradition, are becoming insulated from their communities.

To the extent that this occurs, it may undermine the news-gathering and reporting process, as well as erode journalists' ability to critically evaluate their product.[19] This growing professional dissatisfaction and concern for responsible and involved news coverage has given birth to a grassroots reform movement known as "public journalism." Public journalism treats readers as citizens and assumes that readers want to *be* citizens. Therefore, the reporter's and editor's task *isn't* to report facts in a vacuum, but to "figure out (as only a good journalist can) how to round up a whole community's agenda and questions, and then to put out (as only a good journalist can) a readable newspaper with just the answers citizens are looking for."[20] Consequently, public journalists aim to print all the news that responsible citizens want to know. The mortal sin for a public journalist is falling out of touch with the community he or she serves.

Walter Lippmann described the press as a "search light that restlessly prowls across the expanses, never staying on any feature for very long."[21] The press today is still the most economical way to transmit large volumes of information and news to the millions of citizens of this nation. The power of the press has never faltered through three centuries of scientific advancement—it still maintains its original virtues and strengths. It is staffed by many dedicated, hard-working, and socially interested employees, who would all agree that the method by which the news is delivered is no where near as important as the content of the news itself. The founding fathers didn't know about T.V. or computers. The words of the first amendment make it clear that they knew something far more important—that whether the news is delivered by an ink-stained printer or a stream of electrons, there is no way for a democracy to survive without a free and uncontrolled press.

*   *   *   *   *

Was the *Journal Star* acting in the fine tradition of journalism when it published a story declaring: "NMP Nuclear Power Project in Trouble"? Charles Creamer elected to investigate a topic that certainly had news value and conformed to the intent of public journalism. The nuclear power facility under construction by Northern Michigan Power was timely, of local significance, and potentially consequential. He had conducted background research and interviewed NMP officials, as well as site construction workers. This was a newsworthy story rather than a journalistic creation or pseudo-event. However, did Charles tell all the facts essential to a clear understanding of the story? A story can be true in detail and yet work an injustice by omission. Moreover, such statements as "a China Syndrome of cost" or "horrendous and endemic cost overruns" question his impersonal reporting and spirit of fairness. Also, failure to observe the traditional conventions of on-record and off-the-record colored his investigative reporting. It appeared that Charles was trying to accuse, condemn, and indict rather than investigate. A journalist's personality counts, but he or she must use it wholly as an instrument belonging to the newspaper and the public. While the *Journal Star* was not perpetuating "yellow journalism" in its strictest sense, it was advancing a singular point of view. Beverly Brinkley, NMP public affairs director, reasonably challenged the dramatic privilege taken and sensational spirit displayed.

Defining the Journalistic Interview

Despite their mastheads, *The New York Times* does not give us "All the news that's fit to print," and *The Atlanta Journal* does not "cover Dixie like the dew." Instead, readers receive *all the news that fits the space constraints of the newspaper.* What, then, is news? News has been roughly defined as that which interests people. However, the importance of a story in the eyes of an editor depends on one or more of several considerations: (a) immediacy, (b) proximity, (c) consequence, (d) prominence, and (e) drama. A story is valuable as news if it instructs, informs, or entertains that large cross section of humanity known as the reading public.

However, a new definition of "news you can use" is emerging. The *Boca Raton News* in South Florida unveiled in 1990 the results of their 25/43 Project designed to reach the 25 to 43 age group by presenting interesting stories these readers could digest quickly and easily. The stories were short with visuals and graphics used throughout the paper. Also in 1990, the Gannett Company, which owns the highly successful *USA Today* and more than eighty other newspapers, undertook a major effort to explore ways of changing the content and presentation of news. Their News 2000 program emphasized identifying community interests, making the news relevant to readers in local communities, and finding ways to get readers involved. The results were stories that people care about and that make people care.[22] Newspapers will continue to seek ways to adapt to changing patterns of readers, and journalists need to be receptive to innovative concepts. No matter how the content and delivery of print news might change, *reporters will still rely upon the interview as a primary news gathering device. Interviewing in its broad sense will always be at the core of nearly all newspaper reporting, because nearly all stories deal with people—their doings and opinions.*

What is a journalistic interview? The typical definition considers it to be a formal or informal conversation between two parties for the purpose of obtaining opinions or gathering information for publication. However, while a successful interview may look and feel like a casual conversation, it is not. The interviewer has a specific purpose for conducting the interview and guides the interview with this purpose in mind. The journalist is the reader's surrogate and as such is obligated to carefully form questions, to probe, and to listen intently to the interviewee's answers.

While interviewing is one of the main techniques reporters use to get information, the question-and-answer method as a journalistic tool is a relatively new phenomenon. James Gordon Bennett is given credit for being the father of the interview and publishing someone's views related verbatim with indirect quotations. The first interview in American journalism appeared in the *New York Herald* on October 11, 1835, when Bennett published a conversation between himself and the former postmaster of Buffalo, New York, regarding an alleged mistake made by the *Herald.* Later, in 1836, Bennett published a formal interview with Rosina Townsend, a key witness in a sensational murder case. The questions and answers were related verbatim, and at the end of the article, Bennett summed up his own opinion by analyzing the murder case and Mrs. Townsend's answers in a detective style.[23] While the 1830s gave rise to the direct interview, today about 90 percent of everything in a news story is based on some form of interviewing with the other methods of information gathering being documentary research and observation. However, even when covering a story which the reporter is fortunate enough to observe, a certain amount of interviewing or sympathetic questioning is usually necessary to make the story complete.

There are several ways of classifying journalistic interviews. One of these is by purpose: Why did the interview take place? The interviewer's role is to be a "public reactor" who provides the right questions at the right time to confirm facts, get quotes, collect anecdotes, and characterize the situation. However, since interviewers often seek to achieve each of these ends, it may be better to classify interviews according to their form: How, in what manner, did they take place? While interviews are rarely so mechanical that they can be reduced to standard formulas or categories, there are frequently used styles that deserve attention. The **in-person news interview** is based on "hard news," some event or development of current, immediate interest. The **telephone interview** is a modified version of the news interview, with a phone conversation substituting for a face-to-face exchange. It poses certain challenges, which will be further discussed later in this chapter. The **prepared question interview** is also used when in-person interviewing is difficult. The reporter prepares a set of written questions for submission to an important news source with a request for a reply. More often than not, the questions go unheeded. The **inquiring reporter interview** is casual in nature, with only one question on some topical item being randomly asked of a number of individuals at some specified place and time. This "on the street" style of interview can bring out opinions of importance or merely personal views on some subject of general interest. The **personality interview** is built around the views, personality, or exploits of an individual or group. It is an effort to let readers see the personality, appearance, mannerisms, background, and character of the subject or group. Finally, the **casual interview** is an accidental encounter between a reporter and a news source that arouses curiosity and results, with some digging, in a major news story.

Regardless of the interview assignment or style, the objective is always the same—to ferret out as much news, details, significance, and color as possible. Consequently, competent reporters must understand the stages of the journalistic interview, acquire a degree of skill in question asking, and learn how to handle different kinds of people—how to draw some out, keep others on the topic, and evaluate the motives or honesty of still others. The reporter is a conduit and must never forget that news, in large part, is measured by his or her ability to gain and conduct good interviews. The success of any story depends on the quantity and quality of the information gleaned and the journalist's sense of news values and writing ability.[24]

*   *   *   *   *

Charles Creamer identified the salient issues of interest to his readers. Sources were identified and attribution accorded. On the surface, Charles's story appeared to document the news, but closer examination revealed that he created a prevailing point of view. This controlling outlook denied alternative positions. Such biased storytelling created false impressions, which could flaw reader judgment and imperil decision making. As Sherlock Holmes remarked to Watson in *A Study in Scarlet:* "It is a capital mistake to theorize before you have all the evidence. It biases the judgment."[25]

Charles and the *Star Journal* would probably argue that they went to considerable lengths to get the facts, and despite a couple of minor errors, the evidence was fairly presented. The story accurately described the situation and reasonably projected those issues that the public should seriously consider. The analysis was sound and the conclusions were fundamentally correct. In sum, the insignificant mistakes made were not done out of malice or deliberate disregard of the truth, and the story essentially represented balanced and unbiased journalism.

The Stages of the Interview

The typical journalistic interview runs through seven stages: (1) defining the purpose of the interview, (2) conducting background research, (3) selecting a subject and requesting an interview appointment, (4) structuring the interview and preparing questions, (5) meeting the subject and establishing an easy rapport, (6) asking questions and probing for information, and (7) ending the interview. Understanding each of these stages can lead to a productive exchange and successful interview.

Defining the purpose of the interview. Before deciding whom to interview, the purpose of the interview must be defined, which requires knowing what kind of story is to be written. While stories may vary, the basic types include the news story, the news feature, the profile, the investigative report, and the round-up.[26] The **news story** routinely focuses on daily events and typically reports the traditional who, what, where, when, and sometimes how the events occurred. The **news feature** more carefully explores selected news stories and provides elaboration by giving background details about the who or what, or examining in depth the how or why. The goal of the **profile** is to focus on one person or group and vividly paint a word portrait. The **investigative report** requires taking the time and energy to go beyond what is generally known about an event or issue and relentlessly answering the how and why. Finally, the **round-up** is a symposium-style story that provides perspective on a current issue by combining several people's opinions. Determining the type of story helps define the purpose of the interview and gives direction to the conducting of background research.

Conducting background research. Richard Meryman of *Life* magazine keenly observes that the key to fruitful interviewing "is homework," and experienced reporters agree that for every minute spent in an interview, at least ten minutes should be spent in preparation.[27] Interviews that follow, rather than precede, careful research are nearly always more productive. Homework can be broken into two parts—reading about the issue or subject and preparing a game plan. Careful, systematic research makes the difference between a story that merely records and a story that teaches, explains, and enlightens.

While conducting the necessary background research, the pieces will begin to come together into some kind of organizational pattern. As these elements settle and certain questions emerge, develop a game plan or story angle. This reveals who needs to be interviewed and helps guide the preparation of questions along lines that will provide a publishable story with substance. However, be flexible and receptive to any new angle that may be better than the one originally planned. Always be open to traveling down new conversational pathways.

Selecting a subject and requesting an interview appointment. Journalists select people as interviewee's for one or more of the following reasons: accessibility, reliability, accountability, and/or quotability. It's desirable that the interviewee be readily accessible, and if not, could the interview possibly be conducted by phone or mail instead of in person. Reliable and accountable sources help prevent the reporting of rumor and speculation, which could jeopardize a story. Finally, an expert who is articulate, well informed, and capable of orchestrating quick quotes can enhance a story. The "ideal" interviewee combines all of these characteristics.

After determining the purpose of an interview and possible subject, how is an interview arranged? The answer to this question is simple enough—personally ask, telephone, or write the person to be interviewed. When asking for an interview, the journalist should (1) identify him or herself, (2) identify the news organization the journalist represents, (3) state the purpose for the interview, (4) tell how the interview will be used, and (5) confirm where the interview will take place. When arranging an interview, be realistic about how much time will be needed, since busy people carefully allocate each appointment.

Structuring the interview and preparing questions. Before deciding which questions to ask, the journalist must structure the interview to meet the desired objectives. The interview outline may take one of several shapes: funnel, inverted funnel, tunnel, covertly sequenced, or freeform. The **funnel interview** opens with generalities and then pins down the generalizations with detailed observations. The approach increasingly narrows the interviewee's alternatives until eventually the interviewee cannot avoid specific questions. On the other hand, the **inverted funnel interview** begins with a narrow topic and broadens to a wider subject. Using a specific incident or fact as a foundation, the purview of the interview gradually expands, with the reporter eventually encouraging the interviewee to offer an expert opinion or comment that might explain the story. The **tunnel interview** is meant for quick observations about a specific incident and strings together either all open-ended or all closed-ended questions on a single topic. It is useful for on-the-scene reactions, since the questions do not invite lengthy reflections. A **covertly sequenced interview** attempts to trick the interviewee by interspersing difficult with simple questions, open-ended with closed-ended questions, and friendly with antagonistic questions. By alternating different types of questions in a random sequence, the interviewer hopes to juxtapose earlier responses with later answers and surprise the interviewee into making an unexpected revelation. Covert sequencing can be an especially useful approach when the person being interviewed is defensive, uncooperative, or otherwise avoiding the issue. Finally, the **freeform interview** invites open-ended responses, permitting the interviewee an opportunity to provide the quotes, anecdotes, and colorful details that satisfy readers. Although the interview is open-ended, it is not without direction, and follow-up questions are essential to getting the story. An interview is a journey of discovery, and its structure gives direction to the journey.

Meeting the subject and establishing an easy rapport. Some interviewers come away with a flurry of quotes, anecdotes, and hard facts, while others barely get the story. Why? The answer rests in immediately establishing a relaxed, easy rapport with the subject. A simple smile; a quick, firm handshake; and a direct gaze can provide a positive first impression and indicate a friendly disposition. There is no substitute for the initial impression created, and an effective interview often depends less on the questions asked than on the spirit of questioning. A conscientious interviewer promotes and encourages a candid, thoughtful, and open climate or spirit.

Asking questions and probing for information. One of the best ways to begin an interview is to quickly remind the interviewee of the purpose of the interview. Then, ask questions in a natural, informal fashion always keeping the conversation moving at a productive pace. Probing is the key to skillful interviewing. By asking reflective questions and interpretive or summary questions, the interviewee is encouraged to explain or elaborate on something already said. However, these follow-up questions do more than secure specifics, they also help reinforce rapport by indicating a genuine interest in the subject.

When conducting an interview, the worst thing an interviewer can do is talk a lot. Most of the interview time should be given to listening. Indeed, this is one of the most important things to know how to do, and doing it well requires intense concentration. The successful interviewer must learn to listen with a "third ear," hearing more than the words the interviewee speaks. In many ways, this kind of listening is really watching. Note physical characteristics, head nods, gestures, and nuances, as well as expressions to catch any hidden feelings, reactions, or meanings. Listen for the lead, the main thrust of the story, and be alert for significant quotes or anecdotes, as well as for any unexpected shift in the conversation that may reveal new information and a new angle that might make the story better.

Ending the interview. The close of the interview should be as smooth as the opening stages; therefore, it is advisable for the interviewer to assume responsibility for ending the interview gracefully. Saying, "I have just a few more questions?" can signal the close and help draw the interview to a fast finish. Then, summarize the conversation, and as protection against later criticism that something important was overlooked, add "Is there anything you think is important that I haven't asked?" This can sometimes be very revealing as evidenced when presidential candidate Jimmy Carter admitted to having "lust in his heart" in a 1976 *Playboy* interview.[28] This is also the time to verify information, double check quotes, and assure the interviewee that any unclear technical or statistical information will be checked with them. Finally, politely thank the interviewee, expressing gratitude for the time willingly given, and promptly leave.

* * * * *

Charles Creamer conducted background research and engaged in planning prior to conducting his interviews. He documented national concerns regarding the construction of nuclear power facilities and then localized the story. He carefully selected interviewees to acquire a balanced perspective, including both Northern Michigan Power officials and on-site construction workers. However, while NMP officials confined their remarks to their area of authority, the selected construction workers offered opinions beyond their expertise. Charles could have used telephone interviews with others recognized in the nuclear power field to clarify and elaborate on observations. Also, he might have surveyed public opinion to broaden his investigation and reflect local feelings. This would have taken him down new pathways, which might have modified the story angle pursued.

When conducting the interviews, Charles sought to establish and maintain a cordial rapport while not neglecting to ask the tough questions. He sought answers to the basic who, what, when, where, why, and how, and tenaciously explored local significance. Even when confronted with an occasional "no comment," he was determined to find answers. After concluding the interviews, he followed up, when necessary, with the involved parties. The information gathered reflected an understanding of the stages comprising the interview process.

Asking and Answering Questions

Voltaire said, "Judge a man by his questions rather than by his answers." Journalists ask questions to reveal the underlying causes or principles behind any event or situation, and this can be a difficult and complex task. However, if they know the right questions to ask, they have an unbeatable edge on the competition. A useful pattern for this conceptual level of interviewing, which can assist in the framing of questions, has been suggested by LaRue W. Gilleland called GOSS, an acronym for: Goals, Obstacle, Solutions, and Start.[29] During the **goal stage** of questioning, the interviewer attempts to delineate purpose and discern the motivation behind actions by asking: What are or were some of your goals? What are you trying to accomplish? Why do you want to do this? The **obstacle stage** of questioning focuses on the difficulties or barriers encountered, with the interviewer asking: What are or were some of the obstacles you faced or are facing? What is one example of a difficult problem you experienced? The **solution stage** of questioning explores how the obstacles or barriers were overcome by asking: How did you overcome these obstacles? How did you achieve your goal or how do you plan to achieve it? The final **start stage** of questioning astutely suggests that understanding concepts comes more easily by returning to the beginning of any event or situation. Here, the interviewer attempts to establish the chronology of events necessary for the reader to understand the story and asks: How and why did it all begin? How did you or the program get to this point? Many interviews can be designed around the GOSS model, and it is suitable for a variety of stories, especially profiles, features, and stories about programs or issues.

Factual questions are basic to any interview: who, what, when, where, why, how, and significance or what does it mean? Answers to these questions establish a foundation of knowledge and provide a sense of the story's dimensions. However, probing questions are at the heart of an interview. Asking open-ended questions, reflective questions, interpretive or summary questions, and problem questions give the interviewee room to breathe and the interviewer room to grapple. Questions, such as "What do you think about?" "Can you tell me a bit more about how you feel?" "You're saying then that?" and "Let's suppose that you're faced with the following situation?" provide personal insight, depth, and color. Although the interviewee may seem more comfortable spinning generalities, probe and insist on anecdotes. One key word which will incite anecdotes is "when." "When" takes the subject to a scene, a setting, and thence to a story as in "When did you realize?" If interviewers ask only narrow, specific, direct questions and fail to effectively follow up and probe, they risk ending up with an article that reflects their own preconceptions, an article they could have written in large measure before conducting the interview.

The more probing an interview, the more likely it is that an interviewer will have to get tough. Most journalists get tough when subjects refuse to specifically answer their questions or when it's necessary to broach a sensitive issue. However, the importance of being tough or stern should not be overemphasized. Remember, interviews are conversations, not inquisitions, and even when interviewers must be tough, they needn't be cruel. The purpose is not to provoke or antagonize but to serve as a skeptical observer digging behind the event or situation for its meaning. The trick to tough questions is saving them for the last third of the interview, after rapport has been established, and asking them in a conversational tone, thus making them appear like all other questions previously asked. If the interviewee becomes angry and terminates the interview, the majority of information for the story has already been gathered. Getting tough in an interview means never having to say you're sorry that you didn't get the story.

When covering a story and conducting interviews, it is vitally important that journalists deal with people as individuals. Today, in a multicultural society, this means that whenever there are racial, ethnic, or cultural differences between an interviewer and interviewee, the interviewer should seek to understand those known differences more fully prior to the interview. Reporters need to develop an investigative, nonjudgmental attitude and a high tolerance for ambiguity when trying to expand cross-cultural understanding. Stereotypes and labels interfere with objective viewing and the sensitive search for cues to guide the reporter toward seeing the other person's reality or point of view. The presence of anxiety and tension is common, and both parties to the interview can feel threatened and vulnerable. However, competent interviewers will seek to lower tension by suspending judgment and expressing empathy. They make a concerted effort to get along with and to try to understand people whose beliefs and backgrounds may be vastly different from their own. Multiculturally conscious journalists will be alert to diversity and "respect the dignity and personhood of others."[30] Acting as facilitators, they can build bridges of understanding that span our commonalties. Journalists are in a unique position to serve as "cultural barometers," monitoring the changing relational climate between diverse social groups and sharing positive insights that can promote cultural harmony. As inhabitants of the twenty-first century, we will no longer have a choice about whether to live in a world of many cultures, since racial and ethnic groups will outnumber whites for the first time.[31] The journalistic interview, characterized by its mutual asking and answering of questions, embodies our "utopian hope that people can talk about, through, across, and around their differences and that these exchanges will help us live together justly."[32]

Reporters need to develop an investigative, nonjudgmental attitude and a high tolerance for ambiguity. People buy the paper for information put in a way they can get quickly.

While no interview is alike and all journalists develop their own unique style of interviewing, there are some useful tips to asking questions that can help make any interview more effective. Successful interviewers

- Ask questions the interviewee is qualified to answer.
- Space questions singly, following logically from the stated purpose.
- Put questions in a nonthreatening order, saving tough questions for the end.
- Establish rapport and a pattern of question and response before asking tough questions.
- Ask basic background questions, the who, what, when, where, why, and how.
- Concentrate on "how" and "why" questions that ask for opinions and reveal a point of view.
- Determine chronology or the sequence of events.
- Ask for specifics and verify information.
- Are on the outlook for quotes, anecdotes, and color.
- Ask follow-up questions and probe for details.
- Ask for definition and clarification.
- Consider the interviewee's point of view and ask about pros and cons.
- Are aware of what hasn't been said and ask about omissions.
- Maintain a critical sense while asking questions.
- Avoid asking unfocused or clichè questions.
- Avoid asking yes or no questions or questions including simultaneous opposites.
- Avoid asking leading questions or loaded questions.
- Don't talk too much.
- **Listen and learn!**[33]

Beginning journalists often worry about appearing ignorant or dumb and hesitate to ask simple questions, yet these questions may lead to interesting, quotable answers. It is better to ask too many questions than too few.

The other side of asking questions is answering questions. The interviewee or source is not a passive pawn in this exchange with reporters but is an active participant at the center of journalistic interviewing. Reporters depend on sources for the story; however, the relationship is often symbiotic in that sources may find it beneficial to share information and influence that story. Together, reporters and sources can fulfill mutual needs through the asking and answering of questions.

Return a reporters call as quickly as possible, asking the purpose of the interview, what information will be requested, who else is being contacted, the estimated length of the interview, and the story deadline. Then, take time to carefully prepare for the interview. Gather the necessary facts, statistics, or background information, and determine the important two or three (no more than five) key points that need to be expressed. Also, spend some time anticipating difficult questions and practicing answers that clearly articulate the desired point of view but do not sound contrived or self-serving. As a source, always look for ways to assure that your own agenda is effectively communicated.

During the interview, express confidence and assurance, seeking to appear friendly, courteous, and cooperative. In order to answer questions well, the interviewee must listen closely to each question, being sure to understand it before attempting to answer. Then answers should be concise, accurate, and truthful. Do not lie or exaggerate the facts, and if you do not know the answer to a question, admit it—never guess or speculate. You might offer to call back with the answer or refer the reporter elsewhere if you are not the appropriate spokesperson. When answering questions, keep responses simple, and state the important facts first. Use examples, comparisons, or statistics for follow-up questions. Provide anecdotes and human interest examples to illustrate main points and avoid complex explanations. Speak in personal terms whenever possible rather than using technical terms or jargon. When tough questions are asked, keep your cool and calmly maintain a positive attitude—don't argue with the reporter. If you can't discuss an issue for legitimate reasons, explain as much as you can rather than saying "no comment," which sounds evasive and suggests that you are hiding the facts. Never speak "off the record," if you don't want a statement quoted, do not make it. Dan Rather succinctly advises that when "dealing with the press . . . stick with one of three responses: (a) I know and I can tell you, (b) I know and I can't tell you, and (c) I don't know."[34]

After the interview is over, both parties to the journalistic interview should examine the interview in light of the questions asked and the answers given. Reporters must ask themselves two essential questions: Was the necessary information obtained from this interview? Is it the information my audience needs? The subjects being interviewed must ask: Was my agenda presented and message clearly articulated? Were my answers precise, logical, well-supported, and to the point? Any failure to accomplish these objectives leaves the parties with room to insightfully explore areas for improvement.

*   *   *   *   *

Charles Creamer apparently followed a funnel sequence of questioning when interviewing Northern Michigan Power officials, asking open-ended questions that narrowed to more specific inquiries. This helped ensure his getting the basic information before pursuing more sensitive topics, which might have resulted in NMP terminating the interviews. Throughout these interviews, he probed for information and actively listened to answers.

When interviewing the construction workers in his office, Charles chose a more informal, freeform sequence of questioning. They casually "chatted" about the rumors surrounding the construction of the nuclear facility, and Charles assumed less control of the interview. A more covert sequencing of questions could have revealed their hidden motives and prompted Charles to further investigate their backgrounds.

The parties to the interviews were agreeable and promoted personal agendas, even though some were concealed. The NMP officials displayed a willingness to cooperate and sought to paint a positive picture of their new nuclear power facility. Howard Nottingham, NMP executive vice president, shared confidences with Charles, and Beverly Brinkley, NMP public affairs director, used charts and graphs to show the long-term benefits of the new nuclear facility. While they refused to directly comment on construction schedules and cost overruns, they did assertively express the position of Northern Michigan Power Company. The point of view they hoped to convey to the public was openly displayed and presented. However, speculation and off-the-record comments should have been avoided. It would have been better to consider all answers and statements on record even though journalists normally honor confidentiality when requested.

The construction workers were frank and forthright but less than honest in promoting their agenda. They candidly shared their opinions while concealing the personal grievances motivating their participation. Charles's eagerness to pursue a singular story angle resulted in his failure to listen with a "third" ear or thoroughly probe and follow up answers. Testing for deception might have disclosed their motives. However, since Charles anticipated the NMP message line, he was unaware of the reasons prompting the construction workers to agree to be interviewed. Thus, facts and rumors were blurred contributing to the inaccuracies that occurred in his story as a result.

Telephoning, Note Taking, and Taping

The three most dreaded words for a journalist are, "I've been misquoted." A major misquote not only renders the interview worthless but also damages the reporter's credibility and places the newspaper in jeopardy of a law suit. To resolve this problem, journalists develop over time their own solutions to accurate note taking. Reporters using the telephone often take notes on a word processor, using a shoulder hook to hold the phone to their ear, thus freeing both hands for typing. All experienced journalists take notes on a steno pad or in a personal reporter's notebook, although some are now carrying light-weight, battery-operated laptop computers for note taking in the field. Still other reporters prefer to use compact cassette tape recorders to take notes. These techniques are by no means the perfect solution, and note taking continues to be the bane of reporters in interview situations. However, the telephone, pencil and pad, and tape recorder still remain a reporter's best options to note taking given the alternative of relying on memory, which is always risky.[35]

Not all interviews take place face to face. One special kind of interview is the telephone interview. Newspaper reporters estimate that they spend 50 to 80 percent of their interviewing time on the phone, and reporters for national newspapers have developed long-distance phone interviewing to a fine art. The telephone is often used because they need information almost immediately and do not have the time to set up a face-to-face interview. This can be a quick and efficient information-gathering method for both the interviewer and interviewee. However, there are some important questions reporters must address when deciding whether to use the telephone rather than the face-to-face interview.

How many questions will be asked during the interview to obtain the necessary information? Telephone interviews tend to be much shorter than face-to-face interviews; therefore, if more than eight or ten questions are to be asked, it would be better to see the party in person. To look at the matter another way, if the conversation will last more than fifteen minutes, give serious consideration to seeing the interviewee in person. Consequently, telephone interviews are best used for short stories or for filling in information gaps for a longer story.

How important and how complex is the story? The telephone is an intruder that may disrupt the other party's usually busy day, resulting in an interview which is superficial and touches only on the highlights of the matter under discussion. Also, the interviewee may be more reserved and inclined to terminate the interview at the earliest opportunity. However, in a face-to-face interview, the journalist can better establish rapport and more readily ascertain how the interviewee is reacting to the questioning. Moreover, the reporter can more easily determine the interviewee's meaning by observing facial expressions and gestures. Highly technical matters and complex issues requiring considerable orientation do not lend themselves to telephone interviews. When the story is important and the concepts are complicated, be hesitant to resort to the telephone.

How many people will be interviewed for the story? If a single individual is to be used as the primary source for a story, reporters should be wary of using the telephone. However, if the plan is to conduct brief interviews with a number of individuals, telephone interviews are more apt to produce all the necessary information for a well-rounded story. Sometimes several telephone interviews can yield more information than a single in-person conversation.

Foster Davis, managing editor of the *St. Louis Post-Dispatch,* observes that "the quality of the stories has something to do with the quality of notes."[36] Careful note taking gives reporters an advantage when they begin to write their story, since a good interview is rich in the tiny details that give it texture. Gestures, physical appearance, and verbal inflections all help to personalize an individual and contribute to the "feel" of the interview. When striving for color and mood in an interview, reporters must consider the little details that add up to the dominant impression a subject creates. Little things mean a lot for the observant journalist jotting it all down, especially in a personality interview.

Most interviewees readily permit note taking and *like* to see an interviewer jotting down notes. In fact, they are wary of the reporter who hardly appears to be taking notes at all, especially when they want to get across a complicated or important point. However, people who are not accustomed to being interviewed often become nervous when the journalist starts writing things down. When dealing with these individuals, start the interview slowly by asking nonthreatening questions, and after some rapport has been established, ease out the notepad at a routine stage of the interview. Also, a reporter can ease concern during the interview by offering sincere praise or using gentle flattery. While note taking is important, it should not be so profuse as to interfere with the simple act of listening attentively—the interviewer's first function.

Notes can sketch a person's *message*, but message is nothing without nuances—its inflections of voice and vocabulary—and the tape recorder can capture these with remarkable fidelity. Still, whether to use a tape recorder or simply to take notes during the interview continues to be a somewhat controversial issue. The biggest advantage is self-evident. The tape recorder records everything, while even the best reporter taking notes can only capture *almost* everything. Consequently, verbatim quotes can more easily be extracted, and in legally touchy stories, a tape recording may offer protection against claims of misquotation. In addition, in sensitive interviews, reporters may repeatedly listen to the tape to catch the fine nuances of personality and character that they might have missed originally. Moreover, there is one advantage of the tape recorder that is rarely mentioned or considered. A tape recorder enables journalists not only to rehear the persons interviewed but also to rehear themselves, thus learning poignant lessons about their interviewing techniques.

However, there are several legitimate reasons *not* to use a tape recorder. They are generally inefficient for tight-deadline reporting, since transcribing tapes is time consuming. Also, taped interviews tend to ramble more than those guided by note taking unless the reporter carefully controls the interview. Finally, given the routine nature of most news interviews, there simply is no reason to listen to the conversation again. Ultimately, using a tape recorder or pencil and pad to take notes is largely a mater of journalistic preference.

The telephone, pencil, and tape recorder are basic organizing tools that accomplished reporters use to bring order to the dynamic chaos of covering the news. They are an integral part of the reporting process, since the interviewer is there not only to note what is said, but also *how* it is being said. Those journalists who fail to take careful notes shirk their professional responsibility and run the risk of hearing, "I've been misquoted!"

*   *   *   *   *

The case study did not exactly indicate how Charles Creamer took notes for this story. We do know that he used the telephone to arrange the interviews and did call Northern Michigan Power officials back to clarify specific information. Apparently, during these call-backs, however, he elected to rely on journalistic privilege and did not reveal all his sources of information. Had he mentioned the site construction workers, their questionable backgrounds might have been exposed. This certainly would have allowed NMP officials an opportunity to confirm or deny the accusations.

We further know that during the interviews with NMP officials Charles used a pencil and pad to take notes. He probably should have used a tape recorder when interviewing the construction workers in his office. The individuals he interviewed were certainly not averse to note taking or potential recording. Still, Charles's note-taking practices did not account for the inaccuracies, which were largely due to the calculated use and omission of selected information. Refusal to permit the previewing of a story is common.

Writing the News

News stories used to be typed on cheap paper called newsprint, and it was this typewritten page that ultimately found its way through the hands of many editors to the backshop where it was converted into type for the printed page. Today, more and more newspapers have joined the "electronic generation," and reporters don't even use paper for their stories but put them in a computer before being scanned by editors and copyreaders. At an all-electric newspaper, reporters write their stories on an electronic keyboard, and the stories appear on a monitor above the keyboard. The reporters make corrections with a cursor, a kind of electronic pencil, and when the stories are completed, they go into a computer for storage. When the city editor or the copy editor wants to see them, they can call them up electronically on their video display terminals. Again, the stories are electronically edited, headlines added, and lines set to the specified column width used by the newspaper. It is even possible for a newspaper to have printing plants miles outside the city where a large portion of each day's edition is printed after the news copy arrives electronically. Moreover, the Dijit printer makes it possible for a newspaper to change the news stories in the paper without stopping the presses. The device is hooked to a computerized database, and as a story is breaking, the new information can be fed into the computer which will result in changes in the story in the newspaper.[37]

However, despite all these changes in technology, the basics of writing the news remains the same. After having obtained the material for a news story, reporters still must decide which few of their many available facts are the most important and what to discard as extraneous. They must decide in what order the facts will be introduced and how best to present the material. All news stories must still conform to a fundamental organizational structure and contain three parts: lead, body, and close.

News Story Structure

The structure or arrangement of the news story differs from that of a short story, play, essay, or novel in that the climax is reached at once instead of after considerable delay. The suspended interest element that plays a large part in most forms of writing is almost entirely absent from news stories. The news story, unlike other literary forms, begins at the end. This structural distinction (see figure 14.1) may be visualized as an **inverted pyramid,** representing the news story, as contrasted with an upright pyramid, representing the traditional chronological arrangement.

The inverted pyramid organizes the story from the most important information to the least important. It usually starts with a summary lead that gives some of the basics: who, what, when, where, and why. Backup quotes and facts along with supporting points comprise the body of the story with any final details being included in the close. The advantage of this form is that readers get the crucial information quickly. Consequently, this is one of the most common forms for hard-news stories.[38]

However, variations from the inverted pyramid are being explored, since this traditional structure may not sufficiently entice readers to read past the crucial information contained in the top of the story. Some of these alternative structures include a modified inverted pyramid or hourglass structure, Lionel Linder's "high fives formulas," *The Wall Street Journal* formula, and *USA Today's* list technique.[39]

The **modified inverted pyramid or hourglass structure** is a combination of the basic news story form and the literary form. The basic story information is presented in the first two or three paragraphs and then, similar to flashbacks in the movies, is followed by a chronological or sequential account of events leading up to it. This structure is useful when stories have dramatic action that lends itself to chronological order, such as investigative reports. However, while it adds drama to the story, it also makes the story longer.

The *USA Today's* **list technique** is a modification of the inverted pyramid that conserves space while emphasizing a number of important points. A summary lead and limited backup are followed by a list highlighting the important

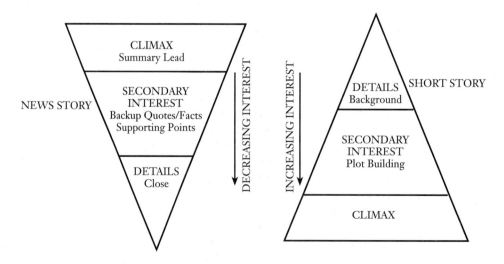

FIGURE 14.1   The News Story (Inverted Pyramid) vs. the Short Story

points with some elaboration in the close of the story. This technique works well for stories about studies, meetings, or programs. Investigative reporters can use lists to itemize the findings of their investigation.

Lionel Linder, while editor of *The Commercial Appeal* in Memphis, Tennessee, devised the **"High Fives" formula,** still another alternative to the inverted pyramid. The opening paragraphs, focusing on the five elements of news, context, scope, edge, and impact, address the basic questions of interest to readers: What happened? What is the background for the event? Is this local event part of a larger, national set of events or trends? Where is this news leading? Why should anyone care? Does the news have any meaning? The remainder of the story provides the details—description, supporting information, quotes, and explanation. This alternative structure is both flexible and interpretive. The five elements may be variably ordered depending upon the story, and taken together, they reveal story significance. The "High Fives" formula gives readers the important information quickly and lets them know how the news immediately affects them.

The Wall Street Journal **formula,** as an alternate structure to the inverted pyramid, personalizes the news story by initially focusing on a person, scene, or event and then providing readers with the general background information and implications. The lead may be anecdotal, descriptive, or narrative, with the body of the story being organized around it. The close is often a quote or anecdote from the person featured in the lead. This is a very versatile formula that can add interest to many news and feature stories. The investigative reporter should also consider using this formula, focusing on a person or event exemplifying the story and illustrating the main points of the investigation.

Regardless of the structure selected, the primary purpose of the newspaper is to give the news, and as much of it as possible, to its readers in the limited time they have to spare. Americans read fast, especially their morning papers. Thousands scan their newspapers over breakfast coffee or on a commuter train *en route* to work. Every line of print, therefore, should be written and arranged with a view to conserving the reader's time.

Headlines and Leads

Headlines announce stories, telling readers what the stories are about. They are usually written by a copy editor or editor, *not* the reporter, except at very small newspapers where the editor may also be the reporter/writer. For most news stories, the copy editor bases the headline on the lead or main points of the story contained in the first few paragraphs.

The **lead,** then, is the first paragraph of the news story. It gives readers the essential facts contained in the story and arouses their interest so they will continue reading. Donald Murray, in his book *Writing for Your Readers,* observes: "Three seconds and the reader decides to read or turn to the next story. That's all the time you have to catch a reader's glance and hold it; all the time you have to entice and inform."[40] Therefore, the lead is crucial, and one of the best tests of a reporter is his or her ability to create an interesting, well-rounded lead.

The **direct lead** or **summary lead** is the simplest, safest, strongest, and most commonly used opening. As the name implies, this type of lead gets directly to the point, summarizing the story and setting forth the salient facts in one or two compact sentences. The summary lead briefly answers the basic questions: Who? What? When? Where? Why? How? and So what?[41]

Although the hard-news summary lead is the type most generally used in American newspapers today, some papers are consciously trying to get away from using such leads for all stories. The **soft lead,** called a feature lead or delayed lead, opens with anecdotes, quotes, or personal narratives. It may take several paragraphs before readers get to the "what's it about" point of the story. Soft leads avoid the otherwise trite recital of facts by introducing a feature angle while answering the basic questions essential to all news stories. However, critics object to soft leads because they introduce extraneous material and take too long to get to the point of the story. New York University journalism professors Gerald Lanson and Mitchel Stephens label soft leads "Jell-O journalism."[42] Consequently, soft leads will never replace summary leads, but they can be judiciously used to create interest, given the subject matter of the story. The choice is really a matter of judgment and the editor's preference.

Body Building

Facts cited in the lead usually are brief and require explanation and elaboration in order to bring out the complete story. The **body** of the news story adds concrete details to support the lead and builds the narrative from the top down. The ideal news story could be cut off at almost any paragraph and yet remain self-explanatory. This is the direct result of telling the facts in the order of their importance and making the story explain itself as it proceeds. Thus, the story may be easily shortened to conform to space limitations by simply taking off paragraphs from the bottom up.

Remembering that simplicity is key, the body of a good news story should be clear, forceful, and concise. Simplicity of structure and diction contributes to clearness. The average newspaper reader has neither the time nor inclination to puzzle over an involved sentence or to consult a dictionary for the definition of a word or technical term. Sentence structure, word choice, references, mood, and grammar must concretely contribute to the clarity of the story. Reporters must know and use fine distinctions in their writing. For example, they must know the shades of difference between said, declared, stated, confessed, admitted, proclaimed, averred, and alleged. Moreover, since gender, race, and geographical and ethnic background can also influence interpretation, clarity requires being sensitive to the diverse readers comprising our multicultural society. Confucius observed centuries ago: "In language, clearness is everything."

Active verbs, colorful adjectives, and concrete nouns lend force to a news story. Verbs inject action, movement, and life. With them reporters can make their ideas sparkle, glow, sing, alarm, soothe, blister, and delight. Vigorous verbs can also make it easier for the headline writer to write an attractive headline. Adjectives, like spice and sugar, add flavor to the story. As with any seasoning, however, they should be used sparingly. Therefore, adjectives should be carefully scrutinized and their effect on the story considered before use. Nouns contribute firmness and specificity. This requires carefully choosing the exact noun needed to express a thought or idea. As Jonathan Swift observed, "Proper words in proper places make the true definition of style." Finally, combine these with interesting anecdotes, stories, quotes, or dialogue, and otherwise "boring but important stuff" becomes a fundamentally forceful news story.

The Kicker Close

The **close** or **kicker** to a news story should be given just as much care and consideration as the lead. The close to a story should leave a lasting impression on the reader. Reporters often return to the lead and use the same concept in the ending but focusing on a different person or situation. Some other closing techniques used by reporters include ending on a quote, a strong factual statement, an indication of future action, or a cliff-hanger. A quote can sum up the mood or main idea of a story. A strong factual statement can also give the reader a powerful punch and leave a lasting impression if it captures the character of the story and is a short, simple sentence that states a *meaningful* fact. Some stories lend themselves to future action and end with the next step in the development of the reported issue. Finally, cliff-hangers might be used as an ending, particularly in a series that will continue to another day. This technique can also be used in stories written in sections, with the cliff-hanger at the end of a section so the reader is compelled to continue. The concept is "What will happen next?" Still, many hard-news stories, particularly those structured with a summary lead and arranged with supporting points in descending order of importance, simply end when there is no more new information to reveal. This, too, is an appropriate close following the dictate to "be plain and simple, and lay down the thing as it was."[43]

Editing is difficult and time consuming but necessary. First drafts are usually incomplete or inadequate in some important phase of writing. Essential points can be inadvertently omitted, and others might be insufficiently developed. Grammar and style often need polishing at the very least. Donald Murray notes that "writing is rewriting . . . rewriting is the difference between the dilettante and the artist, the amateur and the professional."[44] Good reporters recognize the importance of revision and make it a normal part of their writing strategy.

Reporters are expected to display language competence in reporting the day's news. In spite of the movie and T.V. caricature of working conditions in a city news room, efficient newspaper reporters will usually have sufficient time to write and edit their assigned stories. The fictionalized reporter, rushing into the city room and shouting, "Stop the presses! Tear down page one while I knock out a *real* story!" is certainly dramatic—but untrue. Good reporting requires energetic thinking and the ability to weave facts into coherent stories that will hold readers' attention at every point. The best news stories move with a swing that carry readers swiftly and easily along from the lead to the close and leaves them with a clear idea of what they have read. There is always room for reporters with clever leads and individuality of style, those qualities of originality and charm that distinguish the best writing from merely good writing.

* * * * *

It would seem that the story written by Charles Creamer conformed to fundamental journalistic structure and style. Using an inverted pyramid or perhaps a modified inverted pyramid structure, he focused on the important issues and developed a chronology of events. His summary lead immediately directed the reader's attention to the significance of the story, and his kicker close returned to the immediate concerns of the reader. The story was dramatically presented, hinting at clandestine purposes and personal profit at the expense of the public. Veiled threats to public safety and shrouded cost overruns were used to titillate readers. The goals of Northern Michigan Power Company and the obstacles confronting them were narrowly focused to reflect a singular story angle. The cooperative efforts of NMP officials to provide all the facts were for naught. Charles's suspect attitude and cynical outlook resulted in a less than insightful story. Costly inaccuracies degraded story confidence, and breached confidentiality threatened good faith reporting. Discernment and discretion were sacrificed while Creamer tried to rout perceived amoral forces. Personal passion and conviction eclipsed good storytelling. It would appear that Beverly Brinkley, NMP public affairs director, was justified in requesting an advance copy of the story.

Investigative Reporting

Reporters are the eyes and ears of a newspaper. These men and women must get the news, or it will never be printed. A newspaper with a competent staff of reporters is always a good newspaper, while a paper with a poor staff is always a poor one. Prominent in this news gathering milieu and pivotal to any successful newspaper are investigative journalists who rely on their intense curiosity about how the world works—or fails to work—to expose matters of critical importance to readers. Rather than providing a daily deadline account of events, they follow their own agenda, pulling together information from various sources to enlighten their audience. Gene Roberts, while editor of *The Philadelphia Inquirer,* observed that investigative reporting is "not so much catching the politician with his pants down or focusing on a single outrage, instead, it is digging beneath the surface so we can help readers understand what's going on in an increasingly complex world."[45]

A willingness to research thoroughly and dig for facts is critical to successful investigative reporting. Paul Williams, a former professor of journalism at Ohio State University, notes that many would-be investigative journalists fail "the test of finding out everything their readers need to know . . . fail to pull everything together."[46] This cardinal "test" requires investigative journalists to focus their research and ask some fundamental questions: Is the target of the research a fact, a person, or an issue? What information is needed? Why is this information needed?

Where can this information be found? How will this information be used? What is the time frame or deadline for gathering this information and writing the story? The goal of most factual research is a specific number, statistic, date, expert, or place, and after learning where the knowledge genie hides, this information can be easily retrieved. The personal profile requires deeper scrutiny of a subject and demands a breadth of research that goes beyond the reporting of known facts and cliché views. Well-researched profiles glitter with new information, quotes, anecdotes, and description. More than any other type of research, issues command exploring diverse points of view and identifying a local angle. Insightful issue research addresses the salient concerns of the public and presents a fair and accurate report. Thoroughness is central to all research and requires reviewing primary, as well as secondary sources and directly interviewing those persons considered critical to the investigation. Research takes time, and investigative reporting is fraught with obstacles ranging from refusals to release information to uncooperative subjects avoiding interviews. Therefore, it is important to seriously think about the time frame needed for research and to set a realistic deadline for the story.

Today, reporters in hundreds of news organizations are using electronic libraries, computer tapes, tape cartridges, CD-ROMs, and other technology as part of their information gathering. With these new electronic systems, they can quickly access electronic files, usually from their own computers, by typing commands, which retrieve materials and display them on their computer screens. These systems can help investigators conceptualize "the story" and are particularly useful in doing background research, retrieving details, analyzing materials, and identifying interviewees. An electronic filing system is especially helpful to a group of reporters working on a series since it can prevent duplicating work that has been done by other members of the investigative team.[47] This change in the way journalists acquire information for their reports has substantial potential both to influence news production and to change the character of news stories.[48] However, regardless of how information is gathered, it takes a mind trained to discern connections for the information to yield its meaning. Investigative journalists must still ascertain the "so what," as well as answer the who, what, when, where, why, and how.

Keen observation and an incredulous nosiness are essential to investigative reporting and are the traits that distinguish all successful investigative journalists from the others. Such traits lead to perceptive exposés, not because of luck, but because chance favors the observant investigator. What is observed? In a word, detail, massive amounts of it, methodically organized in a way that discloses the whys of what is found. Ken Metzler proposes a systematic set of procedures called SCAM that can promote perspicacious observation and reveal the discriminating details needed to impart the essence of an investigative story. The SCAM concept borrows from those elements comprising good drama: scene, character, action, and meaning. Starting with the scene, the investigative reporter must systematically take note of the surrounding environment and overall setting. However, static descriptions of scenes are dull and come to life only when characters enter. Character observations may range from merely noticing the physical aspects to perceiving the deeper human values and motivation accounting for actions. Observing actions or activities further illustrates character and divulges meaning or purpose. Actions also reveal the emotional climate of the situation which must not be trivialized. Details gained through observing the setting, character traits, and action coalesce to divulge a central theme or purpose. Taken together, the foregoing elements give direction to observation, which can lead to discovery. Whether the subject of inquiry is an issue of some importance or a personality of some significance, this procedure contributes to orderly observation.[49]

The value of interviewing to investigative reporting may, in general, be judged by the same scale of news factors found in other stories. Investigative journalists will want to interview authoritative sources and localize whenever possible. However, the order in which the investigator asks the questions can be crucial, and some time should be spent before the interview carefully ordering the questions. Sometimes chronological ordering makes the most sense, allowing sources to explain their actions sequentially. A chronological account also might help the investigator discover lapses and gaps in logic. It can also be prudent to move from non-threatening to more threatening questions. However, never avoid asking unpleasant questions or raising a disagreeable subject—this is part of an investigator's job. Remember, there are no embarrassing questions, just embarrassing answers. An intemperate response or even a refusal to comment can contribute to writing a compelling story.

The goal of any interview should be to understand people as they understand themselves. Walt Harrington of *The Washington Post* says, "I try to approach each subject . . . from the same cast of mind—the belief that each person, famous or obscure, is at once ordinary and extraordinary in his own way. My job is to discover those ways."[50] This means approaching every interview in a spirit of open-mindedness, remembering that nearly all stories have two or more sides. However, while the interviewee should be allowed an opportunity to fairly state their point of view, the interviewer must carefully listen for omissions and possible deception. Asking some questions to which the answers are known is one way to test for truthfulness. Still, it is important never to approach subjects as though they will be menacing or likely to lie. The investigative journalist should appear innocent, friendly, unafraid, and curious, always respecting confidences shared during the interview.

Sometimes investigative journalists find their request for an interview with a key source repeatedly being ignored or producing a "no comment" or rude rejection. When persistent, more traditional, and polite requests fail, they might consider the "ambush interview" or obtaining information covertly.[51] The ambush interview catches the source unaware, usually in a public place. While it usually results in an angry refusal to speak on the record, it occasionally leads to a productive discussion. The unexpected appearance of the investigative reporter makes it difficult to avoid the interview and leaves no easy way out. Still, this practice raises the issue of sensationalism and the ethical consideration of respecting a source's privacy.

Investigative journalists usually identify themselves accurately and have their recording equipment in plain sight. However, there are instances when they may keep their identity secret or capture information through secret audio taping. Covert conduct raises many ethical questions that all investigative journalists must answer for themselves: Does this story warrant covert behavior? Can the potential harm to an individual or institution be justified by the good that comes to the society at large? Is going undercover or surreptitious recording the only way to gather the information? Is the information vital to the story, or is this largely "news theater?" Until there are ethical guidelines regarding the use of covert information gathering, perhaps investigative journalists are best advised to be guided by the common sense, conscience, and integrity one normally expects from responsible professionals.[52]

Ultimately, the story is the all-important thing. When writing the investigative report, tell all the facts essential to a clear understanding of the story. Jon Franklin, a two-time Pulitzer prize winner, suggests writing the ending first: "The story doesn't pivot on the beginning, it pivots on the ending. So write that first. That way you know exactly what it is that you need to foreshadow."[53] Regardless of how investigative journalists craft the story, even the most thorough research and best outline cannot overcome a fuzzy focus. The highest rewards are reserved for those who hone the focus and tell old facts in a new way. The story should show rather than tell, entertain as well as explain, and involve instead of simply interest the readers. A story is not just facts, and if investigative journalists hope to lure and hook readers, they must find ways to weave human experience throughout their stories. Finally, the ending should leave deep thoughts and emotions in the minds of readers without editorializing or preaching.[54] The ideal story is fair, both in spirit and in detail, and is written from an impersonal, objective viewpoint.[55] Clear thinking, clear statement, accuracy, and fairness are fundamental to good investigative journalism and help to reasonably ensure that the story is libel-proof.

*   *   *   *   *

Charles Creamer was following the instincts of investigative journalists when reporting on the nuclear power facility under construction by Northern Michigan Power Company. In pursuing this story, he had reviewed the national scene, identified NMP officials to interview, and used his curiosity to uncover several outspoken construction workers. His intent was to submit a fair and accurate report, but one which would not shirk exposing problems and difficulties of public concern. Fundamental questions and uncertainties addressed included pubic safety, need, and cost. However, Charles failed to carefully observe the actions and motives of those involved with building the nuclear power facility. He neglected to reference check sources and approached NMP officials with suspicion. The greatest difficulty confronting investigative reporters can be the tendency to guess at facts instead of getting them exactly. Corroboration and confirmation of information was ignored or disregarded. The desire to expose public wrongdoing impeded his investigative conduct and obstructed open-minded inquiry. Getting the "big story" led to reckless and abandoned reporting with diverse points of view being overlooked, as well as professional courtesies. Fairness and accuracy were jeopardized, with the ultimate casualty being the public, which was left uninformed. Charles's cynicism caused him to lose the investigative reporter's greatest asset—perspective. Admittedly, Northern Michigan Power was encountering obstacles and costly delays in constructing the nuclear power facility, but these circumstances needed to be impersonally reported and specifically documented by unimpeachable sources. Before making damaging statements about a person, group, or business, a "good" investigative reporter has hard evidence with no loopholes. "Good" investigative journalism furthers public dialogue by forthrightly presenting the facts necessary to making informed decisions. It should be frank, candid, and accurate, and anything less stifles investigative reporting.

Libel and Journalistic Privilege

Libel may be defined as an untruthful printed or written statement that exposes a person or group of persons to public hatred, contempt, or ridicule.[56] More simply stated, it is anything that unjustly defames character or hurts business. All fifty states have adopted libel statutes, although the specific requirements of the law of each state may vary. It, therefore, behooves newspapers to check and double-check, to make certain that the news being published to thousands of readers daily is fact and not gossip or hearsay or unverified report. Every one of the thousands of sentences in a newspaper, and the dozens of pictures, is potentially libelous if not carefully edited. The law holds that newspapers should establish the truth of their statements on their own behalf. Professor Steve Pasternack of New Mexico State University warns editors that "the author of a libel bears the ultimate responsibility for it, and that everyone who takes part in publication of a libel may be held responsible for it."[57] Courts have held repeatedly that newspapers are subject to the same legal restraints in their publication of news as individuals are in their conversations. Where individuals can be sued for slander for their loose talk, newspapers can be sued for libel.

Laws against libel help protect an individual's good name from statements that damage reputation, cause the person to be shunned, or expose the person to hatred, contempt, or ridicule. Defamation is of two types: *libel per se*, consisting of statements defamatory on their face, such as charges of criminality or dishonesty, and *libel per quod*, consisting of statements not obviously damaging to the reputation but can be shown to be defamatory within the context in which they were written. Traditionally, libel was *presumed* to have occurred if three conditions were met: defamation, publication, and identification. The message must be perceived as insulting or harmful among "right thinking persons," the alleged libel must be communicated to a third party, and the plaintiff to the action must be identifiable as the person defamed. The 1964 landmark case of *The New York Times* v. *Sullivan* added another condition—namely, fault or malicious disregard. This case holding was initially restricted to "public officials," but the 1971 *Rosenbloom* decision broadened the freedom of the media to report by including "public figures" as well. Now, not even a private citizen, a "little person," could successfully sue if that person became involved in a public issue, unless he or she proved actual malice or reckless disregard for truth. No similar requirement was applied to private plaintiffs until the 1974 case of *Gertz* v. *Welch*, where the Supreme Court did include private plaintiffs to this extent: private individuals who sue publishers or broadcasters for defamation must prove a minimum standard of fault known as "negligence."[58] Thus, the degree of fault required varies from simple "negligence" to "actual malice" depending upon the circumstances of the case. Still, it should be an ironclad rule of reporters that whenever they cannot absolutely verify a fact, they should not write it rather than take a chance on it. Few stories are important enough to warrant the risk of a libel suit.

Trained journalists must be right in every particular, therefore, "be Accurate, be Accurate, be Accurate" is the best advice and only defense against libel.

When libel does occur, it should be immediately retracted. This shows good faith on the part of the newspaper or broadcaster and a desire to rectify the error. However, the retraction must not try to exculpate the newspaper or broadcaster. They must simply withdraw or correct the original statement and express regret.

Journalists often use confidential sources to extract sensitive information and are disturbed by the use of court-ordered subpoenas requiring them to reveal these informants. District attorneys, defense lawyers, grand juries, and others have demanded that journalists disclose their sources of information, as well as hand over their notebooks and any tape recordings or film. To refuse has meant going to jail, sometimes for indefinite periods of time. Consequently, journalists have claimed privilege under the First Amendment. Their position is that no government or individual has the right, where controversial news is presented, to demand anything beyond what is presented, for this amounts to harassment and violates the rights of free speech and free press. In seeking protective privilege, journalists argue that journalist-source communications deserves the same legal umbrella, absolute Constitutional privilege, given to attorney-client communications or the qualified privilege given to doctor-patient, priest-penitent, and husband-wife communications. Opponents are quick to point out, however, that unlike the other relationships where the source is known and the information is confidential, here the source is confidential, while the information is freely available to anyone.

Recent years have produced quite a number of "Deep Throat" sources, especially in government, who have revealed corruption in high places. Journalists express concern that the current disclosure requirements will produce a "chilling effect" on the reporting of controversial stories because news sources will dry up. Still, the Supreme Court has consistently ruled that no absolute journalistic privilege exists. However, a number of states have adopted shield laws to protect a reporter's right to keep private sources confidential, and many jurisdictions recognize a qualified privilege.[59] The efforts by journalists to thoroughly investigate and report the news, even when controversial, has continued unabated. They remain a potent social force pledged to protecting a remarkable Constitution that defends their rights to responsibly inform the public.

*   *   *   *   *

Was the *Star Journal* subject to libel charges by Northern Michigan Power Company? Yes! This story damaged Northern Michigan Power's rate increase case pending before the Michigan Commerce Commission, as well as public support for the nuclear power facility under construction. Moreover, questionable sources provided incorrect information that challenged the accuracy of the story. Finally, off-the-record confidences were violated and reported. Charles Creamer was negligent in conducting reference checks, careless in his investigation, and reckless in his reporting. However, does the story reveal malicious intent? No! There is no evidence that Charles or the *Star Journal* deliberately set out to injure Northern Michigan Power Company or jeopardize the construction of the nuclear power facility. Statements were accepted on face value, and there was no knowledgeable intent to falsify information. Moreover, NMP was a public enterprise subject to journalistic inquiry, and this was a controversial issue deserving fair comment. Charles was under no legal requirement to honor off-the-record statements and chose to report them despite journalistic tradition and ethical conduct. Thus, Northern Michigan Power Company would have difficulty prevailing in a libel suit. However, Beverly Brinkley's efforts to "defuse" the impact of the story were an effective challenge to the accusations reported. By identifying the inaccuracies and refuting the allegations, she supported the NMP position while questioning Charles's credibility, as well as the integrity of the *Journal Star*. Her attacks on misleading comments revealed the overstatement and unfaithful reporting that characterized this story. It would be advisable for the *Journal Star* to print an apologetic retraction, correct its inaccuracies, and provide a statement from Northern Michigan Power Company. This would help restore their public confidence while updating the public and allowing Northern Michigan Power a fair opportunity to present their point of view. A lengthy libel suit could be avoided.

Critical Focus

Analyze the following case involving the disappearance of Malcolm Millsap, CEO of Creve Creek Engineering, to discover how reporters gather information and write their stories. Eleven days ago, Malcom Millsap checked into a plush New York hotel, and his phone call home that evening was the last communication from him. This was unusual since Malcolm routinely called his office whenever he was on the road, whether in Alaska or Thailand, and until this incident, no one was more visible at Creve Creek Engineering than this forty-year-old chief executive officer. FBI investigators learned that he had transferred $24,000 from one of his personal accounts to Chicago, but there was no evidence that he knew anyone in Chicago. Friends said they can't remember him having personal dealings in Chicago. His wife, Megan, further confirmed this while expressing remorse and concern regarding his disappearance but has declined interviews with reporters. Colleagues said his last words were that he might have an investor or buyer who could help solve some of the company's financial woes.

Creve Creek Engineering recently emerged as a public company and is experiencing some financial difficulties. However, company officials have ruled out the possibility that Malcolm embezzled funds, and few think he was leading some sort of double life. Most believe that the company's troubles simply became too much for him, and he ran off or checked himself into a health spa to get away from the pressures and will return in a couple of weeks claiming recovery from mental and physical exhaustion.

So what happened to him? Speculation runs the gamut. Was he murdered? There isn't any body or indication that he associated with unsavory characters. Was he kidnapped? No one has made any ransom demands. Was he despondent over the company's recent financial troubles? No one knows for certain. Investigators are baffled, and his vanishing has left the 150 employees of Creve Creek Engineering perplexed and the company besieged by stockholders as stock price falls.

Karen Smart, Director of Investor Relations, and Bill Walters, Public Information Director, jointly prepared the following news release:

PRESS RELEASE
Creve Creek Engineering

There has been a great deal of concern due to the disappearance of Malcolm Millsap, CEO of Creve Creek Engineering. We want to assure the public, shareholders, employees, and friends that everything possible is being done to aid law enforcement agencies in their investigation.

Creve Creek Engineering, a publicly traded Missouri firm, remains committed to their customers and will continue to provide quality service. The company will provide all necessary assistance to the investigation and still remain a viable force in the engineering field.

Even though Creve Creek Engineering stock has suffered a drop in value since Mr. Millsap's disappearance, we remain financially sound. We ask that our stockholders continue to have faith in Creve Creek Engineering and support our plans to provide premium engineering services far into the future.

A press conference is scheduled and will be conducted to provide any further information, as well as answer any inquiries.

Together, Karen Smart and Bill Walters conduct a press conference for the purpose of containing rumors and damage control. Malcolm Millsap and Creve Creek Engineering have become front page material.

The following critical questions can direct and guide your analysis of this incident:

1. What makes this incident "news?" How would an investigative reporter pursue this story? Make a list of sources you would contact to get the necessary information in this story.

2. How would you prepare for this interview? Make a list of questions you would ask at the press conference. Identify the who, what, when, where, why, and how. Can the SCAM procedure guide your observations? What do readers want to know? Stockholders? Employees?

3. Were Karen Smart and Bill Walters cooperative? Defensive? Openly hostile? How well did they handle the tough questions?

4. As you watch the video, take notes and write down some direct quotes. Are your notes legible? Do they have names, dates, titles, and details? Check for accuracy. How might you improve your note taking to help your story?

5. Write a basic news story based on excerpts from the press conference, as well as the background information provided. When you write the story, include material from both the prepared remarks and the questions and answers. What story structure will you select? What will you use as your lead? Your kicker close?

Summary

The daily newspaper is one of the most familiar objects in the everyday life of the average American, and its reading forms almost as regular a part of the daily routine as does the eating of three meals. "People get into them every morning like a hot bath," says Marshall McLuhan, "the breakfast-reader, like the subway-reader, uses his newspaper as a wrap-around environment—he steps into the news."[60] Familiar as it is to the majority of citizens, however, only a few give thought to the effort that goes into producing the paper that lays on their doorstep. A formidable organization of men and women regularly contribute to processing the news, and central to this enterprise is the professional journalist. Reporters must gather and write the news. They are the individuals who make the contacts with the news sources, and it is upon their personality, ability to make and to keep contacts, resourcefulness, and integrity that a large part of a paper's success as a news medium depends.

Alert reporters with a good news sense do not wait for news to happen. They make it happen by digging up facts and then interviewing news sources who may confirm, deny, or elaborate on them. The journalistic interview is an integral part of the news reporting process and the primary way of gathering quotes, anecdotes, and those bits and pieces of information that form a news story. The key to successful journalistic interviewing is the preparation and use of a structured approach to the interview process. Preparation forces journalists to define their purpose, conduct the necessary background research, identify interviewees, and plan the interview. Tactfully asking questions in a strategically structured manner produces the necessary information to carry a story. However, throughout the interview, the journalist must remain flexible, listening with an inner ear to not only what is said but also to what is unsaid.

Skillfully using the telephone, taking notes, and tape recording also need to be part of a journalist's repertoire. Each of these tools pose special challenges or problems, but their use is vital in accurately documenting information. Anybody can file a lawsuit against journalists for libel. Even if the lawsuit is obviously frivolous, the defendants will have to spend a minimum of a few months and thousands of dollars to win a summary judgment. The best journalists can do to deter libel suits is be thorough and accurate in their reporting.

Interviewees need not be passive participants during the journalistic interview. They should share control with the interviewer and not submit meekly to whatever is asked or demanded. This requires preparing their own agenda and providing specific answers supported by examples, anecdotes, and stories. Practicing the principles and procedures of effective answers results in a better interview for both parties.

Ultimately, the information gathered through journalistic interviewing must be distilled into a story. All story structures involve a compelling lead, a detailed body, and a kicker close. At every step, journalists must be cognizant of the impatient reader. Readers do not like dense, endless stories. Skillfully written stories make the who, what, when, where, why, and how relevant and readable. The journalist's goal is to captivate like the most artful novelist while telling the truth as well as humanly possible.

Resourceful reporters are always on the outlook for news stories, and investigative journalists, using their keen skills of observation and intuitive curiosity, ferret out those facts, profiles, and issues that hold particular public import or significance. Following their own agenda, they intensely delve into topics of concern, insightfully interview subjects, and with fairness and accuracy write their stories. However, sometimes their inventive information-gathering methods present ethical dilemmas. Ambush interviews, covert conduct, and surreptitious recording raise questions that professional journalist's have still to answer.

News, news gathering, and news processing are all changing. In the future, the newspaper may not even be a paper. Several media companies are experimenting with "telecomputer" news delivered to subscribers by telephone lines hooked to computers or television sets via modems. Regardless of the changes that may occur, an independent and unfettered press will remain a powerful force shaping and influencing a free and democratic citizenry. Nearly two centuries ago, Edmund Burke, English statesman and patriot, recognized the power of the press when, in the midst of a speech in Parliament, he turned and pointed toward the reporters' gallery in which sat the newspaper reporters of that day and declared that it contained a *Fourth Estate,* more powerful than the generally recognized three estates, the lords spiritual, the lords temporal, and the commons. The term clings to the profession today and will continue to adhere tomorrow. Davis Merrit, Jr., the pioneering public journalist of the *Wichita Eagle,* likes to describe a successful newspaper as "a fair-minded participant in a community that works."[61] George Sutherland, former associate justice of the United States Supreme Court, observed: "A free press stands as one of the great interpreters between the government and the people, to allow it to be fettered is to fetter ourselves."[62]

SHARPENING YOUR FOCUS

1. Newspapers are a business and exist to make a profit. Recently, *The New York Times*, "the old gray lady" added color. Do newspapers today sacrifice their responsibility to the public in order to promote sales and make a profit?

2. Early newspaper editors fought censorship and defended "freedom of the press." Later editors engaged in "yellow journalism" and sensationalism. Are censorship and sensationalism still relevant issues today? Are journalists society's "watch dog" or "junk-yard dog?" Explain.

3. David Halberstam in *The Powers That Be* presents a powerful historical drama of how *The Washington Post*, *The LA Times*, *Time* magazine, and CBS functioned and gained tremendous power within our culture. He examines the tumultuous issues occurring between 1950 and 1972 to illustrate how these media giants shaped the news and created as well as destroyed political careers. Do you believe the media is manipulative? Do the "personalities" of editors and journalists influence their reporting? What should public figures be aware of regarding journalistic/broadcast interviewing and reporting?

4. Select a public figure and outline a potential interview with the person. Include (a) a definition of purpose, (b) interview strategies, and (c) sample questions. Note possible problems.

5. How does the investigative reporter dig beneath the surface of a story to help readers understand what's going on in an increasingly complex world? What ethical considerations should guide their investigation and reporting?

6. Compare and contrast the traditional inverted pyramid structure for writing a news story with such alternative approaches as the hour glass structure, *USA Today's* list technique, *The Wall Street Journal* formula and "High Fives" formula. Note advantages and disadvantages of each. What configuration or form does your campus newspaper employ?

7. List the defenses in libel or slander actions. How can journalists avoid libel actions? What should be done when libel does occur? Should reporters be granted "journalistic privilege" and permitted to protect their sources? Why? Why not?

NOTES

1. This case is based on an actual incident where Illinois Power successfully challenged a derogatory *60 Minutes* investigation. However, when the nuclear power plant went on-line, following the investigative report and public challenge, it was eight to ten years past its originally scheduled completion date, and nearly ten times above its original reported budget estimates. See Richard Campbell, *Sixty Minutes and the News* (Urbana: University of Illinois Press, 1991).

2. Douglass Cater, *The Fourth Branch of Government* (Boston: Houghton Mifflin, 1959), 25.

3. Bryce W. Rucker, *The First Freedom* (Carbondale, Ill.: Southern Illinois University Press, 1968), 87.

4. Ronald T. Farrar and John D. Stevens, *Mass Media and the National Experience* (New York: Harper and Row, 1971), 45.

5. Jonathan Daniels, *They Will Be Heard: America's Crusading Editors* (New York: McGraw-Hill, 1965).

6. Michael Emery and Edwin Emery, *The Press and America,* 6th ed. (Englewood Cliffs, N.J.: Prentice-Hall, 1988).

7. James L. Crouthamel, *Bennett's New York Herald and the Rise of the Popular Press* (Syracuse, N.Y.: Syracuse University Press, 1989), 103. See also Don Carlos Seitz, *James Gordon Bennett* (New York: Beckman, 1974) and Oliver Carlson, *The Man Who Made News: A Biography of James Gordon Bennett* (New York: Duell, Sloane and Pearce, 1942).

8. See William H. Hale, *Horace Greeley: Voice of the People* (New York: Harper and Brothers, 1950) and Henry L. Stoddard, *Horace Greeley* (New York: G. P. Putnam's Sons, 1946).

9. Edwin Diamond, *Behind the Times: Inside the New York Times* (Chicago: University of Chicago Press, 1993). See also Harrison Salisbury, *Without Fear or Favor: An Uncompromising Look at The New York Times* (New York: Times Books, 1980); Gay Talese, *The Kingdom and the Power*(New York: World Publishing, 1969); Meyer Berger, *The Story of the New York Times* (New York: Simon and Schuster, 1951); Francis Brown, *Raymond of the Times* (New York: W. W. Norton, 1951); and Gerald W. Johnson, *An Honorable Titan: A Biography of Adolph S. Ochs* (New York: Harper and Brothers, 1946).

10. Don R. Pember, *Mass Media In America,* 2d ed. (Palo Alto, Calif.: Science Research Associates, 1977).

11. See William Randolph Hearst, Jr., *The Hearsts: Father and Son* (Niwot, Colo.: Roberts Rinehart Publishers, 1991); Lindsay Chaney and Michael Cieply, *The Hearsts: Family and Empire* (New York: Simon and Schuster, 1981); W. A. Swanberg, *Citizen Hearst* (New York: Charles Scribner's Sons, 1961); Edmund D. Coblentz, *William Randolph Hearst: A Portrait in His Own Words* (New York: Simon and Schuster, 1952); and John Tebbel, *The Life and Good Times of William Randolph Hearst* (New York: E. P. Dutton, 1952).

12. Roy Nelson, *Cartooning* (Chicago: Henry Regnery, 1975).

13. Ellen F. Fitzpatrick, *Muckraking* (Boston: Bedford Books, 1994), 11.

14. John Tebbel, *The Compact History of the American Newspaper* (New York: Hawthorn Books, 1969).

15. See James Ford, *Magazines for the Millions* (Carbondale, Ill.: Southern Illinois University Press, 1970); John Tebbel, *The American Magazine: A Compact History* (New York: Hawthorn Books, 1969); and Theodore Peterson, *Magazines in the Twentieth Century* (Urbana, Ill.: University of Illinois Press, 1964).

16. Loren Ghiglione, *The Buying and Selling of America's Newspapers* (Indianapolis, Ind.: R. J. Berg, 1984).

17. George Munster, *Rubert Murdoch: A Paper Prince* (New York: Penguin Books, 1985).

18. Larry Sabato, *Feeding Frenzy: How Attack Journalism Has Transformed American Politics* (New York: The Free Press, 1993), 10.

19. Judee K. Burgoon, Michael Burgoon, David B. Buller, and Charles K. Atkin, "Communication Practices of Journalists: Interaction with Public, Other Journalists," *Journalism Quarterly* 64 (Spring 1987): 125–32.

20. Arthur Charity, *Doing Public Journalism* (New York: Guilford Press, 1995), 19.

21. Walter Lippmann, *Public Opinion* (New York: The Free Press, 1965), 229.

22. Carole Rich, *Writing and Reporting the News,* (Belmont, Calif.: Wadsworth, 1994), 21–24.

23. Nils Gunnar Nilsson, "The Origin of the Interview," *Journalism Quarterly* 48 (Winter 1971): 707–13.

24. Jack Fuller, *News Values* (Chicago: University of Chicago Press, 1996).

25. Sir Arthur Conan Doyle, *The Complete Sherlock Holmes* (New York: Barnes and Noble,1992), 27.

26. Shirley Biagi, *Interviews that Work: A Practical Guide for Journalists,* 2d ed. (Belmont, Calif.: Wadsworth, 1992).

27. Richard Meryman, "Editor's Note," *Life,* 17 July, 1972.

28. "Interview with Jimmy Carter," *Playboy,* November 1976, 86.

29. LaRue W. Gilleland, "Gilleland's GOSS Formula," *Journalism Educator* 26 (1971): 19–20.

30. Carley H. Dodd, *Dynamics of Intercultural Communication,* 4th ed. (Dubuque, Iowa: Brown and Benchmark, 1995), 57.

31. William A. Henry III, "Beyond the Melting Pot," *Time,* 9 April, 1990, 28.

32. Catharine R. Stimpson, "A Conversation, Not a Monologue," *Chronicle of Higher Education,* 16 March, 1994, B1.

33. See Jeanne Tessier Barone and Jo Young Switzer, *Interviewing: Art and Skill* (Boston: Allyn and Bacon, 1995); Shirley Biagi, *Interviews that Work: A Practical Guide for Journalists* 2d ed. (Belmont, Calif.: Wadsworth, 1992); John Brady, *The Craft of Interviewing* (New York: Vintage Books, 1977); Raymond L. Gordon, *Interviewing: Strategy, Techniques, and Tactics,* 3d ed. (Homewood, Ill.: The Dorsey Press, 1980); George M. Killenberg and Rob Anderson, "Sources Are Persons: Teaching Interviewing as Dialogue," *Journalism Educator* 31 (1976): 16–20; Ken Metzler, *Creative Interviewing,* 2d ed. (Englewood Cliffs, N.J.: Prentice-Hall, 1989); and Robert F. Royal and Steven R. Schutt, *The Gentle Art of Interviewing and Interrogation* (Englewood Cliffs, N.J.: Prentice-Hall, 1976).

34. Irving E. Fang, *Television News, Radio News* (St. Paul, Minn.: Rada Press, 1980), 120.

35. Mark Fitzgerald, "Don't (Mis)quote Me on That!" *Editor and Publisher,* 9 May, 1987, 114.

36. Rich, *Writing and Reporting the News,* 118.

37. See David Crowley and Paul Heyer, *Communication in History: Technology, Culture, Society* (New York: Longman, 1991); E. E. Dennis, *Reshaping the Media: Mass Communication in the Information Age* (Newbury Park, Calif.: Sage, 1989); and Frederick Williams, *The New Communications* (Belmont, Calif.: Wadsworth, 1992).

38. Holly S. Stocking and Paget H. Gross, *How Do Journalists Think?* (Bloomington, Ind.: ERIC Clearinghouse, 1989).

39. See George Kennedy, Daryl Moen, and Don Ranly, *Beyond the Inverted Pyramid* (New York: St. Martin's, 1993); Theodore A. Rees Cheney, *Writing Creative Nonfiction* (Berkeley, Calif.: Ten Speed Press, 1991); and Carole Rich, *Writing and Reporting News* (Belmont, Calif.: Wadsworth, 1994).

40. Donald Murray, *Writing for Your Readers* (Chester, Conn.: The Globe Pequot Press, 1983), 44.

41. Brian Brooks, George Kennedy, Daryl Moen, and Don Ranly, *News Reporting and Writing* (New York: St. Martin's, 1992).

42. Gerald Lanson and Mitchel Stephens, "Jell-O Journalism," *Washington Journalism Review* 3 (April 1982): 10–21.

43. Edward J. Friedlanda and John Lee, *Feature Writing,* 3d ed. (New York: HarperCollins, 1996).

44. Donald Murray, "Internal Revision: A Process of Discovery," in *Research on Composing,* ed. Charles R. Cooper and Lee Odell (Urbana, Ill.: NCTE, 1978), 85–86.

45. Steve Weinberg, *The Reporter's Handbook,* 3d ed. (New York: St. Martin's Press, 1996), xvi.

46. Paul N. Williams, *Investigative Reporting* (New York: Englewood Cliffs, N.J.: Prentice-Hall, 1978), 15.

47. Jean Ward, Kathleen A. Hansen, and Douglas M. McLeod, "Effects of the Electronic Library on News Reporting Protocols," *Journalism Quarterly* 65 (Winter 1988): 845–52.

48. See Fredric F. Endres, "Daily Newspaper Utilization of Computer Data Bases," *Newspaper Research Journal* (Fall 1985): 29–35; John Kerr and Walter E. Niebauer, Jr., "Use of Full Text, Database Retrieval Systems by Editorial Page Writers," *Newspaper Research Journal* (Spring 1987): 21–32; and Robert I. Berkman, *Find It Fast* (New York: HarperCollins, 1994).

49. Ken Metzler, *Newsgathering,* 2d ed. (Englewood Cliffs, N.J.: Prentice–Hall, 1986).

50. Walt Harrington, *American Profiles* (Columbia: University of Missouri Press, 1992), 35.

51. Louis J. Rose, *How to Investigate Your Friends and Enemies* (St. Louis, Mo.: Albion Press, 1992).

52. See Deni Elliott, *Responsible Journalism* (Beverly Hills, Calif.: Sage, 1986); Tom Goldstein, *News at Any Cost* (New York: Simon and Schuster, 1985); John Kultgen, *Ethics and Professionalism* (Philadelphia: University of Pennsylvania Press, 1988); Edmund B. Lambeth, *Committed Journalism* (Bloomington: Indiana University Press, 1992); Philip Meyer, *Ethical Journalism* (New York: Longman, 1987); and Philip Patterson and Lee Wilkins, *Media Ethics* (Dubuque, Iowa: Brown and Benchmark, 1994).

53. Jon Franklin, *Writing for Story* (New York: Atheneum, 1986), 95.

54. Barbara Lounsberry, *The Art of Fact* (Westport, Conn.: Greenwood Press, 1990).

55. John Ullmann, *Investigative Reporting* (New York: St. Martin's, 1994).

56. Donald Gillmor, Jerome A. Barron, Todd F. Simon, and Herbert A. Terry, *Mass Communications Law: Cases and Comment* (St. Paul, Minn.: West Publishing, 1990).

57. Kenneth Rystrom, *The Why, Who, and How of the Editorial Page,* 2d ed. (State College, Pa.: Strata Publishing Company), 255.

58. See Evan Hendricks, Trudy Hayden, and Jack D. Novik, *Your Right to Privacy: A Basic Guide to Legal Rights in an Information Society,* 2d ed. (Carbondale: Southern Illinois University Press, 1990); Anthony Lewis, *Make No Law: The Sullivan Case and the First Amendment* (New York: Random House, 1991); and Thomas L. Tedford, *Freedom of Speech in the United States,* 2d ed. (New York: Random House, 1993).

59. See Bill F. Chamberlin and Charlene J. Brown, *The First Amendment Reconsidered: New Perspectives on the Meaning of Freedom of Speech and Press* (New York: Longmans, 1982); Deni Elliott, *Responsible Journalism* (Beverly Hills, Calif.: Sage, 1986); Louis G. Forer, *A Chilling Effect* (New York: W. W. Norton, 1987); Philip Meyer, *The New Precision Journalism* (Bloomington: Indiana University Press, 1991); and Don Pember, *Mass Media Law,* 2d ed. (Dubuque, Iowa: William C. Brown, 1981).

60. Robert Disch, *The Future of Literacy* (Englewood Cliffs, N.J.: Prentice-Hall, 1973), 169.

61. Charity, *Doing Public Journalism,* 17.

62. Quote etched inside the lobby of the *Chicago-Tribune* building.

15 The Broadcast Interview and News Conference

With few exceptions, everything in a daily newscast on radio and television—every audio tape, film clip, videotape, still photo, and map—is prepared and assembled on the day it is aired, all done within the space of a few hours. In a few minutes it is over, and tomorrow it must be done again with fresh news, and the tomorrow after that with still other news. The broadcast interview and news conference are critical to the gathering of news for our electronic media, a medium Marshall McLuhan and Quentin Fiore note "is reshaping and restructuring patterns of social interdependence and every aspect of our personal life."[1]

Chapter 15 differentiates broadcast news from newspaper news; examines the types, characteristics, and purposes of the broadcast interview; explores ways of conducting the broadcast interview, noting potential hazards; and discusses the participants' role in the broadcast interview. The news conference represents a unique type of broadcast interview popularly employed. This chapter is designed to accomplish three objectives:

1. *Awareness.* You will understand the nature of broadcast interviewing, its types and purposes, as well as potential constraints.

2. *Assessment.* You will be able to assess the critical factors comprising the broadcast interview situation, as well as the news conference.

3. *Application.* You will be able to effectively conduct and participate in a broadcast interview and news conference.

* * * * *

One Story—Two Mediums

Mark Mayflower is a reporter for the *Los Angeles Sentinel* and assigned the emergency services news beat. Shortly before 11 A.M. on July 31, 1994, he is dispatched to a fire engulfing the Central Los Angeles Library.

While the scene is chaotic and firefighters are busy trying to control damage, Mark manages to briefly interview Fire Chief Donald Manning and Commissioner Tom Bradey. Later, he conducts a telephone interview with Robert Reagan, the library's public information director. By evening deadline, his story is ready to run and reads as follows:

LOS ANGELES—More that 250 firefighters battled a stubborn, smoky fire that swept through the Central Los Angeles Library today, injuring 22 firefighters and destroying thousands of books in the downtown landmark building.

Fire Chief Donald Manning could not say what caused the fire, which broke out shortly before 11 A.M. in the book stacks. It was declared under control six hours later, after 49 fire companies from across the city fought the blaze. Firefighters were hampered by two factors: the desire to keep water at a minimum to decrease the water damage to the books and the fact that, for several hours, they were unable to bore a hole through the library's concrete roof to let the heat and smoke escape. "This is the most extremely difficult fire we have ever fought," Chief Manning said. "The men could not advance without the fire flaring up behind them."

The 60-year-old library, which had 2.3 million volumes, was listed on the National Register of Historic Places and was declared a historic cultural monument by the Los Angeles Cultural Heritage Board in 1967.

But the three-story building had also been designated as unsafe by the Los Angeles Fire Department and had a long history of fire violations. Some of the violations had been corrected, and library officials said fire doors were being installed when the fire broke out.

The interior of the library, which is situated amid a canyon of glass skyscrapers in downtown Los Angeles, was severely damaged. But its facade, although blackened and scorched, remained intact, in part because it was built of concrete, fire officials said.

About two years ago, a complicated plan involving the construction of three major buildings and the expansion of the library was worked out among private and public officials. The library staff was scheduled to move out next year for the expansion to begin.

Commissioner Tom Bradley, who arrived at the scene thirty minutes after the fire broke out, told reporters: "This magnificent building is something we have tried to save. We tried to get it up to safety standards."

Library officials said more than 300 employees and visitors were evacuated within minutes of the fire alarm sounding. Despite its landmark status, Chief Manning said the building had no modern sprinkler system.

According to Robert Reagan, the library's public information director, the major violations were in the stacks that contained 85 percent of the library's books. The public has no direct access to the stacks. Reagan said the library, the largest in the West, was "designated unsafe by the Fire Department as early as 1979, and violations were not corrected largely because of a lack of funds and uncertainty about its future."

The building, designed by the architect Bertram Grosvenor Goodhue and dedicated in 1926, was one of the few remaining buildings with open space in what is now the city's financial district.

From balconies and plazas of the glass skyscrapers that envelop the library, hundreds of office workers spent their lunch hour watching as smoke poured from the library's windows.

By day's end, neither fire officials nor library officials could estimate the amount of damage. The rare book collection, which is kept in a fireproof vault in the building's basement, was believed to be unharmed. But the general collection of books, many of which Reagan described as "irreplaceable," were probably ruined.

Until the damage can be examined, the library's future is in doubt, Commissioner Bradley said, adding, "We will then decide whether to try to save it or to go forward with the remodeling."

Tiffany Newhart, a reporter for KHBC Channel 2, Eyewitness News, and a camera operator were also dispatched to the Central Los Angeles Library fire scene. They quickly determined a location for the broadcast that visually captured the firefighters battling the flames. She located Captain Anthony Didomenico of the Los Angeles Fire Department and Commissioner Tom Bradley to interview for the broadcast and began her segment for the noon news update:

A fire swept through one of the nation's biggest libraries today. The Central Los Angeles Library was damaged severely, and thousands of books were destroyed. Two-hundred-fifty firemen fought the fire, and 22 of them were hurt. Captain Anthony Didomenico of the Los Angeles Fire Department helped coordinate the fire fighting effort. Captain Didomenic, what was it like?
"It was like walking into a solid brick oven."
Commissioner Tom Bradley is also on the scene. Commissioner, how do you feel about the fire?
"Devastated! This was a great collection of books."
Firemen were hampered because they tried to hold down the use of water—to minimize water damage to books. The cause of the fire is under investigation.
In downtown Los Angeles, I'm Tiffany Newhart reporting for Channel 2, Eyewitness News.

Tiffany's story was taped and replayed as a part of the evening and late evening news broadcasts. Later, Mark Mayflower watched Tiffany's two-minute coverage of the fire, while Tiffany read a more detailed report in the *Los Angeles Sentinel*.

Discussion Questions

1. How do the two stories differ? Does the news medium selected contribute to these differences? What is the focus of each story? Do you prefer one story over the other?
2. What is Tiffany's primary purpose when covering the Los Angeles Central Library fire? How does she conduct the interviews with Captain Didomenic and Commissioner Bradley? Should others have been interviewed?
3. What constraints influenced Tiffany's broadcast of the fire? Could these potential hazards have been avoided?
4. Were the interviewees able to communicate their respective messages? Did one medium lend itself to more active participation than the other? Which would you prefer?
5. Should a news conference be scheduled regarding the fire? Who might conduct such a conference? Commissioner Tom Bradley?

Fire Chief Donald Manning? Library Public Information Director Robert Reagan? Whose interests would be served?

A Brief History of American Broadcasting

The first transmission of an electromagnetic message over a wire in 1844 by Samuel F. B. Morse demonstrated the immense potential of the telegraph. More importantly, his historic message—"What hath God wrought!"—opened the age of electronic communications and started a powerful process that is still unfolding. America was to become a "wired nation" and forever changed as a result.[2]

On December 12, 1901, Guglielmo Marconi stunned the scientific community by spanning the Atlantic with wireless dot-dash transmissions. With the invention of the audion tube by Lee DeForest in 1907, high-quality, wireless voice communications carried by electromagnetic waves set the stage for a radio industry. On November 2, 1920, regular radio programming began with the broadcast of the Harding-Cox election returns over KDKA-Pittsburgh. With less than 1,000 radio sets in the entire nation, others took to the air, and by 1923, over a million American people a year listened to politics, sports, news, music, and drama in their homes.[3] As programming grew, the public bought more radio sets, and as the audiences increased, stations expanded their program schedules. As additional hours of programming became available, the evergrowing audience became more discriminating, with listener tastes changing, causing broadcasters to provide a greater variety of entertainment. With improved listening fare, the industry expanded. The public appetite had been whetted to create a demand for the radio medium, and for the first time, the Gutenberg technology had serious competition.

Now that radio was becoming big business, something had to be done about the chaotic state of the art so that it could more efficiently serve the public and the economic interests involved in broadcasting. Congress passed the Radio Act of 1927, which created a Federal Radio Commission to bring order to the situation. The Radio Act set forth two key principles that continue as public policy governing broadcasting in the United States: (1) the airwaves belong to the people of the United States, not to the stations using them, and (2) broadcasting is to serve the "public convenience, interest, or necessity." The Federal Communications Act of 1934 expanded and clarified the Act of 1927, when the Federal Communications Commission (FCC) was created to regulate telephone, telegraph, as well as radio communication systems. This act remains in effect today, modified, of course, by expanding technology and the prevailing political, social, and economic conditions.[4]

During the 1930s, radio made living rooms the entertainment centers of a nation locked in the squeeze of the Great Depression. Programs were refined and polished, with commercials and spot announcements emerging as a major type of radio ad. People thrilled to the adventures of the Green Hornet, the Shadow, and

Johnny Dollar; laughed with Fred Allen and Jack Benny; and listened to Rudy Vallee or Al Jolson sing while the big bands played on, creating an advertising bonanza. This has affectionately become known as radio's "golden age."

World War II brought a public demand for news. Radio correspondents could bring anxious listeners information about events almost the instant they happened. Edward R. Murrow, Eric Sevureid, Walter Cronkite, and others vividly conveyed war information. Eventually, however, war weariness set in, and entertainment programs began to squeeze the news out of time slots as Americans sought to escape from reality. When the war ended, radio continued to dominate, with FM frequencies being made available for commercial use, but at the same time, the new medium of television haltingly began its phenomenal rise to preeminence as America's major news and entertainment source.

Edward P. Morgan, former ABC commentator, said in a speech delivered at American University entitled "Who Forgot Radio?" that "the public eloped with a brazen but seductive hussy called television and radio suddenly became an abandoned orphan."[5] The once all-powerful radio networks were suddenly relegated to minor programming roles and local-station programming rapidly developed around the omnipresent disk jockey, a stack of records, a skeletal news and sports operation, and anything else that provided for and attracted audiences at a low cost. The 1960s, however, gave birth to a revitalized radio when the Federal Communications Commission permitted FM stereo broadcasting and ruled that AM-FM combinations in cities of over 100,000 population could no longer duplicate more than 50 percent of either station's programming. In 1970, the Public Broadcasting Service (PBS) began the development of a network radio service designed to provide programming for noncommercial, educational stations. By the 1970s, a tough hybrid had emerged from the ashes of radio's golden age, and using any measure as a means of comparison, radio is more massive today than at any other time in its history. Over 98 percent of all U.S. households are radio equipped. There are five radios for every home and over 1.3 radios for every man, woman, and child. Radio reaches nine out of ten people over twelve years of age every week, and studies indicate that the average adult listens to the radio 2.5 hours each day.[6]

While the "new radio" is more massive than "old radio," the characteristics and role of radio in American society has changed. Radio is a local rather than a national medium, with stations selectively programming to satisfy individual needs within a relatively homogeneous group. Until the 1950s radio, as the prestige mass medium, had been controlled by national advertisers and networks, but today it is essentially a local medium in terms of its sources of audiences, income, and programming. Although network radio provides a valuable news service, local broadcasters program selectively to serve certain portions of their population. For example, the FCC granted licenses for racially and ethnically oriented stations that specifically set out to establish themselves as radio service for minority groups within the community. Today, every station seeks to create a distinct personality in order to corner a special segment of the listener-consumer market.

The first experimental license for T.V. broadcasting was granted in April 1928, with seventeen stations operating under noncommercial experimental licenses by

1937. Franklin D. Roosevelt's appearance on television at the 1939 World's Fair in new York City was the setting for televisions coming-out party. In 1952, however, television witnessed the most fantastic growth spurt ever experienced by a mass medium—T.V. began to fulfill its destiny as the dominant leisure-time activity for most Americans.[7] During the early years of television network and station development, most of its content came from radio programming formats. Eventually, however, T.V.'s own particular pattern of adoption in society coupled with its unique properties resulted in changing patterns of programming.[8]

The 1960s were characterized by further technological progress and evidenced the emergence of an intense and dynamic media-society relationship. This was the first full decade of videotape and color television programming replacing black and white. Educational television (ETV) took on a new name, "public broadcasting," and the Public Broadcasting Act of 1967 provided not only the first interconnected network of stations but also the needed financial support necessary for them to become a vital force in American life. With the passing of the Communication Satellite Act of 1962, the United States officially got into international television, and by 1969, satellite usage had become common.[9] During this stormy period, television was said to have created a "new" politics, a "new" generation, and a "new" society.[10] The 1960s were anything but peaceful, and television was on hand providing witness, perhaps even dramatic stimulation to the turmoil. Much of the world was watching and forever being changed in the process. Outspoken critic and former FCC Commissioner Nicholas Johnson observes that "everything we do, or are, or worry about, is affected by television."[11]

The terms *progress, criticism,* and *alternatives* sum up much of what television is all about in the period since 1960. While commercial over-the-air programming remains the standard broadcasting fare in America, several important alternatives have emerged with some force and are responsible for major changes in the industry. The first, a public broadcasting network, has provided the national television audiences with a refuge from commercial television. A second alternative, cable television or Community Antenna Television (CATV), has made more dramatic strides. Cable T.V. today seeks to expand programming offerings to subscribers and has emerged as a huge industry challenging even the commercial networks. Finally, C-SPAN or the Cable-Satellite Public Affairs Network has provided twenty-four-hour alternative programming on two channels for almost two decades. Some 27.3 million Americans seek out C-SPAN programming, with 3.25 million people spending twenty hours or more each month watching C-SPAN telecasts. What C-SPAN has done is make public affairs readily accessible. C-SPAN is part of a quiet information revolution underway in America, and many perceive it as an oasis in "a vast wasteland."[12]

Criticism of television has become the "in" thing as politicians, educators, social scientists, minority and special interest groups, and parents all take turns attacking the medium. Politicians criticize it for its sensationalism and failure to cover critical issues, minorities for its stereotyped representations, special interest groups for its unbalanced coverage, and parents for its failure to present children's programming and promote wholesome family values. This criticism has led many

Americans to dub television the "boob tube," while British intellectuals are fond of calling it "the idiot's lantern." However, like all machines, television's virtues are the virtues of those who use it, and its weaknesses are human weaknesses. It is best that we learn to live with it and to use it, because T.V. is here to stay.

Progress in electronic technology, such as the VCR, and computer development of the "information highway" are further changing the nature of television. It may well move beyond its information and entertainment functions to become a much more interactive medium. For example, MS-NBC Internet News in collaboration with Microsoft agreed to produce on July 15, 1996 24-hour *involved* reporting *involving* a more participative public. Now, not only could Steve Forbes's flat tax be reported by interviewing Forbes and noted economists, but viewers could also personally *interact* with the story by plugging in their own income figures to see how a flat tax might affect their financial situation. Rather than criticizing television for what it is not, these changes focus on what television can become and more positively address the Carnegie Commission's charge in 1967 that "the problem is not so much what has been done with it so far as what has not been done—yet."[13]

Television today is huge, complex, costly, continuous, and competitive. It is a mass entertainer, mass informer, mass persuader, and mass educator. However, as John Chancellor, late NBC senior news correspondent and anchor, observed with his characteristic clarity and simplicity: "Television news is important only when what it is reporting is important. Then, it can make history move much faster." Without a doubt, television is a dominant force in American society, and only now are we beginning to teach media literacy. Still, print is neither dead nor dying but it is "being forced to make a place in the family of human communication for a new way of transferring information and emotion, the electronic reproduction of scenes and sensations."[14]

*   *   *   *   *

These two stories permit us to compare and contrast the two principal mass mediums available today and reflect the differences between print journalism and broadcast journalism. Mark Mayflower's story in the *Los Angeles Sentinel* presented the basic facts regarding the Los Angeles Central Library fire. Readers could quickly learn what happened, as well as where, when, and why. However, the story further explores the historic significance of the library and the importance of its rare book collection. Interested readers were provided insights that went beyond the immediate headlines. The interviews with Commissioner Tom Bradley and Library Information Director Robert Reagan revealed information that contextually added to the comments offered by Fire Chief Donald Manning. While the story vividly described the scene, it also offered interpretation, coherence, and understanding. Readers could envision the smoke, flames, and frenetic activity of the fire firefighters, as well as gain an appreciation of the significance of the event, becoming mindful of how it might influence their lives.

Tiffany Newhart's broadcast from the scene recorded the event as it happened. Viewers could see the Los Angeles Central Library engulfed in smoke and flames and hear Captain Anthony Didomenico of the Los Angeles Fire Department say, "It was like walking into a solid brick oven." The visual imagery of the fire dominated their attention, with little concern being given to the architectural significance of the library or its priceless collection of books. Tiffany's short broadcast focused on the actions surrounding the event and the personal emotions or reactions experienced by the people present. It was a singular moment in a montage of news events presented by KHBC Channel 2, Eyewitness News. The Los Angeles Central Library fire was only a small part of their "entertaining" mosaic.

Both stories provided information, and each offered shared yet distinctive perspectives. Do you prefer one story over the other? Why?

The Nature of Broadcast News and Interviewing

Broadcast news is not newspaper news read aloud. Broadcast news differs from newspaper news in content, arrangement, style, and delivery. The receiver of the information is also different, although in many cases, the radio news listener and the television news viewer do read the daily newspaper. They are different because the media require different degrees of attention and participation. Print is a medium in which readers must be actively involved to get the message. They must concentrate and focus attention on the printed word, using their imagination or mind's eye to fill in the picture the text describes. Quite the opposite demands are made by the broadcast media. The listener or viewer sits passively or may be otherwise engaged in a conversation or glancing through a magazine while hearing or watching the news, depending upon the degree of interest at the moment. Consequently, broadcast journalists have a more elusive target at which to aim their information than do newspaper journalists. If broadcasters offered audiences nothing but newspaper news read aloud, they would not keep their audience.

The ability of radio and television to take audiences to where events are occurring is their unique quality. They let the public share in the moment and experience what historians will later write about. Moreover, as a window on the world, they have the ability to create a massive awareness in a single instant and create or set a public agenda.[15] The massive exposure needed to generate national action can often only be gained through radio and television.

The visual aspect of T.V. is perhaps its greatest strength, as well as its greatest weakness. The viewing audience can be privy to events and witness them as they take place. However, the news events that make the best news film are sometimes not the most important. Conversely, often the most important news of the day does not lend itself to visual explanation. The collapse of the savings and loan industry, the slow pollution of the Great Lakes by industry, and a Supreme Court decision are all important stories, but they are difficult to film. While broadcast journalists do attempt to cover stories beyond those that can be filmed, visual effects dominate their thinking. The medium often concentrates on action rather than thought, on happenings rather than on issues, on shock rather than on explanations, on personalities rather than ideas.[16]

This visual aspect of the television medium creates other problems as well. Television can deceive an audience into believing it is viewing what actually happened and all that happened, when in actuality the viewer sees only what takes place within the range of the camera's eye. Often much more takes place. Eric Sevareid has compared television coverage of an event to searching a dark room with a flashlight. The light, like the T.V. camera, most often picks up what is moving. When it focuses on one part of the room, it does so to the exclusion of the rest of it.[17] Sometimes the magic of television presents the viewer with a picture that exceeds the reality of the event being broadcast. Moreover, it takes time to get a film crew out to a breaking story, so the cameras will go where they're welcome—regardless of where the most important story is. Finally, it is costly to maintain film crews, so when a news director sends out a camera team to shoot a news event and it turns out nothing very important happens, chances are the story will be broadcast anyway. There is too much of an investment to abandon the footage. The fact that television is an electronic medium wedded to T.V. and film cameras dictates in large measure what it can and will cover.

Broadcast news is further differentiated from newspaper news in that radio and television cannot provide the number of facts a newspaper provides. Their audience could not absorb that much detail without becoming bored, and the electronic medium is designed to present a series of events that occur in sequence, and the sequence is the same for all. This is not true for newspaper readers who are exposed to many items simultaneously and may choose the order in which they read them, as well as the degree of depth. David Brinkley expressed this difference when he said:

> The basic reason we are different is that in a newspaper you can skip around, read what is interesting to you, and ignore the rest. While on a news broadcast, you have to take it as it comes, in order.
>
> So what does that mean? In my opinion, it means we should not put a story on the air unless we honestly believe it's interesting to at least 10 percent of the audience. Preferably more. But at least 10 percent. . . .
>
> . . . the right question to ask is: who really cares about this? Does anyone care and should anyone care?[18]

Thus, broadcast news seeks to "include everyone," which means that anything of narrow interest is unlikely to be included. NBC News executive Reuven Frank explains that a newspaper "can easily afford to print an item of conceivable interest to only a fraction of its readers . . . and assume it is adding at least a little bit to its circulation," but a radio or television news broadcast "must be put together with the assumption that each item will be of some interest to everyone."[19] Consequently, broadcast journalism in general concentrates on the surface of events rather than underlying conditions, revealing the world as a series of unrelated, fragmentary moments.

Another distinction and constant obstacle in broadcast journalism is the pressure of time. In broadcasting, time is indeed money, and the pressure of time works against understanding, coherence, and sometimes even meaning. Certainly newspaper journalists have deadlines to meet, but their primary objective is to write a column or fill space. Broadcast news airs at a specific time and broadcast journalists have a limited amount of time to present their stories as well as a limited number of stories they can present. Walter Cronkite admitted many times that T.V. news is a mere sketch of the headlines, a most incomplete picture of the day's news, yet he still ended his nightly news program with the assurance, "That's the way it is." Neil Postman and Steve Powers observe in *How to Watch T.V. News* that "given the limited time and objectives of a television newscast, a viewer has to realize that he or she is not getting a full meal but rather a snack. And depending on the organization presenting the news, the meal may contain plenty of empty calories."[20]

Finally, because of radio and television's unique ability to come into the home and entertain, broadcast journalism takes on an entertainment aspect that is usually not found in standard newspaper journalism. This quality has contributed to the emergence of several "show biz" formats. However, despite this show business element that concentrates as much on ratings as reporting, there is a serious commitment to news, and interviewing is a critical part of broadcast news.

Interviewing is basic to broadcast news, and there are many different formats currently in use to fit radio and television schedules. **News programs** use interviewing as an essential part of gathering information to generate news stories for broadcast. News programs on radio or television typically contain some type of recorded material (audio tape, videotape, or film), and much of this will be short excerpts of interviews conducted by reporters over the telephone or in the field where the news is happening. These brief interviews seek to provide answers to the who, what, when, and where of the event in question.

Magazine programs feature several unrelated segments or events held together by a host or several hosts. *Prime Time, Dateline NBC, 60 Minutes, 48 Hours,* and *20/20* are examples of the magazine format. In all magazine-type programs, the interview is an important element focusing on personalities, as well as exploring selected issues. These interviews seek to profile individuals in the news and go beyond fact finding to seek some understanding about the how and why of a story. The various segments can personalize public figures and arouse public interest.

Interview programs rely on recognized and dynamic interviewers to provide in-depth portraits of public figures or an analysis and coherent explanation of controversial events. Barbara Walters's personality profiles of political figures, movie stars, and sports heroes and Ted Koppel's *Nightline* news show are good examples of this type of programming. The plethora of daily "talk shows" concerned with sensationalism are more disappointing examples of the straight interviewing format. For this format to work best, the selection of people to be interviewed is extremely important. They must be knowledgeable, able to talk intelligently, and capable of sustaining the pressure of an extended interview. When effective, these programs can be informative, insightful, and revealing.

Roundtable news programs bring broadcast journalists together to present their personal perspectives on the range of issues comprising current affairs. David Brinkey's *This Week* and the *McLaughlin Group* are representative of this type of format. The goal of this roundtable interviewing is to bring coherence to events by having competent journalists share their diverse views on timely topics of public concern.

Finally, most radio and television stations produce some type of **public affairs program** that deals with national news topics or delves into local/regional social, political, and economic issues. A host/interviewer may question several guests about a particular issue as is done on many locally produced public affairs programs, or several reporter/interviewers may question one guest on several topics as is done on *Meet the Press* and *Face the Nation*. This format relies on competent interviewers questioning experts and is informational in nature.

Today, there is more news being presented on radio and television than ever before because the cost of news is relatively inexpensive, and new technology has speeded the transmission of news. News programs are now profit centers for the networks, and the news audience is a highly desirable one since people who watch news tend to be more attentive to what is on the screen, tend to be better educated, and tend to have more money to spend than the audiences for other shows. Every night an estimated 40 million people watch the news on the major networks, and millions more watch local news coverage.[21]

*   *   *   *   *

Tiffany Newhart's primary purpose was to publicly report the fire at the Los Angeles Central Library for KHBC, Channel 2, Eyewitness News. Her broadcast from the scene testifies to the occurrence of this unfortunate incident. The interviews with Captain Anthony Didomenic of the Los Angeles Fire Department and Commissioner Tom Bradley further confirmed the tragedy and reflected the personal drama of the event. Viewers learned of the fire and could vicariously experience it but had to decide for themselves its significance. What it meant and how it fit into the larger picture of news events were not the concerns of this "live" at the scene report—and rightly so. Time constraints and the immediacy of the event prevent intensive interviewing and detailed commentary that could be included in a newspaper account. Viewers who wanted news snapshots would probably become disinterested or bored. Consequently, we were informed only that a devastating and upsetting fire occurred today at the Los Angeles Central Library and that it was under investigation. However, people watch television news, in large measure, because it brings "action events" into their homes. They do not watch television to necessarily get the latest news. Radio does a better job. They do not prefer television because they want to get all the news—local, national, and international. The newspaper does a better job. They do not prefer television for depth of coverage or penetrating analysis. A news magazine does it better. What television does do is take viewers to the scenes of the action and show them what is happening or what has recently happened.

This is not to suggest that all broadcast news programs have to be limited and narrow in their focus. Broadcast journalists who conduct in-depth interviews and participate on multi-interview documentary projects can provide substance and context. The time constraints are more flexible, permitting background research, interpretation, and judgment. Viewers can be informed and meaningfully made aware of people, places, and events or issues. Here the electronic medium of broadcasting can both expose and impart while entertaining.

The Types, Characteristics, and Purposes of Broadcast Interviewing

There are four main types of broadcast interviews and each type imposes unique needs and constraints on the interviewer. These four types are (1) the news interview, (2) the in-depth live studio interview, (3) the in-depth recorded studio interview, and (4) the multiple-interview documentary.[22] The characteristics of each must be considered in relation to the story and the challenges of the medium.

The **news interview** is fundamental to radio and television news programs that rely on eyewitness accounts of events. Broadcast journalists, who often report directly from the field, must get to the scene quickly, gather essential facts, and briefly interview actual participants or eyewitnesses. If there is a hierarchy of believability in broadcast news, it would be (1) a live report from the scene with interview excerpts from those involved, (2) a live report from the reporter at the scene of the event, (3) an in-studio report from the reporter who gathered the information and talked with those present at the scene, (4) the newscaster or anchor reading the story over taped video coverage, and (5) the story simply being read. One of the most important ingredients for any news department is live, local coverage. Consequently, broadcast journalists are seldom able to reconstruct and evaluate the event. Fred Friendly, a CBS news pioneer, observed that "reporting the news on television is like writing with a one-ton pencil."[23]

The **in-depth live studio interview** is exhausting, risky, and intense, which leads Richard Reeves to observe that "well done, live . . . interviewing is simply more difficult than print interviewing."[24] The interviewer must observe time constraints, be cognizant of commercial cues, and always be poised for the unexpected response.

However, for broadcasters who "do it right," the in-depth live interview can be both informative and entertaining. They can impart insight and heighten awareness by asking questions that elicit news.

The **in-depth recorded studio interview** is much safer than live interviewing, and there is considerably less pressure involved. Both the interviewer and the interviewee can be more relaxed because cameras can be stopped and started, and they do not have to worry about errors, long pauses, timing, or pacing. All of these elements can be cleaned up by editing. The result is that both parties to the interview can engage in a more conversational exchange that listeners or viewers will find involving.

Finally, the **multi-interview documentary** involves numerous interviews from a variety of sources to form a comprehensive report. Broadcast journalists probe, analyze, and interpret an issue or event, and conduct many interviews, some taped, others done merely for background research. The fact that many sources contribute insights and drama gives the documentary a more solid, authoritative feel. It is the counterpoint to investigative reporting in print journalism and can have a powerful effect, particularly television documentaries, which use the full range of the electronic medium. While at one time documentaries were "tucked away at unwanted hours" and a part of the so-called "Sunday ghetto" of broadcasting,[25] today they are a regular part of programming schedules, exploring such topics as race relations, discrimination, drug addiction, crime, court procedures, business ethics, the job market, political campaigns and elections, and even the influence of media itself.

Mitchell Charnley once said, "News . . . is news, and reporting—through any medium—is reporting."[26] The purposes of broadcast interviewing in many ways parallel those of journalistic interviewing—to fetch facts; dig for details; collect colorful quotes; anecdotes, or stories; and search for significance. A common denominator linking broadcast and print journalists is that each is a translator, not of language but of complexity. Each must competently ask questions that raise understanding and intimately connect them with their community. Speaking about all journalism, Howard K. Smith said, "I would guess that, after formal schooling is over for the average citizen, at least four-fifths of what he continues to learn about his community, about his state and city, and about his nation and the world, come filtered through the observations of a journalist."[27]

*   *   *   *   *

Accidents, fires, and crime figure significantly in most local newscasts because many news directors believe that audience interest in these events never flags. If these violent events appear to dominate local newscasts, it may be that the assignment editor lacks imagination or it may be because the electronic medium is uniquely adapted to covering them. Tiffany Newhart, like many broadcast journalists, found herself rushing from one scene to another with little time to seriously assess a situation or conduct interviews. Therefore, readily available information was reported and the conveniently available interviewed.

However, a number of broadcast stations have developed special segments or unusual kinds of news coverage in a continuing effort to give meaning to the news and to tap audience interest. Live, in-depth studio interviews, taped studio interviews, and multi-interview documentaries permit broadcast journalists to present personal profiles and explore issues. At a later date, Tiffany Newhart could interview others and, combined with this footage, develop a news special focusing on the fire and its aftermath. Still, what makes television news special is the moving picture of events.

Conducting the Broadcast Interview

Although broadcast interviews are conducted in much the same way as journalistic interviews, the circumstances and the time constraints make it essential for broadcast interviewers to focus and define the interview, selectively choose interviewees, carefully control the questioning, understand the demands of the medium, and be conscious of "mike" fright and technology shock. Regardless of the type of broadcast interview, these remain the critical concerns, and all of this requires a great amount of concentration and skill.

Focus and Define the Interview

Broadcast interviewing requires a firm sense of purpose, which means determining a central theme and defining the parameters of the interview. Mike Wallace, veteran CBS News journalist, says that all broadcast interviews must have a "story line" or structure.[28] What topics will be discussed? What issues will be explored? What questions will be asked? What points must be stressed or emphasized? What information needs to be conveyed? Broadcasters are obliged to answer these questions quickly if they hope to present a focused and tightly structured interview. Whether in the field or a studio, they must go into an interview with a sense of what is going to happen and expeditiously get to the heart of the interview.

Selectively Choose Interviewees

Who should be interviewed? Interviewees in the field fall into three categories. First are those in authority, directing the action at the scene and coordinating events. They are recognized by their commanding presence and for their knowledge, expertise, and skills. Second are those caught up in the circumstances, the individuals immediately effected and other participants. These are the people who are intimately connected with the story or involved in its unfolding and otherwise are concerned with the outcome. The third category consists of outside observers who can provide an eyewitness account or informed point of view. When at the scene, the selection of interviewees must be done quickly, and the severe conditions can make accessibility difficult. However, those chosen to be interviewed contribute much to the success of the story, since they can best portray the emotion and drama experienced. Reuven Frank, in a memo to the NBC News Staff said "The best interviews are of people reacting—not people expounding. Joy, sorrow, shock, fear—these are the stuff of news. No important story is without them."[29]

In a studio interview, whether live or taped, the choice of interviewee is equally crucial; however, they can be prearranged and better planned. The interviewer can be briefed in advance and the interviewee made ready by outlining the program and discussing generally the parameters of the interview. However, while the program is planned and the interviewee is prepared, it is important that the interview seem conversational and spontaneous. Still, David Brinkley observes, "If the person has no interesting thoughts, no interesting information, or is unwilling to give you whatever thoughts or information he has, you're stuck."[30]

Since multi-interview documentaries take weeks or months to prepare, they give the interviewer time for essential research and background fact finding. Moreover, potential interviewees can be carefully reviewed and strategically screened for their expertise, knowledge, outlook, or perspective. This can help ensure selecting individuals who are articulate, outspoken, and willing. However, to avoid charges of bias and tabloid sensationalism, it is important to choose individuals representative of varying viewpoints.

Broadcast interviewers quickly learn that there are certain professional people who generally are more difficult to interview than others. Professors, doctors, lawyers, scientists, economists, and business analysts are often awkward to interview because they use technical jargon and are very concerned with how they are viewed by the public, as well as other members of their profession. Moreover, interviewees often come to an interview with personal motives, which can pose a problem. Politicians may be seeking to advance their careers, authors to generate book sales, actors/actresses to promote films, educators to laud programs, and business consultants to garner new clients. Thus, broadcast interviewers must be aware of these problems while diligently pursuing their own agenda.

Carefully Control the Questioning

Broadcast interviews demand a careful control of questioning by the interviewer. In a newspaper interview, the interviewer can allow the interviewee to wander over many topics and discuss seemingly tangential issues and then return to the newsroom to edit and structure the story. In contrast, the broadcast interview is edited and structured as it occurs, and the editor is the interviewer. Mike Wallace notes that the live broadcast interviewer "is not only reporting, he is actually editing and publishing at the same time."[31] Consequently, the broadcast interviewer must carefully maintain control and keep the interview on track, yet not appear pushy or ignore follow-up leads given by the interviewee. This involves a great amount of concentration and skill.

Questioning should be focused, succinctly stated, and reflect what most people would ask if they met the interviewee or had a chance to conduct the interview themselves. This means pursuing difficult questions even if the interviewee says, "I don't want to comment on that!" While a broadcast interviewer's qualities should include sensitivity, they should also include toughness. Ralph Paskman, a former CBS News editor, points out that as broadcast news interviewers "we are not covering a story if we get somebody to say . . . what has already been published in the press."[32] This may require asking leading questions, which telegraphs expected answers, or loaded questions, which pose provocation. While these types of questions are generally avoided in print journalism, here they can add spirit and drama. Above all else, when assuming the lead in questioning, let the interviewee do most of the talking.

Broadcast journalists are the public's representatives at newsworthy events—their ears, their eyes, and sometimes their conscience. As such, they are obligated to ask the "right" questions. Michael J. Arlen, in the *Living-Room War*, elaborates on the proliferation and uselessness of the "how do you feel" school of broadcast interviewing. In his examination of the effects of news reports on society's attitudes, he notes that the "how-do-you-feel stuff would be okay if it led anywhere, if it were something people could respond to . . . but in a professional interview what it really amounts to is a sort of marking time while the reporter thinks up some real questions, or maybe while he hopes that this one time the personage will actually include a bit of genuine information in his inevitably mechanical reply, which the reporter can then happily pursue."[33] This line of questioning is usually ridiculous or unanswerable and a betrayal of the public trust. The point is simple: ask pertinent questions. Give listeners or viewers a chance to get an insight they didn't have before. The job of broadcast journalists is a demanding one and requires responsible questioning that elicits substantive information.

Understand the Demands of the Medium

Broadcast journalists must be aware of the demands of their medium and be able to adjust to the technical requirements of their equipment. Radio news broadcasters need to remember always that the listener is just that—a listener who cannot see the story. Moreover, they should be well versed in proper phone use, since much of their time will be spent interviewing people by telephone. Most radio newsrooms are arranged for easy telephone interviewing.

Television is primarily a visual medium, and because it is virtually the only medium that is able to show action, television journalists must always be cognizant of the camera. While important news without visuals should take precedence over film of minor news value, good newscasts often depend upon good visual stories. Attention must be given to personal appearance, setting, and location; camera angles, focal lengths, lighting, and sound become critical concerns. Television interviewers also must be able to go *through* the camera lens and talk with their audience.

Be Conscious of "Mike" Fright and Technology Shock

A microphone, tape recorder, or camera often intimidates and frightens people, inhibiting an interview. Moreover, the bewildering and chaotic atmosphere of a broadcast studio filled with highly sophisticated electronic equipment can be overwhelming and shocking, causing even the more intrepid interviewee to become nervous. Broadcast interviewers must be aware of this problem and patiently strive to relieve this fear and apprehension experienced by interviewees. Therefore, it is advisable to outline the proposed interview, format with interviewees in advance, and familiarize them with what is going to happen and how things are going to progress. Help them understand that the apparent chaos engulfing them is actually an orderly haste, an organized system going at top speed.

*   *   *   *   *

Tiffany Newhart's broadcast focuses on property and people. She reported the damage done to thousands of books and interviewed Anthony Didomenico, an involved firefighter, and Tom Bradley, a concerned observer. While the hectic environment, severe conditions, and time constraints were unavoidably inhibiting, a more complete story could have been reported. The story exaggerated the size of the library and said not a word about fire safety violations or saving the rare book collection. The interviews were shallow and meaningless, reflecting the "How do you feel?" line of questioning. The pause (indicated by the dash following "tried to hold down the use of water") was used only for dramatic effect, and the closing sentence indicating that "the cause of the fire is under investigation" teased viewers into suspecting ulterior motives. In sum, it was a picture story communicating very little substantive probing, and specific questions could have elicited more information. The value of a story is exposed only when the journalist probes for it. A camera and a microphone are not the only tools of a broadcast journalist's trade—the notebook and pencil should go along as well—yet the likes of this news broadcast can be found everyday. Except for major news, most of the longer television news items establish relationships through the visual.

The "nut" Tiffany Newhart had to crack was should a broadcast journalist give people "what they want" or "what they ought to have?" This problem has confronted broadcasting almost since it began. In terms of broadcast journalism, "what people want" may be defined as those elements that would attract a large audience to a newscast, giving it high ratings in its market. "What people ought to have" may be defined as the experienced journalist's perception of news that is important to the community. There is no answer except on an individual basis.

However, Edward R. Murrow once said, "If television and radio are to be used for the entertainment of all of the people all of the time, we have come perilously close to discovering the real opiate of the people."[34]

Participating in the Broadcast Interview

For most of us, no other form of interviewing is more familiar than broadcast interviews, since we see them conducted every night on the evening news and frequently hear them on the radio. We watch or listen with interest, laughing at funny moments or comments, feeling discomfort as the interviewee gropes for an answer, and experiencing the tension when the interviewee must answer a tough question. However, seeing and hearing broadcast interviews on television or radio is very different from participating in them. Participants must give care and attention to the message they want to convey, as well as the particular qualities characterizing the broadcast medium.

Participants must clearly identify their objectives and determine the two or three key points that will comprise their message. Facts, statistics, and examples must then be used to illustrate these points. Moreover, since their agenda may not coincide with that of interviewers, participants must be persistent in getting their message across. This often requires them to diplomatically assert themselves. They must not allow journalists to intimidate or inhibit them but must concentrate on tactfully including their message in the interview. Participants who are successful in achieving their purpose state important facts first and make their key points.

During the interview, participants should answer questions truthfully, keeping responses simple and avoiding complex explanations. They must beware of being lulled into rambling and diluting their original message. Delivering responses in twenty seconds or less is desirable during at-the-scene interviews since ten-second sound bites are the building blocks of radio and television news stories. Participants should also avoid jargon and speak in personal terms whenever possible, remembering that the reporter is a conduit to the general public. Tough questions require participants to remain relaxed and calm while answering with confidence and reserve. While they can express differences of opinion and should correct the record if journalists have made an error, participants must never publicly argue with reporters. Moreover, participants must never speculate on answers or speak "off the record." Throughout the questioning, it is important for participants to maintain a positive attitude.

Finally, participants need to continually be aware of those features that distinguish the broadcast medium and how such factors influence the interview. For television, participants need to be conscious of their physical appearance and realize that their facial expressions, gestures, and actions will be captured by the camera. Radio, on the other hand, demands that interest, trust, confidence, and believability be conveyed by participants through their voice alone, since visual and body language cues are not available to listeners. Consequently, careful attention must be given to volume, pitch, vocal inflection, and auditory pauses. The point is simple: participants must remember that both what they say and how they say it are important.

Broadcast interviewing also involves all who listen and watch. Therefore, as regular consumers of broadcast news, we all also may be considered participants in broadcast interviews. Neil Postman and Steve Powers advance specific recommendations that can make us all more competent broadcast news recipients and responsible participants. They suggest that we (1) come with a firm idea of what is important and judge the importance of what is reported, (2) keep in mind that it is a "show" to be sold to advertisers and is produced and delivered as entertainment, (3) learn about the economic and political interests of those who run the stations and construct the news, (4) pay special attention to the language of newscasts and not become overly engaged by the "imagery" presented, and (5) reduce the amount of broadcast news consumed, remembering that broadcast news does not reflect normal everyday life.[35] The best way to prepare oneself, as an interviewee or observer, for the broadcast interview is to know exactly what is happening and why.

* * * * *

Captain Anthony Didomenic of the Los Angeles Fire Department and Commissioner Tom Bradley only answered the questions put to them but certainly could have provided more information. Captain Didomenic was understandably reserved, not wanting to speculate on the fire; however, Tom Bradley might have been more assertive in presenting his views, given the possible community exposure. In fact, Tom Bradley and Fire Chief Donald Manning did communicate their respective messages when interviewed by Mark Mayflower of the *Los Angeles Sentinel.* Moreover, their interviews with Mark, along with that of Library Public Information Director Robert Reagan, yielded substantive information, which helped sustain his story. Still, the brief interviews conducted by Tiffany Newhart provided her with the sound bites she needed to support the visual imagery of the fire. What the television news delivered best was impression.

Perhaps, later in-depth interviews could profile the views of Tom Bradley and Robert Reagan. Then, the significance of the library and its future could be highlighted. Also, an investigation into the causes of the fire and similar hazards existing in other public facilities could follow up on the comments offered by Captain Didomenico and feature Los Angeles Fire Chief Donald Manning. These venues more easily permit communicating a personal agenda and offering a private perspective. The broadcast medium, despite its concern with brevity, can provide opportunities for active participation. As a participant, which medium would you prefer?

As consumers of broadcast news and targets of newscasts, we may all be considered participants. Responsible participants need to be able to recognize what is new and interesting and important, realizing that the broadcast medium can create its own reality. Therefore, how should Tiffany Newhart's coverage of the Los Angeles Central Library fire be evaluated? Judged?

Thucydides carved some of his accounts of the Peloponnesian War on wax-covered tablets with a stylus, which incidentally had a blunt end to erase errors, quite a stretch to the electronic equipment necessary to get a broadcast news program on the air today. Still, the vital question is whether all this paraphernalia is helping us to get a more understandable account of current history.

The News Conference

Historian Daniel Boorstin coined the term *pseudo-event* when referring to events that would not occur if not for the media:[36] An event *created because the media will cover it.* Every news conference is a pseudo-event. They are designed and planned to lure media interest and hopefully generate positive press coverage.

In a news conference, both newspaper and broadcast journalists surrender considerable control to the interviewee. The location and the time are decided by the interviewee. The content of the conference is focused by the interviewee. The length, number, and order of the questions, and even who will ask them are determined by the interviewee, with interviewers competing for attention. Consequently, journalists must understand the group dynamics of the situation and realize that news conferences are one-dimensional. The story is probably *not* at the press conference. The best advice for journalists is to cover news conferences but use the information as background and then diligently work to get the rest of the story.

Formal news conferences are arranged for a variety of reasons. Some of the reasons are in the public interest, whereas others are self-serving or egoistic. The purposes for news conferences may include conveying legitimate news or information of general interest, presenting a particular side to a controversy, rebutting rumors, defusing a crisis, or generating publicity for an event, person, product, or idea. Sometimes news conferences are not prearranged and come about spontaneously, with the impetus being derived from members of the news media. General media pressure to cover public figures and those at the center of controversy often results in unplanned news conferences where interviewees may have less control.

Meeting the press in a public forum allows an immediate response to the many journalists who may be individually attempting to arrange interviews, so a news conference can be an efficient and time saving device. It allows for one statement, one consistent message, and one forum, yet exposure to the news media can be risky, so the decision to call a news conference should be made carefully, and the conducting of a news conference should not be left to chance.

The timing of a news conference, as well as determining who will be invited and the physical setting, are initially important concerns. A news conference should be called only after identifying its purpose and determining what is to be achieved. It should then be scheduled such that print and broadcast journalists can meet their various news deadlines. In a crisis situation, it is essential that news conferences be arranged as soon as practical, but not "so early in the crisis that little or no credible information can be provided."[37] In a prolonged crisis, several news conferences may be required. The interviewee may also want to ask outside experts to assist in conducting the news conference. The setting should permit the interviewee to maintain control and address the needs of the various news media. Rooms with a lot of windows or fluorescent lights should be avoided because this poses problems for the television photographers who must control lighting. Also, make sure there is no outside noise or interference that might disrupt the proceedings.

The opening statements are critical to the success of any news conference. They should succinctly convey timely, accurate information and be designed to focus questioning on the areas that necessitated calling the conference. The aim of a news conference is not to lecture the press or public but to precisely state one's purpose, and since journalists are often eager to get beyond "canned" news to the more spontaneous question-and-answer session, brevity is crucial. A copy

The opening statements are critical to the success of any news conference.

of the prepared opening statements should be included in the press kit made available to attending journalists. A press kit should contain news releases and any other items that can help journalists understand and visualize the story. It can be useful in reinforcing the content of the news conference and illustrating items that are difficult to explain orally during the news conference.

Clearly, the balance of power in a news conference rests with the interviewee; however, journalists are free to ask their questions which are rarely provided in advance and often prove to be challenging. Therefore, being able to handle tough or problem questions and remaining calm under pressure are essential qualities when conducting a news conference. Tough questions cannot be ignored and must be answered. The best way to handle tough questions is to have anticipated them and have prepared answers. Also, if outside experts are assisting in conducting the news conference, they can respond to the ticklish technical questions. Throughout the questioning, the interviewee conducting the news conference must not become defensive or confrontational, but needs to remain relaxed and composed. While a news conference can be a lively encounter, fury and rage only engender negative press, defeating any positive purposes for calling the conference.

Finally, a news conference should be brought to a formal close. The best way to end a planned news conference is to have a press aide or public relations person stop the questioning at a predetermined time or at a predetermined signal from the interviewee. Remember, the lengthier the news conference, the more likely the chance for error. People in business, government, and other professions who know that they will have to regularly meet with news journalists should learn how to conduct effective news conferences, acquiring the necessary skills, strategies, and techniques. This is one area where learning on the job can be disastrous.

*   *   *   *   *

Should a news conference be scheduled regarding the Central Los Angeles Library fire? Yes! This is a historic building that had been at the center of civic attention and public concern for some time, and the consequences of the fire would attract media attention. A news conference could be an efficient method to dispel rumors and address the questions raised by print and broadcast journalists. Commissioner Tom Bradley, as a recognized public figure and civic authority, should probably call a news conference as soon as the particular circumstances of the fire become known, the degree of damage is assessed, and preliminary considerations regarding potential reconstruction have been weighed. He would also want to have Fire Chief Donald Manning and Library Public Information Director Robert Reagan assist him in conducting the news conference. Together, they could present a single unified and consistent message concerning the fire and its consequences.

Fire Chief Manning could address the technical questions regarding the causes of the fire, Robert Reagan could discuss the restoration of library services, and Commissioner Bradley could shed light on possible reconstruction efforts in the aftermath of the fire. They should also be prepared to answer tough questions concerning the disregard for safety standards and the earlier proposed plans for expansion of the library. Indeed, this would be a difficult news conference to conduct with charges and allegations being made and public assurances being demanded. Those conducting the news conference must remember to remain calm and composed, not becoming defensive or involved in a "blame game." Their common goal should be to share all available information, ease public concerns, and show a united effort to progress beyond the fire. It would be in their best interest and the public's best interest to display a positive attitude in the face of this unfortunate fire. Commissioner Bradley should probably conduct additional news conferences to update the press and the public.

Journalists covering the news conference would ask tough questions and seek answers to public concerns. However, they must realize that news conferences are only one dimension of the story, a dimension largely controlled by those who conduct the news conference. They would want to pursue the historic significance of the library and its rare book collection to the community and investigate possible fire code violations existing in other older public facilities. Moreover, they should continue monitoring progress toward restoring the library and any planned expansion. The difficult task confronting all journalists is setting up a conversation in which experts and citizens really talk with each other in a constructive way—contribute each according to their abilities, in a language all of them can understand.

Critical Focus

Review again the Critical Focus presented in Chapter 14 involving the disappearance of Malcom Millsap, CEO of Creve Creek Engineering, and replay the videotape segment, analyzing the news conference and examining how a broadcast journalist might cover it. The following critical questions can direct and guide your analysis of the news conference conducted by Karen Smart and Bill Walters.

1. Was a news conference necessary? What alternatives to a news conference exist? What responsibility does Creve Creek Engineering have to its constituencies and the public to address this problem or respond to press inquiries?
2. Does providing a prepared statement at the beginning of the news conference help clarify complicated issues? Do Karen Smart and Bill Walters know

what they want to say or are they merely communicating because it seems like the right thing to do? Should outside experts have been included in conducting the news conference? Who has control of the interview—the interviewee or interviewer? Is the same control maintained throughout the news conference?

3. Does providing answers to reporters' questions help mitigate the problem, or does it add to further confusion? Did Karen Smart and Bill Walters effectively respond to the immediate crisis, or did they react to irrelevant problems and questions? Were tough questions addressed, or did they avoid giving answers? Were there any specific questions that were predictable? What was the tone or climate of the news conference—positive, upbeat, concerned, or a mixture of these and others?

4. Will this crisis invite further dialogue with the press? Does the news conference discourage any further communication?

5. As you watch the video, consider how a broadcast news journalist might cover this news conference. What main points should be made in a short newscast? What sound bites, if any, should be included? What visual considerations should be weighed? How can the news conference be made informative, interesting, and entertaining?

6. What is the rest of the story?[38]

Summary

Broadcasting left its childhood a long time ago, and whether we like it or not, the electronic media is a part of all our lives. There are more radios in America than people, and more people have T.V. in their homes than have indoor plumbing or telephones. If something important or sensational has happened on nearly any part of the globe, we can find out about it while we eat breakfast, lunch, or dinner. Broadcast media plays a distinct and important role in American culture. Broadcast news influences millions, and broadcast interviews connect us with people, places, and events.

The technological and live demands of broadcast interviewing set it apart from the typical journalistic interview. Live news interviews, in-depth studio interviews, and multi-interview documentaries each present difficult and querulous problems. While some of the basic strategies and techniques are similar to the journalistic interview, broadcast interviewers must always be aware of the entertainment element. When conducting broadcast interviews, they must focus and define their purpose, selectively choose interviewees, carefully control the questioning, understand the demands of the medium, and be conscious of "mike" fright and technology shock. Throughout the interviews, they must be alert to the performance dimension, creating a casual, relaxed atmosphere that belies considerable planning and preparation.

Those features that distinguish broadcast interviewing from the journalistic interview also uniquely influence participation. Participants must always be alert to the element of time, assertively working to include their personal agenda and presenting their message. They, too, must understand the demands of the medium and positively address those challenges, realizing that everything they say and do influences listeners and viewers. As listeners and viewers, we are an integral part of broadcast interviewing and must be responsible consumer-participants.

The news conference is a special type of broadcast interview, planned and controlled by the person who will be the focus of the interview. It is a public relations event designed to generate positive publicity. The journalist-interviewer is basically a conduit who passes along information and acts as a gatekeeper in the flow of information between the news maker and the public. Still, to be successful, a news conference requires considerable planning and preparation. The reasons for conducting it must be clearly determined, control must be maintained, and the interviewee must remain cool and calm throughout. These are challenging and formidable tasks, which should not be recklessly undertaken without requisite training.

Neil Postman, author, social critic, and communications theorist, notes that "we have transformed information into a form of garbage, and ourselves into garbage collectors. . . . We are awash in information without even a broom to help us get rid of it. . . . There is no loom to weave it all into fabric."[39] This is a problem print and broadcast journalists share and must confront with as much intelligence and imagination as they can muster. They must give meaning to our history, elucidate the present, and give direction to our future. They have the looms to weave us a pattern for our lives. Public journalists would suggest that newspapers and broadcasters must work together, helping people judge events wisely and finding ways of bringing them together.

SHARPENING YOUR FOCUS

1. We are regularly bombarded by some sort of media, being exposed to radio, television, and print media. Pearl Aldrich observes in *The Impact of the Mass Media* that "one of the problems facing us today is being reached by the media when we really don't choose to be." Do you agree? Disagree? Why?

2. Broadcast journalists, in the past, have been particularly effective during periods of crisis. Today, many media critics, today, believe broadcast journalism is entertainment oriented and scandal driven. Do you agree? Disagree? Is Niel Postman correct in his advice regarding a trained and observant public?

3. Broadcast news is not newspaper news read aloud. How does broadcast news differ from newspaper news in content, arrangement, style, and delivery? What demands of the electronic medium must broadcast journalists carefully manage?

4. Select a news story and compare/contrast its coverage by radio, T.V., and newspapers. What are the differences in the coverage? Which does a better job of presenting the story? Why? Who would you say are the "journalists?" What news source do you go to daily? What source do you got to first?

5. Identify the various types of interview programs and the audiences that a television interviewer is trying to address. Discuss how far a reporter should go to get the interviewee to disclose information that the interviewee obviously does not want to disclose. What is the appropriate balance between interviewer and interviewee participation in a broadcast interview?

6. How is a news conference similar to and different from one-on-one interviews? What skills are required of interviewers and interviewees?

7. Observe a Presidential press conference. Who is in control? What is his agenda? How well does he respond to the journalists' questions? What types of questions are asked? Does he effectively handle "difficult" questions? How is the press conference concluded? Are local public figures as effective with their press conferences? Why? Why not?

NOTES

1. Marshall McLuhan and Quentin Fiore, *The Medium Is the Message* (New York: Random House, 1967), 8.
2. Ralph Lee Smith, *The Wired Nation* (New York: Harper and Row, 1972).
3. Erik Barnouw, *A History of Broadcasting in the United States,* 3 vols. (New York: Oxford University Press, 1966, 1968, 1970).
4. John R. Bittner, *Broadcast Law and Regulation* (Englewood Cliffs, N.J.: Prentice-Hall, 1982).
5. Edward P. Morgan, "Who Forgot Radio," in *The Press in Washington,* ed. Ray Hiebert (Washington, D.C.: American University, 1965), 183.
6. Sydney W. Head and Christopher H. Sterling, *Broadcasting in America: A Survey of Electronic Media,* 6th ed. (Boston: Houghton Mifflin, 1990).
7. Erik Barnnouw, *Tube of Plenty: The Evolution of American Television* (New York: Oxford University Press, 1982).
8. Martin Mayer, *About Television* (New York: Harper and Row, 1972).
9. Leo Bogart, *The Age of Television* (New York: Federick Ungar, 1972).
10. See Robert T. Bower, *Television and the Public* (New York: Holt, Rinehart and Winston, 1973); Terry Galanoy, *Down the Tube* (Chicago: Henry Regnery, 1970); and Caleb Gattegno, *Towards a Visual Culture* (New York: Outerbridge and Dienstfrey, 1969).
11. Nicholas Johnson, *How to Talk Back to Your Television Set* (Boston: Little, Brown and Company, 1980), 140.
12. Brian Lamb, *C-SPAN, America's Town Hall* (Washington, D.C.: Acropolis Books, 1988).
13. Carnegie Commission on Educational Television, *Public Television, A Program for Action* (New York: Bantam Books, 1967), 10.
14. Robert Disch, *The Future of Literacy* (Englewood Cliffs, N.J.: Prentice-Hall, 1973), 166.
15. See Jennings Bryant and Dolf Zillmann, *Perspectives on Media Effects* (Hillsdale, N.J.: Lawrence Erlbaum Associates, 1986); David L. Protess and Maxwell McCombs, *Agenda Setting: Readings on Media, Public Opinion, and Policymaking* (Hillsdale, N.J.: Lawrence Erlbaum Associates, 1991); Everett M. Rogers and James W. Dearing, "Agenda-Setting Research: Where Has It Been, Where Is It Going?" in *Communication Yearbook 11,* ed. James A. Anderson (Newbury Park, Calif.: Sage, 1988), p 555–94; Werner J. Severin and James W. Tankard, Jr., *Communication Theories and Origins, and Uses in the Mass Media* (New York: Longman, 1992); and "Symposium: Agenda Setting Revisited," *Journal of Communication* 43 (1993): 58–127.
16. Maxwell McCombs and Donald Shaw, "Structuring the Unseen Environment," *Journal of Communication* 26 (1976): 18–22.

17. Jay E. Epstein, *The News from Nowhere* (New York: Random House, 1973), 65.
18. David Brinkley, speech to the Radio Television News Directors Association conference, Miami Beach, December 14, 1976.
19. Neil Postman and Steve Powers, *How to Watch TV News* (New York: Penguin Books), 112–13.
20. Ibid., 39.
21. Ibid., 4–5.
22. Cal W. Downs, G. Paul Smeyak, and Ernest Martin, *Professional Interviewing* (New York: Harper and Row, 1980).
23. Fred Friendly, *The Good Guys, the Bad Guys and the First Amendment* (New York: Random House, 1976), 43.
24. Richard Reeves, "I Used to Be Dick Reeves," *TV Guide*, 4 October, 1975, 16.
25. William Small, *To Kill a Messenger: Television and the Real World.* (New York: Hastings House, 1970).
26. Irving E. Fang, *Television News, Radio News* (St. Paul, Minn.: Rada Press, 1980), 328.
27. Howard K. Smith, a lecture at Memphis State University, 23 April, 1969.
28. Hugh Downs and Mike Wallace, "The Craft of Interviewing," *Television Quarterly* 4 (Summer 1965): 8.
29. Fang, *Television News, Radio News*, 122.
30. Shirley Biagi, *Interviews that Work: A Practical Guide for Journalists,* 2d ed. (Belmont, Calif.: Wadsworth, 1992), 113.
31. Downs and Wallace, "The Craft of Interviewing," 10.
32. *Television Newsfilm Standards Manual* (New York: Time-Life, 1964), 75–76.
33. Michael J. Arlen, *Living-Room War* (New York: Random House, 1977), 69–70.
34. Alexander Kendrick, *Prime Time* (Boston: Little, Brown and Company, 1969), 411.
35. Postman and Powers, *How to Watch TV News,* 160–68.
36. Daniel Boorstsin, *The Image* (New York: Atheneum Publishers, 1972), 9–12.
37. Laurence Barton, *Crisis in Organizations: Managing and Communicating in the Heat of Chaos* (Cincinnati, Ohio: South-Western Publishing, 1993).
38. This case is based on an actual incident where the CEO suddenly vanished without explanation. However, later the CEO was apprehended by the FBI, and he pleaded guilty to embezzlement. His wife was also arrested and pleaded guilty to bankruptcy fraud and to making statements to the FBI to hide her husband's whereabouts. See "The CEO Vanishes, Leaving a Company Besieged, Perplexed," *The Wall Street Journal,* 15 March, 1991, 1 and "Fugitive CEO Pleads Guilty to Federal Fraud Charges," *The Wall Street Journal,* 3 October, 1994, A5.
39. Neil Postman, "We Have Transformed Information into a Form of Garbage," *UR Currents,* July-August, 1995, 35.

EPILOGUE

Interviewing is an integral part of our lives. From the first time we asked mom whether or not we could have another cookie or stay up a little later than usual, to asking a professor the best way to study for a final exam or getting a job, we learned that asking and answering questions determined the outcome of our success. We participate in many interviews daily, and understanding their dynamics can greatly improve our probability of achievement. They may range from formal to informal; be highly structured, moderately structured, or unstructured; or deal with business, research, media, or personal problems. Although each interview is somewhat different, all require confidence, knowledge of subject matter, and preparation.

We wrote *Results-Oriented Interviewing* mainly because we realized that just about anyone could benefit from understanding the concepts underlying effective interviewing. We have discussed essential principles, practices, and procedures, but more importantly, we have taught you how to *think* about interviewing and about your goals. This should enable you to use the tools that are best for you when you interview.

The concepts presented in *Results-Oriented Interviewing* are intended to stimulate changes in the way you think and act with regard to interviews. Change can be a difficult thing; the first step can seem impossibly high. New ideas might seem simple enough, but actually putting them into practice can be a little intimidating or quite terrifying. You cannot accomplish the goals set out in this book unless you take some bold steps before, during, and after your interviews. Remember, none of this is magic, none of it is mysterious. You can apply this new knowledge to your own life. As you apply the concepts presented in this book and practice the new behaviors learned, you will find that your attitude about interviewing has changed. You will be less anxious and less nervous. You will be more prepared and more in control. You will achieve results—expertly and successfully.

Interviewing demands intellect, patience, empathy, and concern. Skillful interviewing requires training, practice, and perseverance. To be appreciated, the next task is yours—you must practice, practice, and practice to become perfect.

INDEX

Hearst, William Randolph, 357, 359

Hedges, in workplace counseling interview, 160

Hesitation forms, in workplace counseling interview, 160

Hiring. *See* Selection interview

Honesty
coaching with, in workplace counseling interview, 164
in exit interview, 204–205

Hostility, discipline interview and, 187–188

HPP. *See* Health promotion program

Hypothetical questions, use of, 37

"I" *versus* "you" language, in workplace counseling interview, 159

Identification of performance problem, 180–181

Impact, disparate, discrimination by, 56–57

Information power, 233

Inquiring reporter interview, journalistic, 363

Integrity tests, 64–65

Intensifiers, in workplace counseling interview, 160

Interview
appraisal, 8, 119–141
broadcast, 11–12, 394–420
computer-assisted, 11, 329–350
counseling, 9
discipline, 8–9, 174–194
effective, nature of, 3–24
exit, 9, 195–216
focus group, 10, 277–303
follow-up, 74–75, *75*
investigative reporting, 11
journalistic, 11, 353–393
negotiation, 9, 217–250
news conference, 12
organizational audit, 11
process of, 25–48
sales, 9–10, 217–250
selection, 8, 51–79, 81–118
survey, 10, 253–276
telephone, 10, 271–273
types of, 8–12

workplace counseling, 142–173

Interview guide, for focus group interview, developing, 287–288

Interview programs, 403

Interviewee, role of, 15–17
in selection interview, 84

Interviewer
perspective of, 54–55
role of, 15–17, *68*
for survey interview
choosing, 265
training, 265

Interviewing, defined, 5–7

Interviewing situation, defined, 12

"Inundation" tactic, in negotiation, 237

Inverted funnel interview, journalistic, 365

Inverted funnel sequence, in interview, 30–31

Investigative reporting, 11, 353–393

"It's-a-shame-to" tactic, in negotiation, 239

Jefferson, Thomas, 357

Job profile, 58

Journalistic interview, 11, 353–393
American press, history of, 356–362
defined, 362–364
in-person, 363
investigative reporting, 380–384
libel, 384–386
note taking, 372–375
with prepared questions, 363
questions, 367–372
stages of, 364–367
telephoning, 372–375
writing news, 375–380
headlines, 377–378
kicker close, 379–380
leads, 377–378
news story, body building of, 378–379
structure, of news story, 375–377, *376*
taping, 372–375

Journalistic privilege, 384–386

LAN. *See* Local area networks

Language use, in workplace counseling interview, 159–161
disclaimers, 160
hedges, 160
hesitation forms, 160
"I" *versus* "you" language, 159
intensifiers, 160
questioning forms, 160

Large systems interventions, organizational audit, 315–316

Lead, for news story, 377

Leading questions, use of, 20, 37

Leads, in news writing, 377–378

Legal issues, 55–58
in workplace counseling interview, 167–168

Legitimate power, 233

Letter of application, 99–104
content of, 99–101, *100*
cover letter, sample, *100*
style of, 101–104

Libel
journalistic interview and, 384–386
presumed, 384

Libel *per quod*, 384

Libel *per se*, 384

Lippmann, Walter, 361

Listening
analytically, 42–45
in exit interview, 207–210, *209*
skills, 133
in workplace counseling interview, behaviors, 155–156

Loaded questions, 37–38

Local area networks, computer-assisted interview, 340–341

Luce, Henry, 360

Magazine programs, 403

Marconi, Guglielmo, wireless dot-dash transmissions, 397

Mindfulness, in workplace counseling interview, 158

Mirror statements, use of, 36

Moderator, of focus group interview, 290–293